The **Rough Guide** to

Iceland

written and researched by

David Leffman and James Proctor

www.roughguides.com

Contents

The great outdoors
colour section
following p.88

Iceland: a culture apart colour section
following p.248

3

Introduction to

Iceland

Resting on the edge of the Arctic Circle and sitting atop one of the world's most volcanically active hot spots, Iceland's tourist image is of an inspiring mix of magisterial glaciers, bubbling hot springs and rugged fjords, where activities such as hiking under the Midnight Sun are complemented by healthy doses of history and literature.

But even before the country's economic meltdown of 2008–2009, things hadn't always appeared so appealing. Around 870 AD, the Viking **Flóki Vilgerðarson** sailed to this then uninhabited island with hopes of starting a new life, only to suffer a long hard winter that killed off all his cattle. Hoping to spy out a more promising site for his farm he climbed a high mountain in the northwest of the country, but could see nothing on the far side but a fjord full of drift ice. Bitterly disappointed, he named the country **Ísland** (Ice Land) and promptly sailed home for the positively balmy climes of Norway.

A few years later, however, Iceland was successfully settled and, despite frequent volcanic activity and enthusiastic felling of trees for fuel and timber, visitors to the country today will see it in pretty much the same state as it was over a thousand years ago. Aside from the surprisingly modern and cosmopolitan capital, **Reykjavík**, the only decent-sized population centre is **Akureyri**, up on the north coast. Otherwise, the rest of the tiny population is settled around the **coastal fringe** in small towns, fishing villages, farms and minute hamlets – often no more than a collection of homesteads nestling around a wooden church.

If the coast is thinly populated, Iceland's **Interior** remains totally uninhabited and unmarked by humanity: a starkly beautiful wilderness of ice fields, infertile lava and ash deserts, windswept upland plateaux and the frigid vastness of Vatnajökull, Europe's largest glacier. Even in downtown Reykjavík, crisp, snow-capped peaks and fjords hover in the background, evidence of the forces that created the country. And Iceland's location on the Mid-Atlantic ridge also gives it one of the most volcanically active landscapes on Earth, peppered with everything from naturally occurring hot springs, scaldingly hot bubbling mud pools and noisy steam vents to a string of unpredictably violent volcanoes, which have regularly devastated huge parts of the country. It's something that Icelanders have learned to live with: in June 1998, when Reykjavík was rocked by a major earthquake, the ballet dancers at the National Opera performed right through it without missing a step.

▶ Café culture, Akureyri

Fact file

• Though geographically as big as England, Iceland's population is tiny. At barely 310,000, it's no bigger than many towns in other countries. Two out of three Icelanders live in and around the capital, Reykjavík.

• Iceland sits atop the **Mid-Atlantic Ridge**, the fault line where two of the Earth's tectonic plates are slowly drifting apart. As a result Iceland is getting wider at a rate of roughly 1cm per year. Either side of this ridge, from the northeast to the south-west, **earthquakes** and **volcanic activity** are commonplace.

• There are no motorways or railways in Iceland. The country's one and only main road, the **Ringroad** which circumnavigates the island, was completed in the 1970s following several unsuccessful attempts to bridge treacherous glacial rivers on the south coast.

• Iceland is home to the third-biggest **glacier** in the world, Vatnajökull, covering an area equal to that of the English county of Yorkshire. One of the country's greatest sources of **geothermal energy**, the Grímsvötn caldera, sits directly beneath the icecap.

• Thanks to the existence of countless medieval documents, many Icelanders can trace their ancestors back to the time of the **Viking Settlement**, around 800 AD. Low **immigration** over the centuries means that today's Icelanders have one of the purest gene pools in the world, providing an invaluable research opportunity for scientists.

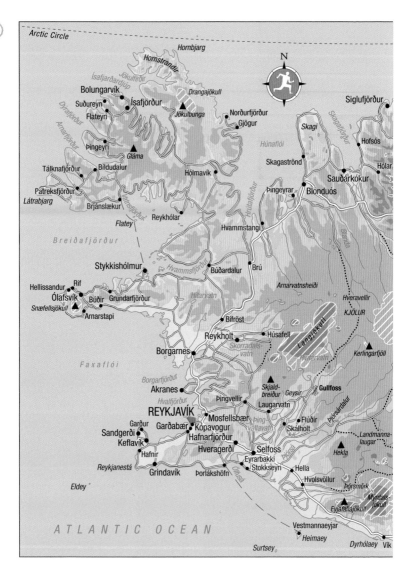

Historically, the **Icelanders** have a mix of Nordic and Celtic blood, a heritage often held responsible for their characteristically laidback approach to life – taps in hotels often drip, buses don't depart to the stroke of the driver's watch, and everybody, including the President and the Prime Minister, is known by their first name. The battle for survival against the elements over the centuries has also made them a highly self-reliant nation, whose dependence on the sea and fishing for their economy is virtually total

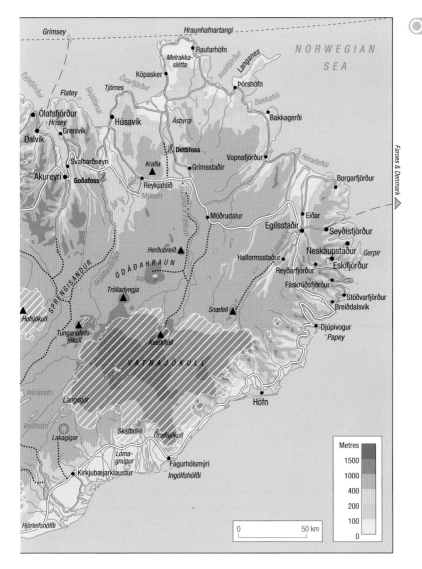

– hence their refusal to allow foreign trawlers to fish off Iceland during the diplomatically tense 1970s, sparking off three "Cod Wars", principally with Britain. Reliance on this more tangible source of income might still be more desirable than the abstract bubble of international banking, as the recent economic crisis has shown. Their isolated location in the North Atlantic also means that their island is frequently forgotten about – Icelanders will tell you that they've given up counting how many times they've been left off maps of

Europe – something that deeply offends their strong sense of national pride. For all their self-confidence though, Icelanders can initially seem reserved – until Friday and Saturday nights roll around, when the *bjór* starts to flow, and turns even the most monosyllabic fisherman into a lucid talkshow host, right down to reciting from memory entire chunks of medieval sagas about the early settlers.

Where to go

nevitably, most people get their first taste of Iceland at **Reykjavík**, rubbing shoulders with over half the country's population. It may be small, but what Reykjavík lacks in size it more than makes up for in stylish bars, restaurants and shops, and the nightlife is every bit as wild as it's cracked up to be – during the light summer nights, the city doesn't sleep. The world's most northerly capital also boasts cinemas, an opera, a symphony orchestra and a dance company, as well as the usual string of museums and galleries. Reykjavík makes a good base for visiting **Geysir**, the original geyser that gave its name to all other such hot springs, the ancient parliament site of **Þingvellir** and spectacular waterfalls at **Gullfoss**. The **Reykjanes Peninsula**, home to the country's main international airport at Keflavík and therefore the first sight most travellers get of Iceland, is renowned for its sublime **Blue Lagoon**, along with teeming birdlife and whales, which are frequently spotted off the peninsula's western tip.

Beyond Reykjavík, Route 1, the **Ringroad**, runs out to encircle the island, and all long-distance buses and domestic planes begin their journeys from the city. Once outside the relatively densely populated **southwestern** corner, the wilder side of Iceland begins – open spaces of vivid green edged by unspoilt coastlines of red and black sands all set against a backdrop of brooding hills and mountains. The main draw of the **west coast** is the towns of **Borgarnes** and **Reykholt** and the surrounding countryside, where there's barely a feature that's unassociated with the **sagas**, such as **Laxárdalur**, a farm where romantic and tragic scenes from *Laxdæla Saga* were played out.

Away from the Ringroad, the **Snæfellsnes Peninsula**, with views of the monster glacier at its tip, is one of the country's most accessible hiking destinations. Arguably Iceland's most dramatic scenery is found in the far northwest of the country, the **West Fjords**, where tiny fishing villages

To whale or not to whale

The Icelandic government's decision to resume **commercial whaling** in late 2006 drove a wedge through Icelandic public opinion. Most of the population views whaling as a virtual birthright and is only too keen to turn a nationalistic blind eye to international protest, but it is also true that the nation's burgeoning **tourism industry** has led to a decline in its near-total dependence on the fishing industry. Consequently, promoters of tourism lost no time in pointing out that foreigners have flocked to Iceland in recent years to **watch whales** in their natural habitat, not to see them unceremoniously sliced up for the dinner table – and despite a seeming nonchalance, Icelanders are painfully aware that their tiny country on the very edge of Europe can ill afford any kind of international boycott.

► Downtown Reykjavik

Getting legless for an arm and a leg

It's one of Iceland's greatest paradoxes: how can a country that charges some of the highest prices for alcohol in Europe also support such an eclectic scene of bars and clubs? Put simply, spending vast amounts of money on everyday items is a fact of life in Iceland, a country where import taxes and inflation have caused prices to soar; and even though alcohol prices in real terms have fallen in recent years, a half-litre of beer in Reykjavík will still cost at least double what you're used to paying at home. Icelanders get round the astronomical cost of booze by drinking at home before hitting the town. Buying beer and wine in the state-run alcohol store, the **vínbúð**, is the home-grown way of cutting costs – and even then, although prices are considerably lower than in bars, the store charges for the plastic bag to take your booty home in.

nestle at the foot of table-top mountains or are tucked away in the neck of narrow fjords which offer protection from the ferocious Arctic storms that batter this exposed part of the country. **Ísafjörður** is the only settlement of any size in the region and makes a good base from which to strike out on foot into the wilderness of the **Hornstrandir Peninsula**. Beautifully located at the head of **Eyjafjörður** on the north coast, **Akureyri** is rightfully known as the capital of the north and functions as Iceland's second city. With a string of bars and restaurants it can make a refreshing change from the small villages elsewhere on the north coast. From here it's easy to reach the island of **Grímsey**, the only part of Icelandic territory actually within the **Arctic Circle**, and nearby **Siglufjörður**, for an insight into the twentieth-century herring boom that once made this tiny village the country's economic powerhouse.

The country's biggest tourist attraction outside the capital is **Lake Mývatn**, an hour to the east of Akureyri. The lake is a favourite nesting place for many species of duck and other waterfowl and is surrounded by an electrifying proliferation of volcanic activity, including long-dormant cinder cones and the still-steaming lava fields at **Krafla**, which last burst forth in the 1980s. North of Mývatn, the small town of **Húsavík** is one of the best places in the country to organize summer whale-watching cruises, while just inland to the east, the wilds of **Jökulsárgljúfur National Park** offer superlative hiking along deep river gorges to the spectacular **Dettifoss**, Europe's most powerful waterfall. Across on the east coast, the **Eastfjords** centre on **Egilsstaðir** and the port of **Seyðisfjörður**, where Iceland's only international ferry docks, and offer further walking opportunities – both coastal and around the fjords, and inland to the volcanic spire of **Snæfell** – in a part of the country which regularly receives the driest and warmest weather. The small town of **Höfn** in the southeast corner is a good base from which to visit Europe's biggest glacier, the mighty Vatna-jökull, either on a skidoo trip or on foot through **Skaftafell National Park**. Further to the west the nearby glacial lagoon, **Jökulsárlón**, offers the surreal chance to cruise alongside floating icebergs which were once part of the glacier itself.

The **south coast** is marked by vast stretches of black, volcanic coastal sands punctuated by tiny villages that unfortunately are prone to some of the country's foulest weather – the town of **Vík** is Iceland's wettest but boasts teeming sea-bird colonies. Iceland's most rewarding hiking route can also be found in this corner of the country: the four-day **Laugavegur trail** between extraordinary hot-springs scenery at **Landmannalaugar** and **Þórsmörk**'s

▲ Snowmobiles on Vatnajökull

lush green slopes. Just off the south coast, and easily reached by ferry, the **Westman Islands** (Vestmannaeyjar) sport the world's largest puffin colonies and were propelled into the world headlines during the 1960s and 1970s by a series of volcanic eruptions that created a new island, **Surtsey**, and also threatened to bury the town of **Heimaey** under lava and ash.

Iceland's barren **Interior** is best tackled as part of a guided tour – it's much easier to let experienced drivers of all-terrain buses pick their way across lavafields and cross unbridged rivers than to try it yourself. Parts of the Interior's fringes are also feasibly explored on foot, however, and even by bus it's perfectly possible to break your journey anywhere and camp – you'll be sharing the stunning scenery with only the ghosts of the early settlers who perished in its bleak, grey-sanded lava deserts.

▶ Icelandic horses

When to go

▲ Church at Núpsstaður

Though milder than you might think, Icelandic **weather** is notoriously unpredictable. In **summer** there's a fair chance of bright and sunny days and temperatures can reach 17°C but these are interspersed with wet and misty spells when the temperature can plummet to a chilly 10°C. Generally speaking, if it's wet and windy in the southwest it'll be sunny and warm in the northeast, which receives more than its fair share of sunshine in the summer months, much to the dismay of city slickers at the other end of the country. Most budget accommodation is only open from late May to early September, and it's at these times, too, that buses run their fullest schedules. Many bus routes through the Interior don't start until late June or early July when the snow finally melts. Although almost all of Iceland lies south of the Arctic Circle and therefore doesn't experience a true **Midnight Sun**, nights are light from mid-May to early August across the country. In the north the sun never fully sets during June. Between September and January

Sexual equality in Iceland

Regardless of the tongue-twisting name, Vigdís Finnbogadóttir put Iceland on the map when she became the world's first female president in 1980, high-profile proof of Iceland's approach to **sexual equality**. However, treating women as equals was nothing new in Iceland. Ever since Viking times, when every pair of working hands was required to farm, fish and simply exist in such a harsh climate, the nation's small population base has catapulted women into positions that for centuries were seen solely as a man's preserve in many other countries. Today, things are no different; both women and men often work long hours, fulfilling several roles, to keep the Icelandic economy ticking over. Generous childcare facilities provided by the Icelandic welfare state have also enabled women to re-enter the labour market shortly after having children, and work their way up the career ladder, often to the very top. Even the Icelandic **language** reflects the equal nature of society; there's often no specifically male or female word for a profession – just one term applied to both men and women.

▲ The Blue Lagoon hot pool

the Aurora Borealis or **Northern Lights** can often be seen. They appear as an eerie, oscillating curtain of green, blue or pale orange light in the night sky.

Winter temperatures fluctuate at 7–8°C either side of freezing point and heavy snowfall and avalanches block many of the roads. There's little chance of accommodation other than in the large hotels in Reykjavík and the other main towns, and hiking and camping are out of the question. However, a stay in the capital at this time means a lack of crowds and at Christmas its streets are bathed in the glow of candles burning behind every window. Bear in mind though that daylight in midwinter is limited to a few hours – in Reykjavík, sunrise isn't until almost 11am in December; the sun is already sinking slowly back towards the horizon after 1pm; and by 3.30pm, it'll be dark again. Further north in Ísafjörður, reckon on around one and a half hours' less daylight than in Reykjavík.

Reykjavík temperatures

	Jan	Feb	Mar	Apr	May	Jun	Jul	Aug	Sep	Oct	Nov	Dec
Average daily temperatures (°C)												
Max	2	3	4	6	10	12	14	14	11	7	4	2
Min	-2	-2	-1	1	4	7	9	8	6	3	0	-2
Rainfall (mm)												
	89	64	62	56	42	42	50	56	67	94	78	79

23

things not to miss

It's not possible to see everything that Iceland has to offer on a short trip – and we don't suggest you try. What follows is a selective taste of the city's highlights: fascinating museums, spectacular buildings and a few ways just to indulge yourself. They're arranged in five colour-coded categories, which you can browse through to find the very best things to see and experience. All highlights have a page reference to take you straight into the Guide, where you can find out more.

01 Dettifoss Page **271** • Encounter nature in the raw at Europe's biggest waterfall, Dettifoss.

02 **The Blue Lagoon** Page **101** • A dip in the sublime waters of the Blue Lagoon is a quintessentially Icelandic experience.

03 **Askja** Page **317** • The Askja caldera in the Interior, containing a geothermal lake, Víti, is perfect for a quick dip.

04 **Sprengisandur** Page **314** • A trip into the desolate, uninhabited Interior is a humbling experience.

05 **The Settlement Exhibition** Page **72** • Travel back in time to the year 871 and see the remarkable remains of one of Reykjavík's earliest houses.

07 **Flatey** Page **176** • Admire the drama of the Westfjord mountains from the green, flat meadows of this tiny, peaceful island haven.

06 **Geysir** Page **113** • See Strokkur erupting at Geysir, after which all geysers are named.

08 Whale watching Page 266 • Set off in search of minke and humpback whales on a boat trip from Húsavík.

09 Þórsmörk Page 134 • Awe-inspiring scenery in Iceland's most popular national park.

10 Látrabjarg Page 207 • These perpendicular cliffs at the very edge of Europe are the best place to spot all kinds of birds.

11 **Lake Mývatn** Page **253** • Curious geological features and rich birdlife come together to make Lake Mývatn one of Iceland's biggest draws.

12 **Phallological Museum** Page **266** • A distinctly Icelandic take on how to present a wildlife museum – an eye-opening exhibition of penises, big and small, from every species of Icelandic mammal.

13 **Join the rúntur** Page **86** • Sample Iceland's legendary nightlife, starting with a pub crawl round some of Reykjavík's bars.

14 **Breiðavík** Page **207** • This sweeping stretch of pristine golden sand and turquoise water is Iceland's most beautiful beach.

15 **Skaftafell** Page **303** • Waterfalls and great hiking make this national park a favourite among Icelanders.

16 **Akureyri** Page **230** • The best place outside Reykjavík to enjoy a spot of urban sophistication.

17 **The sagas** Page **77** •
Reykjavík's Culture House boasts some of Europe's oldest and finest medieval manuscripts.

18 **Hiking in Hornstrandir**
Page **197** • The complete remoteness and majestic landscape make isolated Hornstrandir a luring destination for dedicated hikers.

19 **Landmannalaugar** Page **123** • The Interior's best known feature, Landmannalaugar offers terrific hiking and a chance to bathe in naturally heated waters.

20 Hallgrímskirkja Page **78** • Hallgrímskirkja is undoubtedly Reykjavík's best known landmark and offers unsurpassed views of the world's most northerly capital from its tower.

21 Grettislaug Page **227** • Don't leave Iceland without taking a dip in a geothermally heated hot pool.

22 Þingvellir Page **106** • Human history and geological activity meet at Þingvellir, site of both Iceland's ancient parliament and the rift between the European and North American plates that form the earth's crust.

Fulmars

23 Iceland's birds Pages 335–338 • Iceland has around three hundred bird species, and while it's unlikely that you'll be able to spot the lot, you'll probably see some of the following at the very least.

Pink-footed geese

Razorbill

Golden plover

Gannet

▼ Oystercatcher

▶ Red-necked phalarope

▼ Whooper swans

▶ Kittiwakes

▶ Puffins

▼ Arctic tern

▼ Redshank

▼ Ptarmigan

▼ Harlequin duck

▲ Snipe

▲ Eider

Basics

Basics

www.roughguides.com

Getting there

Iceland's Keflavík International Airport, about 40km west of Reykjavík, is connected by direct flights to many places across Europe, the UK, Scandinavia, the US and Canada. It's also possible to reach Iceland by sea all year round on board the Faroese superferry *Norröna*, which performs a once-weekly crossing of the North Atlantic.

Airfares always depend on the **season**, with the highest being around June to August, when the weather is best; fares drop during the "shoulder" seasons – September to November and April to June – and you'll get the best prices during the low season, November to March (excluding Christmas and New Year).

An all-inclusive **package tour** can sometimes turn out to be the cheapest way of doing things. Deals range from a weekend city-break to Reykjavík and its surrounds to all-singing, all-dancing adventure holidays involving snowmobiling across Vatnajökull and whale watching in Húsavík. Check the specialist tour operator websites below.

The cheapest airfare deals are always available **online**, either direct through the airline website or via a discount travel website. To get the best value from airline websites, book in advance; most allocate a certain number of cheap seats per flight which are available until sold. These deals are fairly flexible, often allowing changes to the dates of departure and return, though sometimes a fee is charged. Discount travel websites offer similar low-cost flight tickets and packages and can turn up some real bargains, but tend towards non-refundable, non-changeable deals.

Compared with the web, the advantage of using a **high-street travel agent** or specialist is finding a more flexible, fully refundable or alterable ticket, plus a range of travel-related services such as travel insurance, rail passes, car rental, tours and the like.

From the UK and Ireland

Iceland Express (☎0118/321 8384, ⓦwww.icelandexpress.com) currently flies from London Stansted to Keflavík (2hr 50 min) all year round, with the lowest return fares starting at £180. Flights generally operate twice daily from April to September, and once daily during the rest of the year.

Icelandair (☎020/7874 1000, ⓦwww.icelandair.co.uk) operates from London Heathrow, Glasgow and Manchester to Keflavík. From April to September, the Heathrow flights (3hr) operate twice daily; from October to March, the frequency is generally reduced slightly. From Glasgow (2hr), Icelandair flies 4–5 times a week, and from Manchester (2hr 30min) just twice a week. Return fares from London Heathrow start at £240, whereas from Glasgow and Manchester they cost from £212.

There are no direct flights between **Ireland** and Iceland, so you'll need to travel first to London, Manchester or Glasgow with Aer Lingus (ⓦwww.aerlingus.com), bmi (ⓦwww.flybmi.com) or Ryanair (ⓦwww.ryanair.com), and then pick up an Icelandexpress or Icelandair flight to Keflavík.

The Norröna ferry

Although it's possible to travel by sea to Iceland, the journey is recommended only to those with a cast-iron stomach, since the frequent gales, storms and unsettling swell of the North Atlantic can well and truly quash romantic images of riding the waves to your destination. Even so, the luxurious *Norröna* ferry (@www.smyril-line.com) runs year-round to Seyðisfjörður from **Esbjerg** and **Hanstholm** in Denmark via **Tórshavn** in the Faroe Islands, offering en-suite cabins, a swimming pool, a shopping arcade and even a fitness centre.

Sailing schedules are complicated and times vary between even and odd-numbered weeks. **High season** is defined as between late June and mid-August, when one-way fares from Denmark to Seyðisfjörður are €286 for one vehicle and up to two people sleeping in a couchette; a cabin costs upwards of an additional €23.

From the US and Canada

Icelandair (@www.icelandair.com) flies out of several US and Canadian cities. The **frequency** of flights is reduced during the winter months; exact details change each year, depending on demand, and some routes are suspended altogether.

From the US, Icelandair flies several times weekly each from Boston (US$550; 5hr), Minneapolis (US$560; 6hr), New York JFK (US$440; 5hr 35min); Orlando (US$900; 7hr 10min; Oct–Mar only) and Seattle (US$600; 8hr). **From Canada**, there are flights from Halifax (C$700; 4hr 15min) and Toronto (C$660; 4hr).

As of summer 2010, Iceland Express is also planning to start flights from New York to Reykjavík – check @www.icelandexpress.com for details.

From Australia, New Zealand and South Africa

There are no direct flights to Iceland from Australia, New Zealand or South Africa, so you'll need to find a discounted airfare to somewhere that does – such as London – and arrange a flight to Reykjavík from there. As London is a major destination for most international airlines the high level of competition ensures a wide choice of routes worldwide.

All airfares to London **from Australian East-Coast gateways** are similarly priced, with the cheapest deals via Asia costing around AU$2000/2400/2800 (low, medium or high season). From Perth or Darwin, scheduled flights via Asia cost AU$110–220 less than if departing from eastern gateways, while flights

via the USA cost around AU$400 more. **From New Zealand** you can fly from Auckland to London via mainland USA or Asia for NZ$2600/2900/3200. From Wellington and Christchurch all options cost NZ$200–$300 more. To get to London **from South Africa**, count on around 6000/6400/6800 ZAR for a Cape Town–London return.

Airlines from Australasia to London

Air New Zealand @www.airnz.co.nz.
British Airways @www.ba.com.
Cathay Pacific @www.cathaypacific.com.
Garuda Indonesia @www.garuda-indonesia.com.
Malaysia Airlines @www.malaysiaairlines.com.
Qantas @www.qantas.com.
Singapore Airlines @www.singaporeair.com.
Thai Airways @www.thaiair.com.
Virgin Atlantic Airways @www.virgin-atlantic.com.

Specialist agents and tour operators

Adventure Center US ☎00800/6650 3998, @www.adventures-abroad.com. Cycling, whale-watching and hiking breaks from this company, specializing in small group tours.
Borton Overseas US ☎1-800/843-0602, @www.bortonoverseas.com. Adventure-vacation specialists, offering a variety of Iceland tours with biking, hiking and rafting activities, plus farm and cabin stays.
Discover the World UK: Arctic House, 8 Bolters Lane, Banstead Surrey SM7 2AR ☎01737/218 800, @www.discover-the-world.co.uk. Well-established Nordic holiday specialist, with groups led by naturalists to Iceland, plus city breaks, fly/drive holidays and independent travel.
Explore Worldwide UK: 1 Frederick St, Aldershot, Hants GU11 1LQ ☎01252/760 000, @www.explore.co.uk. Small-group tours and super-jeep expeditions.

Iceland Adventure US ☎1-888/686-6784, ⓦwww.icelandadventure.com. Small escorted tours to Iceland including rafting and horseriding holidays.

Icelandair Holidays US ☎1-800/779-2899, ⓦwww.icelandair.com. Iceland tour specialists, offering a variety of tours from basic airfare plus hotel packages to fully escorted tours.

My Planet (Bentours) Australia: Level 7, 189 Kent Street, Sydney NSW 2000 ☎02/9241 1353, ⓕ9251 1574, ⓦwww.myplanetaustralia.com.au. Handles Icelandair ticket sales; also offers fly/drive and seven-day Iceland packages.

Nordic Travel Australia: 600 Military Road, Mosman, NSW 2088 ☎02/9968 1783, ⓦwww.nordictravel.com.au. Another Icelandair agent and representative for most Icelandic tour agents, this long-established operator can book you onto pre-existing tours within Iceland or tailor special-interest packages – from driving, hiking or cycling around the highlights to snowmobiling across Vatnajökull.

North South Travel UK ☎01245/608 291, ⓦwww.northsouthtravel.co.uk. Friendly, competitive travel agency, offering discounted fares worldwide. Profits are used to support projects in the developing world, especially the promotion of sustainable tourism.

Passage Tours US ☎954/776-7070, ⓦwww.passagetours.com. Nine-day "Icelandic Quartet" tours, from $2018 including airfare. Optional five-day extensions to Greenland.

Regent Holidays UK: 15 John Street, Bristol BS1 2HR ☎0845/277 3301, ⓦwww.regent-holidays.co.uk. Good package operator specializing in Iceland and Greenland.

Reykjavík Tours US ☎1-866/423-7242, ⓦwww.reykjaviktours.com. Specializes in short breaks to the Icelandic capital including trips to the Golden Circle attractions and the Blue Lagoon.

Scanam World Tours US ☎609/655-1600, ⓦwww.scanamtours.com. Group and individual tours and cruises, plus cheap weekend breaks.

Scantours UK: 73 Mornington St, London NW1 7QE ☎020/7554 3530, ⓦwww.scantours.co.uk; US ☎1-800/223-7226, ⓦwww.scantours.com. Good deals on city breaks and fly/drive holidays.

STA Travel US ☎1-800/781-4040, UK ☎0871/230 0040, Australia ☎134 782, New Zealand ☎0800/474 400, South Africa

Six steps to a better kind of travel

At Rough Guides we are passionately committed to travel. We feel strongly that only through travelling do we truly come to understand the world we live in and the people we share it with – plus tourism has brought a great deal of **benefit** to developing economies around the world over the last few decades. But the extraordinary growth in tourism has also damaged some places irreparably, and of course **climate change** is exacerbated by most forms of transport, especially flying. This means that now more than ever it's important to **travel thoughtfully** and **responsibly**, with respect for the cultures you're visiting – not only to derive the most benefit from your trip but also to preserve the best bits of the planet for everyone to enjoy. At Rough Guides we feel there are six main areas in which you can make a difference:

- Consider what you're contributing to the **local economy**, and how much the services you use do the same, whether it's through employing local workers and guides or sourcing locally grown produce and local services.
- Consider the **environment** on holiday as well as at home. Water is scarce in many developing destinations, and the biodiversity of local flora and fauna can be adversely affected by tourism. Try to patronize businesses that take account of this.
- Travel with a purpose, not just to tick off experiences. Consider **spending longer** in a place, and getting to know it and its people.
- Give thought to how often you **fly**. Try to avoid short hops by air and more harmful night flights.
- Consider **alternatives to flying**, travelling instead by bus, train, boat and even by bike or on foot where possible.
- Make your trips **"climate neutral"** via a reputable carbon offset scheme. All Rough Guide flights are offset, and every year we donate money to a variety of charities devoted to combating the effects of climate change.

☎0861/781 781, ⓦwww.statravel.com.
Worldwide specialists in independent travel;
also student IDs, travel insurance, car rental,
rail passes and more. Good discounts for students
and under-26s.

Taber Holidays UK: 30A Bingley Road, Saltaire,
Shipley BD18 4RS ☎01274/875 199, ⓦwww
.taberhols.co.uk. With over thirty years experience,
this company specializes in regional tours of Iceland
as well as city breaks to Reykjavík.

Trailfinders UK ☎0845/058 5858, Ireland
☎01/677 7888, Australia ☎1300/780 212,

ⓦwww.trailfinders.com. One of the best-informed
and most efficient agents for independent travellers.

Travel CUTS Canada ☎1-866/246-9762, US
☎1-800/592-2887, ⓦwww.travelcuts.com.
Canadian youth and student travel firm.

USIT Ireland ☎01/602 1906, Northern Ireland
☎028/9032 7111, ⓦwww.usit.ie. Ireland's main
student and youth travel specialists.

Yes Travel UK ☎01778/424 499, ⓦwww
.yes-travel.com. Iceland specialist with camping
and caravan holidays, city breaks, fly/drive and
tailor-made tours on offer.

Getting around

Iceland's small scale makes getting around fairly straightforward – at least
during the warmer months. From Reykjavík, it's possible to fly or catch a bus to
all major centres, and in summer there are even scheduled buses through the
interior. In winter, however, reduced bus services and difficult road conditions
might make flying the only practical way to travel. It's also easy enough to hire
cars or four-wheel-drives, though those on a budget will find cycling a cheaper
alternative.

On the ground, you'll probably spend a good
deal of time on Route 1, or *Hringbraut*, **the
Ringroad**, which largely follows the coast in
a 1500-kilometre circuit of the country
via Reykjavík, Akureyri and Egilsstaðir. The
entire Ringroad is sealed, and in winter
snowploughs do their best to keep the route
accessible to conventional vehicles, though
you'll still need to take care and use snow
tyres.

Elsewhere, while stretches around towns
might be surfaced, the majority of Icelandic
roads are **gravel**. Some of these are
perfectly decent if bumpy to travel over,
while many others – such as most **roads
through the Interior** – are only navigable in
high-clearance four-wheel-drives. Note that
interior roads are only open between June
and August; exactly when each opens and
closes each year – or whether some open at
all – depends on the weather, and the going
can be difficult even then.

By air

Flying in Iceland is good value: the single
airfare from Reykjavík to Egilsstaðir, for
instance, is 12,630kr, far less than the price of
the bus fare for the same journey – and takes
just one hour instead of two days. As an
added bonus, you'll get a different take on
Iceland's unique landscape from above –
flying over Vatnajökull's vast expanse of ice is
about the only way to get a grasp of its scale.

The main **domestic airline** is Flugfélag
Íslands and its subsidiary Landsflug (both
ⓦwww.airiceland.is), which flies all year from
Reykjavík to Akureyri, Bíldudalur, Egilsstaðir,
Gjögur, Ísafjörður, Sauðárkrókur, Westman
Islands and Höfn (Hornafjörður) almost daily.
From Akureyri, they have less frequent
connections between April and October to
Grímsey, Vopnafjörður and Þórshöfn. They
offer various **ticket types**: Priority, which are
the most expensive and valid for a year;
Value, which offer less flexibility, but are

Road and weather websites

If you're driving, hiking, cycling or doing anything else outdoors, you'll need to get advance information about **road and weather conditions**. Being unprepared for the weather has the most capacity for ruining your enjoyment of Iceland, and conditions can change very quickly: sunny summer days will be spaced by rain, storms and the real possibility of snow on high ground or in the Interior – you can get caught out even on brief excursions.

Weather forecasts can be found at ⑩ en.vedur.is, which predicts national and local conditions over the forthcoming week. Check on the **current road conditions** anywhere in Iceland by logging on to ⑩ www.vegag.is, a continually updated website in English and Icelandic that shows maps of the country with roads colour-coded according to their condition.

twenty percent cheaper; Bonus, valid for a month and some forty percent cheaper than Priority; and various Net fares, which are cheaper again but can only be booked through the website and can't be altered. Note that bad weather can cause cancellations at short notice and that it's best to book well ahead for summer weekends and holidays. **Luggage allowance** is 20kg, and you need to **check in** thirty minutes before departure.

Sample **Value fares** for one-way tickets from Reykjavík are: Akureyri 11,370kr; Egilsstaðir 12,630kr; Ísafjörður 11,370kr; and Westman Islands 8090kr.

By bus

Buses are pretty much the most convenient way to get around a large chunk of Iceland. Between May and October, services cover the entire Ringroad and many other routes, with regular tours tackling interior destinations once the roads open around June – about the only way you'll get to see these remote places unless you've considerable off-road driving experience and the right vehicle.

The country's umbrella long-distance bus organization is **BSÍ** (⑩ www.bsi.is), based at the bus station in Reykjavík, whose website has a comprehensive **timetable** of scheduled departures and tours run by the country's half-dozen bus companies – you can also find them at ⑩ www.nat.is. The main companies are **Trex** (⑩ www.trex.is or ⑩ www.bogf.is), which operates round-Iceland services, including to the Westfjords, the Kjölur Route across Iceland and the

seasonal Höfn-Egilsstaðir link; and **Reykjavík Excursions** (⑩ www.re.is) and **SBA-Norður-leið** (⑩ www.sba.is), which between them run the **airport bus** and more cross-Iceland routes, plus local services out of Akureyri.

On the down side, bus travel is expensive: one-way **fares from Reykjavík** are 9000kr to Akureyri; 11,200kr to Höfn; 11,800kr to Mývatn; and around 15,500kr to Egilsstaðir. In purely point-to-point terms it costs less to fly (see above), and if you can get a group together, car rental (see p.33) might work out cheaper, depending on how far you're going and for how long. Between October and May, the range of buses is also greatly reduced: interior roads close, local services dry up, and even along the Ringroad buses only run as far east as Höfn and Akureyri.

Bookings for main-road services can be made at the BSÍ terminal in Reykjavík, though they're not really necessary as you can always pay on board, and – according to BSÍ – extra buses are laid on if more than one busload of passengers turns up. Buses into the Interior, or local tours (even if advertised through BSÍ), will require advance booking, however.

Bus passes

Bus passes available from BSÍ and other outlets in Akureyri, Seyðisfjörður and Egilsstaðir will save you money on extended bus travel, though they're only available throughout the summer and are subject to roads being open.

Trex has the most useful passes. Its **Full Circle Pass** (valid 1 June–31 Aug; 30,000kr) lets you orbit the country using scheduled services in either direction along the Ringroad. However, you're not allowed to double back on your route, and have to pay extra if you detour off the Ringroad – through the Golden Circle, Interior or Westfjords for instance – but overall you save around a third of the cost of simply paying fares as you go. The **Full Circle & Westfjords** (1 June–31 Aug; 44,500kr) is the same as the Full Circle, with a Westfjords extension that also covers passage on the Stykkishólmur–Brjánslækur ferry. The **East Circle via Kjölur** (1 July–31 Aug; 31,500kr) travels from Reykjavík to Akureyri via the Kjölur Route across central Iceland, then circles clockwise via the Ringroad back to Reykjavík. Trex also offers passes – tours, really – around the Golden Circle (6500kr), Reykjavík to Landmannalaugar and Skaftafell (17,000kr), West Iceland and the Westfjords (21,000kr) and Snæfellsnes National Park (13,800kr).

Reykjavik Excursions also offers a less extensive range of passes, best of which is the **Highlights Passport**, valid for between one and two weeks (33,000–58,000kr) of unrestricted travel along a set route covering Reykjavík to Akureyri via Kjölur; Mývatn and Húsavik; back south via Sprengisandur to Landmannalaugar; east to Skaftafell and Höfn, including the side-trip to Lakagígar; and back to Reykjavík along the south coast.

Bus tours and buses through the Interior

Trex and Reykjavík Express also run **tours**, from year-round excursions along the Golden Circle (see p.106), to explorations of the Interior in summer. Though most tours only last a single day, you can get off along the way to camp or make use of mountain huts, and pick up a later bus – tell them your plans in advance so a space can be reserved for you. Make sure too that you know when the next bus is due, as only the Kjölur route is covered daily.

Interior routes covered by bus tours from Reykjavík include the **Fjallabak route**, which takes you past Landmannalaugar's thermal springs and a wild gorge system (see p.123); and trips across the country to Mývatn either via the impressively barren **Sprengisandur route** (see p.314) or the easier and slightly more scenic **Kjölur route** (see p.315). Local tours also tackle the trip to the mighty **Askja** caldera south of Mývatn (see p.317); easterly

Snæfell, Iceland's highest free-standing peak (see p.286); and **Lakagígar**, site of a massive eighteenth-century eruption in the south of the country (see p.307).

By car

Driving around Iceland allows far greater flexibility than taking the bus. **Car rental** is expensive for solo travellers but might work out a reasonable deal in a group, and it's also possible to **bring your own vehicle** in to the country by ferry (see p.28). UK, US, Canadian, Australian and New Zealand **driving licences** are all valid for short-term visits.

In summer you don't necessarily need a four-wheel-drive to experience the heart of the country, when both the Kjölur (Route 35) and the Kaldidalur (Route 550) open up to carefully driven conventional vehicles; these roads, however, are still very rough, and you'll need to check with your car-rental policy to ensure you're covered for them. Four-wheel-drive is essential for other Interior routes, but, most often because of sticky sand and numerous river crossings. Whatever you're driving, and wherever you are, note that you must not drive or pull off the road or track, apart from at designated passing places or car parks – aside from often unstable verges, you can cause serious erosion damage to the landscape.

All **fuel stations** have at least some **automatic pumps** where you pay using your credit/debit card with PIN; some rural fuel stations are completely automated and unstaffed for much of the time. If you don't have a credit/debit card, buy a **dedicated card** for a particular brand of station (N1 is probably the most widespread). Annoyingly, automatic pumps are designed so that you have to select the amount you want in litres and pay before filling up, which means you risk buying too much. Fuel currently **costs** 190kr per litre for standard unleaded petrol (95 Octane, or *blýlaust*).

Car rental

Car-rental agencies, offering everything from small economical runarounds to motor homes and gas-guzzling four-wheel-drives,

are found right around Iceland, though in smaller places the selection will be limited. Hiring in Iceland is expensive and you might save money by organizing things in **advance online**: once here, the Reykjavík tourist information offices also have each rental agent's brochures for directly comparing prices.

Rental-rate options boil down to two types: a **daily rate**, which covers the first 100km, after which you pay per additional kilometre; or an **all-inclusive** rate, which fixes a flat daily fee – obviously of benefit if you're planning a relatively short-term, long-range excursion. Check how much of the **CDW** (Collision Damage Waiver) you'll have to pay – it's often very steep and only brought down by paying an extra daily premium. **One-way rental** (hiring the car in Reykjavík and leaving it in Akureyri, for instance) attracts an additional relocation fee. It's always worth **bargaining**, especially if you're planning a lengthy rental period or are in Iceland outside the tourist season, when rental rates drop by a third or more.

Including CDW, prices for a small sedan start around 13,000kr per day for unlimited kilometres, less per day if you rent for a week or more. Even after factoring in petrol costs, this works out favourably over a week for two or more people, compared with bus travel on a Full Circle Pass. For a four-wheel-drive, however, you're looking at 45,000kr per day, plus heavy fuel consumption. **Campervans** – while not cheap at upwards of 55,000kr per day – begin to look better given that you save money on accommodation and eating out.

Car rental agencies in Iceland

Avis ☏591 4000, ⊛www.avis.is.
Budget ☏567 8300, ⊛www.budget.is.
Caravan ☏822 1920, ⊛www.caravan.is.
Europcar ☏591 4050, ⊛www.europcar.is.
Hasso ☏555 3330, ⊛www.hasso.is.
Hertz ☏505 0600, ⊛www.hertz.is.
National ☏568 6915, ⊛www.nationalcar.is.
Saga ☏421 3737, ⊛www.sgcarrental.is.

Bringing your own vehicle

The *Norröna* vehicle ferry from Denmark to Seyðisfjörður in the Eastfjords (see p.28) makes **bringing your own vehicle** into

Iceland fairly straightforward, though obviously you have to get it to Denmark first. Assuming you have been living outside Iceland for the previous twelve months, you're allowed to import the vehicle and 200 litres of fuel duty free for a period of one month starting from the date of entry. You'll also need to produce proof that the vehicle has third-party insurance (this can be purchased on arrival) and to bring along its registration certificate and your driving licence, before a duty-free import permit is granted. Permits can often be extended for up to three months after arrival, but overstay your permit and you'll be liable to full import duties on the vehicle.

Driving regulations and road conditions

Icelanders have a cavalier attitude to **driving** in conditions that most other people would baulk at – they have to, or would probably never get behind the wheel – and take dirt tracks and frozen twisting mountain roads very much in their stride. Native drivers also tend not to indicate and to gravitate towards the road's centre, and don't slow down much or move over for oncoming traffic,

which can be disconcerting. Aside from the weather and potential road conditions, however, low-volume traffic makes for few problems.

Cars are left-hand drives and you **drive on the right** as in the US, but unlike the UK, Australia and New Zealand. The **speed limit** is 50km an hour in built-up areas, 90km an hour on surfaced roads, and 80km an hour on gravel. **Seat belts** are compulsory for all passengers, and **headlights** must be on at least half-beam all the time.

Roadsigns you'll soon become familiar with – even if you stick to the Ringroad – are "Einbreið brú", indicating a single-lane bridge sometimes also marked by flashing yellow beacons; and "Malbik endar", marking the end of a surfaced road. **Bright orange signs** marked "Varúð" or "Hætta" (warning or hazard) alert you to temporary local problems, such as roadworks, ground-nesting birds on the road ("fuglar á vegi") or **sandstorms** – these can be a serious hazard and have been known to overturn vehicles and strip the paint off cars.

Other common problems include having other vehicles spray you with windscreen-cracking **gravel** as they pass – slow down and pull over to minimize this, especially on unsurfaced roads. Most fields are unfenced so always beware of **livestock** wandering about. When there's snow – though you'd be unlucky to come across much around the Ringroad during the summer – you'll find that the road's edges are marked by evenly spaced yellow poles; stay within their boundaries. **Avoid skidding** on gravel or snow by applying the brakes slowly and as little as possible; use gears instead. **In winter**, everyone fits studded snow tyres to their cars to increase traction, so make sure any vehicle you rent has them too. Pack a good blanket or sleeping bag in case your car gets stuck in snow, and always carry food and water.

Rough roads and four-wheel-driving

Iceland's interior routes, plus some shorter gravel tracks off the Ringroad to Þórsmörk and elsewhere, can be really rough. Not all are four-wheel-drive only, but if using them stay on any **marked tracks** to prevent damaging Iceland's fragile environment.

Vehicles easily **bog down** in snow, mud or soft sand, and if that happens it is vital to maintain **forward momentum**: while you're still moving forward, resist the temptation to change gear, as you'll lose your impetus by doing so. If you do stop moving forward, spinning wheels will quickly dig the vehicle in, so take your foot off the accelerator immediately. Hopefully you'll be able to reverse out, otherwise you'll have to start digging.

Four-wheel-drive-only roads – on which you may encounter stretches of sand, boulders, ice or river crossings – are designated with an "F" on road maps (for instance, the Sprengisandur route is F26), and should only be attempted in a suitable vehicle. **Precautions** include not tackling any four-wheel-drive roads alone; being properly equipped with all rescue gear and tools (and know in advance how to use them); and always carrying more than enough fuel, food and water. It's also wise to tell someone reliable where you're going and when you'll be back, so that a rescue can be mounted if you don't show – but don't forget to contact them when you do get back safely. You'll also need **advance information** on road and weather conditions; see box on p.31 for websites or try local tourist offices. Above all **heed local advice** and don't take chances – many people have drowned in their cars attempting to ford rivers in the Interior.

Rivers are potentially very dangerous, and come in two types. **Spring-fed rivers** have a constant flow; **glacial rivers** can fluctuate considerably depending on the time of day and prevailing weather conditions. These are at their lowest during the early morning and after a dry spell of weather; conversely, they can be much deeper in the afternoon once the sun has melted the glacial ice that feeds them, or when it's raining. Some rivers are bridged but many are not; **fords** are marked with a "V" on maps. You need to assess the depth and speed of the river first to find the best crossing point – never blindly follow other vehicle tracks – and to wear a **lifejacket** and tie yourself to a lifeline when entering the river to check its depth. If the water is going to come more than halfway up the wheels, slacken off the fan belt, block the engine's air intake, and waterproof electrics before crossing. Be sure to engage a low gear and four-wheel-drive before entering the water at a slow, steady pace; once in, don't stop (you'll either start sinking into the riverbed or get swept away), or change gear (which lets water into the clutch). If you stall mid-stream in deep water, turn off the ignition immediately, disconnect the battery, winch out, and don't restart until you've ensured that water hasn't entered the engine through the air filter – which will destroy the engine. If in doubt, it's much better to wait for the river to subside or for the weather to improve than to take risks.

Cycling

Bad roads, steep gradients and unpredictable weather don't make Iceland an obvious choice for a **cycling** holiday, but there are plenty of people who come here each summer just to pedal around. And if you're properly equipped, it's a great way to see the country close-up – you'll also save plenty of money over other forms of transport.

You'll need a solid, 18- or 24-speed **mountain bike** with chunky tyres. You can **rent** these from various agents in Iceland for around 2500kr a day. If you're **bringing your own bike** to Iceland by plane, or getting it from one end of the country to the other by air, you'll need to have the handlebars and pedals turned in, the front wheel removed and strapped to the back, and the tyres deflated.

There are bike shops in Reykjavík, Akureyri and a couple of the larger towns, but otherwise you'll have to provide all **spares** and carry out **repairs** yourself, or find a garage to help. Remember that there are plenty of areas, even on the Ringroad, where assistance may be several days' walk away, and that dust, sand, mud and water will place abnormal strains on your bike. You'll definitely suffer a few **punctures**, so bring a repair kit, spare tyre and tubes, along with the relevant tools, spare brake pads, spokes, chain links and cables.

Around the coast you shouldn't need excessively warm **clothing** – a sweater and waterproof in addition to your normal gear should be fine – but make sure it's all quick-drying. If travelling through the Interior, weatherproof jackets, leggings, gloves and headwear, plus ample warm clothing, are essential. Thick-soled neoprene **surf boots** will save cutting your feet on rocks during river crossings.

It's not unfeasible to cover around 90km a day on paved stretches of the Ringroad, but elsewhere the same distance might take three days and conditions may be so bad that you walk more than you ride. Give yourself four weeks to circuit the Ringroad at an easy pace – this would average around 50km a day. Make sure you've worked out how far it is to the next store before passing up the chance to buy **food**, and don't get caught out by supermarkets' short weekend hours (see p.52). **Off-road cycling** is prohibited in order to protect the landscape, so stick to the tracks.

If it all gets too much, put your bike on a **bus** for 1500kr. If there's space, bikes go in the luggage compartment; otherwise it will be tied to the roof or back. Either way, protect your bike by wrapping and padding it if possible.

For help in planning your trip – but not bike rental – contact the **Icelandic Mountain Bike Club** (Íslenski Fjallahjólaklúbburinn, or ÍFHK; Ⓦ www.fjallahjolaklubburinn.is), which organizes club weekends and has heaps of advice for cyclists. You can download most of this and contact staff through the website, which has English text.

Hitching

Hitching around Iceland is possible, at least if you have plenty of time. Expect less traffic the further you go from Reykjavík, and even on the Ringroad there are long stretches where you may go for hours without seeing a vehicle. Leave the Ringroad and you might even have to wait days for a lift, though in either case it's likely that the first car past will stop for you.

Having said this, holidaying Icelanders will probably already have their cars packed to capacity, so make sure you have as little gear as possible – without, of course, leaving behind everything you'll need to survive given the climate and long spaces between shops (see p.52). And though Iceland may be a safer place to hitch than elsewhere in Europe Australia, or the US, it still carries inherent risks, and the best advice is **not to do it**.

If you must hitch, never do so alone and remember that you don't have to get in just because someone stops. Given the wide gaps between settlements it will probably be obvious where you are heading for, but always ask the driver where they are going rather than saying where it is you want to go.

The best places to line up lifts are either at campsites, hostels or the fuel stations which sit on the outskirts of every settlement; it's possible, too, that staff in remoter places might know of someone heading your way.

Tours

Everywhere you go in Iceland you'll find **tours** on offer, ranging from whale-watching cruises, hikes, pony treks and snowmobile trips across southern glaciers, to bus safaris covering historic sites, interior deserts, hot springs and volcanoes or even joy flights over lakes and islands. Some of these things you can do independently, but in other cases you'll find that tours are the only practical way to reach somewhere.

They can last anything from a couple of hours to several days, with the widest range offered between June and September, though some, such as whale watching, are seasonal. **Booking in advance** is always a good idea, especially in the peak tourist months of July and August, when you may have to wait a couple of days before being able to get on the more popular excursions. **Details of tours** and operators are given throughout the guide. In winter – which as far as tourism is concerned lasts from September to May – many operators close completely, and those that remain open concentrate on four-wheel-driving and glacier exploration along the fringes of the southern ice caps, as the Interior itself is definitely off-limits by then. While bigger agents in Reykjavík offer trips almost daily in winter, don't expect to be able to just turn up at a small town off-season and get onto a tour – most will require a few days' advance warning in order to arrange everything.

Accommodation

In summer, almost every settlement in Iceland has somewhere to stay in the shape of a hotel, guesthouse, hostel or campsite. In addition, farms and some rural schools provide accommodation where you might not expect it. Almost all formal lodgings are found around the settled coastal band; if you're heading into the wilds at any stage, you'll need to camp or make use of huts.

Before setting out, pick up the **Áning brochure** from tourist information outlets, which lists most places to stay – though not all – and official campsites, along with their facilities. Hotels tend to stay open year-round, but many other places **shut down** from September to May, or need advance notice of your arrival outside the tourist season. Where places do stay open, winter rates are around 25 percent cheaper than summer ones.

In addition to a range of rooms, several types of places to stay offer budget accommodation. Where **made-up beds** are offered, you basically pay for a bed, not the room, so might end up sharing with strangers but for less than the price of a single room. **Sleeping-bag accommodation** is much the same thing and even cheaper, except only a bare bed or mattress is provided, hostel-style, and you supply all the bedding – so even if you don't intend to camp, it's worth bringing a sleeping bag to Iceland.

Accommodation organizations

Contact details for specific places to stay are given throughout the guide, many of which are run by the following organizations:
Edda Hlíðarfótur 101, Reykjavík ☎ 444 4000, ⓦ www.hoteledda.is. See p.38 for details.
Fosshótel Skipholt 50, 105 Reykjavík ☎ 562 4000, ⓦ www.fosshotel.is. Association of eleven mid-range hotels located at strategic points around the country, including Reykjavík and Akureyri.
Hostelling International Iceland Sundlaugavegur 34, 105 Reykjavík, ⓦ www.hostel.is (see p.38).
Icelandair ☎ 444 4000, ⓦ www.icelandairhotels .com. Seven upmarket hotels, mostly in southern Iceland.
Icelandic Farm Holidays Síðumúli 2, 108 Reykjavík ☎ 570 2700, ⓦ www.farmholidays.is.

Agent for several hundred farms offering accommodation around Iceland; the English-language brochure doesn't include individual farms' contact details, so try to pick up the Icelandic version as well.
Kea Hotels Hafnarstræti 87–89, 600 Akureyri ☎ 460 2000, ⓦ www.keahotels.is. Six top-notch hotels in Akureyri, Mývatn and Reykjavík.

Hotels and guesthouses

Icelandic **hotels** are typically elderly and gloomy or bland, modern, business-oriented blocks, though rooms are comfortable and well furnished as a rule. Bigger establishments might have their own pool, gym, sauna or even casino, and there will always be a restaurant, with breakfast included in the cost of a room. **Room rates** depend on the location and facilities, and start around 20,000kr for a double with en-suite bath, 15,000kr without, and about two-thirds of these prices for a single room with and without bath.

Guesthouses (*gistiheimilið*) tend to have more character than hotels, and they're often family-run. Rooms range from the barely furnished to the very comfortable, though facilities are usually shared, and you'll often find some budget accommodation available too. A breakfast of cereal, toast, cheese and coffee is sometimes included, or offered for an extra 950kr or so; some places can provide all meals with advance notice. As for **prices**, doubles cost 12,000kr or more; made-up beds are around 7500kr per person and sleeping-bag accommodation will be about 3500kr.

Farms

You'll find plenty of **farms** in Iceland (some with histories going back to saga times) which offer accommodation of some kind,

Accommodation price codes

Throughout this guide, prices given for **youth hostels** and **sleeping-bag accommodation** are per person, unless otherwise specified. **Hotel** and **guesthouse** accommodation is graded on a scale from ❶ to ❻, based on the price of the cheapest double room in high season. The price bands to which these codes refer are as follows:

❶ 5000–10,000kr   ❷ 10,001–15,000kr   ❸ 15,001–20,000kr
❹ 20,001–25,000kr   ❺ 25,001–30,000kr   ❻ 30,001kr and over

ranging from a room in the farmhouse to hostel-style dormitories or fully furnished, self-contained cabins. Many also encourage guests to take part in the daily routine, or offer horseriding, fishing, guided tours, or even four-wheel-drive safaris.

For the most part, farm **prices** are the same as for guesthouses; cabins usually sleep four or more and can work out a good deal for a group at around 20,000kr. Come prepared to cook for yourself, though meals are usually available if booked in advance.

Summer hotels and Edda

In Iceland, many country schools open up during the summer holidays as **summer hotels**, fifteen of which come under the **Edda** banner (see p.37 for contact details). They're aimed at the mid-range end of things, though many also provide sleeping-bag accommodation with shared facilities. Most have a thermally heated pool in the grounds and there's always a restaurant.

Prices at summer hotels start from 15,500kr for a double and, if available, 7500kr for a made-up bed and 2500kr for sleeping bags.

Hostels

Hostelling International Iceland (see p.37 for details) runs 33 hostels, ranging from big affairs in Reykjavík to old farmhouses sleeping four out in the country. All are owner-operated, have good self-catering kitchens and either offer bookings for local tours or organize them themselves. Some can also provide meals with advance notice and have laundry facilities. Quite a few are open all year too, though you'd be hard-pushed to reach remoter ones until winter is well and truly over – turn up out of season, however, and you'll often receive a warm welcome.

Whatever the time of year, you should **book in advance**; in summer, hostels are often full, and at other times, even if officially open, owners may simply lock up the house and head off somewhere for a few days if they're not expecting guests. Dormitory accommodation is the norm, either in made-up beds (up to 3600kr) or sleeping bags (2600kr), with around a 25 percent discount for holders of a Hostelling International card – you can buy these at Icelandic hostels, or before you leave home (see contact details below).

Youth hostel associations

A Hostelling International card will pay back its cost within about three nights at Icelandic hostels.

US and Canada

Hostelling International–American Youth Hostels US ☎1-301/495-1240, ⓦwww.hiusa.org. **Hostelling International Canada** ☎1-800/663-5777, ⓦwww.hihostels.ca.

UK and Ireland

Youth Hostel Association (YHA) UK ☎01629/592 700, ⓦwww.yha.org.uk. **Scottish Youth Hostel Association** UK ☎0845/293 7373, ⓦwww.syha.org.uk. **Irish Youth Hostel Association** Ireland ☎01/830 4555, ⓦwww.anoige.ie. **Hostelling International Northern Ireland** Northern Ireland ☎028/9032 4733, ⓦwww.hini.org.uk.

Australia, New Zealand and South Africa

Australia Youth Hostels Association Australia ☎02/9565 1699, ⓦwww.yha.com.au. **Youth Hostelling Association New Zealand** New Zealand ☎0800/278 299 or 03/379 9970, ⓦwww.yha.co.nz.

Camping

Camping is a great way to experience Iceland, especially during the light summer nights, when it's bright enough in your tent at midnight to feel like it's time to get up. You'll also minimize expenditure, whether you make use of the country's 150 or so campsites or set up for free in the nearest field. Camping is, however, a **summer-only** option: in winter, campsites and fields alike will probably be buried beneath a metre of snow.

Official campsites are only **open** between June and some point in September – though you're welcome to use them out of season if you can live without their facilities (just shower at the nearest pool). They vary from no-frills affairs with level ground, a toilet and cold running water, to those sporting windbreaks, hot showers (always 300–400kr extra), laundry, powerpoints, and sheltered kitchen areas. On-site shops are unusual, however, so stock up in advance. Campsites in the Interior are very barely furnished, usually with just a pit toilet. While some town campsites are free, **prices** usually come in at around 750kr per person per day.

A possible way to save costs here is to invest in a **Camping Card** (Ⓦwww .campingcard.is; €95), available online or at N1 fuel stations. This allows the holder, plus spouse and up to four children, to camp for free at 31 participating campsites around the country; two people can cover the cost of a card in around two weeks.

If you're doing extensive hiking or cycling there will be times that you'll have to **camp in the wild**. The main challenge here is to find a flat, rock-free space to pitch a tent. Where feasible, always **seek permission** for this at the nearest farmhouse before setting up; farmers don't usually mind – and often direct you to a good site – but may need to keep you away from pregnant stock or the like. Note, too, that in a few reserves such as Skaftafell and Jökulsárgljúfur camping is only permitted at designated areas. When camping wild, you can bury anything bio degradeable but should carry other rubbish out with you.

Camping equipment

Your **tent** is going to be severely tested, so needs to be in a good state of repair and built to withstand strong winds and heavy rain – a good-quality dome or tunnel design, with a space between the flysheet and the tent entrance where you can cook and store your backpack and boots out of the weather, is ideal. Whatever the conditions are when you set up, always use guy ropes, the maximum number of pegs, and a flysheet as the weather can change rapidly; in some places, especially in the Interior, it's also advisable to weight the pegs down with rocks.

Also invest in a decent **sleeping bag** – even in summer, you might have to cope with sub-zero conditions – and a **sleeping mat** for insulation as well as comfort. A waterproof sheet to put underneath your tent is also a good idea. Unless you find supplies of driftwood you'll need a **fuel stove** too, as Iceland's few trees are all protected. Butane gas canisters are sold in Reykjavík and many fuel stations around the country, but you're possibly better off with a pressure stove capable of taking a variety of more widely available fuels such as unleaded petrol (*býlaust*), kerosene (*steinolía*) or white spirit/shellite ("white spirit").

As for **camping food**, never buy purpose-made stuff from specialist stores – most brands are expensive and barely palatable even when you're too exhausted to care after a hard day's hike. Normal boil/microwave-in-the-bag meals from the nearest supermarket are far cheaper and can't taste any worse.

Mountain huts

At popular hiking areas and throughout interior Iceland you'll encounter **mountain huts**, which are maintained by Iceland's hiking organizations (see p.45). These can be lavish, multistorey affairs with kitchen areas and dormitories overseen by wardens, or very basic wooden bunkhouses that simply offer a dry retreat from the weather, and **cost** 2500–3500kr accordingly. You'll always have to supply bedding and food and should **book well in advance** through the relevant organization, particularly at popular sites such as Þórsmörk and Landmannalaugar (see p.134 & p.123). If you haven't booked – or can't produce a **receipt** to prove it – you may get in if there's room, but otherwise you'll have to pitch a tent; wardens are very strict about this, so if you don't have a tent to fall back on, you might find yourself having to hike to the next available hut late in the day.

Emergency huts, painted bright orange to show up against snow, are sometimes not so remote – you'll see them at a few places around the Ringroad where drivers might get stranded by sudden heavy snowfalls. Stocked with food and fuel, and run by the SVFÍ (Iceland's national life-saving association), these huts are for emergency use only; if you have to use one, fill out the guestbook stating what you used and where you were heading, so that stocks can be maintained and rescue crews will know to track you down if you don't arrive at your destination.

Food and drink

Although Iceland's food is unlikely to be the highlight of your trip, things have improved from the early 1980s, when beer was illegal and canned soup supplemented dreary daily doses of plain-cooked lamb or fish. The country's low industrial output and high environmental consciousness – the use of hormones in livestock feed is forbidden, for instance – means that its meat, fish and seafood are some of the healthiest in Europe, with hothouses providing a fair range of vegetables and even some fruit.

While in Reykjavík and Akureyri the variety of food is pretty well what you'd find at home, menus elsewhere are far less exciting – with sheep outnumbering the people by four to one, there's a lot of lamb to get through. You'll often find some variety to the standby grills or stews, however, even if salads have yet to really catch on; otherwise fast food or cooking for yourself will have to see you through.

Traditional foods

Iceland's cold climate and long winters meant that the settlers' original diet was low in vegetables and high in cereals, fish and meat, with **preserved foods** playing a big role. Some of the following traditional foods are still eaten every day; others crop up mainly at special occasions such as the mid-winter Þorramatur feasts, though restaurants may serve them year round.

Harðifiskur, wind-dried haddock or cod, is a popular snack, eaten by tearing off a piece and chewing away, though some people like to spread butter on it first. Most Icelandic **seafood** is superb – there are restaurants in Reykjavík, Hafnarfjörður and Stokkseyri which specialize in **lobster** – and even everyday things like a breakfast of **sild** (pickled herrings) are worth trying. **Hákarl** (Greenland shark) is a more doubtful delicacy, as it is first buried for up to six months in sand to break down the high levels of toxins contained in its flesh. Different parts of the rotted shark yield either white or dark meat, and the advice for beginners is to start on the milder-tasting dark (*gler hákarl*), which is translucent – rather like smoked glass. Either way, the flavour is likely to make your eyes water, even if connoisseurs compare the taste and texture favourably to a strong cheese. Don't feel bad if you can't stomach the stuff, because neither can many Icelanders.

As for meat, there's ordinary **hangikjöt**, which is hung, smoked lamb, popular in sandwiches and as part of a traditional Christmas spread; **svið**, boiled and singed sheep's heads; haggis-like varieties of **slátur** ("slaughter"), of which blood pudding (*blóðmör*) is a favourite; and a whole range of scraps pressed into cakes and pickled in whey, collectively known as **súrmatur** – leftover svið is often prepared like this, as is súrsaðir hrútspungar, or pickled rams' testicles.

Game dishes include the grouse-like ptarmigan (rjúpa), which takes the place of turkey at Icelandic Christmas dinners; an occasional reindeer (hreindýr) in the east of the country; and puffin (lundi) in the south, which is usually smoked before being cooked. In a few places you'll also come across whale or seal meat, as both are still hunted in limited numbers. Rather more appealing to non-Icelandic palates, lobster, **salmon** (lax), **trout** (silingur) and **char** (bleikja) are all superb and relatively inexpensive. In addition to smoked salmon or trout, try the similar-looking gravað, whereby the fish is marinated with herbs until it's soft and quite delicious.

About the only endemic **vegetable** is fjalla-grös, a type of lichen that's dried into almost tasteless, resilient black curls and snacked on raw or cooked with milk. Home-produced **cheese** and dairy products are very good, and it's worth trying yogurt-like **skyr**, sold all over the country plain or flavoured with fruit. **Pancakes** known as flatbrauð or laufabrauð are traditionally eaten at Christmas, and a few places – notably near Mývatn in northeastern Iceland – bake a delicious **rye bread** called hverabrauð in underground ovens (see p.261).

Drinks

It's been said with some justification that Iceland runs on **coffee**, with just about everyone in the country firmly hooked. There's a definite café culture in the cities – and a national generic café chain, Kaffitar – and decent quality brews are offered even at rural cafés. In some supermarkets, hot thermoses of free coffee are laid on for customers to help themselves, and wherever you pay for a cup, the price usually includes a refill or two. **Tea** is also pretty popular, though not consumed with such enthusiasm. **Bottled water** and familiar brands of **soft drinks** are available everywhere. **Milk** comes in a bewildering range of styles, making a trip to the supermarket fridge quite a challenge if you can't read Icelandic. Mjolk is normal full-fat milk, Lettmjolk is skimmed,

AB Mjolk is plain runny yoghurt, and G-Mjolk is UHT milk.

Alcohol

Alcohol is expensive – bring a bottle of duty-free in with you to save costs – and, with the exception of beer, only sold in bars, clubs, restaurants and state-owned liquor stores known as **vinbúð**. These are often tucked out of sight in distant corners of towns and cities, and always have ludicrously restricted opening hours – sometimes just an hour, five days a week. Most Icelanders drink very hard when they put their minds to it, most often at parties or on camping trips – the August bank holiday weekend is notorious. It's surprising, then, to find that full-strength **beer** was actually illegal until March 1989, when the 75-year-old prohibition laws were revoked. In Reykjavík, March 1 is still celebrated as **Bjórdagurinn**, or Beer Day, with predictably riotous celebrations organized at bars throughout the capital. Beer is available in many supermarkets, and comes as relatively inexpensive, low-alcohol pilsner, and more expensive, stronger lagers.

All wine and most spirits are imported, though hard-liquor enthusiasts should try **brennivín**, a local spirit distilled from potatoes and flavoured with caraway seeds. It's powerful stuff, affectionately known as svarti dauði or "black death", and certainly warms you up in winter – you'll also welcome its traditional use to clean the palate after eating fermented shark.

Restaurants, cafés and bars

Just about every settlement in Iceland has a **restaurant** of some sort. In Reykjavík, and to a lesser extent Akureyri and the larger towns, you can get everything from traditional Icelandic fare to Mexican, Thai, Chinese, and Italian- and French-inspired dishes, and there are even a couple of vegetarian places. This is the most expensive way to dine – expect to pay upwards of 2500kr for a main dish – though keep your eyes peeled for lunchtime **specials** offered, or inexpensive fixed-price meals of soup, bread and stew.

All-you-can-eat **smorgasbords** or buffets also crop up, especially around Christmas, when restaurants seem to compete with each other over the calorie contents of their spreads of cold meats and **cakes** – the latter something of a national institution.

In the country, pickings are far slimmer. Some **hotel restaurants** have fine food, though it's more often filling than particularly memorable; prices can be as high as in any restaurant, but are generally lower. Otherwise, the only place offering cooked food might be the nearest **fuel station café**, which will whip up fast fodder such as **pylsur** (hot dogs), burgers, grills, sandwiches and **pizzas** – virtually Iceland's national dish – for a few hundred krónur.

Found all over the country, **bars**, besides being somewhere to have a drink, also usually sell meals and are frequently decorated along particular themes – decked out 1950s-style, for example, or hung with fishing memorabilia. **Coffee houses** are less widespread, confined mostly to the cities and a couple of towns, offering light meals, coffee and cakes.

Self-catering

Self-catering will save a lot over eating out, though ingredients still cost more than they do at home – again, you might want to bring some supplies (especially camping rations) with you to save money. There are very few specialist food shops besides bakeries, but at least one **supermarket** in all villages, towns and cities. Don't expect to find them attached to campsites, however, and when travelling about, buy supplies when you can, don't get caught short by weekend shop hours, and know where the next supermarket is. There are no shops in the Interior.

Larger supermarkets can be well stocked with plenty of fresh fruit and vegetables – especially in "hothouse towns" such as Hveragerði in southern Iceland – plus fish and meat. Rural stores, however, may have little more than a few imported apples and oranges and a shelf or two of canned and dried food. Iceland grows its own capsicums, mushrooms, tomatoes and cucumbers, plus plenty of berries and a few bananas, but most other things are imported and therefore fairly expensive.

The media

Iceland's main **daily paper** is the right-wing *Morgunblaðið*, available all over the country and giving thorough coverage of national and international news. If your Icelandic isn't up to it, you can get a roundup of the main stories through the **Iceland Review**, an English-language newsheet giving good outlines about main national stories – it's available in Reykjavík's newsagents or online at ⓦwww.icelandreview.com. Reykjavík's bookshops – and libraries around the country – also have copies of **British and US newspapers**, though supply is erratic and sometimes a week or more out of date. International magazines such as *Time* and *National Geographic* are also available from the same sources, and the now defunct **Icelandic Geographic** is worth getting hold of if you can find a copy, for stunning wildlife and landscape photography.

Iceland's **radio stations** play a mind-numbingly repetitive menu of commercial pop, classical music and talk-back shows. The three **television channels** show a familiar mix of soaps, dramas, films and documentaries. All these media are predominantly Icelandic-language only, though films and TV shows are screened in their original language with subtitles.

Festivals

Though Iceland's calendar is predominantly Christian, many official holidays and festivals have a secular theme, and at least one dates from pagan times. Some are already familiar: **Christmas** and **Easter Monday** are both holidays in Iceland and are celebrated as elsewhere in the Western world, as is **New Year**.

Harking back to the Viking era, however, **Þorrablót** is a midwinter celebration originally honouring the weather god Þorri, and became something to look forward to during the bleakest time of the year. It is held throughout February, when people throw parties centred around the consumption of traditional foods such as *svið* and *hákarl* (see p.40), with some restaurants also laying on special menus.

Sjomannadagur, or Seamen's Day (June 4), unsurprisingly, is one of the biggest holidays of the year, with communities organizing mock sea-rescue demonstrations, swimming races and tug-of-war events. This is followed by another break for **Independence Day** (June 17), the day that the Icelandic state separated from Denmark in 1944.

Although not an official holiday, **Jónsmessa**, on June 24, is the day that elves and other magical creatures are said to be out in force, playing tricks on the unwary; some people celebrate with a big bonfire, and it's also meant to be good for your health to run around naked.

Verslunnarmannahelgi, the Labour Day Weekend, takes place around the country on the first weekend in August. Traditionally, everybody heads into the countryside, sets up camp, and spends the rest of the holiday drinking and partying themselves into oblivion; hit any campsite in the country at this time and you'll be sharing it with thousands of drunken teenagers. On Heimaey in the Westman Islands, **Þjóðhátíð** is held on the same day and celebrated in the same way – there's live music, too, and a huge bonfire – though it nominally commemorates Iceland's achieving partial political autonomy in 1874.

One event to look out for, though it's not a single festival, is the annual stock round-up, or **rettir**, which takes place in rural areas throughout September. This is when horses and sheep are herded on horseback down from the higher summer pastures to be penned and sorted; some farms offering accommodation allow guests to watch or even participate.

Sports and outdoor activities

Iceland has its own wrestling style, called *glíma* – a former Olympic sport where opponents try to throw each other by grabbing one another's belts – and there's a serious football (soccer) following; the Reykjavík Football Club was founded in 1899, and an Icelandic consortium owns the English-league club Stoke City. Otherwise, there's not a great obsession with sport, and with most people here go outside not to play games but to work or enjoy the Great Outdoors.

The lava plains, black-sand deserts, glacier-capped plateaus, alpine meadows, convoluted fjords and capricious volcanoes that make Iceland such an extraordinary place scenery-wise also offer tremendous potential for outdoor activities, whether you've come for wildlife or to hike, ride, ski, snowmobile or four-wheel-drive your way across the horizon. Further information on these activities is always at hand in local tourist offices, while you can find out more about the few national parks and reserves from the Department of Forestry or various Icelandic hiking organizations (see p.45). Many activities can be undertaken as part of an organized tour, sometimes with the necessary gear supplied or available for rent. Before you set out to do anything too adventurous, however, check your insurance cover.

Swimming and hot pots

You probably won't be coming to Iceland to **swim**, but in fact this is a major social activity year-round with Icelanders, and it's a great way to meet people or just see them unwinding – it seems mandatory for businessmen to have a dip on their way to work. Just about every settlement in Iceland has a swimming pool, usually an outdoor affair and heated by the nearest hot spring to around 28°C. In addition, there are almost always one or two spa baths or **hot pots**, providing much hotter soaks at 35–40°C – another great Icelandic institution, and particularly fun in winter, when you can sit up to your neck in scalding water while the snow falls thickly around you. Out in the wilds, hot pots are replaced by **natural hot springs** – a great way to relax trail-weary muscles. Note that Icelandic swimming pools have separate

male and female changing rooms but no private cubicles; and at all official swimming pools you are required to shower with soap before getting in the water.

Fishing

As Iceland is surrounded by the richest fishing grounds in the North Atlantic, **sea fishing** has always been seen as more of a career than a sport. The country's rivers and lakes, however, are also well stocked with **salmon** and **trout**, pulling in hordes of fly fishers during the **fishing season** (April 1 to September 20 for trout; June 20 to mid-September for salmon). Both fish are plentiful in all the country's bigger waterways, though the finest salmon are said to come from the Laxá (which means Salmon River), in northeast Iceland, and the Rangá in the south. During the winter, people cut holes in the ice and fish for **arctic char**; the best spots for this are at Þingvallavatn and Mývatn (see p.111 & p.252).

You always need a **permit** to fish. Those for char or trout are fairly inexpensive and easy to obtain on the spot from local tourist offices and some accommodation, but those for salmon are always pricey and often need to be reserved months in advance, as there is a limit per river. For further information, contact the **Federation of Icelandic River Owners**, Baendahöllinni, Hagatorg, 107 Reykjavik (☎553 1510, ⓦwww.angling.is), whose website has a huge amount of English-language information about trout and salmon fishing in Iceland.

Hiking

Hiking gets you closer to the scenery than anything else in Iceland. In reserves and the couple of national parks you'll find a few **marked trails**, and where they exist you should always stick to them in order to minimize erosion. Elsewhere you'll need to be competent at using a map and compass to navigate safely over the lava, sand, rivers and ice you'll find along the way.

Whether you're planning to spend a weekend making short hikes, or two weeks crossing the Interior, it's essential to come properly equipped. Always carry warm, weatherproof **clothing**, food and **water** (there are plenty of places in Iceland where porous soil makes finding surface water unlikely), as well as a torch, lighter, penknife, **first aid kit**, a foil insulation blanket and a whistle or mirror for attracting attention. The country is carpeted in sharp rocks and rough ground, so good-quality, tough **hiking boots** are essential – though an old pair of sports shoes, or a pair of neoprene surf boots with thick soles are useful to ford rivers.

On lava, watch out for **volcanic fissures**, cracks in the ground ranging from a few inches to several metres across, which are usually very deep. These are dangerous enough when you can see them, but blanketed by snow they'll be invisible. Another hazard is **river crossings**, which you'll have to make on various trails all over the country. River levels are at their lowest first thing in the morning, and rise through the day as the sun melts the glacial ice and snow that feed into them. When looking for a crossing point, remember the river will be shallowest at its widest point; before crossing, make sure that your backpack straps are loose so that if necessary you can ditch it in a hurry. Face into the current as you cross and be prepared to give up if the water gets above your thighs. Never

attempt a crossing alone, and remember that some rivers have no safe fords at all if you're on foot – you'll have to hitch across in a vehicle.

When and where to hike

The **best months** for hiking are from June through to August, when the weather is relatively warm, wildflowers are in bloom, and the wildlife is out and about – though even then the Interior and higher ground elsewhere can get snowbound at short notice. Outside the prime time, weather is very problematic and you probably won't even be able to reach the area you want to explore, let alone hike around it.

One of the beauties of Iceland is that you can walk just about anywhere, assuming you can cope with local conditions, though there are, of course, some highlights. Close to Reykjavík, the **Reykjanes Peninsula** (see p.196) offers extended treks across imposingly desolate lava rubble; there are some short, easy hikes along steaming valleys near **Hveragerði** (see p.115), while trails at **Þingvellir** (see p.106) include historic sites and an introduction to rift valley geology. Further east, **Laugavegur** (see p.124) is an exceptional four-day trail; and **Þórsmörk** (see p.134) is one of the most popular hiking spots in the country, a wooded, elevated valley surrounded by glaciers and mountain peaks with a well-trodden network of paths.

Along the west coast, the **Snæfellsnes Peninsula** (see p.170) is notoriously damp but peaks with the ice-bound summit of Snæfellsjökull, the dormant volcano used as a fictional gateway into the centre of the Earth by writer Jules Verne. Further north there's **Hornstrandir** (see p.197), the wildest and

Icelandic hiking organizations

For advance information on popular hiking areas such as Þórsmörk or Landmannalaugar, or simply if you want to sign up for an organized hike, Iceland has two **hiking organizations** to contact: **Ferðafélag Íslands** (The Touring Club of Iceland, Mörkin 6, IS-108 Reykjavík; ☎568 2533, ☏568 2535, ⊛www.fi.is) and **Útivist** (Hallaveigarstigur 1, IS-101 Reykjavík; ☎561 4330, ☏561 4606, ⊛www.utivist.is). Both run guided treks of a couple of days' duration to a week or longer – though groups can be very large – and maintain various mountain huts in reserves and the Interior where you can book a bunk.

most isolated extremity of the Westfjords, a region of twisted coastlines, sheer cliffs and rugged hill walks. Those after an easier time should head to **Mývatn** (see p.252), the shallow northeastern lake where you can make simple day-hikes to extinct craters, billowing mud-pits, and still steaming lava flows; longer but also relatively easy are the well-marked riverside trails around nearby **Jökulsárgljúfur National Park** (see p.268), which features some awesome canyon scenery. Over in the east, the best of the hikes take in the highland moors and glaciated fringes of the massive Vatnajökull ice cap: at **Snæfell** (see p.286), a peak inland from Egilsstaðir; **Lónsöræfi reserve** (see p.297) near Höfn; and **Skaftafell National Park** (see p.303), another riotously popular camping spot on Vatnajökull's southern edge.

Horseriding

Horses came to Iceland with the first settlers, and, due to a tenth-century ban on their further import to stop equine diseases arriving in the country, have remained true to their original stocky Scandinavian breed. Always used for **riding**, horses also had a religious place in Viking times and were often dedicated or sacrificed to the pagan gods; with the advent of Christianity, eating horse meat was banned, being seen as a sign of paganism. Nowadays, horses are used for the autumn livestock round-up, and for recreational purposes.

Icelandic horses are sturdy, even-tempered creatures, and in addition to the usual walk, trot, gallop and canter, can move smoothly across rough ground using the gliding **tölt** gait. The biggest breeding centres are in the country's relatively mild south, but horses are available for **hire** from farms all over Iceland, for anything from an hour in the saddle to two-week-long treks across the Interior. Places to hire horses are given throughout the guide, but to organize something in **advance**, contact Íshestar (ⓦwww.ishestar.is) or Eldhestar (ⓦwww.eldhestar.is), which run treks of all lengths and experience levels right across the country.

Snow and action sports

Snow sports – which in Iceland are not just practised in winter – have, surprisingly, only

recently begun to catch on. Partly this is because the bulk of Iceland's population lives in the mild southwestern corner of the country, but also because snow was seen as just something you had to put up with; cross-country skiing, for instance, is such a fact of life in the northeastern winters that locals refer to it simply as "walking", and were baffled when foreign tour operators first brought in groups to do it for fun.

The possibilities for **cross-country skiing** are pretty limitless in winter, though you'll have to bring in your own gear. **Downhill skiing and snowboarding** are the most popular snow sports, with winter slopes at Bláfjöll (ⓦwww.skidasvaedi.is; see p.90), only 20km from Reykjavík.

Plenty of tour operators offer glacier trips on **snowmobiles** or **skidoos**, which are like jet-skis for snow – the only way for the inexperienced to get a taste of Iceland's massive ice fields, and huge fun. If you're more water-oriented, several of south-western Iceland's larger rivers have caught the attention of **whitewater rafting** enthusiasts (contact Arctic Rafting, ⓦwww.arcticrafting.is, for more information), while

Iceland also has surprisingly good **scuba diving** potential, the prime sites being in Þingvallavatn's cool but amazingly clear waters, at various shipwrecks, and at seal colonies around the coast: Dive Iceland (www.dive.is) can sort out the details, though you'll need dry-suit skills.

Travel essentials

Children

Iceland presents few difficulties for **travelling with children**. Icelanders are very child-friendly people; cities and towns are relatively safe, low-crime places with familiar amenities; and **supermarkets and pharmacies** are well stocked with nappies, formula and anything else you might need (though you do need to keep in mind where the next shops might be in the countryside). **Boredom** might be a problem on long car journeys between sights, though the many **swimming pools** make great places to let off steam once you arrive somewhere.

However, an awareness of the country's **natural dangers** is very much taken for granted in Iceland: there are **few warning signs** or barriers at waterfalls, hot springs, cliffs, crevasses and the like, so children must be supervised at all times in the countryside. Along with everyone else, children also need to come prepared for the **weather**, with plenty of warm, waterproof clothing and tough shoes for use outdoors.

Costs

Due to its small consumer base and dependency on imports, Iceland is an extremely **expensive** country to visit – though the **economic crash** of 2008 has made it slightly more affordable than before. To minimize costs, you need to be as **self-sufficient** as possible: bring food and a sleeping bag if you're intending to use self-catering budget accommodation, along with a tent and all camping gear if camping. Icelandic **bus passes** (see p.31) will minimize transport costs, and a **Hostelling** **International Card** (see p.38) will get you a few hundred krónur a night off official Youth Hostel rates. **Seasons** also affect costs: places to stay and car-rental agencies drop their prices between October and May, though at that time inexpensive summer-only accommodation will be shut, campsites will probably be under snow, and bus services are infrequent or suspended.

Budget travellers who camp out every night, use a bus pass and cook for themselves, can keep average **daily costs** down to around 6000kr (though cyclists can cut this in half). Throw in a few nights in hostel-style accommodation and the occasional pizza and you're looking at 8000kr. Mid-range travel still means using a bus pass to get around, but favouring hostels and eating out cheaply most of the time; this will set you back about 8500kr a day. Staying only in guesthouses or hotels and eating in restaurants for every meal means that you're looking at daily expenses of upwards of 20,000kr.

None of the above takes into account **additional costs** for entertainment such as tours, entry fees, drinking (an extremely expensive pastime in Iceland – see p.41), or alternative transport such as flights and ferries, for which we've given prices in the guide. **Car rental** will add a minimum 13,000kr a day, plus fuel, to daily expenses – see p.33 for more about this.

If you spend more than 4000kr total in any single transaction on goods to take out of the country, you are entitled to a **tax refund** of 15 percent of the total price, as long as you leave Iceland within 90 days. Ask for a **Refund Tax Free form** when you make your purchases, which needs to be filled out by the shop. Money is refunded in cash at **refund points** located in the departure halls at Keflavík, Reykjavík and Akureyri airports; the bank inside the Seðisfjörður ferry terminal; and either on board all international cruise ships two hours before departure, or at Reykjavík port's Visitor Centre. To have the refund made directly into a **credit card account**, ask at the refund point for an Iceland Refund envelope, and then mail the Refund Form back from outside the country. Further details can be found at ⓦwww.eurorefund.com.

Crime and personal safety

Iceland is a peaceful country, and it's unlikely that you'll encounter much trouble here. Most public places are well lit and secure, people are helpful, if somewhat reserved, and street crime and hassles are rare. Needless to say, hitching alone, or wandering around central Reykjavík late at night, is unwise.

Most incidents involve **petty crime** and are largely confined to Reykjavík. Many criminals are drug addicts or alcoholics after easy money; keep tabs on your cash and passport (and don't leave anything visible in your car when you park it) and you should have little reason to visit the **police**. If you do seek them out, you'll find them unarmed, concerned and usually able to speak English – remember to get an insurance report from them if you have anything stolen.

As for **offences** you might commit, **drink-driving** is taken extremely seriously here, so don't do it: catch a taxi. Being **drunk** in public in Reykjavík might also get you into trouble, but in a country campsite you probably won't be the only one, and (within reason) nobody is going to care. **Drugs**, however, are treated as harshly here as in much of the rest of Europe.

Sexual harassment is less of a problem here than elsewhere in Europe; although in Reykjavík clubs you might receive occasional unwelcome attentions – or simply be taken aback by the blatant atmosphere – there's very rarely any kind of violent intent. If you do have any problems, the fact that almost everyone understands English makes it easy to get across an unambiguous response.

Culture and etiquette

Iceland is a modern, egalitarian, outgoing country, and public behaviour is pretty much the same as wherever you've come in from – though perhaps a little less inhibited in Reykjavík's nightclubs. Icelanders themselves are especially proud of their country's modernity, its written culture and the fact that many people can trace their family histories right back to Saga times: they are apt to be thin-skinned about depictions of Iceland as a nation of backwards, axe-wielding Beserkers in horned helmets.

Discussing the **environment** can lead to heated arguments; over-grazing of sheep has caused serious erosion over the centuries, and the right to continue whaling is pursued as a cultural issue. Pride in their heritage occasionally surfaces as low-level **racism**, though with noticeable populations of Chinese, Thai and Philippino migrants settled in Reykjavík, not to mention tourists of all nationalities passing through, this is not a major a issue.

Electricity

Electricity is 240v, 50Hz AC. Plugs are round pin with either two or three prongs; appliances fitted with overseas plugs need an adaptor.

Entry requirements

Citizens from Schengen countries, the European Economic Area, the US, Canada, Australia, New Zealand and many other nations require **no visa** to visit Iceland for up to three months providing that their passport is valid for at least three months after the date of arrival. For the full list, and information on how to apply for a visa if you do require one, contact the Icelandic Directorate of Immigration (ⓦwww.utl.is).

As regards **customs regulations**, all visitors to Iceland, irrespective of country of origin, can bring in the following: up to three kilos of food (but no uncooked meat of any sort); and either one litre of spirits and one litre of wine, or one litre of spirits and six litres of beer, or one litre of wine and six litres of beer or two litres of wine. In addition to this, 200 cigarettes, or 250g of other tobacco products, are also permitted.

Icelandic embassies abroad

Australia and New Zealand Contact the Icelandic Embassy in China: Landmark Tower 1 #802, No.8 Dongsanhuan Bei Lu, Beijing 100004 ☎010/6590 7795, ⓦwww.iceland.org/cn/english.

Canada Constitution Square, 360 Albert St, Suite 710, Ottawa, Ontario K1R 7X7 ☎613/482-1944, ⓦwww.iceland.org/ca. Consulate General, One Wellington Crescent, Suite 100, Winnipeg, Manitoba R3M 3Z2 ☎204/284-1535, ⓦwww.iceland.org/ca/win; plus consulates in Edmonton, St John's, Halifax, Toronto, Montreal and Regina.

Republic of Ireland Contact the Icelandic Embassy in the UK.

UK 2A Hans St, London SW1X 0JE ☎020/7259 3999, ⓦwww.iceland.org/uk.

US 1156 15th St NW, Suite 1200, Washington DC 20005-1704 ☎202/265-6653, ⓦwww.iceland .org/us; Consulate General, 800 3rd Ave, 36th Floor, New York, NY ☎212/593-2700; plus consulates in Phoenix, Tallahassee, Anchorage, San Francisco, Miami, Chicago, Atlanta, Louisville, New Orleans, Boston, Detroit, Minneapolis, Kansas City, New York, Harrisburg, Dallas, Houston, Norfolk and Seattle.

Gay and lesbian travellers

Iceland is a very small and closely knit society, where it's generally said that two Icelanders meeting for the first time can usually find people they know in common – not exactly ideal conditions for a thriving **gay scene** to develop. Indeed, for years many gay people upped and left for the other Nordic capitals, most notably Copenhagen, where attitudes were more liberal and it was easier to be anonymous.

The **Icelandic gay and lesbian association**, Samtökin 78 (Laugavegur 3, ☎552 7878, ⓦwww.samtokin78.is), promotes awareness of homosexuality and gay rights at a political level and also offers a support network, not only in Reykjavík, but also out in rural communities, where attitudes towards homosexuality are not nearly as enlightened. The bar culture that has slowly but surely developed in Reykjavík since the 1990s also means that the city is now confident enough to boast several **gay bars** (see p.87), though there isn't a single gay bar or any gay scene to speak of in the provinces.

Samtökin's efforts have certainly paid off at the political level – after much lobbying, Iceland's politicians not only agreed to allow **gay marriage** in 1996 (in effect the right to register legally a partnership between two same-sex partners thus granting legal parity with straight couples), but also to allow gay men and lesbians to adopt children, making Iceland the first country in the world to pass such progressive legislation.

Health

Iceland's health care is excellent and available in most communities. Tourist offices or accommodation can recommend doctors and hospitals – all of whom will be English speaking. There's at least one **pharmacy**, or *apotek*, in every town, as well stocked as any chemist you'll find at home. Most open during normal business hours, though some in Reykjavík and Akureyri stay open longer. **No vaccinations** are required for visitors to Iceland.

To avoid being charged for **emergency healthcare** in Iceland, Scandinavian citizens must show medical insurance and a valid passport, while citizens of the European Economic Area can simply show their European Health Insurance Card and passport at a health centre or hospital for free treatment (see ⓦwww.dh.gov.uk/travellers). Citizens of other countries need to contact the nearest Icelandic Embassy or representative for information on whether they qualify; if not, you'll have to pay at the time and then claim back the money from your travel insurance.

If you're spending much time outdoors, be aware that the weather and distance might cause difficulties if you need medical attention in a hurry, and it's wise to carry a **first-aid kit**. Two important items to include are a roll of elasticated sticking plaster (band aids) and crepe bandages – both vital for supporting and splinting sprained muscles or broken bones.

Most problems you'll encounter, however, are minor. Though you might not think the northern **sun** would be much trouble, it's still strong enough to cause sunburn and eyestrain – especially when reflected off ice or snow – so use sunscreen and sun glasses. Some sort of hand cream or moisturizer and lip balm are a good idea too, as the **cold dry air**, wind and dust can painfully crack exposed skin. Eye drops will also relieve irritation caused by dust. **Flies** are not the problem in Iceland that they can be in Scandinavia; Mývatn (see p.252) is the only place you'll encounter them in plague proportions, though very few bite. **Water** is safe to drink throughout Iceland.

About the most serious thing to worry about is **hypothermia**, wherein your core body temperature drops to a point that can be fatal. In Iceland, it's most likely to occur if you get exhausted, wet and cold while out hiking or cycling; symptoms include a weak pulse, disorientation, numbness, slurred speech and exhaustion. If you suspect hypothermia, seek shelter from the weather, get the patient as dry as possible, and prevent further heat loss – aside from clothing, a foil "space blanket" available from camping stores will help. Sugary drinks can also help (alcohol definitely doesn't), but serious cases need immediate hospital treatment. The best advice is to avoid hypothermia in the first place: while hiking, ensure you eat enough carbohydrates, drink plenty of water and wear sufficient warm and weatherproof clothing, including a woollen hat – most body heat is lost through the head – and gloves. During the colder parts of the year, **motorists** should always carry a blanket and warm gear too, in case they get stranded by snow.

Insurance

Travel insurance policies provide a certain level of cover for medical treatment and loss of personal items, as well as unforeseen cancellation or curtailment of your journey. Cover for **adventure activities** such as whitewater-rafting, snow sports and trekking, usually incurs an extra premium. Read the small print of prospective policies carefully; cover can vary wildly for roughly similar premiums. Also make sure you check the level of **excess**, the amount of each claim that you have to pay.

With **medical coverage**, ascertain whether benefits will be paid as treatment proceeds or only after return home, and whether there is a 24-hour medical emergency number. When securing **baggage cover**, make sure that the per-article limit – typically under £500 equivalent – will cover your most valuable possession. If you need to **make a claim**, you should keep receipts for medicines and medical treatment, and in the event you have anything stolen, you must obtain an official statement from the police.

Internet

Iceland is one of the highest per-capita users of the **internet**, with most homes and businesses connected. Along with many Reykjavík cafés and some accommodation around the country providing free wi-fi for customers, public libraries or tourist offices often have terminals with access at around 350–1000kr an hour.

Laundry

Outside Reykjavík, which has a public laundromat (see p.91), you'll only find laundry facilities at accommodation or better-equipped campgrounds.

Living in Iceland

European Economic Area nationals may stay longer than three months on condition that they secure **work** for a further period of at least three months. Once in employment, there is no time limit on the length of stay in Iceland but **residence and work permits** are required; check with the Directorate of Immigration (Ⓦwww.utl.is) and the Directorate of Labour (Ⓦwww.vinnumalastofnun.is) for information. Non-EU nationals must apply for residence permits before leaving home, and must be able to prove they can support themselves without working.

Mail

Post offices are located in all major communities and are open from 9am until 4.30pm Monday to Friday, though a few in Reykjavík have longer hours. **Domestic mail** will generally get to the nearest post office within two working days, though a recipient living out on a farm might not collect it so quickly. For **international post** count on three to five days for mail to reach the UK or US, and a week to ten days to reach Australia and New Zealand. Anything up to 20g costs 70kr within Iceland, 110kr to Europe, and 120kr to anywhere else; up to 50g costs 80/170/190kr. International parcels aren't outrageously expensive – check Ⓦwww .postur.is for rates – but not particularly fast; ask at any post office about Express Mail if you're in a hurry, though you'll pay far more than for the normal service.

Post restante facilities are available at all post offices; have mail sent to the relevant office marked "to be collected" in English and turn up with your passport. **Addresses** in Iceland are always written with the number after the street name. If you can't find an expected letter, check that it hasn't been filed, Icelandic-style, under your first name; it might help to have your surname underlined on the letter.

Maps

A range of excellent **maps** of the country, costing upwards of 1300kr, is available for all types of use – if you can't find what you want overseas, you'll be able to pick it up in Reykjavík and Akureyri, or sometimes from local tourist offices and fuel stations. In addition to the maps detailed below, Iceland's hiking clubs (see p.45) and national parks put out a few maps of varying quality for popular nature reserves and national parks (available from park offices on-site).

Landmælingar Íslands, the National Land Survey of Iceland (Ⓦwww.lmi.is), no longer publishes its own maps, but its website is a trove of satellite mapping and online versions of its beautifully drawn but dated *Uppdráttúr* series, covering the entire country at between 1:50,000 and 1:100,000 – it's worth buying old printed versions as a souvenir if you come across copies anywhere.

Printed maps are published by the Reykjavík bookshop **Mál og menning** and **Ferðakort** (Ⓦwww.ferdakort.is). Both produce single-sheet road maps of the entire country, along with four or five separate regional sheets at around 1:300,000. Ferðakort's speciality are detailed maps, suitable for hiking, of specific areas such as Westman Islands, Hornstrandir, Skaftafell and so on at 1:25,000–1:200,000; **Mál og menning** has a few of these too, along with a range of **specialist titles**, such as where to watch birds, a botanical atlas and some geological sheets (including one of Surtsey, the world's newest island). The only **road atlas** available at present is **Mál og menning**'s 1:300,000, which breaks the country down into sixty pages as well as including plans of larger towns.

One final large-scale option is the **Rough Guide map to Iceland** which, while not quite as detailed as the others, has all roads, landforms and settlements marked and is printed on waterproof, tear-proof paper, so it won't fall apart the second time you use it – a big problem with domestic versions.

Money

Iceland's **currency** is the króna (krónur in the plural), abbreviated to either Isk, Ikr or kr. Notes are issued in 5000kr, 2000kr, 1000kr and 500kr denominations, and there are 100kr, 50kr, 10kr, 5kr and 1kr coins, decorated with fish. At the time of writing the exchange rate was approximately 211kr to £1; 182kr to €1; 129kr to US$1; 116kr to CAN$1; 105kr to AU$1; and 122kr to NZ$1. Check **current exchange rates** at Ⓦwww .xe.com.

Banks are found right around the country, including in many single-street villages, and most sport an **ATM**, often located in a weather-proof lobby that can be accessed outside opening hours. Normal **banking**

hours are Monday to Friday 9.15am to 4pm, though a few branches in Reykjavík open for longer. All banks change **foreign currency** (not Australian and New Zealand dollars, however); some stores and accommodation in Reykjavík also accept US dollar, Euro or British notes.

You can just about get around Iceland without ever touching cash: almost everywhere takes **credit cards** (Visa and MasterCard are the most widely accepted), and many businesses' tills – and all ATMs – are wired into the Cirrus/Maestro/Electron network, which allows you to pay, or draw cash from ATMs, direct from your home bank account using a **debit/bank card**. Cash withdrawals will be charged a fee per transaction; check with your bank for more information.

Alternatively, you can use **traveller's cheques** to carry your funds around. On the plus side, you can get them replaced through the issuer if lost or stolen (as long as you have copies of the receipts with you); the downside is that you get charged to buy them in the first place, and then get charged a commission every time you cash one at a bank – the fee for this depends on the bank. Take only Euro, UK sterling or US dollar cheques; Australian and New Zealand cheques are not cashable in Iceland. Some banks now issue **Travel Money Cards**, basically an ATM card which has been precharged to a certain value, and which you can draw on until the funds are exhausted. Again, check with your bank for details, especially regarding compatibility with Icelandic machines.

Opening hours and public holidays

Shops are generally **open** Monday to Friday 10am–6pm and Saturday 10am to mid-afternoon, though you might find that many close for the weekend through the summer. In cities and larger towns, supermarkets are open daily from 10am until late afternoon; in smaller communities, however, some places don't open at all at weekends.

Out in the country, **fuel stations** provide some services for travellers, and larger ones tend to open daily from around 9am to 10pm. **Office hours** everywhere are Monday to Friday 9am to 5pm; **tourist offices** often extend these through the weekends, at least in popular spots.

Businesses are generally closed for the following holidays

Jan 1 New Year's Day
Mar/Apr Maundy Thursday, Good Friday, Easter Sunday, Easter Monday
April 20/21 First day of summer
May 1 May Day
May/June: Ascension Day, Whit Sunday, Whit Monday
June 17 National Day
August Bank Holiday (first Monday)
Dec 24–26 Christmas Eve, Christmas Day, Boxing Day
Dec 31 New Year's Eve

Phones

All **phone numbers** in Iceland are seven digits long, with no regional codes. **Phone book** listings are arranged in order of Christian name – Gunnar Jakobsson, for instance, is listed under "G", not "J". Normal landline **rates** are reduced on domestic calls at weekends and Monday to Friday 7pm to 8am; on calls to Europe daily at 7pm to 8am; and to everywhere else daily at 11pm to 8am.

Payphones can be found outside post offices and at fuel stations. They increasingly accept only credit cards; an alternative are **prepaid cards** from 500kr up, such as those offered by Atlas Fresli (ⓦwww.tal.is), sold at post offices and tourist offices. You dial a free-call number, enter the PIN supplied with the card, then dial the phone number. Note that as the calls are routed through Europe, even Icelandic numbers need to be treated as overseas calls, with all the relevant codes. These cards are good for calls to international and domestic landlines, but awful value to mobiles.

As for **mobile phones**, Iceland uses both GSM and NMT networks. GSM covers most of coastal Iceland, including all communities with over 200 inhabitants. **Pay-as-you-go GSM SIM cards** are available at fuel stations around the country, and also on most **incoming flights**. You'll only need NMT coverage if you're spending a lot of time in Iceland's Interior; you can **rent** both

Operator services and international calls

Operator services in Iceland
Emergencies Fire, ambulance or police ☏112
International directory enquiries ☏114
International operator ☏115
National directory enquiries ☏118

Calling home from Iceland
Note that the initial zero is omitted from the area code when dialling the UK, Ireland, Australia and New Zealand from abroad.
USA and Canada 00 + 1 + area code
Australia 00 + 61 + area code
New Zealand 00 + 64 + area code
UK 00 + 44 + area code
Republic of Ireland 00 + 353 + area code
South Africa 00 + 27 + area code

types of mobile from Iceland Telecom, Ármúli 27, Reykjavík.

Photography

Iceland is staggeringly scenic, as well as being packed with birds and enjoying weird atmospheric effects such as the **northern lights** (best in winter) and the **midnight sun** (seen in late June only in the extreme north of the country). Prime **landscapes** to catch on camera include icebergs at Jökulsárlón; Strokkur erupting at Geysir; the rift valley at Þingvellir; desert along the Sprengisandur route; one of Vatnajökull's glaciers; the West Fjord's flat mountain tops; and Dettifoss, Europe's largest waterfall. As for **birds**, you simply must go home with a snap of a puffin (easiest on Heimaey or at Ingólfshöfði), while Mývatn's ducks, teeming sea-bird colonies anywhere around the coast (though best perhaps at Látrabjarg in the West Fjords) and white-tailed eagles (try on Snæfellsnes) are all worthy targets.

Photo shops selling film, digital accessories, camera batteries and facilities for **film processing** and **downloading cards** to disc are plentiful in Reykjavík and Akureyri; elsewhere, if available at all, they are likely to be located in shopping centres.

Shopping

Icelandic **woollen sweaters** are a practical memento of your trip, and cost around 5000–15,000kr – though only expect the lower end of these prices at non-touristy

country stores. Their characteristic patterns derived around a century ago from Greenland's traditional costumes. As almost all are made in cottage industries, consistent patterns, colours, sizes, shapes and fittings are nonexistent – shop around until you find the right one. Other good clothing buys include woolen hats and mittens, and stylish weatherproof outdoor gear made by local brands **66°N** and **Cintamani**.

Stores in Reykjavík also stock a range of silver and lava **jewellery**, in some intriguing – but always expensive – designs. And Iceland's wild-caught **smoked salmon** is probably the best you'll ever eat, firm-textured and robustly scented without being too oily – it costs much the same as you pay at home for farmed versions.

Time

Iceland is on **Greenwich Mean Time** (GMT) throughout the year. GMT is 5 hours ahead of US Eastern Standard Time and 10 hours behind Australian Eastern Standard Time.

Tourist Information

For information before you go, the **Icelandic Tourist Board** maintains several offices abroad, as does Icelandair and its agents, where you'll be able to pick up brochures of the highlights, plus information on tours, transport and accommodation. Stacks of information is also available **online** – see below for websites.

Once in Iceland, Reykjavík's **tourist information offices** (see p.64) have brochures for the whole country, with independent tourist offices in almost every other town, often housed in the bus station. Wherever you are, your **accommodation** is another good source of local details; for instance, families may have lived on particular farms for generations, and have very thorough knowledge of the region.

Icelandic tourist board offices abroad

Australia and New Zealand There are no Icelandic tourist or airline offices in either Australia or New Zealand; instead, contact My Travel/ Bentours or Nordic Travel (see "Specialist operators" on p.29).

Canada There are no Icelandic tourist or airline offices in Canada; contact the US office instead.

Ireland There are no Icelandic tourist or airline offices in Ireland; contact the UK office instead.

UK Icelandair, 172 Tottenham Court Rd, 3rd Floor, London W1P 9LG ☎020/7338 4499 or 7874 1000, ⓦwww.discover-the-world.co.uk, ⓦwww .icelandair.co.uk.

US Iceland Tourist Board, 655 3rd Ave, 18th Floor, New York, NY 10017-5689 ☎212-885-9700, ⓦwww.icelandtouristboard.com.

Government sites

Australian Department of Foreign Affairs ⓦwww.dfat.gov.au, ⓦwww.smartraveller.gov.au.
British Foreign & Commonwealth Office ⓦwww.fco.gov.uk.
Canadian Department of Foreign Affairs ⓦwww.international.gc.ca.
Irish Department of Foreign Affairs ⓦwww .foreignaffairs.gov.ie.
New Zealand Ministry of Foreign Affairs ⓦwww.mft.govt.nz.
US State Department ⓦwww.travel.state.gov.
South African Department of Foreign Affairs ⓦwww.dfa.gov.za

Iceland online

Explore Iceland ⓦwww.exploreiceland.is. What's on around Iceland, all flight, accommodation and tour bookings, plus information on the country.
Iceland Review ⓦwww.icelandreview.com. Daily round-up of local news stories in English, all reported

with an Icelandic quirkiness – gives a good feel for the country.
Icelandic Tourist Board ⓦwww.icetourist.is. Comprehensive regional run-down of the country, listing the main sights and recommended services.
National Parks ⓦwww.ust.is. Environmental Agency's rundown on Iceland's national parks and special reserves, with some useful practical information.
Natural Iceland ⓦwww.nat.is. Web-guide with regional breakdown of the country; includes info on tours, transport, activities, sights, and has discount online booking.
Outdoor Iceland ⓦwww.outdoors.is. Basic background information on outdoor activities – hiking, skiing, climbing – with contact details for local organizations.
Randburg ⓦwww.randburg.is. Excellent information and booking service covering just about anything you could do in Iceland.
Reykjavík Grapevine ⓦwww.grapevine.is. Website for the irreverent weekly listings magazine, with all upcoming attractions, parties, bands and events, plus archived reviews of accommodation, restaurants, cafés and bars around the country.
Travelnet ⓦhttp://travelnet.is. Tourist brochure with snippets of history, plus practical information on transport, accommodation and tours.
Vatnajökull National Park ⓦwww .vatnajokulsthjodgardur.is/english. Official website for Europe's largest national park.

Travellers with disabilities

Iceland is fairly well prepared for **disabled travellers**. Several hotels in Reykjavík and Akureyri have rooms specially designed for disabled guests, larger department stores are generally accessible to wheelchair users, while transport – including coastal ferries, airlines and a few public tour buses – can make provisions for wheelchair users if notified in advance.

Your first contact in Iceland is **Sjálfsbjörg**, Reykjavík's Disabled Association, at Hátún 12, 105 Reykjavík (Icelandic-only website ⓦwww.sjalfsbjorg.is), whose staff can advise on accessible accommodation and travel around Iceland. Alternatively, contact service operators direct; phone numbers are listed throughout the guide.

Guide

Guide

1

Reykjavík

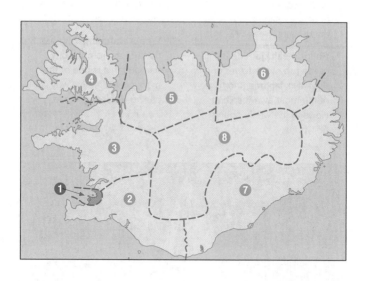

CHAPTER 1 # Highlights

* **Landnámssýningin (Settlement Exhibition)** See how the first Icelanders lived in this underground museum, whose centrepiece is the extensive remains of a tenth-century Viking hall – still in its original location. See p.72

* **Culture House** Get to grips with Iceland's stirring past through this magnificent and accessible collection of ancient sagas and documents. See p.77

* **Hallgrímskirkja** Ride the lift to the top of the tower of this Reykjavík landmark for one of the most awe-inspiring views in the whole country. See p.78

* **Swimming in Nauthólsvík geothermal lagoon** Take a dip in the sublime waters of the capital's open-air lagoon and laze on its golden sands before jumping into the hotpot. See p.80

* **Friday night in Reykjavík** Join the locals on their *rúntur*, a good-natured pub-crawl, and wind your way round some of the city's top bars and clubs. See p.86

* **Whale watching** With handy departures from the city harbour, this is one of the most cost-effective ways of seeing whales up close. See p.89

▲ Hallgrímskirkja

Reykjavík

T he world's most northerly capital, **Reykjavík** has a sense of space and calm that comes as a breath of fresh air to travellers accustomed to the bustle of the traffic-clogged streets of Europe's other major cities, and often literally so. Although unrepresentative of the majority of the country for its relative urbanization, this is a good place to obtain as true a picture as possible of this highly individual, often apparently contradictory society, secluded on the very edge of the Arctic. While it's true, for example, that Friday and Saturday nightlife has earned Reykjavík a reputation for hedonistic revelry, with locals carousing for as long as the summer nights allow – despite the economic collapse of late 2008 – the pace of life is in fact sedate. The tiny centre, for example, is more of a place for ambling around, taking in suburban-looking streets and corner side cafés set against mountain and ocean scenery, rather than somewhere to hurtle around between attractions. Similarly, given the city's capital status, Reykjavík lacks the grand and imposing buildings found in the other Nordic capitals, possessing instead apparently ramshackle clusters of houses, either clad in garishly painted corrugated iron or daubed in pebbledash as protection against the ferocious North Atlantic storms of winter. This rather unkempt feel, though, is as much part of the city's charm as the blustery winds that greet you as you exit the airport, or the views across the sea to glaciers and the sheer mountains that form the backdrop to the streets. Even in the heart of this capital, nature is always in evidence – there can be few other cities in the world, for example, where greylag geese regularly overfly the busy centre, sending bemused visitors, more accustomed to diminutive pigeons, scurrying for cover.

Today, amid the essentially residential city centre, with its collection of homes painted in reds, yellows, blues and greens, it is the **Hallgrímskirkja**, a gargantuan white concrete church towering over the surrounding houses, that is the most enduring image of Reykjavík. Below this, the elegant shops and stylish bars and restaurants that line the main street and commercial thoroughfare of **Laugavegur** are a consumer's heaven. It's within this central core of streets that the capital's most engaging **museums** are also to be found, containing, among other things, superb collections of the medieval **sagas**.

With time to spare, it's worth venturing outside the city limits into **Greater Reykjavík**, for a taste of the Icelandic provinces – suburban style. Although predominantly an area of dormitory overspill for the capital, the town of **Hafnarfjörður** is large enough to be independent of Reykjavík and has a couple of museums and a busy harbour, though it's for its **Viking feasts** that the town is perhaps best known. Alternatively, the flat and treeless island of **Viðey**, barely ten minutes offshore from Reykjavík, is the place to come for magnificent views of the

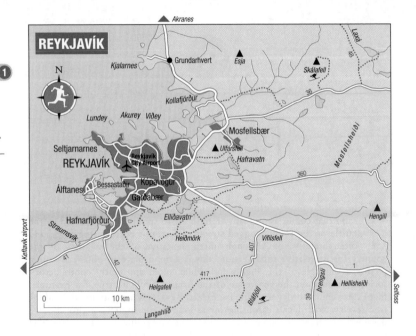

city and of the surrounding mountains – there are also some enjoyable walking trails here, which lead around the island in a couple of hours or so.

The city also makes a good base for excursions around Reykjavík, including to three of Iceland's most popular attractions: the site of the old parliament, **Alþingi**, at Þingvellir (see p.106), the waterspouts and waterfalls of **Geysir** and **Gullfoss** (see p.113), and **Skálholt** (see p.112) cathedral – all within simple reach by public transport – or, more expensively, on day-long guided tours from the city. Also worthwhile is the **Reykjanes peninsula** (see p.196), a bleak lavafield that's as good an introduction as any to the stark scenery you'll find further into Iceland, and home to the mineral-rich waters of the **Blue Lagoon** (see p.101) – the most visited attraction in the country.

If you're only in the city for a short break, or flying on to either the US or Europe, Reykjavík is also the place to fix up adventure activities such as **snowmobile tours** or **jeep safaris** on nearby glaciers or **whitewater rafting** on the Hvitá river in the north (see p.224).

Some history

As recounted in the ancient manuscripts *Íslendingabók* and *Landnámábók*, Reykjavík's origins date back to the country's first settler, **Ingólfur Arnarson**, who arrived in 874 AD, brought here by his high seat pillars – emblems of tribal chieftainship, tossed overboard from his boat – and settling, in pagan tradition, wherever they washed up. He named the place "smoky bay" (*reykja* meaning "of smoke", *vík* meaning "bay", cognate with English *wick*), mistakenly thinking that the distant plumes of steam issuing from boiling spring water were smoke caused by fire. It was a poor place to settle, however, as the soil was too infertile to support successful farming, and Reykjavík remained barely inhabited until an early seventeenth-century **sea-fishing** boom brought Danish traders here, after which a small shanty town to house their Icelandic labour force sprang into existence. Later, in the middle of the eighteenth century, **Skúli Magnússon**, the official in charge of Reykjavík's administrative affairs (*landfógeti*), a man today regarded as the city's founder, used Reykjavík as a base to establish Icelandic-controlled industries, opening several mills and tanneries, and importing foreign craftspeople to pass on their skills. A municipal charter was granted in 1786, when the population totalled a mere 167 – setting the course for Reykjavík's acceptance as Iceland's capital. At the end of the eighteenth century, the city replaced Skálholt as the national seat of religion and gained the Lutheran Cathedral, Dómkirkjan; eighty years later, with the opening of the new Alþingi building, it became the base of the national parliament.

Since independence in 1944, **expansion** has been almost continuous. As a fishing harbour, a port for the produce of the fertile farms of the southwest and a centre for a variety of small industries, Reykjavík provides employment for over half the country's population. The city has also pioneered the use of geothermal energy to provide low-cost heating – which is why you have to wait for the cold water instead of the hot when taking a shower, and why tap water always has a whiff of sulphur.

Over the past fifteen years or so there's been a substantial boom, too, in **tourism**. The ever-increasing visitor numbers to Reykjavík are largely due to the greater number of airlines now operating to Iceland, including a home-grown budget outfit, and the collapse of the country's banking system and currency in 2008 which saw prices drop by half virtually overnight for anyone converting money into the formerly over-valued Icelandic króna. Though it remains to be seen where the exchange rate will settle, Iceland has never provided better value for money.

Arrival and information

Reykjavík is served by two **airports**: Keflavík (airport code KEF; ⓦwww .keflavikairport.com), 52km west of Reykjavík at the tip of the Reykjanes peninsula, where most international flights arrive and depart; and Reykjavík city airport (airport code RKV; ☎570 3030), built by the British when they occupied Iceland during World War II and adjacent to *Hótel Loftleiðir* on the edge of the city centre, served by all domestic flights as well as international services from Greenland and the Faroe Islands, and essentially little more than a glorified bus station. Keflavík, however, is a much larger affair with both **currency-exchange** offices and **ATMs**.

Taxi fares from Keflavík airport into Reykjavík cost you around 12,000kr, which is worth considering if you're with friends. Alternatively, take one of the Flybus **coaches** (ⓦwww.flybus.is), which leave from immediately outside the terminal; departure times, which coincide with arrivals, are displayed on monitors by the baggage reclaim. Tickets for the coach, which can be bought

The Reykjavík Welcome Card

The **Reykjavík Welcome Card** gives you unlimited transport on buses within Greater Reykjavík, access to the main museums and galleries, admission to all swimming pools in the capital, and free **internet** access at the tourist office. Available at the tourist office in Aðalstræti (see below), the youth hostel and campsite (see p.68), the BSÍ bus terminal (see p.62) and the main city bus station at Hlemmur, it costs 1400kr for 24-hours' validity, 1900kr for 48 hours, and 2400kr for 72 hours.

from the Flybus desk and the ticket machines in the arrivals hall, cost 1700kr one way (3000kr return) and are also payable by credit card. The journey lasts around 45 minutes and terminates at the BSÍ **bus station**, Vatnsmýrarvegur 10, around 1.5km from the city centre. Alternatively, Flybus Plus tickets include transfer at the bus station to a **shuttle bus** (2200kr one-way, 4000kr return) which runs to all the major hotels in the city, as well as several guesthouses, the youth hostel and the campsite (see p.68). It's also possible to take taxis into the centre (around

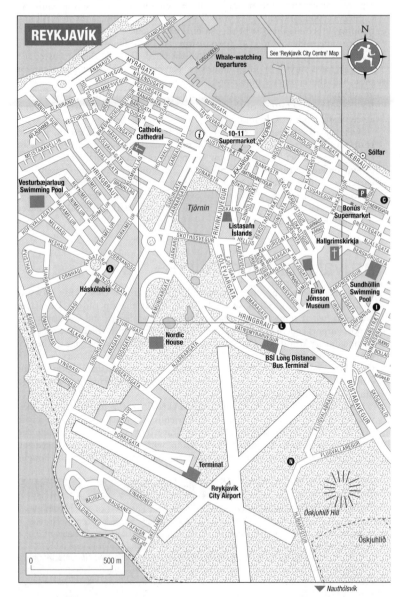

REYKJAVÍK

See 'Reykjavík City Centre' Map

Whale-watching Departures

Catholic Cathedral

10-11 Supermarket

Sólfar

Vesturbæjarlaug Swimming Pool

Tjörnin

Bónus Supermarket

Listasafn Íslands

Hallgrímskirkja

Háskólabíó

Einar Jónsson Museum

Sundhöllin Swimming Pool

Nordic House

BSÍ Long Distance Bus Terminal

Terminal

Reykjavík City Airport

Öskjuhlíð Hill

Öskjuhlíð

0   500 m

Nauthólsvík

1200kr), while buses #1, #3 and #6 (280kr; exact fare only) go directly into town via Lækjargata. Failing that, it's around a thirty-minute walk but bear in mind that bad weather can make this impractical, particularly if you're laden with heavy luggage.

Inside the BSÍ bus station, which is also the terminus for **long-distance buses**, there's a ticket office, a fairly decent café, an ATM, postbox and public telephone here. All bus **timetables** are published on the net at Ⓦ www.bsi.is.

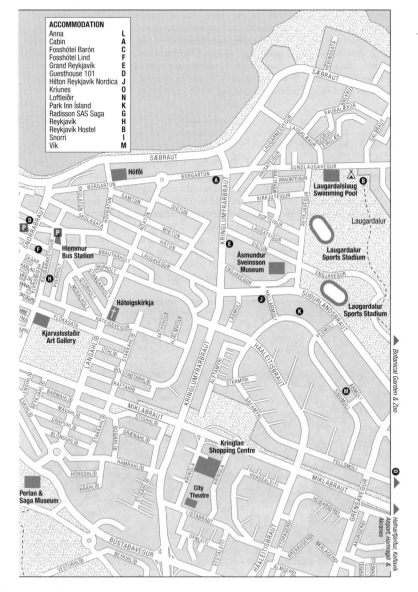

ACCOMMODATION

Anna	L
Cabin	A
Fosshótel Barón	C
Fosshótel Lind	F
Grand Reykjavík	E
Guesthouse 101	D
Hilton Reykjavík Nordica	J
Kríunes	O
Loftleiðir	N
Park Inn Ísland	K
Radisson SAS Saga	G
Reykjavík	H
Reykjavík Hostel	B
Snorri	I
Vík	M

Information

The city's busy **official tourist information office**, at Aðalstræti 2, lies close to the Parliament in the heart of the old town (June to mid-Sept daily 8.30am–7pm; mid-Sept to May Mon–Fri 9am–6pm, Sat 9am–4pm, Sun 9am–2pm; ℡590 1550, Ⓦwww.visitreykjavik.is, Ⓦwww.icetourist.is): it's the best source of up-to-date information on both Reykjavík and the rest of the country, providing untold amounts of brochures and maps, including the useful *What's On* and an Iceland **map**. If you're travelling independently, you can check your itinerary here with the staff before setting off for the more remote regions; there's also **internet access** (500kr per hour) in the same complex (same times). Alternatively, **Trip.is**, at Laugavegur 54 (all year Mon–Fri 9am–6pm; May–Aug Sat & Sun 10am–7pm; Sept–Apr Sat & Sun 11am–4pm; ℡433 8747, Ⓦwww.trip.is), is an unofficial tourist office run by students which is less busy and more friendly than the official tourist office. The office can also book excursion tours for destinations across the country, and there's **internet** access for 300kr per 15min.

City transport

Reykjavík is easy to get around. The heart of the city is the low-lying quarter between the harbour and the lake, busy with shoppers by day and with young revellers by night. Most of the sights are within walking distance of here.

Orange **city buses** known as *Strætó* (℡540 2700, Ⓦwww.bus.is) depart from the city bus station at Hlemmur, at the eastern end of Laugavegur (information office Mon–Fri 8am–8pm, Sat & Sun noon–8pm; ℡540 2701) as well as Lækjartorg. Services run from 7am to midnight Monday to Saturday, and from midday to midnight on Sundays: frequencies are roughly every 30 minutes throughout the day and every hour in the evenings and at weekends. There's a flat, single-trip fare of 280kr that must be paid for with exact change; when boarding, simply throw

▲ Reykjavík city centre

the money into the box by the driver. Tickets are only issued if you're changing buses, in which case ask for a *skiftimiði*, which you then show to the next driver.

Other ticket options include a strip of eleven tickets, called a *farmiðaspjald*, for 2500kr, or a series of cards providing unlimited bus travel in the Greater Reykjavík area, which covers the surrounding satellite towns, including Hafnarfjöruður: the most useful are the **1-day card** (*eins dags kort*; 600kr), **3-day card** (*þriggja daga kort*; 1500kr) and **yellow card** (*gula kortið*; 3500kr), which is valid for two weeks. All these tickets are available at the Hlemmur bus station.

Two useful **routes** are #15, which runs from Hlemmur via Snorrabraut and the BSÍ bus terminal to the city airport; and #19, from Hlemmur via Snorrabraut to *Hótel Loftleiðir* and the Nauthólsvík geothermal pool. If you want to see the city cheaply, bus #15 is excellent – as well as running to the city airport, it also operates in the opposite direction from Hlemmur east via Laugavegur and Suður-landsbraut passing close to the swimming pool, youth hostel and campsite in Laugardalur.

Taxis, parking and cycling

Travelling by **taxi** is not as expensive as you might think – 1300–1500kr should be enough to take you across the city centre. The main ranks are centrally located on Lækjargata, between the junctions with Bankastræti and Amtmannsstígur, as well as opposite Hallgrímskirkja church on Eiríksgata and Hlemmur. It's also possible to call one of the main operators for a taxi: Hreyfill (℡588 5522) is best, or try Borgarbíll (℡552 2440) or BSR (℡561 0000). Remember that Icelandic taxi drivers don't expect tips.

Parking in Reykjavík is a relatively straightforward business and certainly not the nightmare you might expect in a capital city. Most residential streets, although often full with residents' cars, are unmetered, whereas in the city centre parking meters are in use. Multistorey **car parks** are dotted around the city centre, most conveniently at Skólavörðustígur. Once again they're all marked on the tourist office's Reykjavík map. Although the city's **traffic** is generally free-flowing, even at rush hours, it can be busy on Friday and Saturday nights, when it's wise to avoid Laugavegur, which mutates into a long snaking line of slow-moving cars.

Bike rental is centrally available from Borgarhjól, at Hverfisgata 50 (℡551 5653, ⓦwww.borgarhjol.net), or at the youth hostel (see p.68) or the campsite in Laugardalur (see p.68); all charge around 3600kr per 24hr. For more on cycling around the city, see p.83.

Accommodation

Although Reykjavík's **accommodation** options have mushroomed in recent years as the tourist influx has increased, pressure on beds in the summer months is always great and it's a good idea to book in advance, especially in July and August. **Prices** rise by around third between May and September; those given here are for the cheapest double room during the summer months. If you can't find anywhere to stay in the city centre, there are alternatives in the suburb of Hafnarfjörður.

Hotels

Without exception, **hotels** in the city are heavy on the pocket. Standards are uniformly high and a buffet **breakfast** is always included in the price, but the average rate for a double with bath is 15,000–18,000kr, and even a single with private facilities will be around 10,000–12,000kr. If, however, you fancy splashing out for a night or two of luxury, the following are the city's best-value options.

City centre

These are all marked on the Reykjavík City Centre map on p.70

Borg Pósthússtræti 11 ⊕551 1440, ⊛www .hotelborg.is. The city's very first hotel, opened in the 1930s and ever since the unofficial home of visiting heads of state. Now owned by Akureyri's *KEA* group, with a stylish refurbishment only adding to the atmosphere; each room is individually decorated in Art Deco style with period furniture – and prices to match. Breakfast is an extra 2200kr. ❻

Frón Laugavegur 22A ⊕511 4666, ⊛www.hotelfron.is. If you're self-catering, this hotel right in the city centre should be your first choice. Offering stylish, modern studios as well as one- and two-bedroom apartments, each with bath, kitchenette and TV, this place offers exceptional value for money. Studios ❸, two-room apartments ❺

Holt Bergstaðastræti 37 ⊕552 5700, ⊛www.holt .is. Over three hundred paintings by Icelandic artists adorn the rooms and public areas of this luxury, centrally located place which first opened its doors in 1965. Rooms here are of the Persian-carpet, dark-wood-panelling, red-leather-armchair and chocolate-on-the-pillow variety. ❹

Klöpp Klapparstígur 26 ⊕511 6062, ⊛www.centerhotels.is. Despite its bizarre name, one of central Reykjavík's better hotels and a sound choice, modern throughout with tasteful wooden floors, oak furniture and wall panelling in all rooms. Unlike many places, the thick curtains here are effective at cutting out daylight at midnight. The breakfast room, though, is a little cramped. ❹

Leifur Eiríksson Skólavörðustígur 45 ⊕562 0800, ⊛www.hotelleifur.is. Perfect location overlooking Hallgrímskirkja, right in the heart of the city. A small and friendly neatly furnished place; the top-floor rooms, built into the sloping roof, are particularly worthwhile for their excellent views. Good value for the location. ❸

Óðinsvé Þórsgata 1 ⊕511 6200, ⊛www .hotelodinsve.is. Great place that's stylish, relaxed and within an easy trot of virtually everything. The elegantly decorated rooms here have wooden floors, comfortable Scandinavian-style furniture and a homely atmosphere. ❺

Plaza Aðalstræti 4 ⊕590 1400, ⊛www.plaza.is. If you want to stay in the centre of town, this friendly hotel is an excellent choice. The style is Nordic

minimalism meets old-fashioned charm, with the heavy wooden floors, plain white walls and immaculately tiled bathrooms complementing the high-beamed ceilings in this tastefully renovated old building a stone's throw from Austurstræti. Avoid the noisier rooms at the front which overlook the taxi rank. ❹

Radisson SAS 1919 Pósthússtræti 2 ⊕599 1000, ⊛www.1919.reykjavik.radissonsas.com. Housed in the elegant former headquarters of the Eimskip shipping line, this Art Deco hotel in the centre of the city is an excellent choice. All rooms combine old-fashioned charm with modern chic including flatscreen TVs and free broadband. For that special occasion, the penthouse suites with elevated sleeping sections and a separate dining area are arguably the best Reykjavík has to offer. ❹

Reykjavík Centrum Aðalstræti 16 ⊕514 6000, ⊛www.hotelcentrum.is. A curious mix of stylish and homely, this hotel has been built in traditional early 1900s style and is just a stone's throw from the action of Laugavegur. If your budget allows, go for a deluxe room with a queen-size bed and unusually pleasing floral wallpaper. Breakfast is an extra 2200kr. ❻

Skjaldbreið Laugavegur 16 ⊕511 6060, ⊛www .centerhotels.is. The price here is determined less by the plain rooms with floral and net curtains and dull green carpets than by the unbeatable location on the city's main shopping street – a central location rarely comes cheap in Reykjavík. ❹

Out of the centre

These are all marked on the Reykjavík map on pp.62–63

Cabin Borgartún 32 ⊕511 6030, ⊛www .hotelcabin.is. Warm autumn colours are the key here, with lots of restful browns and greys making the décor pleasant if unadventurous. Rooms are all modern and comfortable – try for one at the front with great views out over the sea and Mount Esja. Panoramic views of Reykjavík are afforded from the top-floor breakfast room. ❷

Fosshótel Barón Barónsstígur 2–4 ⊕562 3204, ⊛www.fosshotel.is. En-suite doubles, studios and apartments (all with wooden floors, microwaves and showers), most of which have sea views. There are over thirty apartments varying greatly in size, so look before you choose. Studio rooms 42,300kr May–Sept, just over half that out of season. ❻

Fosshótel Lind Rauðarárstígur 18 ☎ 562 3350, Ⓦ www.fosshotel.is. Bright, modern, functional hotel about a 20min walk from the centre. Rooms are plain and rather too expensive. ❸

Grand Reykjavík Sigtún 38 ☎ 514 8000, Ⓦ www.grand.is. A controversial new glass tower has been added to this top-notch establishment, making it Iceland's biggest hotel with over three hundred rooms. The spacious, stylish rooms with marble floors, chrome fittings and wood panels are sure to delight, though for the money you may wish to be closer to the centre – it's a good 25min walk from here. Rooms in the tower cost about 7000kr more. ❻

Hilton Reykjavík Nordica Suðurlandsbraut 2 ☎ 444 5000, Ⓦ www.reykjavik.nordica.holton.com. One of Iceland's biggest hotels recently incorporated into the Hilton chain, the style here is unreservedly Nordic minimalism: glass, chrome and natural wood everywhere you look. The best rooms are those at the front of the building with views over the sea to Mount Esja. The walk into town from here is a good 30min though buses #2, 15, 17 & 19 pass by. ❻

Loftleiðir Reykjavík city airport ☎ 444 4000, Ⓦ www.icelandairhotels.is. A busy Icelandair-owned hotel whose two-hundred-odd rooms are stuffed with stopover travellers. Rooms, some of which overlook the city airport, have wooden floors and comfortable furnishings though can be a little on the small side. The only hotel in Reykjavík to have an indoor swimming pool, it also has separate-sex saunas. A longish walk into the city centre, however – reckon on about half an hour –

though bus #19 also comes here. Breakfast is an extra 1600kr. ❹

Park Inn Ísland Ármúli 9 ☎ 595 7000, Ⓦ www .parkinn.is. Although a little too far from the centre to be your first choice (about 2.5km though served by the same buses as the Hilton), the stylish, light and airy Scandinavian-designed rooms here, with lots of wood panels and glass and chrome, are a little cheaper than downtown rivals. ❸

Radisson SAS Saga Hagatorg ☎ 525 9900, Ⓦ www.saga.reykjavik.radissonsas.com. This swanky, large business hotel, usually packed with conference delegates dashing up to admire the view from the top-floor restaurant, considers itself one of Iceland's finest. Indeed, the rooms are cosmopolitan in feel and design, with bureaux and comfortable armchairs and a little cheaper than similar establishments. ❹

Reykjavík Rauðarárstígur 37 ☎ 514 7000, Ⓦ www.hotelreykjavik.is. Functional and uninspiring hotel, roughly 20min walk from the centre, worth a look if all else is full. Rooms are plain and simple but clean and presentable, though you might find some disturbingly pink furniture and carpets in them. ❻

Vík Síðumúli 19 ☎ 588 5588, Ⓦ www.hotelvik.is. One of the capital's cheapest hotel options, the simple but pleasant rooms in this hotel are popular with German tour groups. It's oddly located in a business district, 30min walk from the centre but is perfect for good-value, upmarket self-catering, since half the rooms have a kitchen and cost just 1500kr more than an ordinary double. ❸

Guesthouses and apartments

Guesthouse prices have rocketed over the past couple of years and in some instances in July and August can even cost as much as a cheap hotel: count on 16,000–20,000kr for a double, though, unlike hotels, **guesthouses** usually provide kitchens which means it's possible to save by self-catering. Rooms are always on the simple side, with little to distinguish between them. Other than those we recommend, a central location is as good a reason as any to choose one over another, though bear in mind that many are fully booked weeks in advance throughout July and August.

City centre

These are all marked on the Reykjavík City Centre map on p.70

Adam Skólavörðustígur 42 ☎ 896 0242, Ⓦ adam.is. The recently renovated rooms here, all simple but adequate, have a fridge and a basic kitchenette. The reception is not always staffed so be prepared to ring ahead if you arrive without a reservation. There's a

grocery store downstairs for last minute provisions. ❹

Baldursbrá Laufásvegur 41 ☎ 552 6646, Ⓦ http:// notendur.centrum.is/~heijfis. Friendly, modern guesthouse with a fantastic location, right in the city centre and overlooking Tjörnin, though with rather narrow beds and unfortunate floral curtains. ❹

Ísafold Bárugata 11 ☎ 561 2294, Ⓦ www .isafoldguesthouse.is. An excellent choice in a quiet suburban street in the western part of town. The tastefully appointed rooms all have shared bath and are decorated with paintings and stylish furniture. ❸

Luna Spítalastígur 1 ☎511 2800, ⓦwww.luna.is. Good gay-friendly guesthouse in the heart of the city, offering tastefully decorated en-suite apartments, studios (just 14,200kr) and a three-room penthouse. ❸–❺

🏃 **Room with a View** Laugavegur 18 ☎552 7262 or 896 2559, ⓦwww.roomwithaview .is. Another recommended gay-friendly and operated venture, with sixth-floor apartments on the main shopping street that are excellently appointed and have incredible panoramic views from the shared balcony. Kitchen, shower and steambath available. Ten percent discount for stays of seven nights or more. ❷–❹

Salvation Army Guesthouse Kirkjustræti 2 ☎561 3203, ⓦwww.guesthouse.is. The cheapest guesthouse in Reykjavík, often fully booked, despite the narrow rooms with clanking pipes, paper-thin walls and lack of private bath. Although there can be some slightly eccentric local characters in residence, it's a good sensible choice if you're on a tight budget, and it's dead central. Breakfast is included. Sleeping-bag accommodation from 3000kr. ❷

Travel-Inn Sóleyjargata 31 ☎561 3553, ⓦwww .dalfoss.is. One of Reykjavík's top guesthouses in a tastefully renovated old house with good-sized, comfortable rooms overlooking the southern end of Tjörnin and handy for the long-distance bus station

on Vatnsmýrarvegur. The rooms with shared bath are good value. ❷

Out of the centre

These are all marked on the Reykjavík map on pp.62–63

Anna Smáragata 16 ☎562 1618, ⓦwww .guesthouseanna.is. Run by the animated and friendly Anna, who lived in the US for 25 years and speaks excellent English. Good value and very handy for the long-distance bus station, it's definitely one of Reykjavík's better guesthouses with both en-suite rooms and ones sharing facilities. ❸

Guesthouse 101 Laugavegur 101 ☎562 6101, ⓦhttp://iceland101.com. Reasonably priced but soulless place at the eastern end of the main shopping street with cheap furniture and cell-like rooms. ❸

🏃 **Kríunes** Við Vatnsendur ☎567 2245 or 897 0749, ⓦwww.kriunes.is. A 15min drive southeast of the city, this is a truly fantastic lakeside choice, a former farmhouse surrounded by high trees and with views of the lake, painted in warm Mediterranean colours and sporting nice terracotta floor tiles. Self-catering facilities available. ❸

Snorri Snorrabraut 61 ☎552 0598, ⓦwww .guesthousereykjavik.com. A pebble-dashed modern block with uninspiring rooms and an attached tent where breakfast (included in the price) is served; however, it is close to the centre and is useful if elsewhere is full. Sleeping-bag accommodation 4000kr. ❸

The city campsite and the hostels

If money is really tight, you can save cash by staying at the city **campsite** in Laugardalur or one of the city's **youth hostels**, two of which are affiliated to Hostelling International.

Reykjavík Backpackers Laugavegur 28 ☎578 3700, ⓦwww.reykjavikbackpackers.com. With an enviable location on the city's main drag, this smart, new private hostel costs just 3490kr per night per person in small, clinical dorms sleeping 4–8 people, which represents unbeatable value for somewhere so central. Double rooms ❷

Reykjavík Campsite Sundlaugarvegur 32 ☎568 6944, ⓦwww.reykjavikcampsite.is. Open from mid-May to mid-Sept, this is the cheapest place to stay in Reykjavík with a pitch going for just 1000kr. Cooking and shower facilities are available on site, plus there are two-berth cabins for 6000kr per night.

🏃 **Reykjavík City Hostel** Vesturgata 17 ☎553 8120, ⓦwww.hostel.is. More hotel

than hostel, this newly opened central HI place, decorated in subtle pastel colours, is swish and stylish and offers a terrific downtown location (just 10min from Lækjartorg) at unbeatable prices: 2100kr per person in a six-berth dorm, 3000kr in a room sleeping four. Double rooms ❷

Reykjavík Hostel Sundlaugarvegur 34 ☎553 8110, ⓦwww.hostel.is. The city's original and well-appointed youth hostel with dorms sleeping 2–6 people, next to the campsite and Reykjavík's largest swimming pool. For HI members a bed here costs 2100kr per person, plus bed linen at 800kr extra. Bus #12 runs between here and the centre. Allow 14min to walk into town. Double rooms ❶

The City

Although small for a capital (the population is barely 120,000), compared with Iceland's other built-up areas, Reykjavík is a throbbing urban metropolis; the Greater Reykjavík area is home to two out of every three Icelanders. If you're planning to visit some of the country's more remote and isolated regions, you should make the most of the atmosphere generated by this bustling port, with its buzzing nightlife and highbrow museums. The collections in the centrally located **National Museum**, **Culture House** and **Saga Museum**, for example, offer a fine introduction to Iceland's stirring past, while you'll find the outstanding work of sculptors **Ásmundur Sveinsson** and **Einar Jónsson** outdoors in the streets and parks, as well as in two permanent exhibitions – indeed, contemporary art has a high profile in a whole host of art shops and galleries. And yet even with all of this around you, you can never forget that you're bang in the middle of the North Atlantic, with your nearest neighbours being Greenland and the North Pole – a remoteness that is at the core of Reykjavík's appeal.

The city centre is split roughly into two halves by the brilliant waters of the large, naturally occurring lake, **Tjörnin**. To the north and west of this lie, respectively, the busy fishing **harbour**, full of modern hi-tech trawlers and Iceland's whaling fleet, and **Vesturbær**, the city's oldest district, dating back in parts to the Settlement, now largely given over to administration, eating, drinking and entertainment. It's also one of the city's most likeable and picturesque quarters, comprising a spread of well-to-do residential streets, at odds with the concrete apartment blocks on the eastern outskirts of the city. Another gaggle of bars and restaurants are located on **Austurstræti** and **Hafnarstræti** from where **Vesturgata**, bordered by picture-postcard houses with multicoloured roofs and facades, reaches up the hill that begins at Tjörnin's western edge. East of the lake, things become altogether more commercial, as the gently sloping main drag, **Laugavegur**, the city's main shopping street, packed with glitzy designer boutiques and the location for most of the city's bars, restaurants and shops, leads towards the bus terminal, Hlemmur, which marks the edge of the city centre.

Central Reykjavík

You'd be hard pushed to find another capital city as diminutive as Reykjavík, and a leisurely walk of just an hour or two will take you around almost the entirety of the centre. Such smallness accounts for the city's lack of contrasting and well-defined areas: for simple convenience, we've divided the central portion into two sections separated by the lake, **Tjörnin**, and the road, **Lækjargata**, which runs from the lake and Reykjavík's main square, **Lækjartorg**, down towards the harbour. Even the few things of note further out from the centre can be reached in a few minutes on public transport.

Lækjartorg and around

The best place to get your first taste of Reykjavík is the area around **Lækjartorg** and the adjoining pedestrianized **Austurstræti** on its western side – a general meeting place for Reykjavík's urbanites, where people stroll, strut and sit on benches munching cakes, ice creams and burgers bought from the nearby fast-food outlets and the 10–11 supermarket. The square has always been at the heart of Reykjavík life, indeed, it was here that farmers bringing their produce to market ended their long journey from the surrounding countryside and set up camp from where they could carry out their business in town. Lækjartorg was once overlooked from its western end by the headquarters of the main daily newspaper,

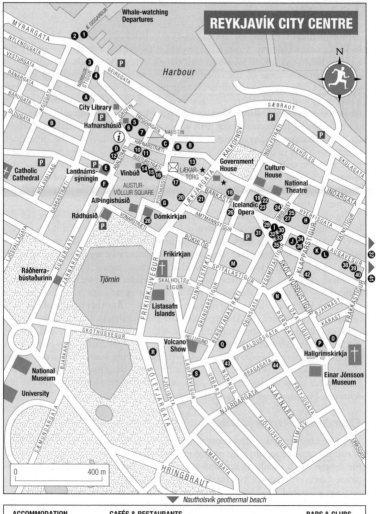

Nautholsvík geothermal beach

ACCOMMODATION

Adam	P
Baldursbrá	S
Borg	G
Frón	K
Holt	Q
Ísafold	B
Klöpp	H
Leifur Eiríksson	O
Luna	M
Óðinsvé	N
Plaza	D
Radisson SAS 1919	C
Reykjavík Backpackers	L
Reykjavík Centrum	E
Reykjavík City Hostel	A
Room with a view	J
Salvation Army	F
Skjaldbreið	I
Travel-Inn	R

CAFÉS & RESTAURANTS

Á Næstu Grösum	30
Argentina Steikhús	41
Basil & Lime	36
Bæjarin's	8
Búllan	2
Café Paris	16
Einar Ben	10
Eldsmiðjan	44
Fish Market	12
Garðurinn	42
Grái Kötturinn	19
Grænn Kostur	31
Grillhúsið	5
Habibi	13
Hornið	9
Icelandic Fish & Chips	3
Indian Mango	40
Jómfrúin	20
Kaffi Sólon	18
Kaffitár	26
Krua Thai	4
Lækjarbrekka	21
Mokka	35
Prikið	29
Restaurant Reykjavík	6
Rosso Pomodoro	39
Sandholt	38
Sægreifinn	1
Vegamót	33
Við Tjörnina	28
Þrír Frakkar	43

BARS & CLUBS

Bjarni Fel	17
Broadway	37
Café Cultura	22
Celtic Cross	25
Dubliner	11
English Pub	15
Grand Rokk	27
Hverfisbarinn	24
Kaffibarinn	32
Nasa	14
Oliver	34
Samtökin	23
Sódóma	7

Morgunblaðið, the implication being that journalists needed only to look through their windows to discover what was happening in the city – which was usually very little. Today, however, the area can be one of the most boisterous in the city. On Friday and Saturday evenings, particularly in summer, hundreds of drunken revellers fill the square when the clubs empty out at 5 or 6am, jostling for prime position – although the noise from the throng can be deafening, the atmosphere is good-hearted and not at all intimidating. By day, the area resumes its busy commercial air as people dash in and out of the post office or pop in to one of the city's two main bookshops, Eymundsson. Beyond its junction with Pósthússtræti, Austurstræti gives itself over solely to pleasure, as this is where some of the city's best bars and restaurants can be found (see p.84). This is also the location for the *vínbúð* state alcohol store (see Listings, p.91) a futuristic glass-and-steel structure at no. 10a, where those who want to drink at home have to come and part with vast amounts of cash (see Basics, p.41, for more on this).

Austurvöllur square and the Alþingishúsið

Pósthússtræti, running south from Austurstræti, leads into another small square, **Austurvöllur**, a favourite place for city slickers from nearby offices to catch a few rays during their lunch breaks, stretched out on the grassy lawns edged with flowers. Yet the square's modest proportions and nondescript apartment blocks belie its historical importance. This was the site of Ingólfur Arnarson's farm; it's thought he grew his hay on the land where the square now stands, and it marks the original centre of Reykjavík. Similarly, the square's central, elevated **statue** of the nineteenth-century independence campaigner **Jón Sigurðsson**, entitled *The Pride of Iceland, its Sword and Shield*, faces two of the most important buildings in the country – the Alþingi and the Dómkirkjan – though you'd never realize their status from their appearance.

The **Alþingishúsið** (Parliament House) is ordinary in the extreme, a slight building made of grey basalt quarried from nearby Skólavörðuholt hill with the date of its completion, 1881, etched into its dark frontage – yet this unremarkable structure played a pivotal role in bringing about Icelandic independence. In 1798, the parliament moved to Reykjavík from Þingvellir (see p.106), where it had been operating virtually without interruption since 930 AD. Within just two years, however, it was dissolved as Danish power reached its peak, but with great pride and after much struggle, the Alþingi regained its powers from Copenhagen as a consultative body in 1843, and a constitution was granted in 1874, making Iceland self-governing in domestic affairs. The Act of Union, passed in this building in 1918, made Iceland a sovereign state under the Danish Crown although the act was open for reconsideration at any time after 1940, but by then Denmark was occupied by the Nazis and the Alþingi had assumed the duties normally carried out by the monarch, declaring its intention to dissolve the Act of Union at the end of the war. Today, the modest interior, illuminated by chandeliers, more resembles a town council chamber than the seat of a national parliament.

The adjacent **Dómkirkjan** (Mon–Fri 10am–4.30pm; free), Reykjavík's Lutheran cathedral, is a Neoclassical stone structure shrouded against the weather in corrugated iron, built between 1787 and 1796 after Christian VII of Denmark scrapped the Catholic bishoprics of Hólar in the north, and Skálholt in the south, in favour of a Lutheran diocese in what was fast growing into Iceland's main centre of population. The church may be plain on the outside, but venture inside and you'll discover a beautiful interior: perfectly designed arched windows punctuate the unadorned white-painted walls at regular intervals, giving an impression of complete architectural harmony. The cathedral is now deemed too small for great gatherings and services of state, and the roomier Hallgrímskirkja (see p.78) is

Icelandic people power

Every Saturday between mid-October 2008 and late January 2009, thousands of Icelanders gathered in Austurvöllur to voice their anger over the **collapse** of the Icelandic banking system which, it's estimated, left one in five families bankrupt. The protesters, led by musician, Hörður Torfason, began by burning the flag of Landsbanki, though soon also called for heads to roll. The main target of popular discontent was leader of the Icelandic Central Bank and former long-serving politician, Davíð Oddsson, who was squarely blamed for the economic meltdown. The **demonstrators** became more vocal as the lack of decisive action by the government continued. Three and a half months' of protests, in Austurvöllur and at various locations around the country, finally convinced Prime Minister, Geir Haarde, that his administration had no future; to national jubilation, it fell on January 26, 2009 (see Contexts, p.330).

preferred for state funerals and other such well-attended functions, although the opening of parliament is still marked with a service in the Dómkirkjan followed by a short procession along Kirkjustræti to the Alþingishúsið.

Aðalstræti, the Landnámssýningin and Hafnarstræti

From the southwestern corner of Austurvöllur, Kirkjustræti runs the short distance to Reykjavík's oldest street, **Aðalstræti**, which follows the route taken in the late ninth century by Ingólfur Arnarson from his farm at the southern end of the street down to the sea. It's here, at Aðalstræti 16, that you'll find one of Reykjavík's most remarkable museums, the **Landnámssýningin** (Settlement Exhibition; daily 10am–5pm; 600kr; ⓦ www.reykjavik871.is), whose centrepiece is the extensive ruins of a **Viking-age farmhouse**. Housed in a purpose-built hall directly beneath Aðalstræti, the structure's oval-shaped stone walls, excavated in 2001, enclose a sizeable living space of 85 square metres with a central hearth as the focal point. Dating the farmhouse has been relatively straightforward since the layer of volcanic ash which fell across Iceland around 871 AD, following a powerful eruption, lies just beneath the building; it's estimated, therefore, that people lived here between 930 and 1000. As you wander around the exhibition, look out for the animal spine, probably that of a horse or cow, buried under part of the farmhouse's western wall as a talisman to ward off evil spirits, a common practice during the Viking period. The exhibition's wall space is given over to panoramic views of forest and scrubland to help give a realistic impression of what Reykjavík would have looked like at the time of the Settlement. Indeed, when the first settlers arrived in the area, the hills were covered in birch woods. However, just one hundred years later, the birch had all but disappeared, felled to make way for grazing land or burnt for charcoal needed for iron-smelting. Well-conceived computer graphics cleverly overlay the wallprints and show ghost-like characters going about their daily chores. Incidentally, excavation work now under way outside the museum at the corner of Kirkjustræti and Tjarnargata has already unearthed what's thought to be a small-scale industrial site, also from the 870s, where bog iron was smelted to produce various goods.

A couple of doors further down Aðalstræti, at no. 10, is Reykjavík's oldest surviving building, a squat timber structure which dates back to 1752, formerly a weaving shed and a bishop's residence, where once lived Skúli Magnússon (see p.327), High Sheriff of Iceland, who encouraged the development of craft industries here. On the opposite side of the street, a few steps north towards the sea outside the present no. 9, is Ingólfur Arnarson's freshwater well, **Ingólfsbrunnur**, now glassed over for posterity, which was discovered by fluke when the city council carried out roadworks here in 1992. Just beyond, at the junction with Fischersund, is the tourist information office (see p.64).

Opposite the tourist office, at the junction of Aðalstræti and **Hafnarstræti**, is another of Reykjavík's beautifully restored timber buildings (covered in corrugated iron for protection), **Fálkahúsið**, one of three buildings in the city where the King of Denmark once kept his much-prized Icelandic falcons before having them dispatched by ship to the Court in Copenhagen. There was outrage when the building was converted into a restaurant, inevitably subjecting the ancient timbers to the wear and tear of hundreds of stomping feet. Despite this, its turret-like side walls and sheer size still impress, especially when you consider the huge amount of timber that was imported for the job, as Iceland had no trees of its own. Cast an eye to the roof and you'll spot two carved wooden falcons still keeping guard over the building, either side of a garish modern representation of a Viking longboat.

Many of the buildings on the south side of Hafnarstræti were formerly owned by Danish merchants during the Trade Monopoly of 1602–1855 (for more on this, see p.327), and indeed, this street, as its name suggests (*hafnar* means "harbour"), once bordered the sea and gave access to the harbour, the city's economic lifeline and means of contact with the outside world. Today, though, the street is several blocks from the ocean after landfill extended the city foreshore. Instead, it is home to some excellent bars and restaurants, and, together with Austurstræti to the south and Tryggvagata to the north, makes up a rectangular block of eateries and drinking-holes, well worthy of exploration (see "Eating and drinking", p.83).

Tryggvagata and the harbour

Tryggvagata, one block north of the bustle of Hafnarstræti, is remarkable for two things other than the number of consonants in its name: the imposing multi-coloured mosaic mural close to its junction with Pósthússtræti, portraying a busy harbour scene complete with fishing trawlers and cranes, which livens up the otherwise frightfully dull **Tollhúsið** (Customs House); and the **Hafnarhúsið** (Harbour House), part of the **Reykjavík Art Museum** (daily 10am–5pm; free; Ⓦ www.listasafnreykjavikur.is), at Tryggvagata 17. This large, austere building was constructed in the 1930s as warehouse storage and office space for the Port of Reykjavík but has now been converted into six spacious exhibition halls connected by a corridor running over a central courtyard. Although there's certainly plenty of space here, the layout is less than obvious since the confusing array of corridors, which once linked the former warehouse's storage areas, twists and turns around the museum's supporting concrete and steel pillars, leaving the visitor quite lost at times (there are no guides available). Although the museum plays host to frequently changing displays of contemporary Icelandic and international art, the only permanent exhibition is that dedicated to the multicoloured cartoon-like work of Icelandic artist **Erró**. His vibrant collages, depicting everything from Viking warriors to space-age superheros all seemingly caught up in the same explosive battle, are certainly striking, if somewhat eye-blinding and not to everyone's taste. Born Guðmundur Guðmundsson in Ólafsvík on the Snæfellsnes peninsula in 1932, Erró grew up in Kirkjubæjarklaustur before moving abroad to study at the art academies of Oslo, Florence and Ravenna and finally settling in Paris where he still lives today. In 1982 Erró (even the museum staff are at a loss as to why he chose this name, although he was forced to change from Ferró to Erró in 1967 after being sued) donated about two thousand of his works, including oil paintings, prints and sculptures, to the City of Reykjavík which chose to dedicate this exhibition to him. There's also a **café** on the first floor, where it's worth taking time out to enjoy the view of the harbour and Mount Esja through the floor-to-ceiling windows.

▲ Reykjavík harbour

From the museum, a two-minute walk down **Grófin** leads to **Geirsgata**, the busy main road that runs along the southern side of the **harbour**, which has been built around reclaimed land – the beach where vessels once landed their foreign goods is now inland from here. Street names around here, such as Ægisgata (Ocean Street) and Öldugata (Wave Street), reflect the importance of the sea to the city, and a stroll along the dockside demonstrates Iceland's dependence on the Atlantic, with fishing trawlers being checked over and prepared for their next battle against the waves, and plastic crates of ice-packed cod awaiting transportation to village stores around the country. Above all, you'll see the black **whaling vessels**, each with a red "H" painted on its funnel (*hvalur* is Icelandic for "whale"). Paradoxically, the harbour is also the departure point for **whale-watching tours**; for more information, see p.89.

Tjörnin and around

From the harbour, Pósthússtræti leads south over the pleasure meccas of Tryggvagata, Hafnarstræti and Austurstræti to Vonarstræti and **Tjörnin**, invariably translated into English as "the lake" or "the pond". *Tjörn* and its genitive form of *tjarnar* are actually old Viking words, still used in northern English dialects as "tarn" to denote a mountain lake. Originally formed by a lagoon inside the reef that once occupied the spot where Hafnarstræti now runs, this sizeable body of water, roughly a couple of square kilometres in size, is populated by forty to fifty varieties of birds – including the notorious **arctic tern**, known for its dive-bombing attacks on passers-by, and found at the lake's quieter southern end – whose precise numbers are charted on notice boards stationed at several points along the bank.

Occupying prime position on the northern edge of Tjörnin is **Ráðhúsið** (Reykjavík City Hall; Mon–Fri 8am–7pm, Sat & Sun noon–6pm; free). Opened in 1992, it's a showpiece of Nordic design, a modernistic rectangular structure of steel, glass and chrome that actually sits on the lake itself. Inside, in addition to the city's administration offices, is a small café and a fabulous self-standing **topographical model** of Iceland, to be found in one of the small exhibition areas. It gives an excellent idea of the unforgiving geography of Iceland – marvel at the sheer size of the Vatnajökull glacier in the southeast (as big as the English county of Yorkshire) and the table mountains of the West Fjords, and gain instant respect for the people who live amid such landscapes.

One of the best **views** of Reykjavík can be had from Suðurgata, a street running parallel to the western shore of Tjörnin and reached from the city hall by walking west along Vonarstræti, crossing Tjarnargata. However, before continuing up to Suðurgata have a quick look at **Ráðherrabústaðurinn** (Minister's Residence) at Tjarnargata 32, an impressive wooden structure first built at Sólbakki in Önundarfjörður in the West Fjords and formerly owned by a rich Norwegian businessman who's said to have either given it or sold it to Iceland's first Home Rule minister, Hannes Hafstein, in 1904 for the princely sum of 1kr; today it is used by the Icelandic government for official receptions. One block to the west, Suðurgata is lined with tidy little dwellings, but from it you can see across the lake to the suburban houses of the city centre, whose corrugated iron roofs, ranging in colour from a pallid two-tone green to bright blues and reds, have been carefully maintained by their owners – the familiar picture-postcard view of Reykjavík.

Þjóðminjasafn: National Museum

At the junction of Suðurgata and Hringbraut is the entrance to the **Þjóðminjasafn Íslands** (National Museum; May to mid-Sept daily 10am–5pm; mid-Sept to April Tues–Sun 11am–5pm; 800kr; free on Wed; Ⓦwww.natmus.is), offering a comprehensive historical overview of the country's past from the days of the Settlement right up to the birth of the Republic in 1944 and beyond. The first floor, devoted to the period from 800 to 1600, is by far the most engaging part of the museum, particularly the video presentation devoted to the early Viking period and the use of **DNA testing**. Recent genetic research has shown that whereas around eighty percent of today's Icelanders are of Nordic origin, sixty-two percent of the early Viking era women originated from the British Isles; the conclusion, therefore, is that the first settlers sailed from Scandinavia to Iceland via the British Isles where they took wives. Informative displays show how DNA testing of the pulp cavity of the teeth of these first settlers is being carried out in an attempt to add scientific credence to the recent genetic research results.

Other prime exhibits include a small human figure, about the size of a thumb and made of bronze, which is thought to be over a thousand years old and portray either the Norse god Þór or Christ. More spectacular is the **carved church door** from Valþjófsstaður in Fljótsdalur (Þórsmörk), dating from around 1200, and depicting the medieval tale *Le Chevalier au Lion*: it features an ancient warrior on horseback slugging it out with an unruly dragon. The Danish authorities finally gave up the treasure in 1930 and returned the door to Iceland, together with a host of medieval manuscripts. Check out, too, the impressive Romanesque-style carved **Madonna** dating from around 1200 which hails from northern Iceland.

The second floor of the museum, devoted to the period from 1600 onwards, canters through key events in Icelandic history such as the Trade Monopoly (1602–1787) and the Birth of the Republic. It terminates in a revolving airport-style conveyor belt laden with twentieth-century appliances and knick-knacks featuring everything from a Björk LP to a milking machine.

Norræna húsið

South of the university at Sturlugata 5 is **Norræna húsið** (**Nordic House**; Mon–Fri 8am–5pm, Sat & Sun noon–5pm; free; Ⓣ551 7030, Ⓦwww.nordice.is), designed by the renowned Finnish architect Alvar Aalto in 1961 and buzzed over by aircraft landing at the nearby city airport. Devoted to Nordic culture, with an extensive library of books written in all the Nordic languages, it holds books on virtually any aspect of Nordic life you choose to mention, from Faroese knitting to Greenlandic seal hunting as well as the main Nordic newspapers. There are also temporary **exhibitions** (often photographic) in the hall and basement and frequent evening events, from classical **concerts** to **talks** covering topics from history to politics to music (sometimes in English). Check what's on from the posters inside or at the tourist office (see p.64). For speakers of non-Nordic languages, the best part of Nordic House is its chi-chi **restaurant**, *Dill* (☎552 1552), which serves up expertly prepared Nordic specialities from across the region.

Listasafn Íslands and Lækjargata

A few minutes' walk north from the Nordic House along Sóleyjargata, which runs along the eastern side of Tjörnin towards **Lækjargata**, passing the offices of the Icelandic president (at the corner of Skothúsvegur), is the **Fríkirkjan**, the Free Lutheran Church, a simple wooden structure painted bright white, whose best feature is its tall tower, useful as a landmark to guide you to the neighbouring former ice house, known as **Herðubreið** at Fríkirkjuvegur 7 (Fríkirkjuvegur is the continuation of Sóleyjargata). Once a storage place for massive chunks of ice, hewn in winter from the frozen lake and used to prevent fish stocks rotting, the building has been completely redesigned and enlarged and now houses the **Listasafn Íslands** (National Gallery of Iceland; Tues–Sun 11am–5pm; free; ⓦ www.listasafn.is). Icelandic art may lack worldwide recognition, but all the significant names are to be found here, including Erró, Jón Stefánsson, Ásgrímur Jónsson, Guðmundur Þorsteinsson and Einar Hákonarson – though disappointingly, lack of space (there's only two small exhibition rooms containing barely twenty or so paintings each) means that the works can only be shown in strictly rationed portions from the museum's enormous stock of around ten thousand pieces of art. You can, however, get an idea of the paintings not on display by glancing through the postcards for sale at reception. Drop in, but expect to leave with your artistic appetite no more than whetted; also, note that on entry you have to leave your coat and bag in the lockers provided.

A walk from here back towards Lækjartorg leads on to **Lækjargata** (effectively a continuation of Fríkirkjuvegur), which once marked the eastern boundary of the town; Tjörnin still empties into the sea through a small brook (*lækjar* comes from *lækur*, Icelandic for "brook") which now runs under the road here, and occasionally, when there's an exceptionally high tide, sea water gushes back along the brook pouring into Tjörnin. The cluster of old timber buildings up on the small hill parallel to the street is known as **Bernhöftsstofan** and, following extensive renovation, they now house a couple of chi-chi fish restaurants. Named after Tönnies Daniel Bernhöft, a Dane who ran a bakery in nearby Bankastræti, they're flanked by two of Iceland's most important buildings: the elegant old Reykjavík Grammar School, Menntaskólinn, built in 1844, which once had to be accessed by a bridge over the brook, and housed the Alþingi before the completion of the current Alþingishúsið in nearby Austurvöllur square (see p.71); and a small unobtrusive white building at the bottom of Bankastræti, which is, in fact, **Stjórnarráðshúsið** (Government House), another of Iceland's very parochial-looking public offices. One of the oldest surviving buildings in the city, built in 1761–71 as a prison, it now houses the cramped offices of the Prime Minister. Up on **Arnahóll**, the grassy mound behind the building, a statue of Ingólfur Arnarson, Reykjavík's first settler, surveys his domain; with his back turned on the National Theatre, and the government ministries to his right, he looks out to the ocean that brought him here over eleven centuries ago. Experts believe this is the most likely spot where Ingólfur's high seat pillars finally washed up; according to *Landnámabók* they were found "by Arnarhvál below the heath".

Laugavegur and around

From Lækjartorg, turn right into the short Bankastræti and on, up the small hill, into Laugavegur (hot spring road), the route once taken by local washerwomen to the springs in Laugardalur. This is Iceland's major commercial artery, holding the main shops and a fair sprinkling of cafés, bars and restaurants. Not surprisingly therefore, on Friday and Saturday evenings in summer it's bumper to bumper with cars, their horns blaring, and with well-oiled revellers hanging out of the windows. However, before you give yourself over to extensive retail therapy, there are a couple of more cerebral attractions worthy of your time and attention in this part of town: the grand former National Library, now the **Þjóðmenningargarhúsið** (Culture House; daily 11am–5pm; 300kr; Ⓦ www.thjodmenning.is), at Hverfisgata 15, one block north of and parallel to Laugavegur, has the country's largest and best exhibition of **medieval manuscripts**. What makes this display of treasures particularly engaging is its accessibility; gone is the tedious intellectual pontificating which so often accompanies Icelandic history, instead you can get close up to these documents and see for yourself what all the fuss is about – an erudite account beside each manuscript serving as an adequate summary. A warren of darkened exhibition halls on the ground floor, illuminated only for a few minutes at a time by soft overhead lighting, contains about a dozen ornately decorated documents, themselves in glass cases, including the magnificent *Flateyjarbók*, which was finally returned to Iceland in 1971 after spending three centuries in Denmark. The largest of all medieval Icelandic vellums preserved today, the book was written towards the end of the fourteenth century and recounts mostly sagas of kings. However, it is also the only document to contain the *Saga of the Greenlanders*, which relates Leifur Eiríksson's exploration in Vínland. Look out, too, for the *Staðarhólsbók Grágásar*, one of the earliest existing manuscripts, dating from around 1270, which runs through laws from the period of the Icelandic

Magnusson's manuscripts

Despite so many of Iceland's sagas and histories being written down by medieval monks for purposes of posterity, there existed no suitable means of protecting them from the country's damp climate, and within a few centuries the unique artefacts were rotting away. Enter **Árni Magnússon** (1663–1730), humanist, antiquarian and professor at the University of Copenhagen, who attempted to ensure the preservation of as many of the manuscripts as possible by sending them to Denmark for safekeeping. Although he completed his task in 1720, eight years later many of them went up in flames in the Great Fire of Copenhagen, and Árni died a heartbroken man fifteen months later, never having accepted his failure to rescue the manuscripts, despite braving the flames himself. As he noted at the time of the blaze, "these are the books which are to be had nowhere in the world"; the original **Íslendingabók**, for example, the most important historical record of the settlement of Iceland, written on calfskin, was destroyed, though luckily it had been copied by a priest in Iceland before it left the country.

The manuscripts were to remain apart from their country of origin until long after Icelandic independence in 1944. In 1961, legislation was passed in Denmark decreeing that manuscripts composed or translated by Icelanders should be returned, but it took a further ruling by the Danish Supreme Court, in March 1971, to get things moving, as the Danes were reluctant to see these works of art leave their country. Finally, however, in April that year, a Danish naval frigate carried the first texts, **Konungsbók Eddukvæða** and **Flateyjarbók**, across the Atlantic into Reykjavík, to be met by crowds bearing signs reading "*handritin heim*" ("the manuscripts are home") and waving Icelandic flags. Even so, the transfer of the manuscripts wasn't completed until 1997.

Commonwealth, several of which are still in force today, and for the two grubby pages full of grease stains and dirty finger marks of *Kálfalækjarbók*, which contains fragments of *Njáls Saga*, one of the most widely read of all the sagas and preserved in more than fifty different manuscripts; this version dates from the mid-fourteenth century. The exhibition also contains a video of the original black and white live television coverage of the manuscripts arriving back in Iceland from Denmark; it's easy to see from the sheer size of the crowds that had gathered at the harbour to welcome the ship, the total fascination Icelanders have with this element of their past – just count, for example, how many streets in Reykjavík alone are named after heroes from the sagas. Naturally, the Culture House's other exhibits pale into insignificance; however, it's worth devoting a few minutes to the **Jón Sigurðsson** room on the first floor (entered through the door marked Fundarstofur; Sun only) dedicated to the independence leader Jón Sigurðsson, though you probably have to be a national to appreciate fully some of the finer details of his bitter struggle with the Danes; a glass cabinet contains some of his personal effects. In Iceland at least, the oil painting on the wall here depicting Jón bravely standing up in the presence of the Danish king and other top officials, putting his nation's case for independence, is much talked about and revered. The top floor is devoted to a series of temporary exhibitions; recent ones have included the history of Icelandic film and the birth of the island of Surtsey.

Hallgrímskirkja church

From the lower end of Laugavegur, the tongue-twisting Skólavörðustígur streaks steeply upwards to the largest church in the country, the magnificent **Hallgrím-skirkja** (daily 9am–5pm). This is a modern concrete structure, whose neatly composed space-shuttle-like form dominates the Reykjavík skyline. Work began on the church, named after the renowned seventeenth-century religious poet Hallgrímur Pétursson, immediately after World War II but was only finally completed a few years ago, the slow progress due to the task being carried out by a family firm – comprising one man and his son. The work of state architect Guðjón Samúelsson, the church's architectural style – not least its 73-metre phallic steeple – has divided the city over the years, although nowadays locals have grown to accept rather than love it since its consecration in 1986. Most people rave about the organ inside, the only decoration in an otherwise completely bare Gothic-style shell; measuring a whopping 15m in height and possessing over 5000 pipes, it really has to be heard to be believed. The cost of installing it called for a major fundraising effort, with people across the country sponsoring a pipe – if you fancy putting money towards one yourself, for which you'll receive a certificate, ask the staff in their office on the right as you enter the church. The tower has a **viewing platform** (400kr), accessed by a lift from just within the main door, giving stunning panoramic views across Reykjavík; if you come up here in winter, remember to bring a warm hat and scarf because the viewing platform is open to the elements. Incidentally, don't expect the clock at the top of the tower to tell the correct time – the wind up there is so strong that it frequently blows the hands off course. In fact, it's rare for any two public clocks in Reykjavík to tell the same time because of the differing wind conditions throughout the city.

With his back to the church and his view firmly planted on Vínland, the imposing **statue** of Leifur Eiríksson, Discoverer of America, was donated by the US in 1930 to mark the Icelandic parliament's thousandth birthday. It's a favourite spot for photographs and makes as good a place as any to survey your surroundings – this is one of the highest parts of Reykjavík and on a clear day there are great **views** out over the surrounding streets of houses adorned with multicoloured corrugated-iron facades.

The Einar Jónsson museum

The heroic form of the Leifur Eiríksson statue is found in several others around the city, many of them the work of **Einar Jónsson** (1874–1954), who is remembered more officially by the pebbledash building to the right of the church at the corner of Eiríksgata and Njarðargata, home to the **Einar Jónsson museum** (June to mid-Sept Tues–Sun 2–5pm; mid-Sept to May Sat & Sun 2–5pm; 500kr; ⓦwww .skulptur.is). Einar was Iceland's foremost modern **sculptor**, and this cube-like structure was built by him between 1916 and 1923; he lived here, too, in the upstairs apartment with his Danish wife, Anna, though they had separate bedrooms. He worked here in an increasingly reclusive manner until his death in 1954, when the building was given over to displaying more than a hundred of his works – many based on religious themes and Icelandic folklore – to the public. A specially constructed group of rooms, connected by slim corridors and a spiral staircase, takes the visitor through a chronological survey of Einar's career – and it's pretty deep stuff. Einar claimed that his self-imposed isolation and total devotion to his work enabled him to achieve mystical states of creativity, and looking at the pieces exhibited here, many of them heavy with religious allegory and all dripping with spiritual energy, it's a claim that doesn't seem far-fetched; look out for his *Vökumaðurinn* (The Guardian) from 1902, a ghost keeping watch over a graveyard to make sure the dead receive a decent burial. If the museum is closed, peek into the garden at the rear of the museum, where several examples of Einar's work are displayed alfresco, or admire his most visible work, the statue of independence leader Jón Sigurðsson, found in front of the Alþingishúsið in Austurvöllur square (see p.71).

The Kjarvalsstaðir Art Gallery

From the Einar Jónsson museum it's a fifteen-minute walk east to the main highway, Hringbraut, beyond its junction with Snorrabraut and then north into Rauðarárstígur, to reach another of Reykjavík's excellent modern-art museums. Despite being surrounded by birch trees and pleasant grassy expanses, the **Kjarvalsstaðir Art Gallery** (daily 10am–5pm; free; ⓦwww.listasafnreykjavikur.is) is an ugly 1960s-style concrete structure, though inside it's surprisingly bright and airy. Part of the Reykjavík Art Museum, it's devoted to the work of Iceland's most celebrated artist, Jóhannes Kjarval (1885–1972). After working during his youth on a fishing trawler, Jóhannes moved abroad to study art, spending time in London, Copenhagen, France and Italy, but it was only after his return to Iceland in 1940 that he travelled widely in his own country, drawing on the raw beauty he saw around him for his quasi-abstract depictions of Icelandic landscapes which made him one of the country's most popular twentieth-century painters. Painted in oils, much of his work is a surreal fusion of colour: his bizarre yet pleasing *Krítik* from 1946–7, a melee of icy blues, whites and greys measuring a whopping 4m in length and 2m in height, is the centrepiece of the exhibition, portraying a naked man jauntily bending over to expose his testicles while catching a fish, watched over, rather oddly, by a number of Norse warriors. The museum is divided into two halls – the east one shows Jóhannes's work, whilst the west hall is dedicated to visiting temporary exhibitions. Although it may take a while for his style to grow on you, it's certainly worth dropping by – note, though, that the entrance to the museum is on Flókagata, off Rauðarárstígur.

Öskjuhlíð and the Saga Museum

If you arrive in Reykjavík from Keflavík airport, it's hard to miss the space-age-looking grey container tanks that sit at the top of the wooded hill, **Öskjuhlíð**, immediately south of Kjarvalsstaðir, across Miklabraut and southeast along

Bústaðavegur. Each contains 4000 litres of water at 80°C for use in the capital's homes, offices and swimming pools; it's also from here that water is pumped, via a network of specially constructed pipes, underneath Reykjavík's pavements to keep them ice- and snow-free during winter. The whole thing is topped by a revolving restaurant, *Perlan*, a truly spectacular place for dinner – if your wallet can take the strain. The restaurant is, one of Reykjavík's best-known landmarks and is the best place for a 360-degree panoramic **view** of the entire city; simply take the lift to the fourth floor and step outside for free. On a clear day you can see all the way to the Snæfellsjökull glacier at the tip of the Snæfellsnes peninsula, as well as the entirety of Reykjavík.

On the ground floor the excellent **Saga Museum** (April–Sept daily 10am–6pm; Oct–Mar daily noon–5pm; 1500kr; ⓦ www.sagamuseum.is) housed in one of the empty water tanks is Iceland's answer to Madame Tussaud's; this popular portrayal of medieval Icelandic life uses expertly crafted **wax models** of characters from the sagas and their reconstructed farms and homes to superbly enliven this often confusing period of history. Although the entrance fee is steep in comparison to Reykjavík's other museums, it's worth splashing out to get a genuine sense of what life must have been like here centuries ago; indeed, all the big names are here: Snorri, who even rocks back and forth as he ponders, Eirík the Red, Leifur Eiríksson, and his sister, Freyðis, realistically portrayed slicing off her breast as a solitary stand against the natives of Vínland who, after killing one of her compatriots, turned on her – according to the sagas, however, on seeing Freyðis brandish a sword against her breasts, they immediately took flight. An informative audio guide, included in the admission fee, leads you through the museum, explaining a little about each of the characters on display – and the smells of the period which have been synthetically reproduced inside.

Before leaving, make sure you see the artificial indoor **geyser simulator** that erupts every few minutes from the basement, shooting a powerful jet of water all the way to the fourth floor: it's a good taste of what's to come if you're heading out to the real thing at Geysir (see p.113).

Öskjuhlíð itself was also an important landmark in the days when the only mode of long-distance transport was the horse, as it stood out for miles across the barren surrounding plains – and more recently served as a military base for the British army during World War II. Today, though, it's a popular recreation area for Reykjavíkers who, unused to being surrounded by expanses of woodland, flock here by foot and with mountain bikes to explore the **paths** that crisscross its slopes. In fact, Öskjuhlíð has only been wooded since 1950, when an extensive forestation programme began after soil erosion had left the area barren and desolate. Today the western and southern areas of the hill are covered with birch, spruce, poplar and pine. At the southern end of the hill at **Nauthólsvík**, on Nauthólsvegur road close to the Reykjavík Sailing Club, is an artificial **geothermal beach** of bright yellow sand where it's possible to swim in a sea-water lagoon (the water temperature is generally 18–20C°), thanks to the addition of hundreds of gallons of geothermally heated sea water into the open-air **pool** (free; café and changing room facilities mid-May to mid-Sept daily 10am–8pm) next to the beach, where there are also two hotpots (30–35C°), one of which is built into the sand. As with the rest of Reykjavík, the hot water is piped here from the tanks atop the hill.

The Sun Voyager and Höfði house

From Öskjuhlíð, it's a twenty-minute walk north along Snorrabraut to the seafront at Sæbraut, where, off to the left (opposite the northern end of Frakkastígur), the striking *Sólfar* (Sun Voyager) **sculpture** is worthy of your attention. This sleek contemporary portrayal of a Viking-age ship, made of shiny

▲ Sólfar (Sun Voyager) sculpture

silver steel by Jón Gunnar Árnason (1931–89), sits elegantly atop the city shoreline and is fast becoming one of the most photographed of Reykjavík's attractions.

From here, it's a five-minute stroll back east along Sæbraut to **Höfði**, a stocky white wooden structure built in 1909 in Jugend style, which occupies a grassy square beside the shore, between the roads Sæbraut and Borgartún. Originally home of the French consul, the house also played host to Winston Churchill in 1941 when he visited British forces stationed in Iceland. However, Höfði is best known as the venue of the **Reagan–Gorbachev snap summit** of 1986, called at the suggestion of the former Soviet President, Mikhail Gorbachev, to discuss peace and disarmament between the two superpowers. Although agreement was reached in Reykjavík on reducing the number of medium-range and intercontinental missiles in Europe and Asia, the thornier question of America's strategic defence initiative of shooting down missiles in space remained a sticking point. However, the Summit achieved one major goal – it brought the world's attention on Iceland, which, in the mid-1980s, was still relatively unknown as a destination for travellers, in effect marking the beginning of the tourist boom that Iceland is still enjoying today.

Whether Gorbachev and Reagan were troubled by the resident Höfði **ghost** isn't known, but it's said to be that of a young girl, who poisoned herself after being found guilty of incest with her brother. Between 1938 and 1951 the house was occupied by diplomats, including one who was so troubled by the supernatural presence that one dispatch after another was sent to the Foreign Office in London begging for a transfer until he finally got his way. In recent years, lights have switched themselves on and off, paintings have fallen off walls and door handles have worked themselves loose. Today – apart from international summitry – the principal purpose of the house is as a centre for the city's municipal functions.

The Ásmundur Sveinsson Museum

If sculpture is more your thing, you'll want to check out the domed **Ásmundur Sveinsson Museum** (daily: May–Sept 10am–4pm; Oct–April 1–4pm; free;

Ⓦwww.listasafnreykjavikur.is), part of the Reykjavík Art Museum, at Sigtún, a ten-minute dog-leg walk from Höfði; first head east along Sæbraut, then south into Kringlumýrarbraut and east again into Sigtún where you'll see the peculiar white igloo shape beyond the trees on your right hand side.

Ásmundur Sveinsson (1893–1982) was one of the pioneers of Icelandic sculpture, and his powerful, often provocative, work was inspired by his country's nature and literature. During the 1920s he studied in both Stockholm and Paris, returning to Iceland to develop his unique sculptural cubism, a style infused with Icelandic myth and legend, which you can view here at his former home that he designed and built with his own hands in 1942–50; he lived where the museum shop and reception are currently located. The museum is an uncommon shape for Reykjavík, because when Ásmundur planned it, he was experimenting with Mediterranean and North African themes, drawing particular inspiration from the domed houses common to Greece. The crescent-shaped building beyond reception contains examples of the sculptor's work, including several busts from his period of Greek influence, but the original of his most famous sculpture from 1926, *Sæmundur á selnum* (Sæmundur on the Seal), is not on display here but, appropriately, stands outside the main university building on Suðurgata. It shows one of the first Icelanders to receive a university education, the priest and historian Sæmundur Sigfússon (1056–1133), astride a seal, psalter in hand. A smaller version of the original, though, now stands in the museum grounds where you'll also find many of Ásmundur's other soft-edged, gently curved monuments to the ordinary working people of the country.

Laugardalur and around

After rambling through central Reykjavík for a good couple of kilometres, Laugavegur finally comes to an end at the junction with the main north–south artery, Kringlumýrarbraut, actually Route 40, leading to Hafnarfjörður. Beyond here **Suðurlandsbraut** marks the southern reaches of **Laugardalur**, a valley containing hot springs known since the time of the Settlement as a source of hot water for washing, hemmed in between the low hills of Grensás to the south and the northerly Laugarás, just behind Sundahöfn harbour. Although the springs, Þvottalaugarnar, are still here, the spot commemorated by the Ásmundur Sveinsson statue, *Þvottakonan* (The Washerwoman), it's for Iceland's best **sports ground**, Laugardalsvöllur, superb outdoor **swimming complex** (see "Activities" p.90), Laugardalslaug, and **youth hostel** that the area is best known. The green expanses beyond the sports ground contain the country's most impressive **botanical garden** as well as a **zoo**.

The botanical garden and zoo

Barely ten minutes on foot from the Ásmundur Sveinsson sculpture museum, reached by walking east along Engjavegur, the **botanical garden**, part of the Laugardalur, contains an extensive collection of native Icelandic flora, as well as thousands of imported plants and trees. This place is particularly popular with Icelandic families who come here not only to enjoy the surroundings but also to show kids the adjoining **family park** (Fjölskyldugarðurinn) and **zoo** (Húsdýragarðurinn; both mid-May to mid-Aug daily 10am–6pm; mid-Aug to mid-May daily 10am–5pm; 600kr; Ⓦwww.mu.is), where seals, foxes, mink, reindeer and fish caught in Iceland's rivers and lakes are all on hand to keep them happy. Once the attraction of the animals starts to wane, there's a small duck lake, complete with replica Viking longboat, along with other activities based loosely on a Viking theme: a fort, an outlaw hideout and even a go-kart track in the surrounding family park. Buses #2, 15, 17 and 19 all run here from the city centre.

When the wind isn't blowing too strongly, the flat surrounds of Reykjavík lend themselves to **cycling** and an excellent, well-marked **trail** has been laid from the western suburb of Seltjarnarnes via the city airport, Öskjuhlíð (see p.79) and the Elliðaárdalur valley, named after the Elliðaá, one of Iceland's best salmon-fishing rivers, to Heiðmörk, a forested city park immediately southeast of the city centre declared a nature reserve in 1948 – this route is clearly marked on the excellent Map of Reykjavík available from the tourist office (see p.64); for bike rental, see p.65. The salmon season itself runs from June to September and **fishing permits** can be obtained from the Angling Club of Reykjavík (ⓦ www.svfr.is).

East of Öskjuhlíð, the path itself follows the river as it flows into Elliðaárvatn, the largest lake within Greater Reykjavík. Formed thousands of years ago when an outflow of lava dammed the glacial valley here, the lake is 174m above sea level and therefore surrounded by Arctic flora; a walking trail leads around Elliðaárvatn and takes around three hours to complete. Elliðaárdalur is one of Reykjavík's main **horseriding** areas – riding tours are booked through the tourist office in Reykjavík with trips varying in length from under an hour to a full day. Bordering the eastern shores of the lake, Heiðmörk, the largest and most popular recreational area in the city, is set between mountains, craters and lavafields and offers 2800 square hectares of forested expanses ideal for mountain biking or hiking – extensive planting began in 1949 to try to avert severe soil erosion from overgrazing and the harsh climate. Walking and cycle paths crisscross the wooded expanses, dotted with picnic sites, making the area a favourite spot during summer weekends for Reykjavík's inhabitants.

The Árbæjarsafn Open-Air Museum

From the botanical garden, it's a short ride on bus #5 (starting from Lækjartorg) to the **Árbæjarsafn Open-Air Museum** (June–Aug daily 10am–5pm; Sept–May Mon, Wed & Fri 1–2pm; 600kr; ⓦ www.arbaejarsafn.is), a collection of turf-roofed and corrugated-iron buildings on the site of an ancient farm that was first mentioned in the sagas around the mid-1400s. The buildings and their contents record the changes that occurred as Iceland's economy switched from farming to fishing – the industrial revolution being heralded by the arrival of the fishing trawler – and Reykjavík's rapid expansion. The pretty turf church here, dating from 1842, was carefully moved to its present location from Skagafjörður (see p.227) on the north coast in 1960. Next to it, the farmhouse is dominated by an Ásmundur Sveinsson sculpture, *Woman Churning Milk*, illustrating an all-but-lost traditional way of life.

Eating and drinking

Reykjavík has the best range of **places to eat** in the country, mostly packed into the downtown area around Laugavegur and Austurvöllur square. Aside from those reviewed below, most accommodation offers at least breakfast and major hotels – such as the *Radisson SAS 1919* and *Holt* (see p.66) – often have accomplished restaurants.

With Icelanders being avid coffee fans, Reykjavík has a **café** to suit everyone, from trendy student venues with **free wi-fi** to nationwide generic chains and glass-fronted places where the main point is being seen. Coffee and a cake or snack will set you back about 1000kr, though some offer full breakfasts and light meals for 1700kr or so. Cafés generally open around 9am–6pm, with variable hours at the weekends; many mutate into **bars** after 6pm.

Fast food can be surprisingly good in the capital, too, with some well-above-average burger and pizza joints to stave off hunger pangs during a night on the town; you're looking at between 700kr for *pýlsur* (hot dogs) to 2000kr or more for a sit-down burger with a soft drink.

Restaurants open for a few hours around lunchtime and then again from 6pm until late. Options include Thai, Italian and even Middle Eastern places where you can enjoy a decent feed for under 4000kr; lunch-time **buffets** or **set meals** (say soup, main and coffee) can come in for half of this. More formal affairs tend to focus on **Icelandic cuisine**, with lamb, lobster (langoustine) and other seafood taking centre stage alongside unusual game meats like guillemot and whale. A full blow-out in an upmarket restaurant will cost upwards of 8000kr a head; three-course **set meals** give a taster of the à la carte menu and are again good value, considering what you get; the catch is that everyone on your table has to join in. Always book ahead and dress fairly smartly.

If you're **self-catering** the best **supermarkets** in the city centre include: 10–11, close to the Austurvöllur square at Austurstræti 17, which, confusingly, is open round the clock; the larger Bónus, at Laugavegur 59; and the best-stocked and largest supermarket in the country, Hagkaup, in the Kringlan shopping centre, at the junction of Miklabraut and Kringlumýrarbraut and reached either on foot in about forty minutes or by taking bus #5 from the city centre. For take-away booze, the *vínbúð* **alcohol stores** are at Austurstræti 10a and on the lower level of the Kringlan shopping centre, both open daily 11am–6pm.

All the cafés and restaurants listed below are shown on the Reykjavík City Centre map on p.70 unless otherwise stated.

Cafés

Café Paris Austurstræti 14. Over the years this French-style café has become a Reykjavík fixture, with outdoor seating in summer overlooking the Alþingi. Fine central choice for a cup of coffee or a light snack. Daily 9am–late.

Grái Kötturinn Hverfisgata 16a. Smoky, friendly basement café, good for meeting young Reykjavíkers who come here for the excellent coffee. Open from 7am for a big breakfast featuring pancakes, bacon and eggs, and other fry-up options.

Kaffi Sólon Bankastræti 7a. One of Reykjavík's most popular cafés, enjoying a perfect position for people watching. The contemporary Icelandic design makes for a truly relaxing afternoon over a cafetiere and a piece of chocolate cake.

Kaffitár Bankastræti 8. Icelandic version of *Starbucks*, but with far better coffee, made from expertly blended varieties of beans (now available as a brand in supermarkets). The usual run of cakes and muffins, too, with good croissants.

Mokka Skólavörðustígur 3a. The oldest café in Reykjavík, opened in 1958, with a changing display of black-and-white photographs adorning the walls. The place makes a point of not playing music and was the first café in the country to serve espresso and cappuccino to its curious clientele.

Prikið Bankastræti 12. Plying the masses with excellent coffee since the early 1960s, the café today is a firm favourite with the city's trendy young things and students who come here to chill. Open Mon–Fri from 8am for large cooked breakfast (1750kr), Sat & Sun from noon.

Sandholt Laugavegur 36. Family-run bakery with good coffee and excellent pastries (try the pecan-and-maple-syrup twists), flans, fresh sandwiches and handmade chocolates.

Fast food and cheap meals

Bæjarin´s Tryggvagata. You can't get more Nordic fast food than *pýlsur*, hot dogs served in a bun with lashings of fried onion and artery-clogging remoulade sauce, and *Bæjarin's* mobile wagon delivers in style. A local institution.

Búllan Geirsgata 1, at the entrance to the harbour. Little 1950s concrete bunker of a building serving burgers and nothing else, and doing them very well. Expect to queue. Daily 11.45am–9pm.

Eldsmiðjan Bragagata 38a ☎ 562 3838. The best pizzas in Reykjavík, from 1500kr, made in a pizza oven that burns Icelandic birchwood. There's also a takeaway service available.

Garðurinn Klapparstígur 37. Vegetarian café with a small set menu that changes weekly but always features soup, vegetable stews, pasta and crêpes.

Dish of the day will set you back 1350kr, soup with bread 800kr. Mon–Fri 11am–5pm, Sat noon–5pm.

Grillhúsið Tryggvagata 20 ☎562 3456, ⑭www .grillhusid.is. Popular and informal grill restaurant which runs to steaks, but is best visited for its burgers (1265kr) or fish and chips (1755kr).

Habibi Hafnarstræti 18. Looks greasy-spoon forgettable from the outside, but cooks up authentic-tasting kebabs, chicken shawarma and felafel. There's seating for about four people at the counter, so best seen as a take-away option.

Icelandic Fish & Chips Cnr Geirsgata and Norðurstígur. Proper sit-down restaurant serving exactly what you'd expect from the name. Cod and chips costs around 1500kr, or splash out for something fancy like monkfish (1790kr). Garnishes include onion rings and home-made mayonnaise.

🏃 **Krua Thai** Tryggvagata 14, nr Geirsgata. This cosy, no-nonsense Thai place offers exceptional value with a huge choice of single-dish meals – green curry, *pad thai* and the like – for around 1350kr. Portions are generous and come with rice. Mon–Fri 11.30am–9.30pm, Sat 2–9.30pm, Sun 5–9.30pm.

Restaurants

Á Næstu Grösum Laugavegur 20b ☎552 8410, close to the junction with Klapparstígur. This place has been serving tasty vegetarian food for years, with most of the organic ingredients coming from geothermally heated greenhouses near Lake Mývatn. There's always one vegan and one wheat-free dish on the menu; a full meal here can cost less than 2000kr. Open Mon–Fri 11.30am–10pm, Sat 1–10pm, Sun 5–10pm.

Argentína Steikhús Barónsstígur 11a ☎551 9555. The best place in Iceland to wolf down vast quantities of home-grown, char-grilled steak. Don't forget to order the traditional Argentinian accompaniment – a bottle of red wine. Expect to pay upwards of 6000kr a head.

Basil & Lime Klapparstíg 38 ☎555 3696. Italian place with gloomy décor (despite cheerful yellow front) and a well-presented, moderately priced menu that includes seafood soup, their famous lobster tagliatelli and tiramisu. Mains under 2500kr.

Einar Ben Veltusundi 1 ☎511 5090, ⑭www .einarben.is. Named after the poet Einar Benediktsson, this place leads in elegant dining with chandeliers, heavy red drapes and soft lighting. The monkfish (3690kr) and duck (4850kr) are both superb, and the four-course set menu is good value. Renowned for its comprehensive (and paralysingly expensive) wine selection.

Fish Market Aðalstræti 12 ☎578 8877, ⑭www .fiskmarkadurinn.is. Smart, stylish restaurant

specializing in Icelandic–Asian fusion fare – grilled seafood with oriental spices and first-rate sushi. A good deal given the quality; sushi is 1200kr a serve and mains are under 4000kr.

Grænn Kostur Skólavördustígur 8b, overlooking a multistorey car park off Bergstaðastræti. ☎552 2028. Simple vegan restaurant desperately lacking in style, but with tasty food; dish of the day is 1390kr, and their excellent banana cake just 500kr.

🏃 **Hornið** Hafnarstræti 15 ☎551 3340. Long-time favourite with young Reykjavíkers, who flock here for the excellent pizzas (1920kr) and pasta (from 1800kr). Wine here can be inordinately expensive – check carefully before ordering.

Indian Mango Beautifully presented Indian food – tandoori char, roasted lamb fillet with mango or Lucknow chicken are all excellent. Not too pricey for what you get; the only downsides are erratic service and slender vegetarian menu.

🏃 **Jómfrúin** Lækjargata 4 ☎551 0100. Popular Danish-influenced place specializing in *smørrebrød* (open rye sandwiches). Pick the fillings from a range including smoked salmon, caviar, shrimps, asparagus, smoked eel and scrambled egg. Fried plaice is the house speciality. It can be expensive for what you get – choose carefully.

🏃 **Lækjarbrekka** Bankastræti 2 ☎551 4430, ⑭www.laekjarbrekka.is. Old wooden building with period furnishings, refined atmosphere and fabulous seafood. The lobster feast (8190kr) includes cream of lobster soup with cognac, grilled lobster en croûte and grand marnier ice cream; the puffin feast (6980kr) features a salad of smoked and marinated puffin followed by puffin breast in a blue cheese sauce; while the lamb menu (7290kr) has roast lamb in mountain herbs as a main dish. Overpriced but the food is superb – somewhere for a special occasion.

Restaurant Reykjavík Vesturgata 2 ☎552 3030, ⑭www.restaurantreykjavik.is. Justifiably renowned for its nightly fish buffet (4700kr), and January Þorrablaðborð buffet (4900kr), which includes some hard-core Icelandic delicacies like rams' testicles and fermented shark. Don a fur coat to visit the adjacent *Ice Bar* for a shot of *brennevín*.

🏃 **Rosso Pomodoro** Laugavegur 40 ☎561 0500. A genuinely good southern Italian restaurant drawing inspiration from the cuisine of Naples and around. Pizzas and pasta dishes go for around 2300kr, salads start around 2150kr and grilled chicken with vegetables is 3200kr. Look for lunchtime specials posted on the board outside.

🏃 **Sægreifinn** Verbúð 8, Geirsgata ☎553 1500. This harbourside fishmongers-cum-restaurant (the name translates as "The Sea Baron") is a favourite haunt of locals after the superlative lobster soup and fresh catfish. It's also the place to come for whale kebabs, if your conscience allows. The owner, Kjartan, doesn't speak English, but a bit of pointing and a few words of Icelandic should get you by. Open daily from 4pm.

Vegamót Vegamótastígur 4 ☎ 511 3040. A favourite hangout for Reykjavík's trendy young things, who come here for the good-value brunches and dinner, though the food isn't as good as the lively, sociable atmosphere. Reckon on 2300kr for a main dish.

Við Tjörnina Templarasund 3 ☎ 551 8666. One of the best fish restaurants in Reykjavík, divided into quaint, cluttered, grand-motherly rooms with views of the pond (you get bread crusts to feed the ducks afterwards). Daring and delicious cuisine, featuring everything from honey-braised wolf-fish to sautéed breast of guillemot in port. Mains around 4000kr.

Þrír Frakkar Baldursgata 14 ☎ 552 3939. Strange name (Three Overcoats) for this backstreet French-style bistro with definite leanings towards traditional Icelandic game: whale pepper-steak, horse tenderloin, *plokkfiskur* (fish and potato mash) and smoked puffin. Mains around 3700kr.

Nightlife and entertainment

Thanks to some cunning publicity from the Icelandic Tourist Board, Reykjavík's **nightlife** is now deservedly known across Europe and the US for its partying. Although the scene is actually no bigger than that of any small-sized town in most other countries, what sets it apart is the northerly setting and location for all this revelry – during the light nights of summer, it's very disorientating to have entered a nightclub in the wee small hours with the sun just about to set, only to emerge a couple of hours later (and several thousand krónur poorer) into the blinding and unflattering daylight of the Icelandic morning. Very few people are out much before 10pm, after which time crowds fill the streets and queues develop outside the most popular joints. Partying rarely winds up before early morning, and it's certainly not uncommon to see hordes of youngsters staggering around Lækjar-torg at 4am shivering in the cold air dressed, fashion-consciously, only in their latest T-shirts and jeans – and often in much less.

You'll need plenty of cash for even a few **drinks** (a beer in a club costs upward of 1000kr) – and don't be tempted to leave your drink on the bar while you go dancing, as the chances are it'll have been drunk by the time you return. **Admission fees** to clubs are not too steep, generally around 500–1000kr if there's live music, otherwise free. As you'd expect, things are liveliest on Friday and Saturday nights, when most places swing until 5 or 6am; closing time the rest of the week is around 1am.

Bars, pubs and clubs

The best spots to start **socializing** are bars and pubs, as well as some of the cafés listed on p.84 that turn into bars after 6pm. Remember that, whatever your tradition at home, you won't be expected to buy a round of drinks if you're in company, since that would be virtually ruinous, and that it's quite permissible to nurse one drink through the entire evening. Some of the bars listed below are attached to restaurants but you can always drink without eating.

Don't expect to get into a club in style-conscious Reykjavík if you turn up in full hiking gear – the **dress code** is generally smart and Icelandic men often don a tie to go out clubbing. For foreigners things are more relaxed, but you'll feel more comfortable if you're smart-casual. At some places, jeans and sneakers aren't allowed. However you're kitted out, don't be surprised if you're approached and chatted up as soon as you've set foot through the door – Reykjavík is a small city and new faces will always draw attention.

Wrecked in Reykjavík

A rite of passage for all Icelandic teenagers, the **rúntur** (literally "round tour") is a drunken pub crawl that generally takes place between at least half a dozen bars and pubs, whatever the weather. Intent on searching out the place with the hottest action, groups of revellers, already well oiled after downing several generous vodkas before setting out, maraud the city centre, particularly on Friday nights. If you come across them, expect to be engaged in conversation or to see some rather unrestrained behaviour – but then nightlife in Iceland isn't known for its subtleties.

All the bars and clubs below are shown on the Reykjavík City Centre map on p.70 unless otherwise stated.

Bjarni Fel Austurstræti 20. Sports bar full of memorabilia and TV screens; best place to catch the latest soccer match over a cold beer.

Broadway Inside *Park Inn Ísland*, Ármúli 9 (see map on p.67). One of the country's biggest night-spots prone to Vegas-style singing and dancing spectaculars, though occasionally with more interesting fare and popular with people of all ages, from teenagers to pensioners.

Café Cultura Hverfisgata 18. Popular expat hangout with imported beers and live music most weekends. Good-value light meals and bar food too.

Celtic Cross Hverfisgata 26. Best of the three Brit/Irish pubs in town; the beer is the same (Guinness and lager) but the atmosphere is livelier – especially when bands fire up at weekends.

Dubliner Hafnarstræti 4. Irish theme bar with wooden tables and live music upstairs most nights. A good choice for an evening pint, and there's also a decent selection of whiskies.

English Pub Austurstræti 12. Lager, Guinness and Kilkenny, soccer on TV and weekend live music. Pay 1500kr and spin the wheel of fortune, with a metre of beer as the prize if you win.

Grand Rokk Smiðjustígur 6. Inexpensive, unpretentious bar, reputedly serving Iceland's cheapest beer – so understandably popular. Live bands perform upstairs, generally at weekends.

Hverfisbarinn Hverfisgata 20. Consistently Reykjavík's most popular bar, attracting all the city's young in-crowd who come to pose and pout in the large glass windows overlooking Hverfisgata. If you're young and beautiful, or just think you are, you'll love it here. Often long queues to get in. Entrance 500kr.

Kaffibarinn Bergstaðastræti 1. Unmistakable red corrugated iron front with green window frames and brown wooden blinds; fancies itself as an arty hangout and definitely a trendy place for a beer or two.

NASA Austurvöllur square. Housed in a former theatre, this is Reykjavík's biggest and best club and *the* place to be seen, with wild dance music all night long attracting Reykjavík's well dressed, well heeled and well tipsy.

Oliver Laugavegur 20a. Immediately recognizable by a large red swirl on the front windows, *Oliver* pulls a 20-something crowd at weekends who come to dance and strut on the dancefloor upstairs.

Samtökin Laugavegur 3. The best place for gay men and women to meet – if the other places listed are quiet, the chances are there'll always be someone here.

Sódóma Tryggvagata 22. Bar and live band venue famous for plastering its urinal bowls with pictures of the failed bankers who fled Iceland after the 2008 financial crash. Good atmosphere for a drink and a listen to some music.

Gay Reykjavík

Although a **gay scene** (Ⓦwww.gayice.is) does exist in Reykjavík, it is very small and at times crashingly provincial in style and scale. There are just two exclusively gay **bars** in the capital: *Samtökin*, Laugavegur 3 (Ⓣ552 7878, Ⓦwww.samtokin78 .is), a bar, café and gay library all rolled into one, open Mon & Thurs 8–11pm, which welcomes lesbians and gay men; and the male-only *MSC* leather club (Ⓦwww.msc.is) in the basement at Laugavegur 28, entered via the iron gate off the main street and open from 11pm on Fri & Sat. Alternatively, try the pink-fronted *Barbara*, a predominantly gay bar and club at Laugavegur 22, though whose entrance is actually on Klapparstígur. The only other place to meet gay men is the sauna at the Vesturbæjarlaug **swimming pool** (see p.90).

Gay Pride (Ⓦwww.gaypride.is) always takes place on the second weekend in August. It's a relatively small-scale though fun affair, with a procession of floats along Laugavegur topped by scantily clad drag queens shivering from the cold, an evening of dancing and merrymaking and other cultural activities. For further information contact *Samtökin* (see p.87).

Live music, theatre and cinema

There's been a strong **rock music** network in Reykjavík for over two decades, represented originally by Björk and the Sugarcubes, and more recently by groups such as Sigur Rós, though decent venues have always been thin on the ground, with most gigs taking place in one of the city's bars or restaurants. Besides the local talent, a lot of British and American acts use Icelandair as a cheap way to cross the Atlantic and they often do a show here on the way. Find out what's on by checking with the tourist information office (see p.64) or by looking through their free handout *What's on in Reykjavík*. The following establishments often have live music at weekends, featuring anything from jazz to rock: *Celtic Cross* at Hverfisgata 26; *Dubliner* at Hafnarstræti 4; and the *Hótel Borg* at Pósthússtræti 11.

Remarkably, for such a small city, Reykjavík boasts several **theatre** groups, an opera, a symphony orchestra and a dance company. Unfortunately, major theatre productions and classical concerts, by the **Icelandic Symphony Orchestra**, are a rarity in summer, but throughout the rest of the year there are full programmes of both. Events are chiefly held at the Þjóðleikhúsið (the National Theatre, Ⓦwww.leikhusid.is) at Hverfisgata 19 or the Háskólabíó cinema complex, home to the Symphony Orchestra, at Hagatorg off Suðurgata. The **Icelandic Opera** (Ⓦopera.is) is at Ingólfsstræti 2a, and the **City Theatre** (Ⓦborgarleikhus.is) at Listabraut 3.

The **cinema** is a better bet if you have time on your hands and little money in your pocket: new international releases are screened with subtitles; see any of the newspapers (see Basics, p.42) or check Ⓦwww.bio.is for full listings. The main cinemas are Regnboginn, Hverfisgata 54, and Háskólabíó, on Hagatorg, off Suðurgata. More unusual is the worthwhile **Volcano Show** at Hellusund 6a (☎845 9548), a two-hour set of films in two showings of recent Icelandic eruptions from daringly close quarters filmed largely by the engaging Villi Knudsen. During July and August part-one screenings in English (Villi Knudsen's volcano adventures) begin at 11am, 3pm and 8pm, with part two (Heimaey and Surtsey eruptions) following at noon, 4pm and 9pm; times vary at other times of the year.

Activities

Although there are plenty of attractions in and around Reykjavík to keep even the most demanding visitor occupied for several days, it's easy access to some exceptional **adventure activities** that really makes the Icelandic capital such an appealing and unusual destination. **Whale watching** and **puffin-spotting tours** are available aboard boats which sail from the harbour right in the city centre; **snowmobile trips**, although not possible in the immediate vicinity of the capital, depart regularly from Reykjavík for several of the country's southeastern glaciers, and **horseriding** astride Iceland's very own breed of horse, the Íslandshestur, a short, stocky creature renowned for its unusual gait, is already inordinately popular.

The **swimming pool** is to the Icelanders what the pub is to the British or the coffee shop to Americans. This is the place to come when in Reykjavík to meet

The great outdoors

In a country whose scenery is so iconic, and whose historical events are inextricably wrapped up with its landscape, the only real way to get to grips with Iceland is to get outdoors. It's where many Icelanders choose to spend their free time too, though they often seem to have a fearless disregard for the weather, geological events and other natural hazards that foreigners take sensible precautions against. For most visitors, the walking trails, hot springs and abundant wildlife are reasons enough to explore

Hiking

Iceland's hiking trails are easy to get to, yet feel wonderfully remote and wild: on many of them you can walk for days and not see anyone. The country is also small enough that it's feasible to simply pick two points on a map and walk between them – assuming, of course, that you're suitably equipped for any natural hazards along the way – though there are also many well-marked trails heading off across the landscape. Popular areas have well-equipped campsites and lodge-like "huts" with kitchens, which make good bases for day-hikes – though there are also some superb, totally wild areas where you can spend a week or more camping rough. You always need to take Iceland's changeable weather very seriously, and come equipped with warm, waterproof and tough clothing, cooking gear, relevant maps, and a tent which isn't going to get blown apart by gale-force winds.

Hiking in winter, Vatnajökull glacier ▲

Hot baths at Landmannalaugar ▼

Getting into hot water

One of the byproducts of the country's location on top of a volcanic faultline is that it has limitless supplies of natural hot water, heated down in the earth's crust before coming to the surface – often violently. Scalding mud pools, whistling steam vents and geysers are just part of the landscape here, but in some places these outpourings have been tamed and put to use. Many Icelandic homes enjoy inexpensive hot water and central heating, either pumped directly from the nearest source or through electricity created in geothermal power plants. Icelanders have also been bathing outdoors in naturally heated springs since the country was first settled, and many of these "hot pots" still exist, often in stunningly scenic locations, where you

Top five hikes

▶▶ **Laugavegur** An epic four-day hike over snowfields, moorland and desert between hot springs at Landmannalaugar and the highland valley of Þórsmörk: see p.124.

▶▶ **Hornstrandir** You can spend days hiking across this totally unpopulated peninsula, which is probably the wildest, most remote corner of Iceland that is still accessible: see p.197.

▶▶ **Þórsmörk** Isolated glacier valley in the southwest, covered in dwarf birch and wildflowers, with almost limitless hiking potential: see p.134.

▶▶ **Skaftafell** Easily reached moorland plateau between two glaciers, with plenty of well-marked trails of up to a day's duration: see p.303.

▶▶ **Jökulsárgljúfur** Straightforward though lengthy trails follow a glacier river canyon down to Europe's largest waterfall: see p.268.

▲ Summertime hiking, Jökulsárlón

▼ Arctic fox

can peel off your clothes and soak any aches away while admiring the surrounding mountains, volcanoes and seascapes. The top three spots for an outdoor soak are Landmannalaugar in southwestern Iceland (see p.123), Grettislaug in the northwest (see p.227) and Krossneslaug in the West Fjords (see p.213). And for those who prefer more formal arrangements, just about every settlement across the country has its own geothermally heated swimming pool too.

Wildlife-watching

Given that Iceland is virtually treeless, and that the dominant landscape is lava rubble covered by lichens, or gravel deserts and ice, you wouldn't think that there would be much in the way of wildlife to watch. However, it's still worth bringing along a pair of binoculars: both arctic fox and

Humpback whale ▲

Harbour seal ▼

reindeer are resident mammals, though – as both are also hunted – they tend to be timid and take off the moment that people appear. You'll have better luck with **birds**, however, which group all over the country in phenomenal numbers throughout the summer. For sea birds – including puffins, skuas, gulls and fulmars – head to the nearest coastline, where you'll also find all manner of waders picking over the shore. Wildfowl – such as divers, whooper swans and geese – congregate in the many lagoons, lakes and moorlands across the country, while if it's duck you're after, head to Lake Mývatn in the northeast (see p.253). Most other wildlife is marine, and Iceland is an excellent place to see **seals**, **dolphins** and several species of **whale** – most commonly minke, fin and humpbacked, though occasionally also blue – with numerous whale-watching tours offered, especially at Húsavík (see p.266), Reykjavík (see p.89) and Keflavík (see p.102).

Bird attack!

Throughout the summer, several of Iceland's ground-nesting birds become obsessively protective of their young, should you wander into their colonies. The main culprits here are the diminutive **arctic tern** and larger, bulky brown **greater skua**, and either will dive-bomb you at high speed should you approach too close to their nests, first just as a warning, then delivering a hard stab with their beaks if you don't clear off. Some people advise carrying a stick held upright above your head – the birds will attack the highest point rather than your scalp – though a self-opening umbrella is also good for scaring off attackers. Incidentally, the Icelandic name for the arctic tern, *kría*, is an aptly onomatopoeic word for the sound the bird makes as it comes in for the attack.

people, catch up on the local gossip and to relax in divine geothermally heated waters. The locals loll around in the pools for hours, as there is no time limit on how long you can stay in the pool. Entrance fees are around 350kr; the cost is kept low by subsidies from the Icelandic taxpayer.

Although Reykjavík is surrounded by superb **hiking** terrain, much of it is difficult to reach without your own transport. However, two excellent areas, both accessible by bus, lie within easy striking distance of the capital. Hengill, south of Reykjavík on the Ringroad towards Selfoss, offers the best hiking opportunities around Reykjavík, whereas the slopes of Mount Esja, between Reykjavík and Akranes, offer steep climbs and superb views of the Greater Reykjavík region.

Lastly, there are also several opportunites for **skiing** at Bláfjöll, Skálafell and Hamragill, all of which are suitable for varying levels of expertise, from beginner upwards.

Whale watching and puffin-spotting

Operated by Elding (☎555 3565, ⓦwww.elding.is), **whale-watching tours** leave daily (April–Oct 9am & 1pm, plus 5pm in June–Aug; 9200kr) from Ægisgarður, the main jetty in Reykjavík harbour, between Geirsgata and Mýrargata, sailing for Faxaflói bay north of Reykjavík. On both tours you're most likely to encounter minke whales, orcas, humpbacks and dolphins, although, occasionally, blue, fin and sei whales also put in an appearance. This tour not only offers exceptional value for money but also a chance to go **puffin-spotting** at close quarters since the vessels sail around **Lundey** and **Akurey**, two islands renowned for their large population of these birds which gather here to breed between late May and mid-August. The staggeringly large population of puffins comes in at around 30,000 (the total Icelandic puffin population is put at ten million and the average bird lives for around 25 years). Although it's not possible to go ashore, it's still a truly remarkable experience. From the boat you'll have a great view of the cliffs and grassy slopes which make up the island's sides, and the burrows where the puffins live. The smell of guano here is also very strong. The birds remain on the islands until mid-August when they head out to sea for a period of approximately eight months.

Snowmobiling

The Activity Group (☎580 9900, ⓦwww.activity.is) are the people to contact for **snowmobile tours** (May–Aug), though sadly they're not in everybody's price range. For a steep 34,200kr, you buy nine hours of sheer exhilaration on the Langjökull glacier, Iceland's second largest, south of Húsafell (see p.163), plus a tour round some of western Iceland's other attractions. Although the price is high, if you're intent on seeing this part of the country without your own transport it might be worth splashing out. **Departures** are daily at 9am from Reykjavík; you'll head first for Hvalfjörður fjord before cutting inland to the Deildartunguhver hot spring (see p.162) and the Hraunfossar waterfalls (see p.163). From here the tour takes the Kaldidalur interior route (see p.164) towards the glacier, where you transfer to snowmobile for a tour to the top of the icesheet. On from here you call at Þingvellir (see p.106) before returning to Reykjavík. A shorter, cheaper version (7hr; 24,500kr) of the tour also leaves Reykjavík daily at 9am, though heading straight for the glacier via Kaldidalur.

Horseriding

Horseriding is an altogether less expensive option with several companies offering tours of anything from one hour to one day. The most established operator is Íshestar (☎555 7000, ⓦwww.ishestar.is), based in Hafnarfjörður at

Sörlaskeið 26. Most of their day tours operate all year round and range from a three-hour excursion around the local lavafields (daily 10am & 2pm; 6,500kr) to a seven-hour trip out to Geysir and Gullfoss (10am; 13,400kr).

Swimming

The abundance of natural hot water around the capital means there's a good choice of **swimming pools**, which are always at a comfortably warm 29°C, often with hot pots at 39–43°C. **Opening hours** are generally from 6.30am until around 10pm Monday to Friday, and from 8am or so until 8pm Saturday and Sunday. Remember you must shower without a swimming costume before entering the pools and thoroughly wash the areas of your body marked on the signs by the showers – because pool water in Iceland doesn't contain large amounts of chlorine to kill germs as is common in most other countries. The best three city-centre pools are: Laugardalslaug, on Sundlaugavegur and adjacent to the youth hostel (see p.68), Iceland's largest outdoor swimming complex, complete with fifty-metre pool, four hot pots, a jacuzzi, steam room, waterslide and masseuse; Sundhöllin, on Barónsstígur and close to Hallgrímskirkja, with an indoor 25-metre pool, two outdoor hot pots, plus single-sex nude sunbathing on outdoor terraces; and Vesturbæjarlaug, on Hofsvallagata, with an outdoor 25-metre pool plus three hot pots, a sauna, steam bath and solarium. Swimming costumes can be hired for a small charge at all three.

Hiking

Set in an area of lush vegetation, hot springs (harnessed by the Reykjavík District Heating Company to provide central heating for the capital) and volcanic activity, **Hengill** (803m) has around 125km of well-marked hiking trails, all detailed on free **maps** available at the tourist information centre in Reykjavík (see p.64). Hengill mountain, which dominates the area, is in fact a volcanic ridge (*gill* is an old Viking word that still exists in northern English dialects meaning cleft or ravine) that has erupted several times in the past, and the surrounding area is made up of numerous lavafields, craters, hot springs and bubbling mud pools – it's therefore vital to follow marked paths that have been carefully laid out. To get here, take the 8.30am (daily June to mid-Sept; mid-Sept–May Mon–Fri only; 1hr) long-distance **bus** from the BSÍ bus terminal to Selfoss and ask the driver to let you off at the bottom of the Hveradala hill at Kolviðarhóll from where you can start hiking, choosing a route that fits your time available and physical ability. To return to the capital, head back for the Ringroad and catch the daily all-year 4pm bus coming back from Selfoss.

Proudly standing guard over Reykjavík, **Mount Esja** is a familiar sight to anyone who's spent even a few hours in the capital. At 909m, the mountain appears to change colour – from light purple to deep blue, from light grey to golden – depending on the prevailing weather conditions and the light that reflects on the basalt rock and palagonite minerals which make up the mountain, although locals say it depends on her mood. Several hiking trails wind their way around the mountain – once again, a detailed **itinerary** is available from the tourist office – but it's best to start out at Mógilsá where the Icelandic state forestry station has its base. From here an easy path leads up the mountain towards the rocky higher stretches.

Skiing

Although **skiing** is possible in the Reykjavík area, there's so little daylight during the winter period that the amount of time you can actually spend skiing in the day is severely limited. For winter **bus** times to all of the ski areas below, call ☏562 1011.

Thirty minutes by car or bus outside the capital there are three winter downhill skiing areas. The best of the bunch is **Bláfjöll** (Blue Mountains), 20km away with five ski areas of varying difficulty. For cross-country skiing there are tracks of

3–10km, with night skiing available on a five-kilometre route. Get here by taking the Ringroad east until you see a sign for Bláfjöll – turn right onto Route 417 and follow the signs to the mountains.

Skálafell lies to the northeast of Reykjavík and, once again, has beginner, intermediate and advanced hills though it isn't as extensive as Bláfjöll. Incidentally, if you're a fan of chairlifts, you'll find Iceland's longest here at 1500m. Excellent cross-country skiing is also available. From the capital take the Ringroad north until you see a sign for Þingvellir, turn right onto Route 36 and continue until you see a sign for Skálafell, finally turn left into the ski area.

Heading east on the Ringroad for around twenty minutes until just beyond the turn for Route 39 – don't take this road but continue one minute beyond it and turn into the ski area marked on the left – brings you to the **Hamragill** skiing area with its seven ski lifts. Pistes of varying degrees of difficulty are available here, as are some decent cross-country routes.

Listings

Airlines Air Iceland/Flugfélag Íslands Ⓦwww .airiceland.is; Icelandair Ⓦwww.icelandair.com; Iceland Express Ⓦwww.icelandexpress.com; departure and arrival information for Keflavík airport online at Ⓦwww.keflavikairport.com and on Teletext on the state Icelandic TV channel, Sjónvarpið.
Alcohol store Austurstræti 10a (Mon–Thurs & Sat 11am–6pm, Fri 11am–7pm; Ⓦwww.vinbud.is).
Bookshops Bóksala Stúdenta, Sæmundargata 4; Eymundsson, Austurstræti 18; Mál og Menning, Laugavegur 18. Both Eymundsson and Mál og Menning sell English-language books and videos on Iceland, Icelandic–English dictionaries and foreign newspapers.
Camping and outdoors equipment Útilíf, Kringlan shopping centre.
Car rental Avis, Knarrarvogur 2 Ⓦavis.is; Bílaleiga Akureyrar, Skeifan 9 Ⓦwww.holdur.is; Budget, Vatnsmýrarvegur 10 Ⓦwww.budget.is; Hassó, Smiðjuvegur 34, Kópavogur Ⓦhasso.is; Hertz, Flugvallabraut Ⓦhertz.is.
Currency exchange Forex, Bankastræti 2 Ⓦwww.forex.is.
Dentist For the duty dentist call ☎575 0505. English spoken.

Embassies and consulates Canada, Túngata 14 ☎575 6500; UK, Laufásvegur 31 ☎550 5100; USA, Laufásvegur 21 ☎562 9100.
Emergencies Fire, ambulance and police ☎112.
Ferries Smyril Line, Stangarhyl 1 Ⓦwww .smyril-line.com, for the Smyril Line ferry from Seyðisfjörður to Tórshavn (Faroe Islands), and Esbjerg/Hanstholm (Denmark); Viðey island from Sundahöfn, Ⓦwww.elding.is/videy.
Internet Tourist Office, Aðalstræti 2; Ráðhúskaffi, Reykjavík City Hall; Trip.is, Laugavegur 54; Reykjavík city library (Borgarbókasafn Reykjavíkur; 5th floor), Tryggvagata 15.
Laundry Þvottahúsið Emla, Barónsstígur 3 ☎552 7499.
Lost property Police headquarters, Hverfisgata 113–115 ☎444 1000.
News in English There is an English-language news summary at Ⓦwww.mbl.is/english.
Pharmacies Lyfja, Lágmúli 5 (daily 7am–1am; ☎533 2309); Lyfja, Laugavegur 16 (Mon–Fri 9am–6pm, Sat 11am–4pm; ☎552 4046).
Police Tryggvagata 19 ☎444 1000.
Post office Pósthússtræti 5 (Mon–Fri 9am–6pm; Ⓦwww.postur.is).

Around Reykjavík: Hafnarfjörður and Viðey

Home to two out of every three Icelanders, **Greater Reykjavík** is composed of the neighbouring municipalities of Seltjarnarnes, northwest of the city centre, Mosfellsbær to the northeast, and, in the southwest, Hafnarfjörður, Garðabær and Kópavogur, the last three of which are passed through by the road into the city centre from Keflavík airport.

Comprising row upon row of neat, tidy suburban dwellings of dormitory overspill for Reykjavík, all but **Hafnarfjörður** hold little of interest to the visitor. During the past twenty or thirty years several of these places, in particular Kópavogur and Garðabær, have grown enormously, sending shivers down the spines of city planners and politicians in Reykjavík who admit to fighting a losing battle to stem the flow of people from the villages and towns in the rest of the country, and new tax breaks and other incentives are constantly being dreamed up to prevent population overload – and ever-rising prices – in Reykjavík. Whether these measures succeed in the long term remains to be seen.

Just outside Sundahöfn harbour, to the north of Reykjavík, the island of **Viðey** makes an excellent destination for a short boat trip. It has some enjoyable walking trails and is easily reached on a seven-minute ferry journey from Sundahöfn harbour, northeast of Laugardalur.

Hafnarfjörður

Stealing the limelight from its neighbours thanks to its dramatic setting amid an extensive lavafield, **Hafnarfjörður**, with a population of around 26,000 and just 10km from the capital, is as big as the centre of Reykjavík, although it's not as likeable. However, there are several good reasons to make the 25-minute bus ride out here, the main ones being to sample some real Viking food at the town's Viking village, **Fjörukráin**, and to learn more about the Icelanders' obsession with elves, dwarves and other spiritual beings – Hafnarfjörður is renowned across the country as the home to the greatest concentration of **huldufólk** ("hidden people").

The town's prosperity stems from its superbly sheltered harbour (Hafnarfjörður meaning "the harbour fjord") – 7000 years ago the volcano Búrfell (see p.119), around 5km east of the centre, erupted, spewing lava out along the northern side of the fjord that is now home to Hafnarfjörður, creating a protective wall. At the beginning of the fifteenth century the village became a strategic centre for trade with England, which was then just starting up, and the harbour was often full of English boats profiting from the then rich fishing grounds offshore. Seventy-five years later, a dispute broke out between the English and newly arrived German fishermen who challenged, and won, the right to operate out of the burgeoning town. Their victory, however, was short-lived, since Hafnarfjörður fell under the trade monopoly of the Danes in 1602, which lasted until 1787, when the place fell into obscurity. Today, however, the place is known for its inhabitants, called *hafnies*, the unfortunate subjects of many an Icelandic joke – it's said, for example, that local children take ladders when they start at high school, which their parents also use to go shopping with if they hear that prices have gone up. Needless to say, Icelandic humour can be an acquired taste.

Arrival and information

From Hlemmur and Lækjartorg in Reykjavík city centre, **bus** #1 runs to Hafnarfjörður (every 30min), passing the **tourist information office** (Mon–Thu 8am–5pm, Fri 9am–5pm, also daily June–Aug 11am–5pm inside Hafnarfjörður museum; ☎585 5500, ⓦwww.visithafnarfjordur.is), at Strandgata 6, and the Fjörður shopping centre, halfway along Fjarðargata.

There's a decent outdoor **swimming pool** at Hringbraut 77 and an indoor pool at Herjólfsgata 10. If you've come to Hafnarfjörður to go **horseriding** (see "Activities", p.89), you'll find Íshestar (see p.89), at Sörlaskeið 26, southeast of the town centre along Kaldárselsvegur. The **library** (Mon–Wed 10am–7pm, Thurs 9am–9pm, Fri 11am–7pm, plus Sept–May Sat 11am–3pm), diagonally opposite the tourist office at Strandgata 1, has **internet** access.

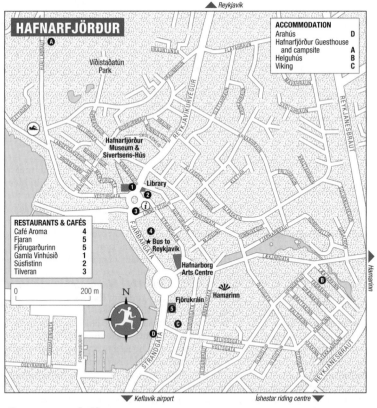

www.roughguides.com

93

Accommodation

There's little reason to stay overnight in Hafnarfjörður, given that Reykjavík is so close, but should you wish to extend your visit here, Víðistaðatún park off Flókagata, north of the centre, has a **campsite** (mid-May to mid-Sept; 1000kr per person) with hot and cold running water, and a **guesthouse**, *Hafnarfjörður Guesthouse and campsite* (same details for both: ☎565 0900, ⓦwww.hafnarfjordur guesthouse.is; ❶) at Hjallabraut 51. Otherwise, in the town centre, at Strandgata 21, *Arahús* (☎555 1770, ⓦwww.arahus.is; ❶) is a pleasant and tastefully decorated guesthouse with shared facilities and two kitchens, whereas, east of the centre, at Lækjarkinn 8, there's another, more dowdy guesthouse, *Helguhús* (☎555 2842, ⓦwww.helguhus.is; ❶) with a handful of rooms, also sharing facilities and a kitchen. Upmarket **hotel** accommodation is available at the *Hótel Viking* (☎565 1213, ⓦwww.fjorukrain.is; ❸) at Strandgata 55, where all 42 rooms have private facilities and a Viking feel to the décor with lots of wooden flourishes and Gothic prints hanging on the walls; there's also a sauna and hot tub for guests.

The Town

The **harbour** is the best place to start your wanderings. Home port for many of Iceland's ocean-going trawlers, it's an interesting spot for watching the bustle as fishermen land their catches, wash down their vessels and mend their nets. From here, it's a five-minute walk south along Fjarðargata to the roundabout to the arts centre of **Hafnarborg** (Wed–Mon 11am–5pm; free) at Strandgata 34. In a fit of generosity the building was donated to the town by a local chemist and his wife in 1983 and today exhibits work by local Icelandic artists as well as doubling as a concert venue – it's worth a quick look, but you're more likely to satisfy your artistic appetite in Reykjavík. Walking south from here, crossing the roundabout into what is now Strandgata, will take you towards the curious steeply roofed wooden structure called **Fjörukráin**, set back from the seafront at no. 55. Although a bit of a tourist trap, this hotel and restaurant is a good place to sample some pretty authentic **Viking food** (see opposite).

From *Fjörukráin*, retrace your steps to the roundabout and follow Strandgata back towards the town centre. This is Hafnarfjörður's diminutive main shopping street, though don't expect the stores here to come close to the selection in Reykjavík – although the capital is only just down the road, this is provincial Iceland. Instead, the interest here lies in the fact that the street of Strandgata and neighbouring Austurgata are, according to Icelandic folklore, home to Hafnarfjörður's population of **hidden people** – elves, dwarves and other spirits who live in entire families between the rocks that are dotted around the town centre. Apparently elves are only visible to those with second sight, though a majority of Icelanders are quite prepared to admit they believe in them. In fact, an alarming number of new roads constructed across the country have been subject to minor detours around large rocks after workers attempted to move the boulders only to find that their diggers and earth movers broke down time and again in the process. Should you be keen to try out your second sight, **tours** (Tues & Fri 2.30pm; 3000kr; ☎694 2785, ⓦwww.alfar.is) lasting a couple of hours and led by guide and storyteller Sigurbjörg Karlsdóttir weave their way through Hafnarfjörður visiting the homes of the *huldufólk*.

A stone's throw from the northern end of Strandgata, one block to the north of the harbour at Vesturgata 8, is **Hafnarfjörður museum** (June–Aug daily 11am–5pm; Sept–May Sat & Sun 11–5pm; free), housed in a wooden warehouse dating from the late 1800s and also known as Pakkhúsið. Inside is a passable if somewhat dull portrayal of Hafnarfjörður's life and times. Next door stands **Sívertsens-Hús**, the town's oldest building, dating from 1803 and once the residence of local trader, boat builder and man about town Bjarni Sívertsen, today home to a folk museum (same times). The interior is stuffed with dreary how-we-used-to-live paraphernalia from the nineteenth century.

More rewarding than Hafnarfjörður's slight attempt at culture are the views from **Hamarinn** cliffs – retrace your steps along the harbour front along Strandgata to the roundabout just before *Fjörukráin*, where you should turn left into Lækjargata, then head east along this road and take the footpath up the hill to the wall of lava you'll see; this leads to the viewpoint. The protected wooded natural area up here offers good views out over the harbour and the surrounding countryside and is a pleasant place to have a picnic when the weather's good. Incidentally, the ugly red- and white-striped towers you can see from here, which dominate the surrounding flat landscape of lavafields, belong to the vast aluminium smelter at Straumsvík, which imports its raw materials from Australia and uses local geothermal power to produce the metal.

Eating and drinking

Unusually for provincial Iceland, Hafnarfjörður throws up more than two **eating** opportunities, but by far the best option is *Fjörugarðurinn* inside the Fjörukráin complex, where you can sample traditional **Viking food**. The best time to visit is during the old Icelandic month of Þorri (from the Friday between Jan 19 & 25 until late Feb) when there are nightly Viking banquets known as *þorrablót* offering the dubious delight of sampling traditional foods – rotten shark, singed sheep's head, pickled rams' testicles, squashed flat and eaten as a topping to an open sandwich – washed down with generous quantities of the potent Icelandic schnapps, Black Death.

Café Aroma Fjarðargata, upstairs in the Fjörður shopping centre. This light and airy café enjoys unsurpassed views over the harbour through giant floor-to-ceiling windows and serves an array of burgers from 1150kr, pasta dishes for around 1390kr plus a wicked chocolate cheesecake at an indulgent 1090kr.

Fjaran Strandgata 55, ☎565 1213. Iceland's answer to a British country pub, replete with a beamed ceiling and brass plates hanging on the walls, serving the same Viking delicacies as *Fjörugarðurinn* (see below), though on proper plates rather than wooden platters.

Fjörugarðurinn inside Fjörukráin, Strandgata 55, ☎565 1213. Designed to resemble a Viking longhouse, this is the place to come for a full Viking dinner (8400kr): fish and seafood soup, shark and dried haddock, lamb shank and *skyr* for dessert, accompanied by a half-litre of beer and some Black Death. Or, more modestly, salted cod with olives (3480kr), braised lamb shank (4550kr) or,

should you conscience allow, grilled minke whale (4550kr). In December there's a smorgasboard-style Christmas buffet consisting of various hams, fish dishes and some of the more unusual fare listed above for 6400kr.

Gamla Vínhúsið Vesturgata 4. The walls of this wooden-beamed place are lined with old wine bottles creating a cosy atmosphere to savour fish of the day (2820kr), loin of beef (4150kr), or just a house burger (1600kr).

Súfistinn Strandgata 9. Hafnarfjörður's main coffeehouse with outdoor seating in good weather, an impressive range of coffees, as well as crêpes (1350kr), panini (1050kr), salads (1320kr) and soup (650kr).

Tilveran Linnetstígur 1. A justifiably popular seafood restaurant with daily lunch specials for 1790kr including soup, the fish of the day and coffee, while in the evening it's 1990kr for a succulent fish dish, 2990kr if you prefer something more meaty.

Viðey

Barely a ten-minute walk north of Reykjavík's Laugardalur area along Dalbraut, which later mutates into Sundagarður, you'll soon see **Viðey** (ⓦwww.elding.is/videy), an island just 750m outside Sundahöfn harbour with a rich historical background. Actually the top of a now extinct volcano and measuring barely 1.7 square kilometres, Viðey (Wood Island – though it's no longer forested) was first claimed by Reykjavík's original settler **Ingólfur Arnarson** as part of his estate. Archeological studies have shown that Viðey was inhabited during the tenth century and that a church was built here sometime in the twelfth century, though it is for the Augustinian monastery, consecrated here in 1225, that Viðey is better known. However, the island's monks fled when, in 1539, representatives of the Danish king proclaimed Viðey property of the Lutheran royal crown. Barely eleven years later, in 1550, Iceland's last Catholic bishop, **Jón Arason**, regained possession of the island through an armed campaign, restored the monastery and built a fort here to defend the island from his Lutheran enemies. Little did that help, however, and in the same year, Arason was beheaded and the Reformation, taking place across mainland Europe, began in Iceland.

Two centuries of peace ensued and in 1751 Viðey was given to the royal treasurer and sheriff, **Skúli Magnússon**, with the **Viðeyjarstofa**, Iceland's first stone building, being built as his residence four years later. In 1817, the island passed into the ownership of the President of the High Court, **Magnús Stephensen**, who brought Iceland's only printing press to Viðey, further enhancing the tiny place's claim as the country's main centre of culture since the establishment of the Augustinian monastery here. Following several more changes of ownership, the City of Reykjavík finally bought the island in 1983.

Around the island

Viðey is easily accessible from Sundahöfn harbour, northeast of Laugardalur, reached by bus #5 from Hlemmur (see p.64). From the harbour, the **ferry** (mid-May to Sept daily every hour between 11.15pm and 7.15pm, but not 6.15pm; 1000kr return; ⓦwww.elding.is/videy) takes just seven minutes.

Between mid-May and September there's also a daily sailing at noon from the main harbour in Reykjavík to Viðey.

A short walk up the path from the jetty where the ferry deposits you is **Viðeyjarstofa**, Skúli Magnússon's residence, now a modest **café**. Designed in simple Rococo style by the architect who worked on the Amalienborg royal palace in Copenhagen, its outer walls are made of basalt and sandstone while the interior is of Danish brick and timber. Standing next to the café is Iceland's second oldest **church**, consecrated in 1774, and worth a glance inside for its original interior furnishings and Skúli's grave beneath the altar. Walk east of here to the site of the old fort, **Virkið**, of which nothing now remains, to see the Skúli Magnússon **monument** (he died here in 1794) and **Danadys** (Danes' Grave), the final resting place for a number of Danish citizens who lived on the island over the centuries. In the opposite direction, off to the left, the unusual wishing-well structure you can see is the **Imagine Peace Tower**. Conceived by Yoko Ono as a beacon to world peace and inscribed with the words "imagine peace" in 24 languages, the structure emits a powerful tower of light every night between October 9 (John Lennon's birthday) and December 8 (the anniversary of his death), illuminating the Reykjavík sky.

There's little else to do on Viðey other than enjoy the spectacular views of the mainland and take a stroll on one of the many **paths** that lead around the island; allow at least two hours to walk all the way round. From Viðeyjarstofa, a road heads beyond the island's schoolhouse to the easternmost point, from where a path takes over, following the south coast back towards the ferry jetty, skirting a protected area (closed May & June) that's home to thousands of nesting birds. Alternatively, from the easternmost point, a track leads back along the north coast past the restaurant and out to the northwestern part of the island, Vesturey, a peninsula connected to the main island by the small isthmus, Eiði. The greatest **coastal rescue** Iceland has ever seen took place off the island's westernmost point in October 1944 after the Canadian destroyer HMCS *Skeena*, with over two hundred men on board, ran aground in heavy seas and blizzard conditions. Although fifteen crew members perished, the remainder were rescued by a team of Icelanders led by Einar Sigurðsson who was later awarded the MBE for his courage and guidance. While in the western part of the island keep an eye out, too, for the **Áfangar**, an alfresco exhibit by the American sculptor Richard Serra, consisting of nine pairs of basalt columns (now covered in bird mess) arranged around Vesturey: when viewed from the correct angle, they frame landmarks visible on the mainland.

Travel details

Buses

The bus details given below are relevant for May–Sept; for winter times, visit Ⓦwww.bsi.is.
Reykjavík to: Akranes (every 2 hours; 50min); Akureyri (2 daily; 6hr); Blönduós (2 daily; 4hr); Blue Lagoon (5 daily; 40min); Borgarnes (4 daily; 1hr 10min); Búðardalur (5 weekly; 4hr); Brú (2 daily; 2hr); Gullfoss/Geysir (2 daily; 2hr 30min); Höfn (1 daily; 8hr); Hólmavík via Brú (3 weekly; 6hr 30min); Ísafjörður via Brú and Hólmavík (3 weekly; 12hr 30min); Ólafsvík (1 daily; 3hr); Sauðárkrókur (daily; 5hr 30min); Siglufjörður (1 daily; 7hr); Skaftafell (daily; 6hr); Stykkishólmur (1–2 daily; 2hr 30min); Þingvellir (2 daily; 50min); Þorlákshöfn (2 daily; 1hr).

Flights

Reykjavík to: Akureyri (7 daily; 50min); Bíldudalur (daily; 40min); Egilsstaðir (4 daily; 1hr); Gjögur (2 weekly; 50min); Höfn (2 daily; 1hr); Ísafjörður (2 daily; 40min); Sauðárkrókur (6 weekly; 45min); Westman Islands (2–3 daily; 30min).

Ferries

Reykjavík to: Viðey (early May to early Sept 8 daily; 7min).

2

Southwestern Iceland

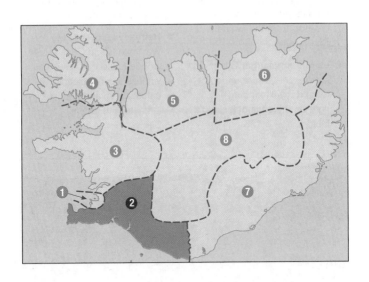

CHAPTER 2 **Highlights**

✳ **Blue Lagoon** Soak outdoors in the steaming waters of Iceland's best known thermal spa, set among the Reykjanes Peninsula's barren lava flows. See p.101

✳ **The Golden Circle** Circuit three of the country's most famous sights – the rift valley at Þingvellir, Geysir's spurting pools, and Gullfoss, the Golden Falls – on a day-trip from the capital. See p.106

✳ **Landmannalaugar** Camp out at hot springs surrounded by rugged rhyolite mountains, right on the edge of Iceland's Interior. See p.123

✳ **Laugavegur** Follow this four-day hiking trail between Landmannalaugar and Þórsmörk, through some exceptional scenery. See p.124

✳ **Þórsmörk** A beautifully wooded highland valley, surrounded by glaciers, that makes a great spot to camp, hike, or just party away the long summer days. See p.134

✳ **Heimaey** Largest of the Westman Islands, this is a wonderful spot to unwind, witness recent volcanic catastrophe, and become intimate with puffins. See p.141

▲ Þórsmörk National Park with Mýrdalsjökull in the background

Southwestern Iceland

S pread either side of Reykjavík, **southwestern Iceland** extends barely 200km from end to end, but nowhere else are the country's key elements of history and the land so visibly intertwined. Here you'll see where Iceland's original parliament was founded over a thousand years ago, sites that saw the violence of saga-age dramas played out, and where the country's earliest churches became seats of power and learning. Culture aside, if you're expecting the scenery this close to Reykjavík to be tame, think again: the southwest contains some of Iceland's most iconic – and frequently explosive – landscapes, compelling viewing whether used as a simple backdrop to a day's drive, or as an excuse to spend a week trekking cross-country.

The region splits into four well-defined areas. Southwest of Reykjavík, bleak, semi-vegetated lava fields characterize the **Reykjanes Peninsula**, site of the international airport at Keflavík, though the famous Blue Lagoon adds a splash of colour. Due east of Reykjavík, a clutch of essential historical and geological features – including the original parliament site at Þingvellir, Geysir's hot water spouts, and Gullfoss' rainbow-tinged cataract – are strung out around the **Golden Circle**, an easy route tackled by just about every visitor to the country. Then there's the **central south**, a broad stretch of grassy river plains further southeast again, whose inland features the blasted landscape surrounding the volcano Hekla and hot springs at Landmannalaugar; while back on its coast the rolling farmland of *Njál's Saga* country is dotted with landmarks from this famous tale. Further east, there's beautiful scenery around the glaciated highland valley of Þórsmörk, along with some spectacular waterfalls down near the highway, which runs out of the region via the coastal hamlet of Vík. Offshore, a short ferry ride or flight from the mainland brings you to Heimaey, the small, intimate core of the **Westman islands**, alive with birdlife and further recent proof of Iceland's unstable vulcanology.

The southwest enjoys good access: most **roads** – with the exception of a few on the Reykjanes Peninsula, around Hekla, and those to Landmannalaugar and Þórsmörk – are surfaced and generally accessible year-round. **Buses** ply the Golden Circle and coastal Ringroad (Route 1) to Vík throughout the year, with Landmannalaugar and Þórsmörk connected over the summer; services around the Reykjanes Peninsula are more restricted, though you can easily get to the Blue Lagoon or Keflavík. The **climate** here is relatively mild, despite being the wettest, windiest part of the country, prone to fog along the coast and potentially heavy snowfalls through the year on higher ground.

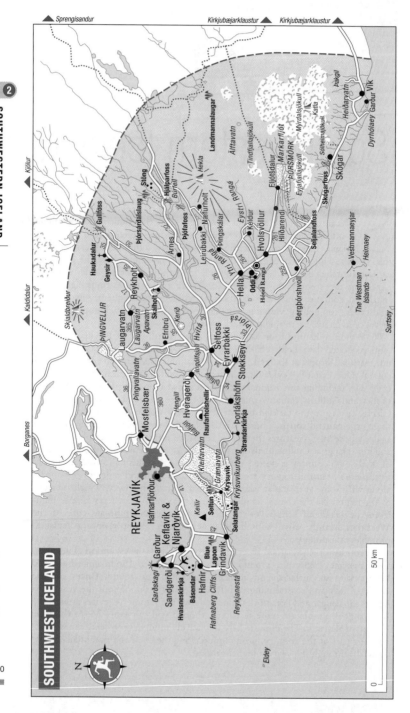

SOUTHWEST ICELAND

▲ Sprengisandur   Kirkjubæjarklaustur ▲   Kirkjubæjarklaustur ▲

▲ Kjölur

▲ Kaldidalur

▲ Borganes

N

50 km

0

Sprengisandur

Landmannalaugar

Álftavatn

Tindfjallajökull

Hekla

Burfell

Hjálparfoss

Stöng

Þjórsárdalslaug

Gullfoss

Haukadalur

Geysir

Reykholt

Skálholt

Laugarvatn

Laugarvatn

Apavatn

Efribrú

Skjaldbreidur

ÞINGVELLIR

Þingvallavatn

Þingvellir

Mosfellsbær

Hengill

REYKJAVÍK

Hafnarfjörður

Keflavík & Njarðvík

Garður

Garðskagi

Sandgerði

Hvalsneskirkja

Básendar

Hafnir

Hafnaberg Cliffs

Reykjanestá

Eldey

Blue Lagoon

Grindavík

Selatangar

Krýsuvíkurberg

Strandarkirkja

Selttún

Keilir

Grænavatn

Krýsuvík

Kleifarvatn

Raufarhólshellir

Hveragerði

Þorlákshöfn

Stokkseyri

Eyrarbakki

Selfoss

Ölfusá

Ingólfsfjall

Hvítá

Kerið

Arnes

Þjófafoss

Næfurholt

Leirubakki

Þingskálar

Ytri Rangá

Eystri Rangá

Keldur

Hella

Oddi

Hóal Rangá

Hvolsvöllur

Hlíðarendi

Seljalandsfoss

Fljótsdalur

Markarfljót

ÞÓRSMÖRK

Eyjafjallajökull

Skógafoss

Skógar

Sólheimajökull

Myrdalsjökull

Katla

Myrdalsjökull

Þakgil

Heiðarvatn

Dyrhólaey Garður Vík

Vík

Bergþórsvoll

Vestmannaeyjar

Heimaey

The Westman Islands

Surtsey

The Reykjanes Peninsula

The **Reykjanes Peninsula**, Iceland's southwestern extremity, provides most visitors with their first look at the country, as they exit **Keflavík**'s international airport and take Route 41 east towards Reykjavík. Unfortunately, local vistas are unremittingly barren – rough, contoured piles of lava and distant peaks, the rocks only coloured by lichen and mosses – and most people leave Reykjanes behind without a second thought. But if you've a few hours to fill in – before a flight, perhaps – the peninsula is conveniently close to the capital and has plenty to offer: there's the **Blue Lagoon**, Iceland's most renowned hot pool; a museum at **Grindavík** to that great Icelandic icon, the cod; a **trans-continental bridge** near Hafnir; plus plenty of wild, rocky coastline with associated birdlife and lonely ruins.

The peninsula is covered in **hiking trails**, taking anything from a few minutes to several days to complete – the most detailed map of the region is Landmælingar Íslands' *Suðvesturland* 1:75,000. Be prepared to carry plenty of **water** (there are few sources anywhere on the peninsula), and note that there's almost no soft ground to pitch a tent on.

The Reykjavík–Keflavík highway (Route 41) is surfaced, as is the road south off this to the Blue Lagoon and Grindavík (Route 43), and much of the coastal stretch between Keflavík and Grindavík. Other roads are mostly gravel, and can be rough going at times. **Buses** run daily all year from Reyjavík to Keflavík and the airport, and from Reyjavík to the Blue Lagoon and Grindavík; and the region is also covered on numerous **tours** from the capital.

The Blue Lagoon and Keflavík

Heading west from the capital, the straight, fast 40km Reykjavík–Keflavík highway is the busiest road in Iceland. After the satellite suburb of Hafnarfjörður (see p.92) drops away, you're confronted with the peninsula's bald vistas: ranges frame the horizon, with the flat, petrified lava flow of Þránsskjaldarhraun in between, blistered with solidified burst gas bubbles and resembling the top of a badly baked cake; the distant conical mountain rising over it all is 379-metre-high **Keilir**. Stay on the highway until you reach the amply signed intersection 8km short of Keflavík, where Route 43 heads down to the Blue Lagoon and Grindavík.

The Blue Lagoon

Known in Icelandic as *Bláa lónið*, the ⚑**Blue Lagoon** (Sept–May daily 10am–8pm; June–Aug daily 8am–9pm; ⓦ www.bluelagoon.com; 4000kr) is Iceland's most trumpeted geothermal spa, a surreal splash of colour and warmth amidst a landscape of black lava rubble. It's also an undoubted tourist rip-off, though worth it once for the experience; on cold days, when thick fog swirls over the warm, milky-blue water, your hair, dampened by vapour, freezes solid.

Blue Lagoon is actually artificial, dug into the middle of a flat expanse of black lava blocks and filled by outflow from the nearby **Svartsengi thermal power station**. Svartsengi taps into steam vents fed by sea water seeping down into subterranean hot pots, and by the time it emerges at Blue Lagoon it has cooled to a comfortable 38°C. There are decoratively positioned caves and arches, a sauna, and the famous silvery-grey **silt**, said to cure skin disorders – Icelanders scoop handfuls off the bottom and smear it all over their bodies, and the shop sells beauty products made from it. Whatever the effects on your skin, hair takes a real battering from the lagoon's enriched mineral content; rub conditioner in as protection before bathing.

Practicalities

Daily **buses** (Wwww.re.is) run here year-round from both Reykjavík's BSÍ terminal and Keflavík's international airport; you can pay for the fare alone or buy a combined fare-Blue Lagoon entry. Large **lockers** at the pool will fit a moderately-sized suitcase if you're travelling via the airport. Blue Lagoon's basic **café** and formal **restaurant-bar** are both expensive. There's on-site **accommodation** at the *Blue Lagoon Health Clinic* (⑥), which also features **spa treatments and massages**; or at the nearby *Northern Light Inn* (T 426 8650, Wwww.nli.is; ④), which offers cosy rooms, a good restaurant and free airport transfers.

Keflavík

Stretching for 5km along the seafront, **KEFLAVÍK** and its adjoining satellite **Njarðvík** – collectively known as Reykjanesbær – between them form the Reykjanes Peninsula's biggest centre, with a population of around 11,000. Keflavík was a trading port as far back as the sixteenth century, but it was World War II that really established the town, when US defence forces stationed here built an **airstrip** to the west. After Iceland joined **NATO** in 1949 – an event that sparked a riot in Reykjavík – the US persuaded Iceland into allowing them to expand the airstrip as a supply and refuelling **base** for their aircraft, and for over fifty years Keflavík flourished alongside as a service centre. Then, in 2006 the US government **closed** the facility, removing the helicopters and fighter jets based here. Although many Icelanders celebrated the news, the country is now defenceless and – rather more importantly – Keflavík has lost its major employer.

As far as tourism is concerned, Keflavík is a functional place, not really a stopover of choice except to catch an early flight from the airport (see p.61) or to visit **Viking World** at Víkingabraut 1 (Wwww.vikingaheimar.com; daily 11am–6pm; 750kr). The centrepiece here is the *Íslendingur*, a full-sized replica Viking long ship built in 1996 and sailed to New York in 2000 to mark a thousand years since the Vikings discovered North America. From May to September you can also hook up for four-hour **whale-watching tours** aboard the *Moby Dick* (T 421 7777, Wwww.dolphin.is; 4000kr), with minke whales, porpoise and dolphin most likely to show; you'll need warm clothing.

Practicalities

The highway from Reykjavík divides on the outskirts of town, the left hand fork heading directly to the International Airport, and the right-hand fork ploughing on for about three kilometres through predominantly residential Njarðvík – marked by the **post office** and Samkaup **supermarket** (Mon–Sat 10am–7pm, Sun noon–7pm) – to the core of businesses that make up Keflavík, before fizzling out at Keflavík harbour. The SBK **bus station** (Wwww.sbk.is) is at the harbour, with irregular daily services to Reykjavík, Grindavík and Hafnir: accommodation can arrange airport or Blue Lagoon transfers, or call a **taxi** (T 421 4141 or 421 1515). Keflavík's services are all around the main road Hafnargata, including **tourist information** and **internet** access (Mon–Fri 10am–8pm, Sat 10am–4pm), both in the library behind the *Flug Hótel*, and **banks**.

The nearest **accommodation to the airport** is 5km from town at *Alex* (T 421 2800, Wwww.alex.is; ②), with beds, self-contained cabins and a **campsite**. Njarðvík's IYHA **youth hostel** (T 421 8889, Wwww.hostel.is; sleeping bag

2200kr), just after you enter town off the highway at Fitjabraut 6A, has a dreary blocky exterior, but is warm and well equipped. Best of the upmarket options is the *Hótel Keflavík* (☏ 420 7000, ⓦ www.hotelkeflavik.is; ⑤) at Vatnsnesvegur 12, a modern transit **hotel** whose staff also run a low-key **guesthouse** opposite (②).

Keflavík's **places to eat** are all near the *Hótel Keflavík* on Hafnargata, and include the culturally confused *Paddy's Irish Bar & Pizzeria*, though the best food is at the long-established *Raïn* – they've got pizzas, fish dishes and salads (the grilled-chicken salad is very tasty) – and it's also a comfortable place for a drink.

Garður

In fair weather, the peninsula west of Keflavík is an easy place to spend a couple of hours trolling around in a car. **GARÐUR** is the first place to aim for, a tiny, scattered community just 7km from town, with a small **folk museum** (May–Sept daily 1–5pm; 500kr) of fishing memorabilia and farm gear. A grassed-over ridge marks the remains of an old wall, apparently the original eleventh-century estate boundary; the discovery of nine Viking graves found south of here in the 1850s supports the theory. Later associations can be found at the nineteenth-century **Útskálakirkja**, a church dedicated to Iceland's only saint, **Þorlákur Þórhallsson**, bishop at Skálholt in 1178–93 (see p.112). Reykjanes' northwestern tip, **Garðskagi**, is marked by two lighthouses; the older, red-striped affair is right on the seafront and was once used to monitor bird migrations. Its base is a sheltered spot to look seawards – with a pair of binoculars you can spot seals, eider ducks, turnstones, gannets and assorted wading birds.

Sandgerði

Heading south for another 6km from Garður brings you to **SANDGERÐI**, a small fishing village with a busy harbour and another lighthouse. At the harbour, **Fraeðasetrið Nature Centre** (Mon–Fri 9am–noon & 1–5pm, Sat 1–5pm; 500kr) is a research centre investigating newly discovered invertebrate marine creatures found off Reykjanes, but there's also a display of larger stuffed animals and, for enthusiasts, extensive files on local botany and geology to sort through. Pick of the exhibits is a huge stuffed walrus in the lobby though, as these are unknown in Iceland, its presence here (and on the town coat of arms) is a bit of a mystery. *Vitinn* **restaurant**, at the harbour entrance, has good seafood and lamb dishes.

A final 7km south past a huge **arctic tern colony**, Hvalsneskirkja church and a grouping of abandoned, century-old stone sheep-pens opposite *Bali* (Washtub) farm, brings you to the end of the road at the orange **Stafnes** lighthouse; views from here take in heavy surf and distant airport buildings. There's a half-day walking trail south along the coast from Stafnes to Hafnir (see p.104), which after about 1km passes the site of **Básendar**, the Reykjanes Peninsula's largest trading town until it was totally destroyed by an overnight storm in January 1799 – killing just one person. Very little remains besides nondescript rubble.

Southern Reykjanes: from Hafnir to Krýsuvík

Coastal roads run from Keflavík around **southern Reykjanes** to the vague locality of **Krýsuvík**, passing the historic fishing settlement of **Grindavík** and some characteristic lava plains, rough shale hills, huge sea-bird colonies and intriguing historical relics along the way. Though Grindavík and Hafnir are served by buses from Reykjavík and Keflavík, services are infrequent and to explore properly you'll need your own vehicle.

Hafnir and Hafnaberg

Just before Keflavík, Route 44 splits off the Reykjavík–Keflavík highway and heads 10km to the coast at **HAFNIR**, another speck of a settlement based around a harbour and old wooden church, by which is a large, rusting anchor, a memento from the 1870 wreck of the schooner *Jamestown*. Hafnir's former fish-processing factory has been painted lilac and green and converted into the **Sæfiskasafnið** (May–Sept daily 2–4pm; 500kr), an aquarium and halibut farm with display tanks full of local fish and crustaceans.

South of Hafnir, the road becomes Route 425 as it crosses a landscape strewn with virtually unvegetated lava rubble – probably through a combination of salt spray and porous soil, which sees rainwater drain straight into the earth. For a closer look, stop at the insubstantial **pedestrian bridge** around 5km from Hafnir which crosses over a narrow fault line between the Eurasian and North American **continental plates** – perhaps the only place in the world you can walk between continents.

Not much further on, **cairns** (locally known as "priests", because they point the way but never go there themselves) mark out the relatively easy fifteen-kilometre **Prestsastígur walking trail** southeast to Grindavík, and also a shorter trail west from a roadside parking bay to some avian real estate on the coastal **Hafnaberg cliffs**. This latter route takes about 45 tiring minutes over sandy slopes, and finally ends on top of forty-metre-high cliffs. From spring through to autumn, these are home to tens of thousands of nesting kittiwakes and fulmars, along with a dusting of shags and black guillemots, all of which you'll hear (and smell) well before you crawl up to look over for a peek – loose soil and strong winds make standing up near the edge extremely dangerous.

Reykjanestá and Eldey

Ten kilometres south of Hafnir, **Reykjanestá** is the Reykjanes Peninsula's south-western extremity, the seascapes here embellished by the white tower of **Reykjanesviti**, one of the area's more interesting lighthouses. To reach it, follow signs off Route 425 past **Reykjanesvirkjun**, a shiny new 100MW geothermal power station, and keep going along the gravel road until you're under Reykjanes-viti around 2km later. Standing some way from the sea atop a knoll, it replaced Iceland's first lighthouse, which for seventeen years stood on high cliffs overlooking the stormy surf until an earthquake knocked it down in 1896.

About 100m further on is a parking area beside the cliff where the lighthouse originally stood; it's an easy walk up the grassy back to enjoy views across the ocean to **Eldey**, a tall platform of rock rising straight out of the sea 15km to the southwest. This is Europe's biggest gannet colony, and has the sad distinction of being where the last known pair of **great auks** (and their single egg) were destroyed on June 3, 1844. These flightless sea birds looked like giant razorbills and were common right across the north Atlantic until being hunted into extinction for their meat and oil. From the mainland at least, it's hard to believe that a flightless bird ever roosted on Eldey's sheer cliffs, but the back of the island has more accessible niches.

Grindavík

GRINDAVÍK is a sizeable town for this part of the country, a well-serviced fishing port of two thousand souls 14km east of Reykjanestá, where coastal roads and Route 43 from the Blue Lagoon intersect. Grindavík has a long history as a trading centre and was important enough to be raided by pirates looking for slaves and plunder in 1627; unlike Keflavík, however, its harbour remains busy and is now given over to a sizeable fishing fleet, whose catches are processed at a factory here.

All this has spawned Saltfisksetur Íslands, the **Icelandic Saltfish Museum** (daily 11am–6pm; 500kr), down near the harbour on Hafnargata, whose motto "*Lífið er saltfiskur*" – "Life is saltfish" – kicks off a fine display of models, videos, dioramas and life-sized photos, all laced with the pervasive aroma of **cod**. It's no exaggeration to say that modern Iceland was built on the back of this fish: the country's original coat of arms, ratified by the Alþing in 1593, was a golden cod, filleted, crowned on a red field. Fishing started off slowly as a seasonal adjunct to farming, however, the catch preserved as wind-dried **stockfish** until salt began to be imported in bulk during the nineteenth century. This coincided with the first large, ocean-going vessels being used in Iceland, increasing catches six-fold and sparking a new industry that undermined Iceland's traditional agricultural economy, drawing people off the land to swell coastal settlements. Today, saltfish accounts for sixty percent of Iceland's exports, the fish ending up mostly in Spain, West Africa and South America.

Fish aside, the town is also strategically placed at the junction of many of the Reykjanes Peninsula's **walking trails**, which start right at the town's boundaries. Local trails include a three-kilometre track heading north off Route 43 to the obvious pinnacle of **Þorbjarnfell** (231m); another good walk follows the coast east from town for 3km to the apex of **Festarfjall** (202m), the remains of a volcano core and splashed with purple, potash-rich rocks.

Practicalities

Grindavík is arranged on the low slopes around its harbour. Route 43 drops south into town as Víkurbraut, where **buses** from Reykjavík via the Blue Lagoon (daily throughout the year) and Keflavík (daily in summer) pull in at a **shopping complex** with supermarket and bank. Ránargata heads 250m down to the harbour from here, and halfway along you cross the intersection with Hafnargata: turn right onto Hafnargata and the Saltfish Museum is just on the left; or turn left for the **fish factory**. There's **accommodation** in town at the **campground** behind the shopping complex; near the museum at *Heimagisting Borg* (℡895 8686, ✉bjorksv@hive.is; ❶), Borgarhraun 2; or at the fish factory's *Guesthouse Fiskanes* (℡897 6388; ❶), Hafnargata 17–19. For **food**, *Brim*, facing the museum on Hafnargata, is a down-to-earth diner patronized by factory workers, with fish-oriented lunchtime specials and a lively evening bar; the *Mama Mía* pizzeria is next door.

Selatangar

Unsurfaced **Route 427** winds east from Grindavík over the back of Festarfjall's volcanic core and then twists down again to run parallel to the coast along the base of a rugged, boulder-strewn range. About 12km along, a signpost to **Selatangar** points 1.7km south, ending at a parking area beside a distinctive **lava field** above the sea. An indistinct **walking track** heads east, defined by rocks and driftwood, bringing you in about ten minutes to the remains of **Selatangar**, a seasonal fishing settlement last used in the 1880s and comprising lava-block dwellings perched above the sea, ranging from buildings the size and shape of a hollow cairn through to large, walled-in caves. There's far more here than you realize at first; poke around and you'll soon find a score or more sites, some almost completely intact, others just foundations. No roofs have survived; these may well have been constructed from driftwood (plenty washes up here) or weather-proofed cloth. With near constant wind howling in from the south, rapidly bringing in and dispersing fog with little warning, Selatangar can be quite spooky – some say that there's even a resident ghost named **Tanga-Tómas** – and it doesn't take much imagination to conjure up what life was like here when the place was last occupied.

Krýsuvík and around

Back on **Route 427**, it's another 9km from the Selatangar junction to **Krýsuvík**, a district farmed since Settlement times. Look for another rough track heading coastwards; conventional vehicles can only manage the first couple of kilometres, leaving a 3km walk to **Krýsuvíkurberg**, a long, curved cliff topped by a crust of green grass (an unusual sight for this part of the coast). This is packed solid all summer long with nesting **birds**: the cliffs are kittiwake grand central, and the turf is riddled with puffin burrows. The east end is topped by a triangulation point, with wonderful seascapes from the red scoria headland behind.

If you don't bother with Krýsuvíkurberg, Route 427 continues, past the site of Iceland's smallest church **Krýsuvíkurkirkja**, which was burned down in 2010, to a junction with Route 42. Follow this northeast for 20km, past **Grænavatn**'s pale green waters, bubbling pools at **Seltún hot springs** and five-kilometre-long **Kleifarvatn** lake, and you'll reach the Reykjavík highway at Hafnarfjörður (p.92). Alternatively, keep heading east and it's 40km to Hveragerði via Strandkirkja – see p.115.

The Golden Circle

The name **Golden Circle** might be a tourist-industry tag, but it's also apt, as this broad circuit east from Reykjavík covers many of Iceland's best-known features and touches on the root of much of its history. The key area is **Þingvellir**, whose dramatic rift valley and associated lake mark the area where the Icelandic state sprang into being in Viking times. East from here on the banks of the Hvítá is the religious centre of **Skálholt**, while following the river northeast takes you past **Geysir**, the original hot blowhole that has lent its name to similar vents worldwide, to **Gullfoss**' powerful twin cataracts.

One popular way of packing all this into one day is by taking a nine-hour **Golden Circle tour** offered by Reykjavík Excursions (Ⓦwww.re.is; 8500kr); they'll collect from Reykjavík accommodation and you get commentary in English en route. For more than one person, however, it's probably cheaper to **rent a car** for the day: head either northeast from Reykjavík along Route 36 straight to Þingvellir, or take the Ringroad southeast via Hveragerði to Selfoss (see p.116), from where separate roads run up to Þingvellir and the Geysir–Gullfoss area. In summer, daily buses heading to Akureyri via the **Kjölur route** (see p.315) pass Þingvellir and stop briefly at Geysir and Gullfoss, so you might not need to make a separate trip to see them.

Þingvellir and around

The region northeast of Reykjavík is scarred by one of the world's great geological boundaries, a **rift valley** marking where the North American and Eurasian continental plates are physically tearing apart. It was in this monumental landmark that Iceland's clan chieftains, or **goðar**, first gathered in the tenth century to formalize their laws and forge a national identity for themselves (see box, p.110). Although

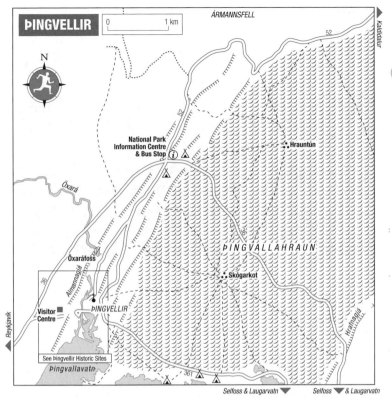

this rift stretches right across Iceland, nowhere else is it so expansively evident – a four-kilometre-wide, forty-metre-deep slash in the landscape, sided in basalt columns and extending for 16km from Iceland's largest lake, **Þingvallavatn**, to the low, rounded cone of the **Skjaldbreiður** volcano in the northeast. **Þingvellir** itself – the "assembly plains" where the chieftains met at the southwestern end of the rift – has been protected since 1930 as a national park.

The main **road** here is Route 36, which runs northeast of Reykjavík to Þingvellir (often dangerously icy in winter) and then south to Selfoss and the Ringroad. In summer, there's at least one daily **bus** (Ⓦ www.bogf.is) in each direction between Reykjavík and Þingvellir. Once here, there are plenty of **hiking** trails around the scenery, along with a couple of **accommodation** options. Þingvellir also marks the southern terminus of the Kaldidalur route through to Reykholt (see p.160).

Þingvellir National Park

Þingvellir National Park encompasses the flat moors at the southern end of the rift valley, with boundaries reaching 6km north from Þingvallavatn to the foothills of **Ármannsfell** – said to be the abode of the region's mythical guardian, Ármann Dalmannsson – and around the same distance east towards the solitary massif of **Hrafnabjörg**. The main focus is, of course, Þingvellir itself, a surprisingly small area at the southwestern corner of the park where the narrow **Öxará** – the Axe

▲ Þingvellir

River – flows down to the lake shore past a **church** and other historic monuments, all hemmed in on the west by the two-kilometre-long **Almannagjá**, the region's most impressive rift wall.

Buses deliver to the **National Park Information Centre** (☏482 2660, ⓦwww .thingvellir.is; May–Sept daily 9am–8pm), just where Route 36 descends into the rift. They have a phone, free hot showers, basic café, sell maps and post weather reports, and issue **camping permits** (June–Oct; 700kr per person) for the park's five campgrounds – the best, with showers and toilets, is next to the Information Centre. Sadly, the grand old *Hótel Valhöll* – Þingvellir's sole **hotel** – burnt down in 2009. **Park rules** protect all plants, animals and natural formations, and prohibit open fires, off-road driving and camping outside designated sites. Finally, you can join free hour-long **tours** of the locality that leave from the church at 10am and 3pm daily throughout summer.

Þingvellir

It's hard to overstate the historical importance of **Þingvellir**, though there are very few specific monuments to see and to capture the spirit of the place you need to familiarize yourself with the buildings and natural formations around which events were played.

Coming from Reykjavík, your first stop should be the **Visitor Centre** (daily June–Sept 9am–7pm), just where Route 36 grazes the top of Almannagjá, which has interactive videos outlining Þingvellir's history. You're right on the edge of the **North American continental plate** here and there's a superb lookout outside: the Alþing site is directly below, with the church over on the far side of the Öxará, which flows south to the lake. Looking northeast up the rift, a flagpole rises in front of where vertical basalt columns topped by rope lava cleave away from the rift wall, while in the distance, Ármannsfell and Hrafnabjörg frame the valley, fist-like and solid. Permanence is an illusion, however – the rift is widening by 1.5cm further each year as the continental plates drift apart. As they move, the valley floor sinks, on average, a couple of millimetres annually, though it fell half a metre in 1789 following an earthquake. Away in the distance, Skjaldbreiður's apparently low summit is easily overlooked, though at 1060m it's actually one of the highest peaks in view.

From the Visitor Centre, a hundred-metre track descends through the deep **Almannagjá** canyon and down to a **flagpole** marking the presumed site of **Lögberg**, the rock where important speeches were made and the lawspeaker recited Iceland's laws to the masses below. Nearby traces of walls outline the remains of **buðs**, the temporary roofed camps raised by participants during assemblies, while the path continues to where the Öxará cascades over Almannagjá as the twenty-metre-high **Öxarárfoss.** Rocks in the river are barely worn, suggesting that the Öxará's path is fairly recent: this supports oral accounts of the river's diversion into the rift around 1000 AD to provide water for the sizeable chunk of Iceland's population who descended at each Alþing. After Danish laws were enforced in the sixteenth century, **pools** near the second falls were used to drown women convicted of witchcraft or sexual offences (men were beheaded for the same crimes), though the idea of a death penalty was repugnant to Icelanders and few such executions were carried out.

Moving down into the valley, cross over the Öxará and follow the road back towards the church. East of here is the splintered wall forming **Flosagjá**, a deep fissure whose southern end has been flooded by underground springs creating **Peningagjá**, an exceedingly clear, deep wishing pool; coins glint silver and electric blue at the bottom. You're now beside the **church**, founded in 1018 after the Norwegian king Ólafur Haraldsson supplied timber for the original building. The current white and blue structure, from 1859, is misleadingly unpretentious, as by the eighteenth century Þingvellir church was wealthy, owning a huge swathe of farmland stretching right up the valley. A raised area behind is reserved for the tombs of outstanding Icelanders; at present the only two incumbents are the patriotic poets **Einar Benediktsson** and **Jónas Hallgrímsson**; the latter especially inspired the

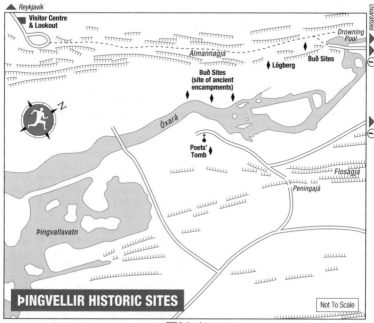

ÞINGVELLIR HISTORIC SITES

Reykjavík

Visitor Centre & Lookout

Almannagjá

Öxarárfoss

Drowning Pool

Lögberg

Buð Sites

Buð Sites (site of ancient encampments)

Öxará

Poets' Tomb

Flosagjá

Peningajá

Þingvallavatn

Selfoss & Laugarvatn

Not To Scale

The Alþing at Þingvellir

With laws shall our land be built up, but with lawlessness laid waste.

Njál's Saga

By the beginning of the tenth century, Iceland's 36 regional chieftains were already meeting at local **assemblies** to sort out disputes, but as the country became more established, they recognized the need for some form of national government. With this in mind, Norwegian law was adapted and the first **Alþing**, or General Assembly, was held in the rift valley north of Þingvallavatn in 930 AD, at a place which became known as **Þingvellir**, the Assembly Plains. Though the Alþing's power declined through the ages, Þingvellir remained the seat of Iceland's government for the next eight centuries.

The Alþing was held for two weeks every summer, and attendance for chieftains was mandatory. In fact, almost everyone who could attend did so, setting up their tented camps – **buðs** – and coming to watch the courts in action or settle disputes, pick up on gossip, trade, compete at sports, and generally socialize. The whole event was coordinated by the **lawspeaker**, while the laws themselves were legislated by the **Law Council**, and dispensed at four regional courts, along with a fifth **supreme court**. Strangely, however, none of these authorities had the power to enforce their verdicts, beyond bringing pressure to bear through public opinion. The adoption of **Christianity** as Iceland's official religion in 1000 AD was one of the Alþing's major successes, but if litigants refused to accept a court's decision, they had to seek satisfaction privately. *Njál's Saga* (see pp.126–127) contains a vivid account of one such event, when a battle between two feuding clans and their allies broke out at the Alþing itself around 1011 AD; while *Hrafnkel's Saga* (see p.285) shows how people manipulated processes at the Alþing, and could, if they wanted, ignore court verdicts.

This lack of real authority undermined the Alþing's effectiveness, creating a power vacuum in Iceland that ultimately saw Norway and then Denmark assume control of the country. By the late thirteenth century the Alþing was losing its importance, with the lawspeaker's position abolished and the courts stripped of all legislative power. They had rather more ability to act on their judgements though, and from the mid-sixteenth century public **executions** – unknown before – were carried out at Þingvellir. Eventually, while still meeting for a few days every year, the Alþing became a minor affair, and the last assembly was held at Þingvellir in 1798, replaced during the nineteenth century by a national court and parliament at Reykjavík.

It was during the nineteenth century that Þingvellir became the focus of the **nationalist movement**, with large crowds witnessing various independence debates here – the Danish king even attended Iceland's millennial celebrations at Þingvellir in 1874. It remained a symbol of national identity through the twentieth century, peaking when half the country turned up at Þingvellir to hear the **declaration of independence** from Denmark and the formation of the Icelandic Republic on June 17, 1944.

nineteenth-century independence movement and drew great inspiration from Þingvellir. The marshlands in front were once possibly an island where **duels** at the Alþing were fought, before the practice was banned in the thirteenth century.

The rift valley

Þingvellir's valley is covered in the overgrown nine-thousand-year-old lavafield **Þingvallahraun**, product of the up-valley Skjaldbreiður (Shield-broad). Though now extinct, this was the first **shield volcano** ever to be classified, a type that spews out high-volume fluid lava in a steady rather than violent eruption, leaving wide, flattened cones. The valley is beautiful in summer and early autumn, carpeted in patchy dwarf forest and heathland plants, with the national park covered in a web of marked **walking trails** – note that some of these cross minor rifts and gorges, which might be dangerously concealed if there has been any snow. To venture further, or climb any of the mountains, you'll need at least basic orienteering skills and Landmælingar Islands' *Þingvellir* 1:25,000 **map**.

Of the **marked trails**, the easiest lead east of Þingvellir's church or north from Þingvallavatn's shore, converging 2km on at **Skógarkot**, a sheep farm abandoned in the 1930s – paths from the church are best, as they cross a couple of interesting rifts and avoid most of the boggy ground you'll find on the other routes. Skógarkot's ruined but strongly constructed **stone buildings** occupy a grassy hillock roughly halfway across the valley, not a high position but still elevated enough for you to take in a panorama of distant peaks and rift walls, and feel dwarfed by the scale of the Þingvallahraun flow. From here you could either continue north to another farm site at **Hrauntún**, and then turn west for the main campsite (another 4km in all); or walk a couple more kilometres across the valley to where Route 36 climbs the eastern rift wall – and onto the Eurasian continental plate – at **Hrafnagjá**, Raven's Rift.

Of the **mountains**, Ármannsfell (765m) is the easiest to climb, though it's still a full-day, eight-kilometre return hike to the summit from the campsite on its southern slopes; there's snow up here until the middle of the year. For Skjald-breiður, you're looking at a two- to three-day hike to the rim of the three-hundred-metre-wide crater, and need advice on the route from the information centre or one of Iceland's walking clubs (see p.45) before setting out.

Þingvallavatn

Immediately south of Þingvellir, **Þingvallavatn** formed nine thousand years ago when fresh lava blocked off the outflow of springs rising in a basin, backfilling it with water to form a fourteen-kilometre-long lake, Iceland's largest. Þingvallavatn and its sole outflow, the **Sog** river, are surrounded by alternately rugged hills and undulating moorland, good for both hiking and bird-watching, while the lake is dotted with three tiny volcanic islands and, on rare windless days, forms a perfect blue mirror to the sky. Three surprisingly unobtrusive **hydroelectric stations** at the head of the Sog provide power for the region, while healthy stocks of char and a dwindling trout population keep the fly population down and anglers happy – winter fishing is especially popular, when holes have to be cut through the ice. In summer, you can buy **fishing permits** and flies at Þingvellir's Visitors' Centre. Þingvallavatn's incredibly clear, blue waters also recently saw the lake – or rather **Silfra**, a nearby flooded chasm – rated as one of the world's top **scuba diving** sites. Wealthy enthusiasts can indulge by contacting Arctic Adventures (℡562 7000, ⓦwww.adventures.is) or ⚐Dive Iceland (℡663 2858, ⓦwww.dive.is), though if the 30,000kr tag seems steep, choose one of the cheaper snorkelling trips.

You can circuit Þingvallavatn in your own transport along a gravel road which runs around the south side of the lake before meeting up with Route 36 about 25km from Selfoss.

Skálholt, Geysir and Gullfoss

One way or another, a tangle of roads east of Þingvellir follow the marshy swards of the Hvítá basin up past the religious centre of **Skálholt**, before converging some 60km later at Iceland's two most famous sights: the erupting hot pools at **Geysir**, and **Gullfoss'** thundering falls, 7km beyond. It's beautiful countryside, fertile, flat, framed by distant hills and – if you've spent any time in Iceland's rougher areas – startling green in summer, thanks to one of Iceland's longest rivers, the **Hvítá**. This starts around 140km northeast at Hvítarvatn, an isolated lake below Langjökull on the Interior Kjölur route (see p.315), and flows swiftly to Gullfoss, where it drops into the plains between here and Selfoss, joins the Sog, and runs the last few kilometres to the sea as the broad-mouthed Ölfusá.

Coming directly **from Þingvellir**, you follow the rough but highly scenic Route 365 to lakeside hot springs at the spa village of **LAUGARVATN**, home to the National School for Sports with its excellent swimming pool (Mon–Fri 10am–9pm, Sat & Sun 10am–6pm; 350kr). There's **accommodation** here at the snug, self-catering IYHA hostel *Dalsel* on the main road (☎486 1215, ⊛www.hostel.is; dorm bed 2200kr), and two summer-only *Edda* hotels overlooking the lake, *ÍKÍ Laugarvatn* (☎448 4820, ⊛www.hoteledda.is; ❷) or the larger *ML Laugarvatn* (☎448 4810, ⊛www.hoteledda.is; sleeping bag 1600kr, rooms with/without bathroom ❷). From here it's a straight run east on routes 37 and 35 to Geysir and then Gullfoss, though it's a bit of a detour on back roads to reach Skálholt.

Coming **from Reykjavík**, turn off the Ringroad just west of Selfoss (see p.116) and follow Route 35 northeast past the sights; this is the trail followed by Golden Circle and **public buses**, which run year-round, and also by summer buses continuing past Gullfoss along the Kjölur route to Akureyri (see p.315). Coming this way, about 15km north of Selfoss you pass photogenic **Kerið crater**, an ancient collapsed scoria cone. The seventy-metre-deep, red-gravel crater is flooded and used for farming fish, and there's an easy, fifteen-minute path around the rim, with a view northwest to the similar **Seyðishólar** crater.

Skálholt

The region of small lakes and streams north of the middle Hvítá is known as **Biskupstungur**, Bishop's Tongue, a name which probably originated after the foundation of the church at **SKÁLHOLT**, which lies around 40km from Selfoss off Route 35. It's easy to overdose on churches in Iceland but Skálholt's definitely warrants a stop: seat of a bishopric as early as 1056 AD, Skálholt's huge wooden **cathedral** developed into a **religious school** and by the early thirteenth century there were two hundred people living here, making it the country's largest settlement. Surviving the Reformation, Skálholt became, along with Hólar in northern Iceland, a major seat of learning, and lasted until the region was hit by a catastrophic earthquake in the late eighteenth century. The bishop subsequently shifted to Reykjavík, and Skálholt was largely abandoned, though a chapel was maintained until the cathedral and school were restored and reconsecrated in 1963.

Today, the cathedral is elegantly underplayed, plainly decked out and unusual only for its size. Inside, a mitre over the door identifies Skálholt as a bishopric; there's a nicely proportioned wooden ceiling, abstract stained-glass windows, and a tapestry-like **mosaic** of Christ behind the altar. Reconstruction work in the 1950s also uncovered a thirteenth-century stone **sarcophagus** belonging to Bishop Páll Jónsson, a charismatic churchman who added a tower and sumptuous decorations to the original building. A wooden crook carved with a dragon's head was found with his remains, and the sarcophagus itself is on view here in the summer. Ongoing **excavations** alongside the church have revealed the foundations of the original bishop's residence – there's a site plan which explains what each area was for – while a rough-cut stone monument, 100m away, commemorates Iceland's last Catholic bishop, **Jón Arason**. Arason was actually bishop at Hólar in the north (see p.228), but rode south in 1550 and captured Skálholt in an attempt to prevent the Danish king from forcing Lutheranism on the country; after a brief struggle he was taken and beheaded by the king's men.

Practicalities

You can **stay** year-round at Skálholt's school (☎486 8870, ✆skoli@skalholt.is; sleeping bag 2000kr, ❶); there's also a summertime **restaurant** across from the cathedral with outside seating in sheltered, attractive gardens. Otherwise, head a further 7km up Route 35 to the greenhouse village of **Reykholt**, whose roadside **fuel station** incorporates a store, café, bus stop and bank. There's **accommodation** at the friendly *Húsið* guesthouse, Bjarkarbraut 26 (☎486 8680; sleeping bag 2600kr, ❶), and pizza/burger meals at the *Klettur* **restaurant**. From here, it's an uneventful 20km to the Geysir–Gullfoss area.

Geysir

Visible from miles away as a pall of steam rising above the plains, **GEYSIR**'s hot springs bubble out over a grassy slope at the foot of **Bjarnfell**, studded with circular pools atop grey, mineral-streaked mounds. The area has been active for thousands of years, but the springs' positions have periodically shifted as geological seams crack open or close down, and the current vents are believed to have appeared following a thirteenth-century earthquake. Just what makes geysers erupt is subject to speculation: some theorists favour gaseous subterranean burps; others believe that cooler surface water forms a "lid", trapping superheated fluid below until enough pressure builds up to burst through as an eruption. What nobody doubts is just how hot the springs are: underground temperatures reach 125°C, and even surface water is only just off boiling point – under no circumstances should you wander off marked paths, step anywhere without looking first, or put any part of your body in the springs or their outlets.

The large, deep, clear blue pool of **Geysir** – the Gusher – is, of course, what everyone comes to see, and in its heyday was certainly impressive, regularly spitting its load seventy metres skywards. After decades of inactivity, a nearby earthquake in 2008 seems to have got things going again, though eruptions are extremely irregular and you'll probably have to be content with the antics of nearby **Strokkur**, the Churn, which fires off a thirty-metre-high spout every few minutes. A split second before it explodes, Strokkur's pool surface forms a distinct dome, through which the rising waters tear. Lesser spouts in the vicinity include **Blesi**'s twin pools, one clear and colourless, the other opaque blue; the unpredictably tempered **Fata**; and **Litli Geysir**, which does little but slosh around violently.

Bjarnarfell and Haukadalur

Near Geysir, you can also climb well-worn **tracks** to the summit of Bjarnarfell (727m) for views down on Geysir's surrounds, though it's a miserable proposition in bad weather. Another option is to follow the signposted, three-kilometre-long gravel vehicle track from Geysir up to a forestry reserve and church at **Haukadalur**. In saga times Haukadalur was an important holding, another famous educational centre that was eventually incorporated into Skálholt's lands. Extensive felling and ensuing erosion put paid to the estate, which was in a sorry condition when turned into a reserve in the 1930s. Since then, the hillsides here have been planted thickly with green pine trees, and thousands of new saplings spread down the valley, coloured in spring by wildflowers. Have a quick look at the nineteenth-century **church**, too, whose brass door-ring is said to have belonged to the friendly giant **Bergþór**, who asked to be buried here.

Geysir practicalities

The Geysir thermal area is right on Route 37, 60km from Selfoss and a bit less than that from Þingvellir. The **Visitor Centre** (⊛www.geysircenter.is) opposite has fuel, a gift shop, basic store and a mediocre canteen; there's a better **restaurant** and accommodation next door at *Hótel Geysir* (℡480 6800, Ⓦwww.geysircenter.is; studio flats with bathroom and kitchen ❷), which also runs the **campsite** (900kr per person), with free showers and barbecue sites. Alternatively, just along the road beyond the hotel, the *Geysir Guesthouse* (℡486 8733, Ⓦwww.geysirgolf.is; ❷) is attached to the **golf course** and tends to get booked out in advance.

All **buses** stop here for around an hour, long enough to catch an eruption and get fed, but not to ascend Bjarnfell or get out to Haukadalur. **Moving on**, there are daily buses all through the year to Gullfoss (and on to Akureyri via Kjölur, see p000), or back to Selfoss and Reykjavík.

Gullfoss

About 6km up the road from Geysir on the **Hvítá** river, **Gullfoss** – Golden Falls – can hardly fail to impress, whether in full flood during the spring thaw or frozen and almost still in the depths of winter. The approach road over moorland follows the top of a two-kilometre-long canyon sided in organ-pipe basalt columns, into which Gullfoss drops in a pair of broad cataracts: the first steps out ten metres in full view, then the river bends sharply and falls a further twenty metres into the gorge's spray-filled shadow. Paths along the edge are dangerous when icy, but at other times they allow you to get thoroughly soaked while viewing spray rainbows above the drop – try and visit in the afternoon, when the western sun lights up the falls.

The falls are a nature reserve, formed after **Sigríður Tómasdóttir**, daughter of the owner of the estate that incorporated Gullfoss, fought first her father and then the government to stop a hydroelectric dam being built here in the 1920s. Permission to build the dam was granted, but, fanned by Sigríður, public feeling ran so strongly against the project that construction never started. The land was later sold to Einar Guðmundsson of nearby **Brattholt farm**, who donated it to the Icelandic Nature Conservation Council in 1976.

The huge **Visitor Centre** at the top of the gorge above the falls has souvenirs, delicious bowls of hearty lamb stew at the **canteen**, and great views north to the peaks and glaciers of the Icelandic interior (though not of the falls themselves). The nearest **place to stay** is 3km down the road at *Hotel Gullfoss* (℡486 8979, Ⓦwww.hotelgullfoss.is; ❸). Gullfoss marks the end of the Golden Circle, though the **Kjölur route** continues northeast across the Interior from here (see p.315), covered by summer buses.

The Central South

East of Reykjavík on the Ringroad, the hothouse town of **Hveragerði** and nearby transit hub **Selfoss** are the gateway to Iceland's **central south**, a swathe of fertile plains watered by the Hvítá, Rangá and **Þjórsá** – Iceland's longest river at 230km – and the clutch of bulky glaciers to its east. The inland here cowers beneath **Hekla**, the destructive volcano whose antics have put paid to regional farming at least twice in recorded history, with tracks past the mountain leading to hot springs and brightly coloured hills at **Landmannalaugar**, right on the edge of Iceland's rugged Interior. Meanwhile, the Ringroad crosses the grassy swards that formed the setting for much of **Njál's Saga** (see box, pp.126–127), Iceland's great medieval epic, beyond which loom the **Eyjarfjallajökull** and **Mýrdalsjökull** ice caps, offering superlative scenery around their wooded edges at **Þórsmörk**. With Mýrdalsjökull squeezing down on an ever-narrowing shore, the Ringroad reaches the mainland's southernmost point near the pleasant coastal village of **Vík**, an area famed for its black sand beaches, eroded cliffs, and birdlife.

The region is one of the best places in the country to get out and about, especially considering how accessible it all is from Reykjavík: if you enjoy camping and hiking, Landmannalaugar and Þórsmörk are worth a trip to Iceland in their own right, as is the four-day **Laugavegur hiking trail** between the two. If you're not that serious, consider less demanding tracks over the hills above Hveragerði, or the coastal paths in the vicinity of Vík. For regional **horse treks**, contact Eldhestar at Vellir, about 2km southeast of Hveragerði (☎480 4800, Ⓦwww.eldhestar.is), who offer anything from one hour to two weeks in the saddle. As far as transport goes, the Ringroad (Route 1) is the regional artery, running east for some 200km via all the main towns, and plied by year-round **buses**. In summer, there are also daily services to Landmannalaugar and Þórsmörk, which are about the only two destinations here that you shouldn't try to reach in a conventional vehicle.

Hveragerði and around

Following the Ringroad southeast from Reykjavík, you cross various flat, lichen-covered lava flows for 45km before the road twists down off the ranges to the coastal plains and the glowing hothouses of **HVERAGERÐI**, a cluster of low buildings on the Varmá (Warm River), nestled beneath steaming fell slopes. Sitting on the edge of a geothermal area, which extends north under the mountains and right up to Þingvellir, a wool mill and hydroelectric dam were already established here when, for the first time in Iceland, subterranean heat was harnessed to grow vegetables in the 1920s. Today, you can enjoy a mud bath at the **Health Clinic** (Grænumörk 10, ☎483 0300, Ⓦwww.hnlfi); or visit Hveragerði's numerous **hothouses**, all involved in the propagation of fruit, vegetables and exotic plants – try *Blómaborg* at Breiðumörk 12, or *Ingibjörg* at Heiðmörk 38. There's also an excellent **pool** (350kr) just north of the centre on Reykjamörk.

Hveragerði practicalities

A small, quiet mesh of streets, Hveragerði is laid out either side of the main drag **Breiðamörk**, which runs north off the highway, past a large **shopping centre** on the right, up through the compact town centre, and out into the countryside and the start of hiking trails. The shopping centre houses a Bónus **supermarket**, **bank** with ATM, post office and the helpful **South Iceland Information Centre** (Mon–Fri 9am–5pm, Sat & Sun noon–4pm; ☎483 4601, Ⓦwww.southiceland .is), which offers internet access at 150kr for thirty minutes. The square outside is where **buses** stop, with plentiful services to Reykjavík and Selfoss, and a daily bus to Þorlákshöfn, the port for the Westman Islands' ferry (see p.140).

For **accommodation**, Hveragerði's **campsite** (mid-May to mid-Sept; ☎483 4601; 850kr per person) is east of the centre on Reykjamörk; it has toilets, showers and a laundry. West on Frumskógar, the *Frumskógar Guesthouse* (☎896 2780, Ⓦwww.frumskogar.is) has cosy doubles in the main building (❶) and self-contained studio apartments with spas (❷); *Frost og Funi* (☎483 4959, Ⓦwww .frostandfire.is; ❷) is a similar operation just north of town off Brieðamörk, with

Hveragerði hikes

Reykjadalur, the steamy heights above Hveragerði, is covered in trails and hot springs, hillsides stained by volcanic salts, heathland plants, and, in fine weather, inspiring views coastwards – not to mention **bathable warm streams**, so take your swim wear. **Maps** of the area, available at the information centre, have all trails and distances marked; on the ground, many routes are staked out with coloured pegs. As always, carry a compass and come prepared for bad weather.

For an easy four-hour circuit, follow Breiðamörk north out of town for about forty minutes to a **bridged stream** at the base of the fells, from where a pegged trail heads uphill. Crossing the muddy top, you descend green boggy slopes into **Reykjadalur**, Steam Valley, named after the hot stream that runs through the middle. You need to wade across this at any convenient point – there's a shallow ford – and then follow the far bank at the base of the forbidding rubble slopes of **Molddalahnúkar**, past a number of dangerous, scalding pools belching vapour and sulphur – stay on the path. At the head of the valley, 3km from the bridge, the stream bends west, with **Ölkelduhnúkur's** solid platform straight ahead and the main trail following the stream west along **Klambragil**, another steamy valley. There are a number of shallow, warm places to soak here – just test the water temperature first before getting in. If you're not ready to head back afterwards, trails continue north for 15km or so to **Þingvallavatn** – see p.111.

---

riverside hot tubs. Pick of the local **farmstays** is *Núpar*, 3km south of town (☎898 6107, ⓦwww.nupar.is; 2–6 person cabins 10,000–15,000kr).

You can get coffee and cakes at the **bakery** on Breiðamörk, though the best place to find pizzas, burgers and beer is the *Kidda Rót* **restaurant** at the shopping centre. If you're self-catering, take advantage of Hveragerði's glut of vegetables (tasting none the worse for their hothouse origins), and hunt out rectangular loaves of dense, dark *hverabrauð*, rye bread baked in underground ovens (for more of which, see p.261) at the bakery or supermarket.

Raufarholshellir and Strandarkirkja

Hveragerði itself makes a good starting point for **hikes** in Reykjadalur (see box, above) and there are a couple of offbeat places within range of a car. **Raufarholshellir** is a subterranean **lava tube** over 1300m long, hidden beside Route 39 some 15km southwest of Hveragerði. It's difficult to explore – there are no lights, the floor is covered in rubble, there are low ceilings and narrow passages – and it's advisable to visit only with experienced guides: Iceland Excursions (ⓦwww.icelandexcursions.is) run tours in summer. For something easier, head 30km southwest down Route 42 to the tiny coastal hamlet of **STRANDARKIRKJA**, named after the pretty, pale-blue **church** here built around 1900 by thankful sailors who had made it ashore after their ship was wrecked in a storm. In summer, there's a **free campsite** and *T-Bær café*, and Route 42 continues westwards along the coast to Krýsuvík (see p.106).

Selfoss

Some 15km east of Hveragerði, the Ringroad passes the junction of routes north towards Þingvellir and the Geysir–Gullfoss area (see p.113), before crossing a suspension bridge over the fast-flowing Öfulsá and running into the bustling town of **SELFOSS**. Caught between the looming bulk of **Ingólfsfjall** to the north and flat grasslands running to the horizon in all other directions, it's been the centre of Iceland's **dairy industry** since the 1930s and now has a population of around four thousand. Although Selfoss has no specific attractions, its crossroads position on the southwest's main roads means that you'll almost certainly pass through on your way around Iceland.

The original English-engineered **suspension bridge**, built in 1891, is the reason Selfoss came into existence. Before then, roads through the region ran further south, to where traffic was ferried across the Öfulsá estuary. Rough waters made these ferry crossings hazardous, and when the bridge was opened it became an immediate success, a focus for shops and homes that gradually coalesced into the country's **first inland town**. The bridge also gave Selfoss the distinction of hosting the country's first **strike**, sparked not over wages but the fact that its builders were given only salmon to eat. The current bridge dates from 1945, built after the original collapsed when two milk trucks crossed it simultaneously.

The view north of town along Route 35 takes in the sharp-lined confluence of the clear, glacier-fed Hvítá river system and the darker **Sog** river, which drains Þingvallavatn lake to the north, to form the Öfulsá – which, in its turn, flows the final 10km to the sea. The two-kilometre-broad wedge of land immediately north of their confluence is a private reserve known as **Þrastaskógur**, the Thrush Forest, which covers a six-thousand-year-old lava field in a low stand of birch and pine woodland. There are several good, easy **walking tracks** around the reserve from the entrance on Route 35, just by the bridge on the north bank of the Sog, around 9km from Selfoss; and you can also **camp** here (see below).

Practicalities

Selfoss is laid out along a kilometre-long stretch of the Ringroad, which runs east–west through town as Austurvegur. At the western end is the bridge and a **roundabout**, near where you'll find the **banks**, post office and library, which also houses the **tourist information** office (May 15 to Sept Mon–Fri 10am–7pm, Sat 11am–2pm; ☎480 1990). The **bus station**, at the N1 fuel station on Austurvegur at the eastern exit of town, is a staging post for services along the Ringroad: there's also a daily bus to Þorlákshöfn, port for the Westman Islands' ferry (see p.140). There's a large **shopping centre** (daily 10am–7pm) opposite the tourist information office, which includes a well-supplied supermarket, and a cut-price Bónus **supermarket** near the bus station. The local **liquor store** is tucked behind the bus station at Vallholt 19.

Accommodation options include the excellent **campsite** and *Gesthús Selfossi* (☎482 3585, ⓦwww.gesthus.is; camping 500kr, ❷) on Engjavegur, two blocks south of parallel Austurvegur, with showers, kitchen facilities and self-contained cabins. You can also camp about 9km up Route 35 in Þrastaskógur woods at *Þrastalundur* (☎482 2010, ⓔtrastaskogur@simnet.is; 1000kr per tent), where there are barbecues, picnic tables, a restaurant and small store. Otherwise, there are further guesthouse-style lodgings above the *Menam* Thai restaurant (☎482 4099, ⓦwww.menam.is; ❶), just off the roundabout on Eyravegur. Also on the roundabout, the stuffy *Hótel Selfoss* (☎482 2500, ⓦwww.hotelselfoss.is; ❹) is the town's conference venue.

Aside from the usual fast food available next door to the bus station, Selfoss boasts two unexpectedly good **places to eat**: *Kaffi-krús*, opposite the library on Austurvegur, is open from 10am until midnight for coffee and excellent cakes in a candlelit ambience; while *Menam* (see above) is a gem – treat yourself to authentic Thai cuisine, such as chicken and green beans in coconut milk for little more than the price of a pizza.

Stokkseyri and Eyrarbakki

South of Selfoss, Route 34 runs straight to the coast across the **Flói**, a ten-kilometre stretch of land so flat that halfway across you can see both your starting point and destination. At the end, the coastal villages of **Stokkseyri** and **Eyrarbakki** offer an insight into the vanished life of Iceland's old fishing communities – Eyrarbakki was also a staging-post for the Viking discovery of North America. There's not much in the way of **accommodation** in the region, and only one **bus** a day in each direction to Selfoss and Reykjavík, so you really need your own transport.

Stokkseyri

Consisting of little more than a few houses, a fish factory, a supermarket and fuel station, the pretty seaside village of **STOKKSEYRI** is a former fishing port set around its church behind a protective storm wall. Over the wall is a windswept, vestigial and unattended **harbour** – though even in its heyday in the 1900s it must have been tough to launch a boat here – and, oddly, a little yellow sand beach nestled amongst black, weed-strewn rocks. Stokkseyri's most famous resident was **Thurídur Einarsdottír**, a nineteenth-century woman who worked on commercial fishing boats and is renowned for successfully defending, in court, her then-illegal preference for wearing men's clothing. The **Cultural Centre**, inside an old fish factory at Hrafnargata 9, houses (among other things) the workshop of Iceland's only **pipe organ** maker, Björgvin Tómasson, who has built instruments for many of Iceland's churches; and the quirky **Ghost Centre** (June–Aug daily 1–6pm; 750kr), where you're guided around dioramas illustrating famous Icelandic ghost tales.

The best reason to visit Stokkseyri, however, is to splash out for an evening meal at ⅍ *Fjöruborðið* **lobster restaurant** (☏ 899 9494, Ⓦ www.fjorubordid.is; bookings essential) beside the Cultural Centre at Eyrarbraut 3a: it's popular with well-off families at weekends – a huge plateful of lobster tails costs 3500kr.

Eyrarbakki

Four kilometres west of Stokkseyri and just past the intersection, **EYRARBAKKI** is a larger version of its neighbour, and has a greater claim to fame: local boy **Bjarni Herjólfsson** sailed from here in 985 aiming for Greenland, lost his way in a storm, and became the first European to set eyes on **North America** – though, displaying an incredible lack of curiosity, he failed to land. After reaching Greenland, he told his story and sold his ship to Leifur Eiriksson, who retraced Bjarni's route, made landfall, and named the place "**Vinland**" after his foster-father reported finding grape vines. The details are recounted in *Greenlanders' Saga* and *Eirik the Red's Saga*, usually coupled together as the *Vinland Sagas* (see "Books", p.342).

Until the early twentieth century, Eyrarbakki's **harbour** was considered one of the best in southern Iceland, though boats had to be launched by dragging them through the surf into deeper water where they could be rowed out. Fishing and a proximity to the Öfulsá estuary ferry ensured Eyrarbakki's prosperity until the Selfoss bridge was completed and the town's harbour was rendered redundant by a safer, man-made effort west across the Öfulsá at Þorlákshöfn. Today, the hamlet's main employer is the local **jail**, one of Iceland's largest.

Despite this downturn of fortune, Eyrarbakki sports an attractive core of early twentieth-century houses, an older timber-sided **church**, and nearby **Husíð**, a Norwegian wooden kit-home dating back to 1765 which, along with adjacent buildings, now serves as a **museum complex** (Ⓦ www.husid.com; June–Aug daily 1–6pm; 700kr). The best section here is the **Maritime Museum**, whose centrepiece is a wooden fishing boat of the kind used until the 1930s; a few photos and weather-beaten oilskins complete the display. Outside, climb the **storm wall** for a look seawards at what fishermen were up against as they set off or returned – a difficult entry over a rocky shore.

Like Stokkseyri, Eyrarbakki boasts an excellent seafood **restaurant**: the 🍴 *Rauða húsið* on Búðarstíg 4 (☎ 483 3330, ⓦ www.raudahusid.is; bookings essential). The only other facilities in town are a small **fuel station** with a store. There's a good drive westwards towards Þorlákshöfn and Reykjavík via a causeway over the Ölfusá's improbably broad estuary, which takes in heathland, coastal flats, vegetated lava flows and a series of brackish marshland pools, all ideal for **bird-watching** – swans, geese, snipe, short-eared owls and godwit are all common.

Þjórsárdalur, Hekla and Landmannalaugar

Upstream along the Þjórsá east of Selfoss, there's a rare relic of Viking times in **Þjórsárdalur**, a once fertile valley laid waste over nine hundred years ago by a particularly violent eruption of **Hekla**, which lies over the river to the southeast. The volcano last let rip in 2000, and the whole region remains patently active, with Iceland's highest concentration of **hot springs** east again from Hekla around **Landmannalaugar**. While Hekla's immediate vicinity is a predictable carpet of rubbly lava fields in various degrees of vegetation, Landmannalaugar – with its bathable springs surrounded by a landscape oozing rugged grandeur – makes a great target, and sits at the northern end of **Laugavegur**, a wonderful hiking trail to Þórsmörk. It's worth noting that cross-country routes on from Landmannalaugar include the **Sprengisandur** (F26) to Mývatn (see p.314) and **Fjallabak** to Kirkjubæjarklaustur and Skaftafell (see p.123), making it a good staging post for wider travels.

Route 30/32 to Þjórsárdalur, and Route 26 to Hekla and Landmannalaugar, are both accessed off the Ringroad east of Selfoss; see below and p.122 for details. **Buses** run past Hekla to Landmannalaugar through the summer; there is no public transport to Þjórsárdalur. While there are a good few kilometres of gravel roads here, Þjórsárdalur and the area around Hekla are accessible to normal vehicles in good weather, though the track from Hekla to Landmannalaugar is for four-wheel-drives only. Take everything you'll need with you, as there are few shops or supplies in the region.

Þjórsárdalur

Around 15km out of Selfoss, Route 30 branches northeast off the Ringroad to follow the west bank of the Þjórsá, mutating along the way into the 32 at the one-horse hamlet of **ÁRNES**, where there's a fuel station, small café-store, and IYHA **hostel** (☎ 486 6048, ⓦ www.hostel.is; camping 750kr, sleeping bag 2000kr) with campsite, kitchen and pool. Past here, there are excellent views from a roadside ridge at **Hagafell** straight across the Þjórsá to Hekla.

Thirty kilometres further on, **Þjórsárdalur** – the Bull River valley – sits north of the road, flanked by grey and orange gravel slopes and framed at its eastern end by the flat tops of **Skeljafell** and larger **Búrfell**. The valley is floored with an eight-thousand-year-old lava flow, and subsequent thick falls of ash from Hekla have regularly wiped out vegetation, making Þjórsárdalur an awesomely sterile place. On the valley's western side, there's an unsurfaced, seven-kilometre signed track to **Þjórsárdalslaug** (June–Aug Wed–Fri 1–7pm, Sat & Sun noon–7pm; 600kr), a

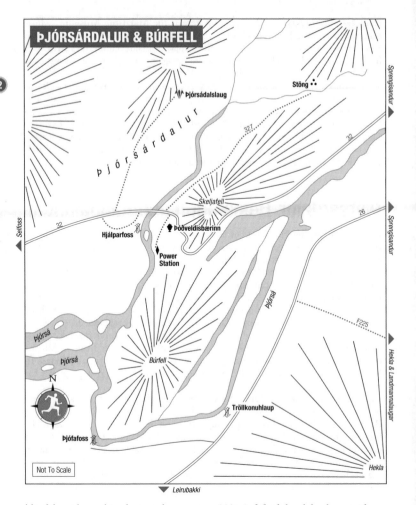

ÞJÓRSÁRDALUR & BÚRFELL

blissful geothermal pool set outdoors among **Þjórsárdalur's** harsh landscape. Alternatively, a brief detour brings you to **Hjálparfoss**, a parallel pair of short, foaming falls 100m south off Route 32. They drop into a round pool, surrounded by thin basalt columns that both spray in all directions and lie piled up like woodstacks; a second, rougher cataract drains the pool towards a power station below Búrfell. Grassy banks make Hjálparfoss a good place to picnic (the water is too cold for a swim), and there are **harlequin ducks** around in early summer.

Stöng and Þóðveldisbærinn

On Þjórsárdalur's eastern side, signposted Route 327 heads 7km north up to the remains of **Stöng**; it's a rough and sometimes muddy road, but you should be able to get within sight of the red-roofed shelter-shed protecting the site. Set on a small stream below the dark slopes of Stangarfjall, Stöng was the home of a chieftain named **Gaukur Trándilsson** until Hekla erupted in 1104 for the first time since Settlement, smothering all of Þjórsárdalur under ash and pumice. Stöng was excavated in 1939 and illustrates a typical **Viking homestead**: a longhouse formed the main hall, with a second, smaller hall and two attached outhouses serving as women's quarters, washroom and pens, all built from stone and timber and sided with turf. Neatly built stone foundations, a central fireplace and post supports provide an outline of the original buildings, but it's the desolate setting – distant orange and green-streaked valley walls, and patches of pasture clinging on along the stream – which really impresses.

For a more complete picture of how Stöng once appeared, return to Route 32 and take the surfaced turning south marked "Búrfellsstöð", roughly opposite the Stöng junction and immediately below Búrfell. This descends 100m down to the power station, but before this follow signs left to **Þóðveldisbærinn** (June–Aug daily 10am–noon & 1–6pm; 600kr), a reconstructed period homestead based on archeological evidence provided by Stöng and other sites, roofed with turf and authentically decked out in hand-cut timber, flagstones and woollen furnishings.

Back on Route 32, the road winds up behind Búrfell and then follows the river upstream for 15km, finally connecting with Route 26 and the Hekla region (see below).

Hekla

Believed to be the literal entrance to hell in medieval times – a fact that left the mountain unclimbed until daring students Eggert Olafsson and Bjarni Palsson scrambled up in 1750 – **Hekla** is Iceland's second most active volcano, with at least eighteen eruptions known to have occurred in the last thousand years. Oriented northeast, the mountain forms a forty-kilometre-long, snow-covered oval ridge cresting at around 1500m; it should be visible for miles around, but a heavy smudge of cloud usually obscures the peak and gives Hekla – Hooded – its name.

Though several thousand years old, Hekla's **earliest recorded eruption** was the one that buried Stöng in 1104, and it has been active, on and off, ever since. The mountain tends to fire up with little warning, spraying out clouds of fluorine-rich **tephra** ash, which blankets the landscape, poisons groundwater, and kills fish and livestock. Lava follows the ash, welling up at various points along a fissure that splits Hekla's crest lengthways for 5km; during the notorious 1768 eruption – before which the mountain had been dormant for seventy years – flows covered over 65 square kilometres. Eruptions often subside relatively quickly, most of the action occurring within the first few days and followed by months of grumbling – the anguished voices of tormented souls, according to legend. Stöng was by no means the only settlement to have been abandoned following such an event and the same eruption is believed to have wiped out twenty similar homesteads. There are only two working farms around the volcano today.

Hekla has erupted every ten years since 1970, the **most recent eruption** occurring on the evening of February 26, 2000. It wasn't much by the mountain's standards – a plume of ash and steam reaching upwards for 15km and a few days' worth of lava spilling east – but it was notable in that most of Reykjavík descended on the area to watch, only to be trapped on Hekla's slopes by a sudden snowfall. This triggered the largest emergency operation in Icelandic history, with over a thousand people having to be rescued. Fortunately, the lava went the other way.

To **climb Hekla** yourself, contact Ferðafélag Íslands, the Icelandic Hiking Association (see Basics, p.45), whose staff can advise about routes; the trailhead for the summit starts off the F225 to Landmannalaugar, and **buses** heading that way can drop you off. If you need a guide, Contact Arctic Adventures (Ⓦ www.adventures .is), leads day hikes to the summit. You can also arrange **quad bike** explorations of Hekla with Unnar Garðarsson of 🏕 Óbygðaferðir (Ⓣ 822 4557, Ⓦ www.icesafari.is) – just don't plan to use your legs much for a couple of days afterwards.

▲ Icelandic horse on the lavafield surrounding Hekla

Around the mountain

About 30km east of Selfoss along the Ringroad, you reach the lonely Vegamót **fuel station**, marking where **Route 26** points northeast towards Hekla and the track to Landmannalaugar. Both Landmannalaugar and Sprengisandur **buses** pass through the region in summer via the Ringroad town of Hella (see p.127).

Buses pull in 30km along Route 26 on Hekla's western edge at *Leirubakki* (☎ 487 8700, ⓦ www.leirubakki.is; camping 800kr, sleeping-bag accommodation 4200kr, ❸), a year-round **hotel** which also supplies fuel, meals and outside hot tubs – including the lava-block "**Viking Pool**" with superlative views of the mountain. The **Hekla Centre** here (May–Sept daily 10am–10pm; 700kr) offers a history of the mountain, with videos of eruptions.

Past *Leirubakki*, Route 26 continues through a wilderness between the Þjórsá river and Hekla's western slopes, the ground covered in tiny pieces of lightweight yellow **pumice** that are collected hereabouts for export. After about 5km there's a road towards the mountain itself and **Næfurholt farm**, one of the area's few functioning survivors – though it actually had to be moved after one eruption – then a roadside ridge blocks in Hekla's foothills while the Búrfell mesa springs up ahead of you. Wheel ruts and guide posts heading off-road towards Búrfell at this point can be followed for 4km to **Þófafoss**, where the river bends right under Búrfell's southern tip in a wide, low waterfall, a friendly splash of colour among the monochrome landscape.

Route 26 presses on northeastwards, passing another waterfall called **Tröllkonuhlaup**, the Troll Woman's Leap, named after one of these unpleasant creatures crossed the river in a single bound while chasing a farmer. Bearing east off this road from here is **Route F225**, the four-wheel-drive-only track to Landmannalaugar; Route 26 continues to parallel the river for 15km up to the junction with Route 32 (which you can follow southwest to Þjórsárdalur – see p.119), before heading northeast across Sprengisandur as the F26 (see p.314).

Landmannalaugar and Laugavegur

Thirty kilometres due east of Hekla, **Landmannalaugar** is an astonishing place, a **hot springs** area set in a flat gravel plain between a glacial river and the front of a fifteenth-century lava flow, all hemmed in by sharp-peaked obsidian and rhyolite mountains, brightly streaked in orange, grey and green. Despite its proximity to Hekla, the area has provided summer pasture for sheep since medieval times, and was once a stage on the **Fjallabak Nyrðri** route (see box below), which ran as an alternative way to the coast if flooding from Katla had closed the preferred southern trails. Today Landmannalaugar is a popular destination in its own right, both for the springs and numerous local **hiking tracks** – not to mention being at the start of the exceptional four-day **Laugavegur trail** down to Þórsmörk.

The main **road to Landmannalaugar** is the four-wheel-drive only F225, which turns east off Route 26 just past Tröllkonuhlaup (see above) via thirty-year-old black ash and lava deposits on Hekla's northern flanks, crosses a couple of rivers and intermittent oases of grassland, and finally reaches a major **ford** immediately west of Landmannalaugar. **Buses** from Reykjavík via Selfoss and *Leirubakki* run here daily from June to mid-September; some continue southeast via the **Fjallabak Nyrðra** route to Eldgjá, Kirkjubærklaustur and Skaftafell (see box below), and northeast via the **Sprengisandur route** to Mývatn (see p.314) – both stop for at least a couple of hours, giving you time for a soak in the springs and a quick walk.

Landmannalaugar's **accommodation** is run by Ferðafélag Íslands, the Icelandic Hiking Association (☎568 2533, Ⓦwww.fi.is), and you'll either be staying in their well-equipped, self-catering **hut** (July–Aug; sleeping bag only, 3300kr), or **camping** (900kr) beside it. Book bunk space in the hut as far in advance as possible, although there are often last-minute cancellations. If camping, be aware that **weather** here can be atrocious, with incredibly strong winds – ominously, the campsite has bins full of rocks for weighting down tent edges. The **ranger's office** is at the hut, where you can buy **maps** of the hiking trails. **Toilets and showers** (400kr) are in a big, separate block. Campers are not allowed to use the hut's kitchen, so bring cooking gear along – though, incredibly, the small *Fjallabúð* **café** in a converted bus (July & Aug 11.30am–8pm) sells drinks and sandwiches. To organize **horse treks** in the region, contact Hraunhestar (☎854 7735).

Around Landmannalaugar

Your first stop at Landmannalaugar has to be the celebrated **hot springs**, which are in a patch of green at the end of a boardwalk up against the lava front. A scalding stream emerges from underneath the lava and merges with a cold flow; you simply wade up the latter to where they mix, find a spot where the temperature is just right, and sit down up to your neck. You have to keep shifting every time a fellow

---

Fjallabak

Fjallabak is an area covering two **old traffic routes** which ran, quite literally, *fjallabak* – "behind the mountains" north of the Mýrdalsjökull glacier. Today, one of these has been resurrected as the F208, which runs from Landmannalaugar to Kirkjubæjarklaustur (see p.307) via **Hólaskjól**, a hut northeast of Mýrdalsjökull, and **Eldgjá**, a deep, forty-kilometre-long volcanic canyon with a spectacular accompanying waterfall, **Ófærufoss**. From June until September, daily **Reykjavík to Skaftafell buses** (Ⓦwww.bsi.is) cover this entire route in just ten hours, though you'll definitely need to stop off along the way at Landmannalaugar and the Eldgjá area to get the most from the journey.

Laugavegur, the 55-kilometre hiking trail between Landmannalaugar and Þórsmörk, is the best of its kind in Iceland, with easy walking and magnificent scenery. Huts with campsites are laid out at roughly fourteen-kilometre intervals, splitting Laugavegur comfortably into **four stages**: six days is an ideal time to spend on the trip, allowing four for the trail and a day at either end, though you could hike the trail in just two days.

The trail is open from early June until the end of August, when **buses** run daily from Reykjavík to the end points at Landmannalaugar and Þórsmörk. Ferðafélag Íslands' **huts** (☎568 2535, ✉fi@fi.is) sleep up to seventy people, cost 3300kr a night for sleeping-bag space, have toilets, kitchens and usually showers, and need to be booked well in advance; make sure you carry the **receipts** to show to hut wardens, as it's the only way you can prove your booking. **Campsites** at the huts cost 800kr, with access to toilets and showers, but not kitchens. Bring everything with you, including food and sleeping bags (you can get water at the huts) and, if camping, a tent, stove and cooking gear.

Weather varies between fair and foul, with gale-force winds a speciality of the region; you need full waterproof gear, warm clothing, solid hiking boots, and some old trainers or surf boots for fording the several frigid **rivers**. Don't wear **denim jeans** for hiking; they become impossibly heavy and abrasive when wet. The trail is well pegged, but carry Landmælingar Íslands' *Þórsmörk-Landmannalaugar* **map** and a compass. Although the overall **gradients** are the same whichever end you begin, in practice it's easier from the north, where you spend a whole day gradually reaching the trail's apex (around 1120m) between Hrafntinnusker and Álftvatn, instead of doing it in one short, brutal ascent from the south.

The trail

The 12km stretch between Landmannalaugar and the first hut at Hrafntinnusker is mostly up. You leave Landmannalaugar via Brennisteinsalda onto the muddy moorland atop the plateau, surrounded by stark, wild hills. About two-thirds of the way along is **Stórihver thermal area**, a steaming gully and rare patch of grass, beyond which there's a scramble onto a higher **snowfield** which peaks at **Söðull**, the ridge above the huge volcanic crater of **Hrafntinnusker**. "Hrafntin" means **obsidian**, and just about all rocks in the area are made of this black volcanic glass. The Hrafntinnusker **hut** has no shower; the campsite here is on scree and very exposed. The tightly folded ridges due west conceal Iceland's densest concentration of **hot springs**, with a pegged walking track (about 40min each way) out to where one set rises under the stratified edge of a glacier, hollowing out **ice caves**, though these mostly collapsed in 2007.

It's a further 12km from Hrafntinnusker to the second hut at Álftvatn. The first stage continues the plateau scenery across snowfields (potentially dangerous in summer due to thinning of snow) to a rocky outcrop just west of **Háskerðingur**, whose sharp,

bather moves, which alters the water currents and temperature, but you couldn't ask for a better place to unwind. Be aware that some unidentified **parasite** in the hot pools has caused paralysis in ducks; the effects on humans are unknown but locals certainly don't care.

For a couple of easy **hikes**, either head south from the campsite for 2km down **Brandsgil**, a tight, colourful canyon full of shallow streamlets and hot springs in the riverbed; or west past the hut and up onto the obsidian-rich **Laugahraun** lava field, following the first couple of kilometres of the Laugavegur trail. You end up on a ridge overlooking the flow, near a concentration of steam vents at **Brennisteinsalda**, from where you can circuit back to the campsite via **Grænagil**, a narrow canyon.

snow-clad peak makes a good two-hour detour – though views northwest from the outcrop, over worn rhyolite hills, patches of steam from scattered vents, and Laufafell's distinctive black mass, are just as good. The plateau's edge at **Jökultungur** is not much further on, revealing a blast of colour below which is a bit of a shock after the highland's muted tones: Álftavatn sits in a vivid green glacial valley, lined with sharp ridges and abrupt pyramidal hills, with Mýrdalsjökull's outlying glaciers visible to the south. The subsequent **descent** into the valley is steep but not difficult, and ends with you having to wade a small stream before the trail flattens out near the **two huts** (one owned by Útivist; ☏562 1000, ⓦwww.utivist.is) and campground on the lakeshore at **Álftavatn**. After getting settled in, hike around Álftavatn's west side and follow the valley for 5km down to **Torfahlaup**, a narrow canyon near where the **Markarfljót river** flows roughly between the green flanks of Stóra-Grænfjall and Illasúla, two steep-sided peaks.

The next stage to Botnar-Emstrur is 16km. Around 5km east from Álftavatn via a couple more streams, **Hvanngil** is a sheltered valley with a privately run **hut and campground** (1900kr/700kr) with showers and toilet; after here you cross a bridge over **Kaldaklofskvísl**, and have to wade the substantial but fairly shallow **Bláfjallakvísl**. The scenery beyond opens up into a grey-brown gravel **desert**, fringed by the surreally green hills and Mýrdalsjökull's ice cap, as you follow a four-wheel-drive track southwest. Part-way across the desert, there's another bridge over the **Innri-Emstruá**, where this chocolate-brown glacial river hammers over a short waterfall with such force that it sends geyser-like spurts skywards. Then it's back across the gravel, up and over various hillocks, until you find yourself descending bleak slopes to the **hut** at **Botnar-Emstrur**, whose campground is in a small, surprisingly lush gully. Otherwise, the immediate scenery appears barren, though there's a short walk west to **Markarfljótsgljúfur**, a narrow, 180-metre-deep gorge on the Markarfljót, and superlative views of **Entujökull**, the nearest of Mýrdalsjökull's glaciers, from clifftops around 3km southeast of the hut.

The final 15km southwest to Þórsmörk is perhaps the least interesting section of the journey, though there's initially another good view of the glacier, just before the path crosses the Emstruá over a narrow bridge. This is followed by a climb onto a gravelly heath, with the Markafljót flowing through a series of deep canyons to the west – easy enough to investigate, though out of sight of the path. As you follow the ever-widening valley, you'll start to encounter a few shrubs before crossing a further bridge over the **Ljósá** and descending to the gravel beds of the **Þröngá**, the deepest river you have to ford on the trail – don't attempt it if it's more than thigh deep. Once across you immediately enter birch and juniper **woodland** marking Þórsmörk's boundary at **Hamraskógar**: shady, carpeted in thick grass, and with colourful flowers everywhere. From here, it's a final 2km into Þórsmörk to the huts at either Húsadalur or Skagfjörðsskáli – for more on which, see p.135.

On a clear day you really should ascend **Bláhnúkur** (945m), the large, bald peak to the south. There's a straightforward, marked trail up the northeast face from near the campsite; it's steep enough but around an hour should see you on the summit enjoying staggering 360 degree views; all around are multicoloured hills, with the campsite edged by moss-covered lava. Off to the northeast is **Tungnaá**, a sprawling area of lakes and intertwined streams at the source of the Skaftá, which empties into the sea near Kirkjubærklaustur. For the descent, either retrace your steps or – if you've good boots and little fear – follow the trail along the peak and off down the steep, slippery scree slope covering Bláhnúkur's west face. You end up at the edge of the Laugahraun lava field as above, with a choice of paths back to base.

Njál's Saga country

Heading southeast from the Þjórsá on the Ringroad, the first thing you'll notice are disproportionate numbers of four-wheel-drives towing boxes, and a wide, rolling expanse of pasture, positively reeking of **horse**. This is one of Iceland's premier horse-breeding areas, with *Oddhóll*, the country's biggest stud farm, near the small town of **Hella**. The countryside between here and the distant slopes of **Eyjafjallajökull** to the east comprises the plains of the two-pronged **Rangá** river system, famed for its salmon and the setting for much of the action of *Njál's Saga* (see box below), though parts of this tale were played out right across southern Iceland. With the highway towns of Hella or **Hvolsvöllur** as a base, getting out to a handful of the saga sites is straightforward enough in your own vehicle, even if you do find more in the way of associations rather than concrete remains when you arrive. Alternatively, you can explore the region on **horseback** with Hestheimar (T487 6666, Wwww.hestheimar.is), just off the Ringroad about 25km from Selfoss. Ringroad **buses** pass through Hella and Hvolsvöllur year-round, with summer services stopping at Hvolsvöllur en route to Þórsmörk and the Fjallabak route.

Njal's Saga

Speared in the belly, Þorgrim dropped his shield, slipped, and fell off the roof. He walked back to Gizur and the rest.

"Is Gunnar at home", asked Gizur, looking up. Þorgrim replied, "You'll have to find that out for yourself – but his spear certainly is." And then he fell dead.

There's nothing to beat the laconic, hard-bitten delivery of **Njál's Saga**, Iceland's gripping tale of Viking-age clan warfare. The story centres on the life of **Njál Þorgeirsson** and his family, who are casually ensnared in a minor issue that somehow escalates into a frightful, fifty-year feud. Bound by their own personalities, fate, and sense of honour, nobody is able to stop the bloodshed, which ends only after the original characters – and many of their descendants – have been killed. But there's far more to *Njál's Saga* than its violence, and the tale paints a vivid picture of Iceland at what was, in some ways, an idyllic time: the power of the Alþing at Þingvellir was at its peak, Christianity was overpowering paganism, and the country's free settlers lived by their own efforts at farming and freebooting.

The tale splits into three uneven parts, beginning in the late tenth century at a point where the fate of several participants is already intertwined. Gifted with foresight and generally respected by all, Njál himself is often a background figure, mediating and advising rather than confronting or fighting, but his sons play a far more active role, especially the proud and ferocious **Skarp-héðinn**. Njál's best friend is the heroic **Gunnar Hámundarson** of Hlíðarendi, whose superb martial skills and physical prowess never get in the way of his generosity or sense of justice. Balancing this nobility is the malevolent **Mörð Valgarðsson**, a second cousin of Gunnar's who grows up hating him for his intrinsic goodness and spends the saga's first third plotting his downfall.

Around 970 Gunnar goes against Njál's advice and marries "Thief-eyed" **Hallgerð**, a thorny character who provokes a violent feud with Njál's household. Njál and Gunnar manage to remain firm friends, but Njál's sons are drawn into the fray by the murder of their foster-father **Þórð**, and the cycle of payback killings begins, quickly spiralling out beyond the two immediate families. Mörð sees his chance, and manipulates various disreputable characters into picking fights with Gunnar, who emerges undefeated yet increasingly worn down from each confrontation. At last, Gunnar is

Hella and around

HELLA, a service centre of six hundred inhabitants where the highway crosses the narrow flow of the **Ytri-Rangá** (also known as the **Hólsá**), grew through the twentieth century to serve **Rangárvallahreppur**, the fertile farming district beyond Hekla's southwestern extremities. Other than hosting the annual Landsmót **National Horse Show** in late June, Hella is really only of interest as somewhere to pause before heading on, either to historic sites nearby, or Hekla, clearly visible 50km to the northeast (see p.121).

The town focuses on a shopping centre on the highway, from where Þrúðavegur runs back along the river. **Buses** – both Ringroad services and those heading to Landmannalaugar – pull in here, where there's also an **information centre** (T 487 5165, F 487 5365; Mon–Fri 10am–5.30pm), fuel station (9am–9pm), supermarket and bank with ATM. **Hotel rooms** can be had at *Fosshotel Mosfell* (T 487 5828, W www.fosshotel.is; doubles without bathroom ❷, with bathroom ❹), behind the fuel station at Þrúðavegur 6; for self-contained **cabins and camping** head over the highway to *Árhús* (T 487 5577, W www.arhus.is; camping 700kr pp, sleeping bag 2200kr; ❷). A good self-catering option is *Gistiheimilið Brenna* (T 861 1662, W www.mmedia.is/toppbrenna; ❶), 500m upstream along the riverbank at

ambushed by **Þorgeir Otkelsson**, whose father he killed earlier as a result of Mörð's scheming; he kills Þorgeir too, but is outlawed for it and banished from Iceland at the Alþing in 990. Torn between his respect for the law and love of his country, Gunnar finds himself unable to leave, and is hunted down to Hlíðarendi by a posse led by Mörð and the upstanding chieftain Gizur the White. When Gunnar's bowstring snaps during the siege, Hallgerð spitefully refuses to give him two locks of her hair to restring the weapon: "To each their own way of earning fame," says Gunnar, in one of the most famous of all saga lines, and is cut down.

After an interlude describing Iceland's **conversion to Christianity** in 1000, the violence sparked by Hallgerð thirty years earlier resurfaces when Njál's sons kill her distant relative, the arrogant Þráin Sigfússon, for his part in Þorð's death. Attempting to placate Þráin's family, Njál adopts his son **Höskuld** and buys him a priesthood, and for a while all seems well. But over the next decade resentment at this favouritism eats away at Njál's sons, and, encouraged by Mörð – who, now that Gunnar is dead, has shifted his vindictive attentions to Njál – they kill Höskuld one sunny morning. Höskuld's influential father-in-law **Flósi of Svínafell** agrees initially to a cash settlement for the murder, but Njál inadvertently offends him at the Alþing in 1011: confrontation is inevitable and the 80-year-old Njál, bowing to fate, retreats with his sons to his homestead **Bergþórshvoll**. Flósi and his men torch the building, killing all but Njal's son-in-law **Kári**, who escapes through the burning roof.

Public opinion against the burning of Njál runs so high that Kári is able to remain free, though a hunted man, and at the following year's Alþing he confronts Flósi and his allies – now known as the **Burners**. Mörð stirs up trouble again and a pitched battle breaks out; in the aftermath, all but Kári accept the Alþing's conditions for peace, which banish Flósi and the Burners from Iceland until tempers have cooled. For his part, Kári swears vengeance, and swiftly tracks down and kills a group of Burners before fleeing the country himself. The action over the next few years follows Kári's peregrinations around northern Europe after his enemies, before he makes a pilgrimage to seek absolution from the Pope. Returning to Iceland, Kári's ship is wrecked at Ingólfshöfði off the southeast coast; walking inland through a blizzard he finds sanctuary at Svínafell and becomes reconciled with Flósi, bringing *Njál's Saga* to an end.

Þrúðavegur 37. Nearby at Þrúðavegur 34, *Kristján X* **restaurant** has decent grills and staples.

If you fancy **salmon fishing** on the Rangá, you need to base yourself 8km east down the Ringroad towards Hvolsvöllur at the ⚶ *Hótel Rangá* (☎478 5700, Ⓦwww.hotelranga.is; ⒼⒼ), a four-star establishment where – if you contact them well in advance – you can arrange licences to cast along the Eystri-Rangá, the Rangá river's eastern branch.

Keldur

Just beyond Hella, Route 264 heads northeast off the Ringroad towards Hekla. Some 20km along, the pretty farm of **Keldur** (June 15 to Aug 15 daily 10am–5pm; 500kr) is named after the "cold springs" (*keldur*) that seep out from under a vegetated lava flow to form a sizeable stream winding off across the plains. There's a modern farm here, but an older string of a half-dozen **turf-covered halls** date, in part, right back to the Viking period – incredibly, it was lived in until the 1930s. The entrance hall is low-ceilinged and flagstoned, leading to a kitchen and store-room; the roof beams and doorway panels are incised with simple **line decorations**, typical of the Viking era. To the left, another room has a **concealed tunnel** leading 25m out into the fields; this dates from the twelfth century and was built as an escape route in case of siege. **Snorri Sturlusson**, Iceland's great medieval man of letters, was raised at Keldur by his foster-father Jón Ólafsson and later built a similar tunnel under his own home at Reykholt (see p.160), in which he was trapped and assassinated by his enemies. Even earlier, Keldur was home to **Ingjald Höskuldsson**, uncle of Njál's illegitimate son, who supported Kári against the Burners.

Once you've looked around inside, take a moment to register Keldur's location, right on the steep front of one of Hekla's flows: the few stone walls defining the fields below were built to limit ash drifts and erosion following periodic eruptions.

Gunnarsstein

Ask at Keldur for directions to **Gunnarsstein**, a boulder 3km east where Gunnar and his allies were ambushed by a group led by local horseman **Starkað of Þríhyrningur**. The battle that followed contains some of *Njál's Saga*'s most savage imagery; when it was over, Gunnar's side had killed fourteen of their attackers, but at the cost of Gunnar's brother **Hjört** (whose name means "heart"). The tale describes Hjört's burial here afterwards, and in the mid-nineteenth century a mound at the site was indeed found to contain a skeleton and a bracelet engraved with two hearts.

Oddi

Not mentioned in *Njál's Saga*, though of a similar vintage, **ODDI**'s couple of houses and prominent, red-roofed **church**, all set on the only hill for miles around, are 5km southwest down the highway from Hella and then the same distance directly south along Route 266. Though you'd hardly credit it today, Oddi was once famous: the French-educated **Sæmundur Sigfússon** became priest here in 1078 and established an ecclesiastical school, whose later alumni included thirteenth-century lawspeaker, historian and diplomat Snorri Sturlusson (see p.161) and St Þorlákur Þórhallsson. Sæmundur himself is the subject of several legends, including one in which the devil – disguised as a seal – offered to carry him back to Iceland from France so that Sæmundur could apply for the post at Oddi. When they were within sight of the shore, the resourceful Sæmundur brained the devil with a psalter, swam to safety, and got the job. Less to his credit, he's also held responsible for causing Hekla's 1104 eruption by tossing a keepsake from a jilted lover – who turned out to be a witch – into the volcano. Built in 1924, the current church is pretty plain, though it has thirteenth-century relics squirrelled away, and a nice modern organ.

Hvolsvöllur

Eleven kilometres southwest down the highway from Hella you reach the broad, open mouth of the **Markarfljót valley**, along which the intricately tangled shallow river flows westwards out from the Mýrdalsjökull and Eyjafjallajökull ice caps. Right on the western edge is the Ringroad town of **HVOLSVÖLLUR**, a few short streets labouring under an unattractive transmitter tower, marking where Route 261 diverges east off down the valley to Fljótsdalur and the Fjallabak route (see p.123). It's a good place to get to grips with *Njál's Saga* country; you're close to the settings for some of the most important scenes in the tale, and Hvolsvöllur itself – or rather the farm, Völlur, 5km north – was the homestead of Mörð Fiddle, grandfather to the tale's archvillain, Mörð Valgardsson. On a practical note, the town is also the last place to stock up on **provisions** before heading eastwards to **hiking** grounds at Flótsdalur or Þórsmörk.

Hvolsvöllur's main attraction is the **Saga Centre** (☎ 895 9160, ⓦ www.njala.is; June–Aug daily 9am–6pm; 700kr), just off the highway down Route 261. The bulk of this is a museum exploring the saga period with models of Viking houses and ships, maps, dioramas and paintings showing the location of local sites and the extent of Viking travels across the northern hemisphere, and replica clothes and artefacts. There's also a Viking-style **Saga Hall** here, complete with wooden beams and horsehide rugs, which is the venue for occasional "saga feasts" – a couple of fun hours' worth of food and storytelling, with the staff dressed up in period costume.

▲ Saga Centre, Hvolsvöllur

Practicalities

Most of Hvolsvöllur is laid out along a hundred-metre strip of the highway, just where Route 261 kinks east. **Buses** along the Ringroad, and also to Þórsmörk and along the Fjallabak route, stop at the easterly Hlíðarendi **fuel station**, also home to the alcohol store. The town's other services – bank, post office and *Kjaraval* **supermarket** (Mon–Fri 9am–9pm, Sat & Sun 10am–9pm) – are all nearby. There are two **places to stay**, both down Route 261: the slightly faded *Hótel Hvolsvöllur* (☎487 8050, ⓦwww.hotelhvolsvollur.is; ❸) is about 50m along, while, 200m further on, *Asgarður* (☎487 5750, ⓦwww.asgardurinn.is; sleeping-bag accommodation 3500kr, ❷) has cabins, dormitories and outdoor hot tubs. Hvolsvöllur's **campground** (750kr pp) is back from the N1 fuel station. **Places to eat** include the *Eldstó* café next to the post office, and the *Björkinn* restaurant-bar next to the Shell fuel station, on the Ringroad at the western side of town.

Bergþórshvoll

South of Hvollsvöllur, follow Route 255 coastwards for 20km off the highway and across the flat, waterlogged countryside to **Bergþórshvoll**, where Njál's homestead sat a thousand years ago. Today, a modern house occupies the low crest 1km from the sea, and there's no visible trace of the original hall, which was besieged by Flósi and his hundred-strong Burners in the autumn of 1011. The two sides (Njál's party consisting of about thirty of his family and servants) met face to face in the open, but, urged by the old man, the defenders retreated into the house, and Flósi – certain that Njál's sons would kill him if they escaped – ordered the building to be set alight. After women, children and servants were allowed to leave, Njál, his wife and sons burned to death; only "lucky" Kári managed to break out. In support of the story, charred remains found here during twentieth-century excavations have been carbon-dated to the saga period.

The Markarfljót valley: Hlíðarendi and Fljótsdalur

It's a beautiful thirty-kilometre run east along Route 261 from Hvollsvöllur up **Fljótshlíð**, the flat-bottomed, heavily farmed northern border of the Markarfljót valley, with the saga site of **Hlíðarendi** and valley setting at **Fljótsdalur** to draw you out this way. It's also the approach road to the **Fjallabak route** around the back of the southern glaciers, and is covered by summer **buses** from Reykjavík. Ahead loom Eyjafjallajökull's black sided, ice-capped heights, while on a clear day the view south extends all the way to the sea; in summer, streams and ponds draining the wetlands in between are alive with birds, especially black-tailed godwits, with their vivid orange and black plumage. **Horseriding** can be arranged about 7km down Route 261 at Torfastaðir farm (☎588 7887, ⓔthorfastadir@emax.is) – check out their collection of exotic chickens too.

Hlíðarendi

The road follows the base of a long line of green hills heading up the valley, whose slopes contrast strongly with the starker-toned mountains opposite. About 17km from Hvollsvöllur, a side road climbs steeply up to where a red-roofed **church** and handful of farm buildings command a splendid view of the area. This was the site of **Hlíðarendi**, home to Njál's great friend Gunnar, the most exemplary of all saga characters; unfortunately his fine character always tended to inspire envy rather than admiration. When Gunnar found that his wife **Hallgerð** had encouraged a slave to steal food from the prosperous farmer Otkel, he fatefully slapped her – hence Hallgerð's refusal to help him later on (see box, pp.126–127) – and offered

Otkel repayment. Otkel's malicious friend Skamkel, however, advised him against accepting, starting the long sequence of blood-letting that led to Gunnar being declared an outlaw. But on the way to the coast to leave Iceland, Gunnar's horse stumbled and he looked back to Hlíðarendi across fields of newly cut hay, and knew he could never leave his homeland – and so, returning to Hlíðarendi, met his end.

Though Hlíðarendi's church is worth a look for it's chandelier and beautiful **blue-panelled ceiling** inset with golden stars, nothing besides the scenery remains from the saga period – though, as Gunnar felt, this can be ample reward (at least on a sunny day). Look on the plains below for the isolated rocky platform of **Stóra-Dímon** (called Rauðuskriður in the saga), where Njál's sons Skarphéðinn and Helgi ambushed Þráin Sigfússon, who had participated in the murder of their foster-father. Þráin spotted them but Skarp-héðinn slid over the frozen river and killed Þráin before he had time to put on his armour, setting in motion events which were to lead directly to the burning of Njál.

Fljótsdalur

East of Hlíðarendi, the hills grow steeper as the valley narrows, with a frill of small, ribbon-like waterfalls dropping down to the roadside. A track pointing south past Stóra-Dimón to the Ringroad marks the start of the gravel, and then you're running alongside the Markarfljót river-system's continually shifting maze of flat, intertwined streams up **Fljótsdalur**, a valley caught between the steep, glaciated slopes of Tindfjöll to the north and Eyjafjöll to the south. Ten kilometres from Hlíðarendi and 27km from Hvolsvöllur, where the road crosses a ford and becomes a four-wheel-drive track, the basic, self-catering **Fljótsdalur youth hostel** (☎487 8498, @fljotsdalur@hostel.is; sleeping-bag accommodation 2050kr) occupies a renovated turf-roofed house, open from April to October – you'll definitely need to book in advance. Fljótsdalur forms the southern boundary of **the Fjallabak region** (see box, p.123), and there are any number of **hikes** to attempt in the area – the most ambitious of which is the nine-hour return trip up Tindafjall to its ice cap, **Tindfjallajökull** (1462m), via a series of mountain huts.

Skógar and Þórsmörk

Southeast across the Markarfljót's sprawl, the highway finds itself pinched between the coast and Eyjafjöll, the mountainous platform for the **Eyjafjallajökull** icecap. Though dwarfed in area by its big sister Mýrdalsjökull immediately to the east, Eyjafjallajökull's 1666m apex is southwestern Iceland's highest point, and the mountain has stamped its personality on the area: an active volcano smoulders away below the ice, which enjoyed major eruptions in the seventeenth and nineteenth centuries and whose sub-glacial melting in 1967 sent a rock- and gravel-laden flash flood – a *jökulhlaup* – west down the Markarfljót.

Back on the coast, melt from Eyjafjallajökull's fringes has created a string of roadside **waterfalls** around the settlement of **Skógar**; while in the highlands north of Eyjafjallajökull, streams feeding into the Markarfljót flow through beautiful valleys at **Þórsmörk**, whose steep, wooded slopes and dark mountains are capped by encircling glaciers. Skógar is on the Ringroad and served by **buses** through the year, while from the coast you can reach Þórsmörk either on summer buses traversing the 249/F249 west of Skógar, or on a popular **hiking trail** which ascends from Skógar via a broad pass between Eyjafjallajökull and Mýrdalsjökull.

Seljalandfoss

Right at Eyjafjöll's western tip, the mostly gravel **Route 249** heads north off the highway and around the back of the mountain to Þórsmörk. Just a few hundred metres along is **Seljalandfoss**, a narrow but powerful waterfall that drops straight off the fellside into a shallow pool; paths run behind the curtain – you'll get soaked but the noise of the falls is impressively magnified – and over to a couple of smaller falls (one of which is almost enclosed by the cliff-face), the meadow in-between thick with a summer crop of cotton grass, kingcups and angelica. There's a **campsite** with modern facilities 500m up the road at Hamra-garðar farm (June–Aug; ☎487 8920; 850kr; showers and washing machines extra), while the last **place to stay** before Þórsmörk is 7km further on at the self-catering *Stóra Mörk III* (☎487 8903, ✉storamork@isl.is; sleeping bag 2050kr; ❷) – the **farm** here featured in *Njál's Saga* as the property of Ketil Sigfússon, a decent man who had the awkward task of being both Njál's son-in-law and brother to Þráin, killed by Njál's sons at nearby Stóra-Dímon (see p.131). Past *Stóra Mörk*, the road becomes the **four-wheel-drive-only** F249 – don't go any further in a normal vehicle.

Skógar, Skógarfoss and the Þórsmörk trail

A further 7km east past Seljavellir along the Ringroad, **SKÓGAR** is an insubstantial, scattered collection of buildings set back off the highway beside **Skógarfoss**, the biggest of the local **waterfalls** and worth a look even if you've otherwise had enough of these things. Other reasons to stop are the entertaining museum and a rewarding **hiking trail to Þórsmörk** up over interglacial passes.

Skógar was settled by the twelfth century, and you'll find a detailed record of the region's farming and fishing communities at the 𝄞 **Folk Museum** (June–Aug 9am–6.30pm; May & Sept 10am–5pm; 1000kr), up against the hills to the east. Guided tours and folk-singing sessions organized by the charismatic curator, **Þórður Tómasson**, are one of the museum's highlights, but even if he doesn't appear the exhibits themselves are interesting enough. Various types of traditional **turf farm buildings** have been relocated to an adjacent field, while inside the main building, the centrepiece is a ten-metre-long wooden **fishing boat** from 1855, tough enough to survive being dragged regularly over miles of sand and gravel to be launched. Pick of the remaining exhibits include a Viking **jade cloak pin**, an edition of Iceland's first printed **bible**, dating from 1584, and a fourteenth-century fragment from the Book of David written in Icelandic on vellum. Ask to be shown (it's easy to overlook otherwise) the **brass ring** found hundreds of years ago, said to have once adorned a chest of gold hidden behind Skógarfoss by the Viking settler **Þrasi** – legend has it he argued with his children and didn't want them to inherit his wealth.

Skógarfoss

Skógarfoss is justifiably famous, looking good from a distance and nothing short of huge, powerful and dramatic close-up, as the curtain of water drops 62m off the plateau. Stand on the flat gravel river bed in front of the rainbow-tinged plunge pool and the rest of the world vanishes into soaking white mists and noise; in full flood the outward blast of air caused by the falling water makes it impossible to get within fifty metres of the falls. A metal staircase climbs to the top, beyond which a muddy trail heads upstream to a much smaller but violent cataract and brilliant views coastwards and up across mossy moorland towards the distant glacier cap. If you're properly prepared, you can follow the river in this direction right up to Þórsmörk – see box on p.134.

The Skógar–Þórsmörk trail

The **Þórsmörk trail** (20km) from Skógar, over the **Fimmvörðuháls pass** between Eyjafallajökull and Mýrdalsjökull, then down the other side to Þórsmörk, is (at least in good weather) a thoroughly enjoyable hike, with spectacular scenery. Although it's feasible to do the whole thing in one day if you're reasonably fit and start early enough, most people spread the trip over two days, overnighting at one of the two mountain **huts** en route run by Útivist, open July and August (bookings essential; ☎562 1000, ⓦwww.utivist.is). The trail is **passable** without equipment usually from around mid-June to September, though a couple of places require a head for heights – outside these times you'll probably need an ice axe to cut steps during the descent to Þórsmörk, and possibly crampons. Whatever the time of year, come prepared for possible rain and snow, poor visibility and cold; the **track** is easy to follow in clear weather, but play safe and carry a compass and Landmælingar Íslands' *Þórsmörk-Landmannalaugar* **map**. If you don't want to walk alone, both Útivist and Ferðafélag Íslands (see p.45) organize **hikes** along the route most weekends from mid-June to late August – June 21 is especially popular, when you'll find hundreds of people making the trek through the midsummer "night".

The trail starts by taking the staircase up Skógarfoss, then simply follows the river uphill over a muddy, shaly **heath** carpeted by thick patches of moss and plants – wild thyme, with its tiny purple flowers and pungent scent, is abundant. There are many, many small **waterfalls** along the way, each of them unique: some twist through contorted gorges, others drop in a single narrow sheet, bore tunnels through obstructive rocks, or rush smoothly over broad, rocky beds. Around 8km along you cross a **bridge** and leave most of the vegetation behind for a dark, rocky plain flanked by the smooth contours of Eyjafallajökull to the west and easterly Mýrdalsjökull. It's another hour from here, following marker poles across gravel and snow fields, to the red-roofed *Balduinsskáli*, the small and rather squalid **first hut** (pit toilet; 1800kr), though almost everybody pushes on for another forty minutes to the far better appointed **second hut**, *Fimmvörðuskáli* (3300kr), near the route's highest point on the **Fimmvörðuháls pass** (1043m).

From here, the trail crosses another snowfield and descends, rather steeply and with a chain to help you along, to **Heljarkambur**, a fifty-metre-long, knife-edge ridge with vertigo-inducing drops off either side. At the far end is the flat, muddy gravel plateau of **Morinsheiði**: head a kilometre north and you'll arrive at its precipitous edges at **Heiðarhorn** and awe-inspiring vistas of Þórsmörk below (see p.134), with Mýrdalsjökull's icy outrunners hemming in the view to the east. The descent here is actually very straightforward, and from then on the path is well marked (if occasionally narrow) for the final 5km to Goðaland and the Básar hut (see p.136) – allow six hours in total from Fimmvörðuskáli.

Skógar practicalities

The kilometre-long Skógar road runs north off the highway, passing a side-road left to the falls and various services, before coming to a T-junction: the grey, box-like building ahead of you is Skógar's **school**, home to the summertime *Hótel Edda* (☎444 4830, ⓦwww.hoteledda.is; sleeping bag 2550kr including breakfast, ❶); turn right and it's 250m to the museum.

Skógar's **information centre** (June–Sept daily 9am–5pm; ☎894 2956, ⓦwww.itm.is) is on the falls road; there's also a **café** here (daily 11.30am–7pm) and a small **store** selling camping essentials – the nearest proper supermarket is 30km east at Vík. Nearby you'll also find a **bank** (no ATM) and two **places to stay**: the self-catering IYHA **hostel** (☎487 8801, ⓦwww.hostel.is; sleeping bag 2050kr) and small, Nordic-chic *Hótel Skógar* (☎487 8988, ⓦwww.hotelskogar.is; ❹), whose amenities run to hot-tubs and a good **restaurant**. The ⚐ **campground**

(June–Aug; ☎ 487 8950; 850kr pp) with toilets and showers is in the big, flat, grassy area in front of the falls – **buses** also pull up here.

Þórsmörk Reserve

Hidden from the rest of the world by encircling glaciers and mountain wilderness, **Þórsmörk Reserve** (generally known simply as "Þórsmörk") covers a highland valley north of Eyjafallajökull, watered by a host of multistreamed glacial rivers that flow west off Mýrdalsjökull's heights and down into the Markarfljót. Greensloped, covered in dwarf willow, birch and wildflowers, with icy peaks rising above, this is one of Iceland's most beautiful spots and, through the summer months, it's a magnet for everyone from hard-core hikers coming to tackle the numerous trails to equally energetic partygoers here to unwind in a bucolic setting.

Orientation and practicalities

Þórsmörk Reserve is laid out west–east along the seven-kilometre-long **Krossá river valley**, the river splitting the reserve into two distinct sections: the area to the north is **Þórsmörk** proper, while south is **Goðaland**. Aside from hiking in from Skógar or Landmannalaugar (see p.132 & p.123), the only way to reach the reserve is via the thirty-kilometre-long Route 249/F249 off the Ringroad at Seljalandsfoss (see p.132). The last half of this is a high-clearance, four-wheel-drive-only route, and can be quite an adventure in itself, crossing a handful of broad glacial

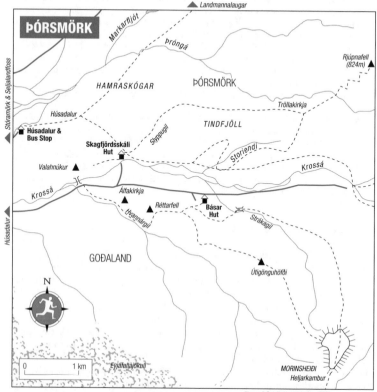

rivers – often impassable in bad conditions – and passing the rapidly shrinking **Steinsholtsjökull**, before reaching the reserve's western end at **Húsadalur**. Daily **buses** to Húsadalur (June to mid-Sept; Ⓦwww.bsi.is) run from Reykjavík's BSÍ terminal via Selfoss, Hella and Hvolsvöllur; some continue further into the park to Básar (see p.136). Iceland's hiking associations (see Basics, p.45) also organize **guided hikes** here every weekend in summer, with less frequent excursions year-round – including over New Year.

Accommodation is at designated campsites (around 850kr), or using your own sleeping bag in hiking huts (2200–3300kr), which need to be booked in advance – as always, make sure you have the receipts to show to wardens. Huts have communal kitchens, with hot showers 300kr extra. The closest places to buy **supplies** are Hvolsvöllur and Vík, so bring all you need with you. Ideally you'll enjoy sunny weather, but come armed for wet, cold conditions. Considering Þórsmörk's popularity, it's incredible that there is no detailed **hiking map** available (though there are rumours of a 1:50,000 sheet in the pipeline): Landmælingar Íslands' 1:100,000 *Þórsmörk-Landmannalaugar* is accurate but the detail is too small, and it needs to be combined with hiking association maps (available from the huts and Húsadalur bus stop). The latter are too inaccurate to use alone, but do show the hiking trails – which are only irregularly pegged on the ground.

North of the Krossá: Þórsmörk

Húsadalur, at Þórsmörk's western end, comprises a **bus stop** and **café** (Ⓣ852 5506) and self-catering wooden bunkhouse **accommodation** at the **Youth Hostel** (Ⓣ894 1506, Ⓔthorsmork@thorsmork.is), which also has a campsite. The scenery here is bland, however, and it's better to follow walking tracks east for twenty minutes to Ferðafélag Ísland's 🏔 **Skagfjörðsskáli hut** and campsite (bookings on Ⓣ568 2533, Ⓦwww.fi.is) – they also have a tiny **store** selling chocolate, biscuits, soap and soft drinks. This is beautifully located at river level beneath knuckle-like **Valahnúkur**: you can sit on the porch and watch vehicles coming to grief on the river crossings (the hut has a photo album of four-wheel-drive disasters), or make a stiff, twenty-minute ascent of Valahnúkur to orient yourself with the view east down the valley of the flat riverbeds with their inter-laced streams between black hills buffed in green, all rising to where the valley is terminated by Mýrdalsjökull's blue-white mass.

The main walk north of the Krossá starts at the next bay east from the Skagfjörðsskáli hut at **Slyppugil**, a gradually widening, wooded gully cutting northeast from the river uphill to the jagged east–west ridge of **Tindfjöll**. The trail then weaves along **Tindfjöll**'s black-gravel, landslip-prone north face to the solitary spire of **Tröllakirkja**, before emerging onto open heath at **Tindfjöll**'s eastern end: the double-tipped cone 2km northeast is **Rjúpnafell**, which can be climbed up a steep, zigzag path to its 824-metre summit – give yourself at least five hours for the return hike from the hut. Alternatively, cross the heath to descend back into the valley down **Tindfjöll**'s southern slopes via **Stóriendi**; the path is intermittently pegged and often seems to be leading off the edge, but always reappears, with some fantastic views of Þórsmörk's eastern end along the way. You end up down at river level approximately 2km from your starting point; this circuit takes around four hours.

South of the Krossá: Goðaland

With Eyjafjallajökull looming above, the landscape south of the Krossá at **Goðaland** is more extreme than that north of the river, and the hiking is harder. To get there, either stay on the bus from Húsadalur, or cross the river using the pedestrian bridge below Valahnúkur's southern face, which leaves you suddenly pathless among shingle and small streams. Head towards the hollowed-out mini-peak of **Álfakirkja**, directly opposite the Skagfjörðsskáli hut, where you can pick up the two-kilometre-long vehicle track east to Útivist's well-equipped, spacious **Básar hut** and campground (bookings on ☎ 562 1000, ⓦ www.utivist.is), which marks the end of the trail from Skógar (see p.132).

The most obvious local excursion from Básar is straight up **Réttarfell**'s ascent via a low saddle is easy to follow and tiring rather than demanding. You can also descend from the saddle down Réttarfell's back into **Hvannárgil**, a steep-sided, narrow canyon, which you can follow westwards for 2km to emerge fairly close to the pedestrian bridge. The next peak east of Réttarfell, and connected by a walkable, five-kilometre-long ridge, is **Útigönguhöfði** – at 805m the highest point in the reserve not permanently ice-bound. Views from the top are stupendous but be warned, the final section is incredibly steep, with chains to help you. Give yourself at least three hours from Básar for the round trip.

The **best hike** in the reserve – which should only be attempted by experienced hikers in good weather – follows the Skógar trail up on to the Morinsheiði plateau (see p.133), from where you need to edge around the plateau's western side until you find marker posts descending towards Útigönguhöfði. Follow them up Útigönguhöfði's steep, scree-ridden eastern face onto the summit – an exhausting twenty-minute scramble – then take the trail west towards Réttarfell and so back to Básar. Allow six hours for the round trip.

From Mýrdalsjökull to Vík

The country's fourth-largest ice cap, **Mýrdalsjökull** protects southwestern Iceland from the scouring effects of the glacial deserts – **sandurs** – further east, though it's also responsible for creating the extensive strips of black, basaltic sand fringing the 30km of coastline between Skógar and **Vík**. Like neighbouring Eyjafjallajökull, Mýrdalsjökull harbours a powerful volcano, 1300-metre **Katla**, which last erupted in 1918 and is worryingly overdue for another blast – they occur once every seventy years on average, and a recent spate of **earthquakes** in the region might be heralding future activity. Katla's *jökulhlaups* (volcanically induced flash floods; see p.306 for more about these) have extended the coastline and devastated the area's farms a dozen or more times since Settlement.

Moving down the coast, mountain ridges supporting Mýrdalsjökull – and occasional outlying glaciers, such as **Sólheimajökull** – intrude further and further towards the sea, finally reaching it around Iceland's southernmost tip, **Dyrhólaey**, where they form impressively sculpted cliffs, home to innumerable sea birds. Past Dyrhólaey, the sleepy village of Vík has more birds and some easy walks, and also marks the beginning of the long cross-desert run into southeastern Iceland. Ringroad **buses** can get you to Vík, though you'll need your own transport elsewhere.

Mýrdalsjökull

Not far east of Skógar, the Ringroad crosses the shallow Jökulsá Fulilækur, a glacial river with origins beneath the ice surrounding Katla. Look upstream from the roadside and you'll see the apparently insignificant, narrow ice tongue of **Sólheimajökull**, one of Mýrdalsjökull's outrunners; a good gravel track heads 4km up the broad river valley to a parking area, a fifteen-minute walk from the glacier front. Close up, Sólheimajökull is steep-faced, blackened with melted-out grit, heavily streaked in crevasses and well worth a look, especially if you haven't seen this sort of thing before. 🎿 **Mountain Guides** (Ⓦwww.mountainguides.is) run 1–3hr ice-walking and climbing excursions here through the summer for 3200–6200kr; you don't need prior experience and they supply crampons and ice axes. Otherwise, don't walk out onto the glacier, as the front is unstable.

To get right on top of Mýrdalsjökull, head 5km further east down the Ringroad and then 10km north along the four-wheel-drive F222 to **Sólheimskáli**, a mountain hut and base for snowmobile tours with Arcanum (☎487 1500, Ⓦwww.snow.is; 20,000kr) – call ahead if you need a pickup, at further cost. For **dog sledding** trips onto Mýrdalsjökull from January until August, contact Dogsledding (☎487 7747, Ⓦwww.dogsledding.is; from 14,900kr), whose tours last from an hour to a full day.

Dyrhólaey

Around 12km down the Ringroad from the Sólheimajökull turn-off, an unsurfaced, bumpy Route 218 slides 5km coastwards past a handful of farms and then over a causeway to where the country reaches its southernmost extremes at **Dyrhólaey** (closed May to June 25 for the nesting season). A set of rugged cliffs rising over a long expanse of black sand, Dyrhólaey is a beautiful place just to watch the sea on a sunny day, though it's also a noted **sea-bird reserve**, with every cliffside crevice occupied from April until the winter sets in, white streaks of guano a sign of tenancy. Stumpy, ubiquitous fulmars – gull-like but related to albatrosses – chatter nervously at you from their half-burrow roosts, or soar in on narrow wings for a closer look; out at sea, rafts of eider duck bob in the waves, while razorbills, guillemots and puffins, bills full of fish, dodge scavenging brown skuas on their way homewards.

Once over the causeway, bear left at the junction and you'll find yourself on a rocky shelf above the sea with the swell hammering into the low cliffs at your feet; there's a surprisingly sheltered bay around to one side, though, where a dense matting of tussocky grass holding the clifftop together is riddled with **puffin burrows** – sit still for long enough and you can get some good photos.

If you bear right at the junction, the road rises steeply to end at a dumpy, orange-topped **lighthouse** on the grassy hill above. From here you can see Iceland's southernmost headland, a narrow face of rock pierced by a large **arch**, said to be tall enough for a sailboat to pass beneath. You can walk out to a cairn here, for views west of black sand beaches stretching up towards Skógar; to the east, the weather-sculpted rocks off Vík stand out clearly, though the town itself is hidden behind round-backed **Reynisfjall**, a ridge that divides the southwest's fertile farmland from the bleak expanses of sand beyond. It also blocks the weather: it's not unknown for it to be snowing one side, and bright and sunny on the other.

Vík and around

Despite averaging the highest rainfall in Iceland, **VÍK** – known more fully as Vík-í-Mýrdal – is a pleasant place of three hundred souls nestling on the toe of Reynisfjall's steep eastern slopes, a last haven before taking on the deadening horizons of **Mýrdalssandur**, the desert laid down by Katla's overflows. Iceland's only coastal village without a harbour, Vík got going as a trading station in the late nineteenth century and today serves a few farms and the tourist traffic, with the *Víkurprjón* **wool factory** and outlet that's making a name for itself with some innovative designs – it's the building next to the N1 fuel station on the Ringroad.

Vík's older quarter is south of the highway along the hundred-metre-long main street of Víkurbraut – though the only sight as such is **Brydebúð** (daily 10am–1.30pm & 2.30–5pm, 750kr), the original nineteenth-century store. This was actually built in 1831 on the Westman Islands (see opposite) and relocated here in 1895; among other things, it houses a small **museum** of photographs (summer daily 11am–9pm; free). A short road and walking track continues along Reynisfjall's lower slopes to a black beach opposite three tall, offshore spires known as **Reynisdrangar**, the Troll Rocks, said to be petrified trolls caught by the sun as they were trying to drag a boat ashore. The headland above is a huge, stratified bird colony: lower down are kittiwakes, with puffins nesting on the steep middle slopes, and fulmar occupying the rocky cliffs near the top; the sky is full of evening activity as birds return from a day's fishing. If the weather is fine, the trail **up Reynisfjall** from the highway also makes for a good hour's climb, ending by the weather station on a muddy hilltop, with views east of Vatnajökull's mighty ice cap floating above the desert haze.

Vík practicalities

Vík is laid out either side of a two-hundred-metre stretch of the Ringroad, with Víkurbraut heading south as you come down the hill from Skógar, and another road more or less opposite leading up to the **church**. **Buses** heading either way along the Ringroad pull in on the eastern edge of town at the N1 **fuel station-roadhouse** (daily 9am–8.30pm); **tourist information** (☎487 1395; June 15 to Sept 1 daily 11am–9pm) is available from the old store Brydebúð on Víkurbraut. There's a well-stocked **supermarket** on Víkurbraut (Mon–Fri 9am–6pm, Sat 11am–1pm), with the village's **bank** (with ATM) and **post office** nearby.

The **campsite** (☎487 1345; 750kr pp, cottages ❶), with showers, a large shelter shed and cooking facilities, is on the eastern side of town opposite the N1 fuel station. Top of Vík's **accommodation** options are the ⚲ IYHA hostel, open April to November (☎487 1106, Ⓦwww.hostel.is; sleeping bag 2600kr), which has wonderful views from its rise near the church, and the characterful ⚲ Hótel Lundi at Vikurbraut 26 (☎487 1212, Ⓦwww.hotelpuffin.is; sleeping bag 2500kr, ❷) – the inn-like main house has the better rooms, while cheaper board is available in an older, tin-sided building with self-catering facilities. The modern, Edda-run Hótel Vík (☎487 1480, Ⓦwww.hoteledda.is; ❸), near the campsite, is a good, pricey back-up if the others are full.

Brydebúð houses a **café-restaurant** called Halldórskaffi (Mon–Sat roughly 11am–8pm), serving good trout, coffee and cakes; for evening grills, burgers and sea views try the Strondin bistro-bar, attached to the N1 roadhouse. For entertainment, there's a sports centre with a **pool** in the street behind the supermarket (Mon–Fri 7.10am–9.30pm, Sat & Sun 10am–5pm; 350kr).

Vík is served by Reykjavík–Höfn **buses**, which run along the Ringroad daily in summer and several times a week for the rest of the year (see Ⓦwww.bsi.is). Heading east from Vík under your own steam, note that it's over 70km to the next town, Kirkjubæjarklaustur (see p.307).

Garður and Þakgil

To see more of the countryside around Vík, drive 5km west along the Ringroad then turn down the far side of Reynisfjall along Route 215 to the coast at the tiny hamlet of **Garður**. This brings you to a polished pebble shingle where the puffins bob offshore; tall cliffs, ridged and twisted with hexagonal basalt columns, drop sheer into the sea at the back of the Troll Rocks, and there are brilliant views westwards to Dyrhólaey's arch (see p.137). It's a beautiful spot on a sunny day, perfect for a picnic.

For a very different take on the area, head east for 5km along the Ringroad, then turn north at **Höfðabrekka** farmstead to follow the rough, twisting Route 214 (check at accommodation that it's open first). This is a slow but beautiful drive, in an occasionally scary sort of way: the road is very eroded but you ascend onto a plateau with superlative views coastwards and inland to the edges of Mýrdalsjökull. About 15km along, the track splits, with one branch heading downhill to a bridge – as far as a conventional vehicle could possibly go – the other continuing a couple of kilometres to Þakgil, a remote valley with an exceptional **campsite** (T 853 4889, W www.thakgil.is; 850kr pp), whose communal dining area is inside a huge cave. Contact them in advance for exact directions and to check on access conditions.

The Westman Islands

The **Westman Islands – Vestmannaeyjar** – are an archipelago of fifteen or so scattered, mostly minuscule volcanic islands around 10km off the coast south of Hvolsvöllur. The only inhabited one in the group, **Heimaey**, is an easy trip from the mainland, and there are two immediate draws: **Eldfell** volcano, still steaming from its 1973 eruption, an event that doubled the width of the island and almost swallowed Heimaey town; and the legendary bird life, especially the large **puffin** population (see box, p.140). Heimaey is small enough to explore thoroughly in a short time, yet it still forms a self-contained community that sees itself as quite distinct from the mainland, where people talk about "going over to Iceland", as if it were another country. Heimaey aside, the other Westmans are difficult to land on and so only infrequently visited by bird or egg collectors, but you may be very lucky and score a rare trip around **Surtsey**, the group's southernmost outpost and newest island, which sprang from beneath the waves during the 1960s.

Geological babies at only 12,000 years old overall, the Westman Islands were inhabited some time before the mainland was officially colonized in the ninth century by Ingólfur Arnarson and his foster-brother Hjörleifur Hróðmarsson. The brothers had brought British slaves with them who, coming from the lands at the west of the Viking world, were known as **Westmen**; Hjörleifur's slaves rebelled, killing him and fleeing to these islands – hence the name – where they were tracked down and slaughtered by a vengeful Ingólfur. Over the succeeding centuries Heimaey became permanently settled, but was generally outside the mainstream of Icelandic history until **Algerian pirates** raided on July 16, 1627, killing or enslaving half the population of five hundred. It took some time to get over this disaster, but by the twentieth century mechanization and the country's economic shift from farming to fishing saw Heimaey becoming a prosperous little haven, well positioned for taking advantage of what are still the North Atlantic's richest cod and haddock grounds.

Fresh problems lay ahead, however. The submarine eruption that formed Surtsey turned out to be the prelude to events a decade later on January 23, 1973, when a two-kilometre-long volcanic fissure suddenly opened up eastern Heimaey beside the long-extinct cone of **Helgafell**. Within 24 hours the entire island had been evacuated and the new volcano Eldfell was gushing lava in

Icelandic puffins

Puffins – *lundi* in Icelandic – belong to the auk family, which includes razorbills and guillemots (murres), and are basically the northern hemisphere's equivalent of penguins. Puffins are, without doubt, the most charismatic of the auks, plump little birds with an upright build and pied plumage, all set off by bright orange feet and a ridiculous, sail-shaped bill striped yellow and red. This comical livery is compounded by an aeronautic ineptitude: their method of landing seems to consist simply of putting out their feet and stopping flying – bad enough to watch on water, but painful to see them bounce and skid on land. Puffins also seem to get victimized by just about every other sea-bird species: when feeding young, they fly back from fishing with their catch carried crosswise in the beak like a moustache, a clear signal for gulls, skuas and even razorbills to chase them, hoping they'll drop their chick's meal.

Each April, around four million puffins arrive to **breed** in Iceland from unknown wintering grounds, a sizeable chunk of which home in on Heimaey, excavating nesting burrows in huge, dense colonies on the island's grassy cliffs – surrounding seas are rich in herring fry, on which puffins raise their young. Watching a colony involves a bit of sensory overload at first, and it takes a while before you can sort through the confusion and concentrate on details: pairs excavating and cleaning up burrows with foot and bill, preening each other, or just sunning themselves on the grass, and the adults' desperate flights back from their fishing grounds. The fledgeling puffins, or **pufflings** – who lack the adults' colourful bill – stay in the burrow until, one night in August, all the adult birds depart Heimaey at the same time, and hunger draws the pufflings out for their first flight. Many then become confused by the town's bright lights and fly, dazzled, into buildings; local cats get fat on this easy prey, but residents round up birds and release them.

Westman Islanders traditionally also **eat** puffins, collecting eggs and netting up to a quarter of a million birds annually as food. However, in recent years Iceland's **puffin population** has declined by around 25 percent – most likely to dwindling food resources – and there's currently a moratorium on hunting them.

violent spasms; houses were buried beneath the flow, set afire by lava bombs, or simply collapsed under the weight of accompanying ash. Worse still, the lava threatened to block the harbour mouth until halted by the novel method of pumping sea water onto the front of the flow. When the eruption ceased in June, Heimaey was two square kilometres bigger, had a new mountain, and, amazingly, a better harbour – the entrance is narrower now, but more effectively shielded from prevailing easterly winds. Only one person was killed during the eruption, but 1700 islanders never returned, leaving a population of around five thousand today.

Getting to the Westman Islands

The most reliable way to reach Heimaey is aboard the *Herjólfur* car and passenger **ferry** (bookings & timetables on Ⓣ481 2800, Ⓦwww.eimskip.com; 2420kr return), which departs twice daily from **Þorlákshöfn**, a small port 20km south of Hveragerði. **Þorlákshöfn buses** from Reykjavík's main bus terminal (1400kr), Hveragerði and Selfoss are timed to connect with the ferries. Þorlákshöfn's **ferry terminal** is left off the main road as you enter town, where you can buy tickets if you haven't done so already – you should arrive at least thirty minutes before departure. An onboard cinema and café make the *Herjólfur* as comfortable as possible, though the crossing (2hr 45min) can be rough.

You can **fly** daily to Heimaey, though weather frequently cancels or delays services. Flugfélag Vestmannaeyjar (Ⓣ481 3255, Ⓦwww.eyjaflug.is) flights leave from Bakki, a tiny airstrip south of Hvolsvöllur; the journey takes just six minutes and costs around 8000kr return. You can also fly from Reykjavík with Landsflug (☎481 3300, ⓦwww.airiceland.is; 9500kr each way), a journey of around thirty minutes.

If possible, pick a sunny couple of days between May and September for your visit, allowing time for walks, intimate contact with puffins and thirty other breeding bird species, plus the chance to see whales and seals. If you want to party, join in the August Bank Holiday Weekend **Þjóðhátíð**, a festival to commemorate Iceland's first steps towards full independence in 1874, which involves bands, fireworks, a huge bonfire and three days of hard drinking with thousands of other revellers. All transport to and from the island for a week either side of the festival gets booked long in advance.

As to the Westmans' **weather**, temperatures are among the mildest in Iceland, but things can get extremely blustery – the country's highest windspeed, 220km an hour, was recorded here.

Heimaey

By far the largest of the Westman Islands, **Heimaey** – Home Island – is only around 6km in length and, except along the east and north coasts, is pretty flat and grassy. At its broad top end you'll find **Heimaey town** and the harbour faced by a narrow peninsula of sheer-sided cliffs; east of here, buildings are hemmed in by Eldfell, the fractionally higher slopes of Helgafell, and the rough, grey-brown solidified lavafield, **Kirkjubæjarhraun**, under which a third of the original town vanished in 1973. Moving south down Heimaey, you pass the cross-shaped

▲ Outskirts of Heimaey Town below the extinct Helgafell

airstrip, beyond which the island tapers to a narrow isthmus, over which the rounded hummock of **Stórhöfði** rises as an end point – one of the best places on the island to watch birds.

Heimaey town

HEIMAEY TOWN is an attractive place, quiet and low-key, with signposts around the place designed to resemble puffins. The **Aquarium and Natural History Museum**, south of the ferry terminal on Heiðarvegur (May 15 to Sept 15 daily 11am–5pm; Sept–May Sat & Sun 3–5pm; 400kr), sports cases of rocks and stuffed animals, as well as more entertaining tanks of live marine fauna. Up the road on the corner with Vestmannabraut, Heimaey's **cinema** hosts the summertime **Volcanic Film Show** in English (daily mid-June to mid-Sept; 600kr), an hour-long account of the eruption and snippets about life in the islands – when they run, the evening show is best as there's a question-and-answer session afterwards. A few minutes away down Hásteinsvegur, there's also a **Folk Museum** at the library (mid-May to mid-Sept daily 11am–5pm; mid-Sept to mid-May Sat & Sun 3–5pm; 400kr), whose extensive collection dates from the Algerian invasion onwards, padded out with cases of stamps and coins.

Down at the **harbour**, you'll find a tightly packed fleet of fishing boats and several warehouses processing their catches, yards piled with kilometres of

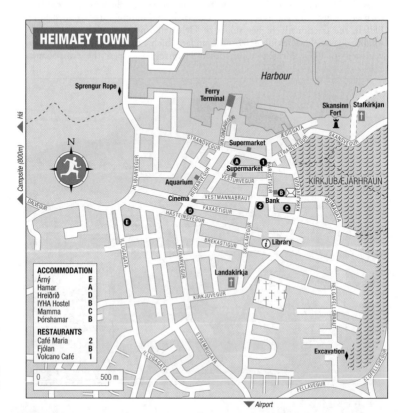

black and green fishing nets being examined and repaired. Around 500m east along Strandvegur, the road crosses the edge of the 1973 flow and passes the neat lava-block walls of **Skansinn fort** built by the English in the thirteenth century and revived after the pirate raid to house Iceland's first and only army. This wasn't the sole occasion that pirates took advantage of the Westmans' isolation: a sixteenth-century rover named Gentleman John once stole Heimaey's church bell. Just across from Skansinn, the extraordinary **Stafkirkjan** is a Viking-era-style wooden church with a steep, black shingle roof, consecrated in 2000 to celebrate a thousand years of Christianity in Iceland. The building faces the presumed site of the country's first purpose-built church, raised by Gizur the White a few years before he championed the new faith at the Alþing in 1000 AD.

Back near the harbour off Strandvegur, you can follow first Kirkjuvegur and then Heimagata and Helgafellsbraut below the two-storey-high, steeply sloping **Kirkjubæjarhraun lava flow** that swallowed up the eastern end of town. Off the south end of Helgafellsbraut, there's an ongoing **archeological excavation** which is expected to uncover some of the houses buried under ash during the eruption; progress is slow, as it's a painful and emotive issue for many locals.

For a final idea of just what Heimaey's population went through in 1973, head south to black-roofed **Landakirkja** on Kirkjuvegur, the island's main church. Enter the cemetery opposite through its arched, wrought-iron gates and on the left you'll find the grave of Theódóra Jónsdóttir, whose two-metre-high memorial is topped by a statuette of an angel, missing a hand. Ash buried this to the angel's thighs; it took Heimaey's residents over a year after the eruption to dig their town out of the black drifts. Markers around town also record the depth of ash along particular streets.

Practicalities

Inevitably clustered around its harbour, Heimaey's small centre is split by the south-running main street **Heiðarvegur**, with most services and attractions in the streets east of here between the harbour and Hásteinsvegur.

The **airport** is a couple of kilometres south of town; a bus or taxi meets all flights. At the harbour you'll find the **ferry terminal**, with daily departures back to Þorlákshöfn, where you can connect with buses to Reykjavík, Hveragerði and Selfoss. The **tourist information office** (Mon–Fri 10am–6pm, Sat 10am–5pm; ☏481 3555, ⓦwww.vestmannaeyjar.is) is at the library, while the **bank** (with ATMs) is on Bárústigur. For **payphones** try either the post office on Vestmannabraut, the town's fuel stations, or the cinema – which also has Heimaey's only public **toilet**. There are two **supermarkets**: Vöruval, which looks like a domed tent, on Vesturvegur (daily 8am–7pm); and the slightly better-stocked Krónan two streets over on Strandvegur (daily 10am–7pm), with the state **alcohol shop** next door (Fri 11am–7pm & Sat 11am–2pm).

Accommodation and food

Heimaey's **accommodation** will either be completely empty or booked solid, depending on local events such as festivals, school soccer matches and the like; always **book ahead**. The **campground** (☏846 6497; 850kr) is dramatically located 1km west of town beside the golf course at Herjólfsdalur (see p.145), where you'll be lulled to sleep by the mutterings of thousands of fulmars roosting above you; it has showers, toilets, laundry and a shelter shed for cooking. If you're here for the August festivities, come a few days early to find a pitch.

The town's only real **hotel** is the plush *Hótel Þórshamar* at Vestmannabraut 28 (☏481 2900, ⓦwww.hotelvestmannaeyjar.is; ❸); use the same contact details for the mid-range *Hamar* on Herjólfsgata (❷), the self-catering *Mamma*, Vestmanna-braut 25 (❶) and the IYHA **hostel**, behind the *Þórshamar* (sleeping bag 2500kr, ❶).

Pick of the island's **guesthouses** are the extremely friendly 🍴 *Hreiðrið*, at the corner of Faxastígur and Heiðarvegur (☎481 1045, ⓦhttp://tourist.eyjar.is; sleeping bag 2500kr, ❶), which can also organize everything you'd want to do on Heimaey; and the long-established *Árný*, a few minutes' walk east of the centre at Illugata 7 (☎&Ⓕ481 2082; sleeping bag 2500kr, ❶).

Places to eat include *Fjölan*, at the Hótel Þórshamar, recommended for its lamb and fish dishes (though the décor is stuck somewhere in the 1970s) and 🍴 *Café Maria*, a cosy upmarket café-restaurant on Vestmannabraut and Skólavegur serving big portions – try the excellent grilled monkfish (3690kr) or savoury crepes (1350kr). There's also the *Volcano Café* at Barústígur and Strandvegur, which does tasty coffee, waffles (550kr) and burgers (1680kr).

Around the island

Heimaey's compact spread of lava and volcanoes – including a still-steaming Eldfell – some stiff cliff-hikes around the north peninsula or easier trails down south, and abundant bird life, need a day or two to do them justice, but try and allow extra time to return to favourite spots. It's possible to **walk** everywhere along tracks and roads, and in summer Viking Tours (☎488 4884, ⓦwww.vikingtours.is) organizes daily **bus and boat tours** around the island. You can also get about by renting **scooters** from Eyjavespur (☎481 1230) or **horses** from Lyngfell (☎481 1509).

Heimaklettur, Eldfell and Helgafell

Steps from Heimagata take you up on top of the 1973 **lava flow**, though it's hard to imagine this huge mass of sharp-sided, weirdly shaped rubble moving at all, let alone flowing. Signs map out the original street plan 16m underfoot, while engraved headstones and collections of little stones painted with windows and doors mark where somebody's home lies buried. There's also a little **garden** hidden away up here, packed full of summertime flowers.

Heading northeast, you cross the road and end up at a lookout opposite yellow **Heimaklettur cliffs**, a good first spot to spy on sea birds: and it's pure chaos, the rocks packed to critical mass with various types of **guillemots**. If you're wondering how they manage to nest successfully on such incredibly narrow ledges, the secret is in the almost conical shape of their eggs, designed to roll in a circle around their tips, rather than in a straight line over the edge.

Both Eldfell and Helgafell are close to town and not too steep, and you won't need too much time or energy to climb them. **Eldfell** is easiest: the north side of the dark red scoria cone was washed away by the outflowing lava, and a path leads up the remains from the road to the west – allow twenty minutes. One of the first things islanders did on returning in 1973 was to start turfing Eldfell's slopes to stabilize the ash; aerial seed drops during the 1990s also helped, and today about half the cone is well grassed. Views from Eldfell's 205-metre-high eastern rim take in the lava flow to the north, the other Westman islands and the mainland's south-western coast and crisp ice caps. The soil is still steaming up here – in fact, a metre down it's over 500°C.

Immediately southwest of Eldfell, **Helgafell** looks similar but is a bit taller (226m) and some five thousand years older. The north and southwest faces present the swiftest routes to the summit, which was used as a lookout post during Heimaey's pirate period; today the crater is almost filled in, a shallow, sterile depression.

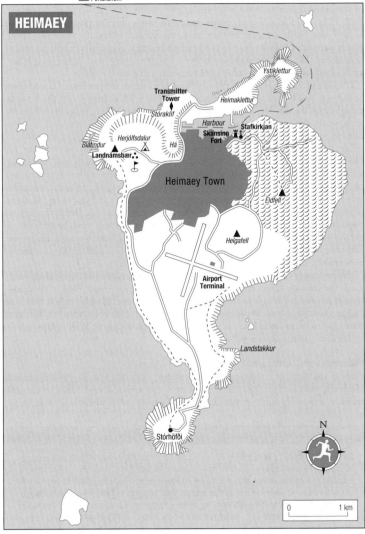

HEIMAEY

Þorlákshöfn

Ystiklettur

Transmitter
Tower

Stóraklif

Heimaklettur

Harbour

Herjólfsdalur

Blátindur

Skansinn
Fort

Stafkirkjan

Landnámsbær

Há

Heimaey Town

Eldfell

Helgafell

Airport
Terminal

Landstakkur

Stórhöfði

N

0   1 km

The north peninsula

Heimaey's **north peninsula** is the wildest part of the whole island, a four-kilometre string of sheer-sided cliffs and hills that includes the island's apex. Be aware that some of the tracks described here are potentially very dangerous, and to tackle them you need to be confident on narrow trails with hundred-metre drops either side.

Start a kilometre west of town by the campsite and golf course at **Herjólfsdalur**, a dramatically scaled bowl formed from a long-dead, partially collapsed volcano. Setting for the August festival and the island's **golf course**, it is also home to the remains of **Landnámsbær**, Iceland's oldest known settlement. While only traces of the original survive at the edge of the golf course, you can see from the nearby timber, lava-block and turf **reconstruction** what this Norse-style longhouse looked like, with separate kitchen area, pigsty and outhouses. Carbon-dating places parts of Landnámsbær in the seventh century, though Icelandic historical records say that the farm was founded two hundred years later. Either way, it was abandoned around 1100, perhaps due to overgrazing on the island.

The hike up the grassy crater slope behind looks much steeper than it is, and once at the top you'll find yourself on a narrow rim, with a drop down the far side straight into the sea. The peak to the west is **Blátindur** (273m), scaled by a slippery path, while east is a very tricky goat-track along the rim to **Há** – tackling either is not recommended.

For an easier ascent of Há, return to the western side of the harbour on Hliðarvegur, where there's a rope dangling down the rocks for practising **sprengur**, the traditional method used on Heimaey by men collecting puffins and birds' eggs; free beginners' sessions are held here in July (ask at the tourist office when to turn up). Walk up the steep grassy hillside behind and you're on Há, from where you can peer down into Herjólfsdalur, or walk north along the rim to opposite the transmitter tower atop **Stóraklif**. Climbing this latter peak is exhausting work; the track again begins down below on the western side of the harbour, ascending first on steps, then scree, then ropes, and finally, a chain – presumably, transmitter maintenance crews are airlifted in.

The peninsula's northeastern heights are far harder propositions, though you can reach the start on the north side of the harbour easily enough. First is **Heimaklettur**, requiring a rough scramble to reach the Westman Islands' highest point of 283m. Beyond is Ystiklettur, regularly visited by puffin collectors but best not attempted without local knowledge and help – make enquiries at the tourist office or *Hreiðrið* guesthouse (see p.144).

Heimaey's coastal trails

Due to the airstrip running over the eastern cliffs, it's not possible to circuit Heimaey completely, though that still leaves you with a decent 12km of **coastal trails** to follow. In summer you'll definitely see plenty of **birds**: wheatear, snipe

---

Surtsey

Surtsey's history proves that Heimaey is by no means the only island in the group to bear volcanic scars. In the late nineteenth century, **Hellisey** unexpectedly popped out of the waves about 5km off Heimaey's southern tip, the first in a series of underwater eruptions that continued at odd intervals for the next few decades. Then, on November 14, 1963, a colossal explosion, accompanied by towering plumes of steam and ash, heralded Surtsey's birth: within a week, there was a volcano rising 70m out of the sea. April 1964 saw lava appear for the first time; and when the eruption finished three years later, what was suddenly the Westmans' second-largest island covered almost three square kilometres. Erosion has since shrunk it by half, but Surtsey remains of great interest to scientists, who are using it as a model to study how islands are colonized by plants and animals. Unexpectedly, they found that larger plants were the first to become established; previous theories had suggested grasses were first needed to hold the soil together.

As it's a special reserve, **landing on Surtsey** is prohibited unless you're part of a scientific team. Your only chance of a trip over is with Viking (see p.144), which makes four- to six-hour circuits from Heimaey – you'll get a good look but they don't land – once or twice each summer, if they get enough people interested and the weather's suitable.

and golden plovers love the island's grassy slopes; ringed plovers, oystercatchers, redshanks and purple sandpipers pick over the shoreline for edibles; while skuas, eiders, gannets and auks patrol the seas. And if you've come to Heimaey hoping to see puffins, you'll be able to get within spitting distance of several million of them.

A clear six-kilometre trail heads down the west coast from the golf course, a pleasant couple of hours following the crumbly cliff tops south to Stórhöfði. Initially there's plenty of bald basalt overlaid by later lava flows, which clearly poured over the edge and into the sea, then the path rises almost imperceptibly over spongy grass until, halfway along, you suddenly realize that you're fairly high up above the water. After crossing several fence lines, you run down to sea level again past frames for preparing that Icelandic delicacy *harðfiskur*, dried fish; you'll get an idea of how windy things are here from the huge bags of rocks weighting the frames down (and how rank the *harðfiskur* smells by this location, far from town). The little beach beyond is good for ducks and waders, then it's a steep, short climb up grassy **Stórhöfði**, its top capped by a transmitter tower. There's a viewing platform on the northwestern side for watching bird activity, while the south cliffs house a sizeable **puffin colony** and are a good spot to scan the seas for whales and gannets, the latter nesting on the sheer-sided islets to the southwest.

From Stórhöfði, carry on up Heimaey's **east coast** to a steeper, rockier and weedier beach, often with some serious surf – this side of the island catches the prevailing winds – and occasional **seals** dodging in and out of the swell. Tidal pools and a couple of interesting caves might slow you down for a while – if you can get to them – otherwise climb the messy scree behind up onto a ridge and follow this north until it reaches a fence line. A stile here gives access to the high, stumpy **Landstakkur** peninsula, complete with another puffin colony and scenic views. Continuing up the coast, you stay high above the sea with a dramatic drop into the deep blue on one side, and a gentle, grassy backslope on the other. Another stiff stretch uphill and you're at a **beacon** above the airstrip, from where you'll have to cut west across country to the road and so back up to town.

Travel details

Buses

The following schedules are valid during summer (approximately June–September). Exact dates and winter schedules are available at W www.bsi.is.
Blue Lagoon to: Grindavík (5 daily; 15min); Keflavík (1 daily; 15min); Reykjavík (6 daily; 45min).
Geysir to: Gullfoss (1 daily; 10min); Hveragerði (1 daily; 1hr 50min); Laugarvatn (1 daily; 1hr 20min); Reykholt (1 daily; 5min); Reykjavík (1 daily; 2hr 30min); Selfoss (1 daily; 1hr 30min).
Grindavík to: Blue Lagoon (5 daily; 15min); Reykjavík (5 daily; 55min).
Hella to: Höfn (1 daily; 6hr 30min); Hveragerði (1 daily; 55min); Hvolsvöllur (2 daily; 30min); Kirkjubæjarklaustur (1 daily; 3hr 30min); Reykjavík (2 daily; 1hr 35min); Selfoss (2 daily; 35min);

Skógar (2 daily; 2hr 20min); Vík (2 daily; 3hr); Þórsmörk (2 daily; 2hr).
Hveragerði to: Geysir (1 daily; 1hr 50min); Gullfoss (1 daily; 1hr 45min); Hella (1 daily; 55min); Hvolsvöllur (2 daily; 1hr 20min); Reykjavík (7 daily; 40min); Selfoss (7 daily; 30min); Skógar (1 daily; 2hr); Vík (2 daily; 2hr 20min); Þórsmörk (2 daily; 2hr 35min).
Hvolsvöllur to: Hella (2 daily; 10min); Höfn (1 daily; 6hr); Hveragerði (1 daily; 55min); Kirkjubæjarklaustur (1 daily; 3hr); Reykjavík (2 daily; 1hr 55min); Selfoss (2 daily; 1hr); Skógar (2 daily; 50min); Vík (2 daily; 2hr); Þórsmörk (2 daily; 1hr 25min).
Keflavík to: Blue Lagoon (1 daily; 15min); Reykjavík (5 daily; 1hr).
Landmannalaugar to: Eldgjá (1 daily; 1hr 15min); Hella (1 daily; 2hr 15min); Kirkjubæjarrklaustur

(1 daily; 3hr 45min); Leirubakki farm (1 daily; 1hr 30min); Reykjavík (1 daily; 4hr); Selfoss (1 daily; 3hr 15min); Skaftafell (1 daily; 4hr 45min).

Selfoss to: Geysir (1 daily; 2hr 30min); Gullfoss (1 daily; 1hr 20min); Hella (2 daily; 35min); Höfn (1 daily; 6hr 30min); Hveragerði (7 daily; 30min); Hvolsvöllur (2 daily; 30min); Kirkjubæjarklaustur (1 daily; 3hr 30min); Laugarvatn (1 daily; 1hr 50min); Reykjavík (6 daily; 1hr); Skógar (2 daily; 1hr 20min); Vík (2 daily; 3hr); Þórlakshöfn (2 daily; 1hr); Þórsmörk (2 daily; 2hr 30min).

Skógar to: Hella (2 daily; 1hr); Höfn (1 daily; 2hr 40min); Hveragerði (1 daily; 2hr); Hvolsvöllur (2 daily; 50min); Kirkjubæjarklaustur (1 daily; 1hr 55min); Reykjavík (2 daily; 2hr 40min); Selfoss (2 daily; 1hr 20min); Vík (2 daily; 1hr 10min).

Vík to: Hella (2 daily; 1hr 25min); Höfn (1 daily; 4hr); Hvolsvöllur (2 daily; 1hr 15min); Kirkjubæjarklaustur (1 daily; 1hr); Reykjavík (2 daily; 3hr); Selfoss (2 daily; 2hr); Skógar (2 daily; 30min).

Þórlakshöfn to: Hveragerði (1 daily; 1hr 10min); Reykjavík (3 daily; 1hr); Selfoss (1 daily; 40min).

Þórsmörk to: Hella (2 daily; 1hr 45min); Hveragerði (2 daily; 2hr 40min); Hvolsvöllur (2 daily; 1hr 15min); Reykjavík (2 daily; 3hr 25min); Selfoss (2 daily; 2hr 30min).

Planes

Heimaey to: Bakki (6 daily; 6min); Reykjavík (6 daily; 30min); Selfoss (on demand; 20min).

Ferries

Heimaey to: Þórlakshöfn: 2 daily; 2hr 45min.
Þórlakshöfn to: Heimaey: 2 daily; 2hr 45min.

3

The west coast

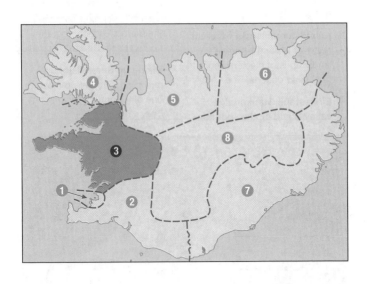

CHAPTER 3   # Highlights

* **Deildatunguhver hot spring, Reykholt** Witness the power of Iceland's geothermal activity at the country's biggest natural hot spring. See p.162

* **Hraunfossar cascades, Húsafell** Iceland's most unusual waterfalls, where subterranean aquamarine water tumbles lazily over moss-dressed rocks. See p.163

* **Kaldidalur valley** An excellent taster of Iceland's remote landscapes of glaciers and grey sand deserts. See p.164

* **Eiríksstaðir, Haukadalur valley** Stand on the spot from which the Vikings set out to discover Greenland and North America. See p.166

* **Stykkishólmur, Snæfellsnes peninsula** Iceland's prettiest town boasting a mêlée of brightly coloured wooden houses set against an island-studded coastline. See p.172

* **Flatey, Breiðafjörður** A night spent in the hotel on this idyllic farming island is the perfect escape from the beaten track. See p.176

* **Hiking up Snæfellsjökull** A rare chance to get up close to one of Iceland's glaciers. See p.180

▲ Hraunfossar waterfalls

The west coast

The panorama of the bay of Faxa Fiord is magnificent – with a width of fifty miles from horn to horn, the one running down into a rocky ridge of pumice, the other towering to the height of five thousand feet in a pyramid of eternal snow, while round the intervening semicircle crowd the peaks of a hundred noble mountains.

Letters from High Latitudes, Lord Dufferin

Reykjavík and the Reykjanes peninsula together form the southern edge of **Faxaflói**, the sweeping bay that dominates Iceland's west coast and any journey north of the capital – the Ringroad clings to its shores as far as the small commercial centre of Borgarnes before striking off inland on its way towards Brú and the north coast. Although the scenery is not Iceland's most dramatic, it provides visitors travelling clockwise around the country with their first taste of small-town Iceland and as such makes a satisfying introduction to the rest of the country. If you can, it's a good idea to break your journey and get a feel for what rural Iceland really is all about – in summer the views of flower meadows dotted with isolated farms sheltering at the foot of cloud-topped mountains are picture-postcard pretty. Travelling north, the first town you come to, the disappointing, ugly **Akranes**, with its concrete factory and fish-processing plants, is best passed over in favour of nearby **Borgarnes**, a small commercial centre with an excellent saga museum that also makes a good jumping-off point for the historical riches of **Reykholt**, Iceland's largest hot spring, Deildatunguhver, and great hiking around Húsafell.

The "pyramid of eternal snow" to which Dufferin, who sailed his yacht *Foam* to Iceland in 1856, was referring is the glacier, **Snæfellsjökull**, which sits majestically on top of a dormant volcano at the tip of **Snæfellsnes**, a long arm of volcanic and mountainous land jutting out into the sea and the highlight of any trip up the west coast. Divided by a jagged mountain ridge, the peninsula not only marks the northern edge of Faxaflói bay but also the southern reaches of the more sheltered **Breiðafjörður**, with its hundreds of islands and skerries, over which lie the table mountains of the West Fjords. On a clear day the snowcap is clearly visible across the water from both Reykjavík and the West Fjords. A gem of a place, **Stykkishólmur**, on the peninsula's north coast, is not only the main town hereabouts but also one of Iceland's most attractive with its brightly painted wooden houses nestling by the vibrant harbour busy with chugging fishing vessels. Indeed, it's from here that the ferry sails for the pastoral delights of Flatey, the largest island in Breiðafjörður. From **Arnarstapi** on the peninsula's southern coast it's possible to take a snowmobile up onto Snæfellsjökull for some of the most exhilarating driving – and vistas – you'll ever experience. For splendid isolation, nearby **Búðir** can't be beaten, its wide sandy bay home only to an unusually charismatic hotel complete with creaking floorboards and ocean views. Occupying a sheltered

3

WEST COAST

25 km

0

N

Blönduós

Hvammstangi

Hólmavík ◄

Bjarkalundur ◄

711

72

704

1

Hrútafjöruur

Holtavörðuheiði

F578

61

Brú

Eiríksstaðir

59

586

60

Baula

Norðurá

F578

Hallmundar-
hraun

Surtshellir

Strútur Eiríksjökull

Kalmanstunga

Langjökull

Fljótstunga

Hraun
fossa

Húsafell

Okjökull

Þórisjökull

Skjaldbreiður ◄

Þingvellir ►

52

F550

Flatey & Brjánslækur ◄

60

599

Laugar

Hvammur

Búðardalur

590

590

Laxárdalur

Hvammsfjörður

Grábrók

Bifröst

Hreðavatn

523

Varmaland
50

Delidartungu-
hver

Borg Á
Mýrum

Reykholt

Kleppjámsreyrkir

AUG

52

Skorradalsvatn

308

Glymur

50

47

48

Hafnarfjall

Hvalfjörður

Reykjavík ►

54

Eldborg

Borgarnes

533

540

50

1

Akrafjall ◄

Akranes

5

Hvalfjörður Tunnel

MÝRAR

SNÆFELLSNES

55

54

54

56

Vegamót

54

Stykkishólmur

58

576

Grundarfjörður

Búðir

54

Ólafsvík

54

Arnarstapi

Hellnar

F570

Snæfells-
jökull ◄

574

Rif

Hellissandur

Dritvík

Djúpalónssandur

Breiðafjörður

Faxaflói

spot in the neck of land which links the West Fjords with the rest of the country, **Laugar** in Sælingsdalur has some hot springs and a few cultural diversions, and makes a good place to break the long journey from Reykjavík to the West Fjords.

What the west coast may lack in scenic splendour, it makes up for in historical and cultural significance – landscapes here are steeped in the drama of the sagas. Close to **Búðardalur**, to the north of Snæfellsnes along Route 586, Haukadalur valley was the starting point for **Viking** expansion westwards which took explorers first to Greenland and later to the shores of North America as heroically recounted in the **Saga of Eirík the Red**. He and his wife lived at **Eiríksstaðir** and, having been outlawed from Iceland, together they pioneered the settlement of Greenland. It's also thought that **Leifur Eiríksson**, the first European to set foot in North America, was born on a farm that has now been expertly reconstructed on the original site. Though tricky to reach, the farm is worth a visit for the unusually tangible remains of saga times – standing beside the turf-roofed farmstead overlooking a barren valley, it's easy to see what inspired the early Icelanders to search for lands anew. Equally rich in history is the tiny village of **Reykholt**, just 45 minutes outside Borgarnes – itself the setting for **Egill's Saga** – and home to the only saga writer known by name, the thirteenth-century politician **Snorri Sturluson**. Here you can still see the outdoor warm pool where the great man bathed and received visitors. More saga history can be found in Laxárdalur valley, northeast of Búðardalur, where characters from the **Laxdæla Saga** lived out their feud-torn lives.

Getting around the west coast

The Ringroad (Route 1) cuts right through the region to Brú, covered year-round by Reykjavík–Akureyri **buses** via Borgarnes. From Borgarnes, Route 54 and more year-round buses head northwest to Snæfellsnes; while for the Búðardalur area you need to turn north off the Ringroad up Route 60 at Bifröst, a route served by buses only in summer.

In some ways it's worth seeing the west coast as a stepping stone **to the West Fjords**: the Reykjavík–Hólmavík/Isafjörður bus follows the Ringroad through the region; there's a regular ferry from Stykkishólmur on Snæfellsnes to Brjánslækur and bus connections to other West Fjord locations; and the Búðardalur bus presses on to the end-of-the-road township of Reykhólar in the southern West Fjords, though you can only travel beyond this in your own vehicle.

Akranes and around

Once beyond Reykjavík and its adjacent overspill town, Mosfellsbær, the Ringroad weaves northwards around the towering form of Mount Esja to Hvalfjörður (whale fjord), the biggest in southwest Iceland and named after the large number of whales seen here by the original settlers. During World War II, the fjord's deep anchorages made it one of the most important bases in the North Atlantic, when British and American naval vessels were stationed here, providing a port and safe haven for supply ships travelling between Europe and North America. As the fjord kinks some 30km inland, however, it was something of an obstacle to road travel, until the opening of an impressive six-kilometre submarine **tunnel** in 1998. It was completed despite concerns from the people of Akranes that the shorter distance to the capital (49km through the tunnel compared with a massive 108km round the fjord) would kill off their local shops and services – fortunately their fears have proved unfounded. Twenty-four-hour **toll booths** are in place at both ends charging 800kr per car, which is worth the expense to save a tedious detour.

Hvalfjörður and whaling

At the head of **Hvalfjörður**, the disused open-air **whaling** station is a poignant reminder of Iceland's days as a whaling nation and of the key role Hvalfjörður played. Right until the late 1980s, tourist buses from Reykjavík would even wiggle their way round the fjord to allow visitors to watch the grisly spectacle of a whale being sliced up alfresco.

Commercial whaling out of Hvalfjörður operated from 1948 until 1989, when specially equipped ships harpooned fin, sei and sperm whales in the deep waters off the west coast of Iceland and towed them back to the Hvalfjörður whaling station. Minke whales were also caught from ordinary fishing boats. In latter years, however, there was immense international opposition to the slaughter from various quarters, not least a boycott of Icelandic seafood instigated by Greenpeace, and direct action, when a Canadian craft sank two Icelandic whaling vessels and destroyed the whaling station here in November 1986.

With its economy declining as a result of the boycott, Iceland withdrew from the International Whaling Commission in 1992, claiming the organization set up to manage whaling had become one devoted solely to preventing all hunts. As an island nation, the Icelanders passionately believe in the right to harvest all living marine resources, and opinion polls at the time showed around eighty percent of the population in favour of whaling. Matters came to a head in March 1999 when, after much debate, the Icelandic parliament voted by a huge majority to **resume whaling** and called on the government to begin preparations. However, since Iceland's most important markets for fish are in Britain, France, Germany and the US, where opposition to whaling is strongest, ministers trod carefully, aware that a country where three-quarters of all exports are fish-related simply cannot risk another boycott. In October 2002 Iceland was readmitted to the IWC, the first step towards the resumption of Icelandic commercial whaling within the jurisdiction of the Commission, and since 2003 has been harvesting minke whales again, although the present left-green government, ushered into power in 2009, may overturn this.

Just beyond the exit from the tunnel, Route 51 strikes off west from the Ringroad for **AKRANES**, the west coast's biggest town and home to 6500 people. Although you'd never guess by wandering around the modern streets today, Akranes traces its history all the way back to 880 AD when the area was first settled by two Irish brothers, Þormóður and Ketill Bresason, most probably monks. Over the following centuries the village grew into a successful agricultural settlement as the name "Akranes", literally "field promontory", indicates – corn was grown on the fertile land around Mount Akrafjall. However, it was when the seventeenth-century bishop Brynjólfur Sveinsson from Skálholt stationed a number of his fishing boats in Akranes that **Iceland's first fishing village** was born, and the town has never looked back: today fishing and fish processing account for roughly half the town's income, and there's a busy, commercial air to the place. Akranes is also renowned for its **sporting** prowess – the local football team, Íþróttabandalag Akraness (ÍA), are frequent national champions – and its two sports halls, swimming pools and soccer stadium are of a correspondingly high standard.

Yet Akranes is hard to like: it's gritty, entirely without architectural charm and a terribly cold spot even in summer as the icy winds straight off the sea howl round street corners, sending the hardiest locals scurrying for cover. However, it's a good base from which to do some decent hikes around the heights of easterly **Mount Akrafjall** or, when the sun is shining, to explore the long sandy beach, **Langisandur**, a fifteen-minute walk from the town centre. The town's one cultural grace is the **Akranes Museum Centre**, where you can get to grips with the history of the 1970s Cod Wars and admire some of Iceland's sporting heroes.

Arrival, information and accommodation

Buses arrive at the Skrúðgarðurinn café on the main street at Kirkjubraut 8, which is also home to the **tourist information centre** (☎431 1780; Mon–Sat 10am–6pm; ⓦwww.visitakranes.is). There's internet access at the **library** at Heiðarbraut 40 (Mon–Thurs 11am–7pm, Fri 11am–6pm, also Oct–Apr Sat 11am–2pm). Following the recent closure of the town's only hotel, there's now only **guesthouse** and youth hostel accommodation in Akranes: *Háholt 11* (☎431 1408, ⓦwww.haholt11.com; ❶, breakfast 700kr) is the name and address of a delightful homestay run by the endearing Ólína; while the new **youth hostel** with two self-catering kitchens can be found in the former pharmacy at Suðurgata 32 (☎868 3332, ⓦwww.hostel.is; 2600kr per bed). To get to Akranes' oceanside **campsite** (May–Sept; ☎431 5100) from the town centre, walk northeast up Kirkjubraut for five to ten minutes to the junction with Kalmansbraut (actually the beginning of Route 509 out of town towards Borgarnes) to the small bay, Kalmansvík.

The Town

Although there are no sights as such in Akranes, sooner or later you'll come across the **Icelandic National Cement Works** (Sementverksmiðjan) close to the harbour at Mánabraut that really gets locals excited, an environmentally friendly plant founded in 1958 which uses crushed shells from the sea bed rather than lime as raw material; mercifully, the cement works are closed to visitors.

Once you've exhausted the harbour area, home in on the town's **Museum Centre** off Garðagrund (June–Aug daily 10am–5pm; Sept–May Mon–Fri 1am–5pm; 500kr

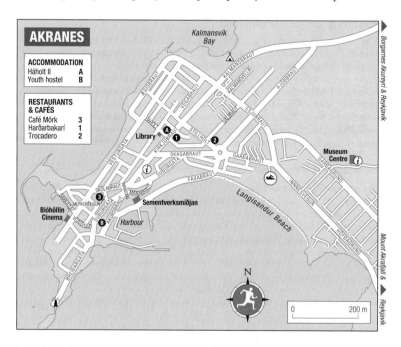

AKRANES

ACCOMMODATION
Háholt II   A
Youth hostel   B

RESTAURANTS & CAFÉS
Café Mörk   3
Harðarbakarí   1
Trocadero   2

all-inclusive ticket; Ⓦ www.museum.is), home to four different museums containing everything from information on the Akranes football team to samples of quartz stone. Outdoor exhibits include several antique buildings; a granite monument inscribed in Gaelic and Icelandic commemorating the Irish role in Akranes' history; and the **twin-masted ketch** *Sigurfari*, built on Britain's River Humber in 1885, which carries the honour of having been the last sailing ship in the Icelandic fleet before being sold to the Faroe Islands where, remarkably, it fished until 1970.

Indoors, your first port of call should be the **Akranes folk musem** located in the building between the granite stone and the *Sigurfari*. The most interesting exhibits are the hook-shaped cutters that were used to sever the nets of British trawlers during the Cod Wars of 1972 and 1975. Though quite ordinary to look at, they proved devastatingly effective when dragged across British trawler wires by the Icelandic coastguard.

The adjacent, low-roofed white building called Safnaskálinn is home to the centre's three other museums. Although the mind-numbing displays of rocks inside the **Mineral Museum** and the **Sports Museum with its countless medals and cups** will delay you no more than a couple of minutes, it's worth devoting more attention to the **Land Survey Museum**, stuffed to the gills with maps and charts of this geologically pockmarked country.

The **swimming pool** (Mon–Fri 6.45am–9pm, Sat & Sun 9am–6pm; ☎433 1100) and sports centre can be found off Garðabraut at Jaðarsbakkar; the changing rooms at the pool contain a steam room, and there's also an outdoor pool and four hot pots. Behind the sports centre complex lies a kilometre-long stretch of sandy beach known as **Langisandur** – a must in Akranes when the sun is shining, since the southern aspect of the shore will do wonders for your tan. Bear in mind, though, that although the water can look tempting on a sunny day it fails the big-toe test by a long way; it's barely 5°C warm at the height of summer.

Eating and drinking

The best bet for **eating** is the popular *Trocadero* at Stillholt 23, essentially a glorified **pizzeria** serving good-value burgers from 1150kr, chicken breast for 1890kr, lamb chops at 1995kr as well as decent pizzas from 1250kr and beer at an amazing 550kr; a takeaway service is also available (☎433 2400). Otherwise, there's the *Harðarbakarí* **bakery** at Kirkjubraut 54, selling the usual range of white loaves, Icelandic flatbread and cakes. Come Thursday, Friday and Saturday evenings, the town's youth can be found drinking at *Café Mörk*, Skólabraut 14, a stylish **bar**-cum-disco where a beer costs 700kr, though there are frequent good-value promotions aimed at pulling in the punters. Snacks such as sandwiches and burgers are also available for around 1100kr.

Mount Akrafjall and Glymur

On approaching Akranes from the Ringroad you'll have driven by **Akrafjall** mountain, which, at 643m, is not only 200m higher than Reykjavík's Mount Esja, but also dominates the skyline east of town. The mountain offers one of the best panoramas in the west of Iceland, with spectacular **views** not only of Akranes but also, on a clear day, of Reykjavík. On a sunny day you'll find most of the town out here either climbing the flat-topped mountain or picnicking in the lush meadows at its foot – during summer you'll also find copious numbers of **sea birds**, especially kittiwakes, nesting on the mountain's craggy sides. Of the mountain's two peaks, the southern one, **Háihnúkur** (555m) is easier to climb thanks to a well-defined **path** leading to the summit from the car park below. The higher northern peak, Geirmundartindur, is split from the other by a river valley, Berjadalur, through which most of the town's water supply flows.

From the mountain, Route 47 winds its way east around the northern shore of Hvalfjörður towards Iceland's highest waterfall, **Glymur**. The falls drop nearly 200m from the boggy ground to the west of **Hvalvatn** lake, but it can be difficult to find a vantage point from where to see the spectacle at its best. A rough **track** leads up through Botnsdalur valley at the head of Hvalfjörður towards the falls – allow about an hour from the road. Incidentally, according to Icelandic folklore, a mythical creature, half-man, half-whale, which once terrified locals from its home in the dark waters of Hvalfjörður, was tricked into swimming out of the fjord, up the river and the Glymur falls, before dying in the waters of Hvalvatn – where, oddly, whale bones have been found.

Borgarnes and around

North of Akranes the Ringroad covers a lonely and exposed 38km before reaching **BORGARNES**, the principal town of the Borgarfjörður region, which not only enjoys a spectacular setting on a narrow neck of land reaching out into the fjord but also has excellent views inland to the glaciers of Eiríksjökull and Langjökull. The stretch of road from Akranes, particularly around Hafnarfjall, on the southern approach to Borgarnes, is one of the most hazardous in the entire country – facing westwards, it takes the full brunt of violent storms which drive in from the Atlantic and not surprisingly closes frequently during the winter months, as cars have been overturned here by the brute force of the wind. In summer things are not quite so severe but it is still an extremely windy spot.

Unlike most other coastal settlements, Borgarnes isn't dependent on fishing – powerful tidal currents in the fjord have put paid to that – but is primarily a service centre for the surrounding dairy farmers who rely on the town's slaughterhouse and good roads for their livelihoods. However, the town's main claim to fame is its historical association with the ninth-century settler, Skallagrímur Kveldúlfsson, father of the pirate, thug and poet **Egill Skallagrímsson**, hero of *Egill's Saga* (see box, p.158). Their lives and times are explored in a first-rate **museum**, while plenty of Borgarnes' streets recall characters from the saga: Skallagrímsgata, Kveldúlfsgata, Böðvarsgata and Egilsgata to name but a few.

Arrival and information

Approaching from the south, the first thing you see in Borgarnes is the lurid yellow Bónus **supermarket**, a clutch of service stations and a modest shopping centre filling **Brúartorg**, the "town square" next to the highway; all **buses** pull up here. There's also a **bank** (Mon–Fri 9.15am–4pm) with ATM, a **supermarket**, the **vínbúð** (Mon–Thurs 11am–6pm, Fri 11am–7pm, Sat 11am–4pm), **pharmacy** (Mon–Fri 9am–6pm, Sat 10am–2pm) and a postbox. The regional **tourist office** (June–Aug Mon–Thurs 9am–4.30pm, Fri noon–8pm, Sat & Sun 10am–3pm; Sept–May Mon–Fri 9am–5pm, Sat 8am–noon; ☎437 2214, ⓦwww.westiceland.is) is a couple of kilometres to the north, located at the junction of the Ringroad and Route 54 towards Snæfellsnes; the staff are a mine of information about west Iceland, sell maps and books about the region, and can provide **internet** access (500kr).

Accommodation

There's plenty of accommodation in and around Borgarnes, so you should be able to find something to suit your pocket, even in summer when the town is still relatively quiet; advance reservations are not necessary.

Egill's Saga

Few characters in literature have been as sharply drawn as the eponymous hero of **Egill's Saga**. The story tells the life of the sullen, brutish and ugly **Egill Skalla-grímsson** (c910–990), whose personality is glimpsed before he even appears in the tale, when both his grandfather and father are revealed as "shape-changers", or werewolves. From his youth through to his dotage, Egill is depicted as relentlessly mean and trouble-making, though also industrious, clever and a gifted poet, and the final picture of him is of a remarkable and complex individual, who never seeks an easy path through life. The saga was probably written by the thirteenth-century politician **Snorri Sturluson**, and it's no coincidence that its central framework, that of a free man stubbornly defying the might of the Norwegian throne, mirrored the political situation in Iceland at the time of its composition, when Norway was attempting to annex the country.

Egill was born to Norwegian parents who had settled in Iceland to escape the wrath of their king, Harald Fairhair. The most telling event of his youth is when his father **Skallagrímur**'s wolfish nature erupts during a ball game, and he tries to kill the 12-year-old. Egill's nurse saves him, but both she and Egill's best friend are killed by Skallagrímur, and Egill's revenge is to murder his father's favourite slave at dinner that night. A few months later, Egill makes the first of many **Viking expeditions**, meeting the man who is to become his arch-enemy: King **Eirik Bloodaxe** of Norway (c895–954), Harald's son. Re-igniting the family feud, Egill falls out with the king and manages to humiliate him publicly, kill his son and survive an attempt by Queen Gunnhildur to poison him – all in one night. Having lost the respect of his subjects and been shamed out of Norway, King Eirik takes up residence across the North Sea in Viking Jórvík (York) only to receive an unexpected visitor – Egill has been shipwrecked on the Yorkshire coast and decides to settle up with his foe. Although condemned to death, he composes a poem in praise of the king and his life is spared.

After many successful years as a Viking, Egill returns to Iceland around 957 and settles down as a farmer. Then tragedy strikes: his **sons** Böðvar and Gunnar die in accidents and Egill is so distraught he decides to starve himself to death. But his daughter Þorgerð tricks him into drinking some milk and composing a **poem** – known as *Sonatorrek*, "Lament for my sons" – and he becomes so caught up in the work that his spirits revive.

According to the saga Egill lived out his **final years** in Mosfell just outside Reykjavík. There, taunted by servants as he sits blind and incontinent by the fire, he plans one last act of mischief: to take his hoard of Viking silver to the Alþing, and start a riot by scattering it among the crowds. Frustrated in this by his daughter-in-law, one night Egill vanishes along with his loot and two servants. He's found the next morning, stumbling blindly alone in the fields, and admits to having hidden his treasure and killed the men. He dies later that year, irascible to the last, and is eventually interred – as befits his violent, pagan life – at the boundary of Mosfell's churchyard.

Bjarg ☎437 1925 or 864 1325, ✉bjarg@simnet .is. Guesthouse accommodation on a working farm a 20min walk out of town along Borgarbraut. There's a rustic studio apartment with kitchen and private bathroom as well as three other regular rooms with shared facilities. Sleeping-bag accommodation 5600kr. ❶

Borgarnes B&B Skúlagata 21 ☎434 1566 and 842 5866, ⓦwww.borgarnesbb.is. Newly opened, no-nonsense guesthouse with plainly decorated rooms, mercifully low on floral flourishes and swirls. ❷

Borgarnes campsite Borgarbraut ☎437 2214. Perched on a little hillock close to Brúartorg at the entrance to the town, this campsite is rather small and has space for just a few tents.

Hótel Borgarnes Egilsgata 12–14 ☎437 1119, ⓦwww.hotelborgarnes.is. A 10min walk from the highway down Borgarbraut, then right, this comfortable, modern hotel has 75 well-appointed rooms with neutral décor and wooden floors. Closed Oct to Easter. ❷

Mótel Venus Hafnarskógur, ☎437 2345, ⓦwww.randburg.com/is/motel_venus. A couple of kilometres south of town across the fjord, in a stunning setting at the foot of Hafnarfjall, there are simple unadorned doubles here with private bathroom and shared facilities; sleeping-bag accommodation 1600kr. ❶

Youth hostel Borgarbraut 9 ☎ 695 3366, ⓦ www .hostel.is. Borgarnes' new youth hostel is perfectly located on the main street and has comfortable dorms where a bed goes for 2100kr. There are also four rooms with private facilities. ❶

The Town

Home to barely two thousand people, Borgarnes is not a big place, comprising little more than a few streets filling a narrow, 1500-metre-long peninsula. The main drag, **Borgarbraut**, runs southwest down the peninsula from the highway to the sea. About halfway along is **Skallagrímsgarður**, a small but pleasant park at the junction with Skallagrímsgata. By the entrance on the left is the **burial mound** of one of Iceland's earliest settlers, **Skallagrímur Kveldúlfsson**, complete with horse, weapons and various other Viking accoutrements. Originally just plain Grímur, he obtained the first part of his name, Skalla ("bald"), because he lost all his hair at an early age. Skallagrímur's son, **Egill**, is portrayed on the accompanying monument carrying home the body of his own son, Böðvar, who drowned in the Hvítá river during a storm: it was in Böðvar's memory that Egill composed his great poem, *Sonatorrek* (see box opposite).

There are a couple of museums in town, but by far the best is the modern, well-designed **Settlement Centre of Iceland**, Brákarbraut 13–15, down at the far end of Borgarbraut (June–Aug daily 10am–7pm; Sept to May daily 11am–5pm; ⓦ www.landnam.is; 1100kr per section, both sections 1600kr). The museum is in two parts, for each of which you can pay separately and are given an audio guide, complete with superb sound effects, which leads you around the exhibits and accompanying video displays. The first section uses interactive models (such as the swaying prow of a Viking longship which you can ride) and audio visual displays to give an idea of what Iceland's first settlers would have found when they arrived to carve up the country between them during the Settlement period (about 870–930). But for sheer gothic atmosphere you can't beat the second exhibition, in the basement, that illustrates *Egill's Saga*, with surreal and often nightmarish figurines, wood carvings and lighting portraying Egill's violent life – look out for his werewolf grandfather lurking in the shadows, and the misshapen skull with Paget's Disease towards the exit – it's thought Egill may have suffered from this abnormal bone condition.

Borgarnes' other attraction is its excellent open-air **swimming pool** and sports centre on Þorsteinsgata, a continuation of Skallagrímsgata, situated right by the water's edge with great views of the fjord and the surrounding hills; there are also a couple of hot pots here, a waterslide, a steam room and a sauna.

Eating and drinking

The most popular **place to eat** is *Hyrnan*, the fast-food restaurant attached to the N1 filling station; it's always full of truckers and holidaying Icelanders wolfing down dishes such as fish and chips with soup and salad (1750kr), pizzas (1090kr), open sandwiches (850kr) and soup (550kr); coffee costs 225kr, while a beer is a whopping 850kr. Alternatively, try the Filipino-run *Matstofan*, near the Settlement Centre at Brákarbraut 3, which dishes up burgers (from 550kr), pizzas (800kr) and a couple of good Asian stir-fries (around 1100kr) daily from 6pm. For more **upmarket** dining, the Settlement Centre itself has a **restaurant** serving good-value lunch specials (1590kr), as well as lasagne (1850kr) and fish of the day (2800kr), while the *Hótel Borgarnes* restaurant has salmon in hollandaise sauce for 2950kr, or fillet of lamb with pepper sauce at 4250kr – expensive but certainly mouthwatering.

Borg á Mýrum

Another site mentioned in the sagas, the farm of **Borg á Mýrum**, just a couple of kilometres north of Borgarnes on Route 54, is easily reached by buses to the Snæfellsnes peninsula. First settled by **Skallagrímur Kveldúlfsson**, Egill's father, this spot is, to Icelanders at least, of double historical significance because of its association with one of Iceland's greatest writers, Snorri Sturluson (see opposite). It's a popular spot with misty-eyed home-grown tourists, though few remain more than ten minutes or so, because the original farmhouse is long gone and there's precious little to see here today other than a small white church, the *borg*, or large rock, after which Skallagrímur's original farm was named, and a sculpture by Ásmundur Sveinsson entitled *Sonatorrek*, after Egill Skallagrímsson's moving poem (see box, p.158).

Like so many of Iceland's historical sites, archeological remains are thin on the ground, so you'll have to arm yourself with the facts and let your imagination do the rest. Skallagrímur ended up here very much by chance after falling foul of his king, Harald Fairhair of Norway. Together with his father, **Kveldúlfur** ("Evening Wolf", so-called because he grew violent and supernaturally strong as dusk came on), he fled the wrath of King Harald and set sail westwards for Iceland. However, during the lengthy and stormy voyage, Kveldúlfur fell ill and ordered that, on his death, his coffin be tossed overboard and his grieving family settle wherever it washed up. Following his father's instruction, Skallagrímur first set foot in Iceland in an area rich in bogs, forests and salmon rivers, at Borg á Mýrum (Rock in the Bogs), where he raised his family, naming the surrounding area, accordingly, Borgarfjörður (Rocky Fjord).

The third great man to live at Borg was **Snorri Sturluson**. At the age of 19 Snorri married the only daughter of Father Bersi the Wealthy, of Borg, and moved to the farm following his father-in-law's death in 1202 to run the estate as his heir. However, his marriage was not a happy one and just four or five years later, around 1206, he decided to move inland to Reykholt, leaving his wife behind.

Reykholt and around

The cultural highlight of any trip up the west coast, **Reykholt** is immediately appealing. Not only does this little hamlet sit amongst the wide open spaces of the fertile Reykholtsdalur valley, enjoying stunning views of dusky mountains and the sleepy Reykjadalsá river, but it also contains tangible memorials to **Snorri Sturluson**. The excellent museum here is by far and away the best place to get to grips with Iceland's rich and, at times, downright confusing history of saga events, characters and writing.

However, don't view a trip here as simply a way of mugging up on Icelandic history. Route 518 runs east from Reykholt to the pastoral hamlet of **Húsafell**, a fantastic place to fetch up for a couple of days of hiking and sightseeing at nearby lava fields, waterfalls and glaciers. In summer, you can also push further out from here for a taste of Iceland's Interior, by following the Kaldidalur route (Route 550) southwest to Þingvellir. **Public buses** can get you as far as Reykholt, but from here you really need your own vehicle to explore.

Reykholt

Lying an hour's drive from Borgarnes, about 40km east off the Ringroad down Route 50 and then Route 518, the tiny hamlet of **REYKHOLT** belies its cultural importance, comprising little more than a few geothermally heated greenhouses and a modern **church**. But a trip to the church – or rather, the critically acclaimed **Heimskringla museum** beneath it (May–Sept daily 10am–6pm; Oct–April Mon–Fri 10am–5pm; Ⓦwww.snorrastofa.is; 600kr) – will leave you in no doubt as to Reykholt's importance in Icelandic minds, packed as it is with exhibits relating to Snorri Sturluson and his writings, along with accounts of Reykholt's role as a centre of learning over the centuries. The large prints of the sagas hung on the walls will give you an idea of what the documents actually looked like, if you failed to see the originals in the Culture House in Reykjavík. The museum's curators are known throughout Iceland for their outspoken views on all things Snorri and have even done battle with the Icelandic government over the taxation of the Snorri estate, quoting a medieval document penned by the great man himself in their defence. Indeed, following meticulous research, staff claim that the handwriting contained on one of the museum prints is actually Snorri's – make sure to see it before you leave. The church itself, with its specially designed acoustic walls, hosts the **Reykholt Music Festival** (Ⓦwww.reykholtshatid.is; 2500kr per concert) in late July when visiting singers and musicians gather for a series of classical music concerts open to the public – look out for details posted around the village.

Across the lawn from the museum and at the foot of the hillock, Snorri's pool, the **Snorralaug**, provides a rare visual example of a piece of medieval Iceland and is even mentioned in the *Landnámabók* (*Book of Settlements*) and the *Sturlunga Saga*. A four-metre-wide geothermally heated pool ringed with stones, this is thought to have been where Snorri would bathe and receive visitors, and next to it are the restored remains of the **tunnel** leading to the cellar of Snorri's farmhouse, where he was assassinated in 1241 (see box below). The pool is fed by an ancient stone aqueduct from the nearby hot spring, Skrifla. Back up the steps from the pool, the Snorri **statue** which graces the front of the former school was presented to Iceland

Snorri Sturluson

Born at the farm of Hvammur (see p.168) near Búðardalur in 1179, **Snorri Sturluson** was descended from some of the greatest figures in early Icelandic history; on his father's side were influential chieftains, on his mother's, among others, the warrior poet Egill Skallagrímsson. At the age of 2 he was fostered and taken to one of Iceland's leading cultural centres, Oddi (see p.128), where, over the years, he became acquainted not only with historical writing but also the court of Norway – a relationship that would eventually lead to his death. In 1206, following his marriage to a wealthy heiress, he moved to Reykholt and consolidated his grip on power by becoming a chieftain, legislator and respected historian and writer; he also developed a distinct taste for promiscuity, fathering three children to women other than his long-suffering first wife, Herdís.

Snorri Sturluson is the most celebrated figure in Icelandic literature, producing first his *Edda* (an account of Norse mythology) then *Egill's Saga* and *Heimskringla* (a history of the Norwegian kings up to 1177), which from its geographical detail shows that Snorri spent several years living in Norway. During this period he developed a close bond of allegiance to the Norwegian earl who reigned alongside the teenage king, Hákon. However, following a civil war in Norway, which resulted in the earl's death, the Norwegian king declared Snorri a traitor and ordered one of his followers, Gissur Þorvaldsson, to bring the writer back to Norway – dead or alive. On the dark night of September 23, 1241, seventy armed men led by Gissur burst into Snorri's farmhouse in Reykholt sending him fleeing from his bed unarmed and defenceless, down into the cellar. Five of the thugs pursued Snorri, and there they hacked Iceland's most distinguished man of letters to death.

by Norway's King Olaf shortly after independence in 1947. It's a clear reminder of the continuing wrangle between the two Nordic nations over Snorri's origins; the Norwegians strongly maintain that Snorri is theirs and claim he was born in Norway. Although the Icelanders have gratefully accepted over three million Norwegian kroner to help set up the Snorri exhibition hall, the new library and Snorri research centre attached to the village church (see opposite), suspicions remain that the Norwegians haven't yet renounced their claims on Snorri.

Practicalities

Buses to Reykholt run just twice a week (Fri and Sun) from Reykjavík via Borgarnes, and terminate at the filling station at the eastern end of the village. Return buses leave on the same days, and also travel via Varmaland (see p.164).

Reykholt's only **place to stay** is the overpriced *Hótel Reykholt* (☎435 1260, ⓦwww.fosshotel.is; ❺); originally built as a boarding school in 1931, it is now completely modernized, with fantastic views of the Okjökull and Eiríksjökull glaciers. The adjoining **restaurant** serves up the dish of the day for around 2500kr. There's a small **shop** at the filling station (daily 10am–10pm) which sells most basics, including food.

Deildartunguhver

While in the Reykholt area, it's well worth checking out the biggest **hot spring** in Europe, **Deildartunguhver**, which lies near the hamlet of Kleppjárnsreykir, 5km west of Reykholt on the side of Route 50. Drawing on the geothermal reserves that lie all around Reykholtsdalur valley, and pumping out a staggering 180 litres of 97°C water a second, the billowing clouds of steam created by this mighty fissure are truly impressive, reaching up high into the cool air – in fact it's water from here that runs via two specially constructed pipelines to heat Borgarnes and Akranes, 34km and 64km away, respectively. As in so many other geothermal areas around Iceland, water from the spring is also used to speed up the growth of plants and vegetables by heating up the surrounding **greenhouses**, and during the summer local farmers often set up stalls here to sell their produce to passing visitors. From the car park, a footpath leads to the spring; it's wise not to get too close to the open pools of bubbling boiling water as it can, and does, splash over the protective fence in front. Incidentally, the area around the spring is the only place in Iceland where the unusual variety of hard fern, *blechnum spicant*, is found.

Húsafell and around

Twenty-five kilometres east of Reykholt and a favourite activity centre for holidaying Icelanders, **HÚSAFELL** is set amid birchwoods and a geothermal area where many Reykjavíkers own summer cottages. Though the main draw here is the vast lavafield **Hallmundarhraun**, there are also some excellent **hiking trails** leading off into the **Húsafellsskógur** forest and, more adventurously, up to the **Eiríksjökull** and **Okjökull** glaciers.

The village itself consists of little more than a **church**, originally built in 1170 but today dating only from 1905, and a hundred or so private summer cottages, mostly owned by the trade unions (whose employees use the cottages in rotation) and individual families. There is also a **service centre** with a food store and filling station, and a fantastic geothermally heated outdoor **swimming pool** offering great views of the surrounding hills and glaciers. From June to October you can pitch a tent at one of several **campsites** (all contactable on ☎435 1550), find a double room in an old **farmhouse**, the *Gamli bærinn* (☎435 1550, ⓦhusafell.is; ❷) with a shared kitchen, or opt for sleeping-bag accommodation in a cabin for 2500kr.

Hallmundarhraun

Some 14km northeast of Húsafell, the **Hallmundarhraun** lavafield – named after the giant Hallmundur of *Grettir's Saga* – is thought to have been formed at the time of the Settlement when magma poured out from beneath the northwestern edge of the Langjökull and entered the Hvitá river. The road there follows first the 518 and then, via **Kalmanstunga farm**, the F578 to the northeastern edge of **Strútur** mountain (939m); you can walk on the lava, but it is hard going and requires tough-soled shoes – take care not to twist an ankle. Off the F578 is **Surtshellir**, a 1970-metre-long cavern thought to have been a hideout of the eighteenth-century outlaw Eyvindur and his friends (see box, p.317). Exercise extreme caution if you decide to go inside as the uneven floor and darkness can prove disorientating; you'll need to bring a torch with you. Nearby **Stefánshellir**, part of the same cave network, is also worth a quick look but is essentially more of the same – together these cave systems measure a whopping 3.5km in length.

In summer the road to Hallmundarhraun is usually passable for all cars as far as the caves, after which point it deteriorates as it continues past the lavafield towards the Arnarvatnhæðir hills, Route 704 and eventually the Ringroad near Hvammstangi; the total distance of this interior route from Kalmanstunga to Núpsárbrú bridge in Austurárdal valley (Route 704) is 42km.

Hraunfossar and Barnafoss

Six kilometres west of Húsafell on Route 518, the waterfalls of **Hraunfossar** and **Barnafoss** are two of the best-known natural features in Iceland. Although both are on the Hvitá, it's Hraunfossar (Lava Falls) that make for the best photographs; however, don't expect thundering torrents of white water – the falls here are gentle cascades of bright, turquoise water, emerging from under the moss-covered lava to tumble down a series of rock steps into the river. From here, a track leads upstream to Barnafoss (Children's Falls), which is far more lively – it was here that two children fell to their deaths when crossing a narrow stone arch that once spanned the river. A modern footbridge now affords an excellent view of the water churning violently as it channels through the ravine below.

Okjökull, Eiríksjökull and Langjökull glaciers

One of Iceland's smaller glaciers, **Okjökull** (Ok) is perfect for a **day hike** from Húsafell. At a height of 1141m, the glacier sits in a dolerite shield volcano and is easily reached from Húsafell by first following the western edge of the Bæjargil ravine up to the Drangsteinabrún ridge. Cross to the eastern side of the small ponds which lie south of the ridge and continue straight up to Ok. On a clear day the **views** from here are truly spectacular – west you can see to the coastline and the town of Borgarnes, inland there are sweeping vistas of the Interior. Allow five or six hours and take enough food and drink to last for a day.

At 1675m the peak of **Eiríksjökull**, on the glacier of the same name, is the highest mountain in western Iceland and the long **hike** here should only be undertaken by seasoned walkers. Before setting out, get detailed information from the service centre in Húsafell, where you can also get helpful **maps**; the following description, however, should help you trace your route along them. Head along the hard, dry grass of the northern slope of Strútur mountain, northeast of Kalmanstunga farm, from where there are difficult trails east across Hallmundarhraun to Hvítárdrög at the foot of the glacier. Begin the climb itself by hiking up the prominent ravine on the westernedge of the glacier, remembering your route to help your descent – it can be very disorientating up here. Beyond the ravine, the going gets considerably easier but watch out for crevasses. Allow a full day and bear in mind that sun-melt can make the hike a lot harder.

The Kaldidalur interior route

From Húsafell, Route 550 (Kaldadalsvegur) winds its way southwest through the haunting beauty of the **Kaldidalur** valley on its way to the information centre and campsite at Þingvellir (see p.106), a distance of around 60km. If you're short of time but want a taste of the barren expanses of the Icelandic Interior, this is a good option: you'll come face to face with four **glaciers** – Eiríksjökull, Okjökull, Langjökull and Þórisjökull, a small oval-shaped ice cap rising to a height of 1350m – and pass through a vast grey **desert** where ferocious sandstorms can appear in seconds, transforming what was once a clear vista of majestic ice caps and volcanic sands into an impenetrable cloud of grit and dirt. As the neck of land carrying the road narrows to pass between the Ok and Þórisjökull glaciers, the route climbs and rides along the straight Langihyrggur ridge affording spectacular views of Þórisjökull opposite.

The Kaldidalur route is unsealed and rough, though generally open to conventional vehicles from mid-June until late August – you'll need to check road conditions in advance through ⓦ www.vegag.is.

Just 20km southeast of Húsafell, but not readily accessible on foot due to its isolated location on the western edges of the Interior, lies Iceland's second-largest ice cap, **Langjökull** (Long Glacier). Covering 950 square kilometres, Langjökull resembles a narrow protruding finger wedged between the Hallmundarhraun lavafield and the Kjölur Interior route (see p.315) – you'll pass its foothills on both the Kjölur Interior route and when tackling the Kaldidalur route (see box above).

North along the Ringroad: Varmaland and Bifröst

Between Borgarnes and Brú, a distance of 85km along the Ringroad, there is little to detain you. However, if you fancy a spot of **hiking** amid lavafields or lush river valleys or scaling a couple of extinct **volcanic craters** before hitting the north coast, there are a couple of diversions worthy of your attention. The first is the village of **VARMALAND**, a small and uneventful place northwest of Reykholt popular with holidaying Icelanders. **Buses** from Reykholt to Borgarnes (but not vice versa) pass through the village, whilst coming in the opposite direction from Borgarnes, you simply take a Ringroad bus to Baula, from where it's an easy five-kilometre walk east along Route 50 then north along the 527. Admittedly, other than its geothermally heated **swimming pool** and the market-gardening centre, Laugaland, where mushroom production began in Iceland, there's little to the place but it does offer a decent **day hike** from here to Bifröst of around 13km. The route follows the course upstream of one of the country's best salmon rivers: the Norðurá. Originating high on the moors of Holtavörðuheiði south of Brú, the river flows southwest to meet up with western Iceland's biggest river, the glacial Hvítá, at the head of Borgarfjörður where it finally empties into the sea. This hike is an excellent way to see off-the-beaten-track Iceland: crystal-clear waterfalls, isolated farms and craggy hilltops surrounded by a carpet of summer wildflowers and rich springy grassland. From Varmaland head north along Route 527 to Einifell farm where the road downgrades into a jeep track as it heads to a T-junction west of Höll farm. From here, head west around the foot of Hallarmúli hill (260m) towards the Laxfoss **waterfalls** in the Norðurá.

Continue past the abandoned farm, Veiðilækur, on to the farmstead at Svartagil and the Glanni **waterfalls**. Here you pick up Route 528 and fork left, crossing the Norðurá and Bjarnardalsá rivers, over the Grábrókarhraun **lavafield** (see below) to join the Ringroad a kilometre or so east of Bifröst.

Accommodation in Varmaland is limited to the predictably named and unadorned *Gistiheimilið Varmaland* (☎430 1516, ✉kof@varmaland.is; sleeping bag 1800kr, ❶) and the **campsite** (June–Sept, ☎430 1520).

Bifröst

Alternatively you could head straight for minuscule **BIFRÖST**, not much more than a filling station, situated on the Ringroad a 25-minute bus ride from Borgarnes. A couple of kilometres south and spread either side of the Ringroad, you'll find the heather-encrusted **Grábrókarhraun** lavafield, formed three thousand years ago when lava spewed from three craters on the north side of the main road: Grábrók, Grábrókafell and a third cone that has now been dug up to provide gravel for road building. Otherwise, the forested shores of **Hreðavatn**, 1km southwest of Bifröst, make for a pleasant stroll and a picnic if the weather's playing along; there's also trout fishing here. Look out for plant fossils in the rocks around the lake.

Northeast of the village, the **Grábrók** crater can be ascended by means of a marked trail, as can the **Baula** rhyolite mountain (934m), 11km from Bifröst and reached along Route 60 or by **buses** heading for Búðardalur if you don't fancy walking from the Ringroad; although the sides of this cone-shaped mountain are steep and scree-covered there are no particular obstacles to the ascent and once at the summit there's a small shelter made of rocks.

Accommodation is located about 3km north up the Ringroad from Bifröst, at *Hraunsnef* (☎435 0111, ❖hraunsnef.is; sleeping bag 2500kr, ❷); they have a restaurant and self-catering facilities. **Buses** from Bifröst's **filling station** head back down to Borgarnes, north via Route 60 to Búðardalur and Reykhólar, and northeast up the Ringroad to Brú (for connections to the West Fjords) and Akureyri.

Búðardalur and around

North of the Snæfellsnes peninsula, the wide and sheltered **Hvammsfjörður** lies protected from the open sea at its mouth by dozens of small islands. Accessed via Bifröst on Route 60, or from Route 54 along the north coast of the Snæfellsnes peninsula, its main service centre is **Búðardalur**, an uninspiring place that is best passed over in favour of the rich **saga country** close by. Running northeast from Búðardalur is **Laxárdalur**, the valley around which one of the best known Viking romances, the **Laxdæla Saga**, was played out. South of here, **Eiríksstaðir**, in Haukadalur, was home to **Eirík the Red**, discoverer of Greenland, and the birthplace of his son, **Leifur**, who went on to discover North America. Although there's plenty of historical significance in this corner of the country, it's not easy to visit by **bus**: only Búðardalur is on a bus route (five times a week from May to September), and there's no service to Laxárdalur or to Eiríksstaðir, though you can reach the minor saga sites around **Laugar**.

Búðardalur

Some 45km from Bifröst, **BÚÐARDALUR** is home to just 250 people, and provides limited banking, postal and retail services to the surrounding rural districts. It's an unkempt place, consisting of little more than a collection of a dozen or so suburban streets, and the only reason to break your journey here is to visit nearby saga sites. The **tourist information office** (June–Aug daily 10am–6pm; ☎434 1441, ⓦwww.dalir.is), housed in a former nineteenth-century warehouse down by the harbour, can help out with information about the local sights. It's also here that you'll find the village's one and only attraction: **Leifsbúð** (same hours; 500kr), a modest museum dedicated to Leifur Eiríksson and his voyage to North America from Greenland. Despite such a rich historical theme to draw upon, the museum will barely whet your appetite with its disappointing collection of wooden models and uninspiring photographs – the key exhibit, a tapestry recounting the discovery of Vínland, is a modern creation and less than accurate in its portrayal of historical facts. Should you wish to stay in the village, in order to visit Eiríksstaðir or Laxárdalur, there's **guesthouse** accommodation with shared facilities available at *Bjarg*, Dalbraut 2 (☎434 1644, ⓦwww.aknet.is /bjarg/english.htm; ❶) and a **campsite** (late May to Aug; ☎434 1132) near the junction of the main Vesturbraut with Miðbraut, opposite the filling station. For food, head for the **restaurant** in the *Bjarg* which dishes up burgers and pizzas from 1050kr or the filling station at Vesturbraut 10 which has burgers for 900kr.

Eiríksstaðir

The country which is called Greenland was discovered and settled from Iceland. Eirík the Red was the name of a man from Breiðafjörður who went out there and took possession of land in the place which has since been called Eiríksfjörður. He named the country Greenland and said it would make people want to go there if the country had a good name.

Extract from *Book of the Icelanders* by Ari the Learned (1067–1148).

Twenty kilometres southeast of Búðardalur and reached by Route 586 (8km from the junction with Route 60) into Haukadalur valley, the former farm of **Eiríksstaðir** (June–Aug daily 9am–6pm; ⓦwww.leif.is; 800kr) is one of the most historically

---

The Vikings, Greenland and North America

Although Icelanders don't like to admit it, **Eirík the Red** and his father were actually Norwegian. According to the Book of Settlements, *Landnámabók*, they left Norway to settle in the Hornstrandir region of the West Fjords where they lived until Eirík's father died. Eirík then moved south to Breiðafjörður where he met his wife and set up home with her at Eiríkstadir, in Haukadalur, and fathered his first child, Leifur. After some run-ins with the neighbours here the couple moved to the island of Öxney at the mouth of Hvammsfjörður, but Eirík committed several murders and was declared an outlaw. Forced out of the country, he sailed far and wide to the west, eventually discovering land in 985 and, according to the sagas, promptly named it **Greenland**, "because it would encourage people to go there if the land had a good name". He settled at Brattahlíð in a fjord he named after himself, Eiríksfjörður, near present day Narsarsuaq. No doubt inspired by his father, Leifur set out to the west from his new home, Greenland, first reaching barren, rocky land that he named Helluland (Baffin Island), from where he continued south to an area of flat wooded land he named Markland (Labrador), in 1000 AD. After another two days at sea he reached more land, where, the sagas have us believe, grapes grew in abundance. Leifur named this land **Vínland**, which some experts believe could mean "Wineland". However, since two days' sailing from Labrador would only take him as far south as current-day New England, not exactly known for its wines, speculation remains as to where Viking Vínland is.

▲ Turfed longhouse, Eiríksstaðir

significant locations in Iceland. This was the starting point for all westward expansion by the Vikings, first to Greenland and later to the shores of North America. Following a couple of earlier failed archaeological digs, a third attempt was made between 1997 and 2000 to excavate this site, which experts believe to be the most likely home of Eiríkur Þorvaldsson, better known as **Eirík the Red** and father of **Leifur**, who became the first European to set foot in North America (see box opposite). During the dig archeologists found the remnants of a fifty-square-metre hall dated to 890–980 AD, and, although no timber was unearthed, they did come across doorways, clearly marked out with stone pavings. It's believed that Eirík moved here from Drangar in Hornstrandir after marrying Þjóðhildur, whose parents already lived at nearby Vatn in Haukadalur. However, he was an unruly man, and, after getting into a row and murdering several of his neighbours, he was driven out of the valley having lived there for ten to twenty years. Eirík then set up home on Suðurey (part of Brokey) and Öxney, two islands east of Stykkishólmur in Breiðafjörður, where he once again fell out with his neighbours who, after further violence, outlawed him from the islands – it was then, with a ship full of friends, that he set sail, charting a course south of Snæfellsnes, for new land and adventure.

An evocative reconstruction of Eiríkur's original **longhouse** now stands in front of the ruins and is a must for anyone interested in the Viking period – turf walls 12m long by 4m wide huddled around a dirt floor and support a roof made of rafters covered over with twigs atop a layer of turf. Story-telling **guides**, evocatively dressed as Vikings, expertly bring the period to life and will also point out the significant features of the ruins. To the untrained eye they can be hard to find (they're located immediately behind the small statue of Leifur; from the statue take the gravel path to the right up the hillside heading towards the waterfall).

The only option for **accommodation** is the comfortable farmhouse at *Stóra-Vatnshorn* adjacent to Eiríksstaðir (mid-May to mid-Sept; ☎434 1342, Ⓦwww .farmholidays.is; sleeping-bag accommodation 1750kr, ❶); breakfast is 800kr and traditional home cooking is also available. There are fantastic views out over the Haukadalsá river to the summit of Jörfahnúkur (557m) from here – the peace and tranquillity of Haukadalur certainly make a night here preferable to one in Búðardalur.

Laxárdalur

The tragedy renowned as one of the great masterpieces of medieval literature, the **Laxdæla Saga** (see box opposite), unfolded in **Laxárdalur**, the valley northeast of Búðardalur and traversed by Route 59. Although there are few remains of the homes of the characters of the tale, the rolling green landscapes are reminiscent of the most romantic scenes in the epic, and the mere mention to an Icelander of virtually any local place-name will conjure up images of forsaken love; handy information boards recounting the main events of the saga are placed at the key sites involved.

Five kilometres out of Búðardalur just to the north of Route 59 lies the farm of **Hjarðarholt**, established by Ólafur the Peacock and later taken over by his son, Kjartan. In the saga, Ólafur moves his livestock from **Goddastaðir**, now a couple of kilometres to the northeast off Route 587, to Hjarðarholt and asks a local chieftain, Höskuldur, to watch the procession from his own farm. The first of Ólafur's animals were arriving at Hjarðarholt while the last were still leaving Goddastaðir – a visual demonstration of wealth which can still be appreciated today by standing at Hjarðarholt and looking at the distant hillside to the northeast. Incidentally, Höskuldur lived next door to Ólafur at **Höskuldsstaðir**, directly located on Route 59 and still inhabited today. Route 59 continues east over the lake-studded moors of Laxárdalsheiði to the fjord of Hrútafjörður from where Route 61 heads north to Hólmavík in the West Fjords and south to the tiny settlement of Brú (see p.220).

Hvammur and Laugar

The other branch of Ólafur the Peacock's feud-torn family lived around 17km north of Búðardalur, at a couple of sites not far off Route 60 – the Búðardalur-Reykhólar **bus** can drop you nearby. **Hvammur** (2km west off Route 60 and then north along a minor road just after Skerðingsstaðir farm) is one of Iceland's oldest settlements and was first occupied by Auður Djúpúðga (Auður the Deepminded) around the year 895, the only woman recorded in the Book of Settlements. Firm but compassionate, she was the matriarch of a leading family in the saga age, though confusingly, the *Laxdæla Saga* refers to her as Unnuras. Auður, the daughter of Ketill Suðureyjajarl (Earl of the Hebrides) and married to King Ólafur Hvíti of Dublin, first came to Iceland with her children and grandchildren around 890 after one of her sons, Þorsteinn, died in battle in Scotland, and she brought with her a large number of Scots and Irish. The land settled by Auður was long occupied by her descendants, one of whom was Þorfinn Karlsefni, who explored America for three years in an attempt to establish a Viking settlement. There's a small memorial to Auður at Hvammur, erected by the University Women of Iceland. She was the first in a long line of prominent Icelanders to live here, the most famous being **Snorri Sturluson** (see p.161), who was born here in 1179; a memorial in his honour stands in the churchyard. **Árni Magnússon**, whose greatest achievement was to persuade Denmark to return many of the sagas to Iceland, was also born and raised here.

A little further up Route 60 from the Hvammur junction and about 2km west, **LAUGAR** in Sælingsdalur valley was the birthplace of Guðrún Ósvífsdóttir. Remains of the **old baths** where she had frequent meetings with Kjartan can still be

The Laxdæla Saga

The *Laxdæla Saga* has three main characters – the tall, blonde and heroic **Kjartan**; the beautiful **Guðrún Ósvífsdóttir**; and Kjartan's cousin **Bolli**, who lurks in the background to complete a classic love triangle. It takes thirty or so chapters before the three figures are centre stage, but before they have met, a wise man predicts that Guðrún will have four husbands. Later that day, seeing Kjartan and Bolli swimming together he predicts that one day Bolli will stand over the dead Kjartan, and be killed for his deeds; and thus the inescapable template for the characters' lives is set out to the reader.

Guðrún is married to her first husband against her will and divorces him after two years. She then marries Þord, who incurs the enmity of a family of sorcerers and is drowned as a result. Guðrún then meets Kjartan, and they become close, but Kjartan decides to seek his fortune abroad, and asks Guðrún to wait three years for him, but she refuses.

While in Norway, Kjartan is held hostage, but still finds time to have an affair with the beautiful princess Ingibjorg. Bolli, who has been with his cousin during his courtship and on Viking expeditions, now returns to Iceland and tells Gudrún that Kjartan intends to settle in Norway, whereupon Gudrún's family persuade her to marry Bolli. Kjartan subsequently returns and marries another woman, Hrefna, giving her a priceless headdress as a wedding gift, a gift actually bestowed on him by Ingibjorg, who had told him to give it to Gudrún as a wedding present.

There is no love lost between the two neighbouring households, and things only worsen when the headdress is stolen. In revenge, Kjartan lays siege to Guðrún and Bolli and humiliates them by not letting them go to the lavatory for three days. Eventually, Guðrún goads Bolli and his brothers to try to kill Kjartan – Bolli is reluctant but eventually joins the fight, dealing a death blow to a barely injured but exhausted Kjartan, who gives himself to be killed by Bolli and dies in his arms. Guðrún gloats over his death but Bolli is inconsolable. Kjartan's brothers avenge him by eventually killing Bolli – Guðrún is pregnant at the time, and one of the killers wipes his sword on her dress.

Eventually Guðrún gives birth to a son whom she names Bolli, after his father. She decides she won't marry again until her husband is avenged, and makes a promise to Þorgils Hölluson that she will marry no other man in the land than him if he kills her husband's murderer. This she does, at which point Guðrún reveals she is betrothed to another, Þorkel Eyjólfsson, who is abroad. She does indeed marry Þorkel, but he drowns, after which Guðrún becomes a nun. She dies a hermit at Helgafell (see p.175) but before she dies, her son Bolli asks her which man in her life she loved the most, to which she replies "I was worst to him I loved the most" – one of the best-known lines of saga literature.

seen at Laugar farm; follow the signs to it along Route 589. This valley is also where her husband Bolli was ambushed and murdered by Kjartan's brothers. In Guðrún's day, the geothermal springs here were an important landmark for travellers on the long journey to and from the West Fjords. Today they feed a wonderful outdoor **swimming pool** and small steam room which forms part of the *Edda Laugar* **hotel** (June–Aug; ☎444 4930, ⓦwww.hoteledda.is; ❶); the hotel also runs the adjacent **campsite**. The hotel **restaurant** serves good fish and lamb dishes from 2500kr and provides breakfast. There's also a school nearby housing a small **folk museum** (June –Aug daily 3–7pm; 500kr), with the usual displays on local history.

Moving on from Laugar, Route 60 continues north, following the course of the Svínadalsá river through Svínadalur, which contains the gorge where Kjartan was ambushed and murdered. Past here, the road reaches the bridge over Gilsfjörður, marking the start of the West Fjords – **buses** in this direction continue only as far as Reykhólar (see p.210), however, and to catch services for the rest of the West Fjords you need to backtrack to Bifröst.

The Snæfellsnes Peninsula

From Borgarnes, Route 54 branches off west past Borg á Mýrum through the sparsely populated **Mýrar** district, a region of low-lying plains and bogs with a few small lakes, heading for the southern coast of the **Snæfellsnes Peninsula**, a rugged yet beautiful arm of the Icelandic west coast that juts out into the Atlantic between Faxaflói bay and Breiðafjörður. The north and south coasts are divided one from the other by a string of spiky mountains which run down the spine of the peninsula and culminate in the magnificent **Snæfellsjökull**, a glacier at the land's westernmost point. Towns – and regional **buses** – are mostly confined to the north coast, where harbours are good and plentiful, and it's from picturesque **Stykkishólmur**, far and away the best place to base yourself on the peninsula, that boat trips can be made across to the peaceful island haven of **Flatey**. From here a road runs west round the tip of the peninsula via uneventful **Ólafsvík**, though, if you're keen to head straight for the glacier, aim for the south-coast township of **Arnarstapi** where **snowmobile tours** of Snæfellsjökull can be arranged. Remember that it's the south coast which more often than not bears the brunt of

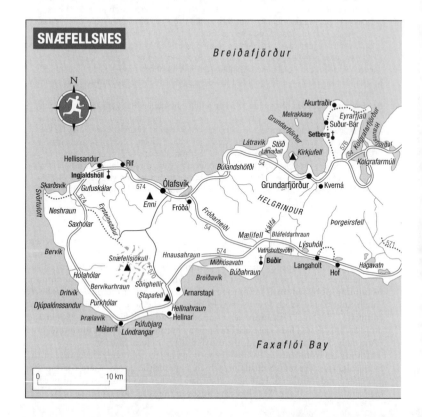

the moisture-laden low-pressure systems that sweep in from the Atlantic, emptying their load here rather than over the mountains on the north coast.

Bus services to Snæfellsnes are fairly comprehensive, though none runs all the way along the peninsula's south coast. Daily between May and September (with a restricted service at other times), services run from Reykjavík and Borgarnes to Vegamót, then head north via Route 55 to the junction with Route 54 (where you change for Stykkishólmur), then along the north-coast towns of Grundarfjörður, Ólafsvík and Hellissandur, returning along the same route. Between June and August, a daily bus also runs a clockwise circuit around the tip of the peninsula from Ólafsvík, via Arnarstapi, Hellnar, Dritvík and Hellissandur. Mál og menning's *Snæfellsnes 1:100,000* is a good **map** of the region, detailed enough for most purposes, including hiking.

To Snæfellsnes' north coast

Approaching Snaefellsnes from the southeast along Route 54, the first place of interest is **Fagraskógarfjall** mountain, once the haunt of Grettir of *Grettir's Saga* (see p.341). William Morris described it as "a savage and dreadful place" during his visit here in 1871, though these days it seems much more green and peaceful. North of here, along Route 55, the caves of **Gullborgarhraun** lavafield are a maze of intricate passageways containing coloured stalagmites and stalactites. It's advisable to seek local advice, though, before exploring them.

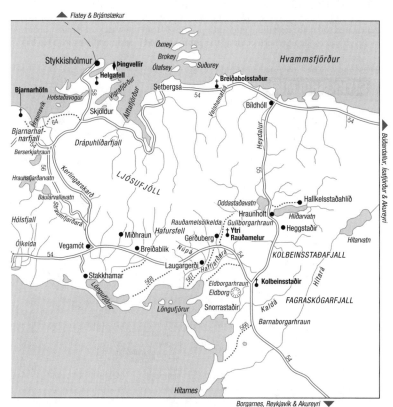

Back on Route 54, the road swings past the oval-shaped **Eldborg** crater, which sits conspicuously amid the flat expanse of the **Eldborgarhraun** lavafield, before reaching an unnumbered gravel road pointing north, signed "Rauðamelur" and "Gerðuberg". This leads in a couple of kilometres to the start of the **Gerðuberg basalt columns**, a two-kilometre-long shattered escarpment of grey, fifty-metre-tall hexagonal columns breaking down into scree – the longest such formation in the country.

A further 20km west along the main road, the pit-stop of **Vegamót** marks the point where Route 56 (and the bus) branches off across the peninsula towards Stykkishólmur and the north coast. Along the way, the road runs parallel to the narrow Kerlingarskarð, a pass named after a female troll who, legend has it, was caught by the sun and turned to stone while on her way home from a good night's fishing. Locals say she can still be seen with a line of trout over her shoulder on a ridge of the Kerlingarfjall mountain. Stories were also rife of drivers experiencing the eerie presence of an extra passenger in their cars as they drove through the pass – not surprisingly perhaps, Route 56 was shifted some years ago and now runs to the west of the pass.

Stykkishólmur and around

The first town of note on the north coast, whether you're approaching on Route 54 from Búðardalur or on Routes 55 or 56 from the south, is picturesque **STYKKISHÓLMUR**, with its brightly coloured harbourside buildings. The largest and most enjoyable town on Snæfellsnes with a population of 1240, it is renowned today for its halibut and scallops landed from the waters of Breiðafjörður, which borders the northern coast of the peninsula and is technically more a sea bay

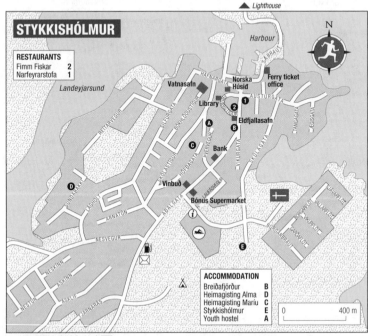

▲ *Lighthouse*

STYKKISHÓLMUR

Harbour

N

RESTAURANTS
Fimm Fiskar 2
Narfeyrarstofa 1

Landeyjarsund

Vatnasafn
Norska Húsið
Ferry ticket office
Library
Eldfjallasafn
Bank
Vinbúð
Bónús Supermarket

ACCOMMODATION
Breiðafjörður B
Heimagisting Alma D
Heimagisting Maríu C
Stykkishólmur E
Youth hostel A

0   400 m

▼ *Þingvellir, Helgafell & Reykjavík*

than a fjord, full of skerries and rocky islets. The Stykkishólmur region was actually one of the first to be settled in Iceland, and the countryside here features in several tales, most notably the **Erbyggja Saga**. This strange story, thick with evil spirits, bloody family vendettas and political intrigue, follows the life of the morally ambivalent Snorri Þórgrímsson, a pagan priest and son of a Viking who finally becomes a champion of Christianity. Easily accessible sites from the period include **Þingvellir**, an assembly ground just south of the town; and the nearby mountain **Helgafell**, the final resting place for Guðrún Ósvifsdóttir, heroine of the *Laxdæla Saga* (see p.169).

Arrival and information

Arriving by **bus**, you'll be deposited at the entrance to town by the **filling station** at Aðalgata 25, which also functions as the town's bus station. From here it's a ten-minute walk along Aðalgata to the harbour, where the **ferry** goes to and from Brjánslækur and Flatey (see box, p.176). On the way you'll pass the Bónus **supermarket** (Mon–Thurs noon–6.30pm, Fri 10am–7.30pm, Sat 10am–6pm, Sun noon–6pm) and excellent outdoor **swimming pool**, at the corner of Borgarbraut, with three hot pots, a sports complex and the **tourist information office** (June–Aug daily 10am–6pm; ☎438 8120, ⓦwww.stykkisholmur.is). The **post office** and **bank** (with ATM) are nearby. **Internet** facilities are available at the library down by the harbour (Tues–Thurs 2.30–6.30pm, Fri 1–5pm) as well as at the tourist office.

Accommodation

Although there's not a great deal of choice when it comes to finding somewhere to stay in Stykkishólmur, there are generally enough beds to go round. However, it's wise to book ahead if you're intent on staying at the youth hostel as it's relatively small and fills quickly.

Breiðafjörður Aðalgata 8 ☎433 2200, ⓦhotelbreidafjordur.is. Right in the heart of the town, this friendly, easy-going hotel has just eleven modern rooms, all with private facilities. There's also a delightful conservatory with good views over the town. **❷**

Campsite Aðalgata ☎438 1075. Located next to the sports field at the entrance to the town, just off the main street, there are plenty of pitches here for tents and caravans.

Heimagisting Alma Sundabakki 12 ☎438 1435 or 848 9833, ⓔalmdie@simnet.is. A small, pleasant guesthouse with just four rooms, all sharing facilities, open all year. **❶**

Heimagisting Maríu Höfðagata 11 ☎438 1258 or 862 9980. A long-established, comfortable

guesthouse, handy for the centre of town, though, once again, with just four rooms. Open all year. **❶**

🏃 **Stykkishólmur** Borgarbraut 8 ☎430 2100, ⓦwww.hringhotels.is. With eighty rooms, this elegant hotel, atop a small hill behind the swimming pool, is the biggest of the town's accommodation options. Rooms here are subtly decorated in warm, autumnal colours and many look out over the green expanses of the golf course. **❺**

Youth hostel Höfðagata 1 ☎438 1417 or 861 2517, ⓦwww.hostel.is. Occupying a perfect hilltop location looking out over the harbour, the cosy dorms (2100kr) and double rooms here are available from May–Oct; there's also a shared kitchen for guests to use. **❶**

The Town

Little more than one long straight main street, **Aðalgata**, which leads to the harbour, Stykkishólmur is the spot where the first settler in the region, **Þórólfur Mostraskegg**, found his high-seat pillars; in true Viking seafaring fashion he'd thrown them overboard vowing to settle wherever they washed up. He named the *nes*, or promontory, after the god of thunder, Þór, hence the name Þórsnes. It wasn't until the beginning of the nineteenth century that things really got moving in Stykkishólmur though, when a man by the name of Árni Thorlacius (1802–91) inherited the town's trading rights from his father. In 1832, he set about building **Norska húsið** (Norwegian House; June–Aug daily 11am–5pm; 500kr) at Hafnargata 5, with coarsely hewn timber from Norway, as was the tradition in the nineteenth century – Iceland then, as now, had little timber of its own with which to build. Today the building is still the town's most impressive, and houses a **museum** that attempts a potted history of Stykkishólmur; look out for the old black and white photographs of Árni and his wife, Anna, with whom he had eleven children, on the second floor, which has been reconstructed as their living room. Rather curiously, Icelanders remember Árni not so much for his commercial success in drawing the town into the modern age but for his pioneering **weather reports** from 1845. From Norska Húsið, it's a short stroll up the hill to the former library at Bókhlöðustígur 17, which now houses the intriguing **Vatnasafn** (Library of Water; May – Aug daily 1–6pm; at other times ask for the key at the library; free), a constellation of tall, glass columns containing glacial water collected from around Iceland, which is the work of the American artist Roni Horn. As natural light is refracted through the columns, unusual shapes and shadows are created on the floor, which is inscribed with Icelandic and English words that describe the weather or human moods.

While down at the harbour it's worth strolling past the Sæferðir shipping office (see below) and continuing around the harbour on Sæbraut to the set of steps leading up to **Súgandisey**, the rocky island which protects the town from the ravages of the open waters of Breiðafjörður. From the bright orange **lighthouse** that sits amid tussocky grass at the highest point of the island, there are unsurpassed picture-postcard-perfect views of the multicoloured houses of Stykkishólmur, with Helgafell in the distance. When the wind is not roaring in from the Atlantic (rare), Súgandisey makes a wonderful place for a picnic; there is a wooden bench halfway up the steps to the island, built into the cliff face, which offers some protection from the wind.

Back in town, the other main place of interest is the newly opened **Eldfjallasafn** (volcano museum; June–Sept daily 11am–5pm; 500kr; ⓦwww.eldfjallasafn.is), a repository of all things volcanic, including an impressive collection of "volcano art", paintings which all portray volcanic eruptions: there's even an original by Andy Warhol from 1985, whose explosive reds and oranges show an erupting Vesuvius. Founded by Iceland's leading volcanologist, local man Haraldur Sigurðsson, the museum also contains samples of the main rocks found in Iceland as well as ancient stone artefacts discovered in Pompeii and Herculaneum. Don't leave without seeing the fascinating English-language film (upstairs) which recounts Haraldur's expedition to the Tambora volcano in Indonesia and his discovery of a buried village in the crater. The only other sight in town is the space-age- looking **church** (daily 10am–5pm; free), a ten-minute walk from the harbour up on a rocky hill off Borgarbraut overlooking the town and with good views on a clear day out towards the waters of Breiðafjörður. Although construction began in 1975, the church wasn't consecrated until fifteen years later; its design includes a vast white ladder-like bell tower rearing up over the doorway and a semicircular domed rear roof. The interior is equally unusual, with hundreds of light bulbs suspended from the ceiling providing the lighting.

Boat trips from Stykkishólmur

Stykkishólmur is an excellent place to take a **boat trip** out into the island-studded waters of Breiðafjörður. Operated from the harbour by **Sæferðir**, Smiðjustígur 3 (ⓣ433 2254, ⓦwww.saeferdir.is), there are two trips to choose from. The most popular is a two-hour **nature-watching tour**, known as the Unique Adventure Tour (mid-May to mid-Sept; 5950kr), which heads out to the dozens of tiny islands northeast of Stykkishólmur, where you'll see plenty of species of birds including puffins, eider ducks, kittiwakes, cormorants and, if you're lucky, the white-tailed eagle. During the tour the crew fish for shellfish using a small drag net and everyone on board gets a chance to taste the contents. The boat passes close to the small and now uninhabited **Öxney** island, east of Stykkishólmur, where Eirík the Red, discoverer of Greenland, and his son, Leifur Eiríksson, who went on to discover North America, lived for several years. A second tour offers the chance to go **sea angling** (mid-May to mid-Sept; 6600kr, plus fishing rod 1550kr); generally, plenty of cod is landed during the tour, which lasts a couple of hours, though there's the chance to catch halibut, redfish and coalfish, too. Sæferðir also operates the car ferry to Flatey (see p.176) and Brjánslækur in the West Fjords (see p.203); for details see the box "Moving on from Stykkishólmur", p.176.

Eating and drinking

For **eating** head straight away to the excellent ✈ *Narfeyrarstofa* at Aðalgata 3, a cosy place with red walls and square white-framed windows that give the impression of eating in a doll's house; take a table upstairs where you can later relax in sumptuous leather armchairs under the steep V-shaped roof. The menu here is equally inspired: loin of lamb with Dijon mustard and garlic (3650kr); fillet of cod with mixed vegetables (2850kr); or tasty solid burgers with salad (950kr). Otherwise you're looking at *Fimm Fiskar* across the way at Aðalgata 4, which serves substantial fish dishes such as grilled monkfish with parsley and garlic (3400kr) and fried catfish with honey (2900kr) – all similar in quality to *Narfeyrarstofa* but with less atmosphere. Sandwiches can also be found at the filling station/bus terminal on Aðalgata. The state liquor store, **vínbúðin** (Mon–Thurs 2–6pm, Fri 2–7pm, Sat 11am–2pm), is at Aðalgata 24, near the swimming pool.

Þingvellir and Helgafell

A couple of kilometres south of Stykkishólmur, a small track leads off Route 58 to the east and running parallel with the Nesvogur inlet leads to the old parliament site of **Þingvellir** at the mouth of the Nesvogur inlet and right on the water's edge. This became a meeting place for the surrounding area following the death of the region's first settler, Þórólfur Mostraskegg. During his lifetime the parliament was on Þórsnes, and, indeed, it was here that Eirík the Red was outlawed following a spate of murders (see box, p.166). A few ruins can still be seen, including a **sacrificial site** that served as an altar to the god Þór, as recounted in the *Erbyggja Saga* – the only mention in any saga that the Vikings practised human sacrifice. The site is located at the end of the track from Route 58.

From Þingvellir, the small mountain you can see to the southwest conspicuous on the flat plain is **Helgafell** (73m), or Holy Mountain which – like many mountains around Iceland with the same name – was regarded sacred in pagan times when it was believed to be an entrance to Valhalla. Indeed, Þórólfur Mostraskegg considered the mountain so holy that he forbade anyone to relieve themselves within sight of it, a decision that later sparked the *Erbyggja Saga*'s central feud, when a neighbouring clan attending the Þingvellir assembly refused to abide by this law. Much later, a **monastery** moved here from the island of Flatey, and stood at the foot of the mountain from 1184 until the Reformation.

It's possible to climb the mountain: the path on the west side is easy enough, but the eastern descent is steep and rocky and you have to pick your way carefully. The ascent is worth making though: at the top there are ruins of a tiny thirteenth-century **chapel**, Tótt, and striking **views** over the islands of Breiðafjörður and to the mountains of the West Fjords. Guðrún Ósvifsdóttir, heroine of *Laxdæla Saga*, spent the last years of her life at the farm at the southern foot of Helgafell and, over nine hundred years on, people still decorate her grave with wild flowers – it's

Moving on from Stykkishólmur

Daily **buses** from Stykkishólmur all run 20km south **to Vatnaheið**, where you can pick up connections west along Snæfellsnes' north coast as far as Hellisandur, or continue south via Borgarnes to Reykjavík.

Heading **to the West Fjords**, you'll cut out a long and tedious detour around the coast by catching Sæferðir's *Baldur* **car ferry** from Stykkishólmur harbour **to Brjánslækur** (3hr; 3850kr single, plus 3850kr per car) in the West Fjords, via the island of Flatey (1hr 45min; 2650kr single, or you can stop for no extra charge en route to Brjánslækur). Sailings are once daily year-round, and twice daily between mid-June and mid-Aug. For more information call ☎433 2254 or check out ⓦwww.saeferdir.is.

By taking the early ferry in summer, it's possible to continue by bus (June–Aug Mon, Wed & Sat only) from Brjánslækur **to Patreksfjörður** (see p.205) and the **Látrabjarg bird cliffs** (see p.207); the journey is possible in the opposite direction on the same days, using the late sailing from Brjánslækur to Stykkishólmur. Similarly, catching the later ferry from Stykkishólmur or the early one from Brjánslækur allows you to continue by bus **to Ísafjörður** (see p.189) or Reykjavík, respectively.

in the simple churchyard marked by a headstone. Even today, local myth has it that anyone climbing from her grave to the chapel remains on top of the mountain will be granted three wishes, on the condition that they climb in silence and the wishes are pure-hearted, kept totally secret and made while standing beside the remains facing east. **To get to Helgafell** it's a four-kilometre walk out of town on Route 58, past the airstrip and beyond the Nesvogur inlet, to the second turn on the left. All **buses** in and out of Stykkishólmur pass this junction.

Flatey

The largest of the Breiðafjörður islands, **FLATEY** is a tranquil haven of two dozen or so restored wooden cottages set amid fields in summer bright yellow with buttercups. If you like the idea of having nothing to do all day but stroll through undisturbed meadows while taking in magnificent vistas of the West Fjord mountains and Snæfellsjökull, then dining by evening on succulent cod caught the same afternoon, this is the place to come. The weather is most dependable in August, but remember if you're coming here out of season the island will be virtually deserted, since most of the houses are only occupied in summer by Reykjavík city slickers; just five people spend the winter on Flatey.

Although low-key in the extreme today, Flatey was once one of Iceland's leading cultural centres, and in 1172 a **monastery** was founded on the island's highest point, a little behind where the present-day church stands, though there's nothing left of it today. The island was also once home to the **Flateyjarbók**, a collection of illuminated medieval manuscripts written on 113 calfskins. Although the book was written at Víðidalstunga in northern Iceland around 1387, it turned up here and remained in the possession of a local farmer's family until they gave it to the Bishop of Skálholt, who in turn sent it by royal request to King Frederik III of Denmark in 1659. The Flateyjarbók finally returned to Iceland in 1971 and is today housed in the Árni Magnússon institute in Reykjavík (see p.77).

The island

From the ferry jetty it's a ten-minute walk down the rough track that passes as the island's one and only road to the **old village**, a restored collection of painted houses nestling around a tiny **harbour**. It's from here that the island's sheep are painstakingly bundled into boats and taken to surrounding islands for summer grazing – quite a sight if you're around to witness it.

Past the harbour the track bears right, turns into a well-trodden path and climbs a little to the diminutive **Lundaberg** cliffs where you'll find plenty of **black guillemot**, **kittiwakes**, **fulmars** and **puffins** from April onwards, when the birds first start to arrive; half of all the different species of bird that breed in Iceland are found on the islands of Breiðafjörður. Beyond the hill, the path continues towards the eastern part of the island, which has been declared a **nature reserve**, marked by the odd sign or two and closed to the public during the breeding season (May 15 to July 20); the birds migrate south in late August or early September. It's possible, though, to pass round the edge of the reserve, following the marked wooden posts, to the island's south coast (also closed May 15 to July 20) where you'll be bombarded by arctic tern who show no mercy for man nor beast – even the island's sheep are subject to regular divebombing raids. If you don't mind this (keeping still seems to deter the birds a little), there are some secluded pebbly coves here, home to the odd wrecked fishing boat, with excellent views on a clear day across to Snæfellsjökull. From the shoreline, the path continues up past the campsite (see below) up to the **church** with its dramatic roof and wall paintings of island life – and puffins — by the Catalan painter, **Baltasar Samper**. Quite the entrepreneur, while visiting the island in the 1960s he suggested painting the church in return for free accommodation; his picture behind the altar shows Christ, unconventionally wearing a traditional Icelandic woolly sweater, standing alongside two local sheep farmers. After much hard work, the yellow building behind the church has been restored to its former glory and proudly claims the title of the oldest and smallest library in Iceland, established in 1864.

Practicalities

For details of the ferry from Stykkishólmur and Brjánslækur, see the box opposite. **Accommodation** on Flatey is limited, so book in advance. Right by the harbour's edge is the island's only **hotel**, ☆ *Flatey* (☎422 7610, ⓦhotelflatey.is; ❸), whose

▲ Flatey island in Breiðafjörður

thirteen tastefully restored rooms (shared facilities) occupy two former warehouses, which date from the island's heyday in the 1800s. The wood-panelled décor of the interior, painted in subtle pastel shades, perfectly complements the sturdy timber structure of the exterior; with its snug rooms oozing rustic charm and generous ocean views, this is one of Iceland's most appealing hotels. Otherwise there's the basic *Krákuvör* farm (T438 1451 or 853 0000, Esjflatey@simnet.is), with a four-person apartment (sleeping bag 2500kr) and a separate six-person cabin (9000kr); they also run the island's **campsite**.

Be sparing with **water** on Flatey since most of it has to be brought from the mainland in tanks. The hotel **restaurant** functions as a small **café** during the day with home-made cakes on offer, as well as a tasty fish lunch for 2000kr, and more substantial evening dishes such as a starter of smoked puffin with horseradish (1800kr), followed by fried cod with lobster (3500kr). In the basement, below the restaurant, the *Saltkjallarinn* **pub**, replete with sturdy stone walls, is a great place for a cold beer after a day's exploring.

Berserkjahraun and Grundarfjörður

From Stykkishólmur, it's 45km west along Route 54 to Grundarfjörður (travelling by bus, you need to change at Vatnaheið). About 15km along, the road crosses **Berserkjahraun**, a 4000-year-old lavafield named after the two **Berserkers** who cleared a route through it in 982 AD. Berserkers, periodically mentioned in the sagas, were formidable warriors, able to go into a trance that made them impervious to wounds; though much valued as fighters they were given a wide berth socially, since they were considered to be very dangerous. Here, as related in the *Eyrbyggja Saga*, local man Víga-Styr gave the two this odd task because one of the Berserkers had fallen in love with his daughter, and completing this well-nigh impossible task was a condition Víga-Styr had set for their marriage. However, with help from the tale's arch-schemer Snorri Þórgrímsson, he later killed the Berserkers and married his daughter to Snorri. Just east of the junction with Route 56, there's a rough but usually navigable five-kilometre-long **vehicle track** (Route 558) heading inland off the main road, which loops west across the centre of the lava field to rejoin Route 57; look carefully and you'll see the path the men cut, known as Berserkjagata, beside which is their burial mound.

Grundarfjörður

Once across the small bridge over Hraunsfjörður, the road soon comes to **GRUNDARFJÖRÐUR**, dominated by the neighbouring **Kirkjufell** mountain. Established in 1786 by the Danish king as one of six commercial centres in Iceland, the place exerted a strong influence on the west coast; in the early 1800s, for example, traders could only operate in the region if they had a branch in Grundarfjörður. From 1800 to 1860, French fishermen also profited from the excellent harbour here and used the town as a base, owning the church, hospital and shipping operations. When they left, they dismantled their buildings and even exhumed their dead, shipping the bodies back to France. Today the village and its 850 inhabitants depend on their position as the commercial centre of western Iceland, and the local freezing plant, for prosperity. Although Grundarfjörður isn't bursting with attractions, the new **Sögumiðstöð** heritage centre (June–Aug daily 10am–6pm; 500kr; Wwww.sagan.is) on the main road at Grundargata 35, is worth a quick look for its lowdown on life in twentieth-century Iceland, though, to be honest, the exhibition featuring a reconstruction of a worker's home from the early 1900s and a local store fail to set the pulse racing. For greater insight into local life, try a **guided walk** around town, offering explanations into how life in rural Iceland is changing and offering a first-hand insight into everything from the local fish factory to the village church; for bookings, contact the tourist information office (see below).

Practicalities

Grundarfjörður's **tourist information office** (T438 1881, Wwww.grundarfjordur .is), inside the heritage centre, also has **internet** access and a small **café**. **Accommodation** can be found at the smart *Hótel Framnes*, Nesvegur 8 (T438 6893, Wwww .hotelframnes.is; ❸), or at the **youth hostel** at Hlíðarvegur 15 (mid-May to mid-Sept; T562 6533, Wwww.hostel.is; 2100kr; ❶), complete with cosy rooms and two kitchens. The **campsite** (T438 6813) is 1km east of the village at the farm located by the Kverná river. For **eating and drinking** look no further than ⅄ *Krákan*, Sæból 13 (signed from the main road); a restaurant, bar and lounge all rolled into one, this place is stylish to a T and is one of the best provincial restaurants Iceland has to offer. Not only is the food top-notch, but the prices are truly amazing: deep fried monkfish (2000kr), lamb fillet (2300kr), succulent burgers from 1400kr and a half litre of beer for a jaw-dropping 450kr. There are plans to open a bakery, too, which will serve breakfast from 7am. The other option, *Kaffi 59*, Grundargata 59, is the place to come for pizzas, burgers and light snacks. If you want to buy **alcohol**, you'll have to time things carefully since the **vínbúð** at Hrannarstígur 3 has ludicrously short opening hours (Mon–Thurs 5–6pm, Fri 4–6pm). The local **swimming pool** with an outdoor pool, two hot pots and sauna is located at the southern end of Borgarbraut.

Ólafsvík

ÓLAFSVÍK is not only the most productive fishing town on Snæfellsnes, it is Iceland's oldest established trading town, granted its charter in 1687. Squeezed between the sea and the towering Enni peak (415m), it's a quiet working fishing village whose population goes about its daily business seemingly unmoved by the groups of travellers who turn up here in search of **Snæfellsjökull**, the nearby glacier (see box, p.180). Indeed, Ólafsvík is the starting point for the summer-only **buses around the glacier**.

Other than the ice cap, Ólafsvík's main sight is the **Gamla Pakkhúsið** on Ólafsbraut, a solid-looking timber warehouse built in 1844 by the town's leading trading firm which, naturally, dealt in fish. Today it houses a **folk museum** (June – Aug daily 11am–5pm; 300kr), which has a few good black and white photographs of the town and the obligatory exhibitions about fishing. The **church** on Kirkjutún is worth a quick look for its three-legged detached bell tower and its sharply pointed spire.

Practicalities

Buses from Ólafsvík run year-round westwards along the coast to Hellissandur; eastwards via Vatnaheið (for Stykkishólmur) to Borgarnes and Reykjavík; and, in summer only, daily around the tip of the Snæfellsnes peninsula via Arnarstapi, Hellnar, Dritvík and Hellissandur.

The **tourist office** (June–Aug Mon–Fri 8am–6pm, Sat & Sun 10am–5pm; T433 9930, Wwww.snb.is/pakkhus) is just behind the Gamla Pakkhúsið at Kirkjutún 2. There's little choice when it comes to **accommodation**: *Hótel Ólafsvík*, at Ólafsbraut 20 (T436 1650, Wwww.hringhotels.is; ❺), has small, rather overpriced rooms with private bathroom; or simpler, unadorned rooms sharing facilities, in the building across the road (❷). The **campsite** (T433 9930) with showers and hot and cold running water is marked by an old fishing boat on the main road beside the Hvalsá river, 1km east of the town centre.

Sadly, a meal in Ólafsvík is not going to be the culinary highlight of any trip to Iceland. The most tasteful place for something filling is the **restaurant** inside *Hótel*

Snæfellsjökull

Enter the Snæfellsjökull crater, which is kissed by Scatari's shadow before the first of July, adventurous traveller, and thou wilt descend to the centre of the Earth.

Journey to the Centre of the Earth, Jules Verne

Made world famous in the nineteenth century by Jules Verne's *Journey to the Centre of the Earth*, **Snæfellsjökull** stands guard at the very tip of the peninsula to which it gave its name (**Snæfell** means "Snow Mountain"; Snæfellsnes means "Snow Mountain Peninsula"). It is from here that Verne's hero, the German geologist Professor Lidenbrock of Hamburg, descends into a crater in the dormant volcano under the glacier and embarks on a fantastic subterranean journey accompanied by his nephew and Icelandic guide with the very un-Icelandic name of Hans. The professor has managed to decipher a document written in runic script that leads him to believe that this is the way to the centre of the earth; rather inexplicably he finally emerges on the volcanic Mediterranean island of Strómboli. This remote part of Iceland has long been associated with supernatural forces and mystery, and stories like this only strengthen this belief – at one time the glacier even became a point of pilgrimage for New Age travellers, though they're not much in evidence today. The 1446-metre-high, three-peaked glacier sits on a dormant volcano marked by a large crater, one kilometre in diameter, with cliff walls 200m high; three eruptions have occurred under the glacier in the past ten thousand years, the last around 250 AD.

Experienced hikers have a choice of **ascents**, though you'll probably need ice axes and crampons, and should also first talk to the national park office about the condition of routes and the likely **weather**. There are two **trailheads**: either east off the four-wheel-drive-only Route F570, which clips Snæfell's eastern flank as it runs for 18km between Ólafsvík and Arnarstapi; or at the ice cap's northwestern corner, via a track running east of Neshraun. **Hiking trails** cross between these two starting points via the glacier's apex, Jökulþúfur (1446m), which sits atop three crags on the crater rim – allow at least four hours to make the crossing, not counting the time it takes to reach the trailheads themselves.

Ólafsvík, where the dish of the day costs around 1500kr at lunchtime, and in the evening they serve up catfish in ginger (2850kr) and fillet of lamb in red wine (3600kr). Across the road, at Ólafsbraut 19, things are altogether more basic and drab: *Hobbitinn* is a grill restaurant-cum-video store serving burgers and expensive pizzas (2380kr), while the bakery next door (Mon–Fri 7.30am–5pm) has a few sandwiches and cakes. The **supermarket** is just up from the harbour (Mon–Thurs 9am–6pm, Fri 9am–8pm, Sat & Sun 1–5pm); the **vínbúð** is at Mýrarholt 12 (Mon–Fri 2–6pm); and the indoor **swimming pool** at Ennisbraut 9.

Rif and Hellissandur

From Ólafsvík, Route 574 continues west past a dramatic beach of black volcanic sand, Harðikambur, on its way towards the minuscule fishing hamlet of **Rif**, which, with a population of just 150 souls, is really nothing more than a well-protected harbour and a few fish-processing plants, and its marginally bigger neighbour **HELLISSANDUR**, 2km further on. Known locally as just Sandur, this is the westernmost settlement on Snæfellsnes and home to most of the fishermen from nearby Rif; it's also the terminus for **buses** from Reykjavík and the summer service around the peninsula's tip from Ólafsvík (see p.179). There's very little to do in Hellissandur other than to pay a quick visit to the two old **fishermen's cottages**, complete with turf roofs, which make up the **Sjómannagarður** (Maritime Museum; June–Aug daily except Wed, 9am–noon & 1–6pm; 500kr) beside the main road, Útnesvegur. In the larger of the two buildings is the oldest rowing boat in Iceland, dating from 1826. Otherwise, Hellissandur makes a good base from which to tackle the various **hikes** around western Snæfellsnes (see box below).

Practicalities

Hellissandur is a thinly spread place with most facilities – **bank**, **post office**, **swimming pool** and **fuel station** – grouped along the main road **Klettsbúð**. The post office also doubles as a modest **information office**.

For **accommodation**, there's the upmarket *Hótel Hellissandur* at Klettsbúð 9 (☎430 8600, ⓦ www.hotelhellissandur.is; ❷), which also has a **restaurant** (evenings only), or the **campsite** (late May to Sept; ☎436 1543), beautifully set by an open meadow on the eastern edge of the village. **Buses** from Hellissandur run daily back along Snæfellsnes' north coast and then down via Vatnaheið to Borgarnes and Reykjavík. In summer, buses also arrive in Hellissandur from

---

Hiking around western Snæfellsnes

Hellissandur makes a good base for exploring the foot of the Snæfellsjökull and the surrounding **lavafields**. A recommended day hike of around 20km leads from the village to Eysteinsdalur valley; take the unmarked secondary road between the campsite and the maritime museum that leads towards the glacier. After around 1km the road becomes a hiking path which strikes out across the **Prestahraun** lavafield, joining up after 4km with the unnumbered road that runs up through the valley. Here, on the south side of the road, a signed path leads up to the hill, **Rauðhóll**, to a red scoria crater. An impressive rift in the lava can also been seen to the east of the hill. Continue another 1km along the road towards the glacier and you'll come to a signposted path to the south of the road, which leads to the prominent basalt spur, **Klukka**, and a beautiful waterfall, **Klukkufoss**, where the Móðulækur river flows through a narrow canyon lined with basalt columns. Back on the main road and another 1km towards the glacier, a path to the north of the road leads to the **Blágil** ravine, where the Ljósulækir glacial river thunders through the narrow rugged gorge. To return to Hellissandur, retrace your steps along the main road, beyond the turn for the waterfall, to the hiking path that heads out to the north across the **Væjuhraun** lavafield for Rif. From here, simply head west along the coastal road to Hellissandur. Maps of these routes should be available from the tourist office in Ólafsvík (see p.179) and the hotel in Hellissandur (see opposite).

Another recommended day hike (18km) leads first to the sandy bay of **Skarðsvík**, walled in by cliffs and crags on its northern and western edges. The lava above the cliffs is overgrown with moss and can be a good place to see rare plants. Excellent **fishing** can be had in the bay's protected waters and it's therefore a favourite spot for local boats. To get here, follow Route 574 west out of Hellissandur to its junction with the unnumbered road signed for Skarðsvík; it's at this point that the main road swings inland, heading for the glacier and the turn for Eysteinsdalur valley. Just 2km west of Skarðsvík the road terminates at the peninsula's westernmost point, **Öndverðarnes**, a dramatic and weatherbeaten spot marked only by a lonely lighthouse and a stone well which legend has it is linked to three springs: one of fresh water, one of sea water and one of wine. The promontory is a favourite destination for basking **seals**, which favour the pebbly beach here. South of the cape the **Svörtuloft** cliffs are worth a visit; swarming with **sea birds** in summer, the cliffs provided a major source of eggs and birds for the tables of local villagers until the 1950s, when living standards began to rise. The free-standing crag in the sea here, **Skálasnagi**, was once connected to the mainland by a natural stone bridge until it fell victim to the pounding of Atlantic breakers in 1973. From the cliffs, a path heads east, inland through the **Neshraun** lavafield to an area of small hillocks known as **Neshólar** before emerging at Skarðsvík.

Arnastapi, having come clockwise around the end of the peninsula – but note that this service doesn't operate in the opposite direction.

Dritvík, Djúpalónssandur and Lóndrangar

As you head west from Hellissandur, the horizon is dominated by the huge mast that transmits the booming 189kHz long-wave signal for Icelandic national radio, anchored down by wire cables against the brute force of Atlantic storms. Beyond this last sign of civilization the landscape becomes increasingly desolate and the road surface more and more potholed – there's nothing but wilderness between here and **Dritvík** bay, 24km southwest of Hellissandur, first along Route 574 then down the 572 signed for Dritvík and Djúpalónssandur. Once home to sixty fishing boats and one of the most prolific fishing villages on the peninsula, today the bay is uninhabited, and centuries of fishing tradition would have been completely lost if it were not for the continuing presence of four mighty lifting **stones** at nearby **Djúpalónssandur beach**, a short stroll south from the bay, all with individual names: the largest, *fullsterkur* (full strength) weighs in at 155kg, next comes *hálfsterkur* (half strength) at 140kg, then *hálfdrættingur* (weakling) 49kg and finally *amlóði* (useless) weighing just 23kg. Any fisherman worth his salt had to be able to lift at least the latter two onto a ledge of rock at hip height to prove his strength. The smallest stone is now broken – perhaps after one too many attempts by weakling tourists.

The lofty rock pillars, **Lóndrangar**, are just 5km southeast of the Djúpalón lagoon and easily reached from Route 574 on the unnumbered road signed "Malarrif". The taller of the two is 75m high and known locally as the "Christian pillar", with its smaller neighbour called the "heathen pillar" although nobody seems to know why; both are remnants of a basalt cinder cone.

Hellnar

Just like its western neighbour of Dritvík, the tiny settlement of **HELLNAR** was once one of the peninsula's most prosperous fishing communities. However, the village is better known as the birthplace of one of medieval Iceland's greatest explorers and travellers, **Guðríður Þorbjarnardóttir**, the wife of Þorfinnur Karlsefni. Together they attempted to settle in Viking Vínland in 1004, and, indeed, Gúðríður gave birth to the first white child to be born in America, Snorri Þorfinnsson. She eventually settled at Glaumbær, near Sauðárkrókur, where a statue in her memory stands in the churchyard (see p.225). Today, though, Hellnar consists of nothing more than a couple of farm buildings, a hotel and the odd holiday cottage either side of a steep, dead-end road that winds its way down to a picturesque hoof-shaped **harbour** and a tiny pebbly **beach** where the occasional fishing boat is moored. To the left of the harbour, the sea cave, **Baðstofa**, is known for its rich birdlife as well as its unusual light shades and hues caused by the swell of the sea.

Practicalities

If you're planning an ascent of Snæfellsjökull, visit the **national park office** here (late May to mid-Sept daily 10am–6pm; ☎436 6888, ⓦwww.snaefellsjokull.is), known as the *Gestastofa*, which contains photographs and information boards about the Snæfellsnes glacier. The office also runs free trips (mid-June to mid-Aug; ask at the office for departure details) to a local foxhole where there's a good chance of spotting **arctic foxes**. **Accommodation** includes the delightful and environmentally friendly ⚑ *Hótel Hellnar* (mid-May to mid-Sept; ☎435 6820, ⓦwww .hellnar.is; ➍), whose rooms enjoy stunning views out over the sea or of the Snæfellsnes mountains; there's a **restaurant**, too, serving locally-caught catfish (2990kr), chicken breast (3550kr) and lentil burritos (2790kr). Guesthouse-style lodgings can be found across the road at *Gíslabær* (☎435 6886, ✉gisting@simnet .is; sleeping bag 2500kr, ❶). The old salting house, dating from 1937, still stands on the harbourside, its walls now housing a charming **café**, the ⅍ *Fjöruhúsið* (late May to late Sept daily 10am–10pm), which sells home-made cakes and great espresso, as well as some excellent fish soup (1690kr) of an evening when the arty interior lighting is provided by a dozen light bulbs suspended on long wire flexes. If the weather's poor, sit inside and savour the uninterrupted views of the Atlantic through the café's small square windows; in fine weather you can sit on the wooden terrace outside, which overlooks the harbour and the boulder-strewn bay.

Arnarstapi and around

Just east of Hellnar along the main road – or a short walk along a clifftop path – the village of **ARNARSTAPI** sits at the foot of Stapafell (526m). It comprises little more than a few holiday cottages and a **harbour**, reached by following the road through the village down to the sea – but beware of the large number of arctic tern that gather here during summer and take pleasure in divebombing unsuspecting intruders. On entering the village, look out too for the large stone **monument** to the pagan-age figure Barður Snæfellsás who, according to local legend, still lives in Snæfellsjökull and protects the area from evil.

The village is a starting point for hikes and jeep drives up to Snæfellsjökull via Route F570 (see box, p.180), but is also known for its **snowmobiling** excursions across the glacier. *Snjófell* (see practicalities below) organizes one-hour trips (10,500kr per person for two sharing one snowmobile, 12,500kr for your own machine); speeding along the ice top is an exhilarating experience, and the views of the glacier and the coastline are breathtaking when the weather is good – but don't be tempted to head onto the ice if it's raining because you'll see nothing. If speed isn't your thing, a slower **snowcat**, a sort of open-top truck on caterpillar tracks, also carries groups of twenty or so across the ice (6500kr).

Practicalities

Buses to Arnarstapi run daily in summer from Ólafsvík, on their way around the tip to Hellissandur. Note that there are **no buses** east from here along the peninsula's south coast.

What little life there is in the village is centred on the red-walled, turf-roofed cottage, *Snjófell* (☎435 6783, ⓦwww.snjofell.is; sleeping bag 3240kr, ❷), which provides **beds** and **camping** space, as well as doubling as the **tourist information office**. Alternative accommodation is available in a well-appointed log cabin opposite (☎435 6820, ✉eddahilmars@vortex.is; 12,000kr per night, discounts for longer stays), which sleeps six and comes complete with its own private jacuzzi. The decent **restaurant** inside the *Snjófell* complex is the only place to eat.

Búðir and Lýsuhóll

Nineteen kilometres east of Arnarstapi, and served by all buses from Reykjavík, **BÚÐIR** is a romantic, windswept location, a former fishing village at the head of the sweeping expanse of white sand that backs the bay here, Búðavík. The settlement, like so many others in this part of the country, was abandoned in the early nineteenth century and today consists of nothing more than a hotel and a church, both situated just a stone's throw from the ocean. Surrounded by the **Búðahraun lavafield**, rumoured to be home to countless elves, and enjoying unsurpassed views out over the Atlantic, the tiny **church**, which dates from 1703, pitch-black and with three white-framed windows, cuts an evocative image when viewed from the adjoining graveyard with the majestic Snæfellsnes mountain range as a backdrop.

Look out too for the unusual wall, made of lava and topped with turf, that surrounds the churchyard.

The wonderful ℀ *Hótel Búðir* (☎435 6700, ⓦwww.budir.is; ❺) was once a favourite haunt of Iceland's Nobel-prize winning author, Halldór Laxness. The original building, built in 1836, was totally destroyed by fire in 2001, but the rebuilding was entirely sympathetic and added a modern touch to the nostalgic wooden decor. Five kilometres east of Búðir and reached on Route 54, the dot on the map that is the farm of **LÝSUHÓLL** is one of the few places on the peninsula with its own source of geothermal mineral water. The spring provides natural algae-rich water for the outdoor **swimming pool** and hot pot (mid-June to late August daily 2–9pm) and offers fantastic views of the surrounding mountains. For a place to stay there are **cabins** (☎435 6716, ⓦwww.lysuholl.is; 10,500kr per night) and a **campsite**, both on the same site as the swimming pool. The farmhouse here has a small **restaurant** which is good for snacks such as soup and home-made bread. It's also possible to go **horseriding** from the farm; reckon on 5000kr for a couple of hours.

East along Route 54 to Borgarnes

From Lýsuhóll, **Route 54** continues east, past several great places to kick back for a couple of days of beachcombing or gentle hiking. Five kilometres from Lýsuhóll, the **guesthouse** *Langaholt* (☎435 6789, ⓦwww.langaholt.is; ❸) also has a restaurant, campsite and sea views over Faxaflói bay; while there's more of the same a few kilometres further on at *Hof* (☎435 6802 or 846 3897, ⓦwww.gistihof.is; ❷).

Beyond here, the major landmark is the powerful Straumfjarðará river flowing down from Seljafell before reaching the lonely Löngufjörur bay; once across it, you pass **Vegamót**, marking where Route 56 heads up over the peninsula to the north coast, and Route 54 heads out of the region towards Borgarnes and Reykjavík.

Travel details

Buses

The bus details given below apply in summer (approximately June to August); for winter times, visit ⓦwww.bsi.is.

Akranes to: Reykjavík (every 2hr; 50min).
Arnarstapi to: Dritvík (1hr 5min); Hellissandur (1 daily; 3hr); Hellnar (1 daily; 15min).
Bifröst to: Akureyri (2 daily; 4hr 10min); Borgarnes (3 daily; 30min); Búðardalur (5 weekly; 1hr 10min); Reykjavík (3 daily; 1hr 40min).
Borgarnes to: Bifröst (3 daily; 30min); Búðardalur (5 weekly; 1hr 35min); Grundarfjörður (2 daily; 1hr 25min); Hellissandur (2 daily; 2hr); Ólafsvík (2 daily; 1hr 50min); Reykholt (2 weekly; 50min); Reykjavík (5 daily; 1hr); Vatnaheið (for Stykkishólmur) (2 daily; 1hr 10min).
Búðardalur to: Bifröst (5 weekly; 1hr 10min); Borgarnes (5 weekly; 1hr 35min); Reykjavík (5 weekly; 2hr 45min).
Grundarfjörður to: Borgarnes (2 daily; 1hr 25min); Hellissandur (2 daily; 35min); Ólafsvík (2 daily; 25min); Reykjavík (2 daily; 2hr 40min); Vatnaheið (for Stykkishólmur) (2 daily; 30min).

Hellissandur to: Borgarnes (2 daily; 2hr); Grundarfjörður (2 daily; 35min); Ólafsvík (2 daily; 10min); Reykjavík (2 daily; 3hr 15min); Vatnaheið (for Stykkishólmur) (2 daily; 50min).
Hellnar to: Dritvík (1 daily; 20min); Hellissandur (1 daily; 2hr 15min).
Ólafsvík to: Arnarstapi (1 daily; 45min); Borgarnes (2 daily; 1hr 50min); Dritvík (1 daily; 2hr 50min); Hellissandur (2 daily; 10min); Hellnar (1 daily; 2hr); Reykjavík (2 daily; 3hr); Vatnaheið (for Stykkishólmur) (2 daily; 40min).
Reykholt to: Borgarnes (2 weekly; 50min); Reykjavík (2 weekly; 2hr).
Stykkishólmur to: Vatnaheið (for connecting buses) (2 daily; 15min).

Ferries

From mid-June to mid-August each ferry runs twice daily; there is one service daily during the rest of the year.
Flatey to: Brjánslækur (1hr 15min); Stykkishólmur (1hr 45min).
Stykkishólmur to: Brjánslækur (3hr); Flatey (1hr 45min).

The West Fjords

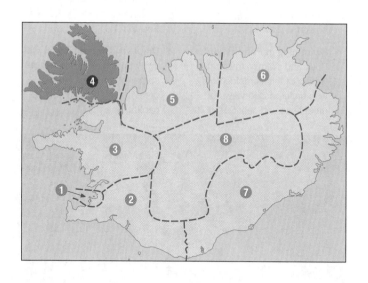

CHAPTER 4 # Highlights

✴ **Hiking in Hornstrandir**
Experience nature in the raw
in this remote and unspoilt
national park of lush valleys
and rocky plateaux on the
very edge of Europe.
See p.197

✴ **Dynjandi, Arnarfjörður**
Meaning "The Thundering
One", this mighty triangular-
shaped waterfall is West
Fjords nature at its most
powerful. See p.203

✴ **Swimming in Patreksfjörður**
Soak and swim in the heated
waters of this fjordside pool
with unsurpassed views of
mountains and sea. See p.206

✴ **Breiðavík beach,
southwestern peninsula** The
white sands and aquamarine
water of this idyllic bay make
the perfect place to chill
out and work on your tan –
weather permitting. See p.207

✴ **Puffin spotting, Látrabjarg**
Seek out Iceland's most
endearing bird along this
vertiginous cliff face, the
westernmost point in Europe.
See p.207

✴ **Djúpavík, Strandir coast** Get
away from it all in this remote
corner of the West Fjords,
once the region's herring
capital. See p.213

▲ Dynjandi waterfalls

The West Fjords

ttached to the mainland by a narrow isthmus of land barely 10km wide, the **West Fjords** are one of the most breathtakingly beautiful and least-visited corners of Iceland – only three percent of all foreign tourists make it out here. This peninsula of 8600 square kilometres, stretching out into the icy waters of the Denmark Strait, with its dramatic fjords cutting deep into its heart, is the result of intense glaciation. Everything here is extreme – from the table mountains that dominate the landscape, plunging precipitously into the Atlantic, to the ferocious storms that have gnawed the coastline into countless craggy inlets. Life up here, on the edge of the Arctic Circle, is tough – even in summer, temperatures seldom rise above 10°C, and drifting pack ice is never far from the north coast.

Since flat land is at a premium in this rugged part of the country, towns and villages have grown up on the narrow strip of lowland that separates the mountains from the fjords. Geologically all but cut off from the outside world, the people of the West Fjords have historically turned to the sea for their livelihood, and today the majority of the 7400 people who still live here are financially dependent on **fishing** and its related industries. However, the traditional way of life is changing, and the effects of rural depopulation are being felt in every village as outlying farms are abandoned and dozens of young people choose the bright lights of Reykjavík over a precarious and uncertain future on the very edge of Europe.

The unforgiving geography of the West Fjords makes travel here difficult and convoluted. Many roads are surfaced with gravel, and they're always potholed and often circuitous. **Route 61**, for example, wiggles its way exasperatingly round no fewer than seven deeply indented fjords en route to the regional capital, **Ísafjörður**. Benefiting from a spectacular setting on a narrow spit of land jutting out into **Ísafjarðardjúp**, the town makes an excellent base from which to explore this 75-kilometre-long arm of the Denmark Strait at the heart of the West Fjords, plus **Drangajökull**, the only glacier in the region, and the outstanding natural beauty of the uninhabited **Hornstrandir** peninsula, which offers some of the wildest and most rewarding hiking in Iceland. From Ísafjörður, Route 60 weaves its way over mountain tops, round several fjords and past a handful of tiny fishing villages on its way to the ferry port of **Brjánslækur**, from where a ferry leaves the West Fjords for Flatey and Snæfellsnes. A brooding, lonely peninsula reaches out into the Atlantic from this point, terminating at **Látrabjarg**, Europe's most westerly point, and one of the world's greatest bird cliffs, with large numbers of puffins, razorbills and other sea birds, and **Breiðavík**, one of Iceland's most stunning beaches with mile upon mile of deserted golden sand. Nearby **Patreksfjörður**, the second town of the West Fjords, is the only place in the region with a population big enough for life to go on independently of Ísafjörður. Meanwhile,

THE WEST FJORDS

Vatnsnes

► *Hvammstangi*

Húnaflói

► *Brú*

Bjarnarfjörður

Drangsnes
Grímsey

► *Búðardalur*

Steingrímsfjörður

Kollafjörður

► *Króksfjarðarnes*

069

Krossneslaug Swimming Pool

Gjögur

Norðurfjörður
Árnes *Naustvík*
Reykjafjörður
Veiðileysa

643

Drangavík

Eyvindarfjörður

Ófeigsfjörður

Djúpavík

645

Hólmavík

61

Trékyllisvík

19

909

Laugarhóll

Vatnsfjörður

60

Bjarkalundur
Þorskafjörður

Reykhólar

607

Gilsfjörður

Open Air Geothermal Pool
Bjarnarfjörður

Reykjanes

Þaralátursfjörður

Hrafnsfjörður

Drangajökull

Kaldalón glacial lagoon

Leirufjörður

Jökulbunga summit (925m)

Snæfjallaströnd

Langadalsströnd

635

Steingrímsfjarðarheiði Plateau

Þorskafjarðarheiði Plateau

809

Langidalur

Skálanes

Kollafjörður

Kaldbaksfjörður

60

Hornbjarg

Hornvík

Hælavík
Hlöðuvík

Hornstrandir

Reykjafjörður

Furufjörður

Aðalvík
Straumnesfjall

Fljótavík

Hesteyri

Jökulfirðir
Grunnavík

Veiðileysufjörður

Hrafnsfjörður

Lónafjörður

Ísafjarðardjúp

Aðey
Unaðsdalur

Vigur

Súðavík

Kaldalón

Mjóifjörður

Ísafjörður

Skötufjörður

Hestfjörður

Seyðisfjörður

633

Álftafjörður

Reykjanes

Mjóifjörður

Skötufjörður

19

Bolungarvík

630

Skálavík

Ísafjörður
Þverfjall

85

Korpudalur

Flateyri
Önundarfjörður

Skutulsfjörður

Glámar

Dynjandi

Vatnsdalsvatn

Vatnsfjörður

Brjánslækur

Suðureyri

Súgandafjörður

624

Dýrafjörður

Þingeyri

622

Kaldbakur

Dýrafjörður

Hrafnseyri

Dynjandisvogur

Borgarfjörður

09

Flókalundur

Kross

Vatnsfjörður

63

Tungumúli

62

Barðaströnd

Breiðafjörður

Denmark Strait

Arnarfjörður

Fossfjörður

Bíldudalur

619

Tálknafjörður

Tálknafjörður

617

Patreksfjörður
Patreksfjörður

612

Hnjótur

614

Bæjarvaðall

Raudisandur

Keflavík

Breiðavík

613

Bird Cliffs

Breiðavík
Hvallátur

Látravík

Látrabjarg
Bjargtangar Point

► *Flatey & Stykkishólmur*

0   25 km

Getting to the West Fjords by public transport

Between June and August, **buses** run three times per week from the Ringroad village of Brú along **Route 61** via Hólmavík to Ísafjörður. From Ísafjörður, there are year-round local buses several times daily to Bolungarvík, Flateyri and Suðureyri. Although there is a year-round bus connection from Reykjavík to Reykhólar via Bjarkalundur, there are no buses into the rest of the region from here.

The most interesting option for reaching the West Fjords, however, is to catch the **ferry from Stykkishólmur** on the Snæfellsnes peninsula (see p.172). This lands you just at **Brjánslækur**, from where buses leave three times a week (June–Aug) for Látrabjarg via Patreksfjörður, and also to Ísafjörður via Flókalundur. The West Fjords' **airports** are at Bíldudalur, Gjögur and Ísafjörður – all connected to Reykjavík; see Travel Details for frequencies.

④

on the other side of the West Fjords, the eastern Strandir coast, which stretches north from the busy fishing village of **Hólmavík**, is hard to beat for splendid isolation, its few villages hardly visited by tourists, and with some of the most dramatic, forbidding landscapes this corner of the country has to offer, particularly around the former herring port of **Djúpavík**.

Ísafjörður

With a population of around 3000, **ÍSAFJÖRÐUR** is far and away the largest settlement in the West Fjords and is where most travellers choose to base themselves when exploring the region, not least because this is the only place from which to reach the Hornstrandir peninsula by boat, a major goal for many visitors. All administration for the area is centred here, too, and there's also a significant **fishing industry**. It's hard to imagine a much more dramatic location; built on the L-shaped sandspit, **Eyri**, which stretches out into the narrow waters of **Skutuls-fjörður** fjord and provides exceptionally good shelter for ocean-going fishing vessels, the town is surrounded by towering mountains on three sides and by the open waters of **Ísafjarðardjúp** on the fourth. During the long winter months, locals are forced to battle against the elements to keep open the tiny airport, which very often provides the only point of contact between the entire region and the rest of the country. Should you arrive in Ísafjörður by plane, however, you'll be treated to an unforgettable experience as you bank steeply around the fjord, then skim past the sheer mountainside of Kirkjubólshlíð before dropping onto the landing strip. In fact, during the darkest months of the year (Dec & Jan), the sheer height of the mountains either side of the fjord prevents the low winter sun from shining directly onto the town for a number of weeks, and the sun's reappearance over the mountain tops at the end of January is celebrated with **sólarkaffi**, "sun coffee" (in fact just normal coffee) and pancakes on January 25.

According to the *Landnámabók*, a Viking by the name of **Helgi Hrolfsson** was the first person to settle in Skutulsfjörður and build his farm here during the ninth century. However, although the sandspit was inhabited from the time of the Settlement, it took several centuries for Eyri at Skutulsfjörður, as Ísafjörður was then called, to emerge as one of the country's main commercial centres, an enviable status due to the establishment of a trading post on the spit by foreign merchants during the late sixteenth century. It was also around this time that the town's most notorious resident, **Jón Magnússon**, a fundamentalist priest, ordered two men on a neighbouring farm to be burned at the stake for sorcery, which was reputed to be widespread in the West Fjords at the time. Finally, in 1786, with the winding-up of the Danish trade monopoly, the town was granted municipal status and became one of Iceland's six official trading posts. Just over a hundred years later, Eyri finally received city status and celebrated by changing its name to the present Ísafjörður, meaning Ice Fjord.

Today Ísafjörður is a quiet and likeable place where you'd be wise to make the most of the shops and restaurants on offer before venturing out into the wilds beyond such as the Hornstrandir peninsula or one of the much smaller West Fjords villages. There's very little of note, though, in the town – Ísafjörður's pleasures are more to be found in strolling through its streets or watching the fishermen at work in the harbour rather than in tourist sights. The **West Fjords Heritage Museum**, one of the very few museums in the region, is worth visiting for an insight into the extreme conditions that past generations have lived under here. That it's located in one of the country's oldest timber buildings, dating from the harsh days of the trade monopoly with Denmark, is unusual in itself, when you consider that the climate here is so severe that anything made out of wood doesn't normally last long at all.

Arrival and information

Long distance buses terminate outside the **tourist information office** at Aðalstræti 7 (June–Aug Mon–Fri 8.15am–6pm, Sat & Sun 11am–4pm; Sept–May Mon–Fri 8am–4pm; ☎456 5121 or 450 8060, ⓦwww.westfjords.is). The **airport**, connected by daily flights to Reykjavík, is 7km out of town on a narrow stretch of land on the eastern edge of the fjord; a bus into Ísafjörður meets all flights, and taxis (1000kr) are also available. **Hornstrandir ferries** (see p.198) use Sundahöfn harbour, at the eastern end of Mjósund, which leads down to the harbour from the tourist office; it's here that the twenty-odd cruiseships, which call in here every summer, tie up.

Most of Ísafjörður's shops and services are within a block or two of *Hótel Ísafjörður*, including **banks** and a **bookshop**, which is handy for hiking maps and English-language books on the West Fjords. Just up the road is the town's main **shopping centre**, with a supermarket (Mon–Fri 9am–9pm, Sat 10am–9pm, Sun noon–9pm), post office and ATM. **Internet** terminals can be found at the library (Mon–Fri 1–7pm, Sat 1–4pm), which is beside the church (see p.192). The **cinema**, at Norðurvegur 1, generally shows several English-language films a week, with Icelandic subtitles. The indoor **swimming pool** (June–Aug Mon–Fri 10am–9pm, Sat & Sun 11am–4pm; rest of the year limited opening), at Austurvegur 9, also has a small **sauna** for men on Monday, Wednesday, Friday and Saturday and for women on Tuesday, Thursday and Sunday. **Tours** around the West Fjords, and bookings for Hornstrandir ferries, can be organized by Vesturferðir (☎456 5111, ⓦwww.vesturferdir.is) at the tourist office.

Accommodation

Given that Ísafjörður sees so few tourists, you shouldn't have any difficulty in finding a bed for the night with a couple of hotels and guesthouses to choose between.

Edda Ísafjörður Skutulsfjarðarbraut ☎444 4960, ⓦwww.hoteledda.is. Open mid-June to mid-Aug, the forty simple rooms in this boarding school (*Menntaskólinn*) in the western part of town have both private and shared facilities. There's sleeping-bag accommodation, too, from 1700kr; breakfast costs 1050kr extra. ❷

Gamla Gistihúsið Mánagata 1 & 5 ☎456 4146, ⓦwww.gistihus.is. Cosy twin-bedded rooms with shared facilities in a former hospital building dating from 1896 are at no. 5, while just down the road at no. 1, there's sleeping-bag accommodation from 2600kr per person, with breakfast at 1000kr. ❷

Gistikofinn Silfurgötu Silfurgata 12 ☏862 5669, ⓦwww.massi.is. Run by the engaging Icelandic–Finnish couple Árni and Mimmo, this superbly appointed studio apartment comes with fully fitted kitchen, high-speed internet and underfloor heating, making a real home from home for longer stays. ❷

Ísafjörður Silfurtorg 2 ☏456 4111, ⓦwww .hotelisafjordur.is. The only hotel in town that's open year-round, located on the town's main square. Don't be put off by the grey concrete exterior; inside the doubles are cosy and well insulated against the biting wind, and breakfast is included. ❸

Ísafjörður Camping Ground Skutulsfjarðarbraut ☏456 4485. Located behind the *Edda Ísafjörður*, the town's campsite is only open from mid-June to mid-Aug.

Litla Gistihúsið Sundstræti 43 ☏474 1455, ⓔreginasc@simnet.is. The four rooms here may be simple, unadorned and share facilities but they are the cheapest in town. There's also a kitchen for guests' use. ❶

The Town

Although there are no specific sights in Ísafjörður, it's a pleasant enough place to stroll round for a couple of hours. It's most logical to start your wanderings in what passes as the town's main square, **Silfurtorg**, in reality little more than the location of the block-like *Hótel Ísafjörður*, ringed by a couple of concrete flowerbeds where the two roads Hafnarstræti and Aðalstræti meet.

Things liven up marginally on Suðurgata as it heads westwards towards the town's only tourist sight: **Neðstikaupstaður**, comprising four of Iceland's oldest buildings, all timber structures dating from the late eighteenth century, located on Suðurtangi. One, the carefully restored **Turnhús**, with its unusual roof tower, was constructed in Denmark before being moved to Iceland in 1784, where it was used as a warehouse and fish-salting house. As the tallest structure in Ísafjörður, it also served as a lookout from where returning fishing boats were spotted – livelihoods depended on being first to the dockside when the boats came in, it being paramount that the fish were processed as quickly as possible. The Turnhús now houses the **West Fjords Heritage Museum** (June Mon–Fri 10am–5pm, Sat & Sun 1–5pm, July & Aug daily 10am–5pm; 500kr; Ⓦ www.nedsti.is). On the ground floor, fishing paraphernalia and old black and white photographs give a good idea of what life was like during the early twentieth century; look out for those depicting the thousands of fish that would be laid out to dry and salted in the open air; in later years, ice cut from the fjord was used to preserve them instead. One photo, from the winter of 1918, was taken when plummeting temperatures and ferocious storms ushered in one of the severest winters for decades, when sheets of ice crept up the fjord, choking up the harbour and freezing the entire fishing fleet – bar one boat – into the ice. Upstairs, there's a rather dreary collection of harmonicas, a reconstructed radio room and a couple of model boats.

Of the remaining buildings on the museum site, the **Krambuð**, immediately to the right of the museum, is the oldest dating from 1757. Used as a storehouse until the early 1900s, it was then converted into a private residence. The **Faktorshús** from 1765, to the left of the museum, was once home to the site's trading manager though now houses, somewhat curiously, the chief librarian at Ísafjörður library. **Tjöruhús**, the fourth building, dates from 1781 and was once used as a warehouse for the store. Today an agreeable café-cum-restaurant (daily June–Aug noon–10pm) with delicious waffles and coffee occupies the heavy wooden interior and makes a splendid place to ponder Ísafjörður's past. Only Tjöruhús and the Turnhús are open to the public.

From the museum, retrace your steps north along Suðurgata turning right into Njarðarsund and then left into Sindragata, to reach the oldest part of town, just north of the harbour. Here, the brightly painted timber houses on **Tangagata** (a continuation of Sindragata) and **Silfurgata**, which crosses it, are particularly beautiful with their mountain backdrop. Back in Silfurtorg, Hafnarstræti leads north to Ísafjörður's highly unusual **church**, at the junction with Sólgata, resembling a folding concertina. Built to replace the former timber church that burned down in 1987, this architectural monster of peach-coloured pebbledash comprises four column-like wedges that seemingly collapse into one another beneath a brilliant metal roof. It was the source of much local controversy ever since its inception, and to add insult to injury, during its construction thirty graves were unceremoniously cemented over to make way for it; a plaque bearing the names of those buried there now stands beside the statue of Christ inside the unadorned interior. Beside the church, in the tussocky field in front of the library, stands a **sculpture** of two burly Ísafjörður fishermen hauling in a net full of cod, a reminder of the town's dependence on the sea; the poignant inscription reads simply, "in honour of those who disappeared, for luck for those who still put out to sea".

Opposite, the diminutive well-tended **town park**, sandwiched between the boarding school and Seljalandsvegur, is remarkable for the arching form of the white-painted whale bone marking the entrance. Dedicated to two local characters, Jón Jónsson and Karlinna Jóhannesdóttir, who painstakingly tended and encouraged all greenery here for several decades, the park is a pleasant place to sit and admire the soaring fjordsides surrounded by angelica and flowering pansies – ultimately, a pure West Fjords experience.

Vigur island

Daily (2pm) between mid-June and late August it's possible to take a **boat to Vigur** (5300kr; book through the tourist information office), a small, elongated island west of Ísafjörður in Ísafjörðardjúp (for more on which, see p.195). The ride over takes about thirty minutes, leaving you a couple of hours to explore the grassy, flat island before heading back to town (there's a café here but nowhere to stay) – you'll definitely see swarms of puffins, arctic terns and eider ducks, plus Iceland's one and only windmill, making for a great afternoon's trip in good weather.

Eating and drinking

Sadly, eateries tend to come and go pretty quickly in Ísafjörður, since they're dependent on the whims and disposable income of just a few thousand people. In the past few years, the number of places serving food has dwindled, leaving a rather meagre selection.

Hamraborg Hafnarstræti 7. This pizza and burger restaurant, crammed into the corner of a video store, is Ísafjörður's answer to an American diner and is inordinately popular with the town's teenagers: pizzas from 1310kr, burgers from 649kr.

Kaffi Edinborg Aðalstræti 7. A great Euro-style brasserie with stark white walls and wooden floors, housed in a former warehouse from 1907 which once did extensive trade with Edinburgh. There's an extensive menu featuring pan-fried fresh fish (2090kr), chicken breast with camembert and bacon (2890kr), as well as burgers, sandwiches and salads.

Kaffihús Bakarans Hafnarstræti 14. A bakery and café all rolled into one, serving sandwiches and crêpes, as well as tasty cakes and a wide range of fresh coffees. Closed Sat.

Krúsin Norðurvegur 1. Although a bit of a drinkers' den attracting a slightly older crowd with its 1960s and 1970s tunes, it's a friendly place where you're bound to be drawn into conversation.

Thai Koon Hafnarstræti 9–13. Excellent Thai restaurant with genuinely tasty chicken, pork and beef dishes accompanied by either rice or noodles for 990kr, 1090kr or 1200kr depending on the size of the portion; beer is 800kr.

Tjöruhúsið Suðurgata. Quite simply, the best fish restaurant in the whole of the West Fjords, located in the Tjöruhús at the Heritage Museum. Though the menu changes daily depending on the morning's catch (catfish, cod and monkfish are usually available), the fish is always fresh, cooked to perfection on a couple of gas rings in the building's rudimentary kitchen and often served with a mouth-wateringly creamy sauce plus salad. Reckon on 2000kr for lunch, 3000kr for dinner. Open June–Aug only.

Við Pollinn Silfurtorg 2. Inside Hótel Ísafjörður, this restaurant is the place to come for fine dining in elegant surroundings: try the gratinated salted cod (2850kr) or the succulent chicken breast with pesto and basil (3500kr). Food, always well prepared, costs around 1000kr less at lunchtime.

North of Ísafjörður: Bolungarvík and Skálavík

Fifteen kilometres northwest of Ísafjörður along Route 61, the fishing village of **BOLUNGARVÍK**, at the mouth of Ísafjarðardjúp, suffers from one of the most exposed locations in the country. Not only does it receive some of the foulest weather in Iceland, but its position at the foot of three mountains, two of which are close to 700m high, means it's also susceptible to avalanches and landslides, and a large section of Route 61 is protected from rock and snowfalls by sturdy metal nets suspended between posts at the roadside; in order to make things safer a new road tunnel is being bored through the mountains to link up with Hnífsdalur and the road to Ísafjörður; the tunnel is expected to open in late 2010.

Although Bolungarvík is the second largest settlement in the West Fjords, with a population of around 960, it's a workaday place with little to entertain visitors. However, it is worth making the twenty-minute trip from Ísafjörður to visit the open-air **Ósvör Maritime Museum** (May & June Mon–Fri 10am–5pm, Sat & Sun 1–5pm; July & Aug daily 10am–5pm; 600kr) at the entrance to town, just before the bridge. The tiny, turf-roofed huts here, with their thick stone lower walls, are reconstructions of structures that were once used to house fishing-boat crews, a salting house and a rack for drying fish, and give a good idea of how cramped conditions were in the early twentieth century. The museum also has a six-oared rowing boat from the 1940s, built to a traditional local design, on display. The landing stage, beyond the huts, was used when the weather conditions were too severe for boats to land in more exposed Bolungarvík itself.

The town's only other attraction, the **Natural History Museum** (Mon–Fri 9am–5pm, plus mid-June to mid-Aug Sat & Sun 1–5pm; 600kr), is a ten-minute walk from the maritime museum following the main road into town, Þuríðarbraut, across the Hólsá river, and straight on into the main street, Aðalstræti. From here, turn right into Vitastígur and you'll see the museum at no. 3 down by the harbour. Inside there's an excellent collection of stuffed seals, arctic fox and various birds – everything from a widgeon to a pink flamingo which oddly turned up out of the blue in eastern Iceland – you name it, they've got it stuffed. The prize exhibit though is the 3-year-old male polar bear (minus penis which was claimed by the phallological museum in Húsavík; see p.266) found floating on spring pack ice off Hornstrandir a few years ago. The bear's death (it was snared by local fishermen who spotted him drifting, exhausted, on the ice), most likely caused by hanging over the side of a fishing boat, needless to say, came in for much public criticism. The museum is also a good place to buy souvenirs, books, maps and postcards, which you can send from the nearby post office at Aðalstræti 14.

Bolungarvík practicalities

The Ísafjörður–Bolungarvík **bus** runs three times daily (all year), terminating at the post office on Aðalstræti. The town's **guesthouse**, *Mánafell* (℡863 3879, ⓦorkudisa.com; sleeping-bag accommodation 1800kr, ❶), at Stigahlíð 2–4, has small, plain apartments with kitchens. The **campsite** is close by at Höfðastíg 1 next to the **swimming pool** and the Hólsá river, where Route 61 from Ísafjörður enters town. Eating is restricted to the delightful **restaurant** *Einarshús*, housed in the former town store down by the harbour at Hafnargata 41, where fresh fish can be had from 2200kr; there's also a bar in the basement which opens every evening.

Skálavík

From the western edge of Bolungarvík, Þjóðólfsvegur (Route 630) continues 12km northwest through the uninhabited Hlíðardalur valley until it reaches the exposed **Skálavík** bay, which takes regular batterings from Atlantic storms as they sweep in mercilessly from the northwest. Although Skálavík is today uninhabited bar a couple of summer houses owned by brave souls who don't seem to mind the weather, at the end of the nineteenth century around one hundred people were living here, ekeing out an existence from the surrounding barren land. Given the village's vulnerable location between the Deild and Öskubakur mountains, avalanches were always a particular hazard and claimed several lives; perhaps not surprisingly therefore, the last farmer gave up his struggle to keep the village alive in 1964 and left.

There's no public transport to Skálavík but it is possible to **walk** from Bolungarvík in around two hours – simply follow Þjóðólfsvegur all the way. The bay offers a real chance to commune with nature and a night spent camping here, battling against the weather, is certainly a memorable experience; bring all the supplies you'll need. There's also some good **hiking** around here; one route (7km) begins at the western edge of the bay and leads west along the shore round Öskubakar to the lonely lighthouse in Keflavík bay, before the Göltur headland. From here, another track (5km) heads inland through the valleys of Norðdalur and Bakkadalur back to Skálavík and the beginning of the track back to Bolungarvík. Details of these routes can be found on the *Vestfirðir & Dalir* **maps**, available from the tourist office in Ísafjörður (see p.190).

Around Ísafjarðardjúp

The largest and most breathtaking of all the West Fjords, the 75-kilometre-long **Ísafjarðardjúp** stretches all the way from the mountains around Bolungarvík at its mouth to the shores of Ísafjörður fjord, the most easterly of the nine smaller fjords that make up the southern coastline of this extended arm of the Denmark Strait. Approaching from the southeast, descending from the Steingrímsfjarðarheiði plateau on Route 61, the views of Ísafjarðardjúp are spectacular – remote, uninhabited, forbidding fjordlands as far as the eye can see. In fact, from the head of Ísafjörður fjord to the regional capital there's just one village along a very lonely road stretching around two hundred kilometres. Look across the waters of the bay and, on the northern shoreline, you'll see the sheer, snowcapped mountains of **Langadalsströnd** and **Snæfjallaströnd**, themselves divided by the glacial lagoon **Kaldalón**, which is fed by meltwater from the only glacier in the West Fjords, **Drangajökull**. Until just a couple of decades ago these coasts were dotted with isolated farms making an uncertain living from sheep farming and growing the odd crop; today though most have been deserted, reminders of how difficult life was up here. In addition to working the land, many farmers also eked out an existence as fishermen on Ísafjarðardjúp, where whitefish was once so abundant. Nowadays the bay is better known for the rich shrimping grounds found at its mouth, as the whitefish have moved further out to sea.

From June to August there are three **buses** a week in both directions along Route 61, via Hólmavík and the Ringroad at Brú, where you can pick up connections to Reykjavík or Akureyri.

Súðavík

Twenty kilometres southeast of Ísafjörður, Route 61 passes through sleepy **SÚÐAVÍK**. This tiny fishing village, with a population of 230 souls, is your last chance to stock up with essentials before the start of the circuitous negotiation of fjords involved in leaving Ísafjörður. There's very little of note in the village, which consists solely of the main road lined on each side by a few brightly coloured homes, and a simple wooden **church**, next to the main road at the Ísafjörður end. Originally built in the now deserted settlement of Hesteyri (see p.198), across the water on Hornstrandir, the church was dismantled when Hesteyri was abandoned in 1952, and brought to Súðavík, where several families chose to begin their new lives. It became a centre for prayer in January 1995, when fourteen people were killed and many homes destroyed by an **avalanche** that crashed down from the precipitous slopes of Súðavíkurhlíð, the steep mountain that rears up behind the village. If you need to stay overnight, try the *Fisherman Hotel*, Aðalgata 14 (☎450 9000, ⊛fisherman.is; ❷). For snacks and burgers, head for the *Amma Habbý* **café** above the harbour where a beer, burger and fries goes for 1940kr. Nearby, on the main road, there's also a **bank** and **post office**.

▲ Fjord landscape near Súðavík

Reykjanes

As Route 61 leaves Súðavík it passes the remains of the **Norwegian whaling station** that provided employment for the village in the early 1900s. The next 150km are remarkable only for their dullness – this section is one of the most infuriating in the West Fjords, as you twist around a horde of little fjords that line the foot of Steingrímsfjarðarheiði, repeatedly driving up to 50km, only to make two or three kilometres of actual headway; around 100km from Súðavík the road finally climbs up and over the Steingrímsfjarðarheiði plateau heading for Hólmavík. A new bridge across the mouth of the penultimate fjord, Mjóifjörður, leads to the tiny settlement of **REYKJANES**, set on a geothermal area located on a spit of land at the mouth of Ísafjörður fjord, and looking out onto the open waters of Ísafjarðardjúp. Virtually the only building is a hotel, the functional *Hótel Reykjanes* (☎456 4844, ⓦwww.rnes.is; sleeping-bag accommodation 3000kr, ❶). Although there's very little to do here, it's an excellent place for a swim in the naturally heated **outdoor pool** (daily 8am–11pm) and **sauna** in the village, to recover from the long drive from Ísafjörður. Alternatively, comfortable accommodation is also available near the head of Mjóifjörður on the horse farm, *Heydalur* (☎456 4824, ⓦwww.heydalur.is; ❷), where there's also a campsite. The farm rents out kayaks (3000kr per hour) and arranges horseriding tours (3500kr per hour), too.

Kaldalón glacial lagoon, Drangajökull and Unaðsdalur

Back on Route 61, another 15km brings you to a **bridge** over the Bæjardalsá river, from where it's a straightforward 70km run east to Hólmavík (see p.211). However, immediately after the bridge, the unsealed Route 635 turns north up along **Langadalsströnd**, Ísafjarðardjúp's southeastern shore, and it's worth exploring in this direction at least as far as **Kaldalón glacial lagoon**, a bumpy thirty-minute drive from the junction (there's no public transport) past lush green fields and a few farms scattered up the coast.

Approaching the lagoon, a U-shaped inlet from Ísafjarðardjúp between the cliffs of Snæfjallaströnd to the west and Langadalsströnd to the east, you spot the trail of brown, muddy meltwater that has come down from the **Drangajökull glacier** as it merges into the saltwater of the bay. From the parking area by the low hills at the head of the lagoon it's possible to walk up to the snout of the glacier along a trail, marked by cairns, in roughly ninety minutes; from the car park head east, following the low hills, to the track leading along the eastern side of the valley up to the glacier. Keep to the eastern side of the cairns and you'll find the going easier, although there are still boulders, stones and streams to negotiate. Note that you shouldn't underestimate the time it'll take to walk to the glacier – the clear air makes the ice appear much closer than it actually is. If you spot the unmarked path leading up the western edge of the snout, past Drangajökull's highest point, **Jökulbunga** (925m), before descending into Furufjörður on the eastern shore of Hornstrandir, don't be tempted to follow it – it's strictly for experienced mountaineers only.

From Kaldalón, Route 635 crosses the glacial river, Mórillá, before continuing northwest for another fifteen minutes' drive to the farming settlement of **UNAÐSDALUR** where there's a small **church** right on the shoreline. From here the mountainous coastline of Snæfjallaströnd stretches to the northwest – although it's hard to imagine, this entire region was once inhabited as far as the cliffs at Bjarnarnúpur, which look across to Bolungarvík on the opposite side of the bay. Historically, Unaðsdalur is perhaps best known for the **massacre** of a boatload of Spaniards who were shipwrecked here in 1614 and then beaten to death by farmers when they tried to leave on a "borrowed" vessel the following year. In 1995 the last locals, perhaps unsurprisingly, upped sticks and left this remote, chilly coast – not even in the warmest summer does the snow melt from the mountains here – abandoning Snæfjallaströnd to the elements alone.

Hornstrandir

Once you've seen the remote snow-covered hills and cliffs of the Snæfjallaströnd coastline, you'll have an idea of what lies immediately north, on Iceland's very last corner of inhospitable terrain. A claw-shaped peninsula of land bordered by the Jökulfirðir fjords to the south and the Greenland Sea to the north, and attached to the rest of the West Fjords by a narrow neck of land just 6km wide, the coastline of **Hornstrandir** is the most magnificent the country has to offer. The rugged cliffs, precipitous mountainsides and sandy bays backed by meadows of wildflowers make up this official nature reserve on the very edge of the Arctic Circle, and hiking here is an exhilarating experience; it's quite common to walk for an entire day without seeing another person. The highlight of any trip to Hornstrandir is a visit to the majestic **Hornbjarg cliff** (533m) at the eastern end of Hornvík bay and the highest point on the peninsula. The cliff is home to one of the country's greatest **bird colonies** and its many ledges are stuffed full with fulmars, guillemots, kittiwakes, puffins and razorbills. Elsewhere, where farmed sheep once devoured everything edible, there is now wild, lush vegetation of unexpected beauty and the wildlife is free to roam – the Arctic fox makes regular appearances – while offshore, seals and whales can be spotted.

Life for settlers on Hornstrandir was always extreme. For starters, the summer is appreciably shorter than elsewhere in the West Fjords and, bar a geothermal spring in remote **Reykjafjörður**, there's no natural hot-water source, no waterfall to generate electricity, no natural harbour, and no road or airstrip. In fact, the fertile valleys and inlets throughout this uninhabited wilderness are littered with traces of derelict buildings where hardy farmers and fishermen once attempted to battle against the inhospitable climate. The peninsula's two main settlements, **Aðalvík** and **Hesteyri**, are now almost completely deserted, their abandonment marking the end of yet another Icelandic community. Founded in around 1894, Hesteyri depended entirely on a Norwegian whaling station – remains of which can still be seen today at the head of Hesteyrarfjörður fjord – until a drastic decline in stocks led to the station being taken over for the processing of herring. At this time, around eighty people lived permanently in Hesteyri, with another hundred temporarily resident at the factory, but a fall in herring stocks led to the closure of the factory in 1940. One by one, farmers and fishermen left, and in 1952 the last families abandoned both Hesteyri and neighbouring Aðalvík. Incidentally, the closing shots of the Icelandic film *Children of Nature* (*Börn Náttúrunnar*), by Friðrik Þór Friðriksson, were filmed on the mountains of Straumnesfjall, which form the northeastern wall of Aðalvík bay.

Today Hesteyri consists of nothing more than a handful of abandoned cottages, disintegrating skeletons of concrete and timber clothed with bits of corrugated iron, broken stone and blocks of turf, with just one or two being renovated by families whose roots lie here. The **ferry from Ísafjörður** (see below) visits almost daily in summer, though the only functioning building is the white and green *Læknishúsið* (☏456 7183 or 899 1515, ✉sossa@bolungarvik.is; sleeping-bag accommodation 2500kr), the former doctor's house, on the western side of the Hesteyrará river, which offers self-catering **accommodation** from late June to late August.

Getting to Hornstrandir

Since there are no roads to or within this area, **approaches to Hornstrandir** are either by passenger ferry or on foot. Once there, most people pick two places that the ferries visit, and hike between them. **Ferry bookings** can be made through Vesturferðir, based at Ísafjörður's tourist office (☏456 5111, ⊛www.westtours.is). Ferries only run in summer – late June until late August at best – and you must **book in advance**.

Ferries **from Ísafjörður** run twice a week to **Aðalvík**, the wide bay at Hornstrandir's western tip; once a week to **Grunnavík**, northeast across Ísafjarðardjúp from Ísafjörður; five times weekly to **Hesteyri**; twice a week to **Hornvík**, on Hornstrandir's northeastern coast; and once weekly to **Hrafnfjörður**, at Hornstrandir's base. There's also a ferry to Reykjarfjörður and Hornvík **from Norðurfjörður** on the Strandir coast (see p.213), which means that by taking this the opposite way, you can leave Hornstrandir without returning to Ísafjörður, though remember there is no public transport to and from Norðurfjörður.

On foot, the main approach is **from Unaðsdalur** (see p.197), where a good path heads north for Leirufjörður following the Dalsá on its way up out of the village. From Leirufjörður it's possible to cross the tidal flats and head towards the mouth of Hrafnsfjörður and on to Hornvík in around four days. Take extra care when crossing Leirufjörður at low tide, however, because the flats are composed of glacial waste washed down from Drangajökull and can be particularly soggy. Alternatively a much longer and more demanding route leads **from Ófeigsfjörður**, northwest of Norður-fjörður, the last main settlement on the Strandir coast (see p.210). The path follows the coast north to Drangavík, Reykjarfjörður (where there's an open-air geothermally heated swimming pool) and Furufjörður, from where it's possible to cut west into Hrafnsfjörður or continue north to Hornvík; for this, you should allow at least a week.

Hornstrandir hiking practicalities

Unfortunately the **weather** in this part of the country, on the edge of the Greenland Sea, is especially unpredictable. Deep snow often lies on the ground until July and snow showers are not uncommon even in July and August. Fog, too, can be a particular problem. Also, remember that there are **no functioning settlements** on Hornstrandir – those marked on maps are farm buildings, or the remains of farm buildings only – and that you must be prepared for emergencies. It's essential therefore to bring the following **equipment**: a sturdy tent and warm sleeping bag, waterproof clothing and boots, more food than you'll need in case of unforeseen delays (there are **no shops** or facilities anywhere on the peninsula, except for the guesthouse at Hesteyri – see p.198), a compass and Landmælingar Íslands 1:100,000 *Hornstrandir* **hiking map**. Although many routes are marked on the map as clearly defined, this is often not the case in reality; in poor weather conditions it can be all too easy to lose the path, so make sure that you can use a compass properly before setting out. Remember, too, that in June and July it doesn't get dark here, which means you can extend your hiking time if needed. **Mobile phones** do not work in Hornstrandir, but there are landline phones for use in emergencies in the orange shelters dotted around the coast and marked on maps. Take extra care if you're crossing **tidal flats**, or rounding headlands at low tide, as the going can often be very boggy. There are no footbridges in Hornstrandir, so bring an old pair of running shoes to cross rivers and streams – and be prepared to grit your teeth against the bitingly cold water.

From Ísafjörður down the west coast: Route 60

Passing through some of the most dramatic scenery the West Fjords have to offer, **Route 60** is the access route for the southern and western sections of this region. It's predominantly a mountain road, winding through narrow passes and deep-green valleys as often as it rounds the heads of fjords, past the handful of tiny villages which mark the way down the west coast from Ísafjörður. It arrives on the south coast at the insubstantial outpost of **Brjánslækur**, where you have the option of continuing south or east and out of the region, or heading down to the West Fjord's southwestern tip at Látrabjarg (see p.207).

Despite Route 60 being one of the West Fjord's main roads, once you're south of the small sleepy fishing villages of **Flateyri** and **Þingeyri**, it's little more than an unsurfaced and badly potholed dirt track, where driving requires slow speeds, much gear changing and even more patience. Things improve after the spectacular descent into minute **Hrafnseyri**, the birthplace of **Jón Sigurðsson**, the man who led Iceland's nineteenth-century independence movement. Beyond here, look out for the most impressive waterfall in the West Fjords, **Dynjandi**, at the head of the eponymously named fjord, and a favourite rest break for buses. One of the main entrance points into the West Fjords lies due south of here, the **ferry** terminal at Brjánslækur for connections to the island of Flatey (see p.176) and on to Stykkishólmur (see p.172) on the Snæfellsnes peninsula.

From June to August, a thrice-weekly **long-distance bus** service follows Route 60 between Ísafjörður and Brjánslækur, stopping at most settlements along the way (except Flateyri) and connecting with Stykkishólmur ferries. It then continues westwards to Patreksfjörður and Látrabjarg on the southwestern peninsula (see p.204 for more about these) before retracing its route to Ísafjörður.

Flateyri and around

Beginning on the southwestern edge of Ísafjörður, Route 60 immediately enters a tunnel to bypass Þverfjall (752m), and after 2km, the tunnel divides in two; the right-hand turn, Route 65, leads to the dreary workaday fishing village of **Suðureyri**, while the main tunnel and Route 60 continue for another 4km before emerging into Önundarfjörður where there's a junction with Road 64 to Flateyri.

The small fishing village of **FLATEYRI**, just 22km from Ísafjörður, is known across the country for its **avalanche** problems, and the colossal **earth dams** separated by fifteen-metre-high walls on the lower slopes of the omnipresent mountains are man-made barriers against the snowfalls which occur here every year. A memorial stone next to the church, at the entrance to the village, bears the names of the twenty people who died in the most recent devastating avalanche in October 1995. The tragedy was a painful loss for this closely knit community where the total population is barely over three hundred, not least because the frozen ground and heavy snow prevented the bodies from being buried in the village cemetery; instead, they had to be kept in the morgue in Ísafjörður until the ground thawed and they could be buried in Reykjavík. Extensive rebuilding was necessary after the accident, including the erection of avalanche defences which now effectively channel all snow-slides into the sea. From the filling station at the entrance to the village, a short path (10min) leads up to a **viewpoint** on the mountainside giving a superb panorama, not only of Flateyri and Önundarfjörður, but down into the lifesaving earth dams.

Founded as a trading centre in 1792, the village was once a base for shark and whale hunting. Today, it's thanks to the **fish-processing factory**, one of the largest in Iceland, that the village has finally shaken off its dependence on Ísafjörður – despite consisting of little more than one main street, Flateyri prides itself on the fact that it has all the major services. However, it's not a good idea to get stuck here since there's very little to do other than marvel at the avalanche defences and the open vistas of the surrounding fjord and mountains.

Flateyri practicalities

Local **buses** operate all year (three daily) from Ísafjörður, stopping outside Flateyri's **post office**, at Ránargata 1. Long-distance buses along Route 60 don't call at Flateyri, but can be caught at the junction of Routes 64 and 60, 7km east of town.

Flateyri has two **guesthouses**: *Brynjukot* at Ránargata 6 with studio apartments (**2**) and *Grænhöfði*, located beside the avalanche defences at Hjallavegur 9, offering double rooms (**1**) as well as apartments (**6**); contact details for both are ☏456 7762 or 863 7662, ✉jens@snerpa.is. The **campsite** (☏456 7878), with toilets and running water, is behind the filling station at the entrance to the village. The **swimming pool** is in Tjarnargata, close to the mountains, north of the church. For eating and drinking there's the pleasant *Vagninn* **restaurant**, at Hafnarstræti 19, serving burgers with fries and salad (900kr), pizzas (1600kr) and steamed haddock (1400kr). Next door at no. 11, the simple summer-only café, *Félagsbær*, has coffee and cakes, as well as a couple of traditional sweaters for sale.

Önundarfjörður

Flateyri sits on the eastern side of the forty-kilometre-long **Önundarfjörður**, and there are a couple of scenic spots to check out nearby. Back at the Route 60 junction, a gravel track leads southeast down to the **Korpudalur** valley at the neck of the fjord. Surrounded by mountains, it's a great place to hike, kayak or just kick back for a couple of days, with accommodation and advice available at

Korpudalur **youth hostel** (☎456 7808 or 892 2030, ⓦkorpudalur.is; sleeping-bag accommodation 3100kr; ❶), which also runs a campsite.

Alternatively, one of the most beautiful beaches in the West Fjords, **Ingjaldssandur** (the settlement here is known as **Sæból**, the name used on most maps) is located at the mouth of Önundarfjörður, across the water from Flateyri at the tip of the mountainous finger of land that separates the fjord from its southern neighbour, Dýrafjörður. Bordered to the west and east by tall, craggy mountains and backed by lush green fields, the beach's grassy foreshore is an idyllic place from which to watch the huge Atlantic breakers crash onto the sand and pebbles below. In summer this is a good place to spot arctic tern and various species of waders; oystercatchers are particularly common here.

Ingjaldssandur is only accessible with your own transport and entails a circuitous drive of 44km from Flateyri, heading first south down Route 60 towards Þingeyri, before taking the unsurfaced and rough Route 624 back northwest to the Önundarfjörður coast. Twenty kilometres before the end of the road at Sæból, the *Alviðra* farm (☎456 8229 or 894 7029, ⓔalvidra@snerpa.is; ❶) is hard to beat for splendid isolation: it offers sleeping-bag **accommodation** and cooking facilities for 2500kr, too.

Þingeyri

Although one of the oldest settlements in the West Fjords, **ÞINGEYRI**, 48km southwest of Ísafjörður along Road 60, is also one of the dullest. The village takes its name from the ancient *þing* (assembly) mentioned in *Gísla Saga*, and the ruins, nothing more than a couple of grassy mounds, can be seen behind the church in the centre of the village. Over the centuries Þingeyri developed into a significant fishing centre thanks to its sheltered location near the head of Dýrafjörður, and even attracted the interest of the French who applied, unsuccessfully, to establish a base here to service their fishing vessels operating in the region.

Today life is centred on the one main street, **Aðalstræti**, where you'll find all the town's **services** and little else. If you've time to kill, head up Sandafell (367m), which stands guard behind the village. This is a favourite place for locals to watch the sun go down as it offers fantastic views out over the fjord and of the mountain ridge, topped by the highest peak in the West Fjords, Kaldbakur (998m), which separates Dyrafjörður from the much larger and multi-fingered Arnarfjörður to the south. Although steep, Sandafell can be climbed from the village – several clear paths lead up the mountainside – and a four-wheel-drive track there heads southwest off Route 60, just 1km south of town.

Practicalities

There's limited information about the town and the surrounding area available at the **tourist office**, Hafnarstræti 7 (☎456 8304, ⓔumthingeyri@snerpa.is) which also sells woollen sweaters and souvenirs. If you get stuck here for the night, try one of two year-round **guesthouses**: *Vera* at Hlíðargata 22 (☎456 8232 and ☎891 6832; ❷) and *Við Fjörðinn* (☎456 8172, ⓦwww.vidfjordinn .is; ❷) at Aðalstræti 26, which have little to choose between them, or a summer-only guesthouse, the bright and airy *Sandafell* (☎456 1600, ⓦwww .hotelsandafell.com; ❷) with both en-suite rooms and shared facilities at Hafnarstræti 7. The **campsite** (☎456 8228) with washing is located next to the modern **swimming pool** at the western end of the village. **Eating out** is limited to the restaurant inside *Sandafell*, which has fish suppers for 2400kr, or lamb dishes at 3700kr, and the **snack bar** at the filling station on the main road, which also functions as the terminus for **buses**.

Hrafnseyri

The seventeen-kilometre drive south from Þingeyri to minuscule Hrafnseyri is one of the most dramatic sections of Route 60. Climbing all the while to squeeze through a narrow pass between mountains over 700m high, the road then makes a stunning descent into Hrafnseyri on the shores of **Arnarfjörður**; when viewed from the hamlet below, the road appears to cling precariously to a vertical wall of rock. Named after the fjord's first settler, Örn (meaning "eagle", *arnar* being its genitive case), who lasted just one winter here, Arnarfjörður is 30km long and up to 10km wide: it forks at its head to form four smaller fjords, Suðurfirðir, to the southwest, and Borgarfjörður and Dynjandisvogur inlet to the northeast. It's widely, and quite rightly, regarded by locals as the most picturesque of all the West Fjords, enclosed by towering mountains.

HRAFNSEYRI itself, consisting of a tiny church and a museum, is one of only two settlements on Arnarfjörður (the other is Bíldudalur, 79km away). It was named after one of Iceland's earliest doctors, **Hrafn Sveinbjarnarson**, who died here in 1213, having trained in Europe then returned home to practice. A memorial stone next to the church commemorates his life, and the grass mound nearby is thought to be the site of his boathouse. This tiny settlement, though, is of much greater historical significance to Icelanders since it was here that **Jón Sigurðsson** (see box below) was born, the man who won independence for Iceland in the nineteenth century. The excellent adjoining **museum** (June–Aug daily 10am–8pm; Ⓦwww.hrafnseyri.is; 400kr) records his life, mostly with photographs, some of his letters and contemporary drawings. Particularly evocative is the painting of the meeting of 1851, which Jón Sigurðsson and a number of Icelandic MPs held with representatives of the Danish state in the Grammar School, Menntaskólinn, in Reykjavík, and which helped pave the way for Icelandic independence. Jón Sigurðsson himself was born in the restored **turf farmhouse**, with three gabled roofs, next to the church. At the rear of the building, his bedroom, containing the desk from his office in Copenhagen, has

Jón Sigurðsson

To Icelanders, **Jón Sigurðsson** (1811–69) is what Winston Churchill is to the British and George Washington to the Americans. This is the man who, through his tremendous skills of diplomacy, achieved independence from the Danes, who had almost bankrupted Iceland during the time of the Trade Monopoly. Born in Hrafnseyri in 1811, Jón spent the first 22 years of his life in his native West Fjords, and after completing the entry examination for university study, he left for Copenhagen where he chose history and political science among his subjects. Although a committed student, he never graduated from the university, opting instead to dedicate his life to the Árni Magnússon Institute, then a powerful symbol of the struggle for recognition against the Danes; this institute fought a long battle to have many of Iceland's most treasured medieval manuscripts, kept in Copenhagen by the Danish authorities, returned home. However, it wasn't until 1841 that Jón Sigurðsson began his political activities, publishing a magazine in which he put forward historical arguments for Iceland's right to independence. A prolific writer about Icelandic history, politics and economics, he was later elected to the Icelandic parliament, which regained its powers as a consultative body in 1843 thanks to his agitation. Further reforms followed as a direct consequence of his influence, including the right to free trade in 1854, and eventually, twenty years later, a constitution making Iceland self-governing in home affairs, though Jón didn't live to see Iceland become a sovereign state under the Danish crown on December 1, 1918. Iceland gained full independence from Denmark on June 17, 1944, the anniversary of his birth.

been kept in its original state and offers an insight into the ascetic life of one of Iceland's most revered figures.

The best time to be in Hrafnseyri is **Icelandic National Day** (June 17), when a special mass is held in the church and prominent Icelanders from across the country travel to the village to remember their most distinguished champion of freedom. Although it's a serious occasion there's a mood of optimism and good humour in the air, with plenty of singing and celebration.

Dynjandi

Twenty kilometres east of Hrafnseyri, at the point where Route 60 weaves around the northeastern corner of Arnarfjörður, the most impressive waterfall in the West Fjords, **Dynjandi**, plunges over a hundred-metre-high cliff-top into the fjord at Dynjandisvogur inlet, forming a triangular cascade roughly 30m wide at its top spreading to over 60m at its bottom. Below the main waterfall a series of five smaller chutes carries the waters of the Dynjandisá to the sea. With your own transport, it's possible to reach the head of the falls – continue south along Route 60 for around 5km, and once the road has climbed up onto the Dynjandisheiði plateau, you'll see the Dynjandisá river, which crosses the road; walk west from here, following the course of the river to the falls.

All long-distance buses make a ten-minute stop at the falls, where there's also a simple, grassy **campsite**, with toilets and running water. Lit by the low sun, it's an incredibly pretty place to spend a summer night, though bear in mind that the waterfall is famously noisy – *dynjandi* means "the thundering one".

Flókalundur and Brjánslækur

South of Dynjandisheiði, Route 60 continues over a spectacular highland plateau, passing **Lónfell** (725m) and the turn-off onto Route 63 for Patreksfjörður via Bíldudalur (see p.204), before finally descending to the south coast and Route 62 at **FLÓKALUNDUR**. Consisting of just a hotel, restaurant and a petrol pump, there's little to note here other than the fact that the Viking **Flóki Vilgerðarson**, who named Iceland, once spent a winter here. He climbed Lónfell, only to be dismayed by the icebergs floating in the fjord and named the land "Ísland", as the inscription on the monument in front of the functional *Flókalundur* **hotel** (late May to mid-Sept; ☎456 2011, ⓦwww.flokalundur.is; ❷), overlooking Vatnsfjörður, reminds modern-day Icelanders. The hotel **restaurant** is nothing special, but it does serve up decent if pricey food (burgers from 1390kr, pizzas 1350kr plus meat and fish dishes around 2800kr) and makes for a good break on the long journey in and out of the West Fjords. The free **campsite** on the same site is run by the hotel and has running water and toilet facilities.

The hotel can also fill you in on the surrounding **Vatnsfjörður Nature Reserve**, which spreads northeast from here and provides endless **hiking** opportunities – one easy trail (8km; 2–3hr) begins at a lake some 5km east along the main road and leads along the eastern shore of **Vatndalsvatn**, a lake known for its rich birdlife and a favourite nesting spot for the dramatically coloured harlequin duck, and the red-throated and great northern diver. Don't attempt to cross the Vatnsdalsá at the head of the lake in order to return down the western shore, since the river is very wide and fast flowing; instead, retrace your steps.

Barely 7km west of Flókalundur on Route 62, **BRJÁNSLÆKUR** is essentially just the jetty for **ferries to Stykkishólmur** via Flatey (see p.171 for schedules). Other than the **snack-bar**-cum-**ticket-office** in the small wooden building on the main road by the jetty, and a free **campsite** with washing facilities (☎456 2011), there are no facilities here. **Long-distance buses** connect three times a week with ferries, then head back along Route 60 to Ísafjörður, or continue westwards to Patreksfjörður and Látrabjarg on the southwestern peninsula (see below).

The southwestern peninsula

From its mountain-top junction with Route 60 by Lónfell, Route 63 descends towards Trostansfjörður, one of the four baby fjords which make up the **Suðurfirðir**, the southern fjords, forming the southwestern corner of **Arnarfjörður**. This section of the road is in very poor condition and features some alarmingly large potholes and ruts. Unusually for the West Fjords, three fishing villages are found within close proximity to one another here – barely 30km separates the uneventful port of **Bíldudalur** from its neighbours, identical **Tálknafjörður**, and the larger **Patreksfjörður**, a commercial centre for the surrounding farms and smaller villages. However, it's the **Látrabjarg** cliffs, 60km beyond Patreksfjörður to the west, that draw most visitors to this last peninsula of rugged land. Here, in summer, thousands upon thousands of **sea birds** including guillemots, kittiwakes and puffins nest in the cliff's nooks and crannies making for one of the most spectacular sights anywhere in the region – what's more, the cliffs are easily accessible from nearby **Breiðavík**, an idyllic bay of aquamarine water backed by white sand and dusky mountains.

From June to August, the **long-distance bus** from Ísafjörður continues on from the Brjánslækur ferry jetty to Patreksfjörður, Breiðavík and Látravík, before terminating at Látrabjarg. Around two-and-a-half hours later, it heads back along the same route to Brjánslækur and then north to Ísafjörður.

Bíldudalur

A thriving fishing port processing vast amounts of local shrimp, there's little to see or do in **BÍLDUDALUR**, a workaday village of just two hundred people at the foot of Bíldudalsfjall mountain on the southern shores of Arnarfjörður. However, the **airport**, 7km south of the village at the mouth of Fossfjörður, has made Bíldudalur a gateway to the southwestern peninsula of the West Fjords with its regular connections with Reykjavík, cutting out the need for the long and tiring journey up hill and down dale from Ísafjörður. The village's only attraction is the curious Memories of Melodies (Tónlistarsafn) **music museum** (June–Aug daily 2–6pm, at other times simply knock on the door; 500kr) at Tjarnarbraut 5. Cobbled together by Bíldudalur's most famous son, singer Jón Kristján Ólafsson (who doesn't speak English), it holds a rambling collection of old 33s and other Icelandic music memorabilia from the 1940–60s: while certainly a worthy tribute to Iceland's past musical greats, it's unlikely to grab the attention of foreign visitors since the featured singers and groups were, mercifully, never big abroad.

Bíldudalur practicalities

Aside from long-distance buses passing through, daily **buses** operate all year round between here and Tálknafjörður and Patreksfjörður from outside the **post office** and **bank** in the main street, as well as to the **airport** to connect with the once-daily flight to and from Reykjavík, operated by Eagle Air (ⓦwww.ernir.is).

The best place to stay in Bíldudalur is the comfortable *Kaupfélagið* **youth hostel** (☎456 2100 or 860 2100, ⓦhostel.is; ❶), a grey pebble-dashed building, complete with guests' kitchen, down by the harbour at Hafnarbraut 2. For the **campsite**, head to the sports field on the southern edge of the village. The only **restaurant**,

Vegamót, at Tjarnarbraut 2, on the main road close to the harbour, has pizzas (from 1000kr) and burgers (750kr) as well as spaghetti carbonara (1590kr) on the menu; there's also beer here for 800kr.

Around Bíldudalur

What Bíldudalur lacks in attractions it more than makes up for with stunning scenery; an excellent fifteen-kilometre **hike** (4–5hr) up the Fossdalur valley to the tiny settlement of Tungumúli on the Barðaströnd coast (Route 62) begins at **Foss farm**, 6km south of the airport at the head of Fossfjörður, following the route taken by local postmen in the late 1800s. From the western side of the farm, the track leads up through Fossdalur towards the small lake, Mjósund, beyond which the route forks. Keep right and take the path over the **Fossheiði plateau**, which has fantastic views over the surrounding rocky countryside, until it descends through Arnbylisdalur valley on the western edge of Tungumúlafjall mountain, to the coast and Route 62 at **Tungumúli**. A couple of kilometres east of here lies the equally small settlement of **Kross**, where there's **accommodation** at *Gistiheimilið Bjarkarholt* (☎456 2025; sleeping-bag accommodation 2500kr, ❶; breakfast is an extra 900kr). The route is shown on the *Vestfirðir & Dalir* maps available from regional tourist offices. From Kross and Tungumúli, it's possible to link up with the three weekly summer **buses** to Látrabjarg or Brjánslækur – check the schedules first at Ísafjörður's information office (see p.190).

Tálknafjörður

Continuing southwest from Bíldudalur on Route 63, it's 15km to where Route 617 heads 4km north to the equally tiny **TÁLKNAFJÖRÐUR**, a stop for the year-round Bíldudalur–Patreksfjörður bus. The only reason to detour here is to ease your muscles at the superb open-air **swimming pool**, which comes complete with hot pots and fantastic views over the surrounding mountains. There are also a couple of natural alfresco hot spots fed by water from a nearby spring just behind the church on the western outskirts of the village; ask for precise directions from the **guesthouses**. *Gistiheimilið Skrúðhamrar* is at Strandgata 20 (☎456 0200, ✉skrudhamar@visir.is; ❶), while *Gistiheimilið Bjarmaland* (☎891 8038, ✉bjarmaland06@simnet.is; sleeping-bag accommodation 2500kr, ❶) is a little further down the main road at Bugatún 8. The **campsite** (☎456 2639) is in the centre of the village next to the swimming pool. Between June and early August, *Kaffi Sæla*, at the corner of Lækjargata and Strandgata, serves up whale steaks (2500kr) as well as seafood soup (1500kr), whilst *Hópið*, at the western end of the main road on Hrafnadalsvegur, offers freshly caught fish dishes for around 2500kr as well as burgers (1030kr) and pizzas (from 935kr) and is open all year round. For snacks, soft drinks and other provisions, head for the food store and **filling station** on the main street.

Patreksfjörður

Located on the shores of the southernmost of all the West Fjords, **PATREKS-FJÖRÐUR** is named after **Saint Patrick**, a bishop from the Scottish islands who acted as spiritual adviser to one of the region's first settlers, Örlygur Hrappson. Today with a population of 770, the village is large enough to exist independently of Ísafjörður, 172km away, and is the only place in the West Fjords, outside the regional capital, to boast more than the odd shop and restaurant. Over the years, this tiny village has won a reputation for pioneering excellence: trawler fishing in Iceland began here; a particular style of saltfish now popular in Mediterranean markets was developed here; and, somewhat less notably, the town also dispatched the only Icelandic vessel ever to hunt seal in the Arctic.

Built on two sandspits, Geirseyri and Vatneyri, Patreksfjörður comprises a main road in and out of the town, Strandgata, which runs along the shoreside to the harbour. Several side streets branch off Strandgata's western end, including Eyrargata, while the main shopping street, Aðalstræti, runs parallel to it. Though there's little to do in the town itself, other than amble up and down the parallel streets peering in windows, the town does have one saving grace: its spectacularly located, open-air **swimming pool**, perched high above the fjord at the western edge of the tiny town centre on Eyrargata. As you swim in the pool, you're treated to uninterrupted views across the fjord to the mountain of Vatnsdalsfjall, which rises on Patrekfjörður's sandy southern shore; soaking in the hot pots, drinking in the views, is equally as pleasurable. Though the pool should have been built a little longer (the neighbouring graveyard is in the way), a swim here is one of the most restorative and relaxing things to do in the whole of the West Fjords region.

Patreksfjörður practicalities

Buses run year-round between here, Tálknafjörður and Bíldudalur. Summer buses to Látrabjarg, Brjánslækur and Ísafjorður depart three times a week from the Esso filling station on Strandgata. The **post office** is at Bjarkargata 10. For cash withdrawals there's an **ATM** outside the small supermarket at Aðalstræti 89.

There are two functional **accommodation** options: the guesthouse *Stekkaból* at Stekkar 19, behind the church off Aðalstræti (June–Aug; ☎864 9675, ✉stekkabol@snerpa.is; sleeping-bag accommodation 2200kr; ❶; breakfast 800kr extra) and the fusty *Eyrar* at Aðalstræti 8 (☎456 4565 or 845 7283, ✉handradinn @simnet.is; sleeping-bag accommodation 2500kr; ❶).

For **eating**, the best choice is *Þorpið*, on Aðalstræti, an airy modern place with excellent views over the fjord and bad local art on the walls inside – the deep-fried catfish with salad and fries is just 1690kr at lunchtime; otherwise there's lamb with broccoli for 2700kr, soups at 750kr, or burgers from 900kr. The only other option is the simple café attached to the *Eyrar* guesthouse which has a few unappetizing cakes. Patreksfjörður also boasts the only **vínbúð** alcohol shop in the entire West Fjords outside Ísafjörður (Mon–Thurs 2–6pm, Fri 2–6.30pm), at Þórsgata 10, down by the harbour.

Hnjótur, Breiðavík and Látrabjarg

Some 59km from Patreksfjörður, the West Fjords reach their southwestern extremity at **Látrabjarg cliffs**, a dramatic and remote corner of the country packed through the summer with nesting **sea birds**. If this isn't enough to tempt you, you could visit an oddly located museum at **Hnjótur** and the quite stunning **Breiðavík beach** – golden, isolated and beautiful – to check out along the way. Without your own vehicle, you can get to all of these places by public **bus** throughout the summer.

Hnjótur Folk Museum

Route 62 runs southeast from Patreksfjörður down to the south coast. Around 12km from town, the unsealed **Route 612** branches westwards to run along the underside of yet another fjord, passing a **beached shipwreck** and the town's now disused airport at **Sandoddi**. After 25km, the road reaches the **Hnjótur folk museum** (mid-May to mid-Sept daily 10am–6pm; 600kr), diagonally across the bay from Patreksfjörður. Its poignant semicircular stone monument is dedicated to the sailors who lost their lives off the treacherous shores of the southwestern peninsula during the early twentieth century – all bar one were from the British ports of Grimsby and Hull.

Inside the museum, two short **films** are worth catching. The first, on the ground floor, features the rescue of the *Sargon* (see p.208); the second, on the upper floor, is a late-1980s documentary on the then 74-year-old Gísli Gíslason, a hermit who lived all of his 79 years in remote Selárdalur at the mouth of Arnarfjörður and only once ventured to his nearest village, Bíldudalur. On the few occasions he spoke, even Icelanders found his bleating speech virtually incomprehensible, and there was general disbelief that such an existence was still possible. Otherwise, the museum contains a jumble of assorted nostalgic paraphernalia, the prize exhibits being two rusting old **planes**: an Aeroflot biplane that landed in Iceland after running out of fuel, having been turned back to Russia from the US, where it was refused permission to land; and an American DC3 that served at the American NATO base at Keflavík and took part in the evacuation of Heimaey during the eruption of 1973. Outside the museum is a replica of a Viking longship, presented to Iceland by Norway to mark 1100 years of settlement. Close by, the *Mummi*, the country's oldest steam-powered fishing boat, is also worth a cursory glance.

Breiðavík

Just after Hnjótur you pass the junction with Route 615, which leads past the farms of Efri Tunga and Neðri Tunga to the comfortable and hospitable ⚒ *Hótel Látrabjarg* (mid-May to mid-Sept; ☎456 1500 or 825 0025, ⓦwww.latrabjarg .com; ❹), 3km from the junction and a good choice if you need local **accommodation**. Rooms, both sharing facilities and en suite, are located in a former boarding school with great views back across the fjord to Patreksfjörður; there's also easy access from the hotel down to the sandy bay, Örlygshöfn, below. Three course dinners are available, too, for 5900kr. Sticking to Route 612 will bring you, after 10km or so, to a **church** and handful of buildings comprising the settlement at idyllic **Breiðavík bay**, with open views westwards over white sand to the aquamarine waters of the Atlantic. This exquisite **beach**, without a doubt one of Iceland's finest, is irresistible, and when the sun shines the sands are seen to their best advantage: kilometres of empty, unsullied white strands, punctuated solely by trickling mountain streams finally reaching the ocean, flocks of squawking sea birds and the odd piece of white-washed driftwood, which can provide welcome shelter from the wind if you're intent on catching the rays.

There's a great **place to stay** here: *Gistiheimilið Breiðavík* (mid-May to mid-Sept; ☎456 1575, ⓦwww.breidavik.is; sleeping-bag accommodation is 3500kr; ❸), which occupies all the buildings apart from the church, and serves legendary home-cooked meals – dinner costs around 3500kr and breakfast is 1500kr. **Camping** is 1200kr per person.

Látrabjarg to Rauðisandur beach

After Breiðavík, the 612 road climbs up and over a plateau (there's an extremely rough 12km gravel road off here to Keflavík – see below) and then steeply down to the coast again before expiring a few kilometres on below the **lighthouse at Bjargtangar**, the westernmost point in Europe. The Ísafjörður–Brjánslækur–Patreksfjörður **bus** spends about two-and-a-half hours here before heading back – don't miss it unless you can afford to wait two days for the next one.

The lighthouse also marks the start of **Látrabjarg cliffs**, which rise up to 441m above the churning sea as they run 14km east from here to the small inlet of **Keflavík**. A footpath leads along the cliff-tops, with excellent views of the thousands of **sea birds** that come here to nest on the countless ledges below. For centuries, locals would abseil down the cliffs to collect their eggs and trap the birds for food – it's estimated that around 35,000 birds were caught here every year until the late 1950s – and, occasionally, they still do.

Although the **guillemot** is the most common bird at Látrabjarg, it's the thousands of **puffins** that most people come here to see. The high ground of the cliff-tops is riddled with their burrows, often up to 2m in length, since they nest in locations well away from the pounding surf, ideally surrounded by lush grass and thick soil. They return to the same burrows they occupied the year before, almost always during the third week of April, where they remain until August or September. The cliffs are also home to the largest colony of **razorbills** in the world, as well as to thousands of other screeching breeds of sea bird including **cormorants**, **fulmars** and **kittiwakes**; the din here can be quite overpowering, as can the stench from the piles of guano on the cliff face.

Incidentally, one of Iceland's most daring **sea-rescue operations** occurred here in December 1947, when farmers from Hvallátur set out to rescue the crew of a British trawler, the *Dhoon*, which had been wrecked off the rocky shoreline during a severe snowstorm. After sliding down the ice-covered cliffs by rope, the Icelanders pulled the sailors to safety using a rescue line they fired across to the stricken vessel – although it took two separate attempts to hoist all the men up the treacherous cliff face from where they were taken by horseback to nearby farms to recover. A year later, a film crew arrived in Hvallátur to make a documentary about the accident, in which several locals were to re-enact the rescue – however, while they were filming, another British trawler, *Sargon*, became stranded in nearby Patreksfjörður, giving the film makers a chance to catch a drama on film for real.

The cliff-top path at Látrabjarg continues east, rounding Keflavík bay and finally descends to the serene red-orange sands at **Rauðisandur** bay after around

▲ Getting close to puffins, Látrabjarg cliffs

20km, where a couple of farming families still live. The lush, open fields that slowly give way to the vast expanse of sand that forms this part of the shore of Breiðafjörður have been cultivated for centuries, and today flocks of hardy sheep wander from field to shore in search of patches of grass. North of the **Bæjarvaðall** lagoon, which marks the eastern end of the sands, you can follow **Route 614** 8km north to join Route 612 between Patreksfjörður and Hnjótur.

The south coast: Bjarkalundur and Reykhólar

East from Brjánslækur and Flókalundur, the south coast of the West Fjords is all but uninhabited. As the unsurfaced Route 60 rounds the head of Vatnsfjörður east of Flókalundur, it's well over a hundred kilometres before civilization reappears at **Bjarkalundur**, itself little more than a hotel and a filling station. Although still dramatic, the mountains along this stretch of road are less rugged and angular than those along the northern and western coasts, and the coastline is dominated by small bays separated by high bluffs, with wide areas of heavily vegetated flatland gently sloping down to the shores of Breiðafjörður. In fact the only village of any significance in this direction is **Reykhólar**, off the main road along Route 607, one of the few settlements in the West Fjords to have a geothermal spring and so a good place to break the long journey in or out of the region with a dip in the outdoor pool. East of here, the dot on the map that is **Króksfjarðarnes** serves as a road junction: from here routes head south to Reykjavík, or via the new year-round road across the desolate Tröllatunguheiði plateau to Hólmavík.

It's not possible to get here **by bus** from the rest of the West Fjords, as there is no service along the Flókalundur–Bjarkalundur stretch. Instead, you'll have to approach from the south, with a service running just twice weekly in each direction between Reykjavík and Reykhólar via Bjarkalundur.

Bjarkalundur

Hiking is just about all there is to do at the small service centre of **BJARKA-LUNDUR**, 126km east of Flókalundur, nothing more than a restaurant and a modern and uninspiring **hotel** bearing the same name (ⓣ434 7762, Ⓦwww .bjarkalundur.is; sleeping-bag accommodation 7000kr; breakfast 1000kr extra; ❶), where they have clean but plain doubles. The **campsite** at the hotel charges 1000kr per tent and has new toilet and shower facilities. Roughly 1km east of the hotel, a four-wheel-drive track marks the beginning of a **trail** (7km) leading to the twin peaks of **Vaðalfjall**, an extinct volcano whose outer layers have eroded away, leaving just a bare chimney from where there are fantastic views out over the fjords and islands of Breiðafjörður. To return to Bjarkalundur, head southwest from the mountains to the old road that leads down to Kinnarstaðir farm, from where it's a couple of kilometres east along Route 60 to the hotel.

Moving on, there are two weekly **buses** each way to Reykhólar and Reykjavík, but none further into the West Fjords. With your own transport, you can also head northeast **to Hólmavík** and the Strandir coast (see p.210) via the new all-season road which has been constructed over the lonely Tröllatunguheiði plateau, starting about 15km south of Bjarkalundur. Route 608 over the Þorskafjarðarheiði plateau, which begins just 8km north of town, is only passable in summer and contains serious potholes and boggy sections.

Reykhólar

From Bjarkalundur, Route 607 and the bus from Reykjavík run 15km southwest to **REYKHÓLAR**, a farming settlement home to just 120 people with attractive views out over Breiðafjörður to the Reykjanes peninsula. Although Reykhólar's history can be traced back to the time of the sagas, there's little reminder today of the village's wealthy past, when it was considered to have some of the best farmland in all of Iceland; the village once made a handsome profit from selling the wheat grown on the three hundred or so offshore islands hereabouts and the surrounding areas on the mainland. It is one of the few places in the West Fjords to have a ready supply of **geothermal energy**, which today has been harnessed and provides the village with its main source of activity – the ugly Þorungaverksmiðja algae plant, located a couple of kilometres south of the village, that extracts minerals from seaweed to make toothpaste, soap and handcream. There's little to do in the village except enjoy a relaxing dip in the warm waters of the outdoor **swimming pool**, which also has two hot pots.

Practicalities

The **tourist information office** (mid-June to mid-Aug daily 10am–noon and 2–6pm; ☎434 7830), located between the guesthouse and the filling station, is friendly but understandably has few suggestions on how to fill your time in this remote corner of the country. Reykhólar's only **accommodation** is the small and pleasant *Álftaland* youth hostel (☎865 9968, ⓦalftaland.is; sleeping bag 2400kr; ❶), on the only main road, Hellisbraut, at the entrance to Reykhólar. The **campsite** can be found at the opposite end of the village next to the swimming pool; it costs 600kr to pitch a tent, and there are toilets, running water and showers. **Food** is available at the store at the filling station, which also serves as the **bus terminal**.

Twice-weekly **buses** run year-round from Reykhólar to Reykjavík via Bjarkalundur.

Hólmavík and the Strandir coast

From Brú in the south to Norðurfjörður in the north, the lonely 220km of the **Strandir coast** form the West Fjords' easternmost extremities and one of the least-visited corners of Iceland – if you're looking to get off the beaten track, this is the place to come.

The main entry point, and the region's only substantial settlement, is **Hólmavík**, accessed along Route 61 from either Ísafjörður or the Ringroad at Brú – **buses** run this route three times a week in summer. North of here, the land is rugged, with snowcapped mountains and deeply indented fjords, the setting for some of the country's most isolated communities, dependent on fishing and sheep farming for their existence. The only thoroughfare, the eighty-kilometre-long **Route 643**, is always in poor condition, prone to landslips and impassable from autumn's first snows until road maintenance crews break through again in late spring. There's **no public transport**, but it's worth making every effort to drive this earth road to really experience the wild and pioneering spirit of Iceland, notably at **Djúpavík**, a former herring-fishing village, now all but abandoned, and home to one of the West Fjords' most welcoming hotels. Beyond here, the road battles on north towards Iceland's most remote airport, **Gjögur**, handy for reaching this forgotten corner of the country, and end-of-the-road **Norðurfjörður**, where it finally expires, marking the jumping-off point for ambitious overland treks north towards the uninhabited wilds of Hornstrandir (see p.198 for walking route).

Hólmavík

A thriving fishing village on the southern shore of Steingrímsfjörður with a population of around 380, **HÓLMAVÍK** was granted municipal status in 1890 but only really began to grow during the twentieth century. Today life is centred around the natural harbour at the northern edge of the village, home to around a dozen fishing boats and the shrimp-processing plant, Rækjuvinnsla, that potent symbol of economic independence in rural Iceland, of which locals are justifiably proud. The village economy is dependent on the **shrimps** the local boats catch – inshore in the fjords in winter, deep-sea shrimping in summer. Hólmavík also functions as a service centre for the surrounding sheep farms and boasts a large **supermarket**, two **banks**, a **post office** (Mon–Fri 9am–4.30pm) and the West Fjords' most offbeat exhibition, the **Museum of Sorcery and Witchcraft** (Galdrasýning á Ströndum; daily 10am–6pm; ⓦwww.galdrasyning.is; 700kr), located in the turf-roofed building behind the shrimp plant at Höfðagata 8–10. An English audio commentary guides you through the various exhibits, which recount the occurrence of witchcraft and sorcery in this part of the country during the seventeenth century. The Strandir region, always one of Iceland's most remote, seems to have hung onto Viking superstitions longer than elsewhere, and even today is reputed as the home of cunning. During the late 1600s, twenty men and one woman were burnt at the stake in the West Fjords for sorcery, which included the practice of wearing *nábrók* ("necropants"), a supernatural means of getting rich quick; having gained the permission of a living man to dig up his body after death, the sorcerer would skin the body from the waist down and step into the skin, which would become one with his own. On placing a coin in the dead man's scrotum, the coin would continually draw money from other living people. A copy of a pair is on display in the museum, alongside other items such as a tree trunk with shackles and birch twigs for whipping offenders. Look out, too, for the eerie stone bowl, kept in a glass cabinet off reception, which is thought to have been used for sacrifices. Discovered at nearby Góðadalur in 2003, the bowl appears to show traces of sacrificial human blood from heathen rituals.

Other than the museum, there are no sights to speak of, though sooner or later you'll undoubtedly come across the oldest building in the village, **Riishús**, on the main street, Hafnarbraut, which runs parallel to the fjord. Built by and named after a local merchant, Richard Peter Riis, the two-storey wooden structure dates from 1897 and now is home to the town's only restaurant (see p.212).

Practicalities

Buses from the N1 filling station at the entrance to the village link Hólmavík with Reykjavík and Ísafjörður – a full 223km away – three times a week between June and August; for Akureyri, catch connecting services at Brú. The **tourist information office** (June–Aug daily 8am–5pm; ☎451 3111, ⓦwww.holmavik.is/info) is located at the entrance to the village, opposite the supermarket and the filling station, and also has **internet** access (250kr for 30min). The new outdoor **swimming pool** is next to the campsite, with two hot pots.

Comfortable self-catering **accommodation** is available at ⚒ *Steinhúsið* (☎856 1911, ⓦwww.steinhusid.is; ❶), Hólmavík's first-ever concrete house, erected in 1911 down by the harbour at Höfðagata 1. Complete with creaking wooden floors, steep steps and period furniture, this guesthouse is a real find and merits a visit to Hólmavík alone. Elsewhere, the newly renovated *Guesthouse Borgabraut* (☎451 3136, ⓦborgabraut4.is; sleeping-bag accommodation 3000kr, ❶) is another sound self-catering choice, overlooking the harbour and the snow-covered mountains on the opposite side of the fjord. It's up on a hill at Borgabraut 4 – from the tourist office, follow the main road into town and you'll find Borgabraut running parallel with the northern end of Hafnarbraut. The **campsite** (℡451 3111) is located at the entrance to the village next to the tourist office and charges 700kr per person; showers and toilets are available in the building housing the tourist office.

The best place **to eat**, and, indeed, one of the most accomplished provincial restaurants Iceland has to offer, is the wooden-beamed ⚜ *Café Riis*, Hafnarbraut 39, whose interior is full of black and white photographs of Holmavík's fishing past. Prices are exceptionally reasonable and the quality of the food is excellent: succulent trout (2490kr), roast breast of chicken (2400kr) or pan-fried puffin breast (2400kr) are all winners. For delicious cakes, muffins and coffee during the day, head for the new café attached to the back of the witchcraft museum, *Kaffi Galdur* – which also serves breakfast. Otherwise, there's just the small **snack bar** inside the filling station with the usual pallid array of burgers and sandwiches.

To Strandir: Laugarhóll and Drangsnes

Eleven kilometres north of Hólmavík, **Route 643** begins its journey along the Strandir coast. After some 15km, it passes through the hamlet of **LAUGARHÓLL**, consisting of little more than a couple of farms grouped around a source of geothermal water, which feeds an **outdoor pool**, natural **hot pot** and a pleasant **hotel**, the *Laugarhóll* (℡451 3380, Ⓦstrandir.is/laugarholl; ❸), with inspiring views of the gentle Hólsfjall mountains, which form a serene backdrop to the place. Even if you're just driving by, stop and have a look at the unusual turf-roofed **sorcerer's cottage** (*kotbýli kuklarans*; mid-June to late June & mid-Aug to late Aug daily noon–6pm; July to mid-Aug daily 10am–6pm; 600kr), just to the left of the hotel; a simple peasant dwelling with stretched sheep's stomachs for windows, it's believed witchcraft was practised here during the seventeenth century.

From Laugarhóll, it's 20km southeast on Route 645 to **DRANGSNES**, a tiny fishing village at the mouth of Steingrímsfjörður overlooking the island of **Grímsey**, the second largest **puffin colony** in the world; you can arrange **boat trips** over there in advance with Ásbjörn Magnússon (℡451 3237 or 896 0337, Ⓔsundhani@simnet.is; 3000kr per person, minimum 4 people). According to legend, Grímsey was formed when three night trolls tried to separate the West Fjords from the rest of Iceland by digging a channel from Húnaflói bay all the way to Breiðafjörður. As the sun rose, the trolls in the west ran east but were turned to stone in Kollafjörður, whereas the troll in the north jumped over Streingrímsfjörður, landing on a rocky peninsula where she had left her ox. In anger she threw down her shovel, breaking off part of the cliff, and creating Grímsey. Locals maintain she, too, was turned to stone, and indeed, a tall rockstack known as **Kerling** (The Old Woman) stands down by the sea (between the swimming pool and *Malarhorn*; see below) looking out at her island and ox.

Drangsnes practicalities

There's a fully-equipped **campsite** above Drangsnes' harbour (June–Sept; ℡451 3207, Ⓔdrangsnes@snerpa.is), as well as a petrol pump and a village shop. However, the best place to stay is *Malarhorn* (℡899 4238, Ⓦwww.malarhorn.is; ❷) at Grundargata 17, a collection of double rooms whose interiors resemble traditional wooden cabins; there are also four smaller rooms (❶) which share facilities, a sitting room and a kitchen. Between June and August, the on-site **restaurant** serves tasty fish dishes from 1590kr. The new open-air **swimming pool** is next door, while there are three **hot pots** on the seafront opposite the church (note the signs requiring all bathers to shower beforehand at the campsite).

Djúpavík

North of Laugarhóll, Route 643 cuts into one of the remotest corners of Europe, where towering rock buttresses plunge precipitously into the icy sea and the coastline is strewn with vast expanses of **driftwood** that originated on the other side of the Arctic Ocean, in Russian Siberia. Tourist facilities in this part of the country are virtually nonexistent, but the region is stunningly beautiful and somewhere to really experience Iceland's rawness close up.

DJÚPAVÍK, a village close to the head of shadowy Reykjarfjörður, is dominated by the huge carcass of its old **herring factory** and the rusting hull of the 100-year-old former passenger and cargo ship *Suðurland*, another victim of the West Fjords weather. When the herring industry was at its height in the mid-1940s, several hundred people lived in this remote outpost, women salting the fish, men turning the remains into animal meal and oil. The factory went bankrupt in 1955 following a disastrous collapse in fish catches, but the enormous costs involved in demolishing the building – once the largest concrete structure in Europe – means that its hulking hollow shell remains, reminiscent of a Hollywood film set; Icelandic band Sigur Rós saw its potential in 2006 and even played a concert in it, attracting over three hundred people, a veritable throng in these parts.

Practicalities

Despite the evident failure of the herring adventure, there's an endearing air to diminutive Djúpavík, consisting of just seven houses and one of Iceland's most charming **hotels**, *Hótel Djúpavík* (☎451 4037, ⓦwww.djupavik.com; sleeping-bag accommodation 2500kr, ❶; breakfast 1100kr extra, dinner around 2000kr). A former hostel for the women who worked on the dockside and in the factory, this remote retreat has rooms (all with shared facilities) at the front overlooking the fjord (dolphins are sometimes spotted from the hotel), while those at the rear have views of Háafell (791m), which bears down on the tiny hamlet. In a separate building there are also a number of simple rooms (sleeping-bag accommodation 3000kr) that share a kitchen. The only way other than driving of reaching the hotel is by **flying to Gjögur** (see below); the hotel will pick you up from the airport by snowmobile if the weather demands, otherwise more conventionally by car, for around 1500kr. The hotel now owns the herring plant and runs **tours** inside (June–Aug daily at 10am or 2pm), which include access to Sögusýning Djúpavíkur (Historical Exhibition of Djúpavík; 500kr) containing evocative black and white photographs from the herring years.

Norðurfjörður

Fifteen kilometres up the coast from Djúpavík, you pass tiny **Gjögur airport** (ⓦwww.ernir.is for fares and schedule), from where it's a further thirteen kilometres to the end of the road at **NORÐURFJÖRÐUR**, one of Iceland's last places. Occupying a stunning position amid fertile farmland at the head of the fjord of the same name, the village is dominated by the mountain Krossnesfjall (646m) to the east. One of the country's most dramatically situated swimming pools, **Krossneslaug**, is just 4km northeast of the village, north of the farm at Krossnes. Here, natural springs provide a continuous source of hot water to feed the **open-air pool** down on the pebble beach, whose walls are barely a couple of metres from the icy waters of the Atlantic; a swim here is one of the most memorable experiences Iceland has to offer.

Norðurfjörður is also an **access point for Hornstrandir**; you can either hike in, or take the **ferry** (ⓦwww.westtours.is), which travels northwards up the Strandir coast to Hornvík via Reykjarfjörður three or four times per week between late

June and mid-August. From Hornvík, you can hike around Hornstrandir and then catch a ferry to Ísafjörður; see p.197 for more about Hornstrandir.

Practicalities

Norðurfjörður's **accommodation** prospects include the *Valgeirsstaðir* hostel run by Ferðafélag Ísland (☎451 4017 or 568 2533, ⓦwww.fi.is; 3300kr), with an adjoining tiny **campsite** (600kr; shared facilities with the hostel), and, by the harbour, the *Bergistangi* **guesthouse** (☎451 4003, ⓔgunnsteinn@simnet.is; sleeping bag 2200kr) and the *Norðurfjörður* (☎554 4089, ⓔgulledda@simnet.is; ❶), both simple but pleasant options. The harbour is also the place to find a small **food store** selling a limited range of fruit and vegetables, and a **petrol pump**. For something to eat, head for *Kaffi Norðurfjörður* (mid-June to mid-Aug only), also at the harbour, offering lamb chops, burgers and soup from 1050kr.

Travel details

Buses

Note that the following long-distance West Fjords buses only operate through the summer. For local services, see main text.

Bjarkalundur to: Bifröst (2 weekly; 2hr); Borgarnes (2 weekly; 2hr 30min); Búðardalur (2 weekly; 1hr); Reykjavík (2 weekly; 4hr); Reykhólar (2 weekly; 30min).

Brjánslækur to: Ísafjörður (3 weekly; 2hr); Látrabjarg (3 weekly; 2hr).

Hólmavík to: Akureyri (3 weekly; 3hr 30min); Brú (3 weekly; 2hr 15min); Ísafjörður (3 weekly; 3hr 40min); Reykjavík (3 weekly; 4hr).

Ísafjörður to: Akureyri (3 weekly; 12hr 45min); Brjánslækur (3 weekly; 3hr); Brú (3 weekly; 9hr); Hólmavík (3 weekly; 4hr); Hrafnseyri (3 weekly; 2hr); Látrabjarg (3 weekly; 4hr 40min); Patreksfjörður (3 weekly; 3hr 40min); Reykjavík (3 weekly; 11hr); Þingeyri (3 weekly; 1hr 30min).

Látrabjarg to: Brjánslækur (3 weekly; 3hr 30min); Ísafjörður (3 weekly; 5hr 30min); Patreksfjörður (3 weekly; 2hr 30min).

Patreksfjörður to: Brjánslækur (3 weekly; 1hr); Ísafjörður (3 weekly; 4hr); Látraberg (3 weekly; 1hr).

Reykhólar to: Bifröst (2 weekly; 2hr 30min); Bjarkalundur (2 weekly; 30min); Borgarnes (2 weekly; 3hr); Búðardalur (2 weekly; 1hr 30min); Reykjavík (2 weekly; 4hr 30min).

Ferries

Brjánslækur to: Flatey (2 daily; 1hr 15min); Stykkishólmur (2 daily; 3hr).

Flights

Bíldudalur to: Reykjavík (1 daily; 50min).
Gjögur to: Reykjavík (2 weekly; 50min).
Ísafjörður to: Reykjavík (2 daily; 40min).

Northwest Iceland

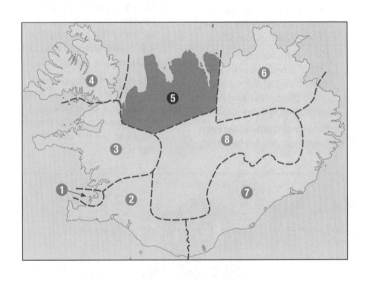

CHAPTER 5

Highlights

✳ **Þingeyrakirkja, Þingeyrar** One of Iceland's most spectacular church interiors, with an intricate wooden pulpit from the late 1600s. See p.221

✳ **Seal watching, Ósar** Get close to a rare seal-breeding colony on the Vatnsnes peninsula. See p.221

✳ **Skagi peninsula, Skagafjörður** Witness the austere beauty of one of Iceland's most exposed coastlines and gain instant respect for the hardy people who live here. See p.223

✳ **Herring museum, Siglufjörður** One of the northwest's best museums, this is the place to get to grips with Icelanders' fascination with fish. See p.229

✳ **Botanical Garden, Akureyri** Seemingly defying the northerly latitude, this delightful garden is awash with colour during the short summer months, containing an example of virtually every Icelandic flower, shrub and moss. See p.235

✳ **Ptarmigan spotting, Hrísey** In summer dozens of these plump game birds waddle through Hrísey's main village with their offspring in tow. See p.240

✳ **Hiking in Í Fjörðum** Hike through uninhabited valleys and mountain passes, all within easy striking distance of Akureyri. See p.243

✳ **The Arctic Circle, Grímsey** Crossing the magic line gives a real sense of achievement, and Grímsey is one of the best places to see the midnight sun. See p.246

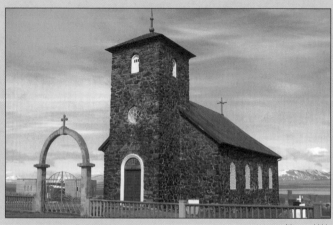

▲ Þingeyrakirkja

5

Northwest Iceland

Compared with the neighbouring West Fjords, the scenery of Northwest Iceland is much gentler and less forbidding – undulating meadows dotted with isolated barns and farmhouses are the norm here, rather than twisting fjords, though there are still plenty of impressive mountains to provide a satisfying backdrop to the whole coastline. However, what makes this section of the country stand out is the location of two of Iceland's great historical sites. Entering the region at the tiny service centre of **Brú** (also known by the name of the filling station here, **Staðarskáli**), strategically located where Route 61 from the West Fjords meets the Ringroad (Route 1), it's a short drive to **Þingeyrar**, once the location for an ancient assembly and monastery where monks compiled some of Iceland's most outstanding pieces of medieval literature. As the Ringroad heads northeast from here on its way to Akureyri, it passes through some of Iceland's most sparsely populated areas and **Blönduós**, an unprepossessing service centre for the surrounding farms and hamlets. The village is, however, the starting point for a worthwhile trip round the **Skagi** peninsula along Route 745, one of the northwest's most enchanting stretches of wilderness coastline and barren moorland. The best place to break the long journey along the north coast is the likeable **Sauðárkrókur**, enlivened by stunning sea views out over **Skagafjörður** and **Drangey** island, once home to saga hero **Grettir**, who bathed here in the nearby natural hot pool now named after him. Just half an hour's drive away is the north's second great historical site, **Hólar í Hjaltadal**, which functioned as the ecumenical and educational centre of the north of the country between the twelfth century and the Reformation. A further detour up Route 76, via the Icelandic Emigration Centre at **Hofsós**, brings you to the fishing village of **Siglufjörður**. Hemmed in on three sides by sheer rock walls, the village more than repays the effort of getting there and is especially worth a visit if you've not managed to make it to the West Fjords since the surrounding scenery is, unusually for the north coast, almost identical.

Slicing deep into the coastline of this part of northern Iceland, **Eyjafjörður**, or Island Fjord, is named after the island of **Hrísey** at its mouth, renowned for its rich birdlife. Bordered by flat-topped perpetually snow-covered mountains, Eyjafjörður is the country's longest fjord and was for centuries **Akureyri**'s window on the world as ships sailed its length to deliver their goods to the largest market in northern Iceland. Today, though, fisheries have taken over as the town's economic mainstay, profiting from the rich fishing grounds found offshore. With a population of fifteen thousand making it the largest town outside the Reykjavík area, not only does Akureyri boast a stunning setting at the head of Eyjafjörður, but it's also blessed with some of the warmest and most stable weather anywhere in the country, a perfect complement to the long white nights of summer. Between June

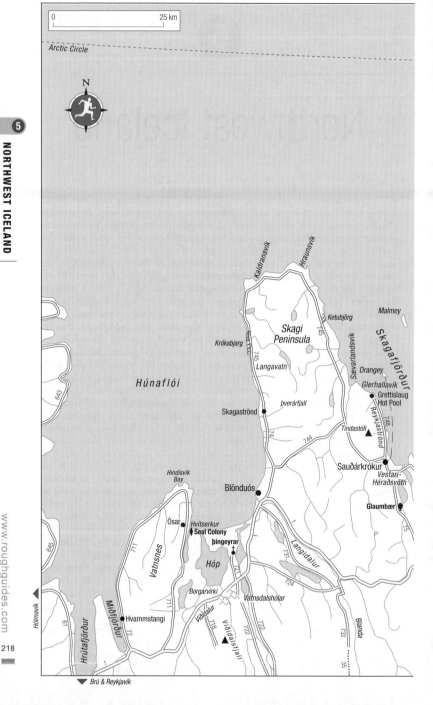

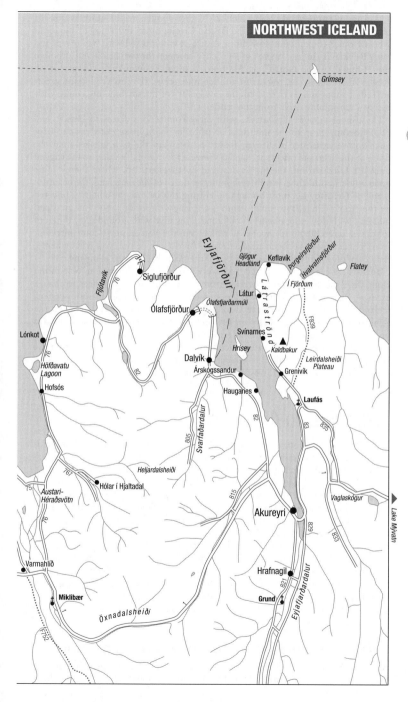

Grímsey

Eyjafjörður

Fljótavík

76

Siglufjörður

Ólafsfjörður

Ólafsfjarðarmúli

Gjögur
Headland

Keflavík

Þorgeirsfjörður

Hvalvatnsfjörður

Flatey

Í Fjörðum

Látur

Láturströnd

F839

Lónkot

76

Höfðavatu
Lagoon

82

Dalvík

Árskógssandur

Hrísey

Svínarnes

Kaldbakur

Leirdalsheiði
Plateau

Hofsós

Haganes

Grenivík

Laufás

83

835

Svarfaðardalur

805

767

Heljardalsheiði

Hólar í Hjaltadal

815

1

Vaglaskógur

15

Austari-
Héraðsvötn

76

Akureyri

829

833

Varmahlíð

Hrafnagil

821

Vaglaskógur

Miklibær

Öxnadalsheiði

Grund

Eyjafjarðardalur

1

F752

Lake Mývatn

www.roughguides.com

and August temperatures can reach 20°C hereabouts, really quite warm for somewhere just 100km south of the **Arctic Circle**, much to the joy of the locals who are quick to point out how sunny Akureyri is compared with windswept and rainy Reykjavík. Indeed, there's great rivalry between the two places and although the "Capital of the North", as Akureyri is often known, can't compete with Reykjavík's eclectic bar, restaurant and nightlife scene, the town's pleasant streets are full of shops and services, with the raw beauty of the surrounding countryside barely a ten-minute drive from the centre.

The fishing villages of **Dalvík**, with ferry connections across to Hrísey, and **Ólafsfjörður**, close to the mouth of Eyjafjörður, both make excellent day-trips once you've exhausted Akureyri; Route 82 between the two villages hugs the shore of the fjord and offers spectacular **views** across the chilly water to the rugged peaks of **Látraströnd**, the fjord's deserted northeastern tip, where there's some good wilderness **hiking**. Just forty kilometres north of the mainland, the beautiful island of **Grímsey** is a must for anyone visiting this part of the country; bisected by the Arctic Circle, this rocky island is a springy carpet of moor and grassland bursting with flowering plants, its cliffs and skies alive with around sixty different species of screeching birds, many of which consider you an unwelcome intruder. Even if you haven't yet been attacked by an Arctic tern before, you will be here – they even divebomb visitors as they board the plane back to the mainland.

Buses between Reykjavík and Akureyri run through the region year-round along the Ringroad; if you're arriving from the West Fjords, you'll need to change buses at Brú. You can also enter the area direct from Gullfoss in southwestern Iceland along the **Kjölur route** through the Interior, which lands you on the Ringroad around halfway between Brú and Akureyri. This summer-only road is open to conventional cars (with extreme care) and is covered by daily buses; see p.315 for more about the route. Once here, there are **local bus** routes from the Ringroad town of Varmahlíð to Sauðárkrókur, and from there to Siglufjörður, as well as from Akureyri northwest to Dalvík and Ólafsfjörður.

From Brú to Akureyri

The 230-kilometre-long stretch of the Ringroad **between Brú and Akureyri** is one of its least interesting, and many travellers speed through it as quickly as possible. But while the Ringroad itself holds few attractions, it is worth detouring off it: highlights include the **Vatnsnes peninsula**, where there's a good chance of seeing seals; the north's great historical sites of **Þingeyrar** and **Hólar í Hjaltadal**; and two fine examples of small-town Iceland, **Sauðárkrókur** and **Siglufjörður**.

Travelling by bus, it's almost impossible to avoid spending some time at the tiny staging post of **BRÚ**, some 120km from Hólmavík in the West Fjords, 85km from Borgarnes on the west coast and 38km from easterly Hvammstangi, the nearest settlements of any size. Brú began life in the 1950s as little more than a telephone exchange, post office and a **bridge** (*brú* in Icelandic) over the Hrútafjarðará, which flows into Hrútafjörður fjord on Húnaflói bay. Today the post office has been downgraded to a postbox and the only other signs of life here belong to the filling station (with an ATM), busy with travellers taking a break at the **restaurant** inside or waiting for an onward bus connection.

Hvammstangi and the Vatnsnes peninsula

About 30km northeast of Brú, the eastern shore of Miðfjörður fjord is the setting for the only town in the area, **HVAMMSTANGI**, although "town" is something of a misnomer since only six hundred people live here. Just 6km north of the Ringroad along Route 72 (buses pull in here on request), the place survives on shrimp fishing, and a couple of brightly coloured fishing vessels are often moored in the tiny harbour, right by the one and only main road which cuts through the handful of houses that pass as the town centre.

From Hvammstangi, you'll need your own transport to follow Route 711 as it heads northeast around the **Vatnsnes peninsula**, a wild and uninhabited finger of land on the eastern side of Húnaflói known for its superb views out over the bay towards the needle-sharp peaks of the Strandir coast in the West Fjords (see p.210). While ascending tiers of craggy, inaccessible hills form the spine of the peninsula, the land closer to the shore is surprisingly green and is given over to grazing land for horses; you'll also spot flocks of **greylag geese**. At **Ósar**, just around the head of the promontory on the more sheltered eastern coast, there's a **seal-breeding ground**, where many of the creatures and their young can be spotted lolling idly on the black volcanic sands during June and July – a rare opportunity to see these appealing creatures at close quarters. A short walking path leads down to the sands from the friendly **youth hostel** *Ósar* (May–Oct; ☎862 2778, ⓦhostel.is; 2000kr per person, bed linen 900kr extra; double rooms ❶), set on a farm, 29km north of the Ringroad along Route 711. This self-catering hostel, complete with snug log cabins as well as regular dorms, is worth seeking out for its peaceful surroundings and undisturbed views of mountains and ocean across to the rugged coastline of the Skagi peninsula, which marks the eastern edge of Húnaflói bay. Ósar is also the location for the fifteen-metre-high rock formation **Hvítserkur**, a striking landmark. Sculpted by the tremendous force of the sea, this craggy rock, just off the coast, looks like a forbidding prehistoric monster rearing up from the waves.

Þingeyrar

As it heads southwards down the eastern shore of Vatnsnes, Route 711 rejoins the Ringroad in **Víðidalur**, one of the area's most populated valleys and dotted with some beautifully located farms, most notably **Auðunarstaðir** (between the junctions of Routes 711 and 716 with the Ringroad), named after the evidently well-endowed settler Auðun Skökull (Auðun the horse phallus), to whom the British royals can apparently trace their family line. The breathtaking backdrop of the brown and green hues of Víðidalsfjall mountain (993m) forms the eastern side of the valley through which one of the northwest's best salmon rivers, the lengthy Víðidalsá, flows from its source at Stórisandur in the Interior.

However, it's not for the scenery that this part of the country is best known, since it's also the location of the ancient site of **Þingeyrar**, which lies just 6km north of the Ringroad along Route 721. If you don't have your own transport, you will find that it's a straightforward walk, if necessary. This was originally the site of a **legislative assembly** during the Icelandic Commonwealth (see Contexts, p.322), and the first Bishop of Hólar, Jón Ögmundarson, pledged to build a church and an associated farm here if God were to relieve a severe local famine. When the land began to regain its productivity, the bishop took things one step further and established Iceland's **first monastery**, Þingeyraklaustur, here in 1133, which remained in existence until the Reformation in 1550. The monks went on to copy and transcribe some of the country's most outstanding pieces of medieval litera-ture, and it was on this spot that many of the sagas were first written down for posterity.

There's nothing left of the monastery, but a superb nineteenth-century church, **Þingeyrakirkja**, now stands adjacent to where the monks once lived and worked. Constructed of large blocks of basalt, brought here on sledges dragged across the nearby frozen lagoon of Hóp, the church was the first building on the site to be made of stone – all previous structures had been of turf – and it brought much admiration from local worthies. Although its grey mass is indeed an impressive sight, clearly visible from miles around, it's the interior that really makes a trip here worthwhile, with its stark white walls setting off the blue ceiling, painted with a thousand golden stars, and simple green pews. The wooden pulpit dates from 1696 and is thought to come from Denmark or Holland, whereas the altarpiece, inset with religious figures made of alabaster, dates from the fifteenth century and was originally made in the English town of Nottingham for the monastery there. The wooden figures of Christ and the twelve apostles lining the balcony were carved in 1983 to replace the original statues from Germany, which are now in the National Museum in Reykjavík (see p.75). The church is **open** from July to September; at other times call in at the adjacent horse farm, Þingeyrar, where the keys are kept.

Blönduós

Clustered around the turn-off to Route 721 for Þingeyrar and Route 722, the extensive area of small hillocks known as **Vatnsdalshólar** is leftover debris from a massive landslide from the Vatnsdalsfjall mountains west of the Hóp lagoon. These conical shaped hills cover a total area of around four square kilometres and are so numerous that they have become one of Iceland's three "uncountables": the other two are the islands of Breiðafjörður and the lakes of Arnarvatnsheiði moors near Húsafell. One of the hillocks, Þrístapar, has gone down in history as the location for Iceland's last beheading, when a couple were executed on it in 1830 for a double murder.

From the Vatnsdalshólar, it's a further 19km along the Ringroad to **BLÖNDUÓS** (84km from Brú), the focal point of Húnaflói bay, with a huge hospital and its modern, multicoloured houses grouped on either side of one of Iceland's longest rivers, the glacial Blanda. Without a good harbour the town is merely a service centre for the locality, pasteurizing milk from the surrounding farms. The centre, consisting of a handful of uneventful streets and the odd shop, straddles both banks of the river, accessed from the Ringroad by the roads of Blöndubyggð on the southern side and Húnabraut on the northern shore.

There's little reason to stop here, as the town's main attraction, its astonishingly ugly concrete **church**, can be seen from the Ringroad anyway. Designed to resemble a volcanic crater, the church sits opposite the tourist office atop a small hill overlooking the town and its charmless grey walls therefore dominate almost any view of Blönduós. The interior is equally austere, with unadorned walls of concrete and excellent acoustics – if the church is locked ask at the tourist office for the key. Otherwise, the only other thing to detain you in town itself is the interesting **Hafíssetrið** (Sea Ice Exhibition Centre; June–Aug daily 11am–5pm; free), housed in Iceland's oldest wooden building dating from 1733, down by the river near Aðalgata. Húnaflói is generally the first bay in Iceland to encounter sea ice during the winter months and the museum, explains fully how this phenomenon occurs – and about the polar bears who sometimes ride the sea ice as it floats from Greenland to Iceland. Indeed, the exhausted and half-starved polar bear which came ashore near Skagaströnd (see p.223) in July 2008, now stuffed, is on display in the museum. It's safe to skip the town's other museum: the **Heimilisiðnaðarsafnið** (Museum of Handicrafts; late June to late Aug daily 2–5pm; ☏452 4067; 450kr) at Árbraut 7, with its dreary collections of knitting and weaving.

Blönduós practicalities

All **buses** from Reykjavík via Borgarnes and Brú to Akureyri stop at the N1 **filling station**. The **tourist information office** (early June to late Aug Mon–Fri

8am–7.30pm, Sat 10am–4pm; ☎452 4520, ⓦwww.northwest.is) is on the northern side of the river on the main street, just over the bridge. There's **accommodation** at the overly pink *Hótel Blönduós*, Aðalgata 6 (☎452 4205, ⓦwww .hotelblonduos.is; ❹), whose staff also run better-value wooden cabins (☎820 1300, ⓦwww.gladheimar.is; 10,000–17,000kr) located next to the tourist office and overlooking the river; each sleeps up to eight, is complete with kitchen and shower and also have their own outdoor jacuzzi on the terrace. Alternatively, there's the **campsite** (June–Aug; ☎452 4520), next to the tourist information.

Eating options in Blönduós are limited to the bright and airy *Potturinn og Pannan*, beside the church, offering fish of the day (2590kr), grilled chicken breast (1890kr) and even seal steak (4800kr), and the homely *Við Árbakkann* café-bar, at the corner of Húnabraut and Holtabraut, which serves up tasty toasted sandwiches (660kr) and soup and salad (1670kr); coffee here is 340kr, a beer is 890kr. The **vínbúð** (Mon–Thurs 2–6pm, Fri 2–7pm) is at Aðalgata 8, next to the hotel.

The Skagi peninsula

Barely a kilometre or so outside Blönduós, where the Ringroad swings sharply inland to follow the course of Langidalur valley towards Varmahlíð, Route 74 (no public transport beyond Skagaströnd) strikes off north for the **Skagi peninsula**, a tooth-shaped chunk of land that forms the eastern side of Húnaflói bay. After 23km the road comes to the peninsula's only centre of habitation (barely 610 people live here), **SKAGASTRÖND**, a terribly ugly place dominated by a hulking fish factory down by the harbour and the brooding heights of the **Spákonufellsborg** (646m) mountain which bears down on the settlement from across the main road. Although trading began here centuries ago, there's precious little to show for it since most buildings today date from the tasteless expansion of the 1940s herring boom. There's no real reason to tarry, and it's a much better idea to press on to the unspoilt nature of the peninsula beyond, unless you're looking for fuel at the **filling station** at the entrance to the village or a bite **to eat** at the enormous log cabin *Kántrýbær*, that most curious of Icelandic establishments – an imitation country-and-western restaurant serving up steaks, burgers and fries (from 1090kr) – next door at Hólanesvegur 11. Upstairs, a radio station, Útvarp Kántrýbær, pumps out country hits on 96.7FM, and 100.7FM in Sauðárkrókur.

From Skagaströnd, the unsurfaced Route 745 begins its circuit of the **Skagi peninsula**, a lonely uninhabited landscape of desolate rocky moorland studded with numerous tarns and tussocky grassland. Although the attraction of the peninsula is primarily its barren landscapes, it's worth stopping for a closer look at one or two points of interest along the way. On the western shore, roughly 15km north of Skagaströnd, the ten-kilometre-long cliffs at **Króksbjarg** and the glittering **waterfall** where the Fossá river tumbles down the cliff-face into the sea are an essential first stop. Beyond Króksbjarg, the road passes several deserted farms before reaching the sweeping bay of **Kaldranavík**, at the tip of the peninsula, one of the best places for truly magnificent ocean vistas. Having weaved past the remote farm of Hraun, at Hraunsvík on the northeastern extremity of the peninsula, the road finally veers south following the coastline of **Skagafjörður** fjord for the rugged sheer sea cliff (signed from the road) **Ketubjörg**, actually the remains of an old volcano, and the accompanying rock pillar, **Kerling**, just off the shore to the northeast. From here it's an uneventful and easy drive on towards Sauðárkrókur.

Varmahlíð and Glaumbær

Continuing east from Blönduós along the Ringroad, it's 25 kilometres to where Route 732 heads south to join the **Kjölur Route** (Route 35) across the Interior to

Gullfoss (see p.114). About the same distance again along the Ringroad, the minuscule settlement of **VARMAHLÍÐ** is of interest only as the junction with Route 75 heading north up to Sauðárkrókur via **Glaumbær**, and for one of Iceland's best activity centres specializing in **whitewater rafting**. Established in 1992, Ævintýraferðir (T453 8383, Wwww.rafting.is) operates rafting tours (May–Sept 2–3 daily) of varying degrees of difficulty on the nearby rivers, Blanda, Vestari Jökulsá and Austari Jökulsá – its office is west of the centre, 150m off the Ringroad near the junction with Route 752. Trips range from four hours of relatively easy rafting (6500kr) to three days of serious rapid-shooting (59,800kr).

Varmahlíð's **accommodation** is limited to the charmless *Hotel Varmahlíð* (T453 8170, Whotelvarmahlid.is; ❹), or the much better-value *Lauftún* (T453 8133; ❶), a simple private farm with just five rooms, 1km or so east of Varmahlíð on the Ringroad, just beyond the bridge over the Húseyjarkvísl river; it also has sleeping-bag accommodation (2500kr) and a **campsite**. **Eating** options are limited to the hotel restaurant or self-catering from the supermarket at the central road junction. The **swimming pool** is up on Norðurbrún above the hotel. All Ringroad **buses** between Reykjavík and Akureyri, plus the Kjölur service, call at the filling station in Varmahlíð; change here for year-round buses to Glaumbær and Sauðárkrókur.

Glaumbær

About 14km from Varmahlíð up Route 75 is the immaculately preserved historical farm, **Glaumbær** (June to early Sept daily 9am–6pm; Wwww.glaumbaer.is; 600kr) – all **buses** to Sauðárkrókur stop here. Though founded in Settlement times, Glaumbær's current row of wood-fronted turf-walled and turf-roofed dwellings date from 1750 to 1879, and were inhabited up until 1947. With their lop-sided, hobbit-like construction (such as wooden-frame windows set into the grassy walls), the buildings are both charmingly rustic and also a powerful

▲ Turfed buildings at Glaumbæ

reminder of the impoverished lifestyle many people led in Iceland during the eighteenth and nineteenth centuries.

The adjacent timber building houses the Skagafjörður **folk museum** (same hours and ticket), with a collection of rustic implements once used on the farm, from spinning wheels to brightly painted clothes chests. Not only does the farm demonstrate centuries-old Icelandic building techniques, it's also where **Snorri Þorfinsson**, the first American born of European parents (in 1003), is buried; Snorri came to Iceland with his parents and lived out his life on the farm here. A simple statue of Snorri and his mother, **Guðríður Þorbjarnardóttir** (see "Hellnar", p.182), by sculptor Ásmundur Sveinsson stands in the graveyard next to the church.

Sauðárkrókur and around

Set at the base of the broad, north-facing Skagafjörður, 25km north of Varmahlíð, **SAUÐÁRKRÓKUR** is the second-largest town on the northern Icelandic coast, with a population of 2600. It's a likeable spot and the only place hereabouts where you'll find signs of life in the streets on summer evenings. While the town's centre takes no longer than an hour or so to see, its main attractions are the boat trips to the nearby island of **Drangey** and a dip in **Grettislaug hot pool**, both connected to Iceland's classic outlaw tale, *Grettir's Saga*, and **horseriding** tours out into the surrounding countryside with Topp Hestar (☎453 5130, ⓦwww.topphestar.is; 6500kr for two hours).

Arrival, information and accommodation

Buses operate all year between Varmahlíð and Sauðárkrókur, stopping at the filling station at Aðalgata 22. Between June and September, buses also run daily except Saturday from Sauðárkrókur **to Siglufjörður**, jumping-off point for some great hikes (see p.230).

For **internet** access, try the **library** inside the Safnahúsið building in Faxatorg square, opposite the Shell station, on Skagfirðingabraut.

Curiously, for such an off-the-beaten-track provincial town, Sauðárkrókur boasts one of Iceland's most charismatic **hotels**, the ⚸ *Hótel Tindastóll* (☎453 5002, ⓦwww.hoteltindastoll.com; ❹), an elegant 1820s listed timber building that oozes old-fashioned charm at every turn. Marlene Dietrich stayed here during World War II, while entertaining British troops stationed in the area, and the room she stayed in – the *Guðríður Þorbjarnardóttir* suite – is reputedly **haunted**, often smelling of cigar smoke although it's a no-smoking room. Each of the ten low-ceilinged rooms has original wooden floors, beams and broadband internet. There's even a copy of Grettislaug (see p.227) at the back of the hotel. Less extravagant is the *Mikligarður* **guesthouse**, opposite the church at Kirkjutorg 3 (☎453 6880, ⓦmikligardur.is; ❷), a pretty house with a white balcony, small but perfectly adequate rooms (with and without facilities) plus a guest kitchen upstairs. Alternatively, the *Hótel Mikligarður* (June–Aug; ☎453 6880, ⓦwww .mikligardur.is; sleeping-bag accommodation 3500kr; ❸), opposite the hospital at Skagfirðingabraut 21, is based in the vast, local boarding school, with numerous institutionalized en-suite rooms. The **campsite** (☎453 8860) is on Skagfirðinga-braut, next to the swimming pool, at the southern end of the town.

The Town

Occupying a triangle of suburban streets bordered by fjordside Strandvegur, Hegrabraut and Skagfirðingabraut, Sauðárkrókur's brightly painted houses and wide open spaces, with views of the bustling harbour on the edge of its centre, lend a pioneering edge to the town. Although there are few sights to speak of, wandering around the streets is a pleasant enough way to pass an hour or two – there's no set route to take, but sooner or later you'll wind up on the main street, **Aðalgata**, which is home to a handful of shops, restaurants and, at no. 16, the **Minjahús museum** (mid-June to Aug daily 1–6pm; free), whose key exhibition throws light on recent, local archaeological excavations, which, among other things, have uncovered several skeletons from an eleventh-century cemetery in nearby Keldudalur. Nearby, **Sauðárkrókskirkja** is an impressive wooden church from 1892, standing amid an area of residential homes and commercial premises, which is worth a look for its fourteen highly unusual stained-glass windows. The futuristic patterns on the centre panes portray a variety of scenes from the Crucifixion to the Holy Trinity. However, more engaging is the story of the errant polar bear, shot just 15km from the town centre in June 2008 and now stuffed for posterity, which is told at the **Nátturustofa** (Mon–Fri 9am–4pm; free), opposite the church, at Aðalgata 2. The hungry bear had swum over from Greenland before roaming the hills above Sauðárkrókur looking for food; check out the alarming photograph inside the museum of the foolhardy cameraman and local farmer, who came within 20m of the bear – they are lucky to be alive today.

Before leaving town make sure you walk down, past **the shrimp processing plant**, to the **harbour** where there's a vast collection of **dried fish racks**. Here, row upon row of wooden frames have been erected and draped in several hundred thousand fish heads and bodies – all awaiting export to various African countries where wind-dried Icelandic fish is considered a delicacy – the stench, though, can be quite overpowering.

Eating and drinking

Sauðárkrókur's few **places to eat and drink** are all located in the centre of town along Aðalgata. *Kaffi Krókur*, at no. 16, is a modern, airy bistro serving burgers (from 1490kr), pasta (from 2290kr) and several tasty fish dishes (from 2450kr) whereas, opposite, at no. 15, a bright blue wooden building houses *Ólafshús*, a fine dining establishment, with top-notch fish and meat dishes – try the excellent roast lamb (3190kr), as well as a good-value lunch buffet (1400kr). The **vínbúð** is at Smáragrund 2 (Mon–Thurs 11am–6pm, Fri 11am–7pm, Sat 11am–4pm).

Drangey

Boat trips, operated by Drangey Tours (May–Aug daily no fixed schedule; 3–4hr; 6000kr; ☏453 6310), leave from the harbour at **Reykir** (see p.227) for the steep-sided, flat-topped island of **Drangey**, which resembles an arrow pointing north. This is undoubtedly one of the best tours in northern Iceland, with an unbeatable combination of birdlife and history – although it's not one for the faint-hearted given the steep climb required once ashore and several dizzying drops.

Although the island is now a bird sanctuary where kittiwakes, puffins and guille-mots can be seen in abundance, it was once the hideout of Grettir the Strong, or **Grettir Ásmundarson**, hero of *Grettir's Saga*. This is Iceland's great outlaw story, about a man who is born out of his time: Grettir has the wild spirit of a Viking, but lives a generation after the country's conversion to Christianity. Outlawed for three years in his youth for killing a man, Grettir spends the rest of his life performing great deeds – often for the benefit of others – yet something bad always seems to result from his actions, isolating him from his fellow men and eventually forcing him into perpetual banditry. In the end, he and his brother **Illugi** settle on Drangey, living off sheep left here by local farmers. Yet even as he is granted a pardon at the Alþing for his past crimes, Grettir is hunted down by his enemies and finally killed after three years on the island.

From the boat moorings a narrow winding path streaks steeply up the island's rocky cliffs to the grassy meadow at the summit of this 180m high plug of palagonite rock. The deep hollow in the turf here, where the bedrock shows through, is where Grettir once lived, with a lookout to the west. The island's **northern summit** is accessible only by climbing a rusty ladder, erected by local bird hunters, which overhangs an area of crumbling rock – definitely not one to attempt if you're afraid of heights. Incidentally, for fresh water Grettir depended on a spring virtually hidden under a steep rock overhang on the island's southern cliff. Even today, the only way to reach the source is to clamber hand over hand down a knotted rope, trying not to look down at the 500m sheer drop beneath.

Reykir and Grettislaug

The stretch of bitterly cold sea between the island and the farm at **REYKIR** on the mainland opposite is known as **Grettir's Swim**, which the outlaw reputedly swam across to fetch the glowing embers he'd spotted on the mainland after his own fire has gone out; its 7.5km are still sometimes swum for sport despite the water temperature in summer barely rising above 9°C. However, if the bawdy humour of the sagas is anything to go by, this feat certainly takes its toll, even on Viking superheroes; according to *Grettir's Saga* two young women, finding Grettir lying naked on the ground numb after his swim through the freezing waters, declare, "He is certainly big enough in the chest but it seems very odd how small he is farther down. That part of him isn't up to the rest of him," to which Grettir retorts, "the wench has complained that my penis is small and the boastful slut may well be right. But a small one can grow and I'm still a young man, so wait until I get into action, my lass."

Indeed, to revive himself after the swim, Grettir jumped into a hot pool now known as **Grettislaug**, located at Reykir. This is reached along the very bumpy twenty-kilometre Route 748 from the harbour in Sauðárkrókur. Greedily, the landowners now charge admission (300kr) to this piece of Icelandic heritage and have cordoned the area off with a series of fences and gates. Although stone slabs now act as seats and the area around it has been paved with blocks of basalt, you can still do as Grettir did and step into the hot water and steam to your heart's content, admiring the twenty-kilometre-long, snow-splashed mountainface of Tindastóll (989m) on one side, the open ocean and views of Drangey on the other – a quintessentially Icelandic experience. Should you want to stay here, there's now a log cabin with **double rooms** (☏453 6310; sleeping-bag accommodation 2000kr; ❶; breakfast is an extra 1000kr) and a simple **campsite**.

At low tide only it's possible to reach the enchanting **Glerhallavík** bay from Grettislaug: from the pool, walk along the beach around the foot of Tindastóll to the bay, where the sight of thousands and thousands of shining quartz stones on the beach, buffed by the pounding surf, is quite breathtaking. Note that it's forbidden to remove them from the bay.

Eastern Skagafjörður

From Sauðárkrókur, it's a hundred-kilometre run along routes 75 and 76 up the eastern side of Skagafjörður to **Siglufjörður**: between May and September several **buses** a week run this way. It's worth making the short detour off Route 76 to **Hólar í Hjaltadal**, which was northern Iceland's ecumenical and educational centre until the Reformation. Today, this tranquil place in the foothills of Hjaltadalur valley consists solely of a redstone cathedral and an agricultural college, a remote and peaceful spot that's worth seeking out – particularly if you fancy **hiking**, since a trail leads from here over to Dalvík (see p.239). Beyond Hólar, Route 76 leads north to **Hofsós**, another diminutive settlement, best known as a study centre for North Americans of Icelandic origin keen to trace their roots, and beyond to **Lónkot**, an ideal choice of accommodation if you want to spend the night out in the wilds – and sample some truly inspiring local cuisine.

Hólar í Hjaltadal

Lying 12km down Route 767, which runs east off Route 76 about thirty minutes from Sauðárkrókur, the hamlet of **HÓLAR Í HJALTADAL**, or simply Hólar, was very much the cultural capital of the north from the twelfth until the eighteenth century: monks studied here, manuscripts were transcribed and Catholicism flourished until the Reformation. Now home to just sixty-odd people, most of whom work at the agricultural college – this and the cathedral are the only buildings remaining – it was the site of the country's **first printing press** in 1530, set up by Iceland's last Catholic bishop, Jón Arason (who was beheaded twenty years later at Skálholt for his resistance to the spread of the Reformation from the south).

A church has stood on this spot since Arason's time, but the present **cathedral** (to enter, ask in the college next door) was built in 1759–63 in late Baroque style, using local red sandstone from the mountain Hólabyrða, and is the second-oldest stone building in the country. Inside, the fifteenth-century alabaster altarpiece over the cathedral's south door is similar in design to that in the church at Þingeyrar (see p.201), and was likewise made in Nottingham, England. The main altarpiece, with its ornate carvings of Biblical figures originated in Germany around 1500 and was given to the cathedral by its most famous bishop, whose memory is honoured in the adjacent bell tower: a mosaic of tiny tiles, by Icelandic artist **Erró**, marks a small chapel and headstone, under which the bishop's bones are buried.

Practicalities

Though the Sauðárkrókur–Siglufjörður **bus** will currently call in at Hólar on request (daily except Sat), it doesn't stop long enough to look around, meaning you're stranded here until the next onwards bus – unless you hike back to Route 76 the following morning to pick up a passing service. You could, however, get in or out along the two-day **hiking trail** to Dalvík (see p.239). If you do need to spend the night at Hólar, you can stay at the agricultural college, which operates as a **hotel** (June–Aug only, ☎455 6300, ⓦ www.holar.is; ❷), with a swimming pool and hot pot attached. The **campsite** is located behind the main building, and the college's **restaurant** serves a variety of dishes, often including locally reared Arctic char.

Hofsós

Seventeen kilometres up Route 76 from the Hólar junction, **HOFSÓS** is a tiny, nondescript village on the eastern shores of Skagafjörður, consisting of one street and a tiny harbour, with a population of around two hundred. It's primarily a base for the hundreds of Americans and Canadians of Icelandic descent who come here to visit the Vesturfarasetrið, or **Icelandic Emigration Center** (June–Aug daily 11am–6pm; other times by arrangement; 500kr; ☎453 7935, ⓦ www.hofsos.is), housed in several buildings beautifully set on the seafront by the harbour. The centre's genealogy and information service is located in the Frændgarður building, while the main exhibition A New Land, A New Life, tracing the history of the Icelanders who emigrated west over the sea, is on display in the red-roofed building just beyond. In the Konungsverslunarhúsið, before the bridge, there's a moving display of black and white photographs recounting the lives of children who emigrated to North Dakota.

Up the hill from the emigration centre, the *Sunnuberg* (☎453 7434 or 853 0220, ⓔ gisting@hofsos.is; ❶, breakfast 1000kr extra) at Suðurbraut 8 has en-suite rooms with sea views. **Eating** is only possible at the *Sólvík*, opposite the centre, with a delightful wooden terrace with sea views, serving fish and chips (1850kr), steak and chips (2890kr) and sandwiches (from 850kr).

However, for truly inspirational local cuisine it's worth pushing on to the **restaurant** and **guesthouse** of *Lónkot* (June–Aug; ☏453 7432, ⓦwww.lonkot .is), 12km further north beyond the Höfðavatn lagoon and opposite the now abandoned island of **Malmey**, where, according to legend, neither mice nor horses will thrive, and if a married couple lives here longer than twenty years, the wife will disappear, never to be seen again. *Lónkot* specializes in cuisine using only the finest local ingredients, for example marinated breast of Skagafjörður puffin, or locally caught pan-fried cod (4 courses for 6500kr). **Accommodation** here comes in various forms inside farm buildings: double rooms (❷) with simple kitchenettes located in a converted sheepshed or larger apartments with beds in curtained-off ship-style berths.

Siglufjörður

Having wound northeast around the convoluted coast for 60km from Hofsós, Route 76 cuts through an unpleasantly dark and narrow single-lane tunnel to land you at the enjoyably remote fishing village of **SIGLUFJÖRÐUR**, a highlight of any trip to the northwest. The country's most northerly town, Siglufjörður clings precariously to the foot of steep mountain walls which enclose an isolated narrow fjord on the very edge of Iceland: the **Arctic Circle** is barely 40km away and you're as far north here as Canada's Baffin Island and central Alaska. Winters can be particularly severe, though in summer, Siglufjörður makes an excellent base from which to **hike** across the surrounding mountains.

From 1900 to 1970, Siglufjörður was the **herring** capital of the North Atlantic, when hundreds of fishing boats would crowd into the tiny fjord to unload their catches onto the rickety piers that once stretched out from the quayside, where **herring girls**, as they were known, would gut and salt them. During a good season, casual labour and the number of fishermen (who were, in the early part of the century at any rate, primarily Norwegian) could swell the town's population threefold to over ten thousand. Their story is brought to life in film, photographs and exhibits at the **Síldarminjasafn Íslands** (Herring Museum; daily late June to mid-Aug 10am–6pm; rest of the year 1–5pm; ⓦhttp://herring.siglo.is/en; 800kr), at Snorragata 15, an old salting station that housed around fifty herring girls – you can still see graffiti, daubed in nail varnish, on the walls of the second-floor room where they once slept, alongside faded black and white photographs of heart-throb Cary Grant. The new wooden-fronted building adjacent to the main museum has been authentically designed to show what a 1930s herring factory looked like.

Today, Siglufjörður's heyday is long gone and the place is considerably quieter with a population of just fourteen hundred people. It's a pleasant spot, consisting of a handful of parallel streets with unkempt multicoloured homes grouped around the main street, **Túngata**, which turns into **Snorragata** as it approaches the **harbour**, busy with the goings-on of a low-key port. Here, you'll see fishermen mending their nets in the shipyard and fish hanging out to dry – the town still produces kippers (smoked herring) from a factory down by the harbour. Once you've seen the herring museum there's some excellent **hiking** to be had along the trails that lead up out of the fjord (see box).

Practicalities

Between May and September, **buses** run back to Sauðárkrókur daily except Saturday, from the Olís filling station at the junction of Aðalgata and Tjarnargata.

Hiking around Siglufjörður

Several excellent day **hikes** can easily be undertaken from Siglufjörður. The trails described below are shown on the hiking **map** of Siglufjörður available at the Síldarminjasafnið herring era museum (see p.229), and you can check out details in advance at ⓦwww.siglo.is/en.

The best of the shorter routes (5–7hr), forming a clockwise circle around the town, begins at the southern edge of Siglufjörður, where the road veers left around the head of the fjord. Follow the walking path up **Eyrafjall**, heading towards the Dalaskarð pass, then over the mountain tops and up **Hafnarfjall**, from where there's an excellent view over the fjord, the surrounding peaks and even Grímsey. From here it's an easy climb up **Hafnarhyrna** (687m), the highest point on Hafnarfjall and the starting point for the easy descent towards the bowl-shaped hollow of **Hvanneyrarskál**, a well-known lovers' haunt during the herring boom. From this hollow, a road leads back down into town.

A second, longer trail (10–14hr) begins beyond the disused airport on the eastern side of the fjord (follow the main road through the village to get there) and leads southeast up the valley of **Kálfsdalur**, which begins just above the lighthouse beyond the airport, past **Kálfsvatn** lake, over the **Kálfsskarð** pass (450m) before descending into Nesdalur valley on the other side of the ridge. The trail then leads north through the valley to the coast and the deserted farm, **Reyðará**. From the farm, the trail leads west along the steep slopes of Nesnúpur (595m) passing a lighthouse and several abandoned huts, built by the American military during World War II as a radar station. Once back on the eastern side of the fjord the path trail continues along the shoreline towards the airport and Siglufjörður.

If you're **driving**, things look set to improve from late 2010 when a new **tunnel** is due to open, linking the town with Ólafsfjörður and avoiding the circuitous summer-only Route 82, which, incidentally, is the highest mountain road in Iceland; expect bus routes to change accordingly.

Accommodation in Siglufjörður is limited. *Gistiheimilið Hvanneyri* (☎467 1506, ⓦwww.hvanneyri.com; ❶), Aðalgata 10, is a monument to bad taste: plastic flowers, garish floral drapes and multicoloured swirls of paint daubed over the staircase. Rooms here all share facilities and are a little on the dark side, though there is a well-equipped kitchen for self-caterers. The other option is the **campsite** on Snorragata (☎460 5600), south of town beyond the harbour.

When it comes to eating, things are not much better: **food** supplies are available at the supermarket (Mon–Fri 9am–7pm, Sat 10am–7pm, Sun 1–6pm) at Suðurgata 2–4, while *Pizza 67* at Aðalgata 30 has a range of decent pizzas around the 1500kr mark, and *Allinn*, next door in the former cinema, has even more pizzas – albeit ones you compose yourself with a choice of toppings.

Other facilities in Siglufjörður are limited although there is a **vínbúð** (Mon–Thurs 2–6pm, Fri 2–7pm) at Eyrargata 25, and a **library** with **internet** access at Gránugata 24 (Tues, Wed & Fri 2–5.30pm, Thurs 2–6pm). The **swimming pool** is located at the entrance to the town at Hvanneyrarbraut 52.

Akureyri

According to *Landnámabók*, the first Viking ships sailed into Eyjafjörður fjord, its mouth barely 40km south of the Arctic Circle, around 890, fifteen years after the Settlement began. The first intrepid pioneers to set foot in the hitherto uninhabited north, **Helgi Magri** (Helgi the Lean) and Þórunn Hyrna, made landfall at

Kristnes, 9km south of where **AKUREYRI** presently stands, believing that Þór had guided them into Eyjafjörður. Their faith seems, however, to have been in a state of confusion since they curiously chose to bestow an unqualified Christian name (Christ's Point) on their new home. Although little more is known about this early period of Akureyri's history, it is thought that Helgi suffered from a nutritional disease he developed as a child in the Hebrides, where he lived with his Irish mother and Swedish father before coming to Iceland.

Several centuries would then pass before mention of what is now Akureyri was made, its name "the cornfield on the sand spit" a clear indication of its current location, the land promontory where **Laxdalshús**, the oldest building in town dating from 1795 and now a private home, stands at Hafnarstræti 11. In 1602, however, Akureyri became a trading post with the establishment of a commercial monopoly which gave the Danish merchants of Helsingør the exclusive right to trade with Iceland. Curiously though, the traders were not permitted to take up permanent residence in the town, forced instead to leave for Denmark after closing their stores in the autumn. It wasn't until 1787 that this punitive monopoly was lifted and Akureyri became one of six towns in Iceland to be granted municipal status, despite the fact that its population then numbered little more than a dozen and most trade remained firmly in the hands of Danish merchants and their families. However, it was to the sea and its sheltered harbour, today located right in the heart of the town between **Drottningarbraut** and **Strandgata**, that Akureyri looked for renewed prosperity. Indeed, from then on the town prospered, and in the late nineteenth century one of Iceland's first cooperatives, **KEA**, was established here, going on to play a key role in the economy (see box below). Iceland's only **university** outside Reykjavík was established here in 1987, giving the town a much needed youthful boost.

Today, the transport hub and commercial centre of the whole of northern Iceland is divided into two distinct areas: the town centre, harbour and commercial district north of **Kaupvangsstræti**, and the suburban areas to its south, where the distinctive **Akureyrarkirkja** church, **museums** and the superb **botanical gardens** can all be found. As far as entertainment goes, the town is a decent enough place to relax in for a day or two, with an excellent open-air swimming pool and enough cafés and restaurants to keep you well fed and watered. That most un-Icelandic thing, the **forest**, makes a welcome appearance just south of Akureyri in the form of **Kjarnaskógur**, easily accessible on foot from the town centre and a popular destination for locals at weekends who come here to walk the many trails that crisscross the forest and to picnic. If you're doing much touring, you're almost certain to find yourself in town sooner or later, as it makes an excellent base from which to explore nearby Lake Mývatn, Húsavík and the Jökulsárgljúfur National Park (all covered in Chapter 6; see p.252, p.264 & p.268).

KEA

Spend any time in and around Akureyri and you can't fail to notice the ubiquitous **KEA** logo, plastered on hotels, fishing boats and even Kaffibrensla Akureyrar, the town's coffee-roasting plant. It's said locally that KEA, the Kaupfélag Eyfirðinga Akureyri (Cooperative Society of Eyjafjörður and Akureyri), owns everything except the church and, while that's not strictly true, KEA does have fingers in many pies. Established in June 1886 by local farmers keen to win a better price for the live export of their sheep to England, ten years later the society opened its first co-op store and never looked back. Still with headquarters on the main street in Akureyri, and still operating despite the economic downturn, KEA now owns shares in virtually any local business you choose to mention, concentrating on the food and merchandise sectors.

Driving in from the west, beyond Varmahlíð the Ringroad makes the steep ascent to the high moorland of **Öxnadalsheiði**, where, legend states, many of the victims of the thirteen-century Sturlung Age battles are buried, close to the road at Miklibær. There are countless stories of the ghosts of lost travellers haunting the pass and in winter it's one of the first in the country to become blocked. The government subsidizes the highest farm here, ensuring not only that it keeps going but also that help is available for anyone stranded.

Arrival and information

The **airport** is stunningly located on a spit of land in the middle of the fjord, three kilometres south of town. From here, it's possible to walk into the centre in around thirty minutes following the highway, Drottningarbraut, northwards as it runs parallel to the fjord; alternatively, taxis (1200kr) are available outside the terminal building. **Long-distance buses** terminate in the station at the southern end of Hafnarstræti, the town's main street.

The friendly **tourist information office** (June–Aug daily 7.30am–7pm; Sept–May Mon–Fri 8am–4pm; ☎553 5999, ⓦwww.visitakureyri.is) is set to move from the bus station to the new Menningarhús Hof (Culture House), currently under construction at the junction of Glerárgata and Strandgata – check locally for the latest details. The pedestrianized part of **Hafnarstræti** (north of its junction with Kaupvangsstræti) is the main shopping precinct and runs to Akureyri's diminutive main square, **Ráðhústorg**. From Ráðhústorg's northwestern corner, Brekkugata leads up to the newlyextended **library** (Mon–Fri 10am–7pm, also Sept–May Sat noon–5pm), a veritable haven on rainy afternoons with numerous books in English about Iceland; **internet** access is also available here.

Accommodation

There's no shortage of **accommodation** in Akureyri and there's no need to book in advance, even in summer, unless you wish to stay at the youth hostel. **Breakfast** is usually included in the price for hotels, but not guesthouses. If you're planning to base yourself in Akureyri and want room to spread out in, it's worth considering renting an **apartment** – the tourist information office can help set this up.

Hostel, campsite and guesthouses

Brekkusel Byggðavegur 97 ☎461 2660, ⓦwww .brekkusel.is. A pleasant suburban guesthouse, handy for the town swimming pool, with its own garden and outdoor hot pot. The clean rooms are simple in style, though some have private facilities. A larger studio apartment is available downstairs. Sleeping-bag accommodation 6500kr for two people per double. ❶

Campsite Þórunnarstræti ☎462 3379. Open June to August, Akureyri's campsite is located

Getting to Akureyri

Akureyri sits on the Ringroad pretty much halfway along the country's northern coastline and is connected by **bus** year-round to Reykjavík. Throughout the summer, bus services also connect the town with Húsavík, Mývatn, Ólafsfjörður and Egilsstaðir, and approximately mid-June to mid-August with southwestern Iceland via the Kjölur track across the Interior (see p.315). You can **fly** year-round from Reykjavík, Grímsey and northeasterly Þórshöfn and Vopnafjörður; and there are also direct summertime **international flights** from Copenhagen and London Gatwick.

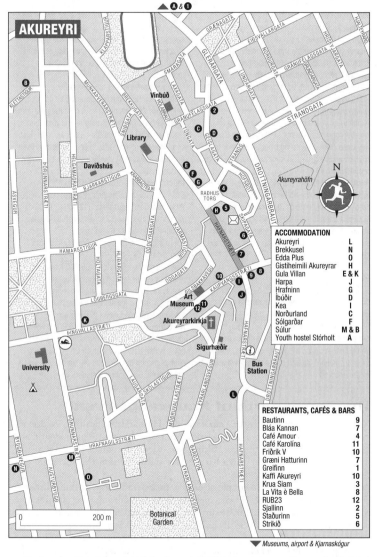

AKUREYRI

Akureyrahöfn

N

ACCOMMODATION

Akureyri	L
Brekkusel	N
Edda Plus	O
Gistiheimili Akureyrar	H
Gula Villan	E & K
Harpa	J
Hrafninn	G
Íbúðir	D
Kea	I
Norðurland	C
Sólgarðar	F
Súlur	M & B
Youth hostel Stórholt	A

RESTAURANTS, CAFÉS & BARS

Bautinn	9
Bláa Kannan	7
Café Amour	4
Café Karolína	11
Friðrik V	10
Græni Hatturinn	7
Greifinn	1
Kaffi Akureyri	10
Krua Siam	3
La Vita è Bella	8
RUB23	12
Sjallinn	2
Staðurinn	5
Strikið	6

▼ Museums, airport & Kjarnaskógur

next to the university and has good toilet and shower facilities on the other side of the street in the school building, plus an on-site playground for kids.

Gistiheimili Akureyrar Hafnarstræti 104 ☎462 5600, Ⓦwww.hotelakureyri.is. Bang in the city centre, this is the budget wing of *Hotel Akureyri* with small but comfy rooms, both with and without (1500kr less) facilities. Breakfast is 1250kr. ❷

Gula Villan Brekkugata 8 & Þingvallastræti 14 ☎896 8464, Ⓦgulavillan.is. A total of nineteen identical rooms in two guesthouses, all with shared facilities, kitchen and TV. Breakfast is 1190kr. Sleeping-bag accommodation 6600kr per double room. ❶

Hrafninn Brekkugata 4 ☎661 9050, Ⓦakureyriguesthouse.is. Under new ownership, this long established guesthouse close to the main square has just five doubles but is a sound choice for elegantly decorated, central en-suite rooms. Dark wooden floors and headboards add a nice touch of class. ❷

Sólgarðar Brekkugata 6 ℡461 1133,
ⓔsolgardar@simnet.is. Three highly agreeable,
bright and spacious rooms with TV and access to a
kitchen, just one minute from the main square.
Breakfast is 1000kr extra. Sleeping-bag accommodation 6000kr per double room. ❶

Súlur Þórunnarstræti 93 & Klettastígur 6 ℡461
1160, ⓔsulur@islandia.is. Pleasant double
rooms sharing facilities and a kitchen are
available all year at Þórunnarstræti 93, while the
four-bedroom apartments at Klettastígur 6 are
only open from June to mid-Aug. Breakfast is
1000kr; sleeping-bag accommodation 6600kr per
double room. ❶

Youth hostel Stórholt 1 ℡ 462 3657 or 894 4299,
ⓦwww.hostel.is. The 65 beds at this hostel, 1.5km
out of town back towards Reykjavík along
Glerágata (closed mid-Dec to mid-Jan), fill quickly
thanks to the low price – the green, leafy location
is an added bonus. Sleeping-bag accommodation
2100kr. ❶

Hotels

Akureyri Hafnarstræti 67 ℡462 5600, ⓦwww
.hotelakureyri.is. Located in a black and white-
painted house virtually opposite the bus station,
this smart hotel is Nordic chic to a T. Plain, tasteful
rooms with minimalist décor and wooden floors, all
with private facilities and some with good views
out over the fjord, though they are somewhat small
for the price. ❸

Edda Plus Eyrarlandsvegur 28 ℡444 4900,
ⓦwww.hoteledda.is. Open mid-June to
Aug, rooms in this newly built glass and chrome
structure, which functions as university accommodation during term time, offer great value for
money. ❸

Harpa Hafnarstræti 83–85 ℡460 2000, ⓦwww
.hotelkea.is. Not quite as upmarket as its
neighbour, the *Kea*, but cheaper. Sharing the same
reception and breakfast room as the *Kea*, this
adjoining hotel provides the best of both worlds:
comfortable communal surroundings and virtually
the same room – all you lack is a minibar and a
hairdryer. ❹

Íbúðir Geislagata 10 ℡462 3727 or ℡892
9838, ⓦwww.hotelibudir.is. Pleasant one- to
three-bedroom apartments (18,900–33,900kr)
with sitting room and kitchen, usefully located
within 2min walk of Ráðhústorg.
There are also a number of one-room studio
apartments. ❷

Kea Hafnarstræti 87–89 ℡460 2000, ⓦwww
.hotelkea.is. The largest and most luxurious hotel in
Akureyri with modern, carpeted en-suite rooms
kitted out with satellite TV and a minibar. Rooms at
the front have good views of the town. ❹

Norðurland Geislagata 7 ℡462 2600, ⓦwww
.hotelkea.is. A good location for this KEA-owned
hotel, within easy striking distance of the main
square, though the carpeted en-suite rooms are
rather plain. Breakfast is included. ❹

The Town: north of Kaupvangsstræti

North of Kaupvangsstræti, the pedestrianized **Hafnarstræti** leads to Akureyri's
main square, **Ráðhústorg**. This modest street, no more than 150m in length, and
its parallel neighbour to the east, **Skipagata**, together contain virtually all the
shops and services that the town has to offer and it's within this rectangle that
you'll spend much of your time.

From Ráðhústorg itself, a couple of diversions are within easy striking distance.
Head northwest up to the library, then south onto Oddeyrargata, take the first
right into Krabbastígur and finally turn left into Bjarkarstígur to reach the austere
building at no. 6 known informally as **Davíðshús** (June–Aug Mon–Fri 1–2.30pm;
500kr), the former home of one of Iceland's most famous poets, novelists and
playwrights, Davíð Stefánsson. Born in 1895 to the north of Akureyri, he
published his first anthology of poems at the age of 24 and went on to write verse
and novels that were often critical of the state. It was only after his death in 1964
that Davíð was finally taken into Icelanders' hearts and he is now regarded as one
of the country's greatest writers. Inside, in addition to his numerous books that
adorn the walls, are many of his personal effects, including his piano and writing
desk as he left them.

From the top of Bjarkarstígur, the long, straight Helgamagrastræti, named after
Helgi Magri, the first settler in the Eyjafjörður region, leads south to Þingvallastræti and the town's excellent outdoor **swimming pool**, which has two large
pools, several hot pots, a steam room and a **sauna** (women only Tues & Thurs;

men only Wed & Fri), and is an absolute treat when the sun is shining. Head east down Þingvallastræti and you'll come to the uninspiring **Akureyri Art Museum** at Kaupvangsstræti 24 (Listasafnið á Akureyri; Tues–Sun noon–5pm; ⓦwww .listasafn.akureyri.is; free). Inside is a collection of works by local artists as well as a number of studios alongside, known as Listagilið, where workshops are occasionally held.

It's worth venturing east of the commercial centre of town to explore the harbourside, best reached along the main road, Drottningarbraut, running parallel to Skipagata. Although the small southern **harbour**, Akureyrarhöfn, is close to the junction of Drottningarbraut and Kaupvangsstræti, it's really along Strandgata, which runs along the harbour's northern edge, that the industrial face of Akureyri becomes more prominent. The shipyard and freighter terminal here make up the largest commercial port outside Reykjavík, a bustling part of town where the clanking of cranes accompanies the seemingly endless unloading and loading of ocean-going vessels at the dockside. In summer it's not uncommon for gargantuan cruise liners to be moored here, too.

The Town: south of Kaupvangsstræti

Although Akureyri is far from ostentatious, you can't miss the dramatic **Akureyrarkirkja** (daily 10am–noon & 1–5pm; ⓦwww.akirkja.is), whose twin towers loom over the town, perched on a hill up a flight of steps from the junction of Hafnarstræti and Kaupvangsstræti. Comparisons with Hallgrímskirkja in Reykjavík (see p.78) are unavoidable, especially since the two were designed by the same architect, Guðjón Samúelsson, and not only tower over neighbouring buildings but are both modelled on basalt columns. Inside, there are some dazzling **stained-glass windows**, the central panes of which are originally from the old Coventry cathedral in Britain – removed, with remarkable foresight, at the start of World War II before it was demolished during bombing raids, and sold to an Icelandic dealer who came across them in an antiques shop in London. The church's other stained-glass windows (also made in England, during the 1970s) depict famous Icelanders, while the **model ship** hanging from the ceiling commemorates a former bishop.

A pathway leads round the church to **Sigurhæðir**, at Eyrarlandsvegur 3 (The House of Verbal Arts; June–Aug Mon–Fri 3–5pm; 500kr), the former home of **Matthías Jochumsson** (1835–1920), the distinguished poet and author of the stirring Icelandic national anthem. Now a museum containing a small and unexceptional collection of his furnishings and a few portraits, the house was built in 1902 and was his home until his death in 1920. Unless you have a burning desire to immerse yourself in obscure Icelandic poetry, however, it's better to walk right on by, and head instead for the glorious **Botanical Garden** (Lystigarður; June–Sept Mon–Fri 8am–10pm, Sat & Sun 9am–10pm; free), at the end of Eyrarlandsvegur. Established in 1912 by Margrethe Schiöth, a Danish woman who lived in Akureyri, the gardens are a rich display of plant life enclosed by that Icelandic rarity, fully grown trees. Besides virtually every Icelandic species, there's an astonishing number of subtropical plants from South America and Africa – seemingly defying nature by existing at all in these high latitudes, the annual mean temperature for Akureyri being barely 3.4°C. In summer, when the fragrance of hundreds of flowers hangs in the air, the gardens, with undisturbed views out over the fjord, are a real haven of peace and tranquillity. The dozens of kids you'll see around the gardens, and indeed the rest of Akureyri, are there on behalf of the town council, keeping the place tidy and earning a little pocket money in the process.

Below the gardens is the oldest part of Akureyri, and many of its wooden buildings, including several along Aðalstræti, to the southeast, have been preserved and turned into museums. The first, however, is the least interesting: the **Good Templars Museum**, or Friðbjarnarhús (July & Aug Sat & Sun 1–5pm; free), at no. 46, where the Icelandic Good Templars Order was founded in 1884 – an occasion recorded inside with singularly uninteresting documents and photos. The museum is named after a local book merchant, Friðbjörn Steinsson, who once lived here.

Further on, at Aðalstræti 54, the black wooden house with white window frames is **Nonnahús** (Jón Sveinsson Memorial Museum; June–Sept daily 10am–5pm; ⓦwww.nonni.is; 350kr, 600kr for combined entry with Akureyri Museum), the childhood home of Jón Sveinsson, the Jesuit priest and author of the Nonni children's books – Nonni is the diminutive form of Jón in Icelandic. Based on his experiences of growing up in northern Iceland, the stories are little known to English-speaking audiences but are inordinately popular in Germanic countries – most were written in German – and are translated into around forty other languages. Nonni lived here until he was 12, when, following his father's death, he moved first to Denmark, where he converted to Catholicism, then moved again to France and then, in 1914, to Austria, where he wrote his first book, before settling in Germany. Inside the house illustrations from his stories decorate the walls and numerous translations of his dozen books are displayed. Dating from 1850, the house itself is one of the oldest in the town and still has its original furniture, giving a good indication of the living conditions at the time of construction; note the low ceilings and narrow doorways, which were designed to keep the heat in. Incidentally, when Nonni lived here the fjord stretched right up to his front door – all the area east of the house, where the main road now runs, is reclaimed land.

A few strides on is the **Akureyri Museum** (June to mid-Sept daily 10am–5pm, rest of the year Sat & Sun 2–4pm; 500kr) at Aðalstræti 58, set back a little from the street behind a well-tended garden. The upper floor of the museum has a good assortment of farming and fishing items from Akureyri and Eyjafjörður's past, plus a spectacular wooden pulpit from 1768, which once proudly stood in the church at nearby Kaupangur, hand-painted in subtle greens and blues and bedecked with painted flowers by local Jón Hallgrímsson. However, it's the skeletons of a middle-aged man with a horse and dog, found in a boat grave at nearby Dalvík, that really impresses. Dating from around the year 1000, this man was one of the first settlers in the Eyjafjörður region. Downstairs, an exhibition detailing how the town has developed from the 1700s to the present day contains a glorious jumble of household items including a mangle, cash till and even a sleigh.

Kjarnaskógur

Not content with the trees that line most of Akureyri's streets, locals have now planted an entire **forest** on former farmland roughly an hour's walk south of the town, the first stage in a much more ambitious plan to encircle Akureyri with forest. **Kjarnaskógur**, easily reached by walking south from the museums along Drottningarbraut out past the airport, is a favourite recreational spot at weekends and on summer evenings, when the air is heavy with the scent of pine. Although birch and larch predominate, there are over fifty species of shrubs and trees here, some of which have grown to over 12m in height, quite a feat for a country where trees rarely reach little more than waist height – hence the long-standing Icelandic joke about what to do when you get lost in an Icelandic forest (answer: you stand up). Within the forest there are easy walking paths complete with picnic sites, a jogging track for the more energetic that doubles as a skiing trail in winter, plus a children's play area. Camping is not permitted here.

Eating, drinking and nightlife

Unless you're arrived directly from Reykjavík, you'll feel quite dizzy at the wide choice of eateries in Akureyri. Thanks to the town's small university and its role as a commercial centre for the entire north of the country, there's a fair choice of **cafés** and **restaurants** – even the odd **bar** or two. In short, indulge yourself before moving on.

Cafés and restaurants

Bautinn Hafnarstræti 92. Always busy and popular with locals as well as visitors, this is essentially a cheap and cheerful dine-and-dash type place. Although the menu does extend to a couple of meat and fish dishes (around 3000kr), it's not going to be the culinary highlight of any visit to Akureyri and is best used for a quick burger and chips (from 1390kr).

Bláa Kannan Hafnarstræti 96. Housed in an old wooden building on the main street, this atmospheric place with grand, old chandeliers serves the best coffee in Akureyri. They also do great cakes, bagels and panini and, consequently, it's popular with local shoppers.

Café Karolína Kaupvangsstræti 23. Akureyri's most stylish café-cum-bar, with works of art hanging from the walls, popular with budding artists and trendy students. Known for its wide selection of coffees and delicious cakes.

Friðrik V Kaupvangsstræti 6. This fine dining restaurant – complete with the cutlery collection of three local old ladies stuck to the white stone walls – is quite simply the best in

Akureyri. Run by the ebullient Friðrik who trained at *Hótel Holt* in Reykjavík and London's *River Café*, the menu goes from strength to strength and is new Nordic cooking at its most inventive: Icelandic herbs and flavours blending perfectly with the best of Italy and Spain. Count on 4000kr and up per main dish, starters around half that.

Greifinn Glerárgata 20. Close to the youth hostel, this pizza, pasta and TexMex joint is worth seeking out for its lively atmosphere; it's the most popular restaurant with locals and is usually busy. Although prices are similar to those of *La Vita è Bella* in town, there's a more extensive menu including salads. Reckon around 2050kr for a large pizza or 3000kr for *fajitas*.

Krua Siam Strandgata 13. Akureyri's only Asian restaurant, serving reasonable if not overly authentic dishes. The weekday lunch buffet for 1350kr is good value; otherwise mains, such as *pad thai*, go 1500–1900kr. Vegetarian options available.

La Vita è Bella Hafnarstræti 92. The most authentic Italian restaurant in town, with pizzas from 1260kr and pasta dishes from 1940kr. There's

▲ Bláa Kannan café, Akureyri

also a choice of good meat and fish dishes, such as grilled salmon, for around 3500kr.

RUB23 Kaupvangsstræti 23. A new, stylish sushi restaurant offering a wide variety of fish all rubbed in a secret blend of spices, seeds and herbs. Fourteen pieces cost 3750kr, or try a mixed seafood platter for 4550kr.

Staðurinn Skipagata 2. Akureyri's new vegetarian restaurant with a changing menu of meat-free dishes – quiche and lasagne (1390kr) are always available, as are gluten-free cakes.

Strikið Skipagata 14. A deservedly popular top floor brasserie with an open-air terrace offering superb views of Akureyri. Reckon on around 2000–3000kr for the brasserie-style mains such as burgers with all the trimmings, pizzas, tortillas and salted cod.

Bars and nightlife

Café Amour Ráðhústorg 7. This place quite fancies itself, all Nordic minimalist, leather chairs and wooden floors undeniably creating a laid-back, trendy atmosphere popular with Akureyri's young things who congregate here from early evening onwards.

Græni Hatturinn Hafnarstræti 96. A popular, evenings-only British-style pub in the basement of the *Bláa Kannan*, and good for a beer or three.

Kaffi Akureyri Strandgata 7. A popular bar with a wooden interior finished off by a parquet floor and window blinds which mutates into a club with occasional live music at weekends.

Sjallinn Geislagata 14. Dance club where you'll find virtually every young person in Akureyri on Thursday to Sunday evenings grooving to the latest tunes or to live music.

Listings

Alcohol store Hólabraut 16. Mon–Thurs 11am–6pm, Fri 11am–7pm, Sat 11am–6pm.

Bookshops Eymundsson, Hafnarstræti 91–93, is good for maps and guidebooks. For second-hand English paperbacks, try Fornbókabúðin Fróði, Kaupvangsstræti 19.

Car rental Budget, Glerárgata 36 ☎462 3400; Hertz, Akureyri airport ☎461 1005; Europcar, Tryggvabraut 12 ☎461 6000.

Cinemas Nýja Bíó, Strandgata 2; Borgarbíó, Holar-braut 12.

Hospital The hospital on Eyrarlandsvegur has a 24hr accident-and-emergency ward ☎463 0100.

Laundry Þvottahúsið Höfði, Hafnarstræti 34 ☎462 2580.

Library Brekkugata 17 ☎462 4141.

Pharmacy Apótekarinn, Hafnarstræti 95.

Police Þórunnarstræti 138 ☎112.

Post office Skipagata 10 (Mon–Fri 9am–4.30pm).

Supermarket Bónus, Kjarnagata, just off the highway past the Youth Hostel, heading towards Reykjavík; Samkaup Strax, Byggðavegur 98, close to the campsite.

Taxi BSO ☎461 1010.

Woollen goods The Viking, Hafnarstræti 104; Fold-Anna, Hafnarstræti 85.

Western Eyjafjörður

Running up Eyjafjörður's western flank from Akureyri, Route 82 affords stunning views over icy waters to the glacier-formed mountains which serve as a protective wall all around the fjord. If you have time, it's well worth making the trip from Akureyri to see not only the mountains but also the rich farmland hereabouts, which is heavily grazed during the summer by cattle and sheep. The long hours of daylight in this part of Iceland, coupled with mild temperatures, make excellent growing conditions for various crops, and the small white dots you'll see in the fields are barrel-shaped bundles of hay, neatly packaged in white plastic, to provide the animals with much needed food during the long months of winter. The highlight of any trip up the fjord is the island of **Hrísey**, noted for its hundreds of wild ptarmigan, found near the mouth of Eyjafjörður and overlooked by the fishing village of **Dalvík**, itself the starting point for some excellent hiking. Nearby the village of **Hauganes** is the place to make for if you fancy a spot of whale watching whilst in the north. Beyond here, a dark tunnel slices through the exposed headland, Ólafsfjarðarmúli, to reach the isolated village of **Ólafsfjörður**. Although with few attractions itself, it does have splendid end-of-the-world feeling about it thanks to its location overlooking the northern reaches of the Atlantic Ocean.

Buses run year-round, several times daily (Mon–Fri) in each direction along Route 82 between Akureyri, Dalvík and Ólafsfjörður, connecting along the way for **ferries** to Hrísey and Grímsey.

Dalvík

DALVÍK, a nondescript fishing village 42km north of Akureyri with just fourteen hundred inhabitants, enjoys a superbly sheltered location on the western shores of Eyjafjörður overlooking the island of Hrísey (see p.240). Paradoxically, though, its poor natural harbour hampered the growth of the fishing industry here until a new harbour was built in 1939 to remedy matters, today used as the departure point for the **ferry to Grímsey**. A major shipbuilding and fish-curing centre early in the twentieth century, today Dalvík has lost its buzz, and its quiet **harbour** front, lined by the main road, **Hafnarbraut**, stands guard over the familiar cluster of uniformly shaped modern homes that are so prevalent in the country's smaller communities. Dalvík's lack of older buildings is due to the devastating **earthquake** of 1934, measuring 7.2 on the Richter Scale, which demolished half the structures in the village and caused serious damage to the ones that did survive – two thousand people lost their homes.

The village is really only visited by people putting to sea for **whale watching** or en route to Grímsey, but should you find yourself with time to kill take a quick look inside the folklore museum, **Byggðasafnið Hvoll** (June–Aug daily 11am–6pm; 500kr), one block back from the harbour at Karlsrauðatorg 7. The museum is divided into four small sections, and it's the collection of photographs and personal belongings of Iceland's tallest man, Jóhann Kristinn Pétursson, born in nearby Svarfaðardalur valley in 1913, that catches the eye. Measuring a whopping 2.34 metres in height (7 feet 7 inches), Jóhann the Giant, as he was known locally, spent most of his life performing in circuses in Europe and America before retiring to Dalvík, where he died in 1984. The museum also contains a collection of birds' eggs, several species of stuffed sea birds and a stuffed polar bear.

The excellent outdoor **swimming pool**, with its mountain backdrop, also has a couple of hot pots and a mixed steam room; it's on Svarfaðarbraut, which runs roughly parallel with Hafnarbraut.

Practicalities

For information on the three-times weekly **Grímsey ferry** call ☎458 8970 or go to Ⓦwww.landflutningar.is/saefari_ferry_english; see also p.247 for times. For

---

Hiking from Dalvík to Hólar

From Dalvík a **long-distance hike**, lasting three or four days, leads over the Heljard-alsheiði plateau to the episcopal seat at **Hólar í Hjaltadal** (see p.228). It leads up through Svarfaðardalsá valley, just south of town, passing the wedge-shaped **Stóll**, a mountain which divides the valley in two. Continuing southwest past a couple of farms, the route then heads up over the flat-topped mountains of the Tröllskagi peninsula, which separates Eyjafjörður from its western neighbour, Skagafjörður, heading for Hólar, passing through some of Iceland's best mountain scenery. It should take two or three days to reach this point, but you'll need another half-day to reach the main road, Route 76 itself reached along Route 767 from here. From June to September, buses run daily except Saturday along Route 76 between Siglufjörður and Sauðárkrókur – see p.225.

online tourist **information**, check out ⓦ www.dalvik.is. The **library** is located in the basement of the town hall (*ráðhús*) at the corner of Kirkjubraut and Goðabraut and has **internet** access.

The best **accommodation** in Dalvík itself is the rambling *Fosshotel* (☎ 562 4000, ⓦ www.fosshotel.is; ❸) at Skíðabraut 18, though it's only open between May and September. Alternatively, Dalvík's **campsite** (June–Sept; ☎ 466 3233; free) is south of town beside the main road, just 100m from the swimming pool.

There are two **places to eat** in Dalvík, with little to choose between them. First up is the *Kaffi Sogn*, opposite the town hall at Goðabraut 3, open for dinner, which serves pizzas, fish and other light dishes for around 1500kr. *Við Höfnina*, meanwhile, further west along the main road at Hafnarbraut 5, has a pleasant outside terrace overlooking the harbour, and serves simple sandwiches, light snacks and coffee. The **vínbúð** (June–Aug Mon–Thurs 11am–6pm, Fri 11am–7pm, Sat 11am–2pm; Sept–May Mon–Thurs 2–6pm, Fri noon–7pm) is on the main road at Hafnarbraut 7.

Hrísey

No trip to the north coast of Iceland is complete without seeing the hundreds of **ptarmigan** on **HRÍSEY**, a flat, teardrop-shaped island at the mouth of Eyjafjörður, reached by ferry from Árskógssandur, about 10km southeast of Dalvík. Although the country's second-largest island (Heimaey in the Westman Islands is the biggest; see p.139), at 7.5km long and 2.5km wide, it's home to barely two hundred people. However, it does house more ptarmigan than anywhere else in Iceland, since here they're protected by law and there are no natural predators such as mink or foxes. As a result, the birds are very tame and roam the entire island, and you'll spot them in the picturesque village here, laying their eggs in people's gardens or, particularly in August after the breeding season, strolling down the main street with a string of fluffy chicks in tow.

The island's history, however, is more tied to fish than birds and its population peaked at 340 in the mid-twentieth century, when fishing boats from across the country landed their catches in the tiny harbour, making it the second-largest herring port on the north coast, after Siglufjörður. Since then things have declined, and in 1999 the main source of employment, the fish-processing factory down at the harbour that once provided the British supermarkets with fresh North Atlantic fish, closed and over thirty people left the island to look for work in Akureyri and Reykjavík. Today, it's the Icelandic National Quarantine Centre, established in 1974 so that stocks of Galloway cattle could be imported from Scotland, that keeps many islanders in employment. **Reafforestation** has also begun in a couple of areas, in an attempt to protect the thin layer of soil atop the basalt rock of which Hrísey is formed from further erosion.

Hrísey **village** is tiny, consisting of two or three parallel streets perched on a small hill above the walled **harbour**. Brightly painted houses, unfortunately all of them modern and block-like, look out over the fjord and the handful of small boats that bob up and down in the tiny port. Otherwise, there's a minuscule outdoor **swimming pool** on the main street, Norðurvegur, at the eastern end of the village; at just 12.5m in length, it's heated by geothermal water from Hrísey's very own borehole on the west coast. Even though the village can easily be walked around in 10min there's a map down on the harbourside.

Once you've explored the village, there's some wonderful **walking** to be had along tracks that head around the southeastern corner of the island; all three colour-coded paths (green 2.3km; yellow 4.5km; and red 5km) begin just ten minutes from the village near the island's southernmost tip, beyond the couple of colourful private summer cottages that look out over the fjord. The green route traces a circular route up to the hills of Háaborð, dropping towards Beinalág and returning to the village; the red path heads further north along the coast, while the yellow track follows essentially the same routing though further inland; both routes turn south again at the Borgarbrík cliffs. Unfortunately for visitors, Hrísey also has the largest breeding colony of **arctic tern** in Europe, who, should you come too close to its young, will readily divebomb you from on high, which means you'll pretty much need hard hats if you get too close to their nesting sites. The island is also a good place to spot **golden plover** and **eider ducks**, which have a significant breeding colony in the northern part of Hrísey which is out of bounds to visitors.

Practicalities

A **ferry** shuttles to Hrísey on the fifteen-minute journey from tiny **Árskógssandur**, just off Route 82 some 10km south of Dalvík (mid-June to mid-Aug 9.30am–11.30pm hourly; rest of the year 9.30am–9.30pm every two hours; Ⓦ www.hrisey.net; 1000kr return). You can catch a direct **bus** to Árskógssandur three times a day (Mon–Fri) from Akureyri, Dalvík and Ólafsfjörður.

The island's only **guesthouse** is *Brekka*, at Brekkugata 5 (Ⓣ 466 1751, Ⓦ brekkahrisey.is; ❶), a wooden building painted bright yellow up on the hill behind the harbour: it has just three doubles with shared facilities, but if these are full the owners will endeavour to find a room in a private house somewhere in the village. Lunch here, in the **restaurant** overlooking the sea and the jagged mountains of the western shore of Eyjafjörður, is truly excellent; try the salted cod in coconut with a pineapple sauce (2890kr). The **campsite** (900kr) is located beside the swimming pool on Norðurvegur. The only other facilities are a **grocery** store at Sjávargata 2 (Mon–Fri 11am–6pm, Sat 11am–5pm, Sun noon–5pm), which also serves coffee and light meals, and a **bank** (Mon–Fri noon–4pm) with an ATM on Skólavegur.

Ólafsfjörður

From Dalvík, Route 82 winds its way north for 17km to the fishing village of **ÓLAFSFJÖRÐUR**, clinging all the way to the steep slopes of the mountains that plunge into the steely waters of Eyjafjörður, and with superb views of the snowy peaks of the uninhabited Látraströnd coastline on the opposite shore. On a clear day it's easily possible to spot the island of Grímsey (see p.244), northeast of the fjord's mouth, bisected by the **Arctic Circle**. The village is connected to Akureyri by means of a single-lane, claustrophobic, 3.4-kilometre tunnel through the Ólafsfjarðarmúli headland, which divides Eyjafjörður from its smaller cousin, Ólafsfjörður, which gives the settlement its name.

Although the drive to Ólafsfjörður and its setting are breathtaking, the village, unfortunately, isn't: this is an unattractive, workaday place of a thousand people, set behind the working **harbour** on Sjávargata, one block northeast of the main road, **Aðalgata**. There's little here to detain you other than the taxidermist's dream, the well-stocked **Náttúrugripasafn** (Natural history museum; June–Aug Tues–Sun 2–5pm; Sept–May by arrangement with Sparisjóður bank, in the same building; 500kr), at Aðalgata 14, containing the usual suspects – everything from a ringed seal to a stuffed polar bear shot by a local fisherman off Grímsey as he saw it approaching his boat while balancing precariously on a piece of pack ice. With over 140 bird species stuffed for posterity, you'll at least learn the names of some of the living birds you'll see in the wild; pick up the free museum catalogue for the English translations.

Practicalities

Buses to Ólafsfjörður arrive at the only **hotel** in the village, the drab *Brimnes Hótel* (Ⓣ 466 2400, Ⓦ www.brimnes.is; ❸), at Bylgjubyggð 2. Doubles here are cramped and so plainly furnished they resemble a school dorm rather than an expensive hotel. Much better are their eight Finnish-built log **cabins**, all with shower and bathroom, overlooking the lake opposite the hotel; these sleep four to eight people and cost 13,000 (without kitchen) or 18,000kr (with kitchen). The hotel **restaurant** serves tasty fish meals (1700kr), as well as pasta (1550kr) and lamb (2750kr). *Höllinn* at Hafnargata 16, near the harbour, is popular with local fishermen and the best bet for decent food – pizzas for 1400kr, burgers 1200kr, grilled salmon 2600kr. Alternatively, there's a small **supermarket** at the corner of Strandgata and Aðalgata, next to the harbour. The **swimming pool** and the **campsite** are together, just off Hornbrekkuvegur, which heads south from Aðalgata.

Eastern Eyjafjörður

The eastern shore of Eyjafjörður, covered in part by the Ringroad and then Route 83, offers something quite rare in Iceland – remote, uninhabited wilderness that is relatively accessible from a major town. North of the small village of **Grenivík**, now the only centre of population on the eastern side of the fjord, the perpetually snowcapped **Látraströnd** coastline is made up of some of the most rugged mountains in the north of Iceland, including the peak of **Kaldbakur** (1167m), which dominates any view of the eastern shore. Excellent and challenging **hiking** routes lead through the wilderness to now abandoned farms which, until World War II, made up some of the country's most remote and desolate communities, where life was a constant struggle against the elements in this area of unforgiving Arctic fjordland, known here as Í Fjörðum. The region's other attraction, however, is not nearly so remote: the unusual five-gabled turf farmhouse and church at **Laufás**, 10km south of Grenivík and close to the Ringroad.

It's 40km from Akureyri to Grenivík and, though **no public transport** runs this far, buses heading east from Akureyri to Mývatn or Húsavík can drop you at the start of Route 83, some 20km from town – you'll have to rely on your legs or passing motorists beyond this point.

Laufás

Thirty kilometres northeast of Akureyri up Route 83, **Laufás** (mid-May to mid-Sept daily 10am–6pm; 500kr) is a superb example of a traditional turf farmhouse. Dating from 1866, the building is timber-fronted and has five gabled roofs, all made of turf, giving the impression that it's composed of several separate cottages all joined under one roof. The most remarkable feature, however, is the fabulous herringbone arrangement of turf pieces used to make up part of the front wall. Don't miss the unusual carved eider duck that sits on one of the gable ends, serving as a reminder of the local nesting area belonging to the property; the eider down once brought the owners a considerable income. Inside, sadly, is the usual array of mind-numbing how-we-used-to-live paraphernalia, showing household and farm life from the days when the house was used as a manor farm and a parsonage for the next door **church**, which itself dates from 1865 and contains a pulpit with wood carvings from 1698; the local priest shared the building with his labourers.

Grenivík

Ten kilometres northwest of Laufás, **GRENIVÍK** is a modern fjordside village, which only began life in 1910. Although improvements to the tiny **harbour**,

A circular four- to five-day **hike** leads from Grenivík via the Látraströnd coast to the Gjögur headland, guarding the eastern entrance to Eyjafjörður, east through the coastal Í Fjörðum region to Hvalvatnsfjörður and the beginning of Route F839, which then returns towards Grenivík.

From Grenivík, follow the unnumbered road northwest from the village to the now deserted farm, **Svínarnes**, where the road ends and a track continues along the Látraströnd shoreline, passing several more abandoned farms, including **Látur**, which has been empty since 1942. The path then swings inland through the **Uxaskarð pass** (in order to avoid the Gjögur headland) and drops down through Keflavíkurdalur to reach the shore at **Keflavík**, one of Iceland's remotest locations, a now deserted farm that was regularly cut off from the rest of the country for months in the wintertime. At the beginning of the eighteenth century, people on the farm here were taken ill and died one by one as the harsh winter weather set in – all except for an 11-year-old girl, who remained alone here for ten weeks until people from the nearest farmstead finally managed to dig their way through the heavy snowdrifts to rescue her. Passing Þorgeirsfjörður, the path heads southwest for the next fjord, Hvalvatnsfjörður, and the beginning of the mountain road back over the hills up to the Leirdalsheiði plateau and finally down into Grenivík; there can often be snow along this route until the middle of July.

On certain dates in July it's possible to do this hike in the opposite direction as part of an **organized tour**; the trip includes transport to Hvalvatnsfjörður and back from Svínarnes, breakfast and dinner – and most importantly horses to carry all your equipment. It's likely to cost around 41,000kr; contact Jón at the snack bar in Grenivík or call ☏463 3236 or 861 6612, ⓦwww.vip.is/fjordungar.

---

around which the village is situated, brought about a slight increase in trade and thus population, there are still only around 250 people who call the place home. Its principal use is as a starting and finishing point for **hikes** along the fjord to **Látraströnd** and the **Í Fjörðum** region of the north coast (see box above), although there is a snack bar in the centre of the village, at Túngata 3, and a **swimming pool** (☏463 3159) next to the school. For **accommodation**, head to *Miðgarðar*, at Miðgarður 4 (☏860 9999, ⓦmidgardar.net; sleeping-bag accommodation 2900kr, ❶). Simple fish meals are also available in the small **restaurant** here. The **campsite** is next to the swimming pool beside the village school.

South from Akureyri: Eyjafjarðardalur valley

South of Akureyri, beyond the head of Eyjafjörður, the tongue-twisting **Eyjafjarðardalur** (pronounced ay-ya-farther-darler) is the wide fertile floodplain surrounding the Eyjafjarðará river, which flows down the valley from its source near Nýjarbæjarafrétt, up in the country's Interior. An extensive range of crops are grown, and the animals that graze the valley produce twenty percent of Iceland's milk. The farms throughout the valley do good business from the rich soil, too, with most of Iceland's potatoes grown here, and in good years the country is virtually self-sufficient in this crop. However, bad weather can – and all too often does – wipe out entire harvests. The further inland the valley stretches, the wider it becomes, before getting lost in the foothills of the vast highland plateau generally known as Hálendið that forms the uninhabited centre of the country. It's here that the **F821 mountain road** begins, as it heads towards the Sprengisandur area of the Interior (see p.314). If you don't have your own transport, note that **highland tours** arranged through a travel agent in Reykjavík (see p.32) provide the only form of transport to the Eyjafjörður valley from Akureyri.

The drive around the wide Eyjafjarðardalur valley (Routes 821 and 829 run either side of the Eyjafjarðará, meeting up 8km south of Grund; see below) offers a chance to escape the mountains that box in so many Icelandic villages and to enjoy wide open vistas of rolling farmland and undisturbed views of the **midnight sun**; the upper reaches of the valley are one of the most enjoyable spots from which to watch the sun dip to the horizon over some of Iceland's greenest countryside, then skim the North Atlantic before rising again towards the east. There are few specific sights – instead, make a trip here to stay on a farm or to enjoy the open countryside around the valley's only real settlement, **HRAFNAGIL**, a mere dot on the map some 12km along Route 821 that runs up the western side of the valley. Home to barely 95 inhabitants, during the time of the Settlement the area around the hamlet was once a chieftain's estate and, later, the residence of Iceland's last Catholic bishop, Jón Arason, although there's nothing today, unfortunately, to attest to the place's historical significance. Five kilometres further south along the same road, the apparently Byzantine-inspired church in the hamlet of **GRUND**, with its onion-shaped dome and Romanesque mini-spires, is one of the most unusual in Iceland; designed by a local farmer to serve the entire valley, it broke with tradition by being built on a north–south, not east–west, axis. If the church is locked, you'll find the key at the neighbouring farmhouse.

By far and away the best place to stay in the valley is the good *Öngulsstaðir III* **farmstay** (T463 1380, Wwww.ongulsstadir.is; ❷), whose friendly owners will make you feel at home. The pleasant rooms, simply decorated and en suite, are located in the former cow sheds, while the main building, where breakfast (950kr) is served, is a converted barn. Get here by taking Route 829 (signposted to "Laugaland") up the eastern side of the valley. For **hotel** accommodation there's the *Vin* in Hrafnagil (T463 1333, Wwww.vin.nett.is; ❷), where breakfast is an extra 850kr.

Grímsey

Forty kilometres north of the mainland, the five-square-kilometre chunk of craggy basalt that defiantly rears up out of the Atlantic is the island of **Grímsey**, straddled by the **Arctic Circle**, where Iceland ends and the Arctic begins. First settled by the Viking **Vestfjarða-Grímur Sigurðsson**, and named after him ("Grímsey" means Grímur's Island), the island supports one tiny settlement, scruffy **Sandvík**, on the southwest coast. While many come here to cross that magical geographical line, the island also hosts some amazing birdlife, including **puffins**, **razorbills** and **guillemots**, which are resident on the island's cliffs for most of the year – some 36 species breed here. Take special care when walking around the island since you're likely to be attacked by **arctic tern**, in particular, which will stop at nothing to protect their eggs – they are present on the island from early May to early September.

There's just one road on Grímsey, which runs the length of the west coast from the lighthouse at its southernmost point, Flesjar, through the village to the airport

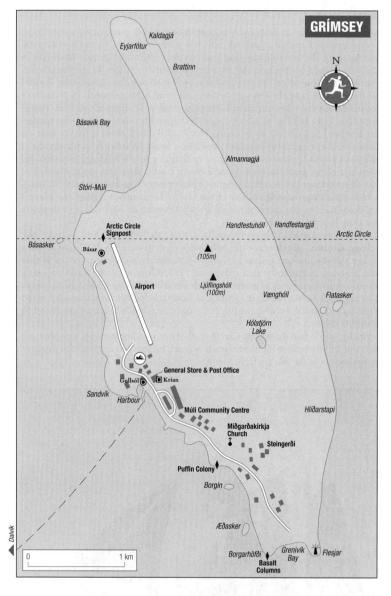

GRÍMSEY

N

Kaldagjá

Eyjarfótur

Brattinn

Básavík Bay

Almannagjá

Stóri-Múli

Handfestuhóll   Handfestargjá

Arctic Circle
Signpost   Arctic Circle

Básasker   Básar ◉

▲
(105m)

Airport   ▲
               Ljúflingshóll
               (100m)   Vænghóll   Flatasker

                        Hólatjörn
                        Lake

                        ✈

Gullsól ◉   ■ Krían   General Store & Post Office

Sandvík

Harbour

                    Múli Community Centre   Hlíðarstapi

                         Miðgarðakirkja
                         Church
                                    Steingerði

Puffin Colony ▸

      Borgin ⬭

                                             Æðasker

                                                Grenivík
                                   Borgarhöfði ▸ Bay ▸ Flesjar
                                       Basalt
                                       Columns

▲ Dalvík

0   1 km

at Básar – a total length of 3km. Landing here in the Air Iceland twin otter that links the island with Akureyri can be quite an experience, as it's often forced to buzz over the runway on the initial approach to clear the hundreds of potentially dangerous birds that gather on it before coming in a second time to land. Taking off is no less hazardous – although one of the island's few cars is driven up and down the runway to achieve the same result.

Sandvík

SANDVÍK, home to 85 people, is essentially nothing more than twenty or so houses grouped around a harbour, which is where the ferry from Dalvík docks. Southeast of the harbour, the road leads to the community centre, **Múli** (ask at the village shop for the key), where every year on November 11 the birthday of the island's benefactor, nineteenth-century American chess champion **Daniel Willard Fiske**, is celebrated with coffee, cakes and a day off work. A prominent journalist during the nineteenth century, and a leading scholar on things Icelandic, Fiske left the islanders US$12,000 upon his death and gave instruction for a school and library to be built. Oddly, Fiske had never once set foot on Grímsey, but it seems the islanders' reputation as the greatest **chess** players in the whole of Iceland (chess was introduced to Grímsey by the Vikings) furthered his own love of the game; he even donated eleven marble chess sets to the island. The last remaining set can be seen, alongside Fiske's portrait, in the library inside Múli, which stands on the original site of the school he financed. Today, the island's children learn to play chess at school and there's even an open-air table opposite the shop if you fancy a game.

A few steps beyond the community centre, the whitewashed walls of the village **church**, which was originally built of driftwood in 1867, cut a sharp image against the heavy skies. It seems to be thanks to one former priest that this isolated community still exists: in 1793, Grímsey came close to being abandoned when a plague swept through the island killing almost all the men. The six healthiest sailed to the mainland to seek help, but were drowned when their boat capsized, leaving the priest the only able-bodied man on the island to fulfil his duties.

Finally, you'll find the **Arctic Circle** marked not by a line but by a **signpost** just past the airport – there's a picnic bench beneath it, and you can read the signpost to find out how far you are from home.

▲ Daniel Willard Fiske memorial, Grímse

Around the island

Setting out from the airport it's possible to **walk round the island** following a rough sheep track all the way. It's wise to use the cliff tops as a guide, as the track soon gets lost amid the many springy tussocks that mark this part of the island, as it heads up the hillside to the east coast, by far the most dramatic aspect of the island; here sheer cliffs plunge down into the foam and the roaring waves of the Arctic Ocean. The promontory you can see from here, **Eyjarfótur**, stretching out to the north, is a good place to watch the birds since it affords views out over the sea and back over the low fields around the guesthouse and airport where so many species congregate. However, there is no area of the island devoid of birds and simply walking around Grímsey, be it on the cliffs or in the village, will bring you into contact with various varieties of sea birds. Heading south from the headland following the shoreline, the path climbs a little as it goes over **Handfestuhóll**, from where you can see the rock fissures **Almannagjá** and **Handfestargjá** in the cliff face. Beyond the small islet, **Flatasker**, the coast swings south heading for the lighthouse at Grímsey's southeastern point, **Flesjar**. Across Grenivík bay from here, on the southwestern point, Borgarhöfði, a series of basalt columns form a mini-version of Northern Ireland's famous Giant's Causeway. From here the road continues along the west coast into the village and back to the harbour. The headland opposite the church, which you'll pass heading back to the village, is one of the most easily accessible places to spot puffins. Quite remarkably, during the course of just one night (usually around August 10), every puffin heads off out to sea for the winter.

Island practicalities

The *Sæfari* **ferry** (☎458 8970, ⓦ www.landflutningar.is/saefari_ferry_english; 3hr each way; 5800kr return) runs year-round three times a week between Dalvík and Grímsey; **buses** from Akureyri connect with services and take about an hour. Alternatively, you can **fly** in from Akureyri three times a week (daily mid-June to mid-Aug) in just 25 minutes.

In summer, day-trippers can make the island relatively busy, so it's nice to linger overnight and have the island to yourself. There are two places to stay: the charming *Gullsól* **guesthouse** down by the harbour (☎467 3190, ⓔstellagella@hotmail.com; sleeping-bag accommodation 2000kr, ❶) is housed in an aluminium-sided home, while the equally pleasant 🏕 *Básar* guesthouse (☎467 3103, ⓔgagga@simnet.is; sleeping-bag accommodation 2000kr, ❶) overlooks the tiny runway and the sea. Breakfast here is an extra 1000kr, lunch is 2000kr and dinner 3000kr. **Camping** is permitted anywhere on the island away from the village. The other place to eat is at the *Krían* **café** above the harbour, which serves burgers and chips (around 1300kr) from noon until 8.30pm. Next door, the **general store** is pretty well stocked, and closes any time after 5pm. The indoor **swimming pool** is located in the grey building at the southern end of the runway; it opens if three or more people want to swim – enquire at the store.

Travel details

<table>
<tr><td>Buses</td><td>**Akureyri** to: Árskógssandur (Mon–Fri 4 daily; 35min); Blönduós (2 daily; 2hr); Brú (2 daily; 4hr); Dalvík (Mon–Fri 3 daily; 45min); Egilsstaðir (1 daily; 3hr 30min); Húsavík (4 daily; 1hr 10min); Ísafjörður (3 weekly; 11hr); Mývatn (1 daily; 1hr 30min);</td></tr>
</table>

The bus details given below are relevant for May to September; for winter times, visit ⓦ www.trex.is.

Ólafsfjörður (Mon–Fri 3 daily; 1hr 30min); Reykjavík (2 daily; 6hr); Varmahlíð (2 daily; 1hr 20min).

Árskógssandur to: Akureyri (Mon–Fri 3 daily; 35min); Dalvík (Mon–Fri 3 daily; 10min); Ólafsfjörður (Mon–Fri 3 daily; 1hr).

Blönduós to: Akureyri (2 daily; 2hr); Brú (2 daily; 1hr 45min); Reykjavík (2 daily; 3hr 45min); Varmahlíð (2 daily; 45min).

Brú to: Akureyri (2 daily; 4hr); Blönduós (2 daily; 1hr 45min); Hólmavík (3 weekly; 2hr 30min); Ísafjörður (3 weekly; 7hr); Reykjavík (2 daily; 2hr); Varmahlíð (2 daily; 2hr 25min).

Dalvík to: Akureyri (Mon–Fri 3 daily; 45min); Árskógssandur (Mon–Fri 3 daily; 10min); Ólafsfjörður (Mon–Fri 3 daily; 45min).

Hofsós to: Sauðárkrókur (Sun–Fri daily; 45min); Siglufjörður (Sun–Fri daily; 1hr).

Ólafsfjörður to: Akureyri (Mon–Fri 3 daily; 1hr 30min); Árskógssandur (Mon–Fri 3 daily; 1hr); Dalvík (Mon–Fri 3 daily; 45min).

Sauðárkrókur to: Hofsós (Sun–Fri daily; 45min); Siglufjörður (Sun–Fri daily; 1hr); Varmahlíð (2 daily; 30min).

Siglufjörður to: Hofsós (Sun–Fri daily; 1hr); Sauðárkrókur (Sun–Fri daily; 1hr 45min).

Varmahlíð to: Akureyri (2 daily; 1hr 20min); Brú (2 daily; 2hr 25min); Reykjavík (2 daily; 4hr 25min); Sauðárkrókur (2 daily; 30min).

Ferries

Árskógssandur to: Hrísey (May–Aug hourly; Sept–April every 2 hours; 15min).

Dalvík to: Grímsey (3 weekly; 3hr 30min).

Flights

Akureyri to: Grímsey (3–7 weekly; 25min); Reykjavík (7 daily; 50min); Vopnafjörður (5 weekly; 45min); Þórshöfn (5 weekly; 40min).

Iceland: a culture apart

Geographically isolated from mainland Europe, Iceland has developed a very different culture from the rest of the Continent. A lack of communication with the outside world for centuries has set the country apart and preserved many aspects of its stirring Viking past, such as a widespread belief in spirits, heathen gods and the omnipotence of nature, in particular the sea. Even today, most Icelanders retain an unparalleled respect for their history and forebears which, at times, can seem to contradict the modern nation's cornerstones of peace, prosperity and equality.

Hafnarfjörður viking festival ▲

Winter festival on Heimaey ▼

Practising traditional crafts ▼

Keeping the past alive

Icelanders are fiercely proud of their **Viking** heritage. Links with the past are especially tangible during þorri, the fourth division of the old Icelandic calendar, which developed out of seasonal and climatic factors and today falls between late January and late February. According to the sagas, it was common practice during pagan times to hold a sacrifice or þorrablót as a midwinter celebration. Preserved foods such as rotten shark, which sustained people through the long winter months, were offered to the gods, along with delicacies such as squashed rams' testicles and singed sheep heads; in Viking times no part of an animal was wasted since food was a precious commodity. Today's Icelanders honour their forebears by feasting on these traditional foods at special þorrablót banquets, the best known of which is held in Hafnarfjörður near Reykjavík (see p.94). These orgies of medieval indulgence are, in part, held for tourists, but since most families can trace their ancestors back to the time of the Settlement, remembering þorri is just one way today's Icelanders keep in touch with their past.

The importance of the climate and the seasons to Icelanders is difficult to overestimate. If þorri is a celebration of winter, then *Jónsmessa* is its antithesis. Marking the **summer solstice**, this festival is associated with white nights when the air is full of magic. Indeed, it's easy to see how tales of magical deeds spread through medieval society, since it was around **Midsummer Day** that the Alþing (General Assembly) held its annual gathering at Þingvellir drawing people from across the country. Indeed, it's folklore rather than specific events that govern this day; cows are said to gain the ability of speech and seals, which are believed to be people under a spell of enchantment, cast off their skins and take on their human form again. Another belief associated with *Jónsmessa* is that anyone who rolls naked in the dew at midnight will be cured of all ills and live happily ever after. Beyond Iceland's borders it's easy to scoff at such convictions, but talk to any Icelander and they'll assure you that this is the most magical time of the year in the north and that anything is possible. Reykjavík's Nordic House (see p.75) is a good place to catch the *Jónsmessa* celebrations.

▲ Folk dancers in national costume

▼ Troll head carving, Bakkagerði

Huldufólk: the hidden people

It seems remarkable in today's modern age that anyone still believes in **elves and spirits** at all, let alone in any large number. In Iceland, however, there is no doubt that the *huldufólk*, or hidden people as they're known, do exist: surveys repeatedly show that eight out of ten Icelanders believe in elves, and in Hafnarfjörður, the reputed **centre of the elf kingdom**, one in four people even claims to have seen them. The town has been quick to realize this hidden potential and it's now possible to take a tour of Hafnarfjörður visiting the spots where elves are said to appear (see p.94). To the non-believer, it may sound odd to hear that housing and road construction companies sometimes consult local clairvoyants over the presence of elf dwellings on the site of a proposed development. Nor is it unusual for straight roads to be diverted around large rocks where elves are said to live in order to avoid upset among the *huldufólk*; the Ringroad in Reykjavík, for example,

Rock formation inhabited by elves, Reykjavík ▲

The Icelandic alphabet has 32 letters ▼

has been moved twice in Grafarholt in the southeast of the city for this very reason. Pinning down the belief in elves and spirits, which goes back centuries, is no easy task, though one theory suggests that it stems from ancient pagan convictions, which grew out of the fantastic shapes and forms that the omnipresent lava landscape can create.

The language of the Vikings

Notwithstanding the odd change in pronunciation, today's **Icelandic** is essentially the same language the Vikings spoke over 1300 years ago. Few other European languages can claim such a pure and unsullied past. The importance of fishing to Iceland's economy is evident in its language: *þín þorskur!* ("you cod!") is a term of abuse, while "to give up" is often rendered as *leggja ára í bát*, "to lay one's oars in the boat". If something isn't up to much, it's *ekki upp á marga fiska* – "not worth many fish". Rural life has also left its mark on the language: on Friday nights in Reykjavík you'll find plenty of people who're *sauðdrukkinnn* – "as drunk as a sheep"; the word for sheep, *fé*, is also the generic term for money.

Icelandic names

In Viking tradition, Icelanders have a given name, plus the name of (usually) their father with an attached "-son" for boys and "-dóttir" for girls. So, Jón's son Gunnar is called Gunnar Jónsson, and his daughter Njóla is called Njóla Jónsdóttir. Because of this lack of family names, telephone directories are arranged by given names, sometimes with the addition of a profession for clarity.

6

Mývatn and the northeast

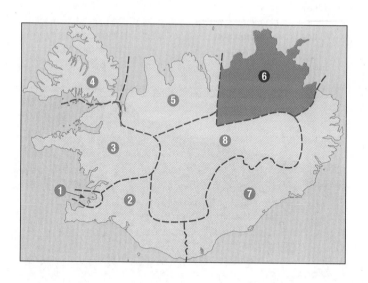

CHAPTER 6 # Highlights

* **Lake Mývatn** Clock up
the birdlife and explore
surrounding craters, and hot
mud pools, and bathe in the
northeast's only geothermal
spa. **See p.253**

* **Krafla and Leirhnjúkur**
Spend a half-day hiking
around this volcano crater
and rugged lava flow, still
steaming after an eruption in
the 1980s. **See p.262**

* **Húsavík** Iceland's premier
whale-watching venue, where
you're almost guaranteed
sightings through the summer.
See p.264

* **Jökulsárgljúfur** Superb
camping and hiking among
heath and weird rock
formations at this deep river
gorge and National Park.
See p.268

* **Ásbyrgi** Huge horseshoe-
shaped cliff face, reputedly a
hoofprint made by the Norse
god Oðinn's eight-legged
horse. **See p.270**

* **Dettifoss** Europe's most
powerful waterfall is spectacular at the start of summer,
as glacial melt upstream turns
the river into a furious brown
torrent. **See p.271**

▲ Ásbyrgi cliffs, Jökulsárgljúfur National Park

6

Mývatn and the northeast

Northeast Iceland forms a thinly populated, open expanse between Akureyri and the Eastfjords, half of which is dominated by the lava-covered Ódáðahraun plateau, which slopes gently from the Interior to the sea, drained by glacial rivers and underground springs. Tourists, along with most of Iceland's wildfowl population, flock to **Mývatn**, an attractive lake just over an hour's drive from Akureyri, whose surrounds are thick with hot springs and volcanic formations – many of them still visibly active – as well as a sublime **geothermal spa** that is the northeast's less-touristy answer to the Blue Lagoon. North of here, the pleasant town of **Húsavík** offers summer **whale-watching** excursions, and is just a short jaunt from **Jökulsárgljúfur**, a broad canyon cut into the wilderness by one of the region's glacial rivers, which thunders through a series of gorges and waterfalls – a superb place to spend a few days hiking or camping.

The eastern half of the region has far less obvious attractions; indeed, the only real access to this mix of mountains, lava desert and boggy lowlands is along the coastal road between Húsavík and **Vopnafjörður**. However, it's a great place for purposeless travel, bringing you close to some wild countryside, breezy coastal walks, and small, isolated communities – plus the chance to reach the mainland's northernmost tip, which lies fractionally outside the Arctic Circle.

The northeast's **main roads** are the Ringroad (Route 1), which crosses east from Akureyri to Mývatn and then heads out of the region to Egilsstaðir; and Route 85, which mostly follows the coast via Húsavík and Jökulsárgljúfur to Vopnafjörður, before cutting inland and down to the Ringroad. **Buses** cover both routes in peak season – roughly June through to September – though at other times services are limited or nonexistent; there are also **tours** of the regional highlights, primarily out of Mývatn. If taking your own transport, note that as there are few fuel stations between towns it's best to top up the tank whenever you can. The main roads are sound, though not always surfaced and sometimes closed at short notice by snow. Minor roads in the area, while not necessarily needing four-wheel-drives, may only be open for a month or two in summer, so you'll need to find out their condition by asking other visitors or by contacting local information centres before tackling them.

Away from Mývatn and Húsavík, services are thinly spread, though most settlements have at least a bank, a supermarket and somewhere to stay; elsewhere, there

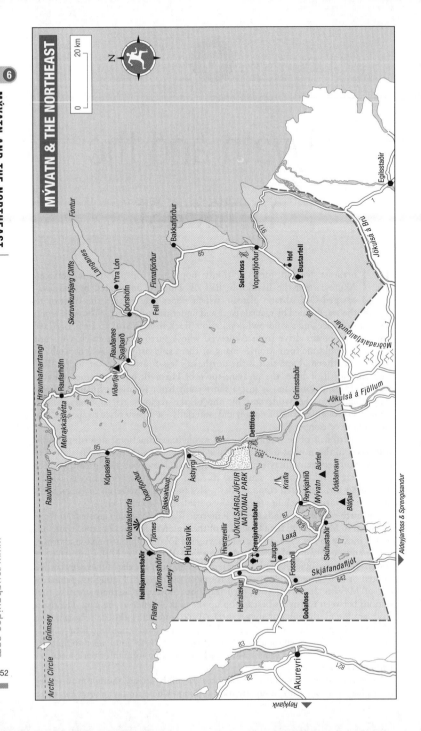

N

0   20 km

Egilsstaðir

Jökulsá á Brú

Bakkafjörður

85

Selárfoss
Vopnafjörður   ✝ Hof
116   ♨ Bustarfell

Fontur

Ytra Lón
Þórshöfn
Fell
Finnafjörður

Langanes

Skoruvíkurbjarg Cliffs

85
Rauðanes
Viðarfjall Svalbarð

Móðrudalsfjallgarðar

85   1

85

Hraunhafnartangi

Raufarhöfn

Grímsstaðir

Jökulsá á Fjöllum

Melrakkaslétta

1

864   Dettifoss

Rauðinúpur

Kópasker

Öxarfjörður

298

Bakkahlaup   Ásbyrgi

JÖKULSÁRGLJÚFUR
NATIONAL PARK   Krafla
                                        Mývatn Búrfell
85   Reykjahlíð   Óðáðahraun
Voladalstorfa   Bláfjall
Tjörnes   87
Hljóðaklettar   Hveravellir Grenjaðarstaður
Tjörneshöfn   87   Laugar Laxá Skútustaðir
Húsavík   862
Hallbjarnarstaðir   87   Fosshóll
Lundey   Hraðalækur 98   Skjálfandafljót 842
Flatey   Goðafoss

Arctic Circle   Grímsey

Reykjavík

Aldeyjarfoss & Sprengisandur

83
Akureyri
82   821

are farmstays, a few hostels, and limitless camping opportunities. The northeast's **weather** is much drier and often sunnier than southern Iceland's – and this far north it barely gets dark for three months of the year – though winters are bitterly cold, with heavy snowfalls throughout.

Mývatn and around

Around 100km east of Akureyri on the Ringroad, **Mývatn**'s placid, shallow spread of water belies its status as one of the country's most touristed locations. Admittedly, Mývatn has had its detractors ever since the Middle Ages – when the lake and its steaming surrounds were fearfully dismissed as a pool of the devil's piss – though now it's the summertime swarms of tiny black **flies** (Mývatn means "Midge Lake") that are most likely to get up your nose. While visitors seek sanctuary behind gauze netting, the flies and their larvae provide an abundant food source for both fish and the hundreds of thousands of **wildfowl** which descend on the lake each year to raise their young. All of Iceland's duck species breed either here or close by on the **Laxá**, Mývatn's fast-flowing, salmon-rich outlet, and one – **Barrow's goldeneye** – nests nowhere else in Europe.

There's plenty more to hold your attention beyond the birds and bugs. Covering over 36 square kilometres, Mývatn sits on the western side of a major tectonic fault, eruptions along which not only created the lake itself by damming local springs, but also the collection of hulking, flat-topped mountains away to the southeast, and the cones, craters and oddly contorted lava which surround the lakeshore. Due east of Mývatn, the land is still smoking and bubbling away at **Bjarnarflag** where the **Jarðböðin nature baths** harness the earth's subterranean power to create Iceland's most agreeable **geothermal spa**. Northeast, in the highlands beyond **Hverir**'s bubbling mud pits, **Krafla** and **Leirhnjúkur** mark an area of intense volcanism, where explosively violent fissures were fully active through the 1980s.

Most people base themselves on the northern side of the lake at **Reykjahlíð**, Mývatn's small service centre and home to most of the region's facilities, though a few alternatives are dotted elsewhere around the shore – especially at southerly **Skútustaðir**. A good **road** circuits Mývatn, with tracks and footpaths elsewhere, and two busy days are enough to take in the main sights – some people even day-trip from Reykjavík by plane.

Mývatn looks its best in summer, but can get very crowded then, when beds are in short supply and it's a toss-up to decide whether there are more tourists, insects, or ducks. As for the flies: a few bite, but most just buzz irritatingly around your face – keep them off by buying a hat with attached netting. Alternatively, hit a few good days in late spring and, while you'll miss out on some of the bird life, there are no flies and you'll have the place to yourself – though facilities are limited out of season.

Getting to Mývatn

Between May and September **buses** (Ⓦwww.sba.is) run daily to **Rekjahlíð**, Mývatn's main township, from Akureyri, Húsavík and Egilsstaðir; for the rest of

Mývatn's ducks

In summer, plentiful food and nesting space make Mývatn the best place to see **wild ducks** in northern Europe and, armed with a pair of binoculars and a little patience, you should be able to clock up eighteen species during your stay. Their favourite **nesting area** is in spongy heathland on the northwest side of the lake (given the country's often treeless environment, all Icelandic ducks are ground-nesting), though more accessible places to spy on them include Mývatn's southeastern corner (especially good for Barrow's goldeneye); the Laxá outflow on the western side of the lake (for harlequin ducks); and even the shore at Reykjahlíð (anything). Female ducks tend to be drably coloured, to blend in with vegetation while incubating their eggs, and unless otherwise stated, the following descriptions are of breeding males.

Several types of duck at Mývatn have a black head, and black and white body (females with a brown or russet head and grey elsewhere). The most celebrated is the locally abundant – though otherwise rare – **Barrow's goldeneye**, easily identified by a characteristic white comma-shaped patch between the manic golden eye and bill. They live here year-round, and their courtship displays start in late April: males stretch their necks out towards a potential partner until their beak touches the water, then flick their heads backwards; females respond in a similar manner. Keep an eye open too for their cute, black and white striped chicks. Barrow's goldeneye are most likely to be confused with either the similar-looking **tufted duck** or **scaup**, though neither share its "comma" – tufted ducks also have a droopy back-swept crest, while the scaup has a grey, not white, back.

Mývatn's other speciality is the **harlequin duck**, which sports unmistakable chestnut, white and blue plumage, though as indicated by its Icelandic name – *straumönd*, stream duck – is less likely to be seen on the lake than bobbing in and out of rough water on the Laxá. In fact, adult harlequins prefer the sea and spend as little time inland as possible, arriving to nest in late April and moving on by mid-July. Other marine ducks spending their summers at Mývatn include the **scoter**, a uniquely all-black diving duck, which in Iceland breeds only at Mývatn, and the **long-tailed** or **old squaw**, another strikingly patterned bird with a summer plumage including a black neck and crown and very long, pointed tail (the similar **pintail** has a white throat, though so does the long-tail in winter).

One species absent from the lake is the **eider**, which nests mostly up along the Laxá – both sexes have wedge-shaped bills and a distinctive low posture in the water; the two-tone males have subtle pastel pink and green touches on their chests and napes. The eider's bulky build comes into its own at sea, where the birds gather into huge "rafts" and calmly ride out heavy swells, as unsinkable as a fleet of lifeboats. They pad their nests with special down, and it's this which is commercially collected (after the ducks have moved on) for stuffing cushions, sleeping bags and the like – a small but profitable business in Iceland.

Otherwise, you'll be fairly familiar with most of Mývatn's ducks, which are primarily freshwater species. Some of the more plentiful include the **mallard**; the red-headed **pochard**; the long-beaked **merganser** and **goosander**, and the wide-beaked **shoveler**; **widgeon**, with their coppery heads and vertical blond streak between the eyes; the uniformly nondescript **gadwall**; and **teals**, which sport a glossy red head and green eyepatch.

the year, just four services a week call in on their way between Akureyri and Egilsstaðir. From late June until mid-August, there are also direct buses from Reykjavík via the remote **Sprengisandur route** (see p.314), though this requires an overnight stop at Landmannalaugar.

Driving in from Akureyri along the Ringroad, it's worth stopping after about 40km at tiny **FOSSHÓLL**, where the ice-blue Skjálfandafljöt (which originates way down south at Vatnajökull) tears through horseshoe-shaped basalt canyons in a pair of cataracts. The largest of these, **Goðafoss** (Waterfall of the gods), is where Þorgeir Ljósvetningagoði – the lawspeaker who decided that Christianity should be Iceland's official religion at the historic Alþing in 1000 – destroyed his pagan statues by pushing them over the falls. It's a beautiful spot to stop overnight, and Fosshóll itself comprises a roadhouse with a filling station, a café-restaurant and the **Fosshóll guesthouse** (☎464 3108, ✉fossholl@nett.is; ❷), which also has space for campers. Some 35km downstream of Fosshóll along a seasonal gravel road – check at the roadhouse to see if it's open – **Aldeyjarfoss** is another spectacular waterfall right at the top of the **Sprengisandur Route** from Reykjavík.

Back on the Ringroad, the other place to pause before Mývatn is **LAUGAR**, a small town with a fuel station, bank with an ATM, post office (Mon–Fri 9am–4pm) and a school where *Fosshótel* runs a **summer hotel** (☎464 6300, ⓦwww.fosshotel.is; sleeping bag; ❹). From here, it's another 45km to Reykjahlíð, either along the Ringroad via **Skútustaðir** (see p.260) at the south end of the lake, or direct to Reykjahlíð along Route 848.

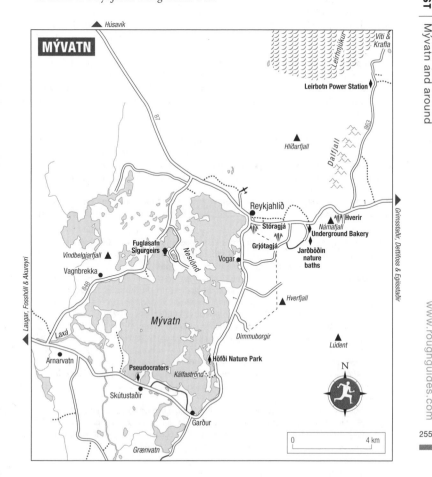

Reykjahlíð and the lake

Given the number of visitors who invade each summer, **REYKJAHLÍÐ** is surprisingly insubstantial – just a handful of services and a couple of residential streets up at Mývatn's northeastern corner, where the Ringroad and the Húsavík road converge. Marking the western edge of things, Reykjahlíð's **church** is worth a look, less for the neat white structure itself than the **lava flows** either side. These date to August 1729, when erupting fissures 10km northeast at Leirhnjúkur (see p.263) rounded off a prolonged spell of activity. Fast-flowing lava descended from the hills and covered three nearby farms, but was mysteriously deflected around the low-lying church – some say by the cemetery wall, others (in keeping with similar cases elsewhere in Iceland) by prayer. A carving on the pulpit depicts the church of the time under threat, and check out the lava, too: there are some good stretches of rope-lava pavements, and plenty of fissures caused by escaping gases. Other than this, Reykjahlíð's main attraction is its shallow **swimming pool** (daily 10.30am–7.30pm; 350kr), with the usual complement of hot pots.

On a cold day you'll see steam rising from small cracks in the ground all around Reykjahlíð, and for a closer look walk just southeast of the Húsavík-Ringroad intersection, where you'll find **Stóragjá**, the most accessible of Mývatn's sunken hot springs, hidden in among the rough scrub and lava. A ladder and rope reach down into the two-metre-wide cleft from ground level, and it was a popular bathing hole until it cooled during the 1990s (it's now around 25°C), allowing harmful algae to invade. Some people do still swim here, but at the risk of getting any cuts or grazes infected – best stick to the swimming pool.

The lake shore around Reykjahlíð is flat and good for **bird-watching**, with a few pairs of **slavonian grebes** – sleek diving birds with yellow tufts behind the ears – nesting each year; take the short track to the water from opposite the *Reynihlíð* hotel and you should find them. There's also a fair chance of spotting **red-necked phalaropes**, small waders with pointy beaks and a distinctive red

---

Tours from Reykjahlíð

If you don't want to take the following tours, you'll need to **hire a car or bicycle** from *Hótel Reynihlíð* or make use of the eight-kilometre-long Reykjahlíð–Grótagjá–Hverfell Dimmuborgir hiking trail. The following excursions run in summer only; either contact operators direct or book through Mývatn's Visitor Centre.

SBA **buses** (W www.sba.is) runs return **day trips** from Akureyri round the lake and out to **Krafla** (9500kr), and an extended version out to **Dettifoss** in Jökulsárglúfur National Park (10,500kr). It also operates three-day expeditions to ice caves and glacier traverses at **Kverkfjöll** and **Vatnajökull** (25,000kr; see p.318).

The track south from Mývatn to the Interior at **Askja** (see p.317) is covered by bus with Mývatn Tours (T 464 1920, W www.askjatours.is; 14,000kr); this is a lengthy day-trip, though you can arrange in advance to stay at huts along the way and be collected another day. Mývatn Adventures (T 464 4164, W www.myvatn.is; 28,000kr) does the same thing in super-jeeps, and also heads right down to the fringes of the Vatnajökull ice cap at **Lofthellir Ice Caves** (June–Sept daily; 7700kr), frozen lava caverns discovered in 1989 (35,000kr).

For **scenic flights**, Mýflug Air (T 464 4400, W www.myflug.is) out of Reykjalíð can take you for a spin over Mývatn and Krafla, or out to Askja and Dettifoss, or out to Grímsey – trips last from twenty minutes to two hours and cost 10,000–39,500kr. Finally, you can arrange **horseriding** in the area through *Hlíð* (T 464 4103).

stripe, which perform "pirouettes" on the water; this creates a whirlpool which sucks up bottom-dwelling bugs on which the birds feed. The northeast bit of Mývatn is also the only place that you don't need a boat to go **fishing** on the lake, though you will require a permit (around 3500kr a day; ask at accommodation); stocks of trout and arctic char are generally good. Several people in Reykjahlíð have **smoke houses** for curing fish which you can buy direct or through the store; in the absence of timber they use dried sheep-dung for smoking, and the results are somewhat coarser than wood-smoked fish.

Practicalities

Reykjahlíð is strung out along 500m of road on Mývatn's northeastern shore. The main focus is the well-stocked but pricey Samkaup/STRAX **supermarket** (daily: summer 9am–8pm; winter 10am–6pm) and **fuel station** at the eastern side of "town"; there are also an **ATM** and toilets here. **Buses** pull in next door at the helpful **Visitor Centre** (June–Aug daily 9am–6pm; ☏464 4460, ⓦwww .umhverfisstofnun.is); note that Reykjahlíð is often confusingly marked "Reynihlíð" on bus timetables. Further back, beyond a clutch of houses, is the **swimming pool**. About 250m west along the shore, past several places to stay, is the church, behind which is Reykjahlíð's **airstrip**.

For **food**, make sure you try some smoked fish, along with *hverabrauð* – bread baked in the underground ovens east at Bjarnaflag (see p.261) – both of which are available at the supermarket and a stall outside *Hótel Reynihlíð*. Reykjahlíð's best **eating** option is the 🍴 *Gamli Bærinn* (daily 10am–midnight), a cosy café-bar in a converted farmhouse next to *Hótel Reynihlíð* – packed solid around noon when tour buses pass through – with a good selection of sandwiches (600kr), cooked meals (1900kr), cakes, coffee and beer.

Accommodation

Accommodation is very tourist-season oriented. Prices are high at peak times, falling heavily in winter – if establishments even bother to open. If all of Reykjahlíð is full, there's further accommodation in Skútustaðir (see p.260). Reykjahlíð's two **campsites** are at *Bjarg* and *Hlíð*, with other options around the lake at Vogar (see p.258) and Skútustaðir – camping elsewhere is prohibited.

Bjarg Beside the main road overlooking the lake ☏464 4240, ⓔferdabjarg@simnet.is. As well as a campsite with laundry and kitchen facilities, this lakeside establishment rents out two comfortable double rooms between April and December. Camping 750kr per person, ❷

Eldá Helluhraun 15 ☏464 4220, ⓦwww.elda.is. Friendly, family-run business utilizing four places around Reykjahlíð with the option of single, double and triple rooms. Rates include breakfast. Sleeping-bag accommodation available in low season only at 2250kr per person. Internet access for guests. ❸

🏃 **Hlíð** Off the airstrip road behind the church ☏464 4103, ⓦwww.hlidmyv.is. Good budget option with nice views over lake, town and distant mountains. Spacious campsite with a laundry, bathrooms, hot-tubs and kitchen; a roomy,

self-catering bunkhouse favoured by tour groups with around a dozen four-person dorms, plus a large kitchen and dining area; and self-catering, four-person cabins. Camping 750kr pp, sleeping bag 4500kr, made-up bed 5000kr.

Reykjahlíð On the lakeshore between the super-market and church ☏464 4142, ⓦwww .reykjahlid.is. Low-key bed and breakfast overlooking the lake, whose pleasantly laconic owner and relaxed furnishings make it feel more like a guesthouse. Shared bathrooms only. ❹

🏃 **Reynihlíð** Next to the church ☏464 4170, ⓦwww.myvatnhotel.is. A modern, motel-like affair whose well-furnished tastefully decorated rooms in contemporary Nordic style have the edge over those at the *Reykjahlíð*. Their *Mýllanllan* restaurant is an upmarket version of the adjacent *Gamli Bærinn*. ❻

The lakeshore

Moving clockwise around Mývatn from Rekjahlíð, you follow the Ringroad down around the lake via the hamlets of **Vogar** and **Skútustaðir** to where the Laxá drains westwards, then cross the river and take Route 848 up the west shore and back to town. This circuit is about 35km long in itself, but there are several places to make fairly extensive detours away from the lake, principally **Grótagjá** hot springs; the rough lavafield at **Dimmuborgir** and **Hverfjall** cone, east of the lake; and **Vindbelgjarfjall**, a peak on Mývatn's northwestern side. Aside from the highly visible wildfowl, keep your eyes peeled for ptarmigan, arctic foxes and maybe even rare **gyrfalcons**. Also note that erosion is a serious problem at many popular sites and that you should stick to marked paths where you find them.

As there are few tour options available at present, you really need your own **vehicle** – cars and bicycles can be **rented** through *Hótel Reynihlíð*. You can of course **walk** and should at least tackle the well-marked, eight-kilometre **trail** that links Reykjahlíð with highlights at Grótagjá, Hverfjall and Dimmuborgir. To explore away from here, carry *Landmælingar Íslands* Mývatn 1:50,000 map – the Visitor Centre might have these, otherwise Akureyri's bookshops are the nearest source.

Vogar and Grótagjá

Heading south from Reykjahlíð, you pass sheep pens built of lava blocks, and the first small stands of **birch** that appear in patches all down the eastern lakeshore. Big chunks of lava by the roadside also mark the edge of a vast expanse of volcanic detritus – once out of the woods you'll realize how extensive this is.

Only about 2km from Reykjahlíð, **VOGAR** is a handful of farms with **accommodation** at *Vogar Ferðaþónusta* (☏464 4399, ⓦ www.vogahraun.is; camping 1200kr, sleeping bag 4300kr, doubles including breakfast ❷). There's no store here, but you can eat in the *Vogafjós Cowshed Café* (May–Sept 7.30am–11.30pm) – try the *hverabrauð* and smoked trout, drink coffee or beer, and even watch the cows being milked (7.30am & 5pm).

Detour a couple of kilometres northeast from Vogar along a gravel road and you're at **Grótagjá**, the best-known of Mývatn's flooded fissures. From the outside, the lava is heaped up in a long, five-metre-high ridge; entering through a crack, you find yourself in a low-ceilinged tunnel harbouring a couple of clear blue, steaming pools (one for men at 48°C, one for women at 44°C), lit by daylight through the entrance. The drawback is that unless you're here in winter – when the women's pool is just about bearable for a quick immersion (take care on the rough rocks) – Grótagjá is a bit too hot to get into, though it is cooling down each year. There are more comfortable hot pools elsewhere at Mývatn, however, and if you're lucky locals may show you their favourites – some are superb in winter, when you have to climb down the ice into them.

Hverfjall and Lúdent

Around 3km southeast of Vogar, **Hverfjall** (also marked as Hverfell on some maps) is Mývatn's most easily identified landmark, looking just how a volcano should: broad, conical and strewn with black rubble and rocks, it's a classic **tephra cone**, made of consolidated ash and pumice. At 2500 years old, Hverfjall is also a bit younger than the lake, and its rim (400m) presents a satisfying, straightforward climb from the **parking area** 1.5km east off the highway along a gravel track. Two hours is ample time for a slow ascent and circuit of the kilometre-wide caldera, which is a great way to orient yourself: immediately west lie the lake's flat blue waters, its scattering of islands and convoluted shore; views north take in the town, steaming thermal areas, and the plateau harbouring Krafla; southeast lurks Lúdent, beyond which lava stretches out to the distant string of impressively solid table-top formations of Búrfell, Heilags-dalsfjall and Bláfjall.

If you enjoyed Hverfjall, it's worth trekking the additional 5km out to see **Lúdent**'s similar formations (if you're driving, you'll need a four-wheel-drive for the soft black sand along the way). The track curls around Hverfjall's south side and then bears southeast, rising to cross a line of rough-edged, overgrown volcanic blisters and miniature outlying craters on the abrupt western edge of the Mývatn fault. A further kilometre across the rift and you're on top of the iron-rich, red gravel slopes of Lúdent's main crater; the rim lacks Hverfjall's symmetry, being partially collapsed and invaded by several secondary cones – the one directly north is almost as wide as Lúdent, and slightly higher at 490m. Look back the way you've come and there's a superb line of sight right along the rift wall.

Dimmuborgir

Back on the lake road a kilometre or so south of the Hverfjall junction, another access road runs 1500m east to a car park at **Dimmuborgir**, a collection of crumbled and contorted lava towers set amongst the birch scrub. This was once a **lava lake**, whose crust had solidified by the time its containing wall collapsed, allowing the liquid underneath to drain out but leaving the crust as a broken-up mess behind. Taller formations may have been where steam erupted through the deep pool of molten rock, cooling it enough to form surface-high columns which were left standing on their own once the lava drained away.

You could easily spend a couple of hours on Dimmuborgir's marked paths, examining the rocks' unexpected and indescribable shapes; none of the forms is very tall but every inch is differently textured, all finished in tiny twists and spires. Dimmuborgir's highlight is the lava cave known as **Kirkja**, the Church, about half an hour east from the entrance – what looks like a giant burst bubble of lava, into which around twenty people could comfortably squeeze. Next to the car park, there's a **café** (daily 10am–10pm) serving cakes, coffee and home-made soup, and a **viewing area** where you can take in Dimmuborgir's weird formations from above.

Höfði, Kálfaströnd and Grænvatn

A couple of kilometres south past Dimmuborgir on the lake road, the private nature park **Höfði** marks the first specific lakeside stop. Stack-like formations and tiny islets in the crystal-clear waters here attract birds in some numbers, while the flower-strewn birch woodland along the shore offers good cover for watching them. A local speciality is the **great northern diver** (known as "loon" in the US), which nests here; with luck you'll see the less common red-throated variety, too, along with countless Barrow's goldeneyes – this area is their main hangout. Across the inlet at Höfði, **Kálfaströnd** is a long peninsula with similar appeal; get here by taking the next turning after Höfði, then walking around the shoreline from the farm area.

Rounding Mývatn's southeastern corner, you pass where the lake's **springs** well up below the waters, though this is invisible except in winter, when their warmth stops the surface from freezing. A kilometre further on, the tiny hamlet of **GARÐUR** marks a two-kilometre road south to **Grænvatn**, a much smaller satellite lake of Mývatn. The lake isn't that interesting but the **turf-roofed farmhouse** here is: built in the late nineteenth century and now one of the oldest buildings in the region, it's still lived in.

Skútustaðir

Three kilometres west of Garður, **SKÚTUSTAÐIR** is an alternative base to Reykjahlíð, a small knot of buildings right by the lake comprising a **church**, a **store** with basic supplies, a **café** and **fuel pump**, plus several **places to stay**. Running most of these amenities is the indifferent *Hótel Mývatn* (☎464 4164, ⓦwww.myvatn.is; ⑥), which also rents out bikes; diagonally opposite, its more modern rival *Hótel Gígur* (☎464 4455, ⓦwww.keahotels.is; ④) has excellent views from its restaurant though rooms are nothing special. Budget accommodation is provided by the *Skútustaðir* guesthouse, next to *Hótel Mývatn*, which has self-catering rooms (☎464 4212, ⓦwww.skutustadir.com; sleeping bag 2500kr, ③). If you're after **smoked fish**, visit the smoke house Reykhúsið Skútustöðum, on the road in front of the church, which sells superb salmon, char and trout at around 3000kr per kilo.

Whether or not you stay the night, Skútustaðir's **pseudocraters**, on the lakeshore right in front of the hamlet, warrant a close look. Looking like bonsai volcanoes, pseudocraters are created when lava pours over marshland, boiling the water beneath, which bursts through the solidifying crust to form a cone. They tend to occur in clutches around the lake shore, though most of Mývatn's islands are also pseudocraters, including the largest, **Geitey** – a mere 30m high. There are about a dozen closely packed together at Skútustaðir, known as **skútustaðagígar**, and it takes about an hour to walk from the campsite around the collection of grassy hillocks, following paths and boardwalks.

The west shore: the Laxá, Vindbelgjarfjall and Neslönd

Another 4km west from Skútustaðir the **Laxá** drains quickly out of Mývatn through a collection of low, marshy islands and starts its journey northwest towards the sea at Húsavík. The Ringroad continues west towards Fosshól and Akureyri, but for the western side of the lake, turn over the **bridge** here onto Route 848. Immediately across the Laxá there's a rough parking area, from where a walking track follows the river's rapids upstream for about 1km – before they head seawards in late June, you'll almost certainly see big groups of **harlequin ducks** here, along with geese, phalaropes and whooper swans.

Past here, the lake circuit continues north for 12km along Mývatn's western shore, passing small, black-sand beaches. Beyond rises the unmistakably tall **Vindbelgjarfjall** (529m), whose access track leaves the main road at a sharp bend just before Vagnbrekka farm – don't attempt driving this in anything less than high-clearance four-wheel-drive. On foot, it takes about twenty minutes along this track to reach an obscure path up the back of the mountain, marked with white pegs; if you find yourself in a seriously boggy patch, you've gone too far. Once through lowland heather and scrubby thickets, it's scree all the way around the top – quite slippery and steep – but the scramble to the cairn marking the summit only takes around thirty minutes, from where there are dramatic **views** of the mountain's steep east face and over the lake.

Past the mountain, the main road clips more **pseudocraters** – less visited and more tightly packed than Skútustaðir's – before passing a track eastwards into **Neslönd**, a marshy, scrubby bird-breeding area. Access is restricted to the track in summer, though you can see plenty of birds on nearby ponds, including divers and grebes. At the end of the road is **Fuglasafn Sigurgeirs** at **Ytri-Neslönd farm** (ⓦwww.fuglasafn.nett.is), a truly extraordinary collection of stuffed birds covering just about every species that it's possible to see in Iceland. Beyond the Neslönd turning, it's another 8km back to Reykjahlíð.

Northeast of the lake

While Mývatn's immediate surrounds appear fairly stable, the plateau rising just outside town at **Bjarnarflag** and extending northeast is anything but serene, the barren, pock-marked landscape pouring out lively quantities of steam and – when the mood takes it – lava. Even so, this being Iceland you can see not only how destructive such events have been, but also how their energy has been harnessed by the local community. Alongside power stations and even an underground "bakery", this is also the location for the **Jarðböðin nature baths**, building on the centuries-old tradition of using the area's plentiful geothermal water for bathing. Beyond here, still on the Ringroad, the bubbling mud pools at **Hverir** are definitely worth a stop en route to the **Krafla volcano**, reached by a detour north along a sealed track. The mountain and the neighbouring plains at **Leirhnjúkur**, still dangerously hot after a particularly violent session during the 1980s, are Mývatn's most geologically active region.

From mid-June until August a daily **bus to Krafla** from Skútustaðir and Reykjahlíð stops at these sights then continues on to Dettifoss (see p.271). There's also a marked, though tiring, twelve-kilometre **hiking track** direct from Reykjahlíð to Krafla. With your own vehicle, follow the Ringroad east to Bjarnarflag (4km from Reykjahlíð) and Hverir (6km), and then turn north to the Krafla area (13km).

Jarðböðin and the underground bakery

Only 4km from Reykjahlíð, **Bjarnarflag** is a thermal zone on the lower slopes of Dalfjall, a long faulted ridge pushed up by subterranean pressures that runs northeast to Krafla itself. Bjarnarflag has a small geothermal power station – Iceland's first, built in 1969 – whose outflow has been harnessed to create the ⚒ **Jarðböðin nature baths** (June–Aug daily 10am–midnight; Sept–May daily noon–10pm; 2000kr; ⓦ www.jardbodin.is), the local version of Reykjavík's Blue Lagoon. It's an exceptional setting – fractured orange hills rise behind and the poolside overlooks Mývatn itself – where you can loll to your heart's content in milky-blue waters heated to 38–40°C. Just remove any copper or silver jewellery before entering the water, since the high sulphur content of the water can cause discolouration. In addition to the pool, there's a hot pot and a couple of steam saunas which are perfect for whiling away a couple of hours.

The underground bakery

Next door to the nature baths, still on the south side of the highway, a brickworks makes a good landmark for locating Bjarnarflag's **underground bakery**. This sounds much more technical that it really is; the "bakery" is simply a few small pits dug into the superheated, steaming soil between the road and brickworks, each covered with weighted dustbin lids or sheets of scrap metal. Rye dough is mixed with yeast and molasses in a cardboard milk carton and left underground for a day, where it transforms into neat, rectangular loaves of heavy **hverabrauð** – "steam bread" – which is especially delicious eaten hot with butter. This isn't the only such bakery in Iceland, but it is one of the largest; what isn't made for private consumption is sold through various outlets in Reykjahlíð. People sometimes cook other things in here too – such as the Icelandic speciality of boiled sheep's head – so prepare for a shock if you lift the lids for a look (though residents would rather you left their ovens alone).

Námafjall and Hverir

Immediately east of Bjarnaflag, the road twists up and over Dalfjall; on the way, look for a big split in the ridges north, marking the line of the Mývatn rift. The

▲ Steam vent, Hverir

high point south of the road's crest is **Námafjall**, streaked in grey gypsum and yellow **sulphur deposits** – these were once mined and exported for use in gunpowder – and there's an easy twenty-minute track to follow through soft mud to the summit's stony outcrop. The whole Mývatn area is spread below; in particular, look for Hrossaberg to the southwest, a large exploded vent with ragged edges simmering quietly away between here and Hverfjall.

The road meanwhile descends Námafjall's eastern face, and at the base you'll find **Hverir**, a large field of **solfataras**, evil-smelling, blue-grey belching mud pools. These are caused by groundwater percolating downwards for over a kilometre to magma levels; heating then forces it back to the surface, where it exits through the sticky red soil at 200°C. It's essential to follow boardwalks and guide ropes here; every year someone leaves them and sinks knee-deep into the scalding pools. These, however, are docile compared with the accompanying **steam vents**, where rocks, gravel and earth have been burst upwards like a bubble to form waist-high, perforated mounds through which vapour screams out ferociously.

Krafla and around

Up in the hills north of Hverir, the area around the Krafla volcano has been intermittently erupting for the last three thousand years and shows no signs of cooling down yet. **Krafla** itself (818m) was last active in the 1720s during a period known as the **Mývatn Fires**, which began when the west side of Krafla exploded in 1724, forming a new crater named **Viti** (Hell); earthquakes over the next five years opened up a series of volcanic fissures west of Krafla at **Leirhnjúkur**, producing the lava flows which so nearly destroyed Reykjahlíð's church. More recently, a similar spate of earthquakes between 1977 and 1984 reopened the fissures running north from Leirhnjúkur in what came to be called the **Krafla Fires**, and it's this mass of still-steaming lava rubble that is the main draw today.

A marked **hiking trail** connects Reykjahlíð with Leirhnjúkur, while the vehicle access road runs north off the Ringroad beyond Hverarönd, passing right under piping from **Leirbotn power station** on the way. By harnessing steam vents in the area it was hoped to achieve a 60 megawatt output, but – aside from construction of the plant unfortunately coinciding with the Krafla Fires – one of the boreholes exploded during drilling to form an artificial crater (dryly known as Sjálfskapar Víti, "Home-made Hell"). For years the station ran at half capacity, though newly opened bores have put things back on track; these are what you can hear roaring away like jet engines up on Krafla's flanks.

Víti and Leirhnjúkur

After Leirbotn, the road heads steeply uphill to a plateau; at the top, continue straight ahead for 500m to Víti, or turn left for walking tracks to Leirhnjúkur. **Víti** is a deep, surprisingly attractive aquamarine crater lake on Krafla's steep brown gravel slopes; a slippery track runs around the rim through atmospheric low cloud and plenty of real steam hissing out of bulging vents. **Leirhnjúkur**, on the other hand, is compellingly grotesque, and a testament to the lasting power of molten rock: thirty years on, and the ground here remains, in places, too hot to touch. Tracks from the parking area cross older, vegetated lava before climbing onto the generally darker, rougher new material, splotches of red or purple marking iron and potash deposits, white or yellow patches indicating live steam vents to be avoided – not least for their intensely unpleasant smell. Pegs mark out relatively safe trails around the field, between giant, solidified bubbles, smooth lava pavements, and impossibly cracked, split and twisted mounds. From the high points you can look north towards where the main area of activity was during the 1980s at **Gjástykki**, a black, steaming swathe between light green hills. As usual, apply common sense to any explorations.

The northeast

Just a brief drive from either Akureyri or Mývatn, **Húsavík** is northeast Iceland's largest town, and the start of the 290-kilometre run eastwards around the coast on Route 85 to **Vopnafjörður**, through a barren, underpopulated countryside (most people left in the late nineteenth century following the volcanic activity at Askja). The regional highlights are **whale watching** out from Húsavík itself, and the gorges, waterfalls and hiking at **Jökulsárgljúfur National Park**, while elsewhere the scattering of small fishing towns and understated landscape of moorland and small beaches have their own quiet appeal. Don't forget that you're almost inside the **Arctic Circle** here, and summer nights are virtually nonexistent, the sun just dipping below the horizon at midnight – conversely, winter days are only a couple of hours long. From mid-June until the end of August, **buses** run daily from Mývatn, Akureyri and Húsavík to Jökulsárgljúfur; for Route 85 along the northeast coast, there's a year-round service via Húsavík as far as the town of **Þórshöfn**.

To Húsavík

Coming **from Akureyri**, Húsavík is a straightforward 90km or so northeast along Route 85; **from Mývatn**, the quickest way is by following Route 87 for 55km northwest from Reykjahlíð. Either way, the journey ends up by following the Laxá and its tributaries, with a chance to detour along the way to **Grenjaðarstaður**, around 35km from Mývatn, where a nineteenth-century church and block of turf-roofed farmhouses – the largest such collection in Iceland – are well insulated from the icy prevailing winds. Now a **museum** (June–Aug 10am–6pm; 500kr) containing household items and farming implements from days gone by, the estate was founded in medieval times, when it counted as one of the best holdings in all Iceland – a contemporary altar cloth from the original church is now in the Paris Louvre.

North of here, Route 85 touches the edge of the prehistoric **Aðaldalshraun lava flow**, which runs almost all the way on up to the coast via a landscape of lava rubble, exploded bubbles and pseudocraters. Alternatively, Route 87 passes **Hveravellir**, a spread of steam-heated greenhouses growing and selling house plants and vegetables. Both routes join up north of these places and run up to Húsavík in around 20km.

Húsavík and around

Approaching **HÚSAVÍK** from the south, you come over a crest and see the town sitting below Húsavíkurfjall on a rare dip in the otherwise high coastline, the blue-green bay out front patched by cloud shadows and a couple of islands. This attractive setting was the site of one of the earliest recorded settlements in Icelandic history, after the ninth-century Swedish rover **Garðar Svavarsson** wintered here while making the first circumnavigation of the country; the shelters he built gave Húsavík (House Bay) its name. It's also said that two of his slaves decamped during his stay and afterwards established a farm, though later historians – looking for nobler lineages than this – tend to overlook the possibility that they were the mainland's first permanent residents.

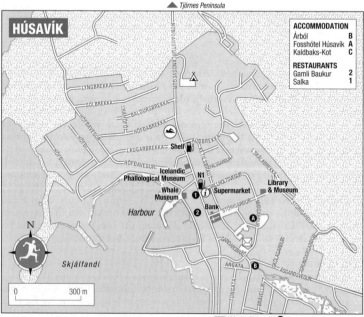

The area's economy focused on sheep-farming until hit by the nationwide **depression** of the late nineteenth century – caused in part by the 1875 eruption of Viti in the Askja caldera (see p.317) – when those who could switched to fishing, or emigrated to Canada or the US. The remaining farmers, who felt exploited by trade monopolies, formed **Kaupfélag Þingeyinga**, a cooperative that bypassed middlemen and traded directly with merchants from Newcastle in England. Nowadays, Húsavík has reinvented itself as one of the best places in Iceland to go **whale watching**; so dependent now is the town on this summer income that Húsavík led criticism within Iceland of the government's decision in late 2006 to resume commercial whaling. The town's other draw is the **Icelandic Phallological Museum**, with its eye-opening collection of penises and all matters penile or testicular. Otherwise there isn't a huge amount to do here, though the town and adjacent coast make a pleasant place to stock up before tackling the northeast's rather less well-supplied stretches.

Arrival and information

Húsavík's population of 2500 is served by a core of businesses grouped around the harbour and church along main-street Garðarsbraut, including **banks** (with ATMs), the KASKO **supermarket** and the **post office**. All SBA **buses** stop at the N1 and Shell filling stations on Garðarsbraut, with services running as far as Akureyri and Þórshöfn (year-round), and to Ásbyrgi and Dettifoss in Jökulsárgljúfur National Park (mid-June to August only). The helpful **tourist information** office (☎464 4300; June–Sept daily 10am–6pm; closed Sun in June; ⓦwww.husavik.is) is inside the supermarket, offers **internet** at 400kr an hour and is good at locating homestay accommodation.

Húsavík's **swimming pool** (June–Aug Mon–Fri 6.45am–9pm, Sat & Sun 10am–5pm; Sept–May Mon–Fri 6.45am–10am & 6pm–9pm, Sat & Sun 10am–4pm; 350kr) is on the main road north about 200m up from the harbour, opposite the sports field. **Horses** can be hired through *Saltvík* farm, about 5km south of town on the Akureyri road (☎847 9515, ⓦwww.saltvik.is); they offer anything from riding lessons for beginners to a nine-day tour into the Interior. For **car hire**, try Bílaleiga Húsavíkur at Garðarsbraut 66 (☎464 1888).

Accommodation

Aside from the following, contact the tourist information about **private homestays** in summer; the usual deal is sleeping-bag accommodation with or without breakfast from about 2500kr. Húsavík's fine **campsite** (May–Sept only; ☎845 0705; first night 750kr per person, then free) is about 300m up the road from the church on the northern edge of town, with toilets, laundry, a cooking area and sheds for sheltering from inclement weather.

Árból Ásgarðsvegur 2 ☎464 2220, ⓦwww .simnet.is/arbol. Friendly guesthouse in an early twentieth-century wooden building, with bright rooms and helpful management. Advance booking recommended; room rates include breakfast. ❷
Fosshótel Húsavík Ketilsbraut 22 ☎464 1220, ⓦwww.fosshotel.is. Welcoming place with seventy cosy rooms and an inhouse restaurant. Try for rooms 304, 320–329 or 404, which all have balconies and reasonable views out over the sea. ❺
Kaldbaks-Kot 3km south of Húsavík at Kaldbakur on the main road ☎464 1504 or 864 1504, ⓦwww .cottages.is. Self-contained pine cabins with TV, kitchen and bathroom on a rise overlooking the sea and town; can arrange horseriding and fishing. Fifth night free, and reductions of 30–40 percent during Sept–May. 4–8 person cabin 9900–12,900kr a night.

The Town

Húsavík's landmark wooden **church** on Garðarsbraut dates from 1907, with complex eaves and a green painted roof, while across the road the **harbour** is

Whale watching in Húsavík

The whale-watching industry in Húsavík started after whalers hit by a 1989 morato-rium realized that there was still good money to be made by taking tourists out to find the creatures. Though the Icelandic government allowed commercial whaling to resume in late 2006, whale stocks remain high, and if you put to sea in summer off Húsavík the chances of seeing at least one species are good. Dolphins, porpoises and medium-sized **minke** whales are seen more frequently, with much larger **humpback** whales runners-up; these are identified by lengthy flippers and their habit of "breaching" – making spectacular, crashing leaps out of the water. Similar-looking **fin whales** are the next most likely candidates, with rarer sightings of colossal **blue whales**; **orca**, or killer whales; and square-headed **sperm** whales. For some reason, only males of the last species are found in Iceland.

Cruises generally head directly across the bay from Húsavík – this can be rough in a northerly wind – where you'll come across puffins and other sea birds fishing; the whales obviously move around a lot but boat crews are expert at locating them. Most of the time you'll see little more than an animal's back, fluke or tail breaking the surface in the middle distance, and perhaps jets of water vapour as they breathe; if you're lucky, whales swim right under the boats, lie on their sides looking up at you, or breach. And you might, of course, see nothing at all – though as tour operators advertise sighting rates, you can check before booking whether recent cruises have been successful.

Whale-watching **trips** run at least daily from May to October (5–6 times daily June–Aug), cost 8500kr and last three hours; it's best to buy **tickets** in advance. Húsavík's two **operators** are Gentle Giants (T 464 1500, W www.gentlegiants.is), based harbourside next to the *Salka* restaurant; and North Sailing Húsavík (T 464 2350, W www.northsailing.is), whose ticket office is above the harbour opposite the church. There's little to choose between the two: both use wooden whaling ships seating around forty people – North Sailing's rigged sailship is the most attractive – and provide essential full waterproof gear, hot drinks and biscuits. Bring binoculars and plenty of warm clothing.

where to book and board a **whale-watching cruise**. Views west across wide **Skjálfandi bay** take in the heights of the peninsula opposite, inhabited until its extraordinarily mountainous terrain prevented roads and power being supplied in the early 1960s, after which its scattered farms were abandoned. Look north up the coast and you may be able to spot **Lundey**, a small, uninhabited flat-topped island famed for its puffins.

Also at the harbour is Húsavík's excellent 🗡**Whale Museum** (daily: May & Sept 10am–5pm; June–Aug 9am–7pm; W www.whalemuseum.is; 900kr), sited in an old slaughter house. Inside, an informative collection of models, photos, relics, and even ten full-size skeletons unnervingly suspended above you – all taken from beached or drowned whales – along with several continually playing videos, fill you in on cetacean biology, the history of whaling in Iceland and today's environ-mental threats caused by pollution. Pick of the exhibits are pieces of tremendously hairy baleen plates, with which filter-feeding species strain their nourishing plankton diet like slurping soup through a moustache.

The Phallological Museum

Just around the corner from the Whale Museum, the **Icelandic Phallological Museum** (May 20 to Sept 10 daily noon–6pm; 600kr; W www.phallus.is) is altogether more earthy, featuring a collection of the penises of virtually every mammal found either in Iceland or its offshore waters. More than ninety specimens are displayed in jars of formaldehyde and alcohol, from the sizeable member that once belonged to a young male blue whale, now hollowed out, salted, dried and placed on a wooden plaque, to that of a rogue polar bear found drifting on pack ice off the West Fjords, shot by Icelandic fishermen and then unceremoniously butchered. Nor have testicles been neglected: a lampshade made of ten rams' scrotums sees to that.

Although a human specimen has escaped the collection to date, the museum does have a certificate signed by Páll Arason, a farmer in his 80s from Bugi near Akureyri, who's agreed to donate his apparently ample wedding tackle to the museum on his death. There are also the misshapen foreskin of a 40-year-old Icelander donated by the National Hospital after an emergency circumcision operation in 2002; and plaster casts and photos of several former museum visitors from Britain, the US and Germany which leave nothing to the imagination.

Húsavík library

To cool down after the Phallological Museum, head 150m behind the church to Húsavík's **library** along Stórigarður and its **town museum** (daily June–Aug 10am–6pm; Sept–May Mon–Fri 9am–5pm, Sun 4–6pm; 500kr; Ⓦwww.husmus .is). Pick of the exhibits are bits of medieval weapons found near the town, the impressive family tree of a local woman born in 1904 showing her descendants back to the time of the Settlement, and another stuffed polar bear, this one killed in 1969 on Grímsey after drifting over from Greenland on an ice floe. Downstairs is devoted to maritime history and includes a collection of rowing and fishing boats, but don't miss the eccentric collection of one hundred thousand **beer bottle labels** zealously put together by a local man who, oddly, was teetotal; the labels are kept in folders by the entrance to the maritime section.

▲ Whale skeleton, Húsavík Whale Museum

Eating and drinking

The **supermarket** itself has a decent range of meat, fish, fruit and vegetables even in winter; and booze is available from the **vínbúð** at Garðarsbraut 21, about 200m south of the harbour and a couple of streets back. If you don't fancy fuel-station burgers, try either of Húsavík's two harbourside **restaurants**, which both open from 11.30am until 9pm: the ⚓ *Gamli Baukur*, a wood-panelled, mid-range place with top marks going to their grilled cod with sautéed vegetables and basil (2650kr) and boiled salmon in butter sauce (3150kr); or *Salka*, next to the Whale Museum, which serves similar fare (fish dishes around 2600kr) but has more of a café-bar atmosphere. The cheapest pizzas in town can be found at the restaurant inside the *Fosshótel*, with a twelve-inch pepperoni number costing an exceptionally good-value 1250kr.

The Tjörnes peninsula and on to Jökulsárgljúfur

North of Húsavík, the **Tjörnes peninsula** is a rather broad, stubby mass with brilliant sea views. A few kilometres from town in this direction along Route 85 there's a roadside monument to the locally born patriotic poet **Einar Benediktsson**, one of the key figures of Iceland's early twentieth-century nationalist movement. Past here, now 5km from town, the headlands drop to low **beaches**, reached along vehicle tracks from the road, where you should find the usual melange of **sea birds**, including purple sandpipers, puffins, black guillemots and gannets; in spring, look out for marine ducks and divers (loons) heading to Mývatn. Walking along the beach, it's not unusual to find yourself being followed offshore by **seals**.

Moving on, the cliffs soon return and 10km from Húsavík there's another track off the main road marked **Tjörneshöfn**, which descends steeply to a tiny boatshed and harbour looking straight out to Lundey. A shingle beach stretches in both directions below the cliffs, though a small river to the north may stop you heading that way; south there's plenty of seaweed and pleistocene-period **fossil shells** in the headland's layered, vertical faces.

Back on Route 85, Tjörnes' northern tip is a further 7km beyond the museum; once past the **Voladalstorfa lighthouse** there's a roadside **viewpoint** with vistas northeast over the often staggeringly blue Öxarfjörður bay to Kópasker (see p.272); on a clear day it's also possible to pick out a very remote Grímsey to the northwest, and **Mánárayjar**, a couple of closer volcanic islets that haven't experienced any stirrings for over a century. From here, the main road continues 40km east across the **Bakkahlaup**, a complex of shallow lakes at the Jökulsá á Fjöllum delta, to Ásbyrgi and the northern end of Jökulsárgljúfur National Park.

Jökulsárgljúfur National Park

Cutting into the northeast's rocky inland plains some 60km east of Húsavík, the tongue-twisting **Jökulsárgljúfur National Park** – an isolated fragment of the enormous Vatnajökull National Park (see p.297) – encloses a 35-kilometre-long stretch of the **Jökulsá á Fjöllum**, Iceland's second-longest river. Originating almost 200km south at Vatnajökull, for much of its journey through the park the river flows through the mighty **Jökulsárgljúfur**, a canyon which is 120m deep and 500m wide in places, forming several exceptional waterfalls and an endless array of rock formations. There are two key sights: the horseshoe-shaped **Ásbyrgi** canyon in the north of the park; and **Dettifoss**, Europe's most powerful waterfall, at the park's southern boundary. In between, the silt-laden river cuts its way between stark grey gorge walls, all set against an unusually fertile backdrop: over half of the country's **native plant** species are found here, and in summer the heathland above the gorge is lush and splashed pink and white with flowers – except in a couple of places, however, trees are rare.

Park practicalities

With three or four days to spare, the park can be thoroughly investigated on foot along marked **hiking tracks**, the longest of which follows the west side of the gorge for 35km between Ásbyrgi and Dettifoss. Two rough gravel **roads** also run from Ásbyrgi to Dettifoss, and then south to the Ringroad east of Mývatn – note, however, that these are open June–August only and may be closed by bad weather even then. The **F862** follows the west side of the gorge and requires a four-wheel-drive; **Route 864** down the east side of the gorge is generally open to all vehicles.

Between mid-June and the end of August, two **bus routes** (W www.sba .is) cover the park: one from Akureyri via Húsavík and Ásbyrgi to Dettifoss; and one from Mývatn via Grímsstaðir (see below) to Dettifoss. Both travel via Route 864 along the eastern side

of the gorge, and their schedules overlap so that it is possible to complete the whole journey in one go.

Within the national park, the sole **accommodation** option is to **camp** at one of the three designated sites (850kr per person), which all get notoriously busy through the summer. The closest alternative outside the park boundaries is 7km north of Ásbyrgi at *Lundur* (T 465 2247, W www.lundurtravel.com; camping 800kr, sleeping bag 2700kr, beds 2750kr; ❶), which also has a pool and restaurant. Otherwise, there are two self-catering **farmstays** 20km south of Dettifoss near the Route 864–Ringroad junction at **Grímsstaðir**: either *Grímstunga I* (T 464 4294, E djupadokk@simnet.is; sleeping bag 2400kr, made-up beds 4200kr) or next door at *Grímsstaðir* itself (T 464 4292, E grimsstadir@simnet.is; camping 750kr, sleeping bag 2200kr). Note that, despite its prominence on maps, Grímsstaðir is not a town and that there are no stores or other facilities here.

Bring along all **supplies**: the nearest shops are wherever you've just come from, though there's a small **store** at the roadhouse just outside the park at Ásbyrgi (see below). The best **map** of Jökulsárgljúfur is the inexpensive national park brochure available from the park headquarters (free if you're camping). Local **weather** is quite cool, though rain is probably the worst you'll experience from July through to September.

Ásbyrgi

Coming from Húsavík along Route 85, there's little sign in the otherwise bare landscape of the natural wonders just south of the road. Look for a **roadhouse** (daily 10am–8pm) marking the Ásbyrgi junction, which sells fuel, fast food and a good selection of bread, cheese, veg, camping gas and other essentials. Behind the roadhouse you'll find a golf course and the **National Parks office** (May & Sept 10am–4pm; June–Aug 9am–8pm; ☎470 7100; ⓦ www.ust.is), where you can pick up a **free map**, find out when the next **bus** is due, and organize **camping**. The two local options are on the other side of the golf course, where the facilities include a laundry with drying cupboards, barbecue and tables, payphone, children's play area and shelter (showers are an extra 300kr); or the overflow area about 5km down the road near Ásbyrgi itself.

At this end of the park the gorge is very broad and waterless, the river having shifted course long ago leaving a flat grassland between low walls. One of these rises behind the park headquarters as **Eyjar**, a long, flat-topped island of rock which can be scaled easily enough from its northern end, giving a good view of this rather open region of the park. Better though is **Ásbyrgi**, where the road dead-ends at a pond fringed in birch and pine woods beyond which rises a vertical, ninety-metre-high amphitheatre of dark rock patched in orange lichens and home to a colony of gurgling fulmars. Legend has it that this is the hoofprint of the Norse god Óðinn's eight-legged steed **Sleipnir**, though geologists believe that the canyon was carved by a series of titanic *jökulhlaups* that flooded out from underneath Vatnajökull. Just avoid it in the late afternoon, when the sun catches the cliffs: it looks great, but half of Iceland descends to watch. The view from the top is spectacular, too, though to get up here you need to follow the Dettifoss trail (see below).

Ásbyrgi to Dettifoss

It takes around two days to walk the largely easy route **from Ásbyrgi to Dettifoss** (35km), with an overnight stop along the way at **Vesturdalur** (11–14km from Ásbyrgi depending on route) – though you'll see plenty even if you just make a return day-trip to Vesturdalur. The easiest way to pick up the trail is to head past the roadhouse and turn immediately south down the *Ás* farm road; about 50m along you'll see a wooden signpost and pegs by the roadside which mark the way. Alternatively, cross from the park headquarters below the golf course to where you'll find a **rope** hanging over an eight-metre ledge, and pull yourself up to the same path. Either way, follow the trail along the clifftop and you soon exit the tight birch scrub onto an open heathland; 3.8km from camp will find you looking north from the rounded rocks atop of Ásbyrgi.

There are two trails to Vesturdalur from here; one short-cuts south (8.5km) but for a fuller view of the gorge, take the longer track (11.5km). This crosses east over the heath for a couple of kilometres – look out for plovers, redshanks, godwits, ravens and **short-eared owls** – suddenly bringing you to the brink of the gorge, where jutting rocks offer a good perch for looking down at the grey river rushing smoothly across a shingle bed. The trail now follows the gorge south, crossing intermittent sections of green heath and dark basalt, joining up with the short cut from Ásbyrgi and then entering a brief, slow section of ashy sand. Once through this, a side track makes the short climb to **Rauðhólar**, the remains of a scoria cone whose vivid red, yellow and black gravel is a shock after the recently monochrome backdrop. Past here you descend to **Hjóðaklettar**, where the noise of the river – which funnels violently through a constriction at this point – is distorted by hexagonal-columned hollows in huge, shattered cliffs. There are some weird formations to poke around in here, and it's one of the few places on the hike where you're almost at river level. The path then crosses a vehicle track, with the **Vesturdalur campsite** (toilets and fresh water) about a kilometre away, sited by a pleasant, if sometimes boggy, meadow.

Vesturdalur to Dettifoss

Over the next 8km, the trail moves above the river and then down to the marshy **Hólmatungur**, where underground springs pool up to create three short rivers which flow quickly into the Jökulsá through some thick vegetation. The trail crosses the largest of these tributaries, the Hólmá, on a bridge just above where it tumbles into the main river. Upstream from here on the Jökulsá's east bank, the prominent face of **Vígabjarg** marks where the formerly mighty Vígarbjargfoss ripped through a narrow gorge, before a change in the river's course dried it to a trickle seventy years ago. From here it's another 8km to the 27-metre-high **Hafragilsfoss**, an aesthetically pleasing set of falls whose path through a row of volcanic craters has exposed more springs, which mix their clear waters with the Jökulsá's muddier glacial flood (there's a particularly good view of Hafragilsfoss off **Route 864**, on the eastern side of the gorge).

A final tricky couple of kilometres of scrambling brings you to the park's southern limits at **Dettifoss**, where the dirty white, violent river rips across a twisted basalt bed before dropping 45m with enough force to send the spray hundreds of metres skywards. Again, the best – and closest – vantages are actually from the eastern side of the river. On the western side, Route 862 meets the end of the hiking trail, where there's a **basic campground** (no amenities) for hikers wanting to overnight here. After Dettifoss, it's worth carrying on a further kilometre upstream to **Selfoss**, where a diagonal fault across the river has created a long, but only ten-metre-high, cascade.

The northeast coast

After Ásbyrgi, Route 85 continues around the northeast coast past a string of small communities – **Kópasker**, **Raufarhöfn**, **Þórshöfn** and **Vopnafjörður** – relying on fish-processing for their main industry. There are a couple of historical echoes here, but mostly it's the landscapes which are memorable: the flat, marshy **Melrakkaslétta** which lies just outside the Arctic Circle; the fells and dales of the foggy **Langanes Peninsula**; and a score of little black sand and shingle beaches strewn with huge piles of driftwood and disproportionate numbers of **whale strandings**. These were once something of a windfall for local landowners (the term *hvalreki*, literally "whale wreck", is used nowadays for "jackpot"), providing meat, oil, bone and various tradeable bits, such as sperm-whale teeth. In saga times, people would actually fight for possession of these riches, but today a whale stranding is a bit of a burden, as the law demands that the landowner is responsible for disposing of the carcass – not an easy matter in the case of a thirty-ton sperm whale.

In summer, the region is also infested with **nesting birds** (you'll see orange warning signs marked *Fuglar á vegi*, meaning "Birds on road"), the well-camouflaged, fluffy chicks guarded by overprotective parents – this can make getting out of the car something of an ordeal at times, as you risk being dive-bombed by terns and plovers. Otherwise, there's good **camping** potential along much of the coast, with plenty of soft grass. **Buses** go as far as Þórshöfn; while Vopnafjörður marks the end of the coastal road, and routes divide here westwards back to Mývatn, or southeast to Egilsstaðir and the Eastfjords.

Kópasker

From the Ásbyrgi junction it's another 40km north to the port of **KÓPASKER**, first following the edge of the Jökulsá's broad delta where fish are farmed in large round ponds, then the gravelly Öxafjörður coast. The village looks small on approach, but is actually tiny, with an outlying church marking a short sideroad off the highway into the town's simple square of streets beside the harbour. The church is next to a Settlement-era **assembly site**, giving Kópasker a surprisingly venerable historical anchor, but otherwise the town is best known for suffering a severe force-eight **earthquake** in January 1976, thanks to activity at Krafla (see p.262). Kópasker has just enough room for a school with sculptures made from local rocks decorating its lawn, a **bank** (Mon–Fri noon–4pm), **supermarket** with attached **café** (Mon–Fri 9.30am–noon and 1–6pm, Sat noon–5pm), **fuel station**, **campsite** just as you enter town and ⚲ **youth hostel-cum-guesthouse** (☏465 2314 or 861 2314; ⓦwww.hostel.is; sleeping-bag accommodation 2600kr, ❶) at Akurgerði 7: although they're officially only open May–Oct, there's a good chance they'll open up for you out of season too if you call ahead.

Melrakkaslétta and towards the Arctic Circle

After Kópasker, the road passes through the partially greened slopes of the low **Leirhafnalfjöll** range, a string of early nineteenth-century cinder cones, and then turns northeast into the empty tundra of **Melrakkaslétta** (literally Arctic Fox plain), which forms Iceland's northernmost peninsula. It might not look that inspiring, but in its own way Melrakkaslétta has as much wildlife as Mývatn: a coastline of shingle and sand beaches pulls in plenty of wading birds; while the tundra and an associated mass of small, fragmented lakes attract big nesting colonies of eider ducks and arctic terns, as well as whimbrel and the otherwise rare **grey phalarope**, along with both of Iceland's diver (loon) species. To cap all this, Melrakkaslétta is also visited by large numbers of non-resident birds, including barnacle geese, arctic redpoll and knot, migrating between Europe and Greenland or Canada – they pass through in late April and early May, and return with young in September.

Hraunhafnartangi and the Arctic Circle

For a quick look at the coast, turn north off Route 85 around 16km from Kópasker, and follow an eight-kilometre track to the abandoned farm Grjótnes, from where a footpath follows gannet-infested cliffs for 3km to the flat-topped, sheer-sided headland of **Rauðinúpur**. Meanwhile, the main road brushes the shore between some long lagoons; climb the small rise here and you can look south along the geological fault that runs all the way down to Mývatn.

Shortly afterwards, look for the square-sided **Þórgeirsdys lighthouse**, which rises 21 metres above **Hraunhafnartangi**, widely regarded as the mainland's northernmost extremity – a mere 2.5km outside the **Arctic Circle**. To get to the lighthouse, leave the road and take the gravel and rock path that follows the bay's shoreline here, heading for the "No Entry" vehicle sign ahead of you; allow an hour for the return walk and watch out for aggressive, ground-nesting birds in summer. Head past the lighthouse and cairn, and up onto the loosely piled stone sea wall to see the grey-blue Arctic Ocean pounding the far side. The harbour here, beside the lighthouse, known as Hraunhöfn, was first used during the Middle Ages when pack ice regularly closed the harbour in nearby Raufarhöfn, forcing boats to put in here instead. According to *Frostbræðingasaga*, the cairn beside the lighthouse is the final resting place of the warrior after whom the lighthouse is named, one Þorgeir Hávarsson; he once slayed fourteen men in defence of this place.

Raufarhöfn

Iceland's northernmost town, **RAUFARHÖFN** sits on the Melrakkaslétta's eastern coast some 54km from Kópasker and 10km beyond Hraunhafnartangi. In the 1960s Raufarhöfn was at the core of Iceland's herring industry and the town's salting plant processed more herring than anywhere else in the country, providing seasonal work that attracted a floating population of thousands. Times have changed, however: the 1990s saw the town's prosperity ebb away as demand for herring dried up and the plant shifted to hiring Polish workers to freeze and export Russian cod to the US. Today the factory limps on freezing fish for export.

The main road runs straight through Raufarhöfn, with the turning to the **harbour** and church on the northern side. On this road by the harbour, at Aðalbraut 2, you'll find the good-value *Hótel Norðurljós* (☎465 1233, ⓦwww .raufarhofn.is; sleeping bag 2200kr, ❸), run by the charming husband and wife team, Erlingur and Ágústa, who can point you in the direction of some good walking trails in the area. The only other accommodation is the **campsite** (☎465 1144) at Raufarhöfn's south exit by the **swimming pool**. In between are the **bank**, card-only **fuel station** and a general **store**. The town's sole **restaurant** is at the hotel, with harbour views from its outdoor terrace.

Rauðanes, Þórshöfn and the Langanes peninsula

Out of Raufarhöfn, it's 65km to Þórshöfn ascending high, rocky heathland as the road heads inland and south. Around halfway you catch a glimpse of the coast before rounding the knife-edge scree atop **Viðarfjall**, then it's down to ground level again around **Svalbarð** – historians reckon the farm here is one of Iceland's oldest, though the modern, nondescript buildings give no visual evidence of this.

Just north on the coast from here, **Rauðanes** is a particularly attractive headland where an easy seven-kilometre marked **footpath** takes you to tall, layered cliffs, caves, a couple of beaches, plenty of surf and birdlife (there used to be a huge puffin colony here too, but they were cleared out by feral minks) – it's a great spot to stretch your legs for few hours. On a good day, views from the road beyond reach out to Gunnolfsvíkurfjall, a ridge of hills at the southeastern end of the goose-necked **Langanes peninsula** – which juts out to the northeast for 35km along the divide between the Arctic Ocean and warmer North Atlantic, and so is frequently fog-bound in a fine, wet mist – and the higher Heljardalsfjoll (931m) to the south, whose summit just brushes the clouds.

Þórshöfn

Likeable **ÞÓRSHÖFN** is a compact, busy little place at the base of the Langanes peninsula, and marks the limit of **SBA buses**, which head back west along Route 85 to Húsavík and Akureyri (ⓦwww.sba.is; year-round Mon–Fri at 2pm). The highway enters Þórshöfn from the south, and runs for 250m past a church, **bank** (with ATM), **post office** and **fuel station** (which has the last fuel for at least 80km), to an intersection. Turn right here, and the road heads uphill to the *Samkaup* **supermarket** (Mon–Fri 8.30am–6pm, Sat 11am–1pm), which also houses the local **vínbúð** and a modern **pool** and sports centre (Mon–Thurs 4–8pm, Fri 3–7pm, Sat 11am–2pm; 300kr); turn left for *Eyrin*, the town's only bar and a **restaurant** serving pizzas from 1900kr, burgers 1500kr, fresh halibut steak at 2890kr and lamb cutlets 2960kr, though the fuel station dishes up hotdogs and coffee.

Accommodation in Þórshöfn is either near the church at the grassy **campground** (free, with toilets and sink – head to the pool for a shower), or at the *Hótel Jorvík* diagonally opposite the pool at Langanesvegur 31 (℡468 1149, ⓔjorvik @netfang.com; sleeping bag 2500kr, ❸), which offers meals, self-catering accommodation, and a fantastic view over the sea.

Ytra Lón and the Langanes peninsula

While Þórshöfn is just somewhere to stock up, the **Langanes peninsula** offers some good hiking across grassy fells and moorland out to an uninhabited coast. To reach it, carry on through town and follow the gravel road 15km northeast to ⚲ *Ytra Lón* farm, a snug and friendly, self-catering **youth hostel** (℡468 1242 or 854 3797, ⓦwww.visitlanganes.com; 1850kr; double room ❶) – it's very small though, so book in advance. Open year-round, this is a working sheep farm (they also collect eider down in season); there's the chance to join in or just observe working life – the annual *rettir*, or sheep round-up, takes place in late September – **fish** local streams for trout, or plan a **hike**. There are a couple of good full-day circuits to be made, though to get to the Fontur lighthouse at Langanes' tip you'll need to camp out overnight; keep your eyes peeled for **gyrfalcons** while you walk. Keen birders also won't want to miss the huge **gannet colony** at Stóri-karl (Big Man), a rock stack off the Skoruvíkurbjarg cliffs on Langanes' northern coast.

Bakkafjörður

Heading on from Þórshöfn, Route 85 crosses the base of Langanes, then rejoins the coast and meets the Atlantic for the first time above the deep bay **Finnafjörður**. Forty kilometres on, **BAKKAFJÖRÐUR** is an isolated cliff-top community of rich, reclusive fishermen, some 5km off the main road. As the region's smallest settlement the village endures much "butt of the world"-type humour, and in truth there's not much here beyond the obligatory salting plant, a self-service **fuel pump** and the Tangi **store** (which also houses the village post office and public telephone), located at the end of the one and only main road overlooking the sea. There's nowhere to eat or stay other than the summer **campground** (℡473 1686) though, if you do stay, a good day's walk can be had over the humpy Digranes headland and around a rocky coastline to the Svartnes lighthouse.

Vopnafjörður

South of Bakkafjörður, the road cuts inland again and suddenly acquires a sealed surface, the first in a long while. About 25km along, a good side road (signed "Selárdalslaug") leads 3km southwest down the **Selá**, to where a small riverside **swimming pool** (daily 7am–11pm; free) complete with basic changing rooms and showers utilizes the northeast coast's only economically viable hot spring. A further kilometre upstream along a jeep track brings you to **Selárfoss**, a five-metre-high tumble of clear, emerald green water – there's a fish ramp beside the falls for the salmon in the river.

It's a final 7km along the main road past Selá, over Nipslón lagoon, to **VOPNAFJÖRÐUR**, a relatively sizeable town famed for its warm weather and salmon fishing arrayed along the narrow, rocky finger of the **Kolbeinstangi peninsula**. The nearby region featured in several interconnected Settlement-era tales of clan feuding known as the **Vopnafjörð sagas** – appropriately enough, Vopnafjörður means "Weapons Fjord". The town was also the **emigration point** to the US and Canada for around two thousand impoverished farmers and their families, after their lands to the southwest were sterilized by the 1875 eruption of Viti in Askja (see p.318). Canada, which at the time had a "populate or perish" policy, offered subsidized passages for anyone wanting to migrate, and sent ships to take them. Vopnafjörður's **Kaupvangur Culture Centre** (daily in summer 10am–6pm; ⓦwww.mulastofa.is), in a restored, yellow-painted corrugated-iron warehouse next to the fish factory on Hafnarbyggð, has a small photo exhibition on the migrants, along with a few stuffed birds.

Practicalities

Vopnafjörður's **Tourist Information Centre** is inside the Cultural Centre (same opening hours; ⓣ473 1331). The exposed **campsite** (ⓣ894 2153) is sandwiched between the top road, across from the school, and the middle road, Lónabraut, which is where you'll also find the **bank** and **post office** near the church. Kauptún **supermarket** (Mon–Thurs 9.30am–6pm, Fri 9.30am–6.30pm, Sat 10am–4pm) and the only central **accommodation**, *Hótel Tangi* (ⓣ473 1840, ⓔhoteltangi @simnet.is; ❸), are one street below again, on the harbour road, Hafnarbyggð. The nearest **farmstay**, *Syðri-Vík* (ⓣ473 1199, ⓦwww.farmholidays.is; sleeping bag 2500, ❷), is about 7km southeast of town on Route 917 and has a guesthouse, self-contained cabins, kitchen, laundry and horses. *Hótel Tangi*'s **restaurant** serves a reasonable, if expensive, range of lamb, fish, chicken, pasta and pizza dishes, and the **fuel station** sells snacks.

From Vopnafjörður to Mývatn and Egilsstaðir

Fill up before you leave Vopnafjörður; to the south, there's no fuel available for at least 120km on the main road, while northwards the next reliable source is Þórshöfn.

The main road is **Route 85** southwest, initially climbing up **Bustarfell**, 18km from town, where there's an open-air **museum** (mid-June to mid-Aug daily 10am–6pm; 500kr) featuring well-preserved, turf-gabled farm buildings, founded in 1770 and lived in by the same family until 1966 – it's worth a look if you haven't seen traditional Icelandic houses before. The heights above are exposed, with sudden snowdrifts possible all through the year, and then the road winds slowly down to join the Ringroad some 70km from Vopnafjörður. Turn west here for a 65-kilometre run across desolate lava plains and gravel deserts to Mývatn via Grimsstaðir and the turning to Dettifoss (see p.271); or east for the last 100km to **Egilsstaðir**, with the Ringroad crossing the **Möðradalsfjallgurðar** range (800m), the highest pass of its entire circuit, before it descends into the long valley of Jökuldalur and passes the turning coastwards to Húsey.

There's also the direct, eighty-kilometre **Route 917** east from Vopnafjörður towards Egilsstaðir, though this mountainous gravel road is only open in summer. Turn off the Bustarfell road just outside town and follow the western side of the fjord up to where the road cuts east across the rugged Hellisheiði – views on the far side are spectacular – then follow the Jökulsá á Brú south to join the Ringroad around 25km west of Egilsstaðir.

Travel details

Buses

Most services below run only from around mid-June until some point in late August or early September, with the exception of buses from Akureyri to Húsavík and then along Route 85 to Þórshöfn, which run Mon–Fri year-round. For further details contact SBA in Akureyri (☎550 0700, ⓦ www.sba.is).

Ásbyrgi to: Dettifoss (daily; 1hr 30min); Húsavík (daily; 50min); Kópasker (5 weekly; 30min); Raufarhöfn (5 weekly; 1hr 30min); Þórshöfn (5 weekly; 2hr 45min).

Dettifoss to: Akureyri (daily; 7hr); Ásbyrgi (daily; 4hr); Húsavík (daily; 4hr 20min); Reykjahlíð/Mývatn (daily; 1hr 30min).

Húsavík to: Akureyri (3 daily; 1hr 10min); Ásbyrgi (daily; 45min); Dettifoss (daily; 3hr 20min); Kópasker (5 weekly; 1hr 25min); Raufarhöfn (5 weekly; 2hr 15min); Reykjahlíð (3 daily; 45min); Þórshöfn (5 weekly; 3hr 30min).

Kópasker to: Akureyri (5 weekly; 3hr 25min); Ásbyrgi (5 weekly; 30min); Húsavík (5 weekly; 1hr 15min); Raufarhöfn (5 weekly; 50min); Þórshöfn (5 weekly; 1hr 55min).

Raufarhöfn to: Akureyri (5 weekly; 4hr 10min); Ásbyrgi (5 weekly; 1hr 15min); Kópasker (5 weekly; 45min); Þórshöfn (5 weekly; 1hr 15min).

Reykjahlíð (Mývatn) to: Akureyri (5 daily; 2hr 45min); Dettifoss (daily; 1hr 30min); Egilsstaðir (4 weekly/1 daily; 2hr 5min); Goðafoss (5 daily; 40min); Grímsstaðir (4 weekly/1 daily; 30min); Húsavík (3 daily; 45min); Krafla (2 daily; 15min).

Þórshöfn to: Akureyri (5 weekly; 5hr 10min); Ásbyrgi (5 weekly; 2hr 35min); Húsavík (5 weekly; 3hr 20min); Kópasker (5 weekly; 1hr 45min); Raufarhöfn (5 weekly; 1hr).

Flights

Vopnafjörður to: Akureyri (5 weekly; 45min).
Þórshöfn to: Akureyri (5 weekly; 45min).

7

The Eastfjords and
the southeast

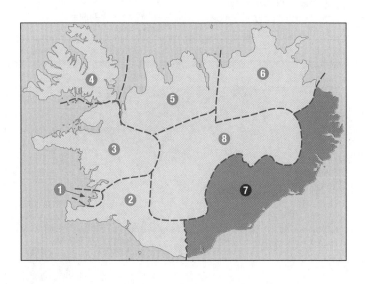

CHAPTER 7   # Highlights

* **Bakkagerði** The most
  isolated and picturesque
  of the Eastfjord towns,
  surrounded by shattered
  mountains and stiff walking
  trails. See p.287

* **Papey** Make a day-trip to
  this tiny, bird-rich island, with
  pre-Viking history. See p.296

* **Vatnajökull** Skid across
  the outrunning glaciers of
  Europe's largest ice cap
  by four-wheel-drive or
  snowmobile. See p.296

* **Lónsöræfi** Spend a week
  hiking through wild and
  remote highlands between the
  south coast and Snæfell.
  See p.297

* **Skaftafell** Prime camping
  and easy walking around this
  heathland plateau, caught in
  between two glaciers.
  See p.303

▲ Snowmobiles on Vatnajökull ice cap

The Eastfjords and the southeast

T he 550-kilometre strip covering Iceland's Eastfjords and the southeast takes in a quarter of the country's coastal fringe, though the scenery divides into just two distinct regions. About as far as you can possibly get from Reykjavík, the **Eastfjords** are necessarily self-contained but also unexpectedly well settled, with a population distributed between eastern Iceland's main town of **Egilsstaðir**, and a handful of relatively substantial coastal communities which are dotted at regular intervals along the fjords' convoluted coastline. The area has been farmed since medieval times, but the coastal villages here only really took off during the herring boom of the early twentieth century, and a few were even used as Allied naval bases during World War II. Today fishing is on the decline, but the port of **Seyðisfjörður** remains important as an alternative entry or departure point for Iceland, via the weekly ferry from the Faroes and Denmark. There's a little bit of history to soak up, though the main focus here is the fjords themselves, a mix of steep-sided hills and blue waters, with some relatively easy hiking trails to explore. Southwest of Egilsstaðir, wild highlands of tundra and moorland host substantial reindeer and wildfowl populations, and peak at the solitary heights of **Snæfell**, the core of an extinct volcano – a once pristine area which has been compromised by the construction of a hydro-electric plant at **Kárahnjúkar**.

South of the Eastfjords, the landscape becomes dominated by the vastness of **Vatnajökull**, whose icy cap and host of outrunning glaciers sprawl west of the town of **Höfn**. With a largely infertile terrain of highland moors and coastal gravel deserts known as **sandurs** to contend with – not to mention a fair share of catastrophic volcanic events – the population centres are few and far between, though you can explore the glacial fringes at the wild **Lónsöræfi reserve**, accessed via Stafafell farm, and at **Skaftafell**, where there are plenty of marked tracks. Further west, the tiny settlement of **Kirkjubæjarklaustur** is the jumping-off point for several trips inland, the best of which touches on one of Iceland's most disastrous eruptions.

Egilsstaðir and Höfn are the regional transport hubs, served by a complement of regular **flights** to Reykjavík and summertime **buses** travelling the Ringroad (Route 1). The Eastfjords are less well covered, though everywhere is within range of local services. Note, though, that between September and May – when Ringroad services **terminate** at Höfn and Egilsstaðir – it is not possible to circumnavigate

Iceland by bus. **Weather-wise**, expect cold winters with heavy snowfalls, though the southeast coast tends towards wet conditions, while everywhere east of Vatnajökull seems to have much sunnier weather than the rest of the country – at least when the westerlies are blowing.

Egilsstaðir, the Eastfjords and around

Far from the flow of things, Egilsstaðir and the Eastfjords form a compact region whose underrated attractions offer a very different view of Iceland from that presented by the country's more famous sights. Set on the Ringroad halfway around the country from Reykjavík, **Egilsstaðir** makes a good base for excursions inland around **Lögurinn**, a narrow, lake-like stretch of river where you'll find some saga history and Iceland's most extensive woodlands; or even for an assault on the highlands around **Kárahnjúkar** and **Snæfell**, eastern Iceland's tallest peak. The **Eastfjords** themselves provide wonderfully convoluted coastal scenery, though the only places unquestionably worth making a special detour to see are **Bakkagerði**, with its sea birds and **hiking trails**; the port of **Seyðisfjörður**, where the international ferry docks; and **Djúpivogur**, from where you can make an excellent day-trip to the tiny island of **Papey**.

The regional **airport** at Egilsstaðir is open year-round, but don't forget that buses from Egilsstaðir to Höfn only operate between June and September. Once here, it's best to have your own transport if possible; Egilsstaðir and the Eastfjord towns are connected by regular **buses**, but you'll have to spend at least a day in each place, waiting for the next service. In winter, only Egilsstaðir is reliably accessible, though you'll find a reasonable amount of accommodation and services remain open.

Egilsstaðir

Wherever you've come from, arrival at the crossroads town of **EGILSSTAÐIR** is a bit of an anticlimax. Egilsstaðir itself dates only to the late 1940s, when a supermarket, a vet, a hospital and a telephone exchange chose to set up shop on a narrow strip of moorland between the glacier-fed **Lagarfljöt river** and the back of the Eastfjord fells, bringing the first services into this remote corner of the country. Today Egilsstaðir has grown to fill a couple of dozen streets but remains an unadorned service and supply centre, important to the regional economy but containing neither a proper town centre nor much in the way of essential viewing.

Egilsstaðir is, however, a major **transportation** hub; the airport has flights to Reykjavík, the international port of Seyðisfjörður is nearby, and anyone travelling by bus has to stop here for at least as long as it takes to change services. It's also a useful springboard for regional attractions: aside from roads out through the Eastfjords, there's forested **Lögurinn** lake (see p.283); routes to the highland plateau around **Kárahnjúkar** and **Snæfell** (see p.286); and overnight stays at the quiet rural retreats of **Húsey** and **Bakkagerði**.

Arrival and information

Egilsstaðir sits on the Ringroad, where separate routes from Bakkagerði, Seyðisfjörður and Reyðarfjörður converge. All services – **banks**, **shops** and **fuel stations** – are clustered east off the highway either side of **Fagradalsbraut**.

The **airport** and airline office (T471 1210, Wwww.airiceland.is) are off the Ringroad a kilometre north of town, with daily services to Reykjavík. The **bus station** is in town, just off the Ringroad beside the N1 **fuel station**, with departures through the year **to Akureyri** (Wwww.sba.is) and from June until August **to Höfn** (Wwww.trex.is). Bakkagerði, Seyðisfjörður and other **Eastfjord towns** are served through the year by separate companies; see the relevant accounts for details.

The bus station also doubles as Egilsstaðir's **tourist information office** (June–Aug daily 8am–8pm; Sept–May Mon–Fri 9am–5pm, Sat & Sun noon–4pm; T471 2320, Wwww.east.is).

For **car rental**, try Hertz (Wwww.hertz.is) or Avis (Wwww.avis.is), both at the airport, or Bílaleiga Akureyrar/National (T461 6070, Wwww.nationalcar.is) at Lagarbraut 4 in Fellabær, north of the airport. **Tours** are operated by Ferðaskrifstofa

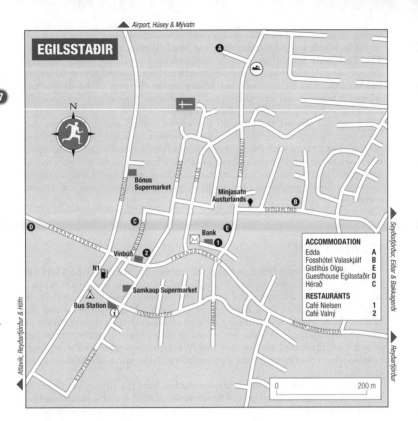

Airport, Húsey & Mývatn

EGILSSTAÐIR

N

Bónus Supermarket

Minjasafn Austurlands

Bank

Vinbúó

N1

Samkaup Supermarket

Bus Station

SKÓGARLÖND

FAGRADALSBRAUT

FAGRADALSBRAUT

ACCOMMODATION
Edda   A
Fosshótel Valaskjálf   B
Gistihús Olgu   E
Guesthouse Egilsstaðir   D
Héraó   C

RESTAURANTS
Café Nielsen   1
Café Valný   2

0   200 m

Atlavík, Reyðarfjörður & Höfn

Seyðisfjörður, Eiðar & Bakkagerði

Reyðarfjörður

Austurlands (☎471 2000, ⓦwww.fatravel.is) near the bus station at Miðvangur 2–4, or the long-established Tanni Travel, based in the Eastfjord town of Eskifjörður (☎476 1399, ⓦwww.tannitravel.is).

Accommodation

Accommodation fills up fast in summer, particularly mid-week, when the ferry docks at Seyðisfjörður. The functional **campsite** is next to the bus station (book through the information office, see above; 900kr per person) with showers, laundry, tiny barbecue shed and potentially boggy tent sites; if you're after scenery, head down to Atlavík (see p.284). For **homestays** with sleeping-bag accommodation, contact the tourist information office.

Edda Tjarnarbraut 25, across from the pool ☎444 4880, ⓦwww.hoteledda.is. Summer-only option, offering en-suite doubles and family rooms, plus conference facilities and a good restaurant. ❷

Fosshótel Valaskjálf Skógarlönd 3, opposite the museum ☎470 5050, ⓦwww.fosshotel.is. The drab exterior won't win any prizes but it's a friendly, organized place inside, with good-sized rooms. ❸

Gistihús Olgu Tjarnarbraut 3, ☎860 2999, ⓔgistihusolgu@simnet.is. Cute and cosy B&B; the most welcoming, laid-back place in town. ❷

Guesthouse Egilsstaðir 250m west of town overlooking Lögurinn's shore ☎471 1114, ⓦwww.egilsstadir.com. Very pleasant option in a converted, solid stone farmhouse with friendly staff and grand views down the lake. ❸

Héraó Miðvangur 5–7, ☎471 1500, ⓦwww.icehotels.is. Icelandair's smart, Nordic-style hotel with all business facilities. ❸

The Town

Egilsstaðir's main distraction is the pedestrian **Minjasafn Austurlands museum**, a ten-minute walk from the bus station on Tjarnarbraut (June–Aug Thurs–Tues 11am–5pm, Wed 11am–9pm; Sept–May Mon–Fri 11am–5pm; 500kr, free on Wed), which aims to give a potted history of the town since its creation in the 1940s. Beside the usual suspects – battered farming implements, saggy woollen clothes and old riding saddles – there's a more interesting reconstruction of an old wooden church plus accounts of nearby archeological excavations from Viking times.

Continue past the museum up Tjarnarbraut and you'll pass within sight of a modern **church**, whose design dimly echoes volcanic rock formations, and then reach Egilsstaðir's **swimming pool**, somewhere to unwind on a wet day (June–Aug Mon–Fri 7am–9.30pm, Sat & Sun 10am–7pm; Sept–May Mon–Fri 7am–8.30pm, Sat & Sun 10am–5pm; 350kr). In better weather, there's a brief **walk** to be made uphill from the bus station to a rocky outcrop overlooking the town, with long views down the lake towards a distant Snæfell. If you've got your own transport, it's also worth checking out **Fardagafoss**, a small waterfall in a twisting canyon about 5km northeast of town on the lower slopes of the Seyðisfjörður road.

Eating and drinking

Eating wise, the N1 fuel station **café** is inexpensive and well patronized for the usual grills, pizzas and sandwiches. Nearby *Café Valný* serves excellent coffee, home-made cakes and light, healthy meals; while up the hill, hidden behind a screen of trees next to the bank, ⊁ *Café Nielsen* is a cosy **café-restaurant-bar** with a bit of charm offering beer, lunchtime buffets (around 1500kr) and more substantial fish and meat dishes (from 2600kr). **Self-catering** is possible by stocking up at either of the two supermarkets: Samkaup (Mon–Fri 9am–7pm, Sat 10am–6pm, Sun noon–6pm), behind N1, is the better stocked of the two and has a good range of road maps; while Bónus (Mon–Thurs noon–6.30pm, Fri 10am–7.30pm, Sat 10am–6pm, Sun noon–6pm), on the Ringroad, is cheaper. The **vínbúð** is diagonally opposite the *Hérað* hotel at Miðvangur 2–4.

Lögurinn

In common with many Icelandic lakes, **Lögurinn**, stretching directly southwest of Egilsstaðir for 30km, fills a glacier-eroded valley. Unusually, however, the valley is fairly well **wooded**, at least along its eastern side. Most people don't get much further than these woods' southern reaches around the bay of **Atlavík**, but a decent road runs right around the lake and elsewhere there's saga lore and medieval remains to take in, along with an impressive waterfall. Deep and green, the lake itself is home to the **Lagarfljótsormur**, a monster of the Scottish Loch Ness and Swedish Storsjön clans, though so elusive that nobody is even very sure what it looks like – a giant snaky form is favoured.

You need only one nice day to appreciate Lögurinn, but if you want to stay longer, note that **accommodation** is concentrated in the more visited stretch between Egilsstaðir and Atlavík. In your own vehicle, Lögurinn takes an easy few hours to circuit, including time for stops along the way; otherwise you'll have to rely on **tours** from Egilsstaðir (see p.281). Alternatively, you might pass through en route to Kárahnjúkar and Snæfell (see p.286), as the road runs off Lögurinn's southwestern shore. In summer, you can also **cruise** down to Atlavík with Ormur

(☎471 2900, ⊛www.ormur.is), whose boats depart from the far side of the wooden bridge 3km north of Egilsstaðir.

Eastern Lögurinn

Iceland's forests were never very extensive and soon fell to human and grazing pressures after the Settlement. To partially remedy the situation, since the early twentieth century the **Icelandic Forestry Commission** has put considerable effort into expanding surviving pockets of woodland around the country, and the eighteen-kilometre stretch along Lögurinn's eastern shore is their showpiece. The woodland is mostly birch (distinguished by its smooth red or silver bark), though mature plantations of much larger ash, spruce and larch are wildly popular with Icelanders, who are struck by the novelty of seeing vegetation that is taller than they are – visitors from lusher climates may feel that the area, pleasant though it is, doesn't warrant so much excitement.

Hallormsstaður and Atlavík

Start by heading south from Egilsstaðir down the Ringroad, then turn west to follow **Route 931** along the lakeshore. About 25km from town you'll find yourself in thick woodland at **HALLORMSSTAÐUR**, a fuel station, small store and **accommodation** at either a lakeshore **campsite** (☎471 1774 or 849 1461) or inside *Hótel Hallormsstaður* (☎471 2400, ⊛www.hotel701.is; cabins ❷, rooms ❸), which offers rooms, self-contained cabins, a restaurant and access to the local **pool**. There are marked walking tracks out of the woods and up onto the fellsides here, the longest of which takes around five hours return; the hotel also hires out **horses** for these trails at around 2500kr per hour.

It's 2km past Hallormsstaður to the **forestry office** and **arboretum**, where there's a half-hour stroll around a labelled collection of century-old native and imported tree species, including the country's tallest (a pine), which towers 22m overhead. A couple of kilometres further brings you to a sharp downhill turn to the water's edge at **Atlavík**, a small bay with a half-kilometre-long gravel beach and granite headland, a jetty and a grassy **campground** (☎471 1774 or 849 1461, ⊛hallormsstadur@skogur.is) with picnic tables and toilets all fringed by aromatic birch forest – somewhere to spend a few days following walking tracks into the hills, or doing nothing much at all.

Hrafnkelsstaðir

Almost immediately after Atlavík, you exit the woods and find yourself well towards Lögurinn's southern end, the slopes above the opposite shore bald and shelved along their length, like very broad steps. A few kilometres later and the road divides, the main stretch heading over to Lögurinn's western shore via a **bridge**; stay on the eastern side and the surface quickly becomes gravel. A couple of kilometres in this direction is **Hrafnkelsstaðir**, the farm that features in the latter stages of **Hrafnkel's Saga** (see box, p.285); there's no trace of saga times in the current buildings but it remains an atmospheric, brooding location. Pressing on past here eventually brings you to another bridge leading over to the far shore at Valþjófsstaður (see below).

Western Lögurinn

Western Lögurinn's attractions are mostly clustered down the southern end of the lake, reached via either of two bridges. Near where the Jökulsá flows into Lögurinn, **Valþjófsstaður** is another historic farm founded by the influential twelfth-century chieftain Þorvarður Þórarinsson. The otherwise unremarkable **church** here, built in

Lögurinn and the lands to the west form the stage for **Hrafnkel's Saga**, a short but very striking story set in the mid-tenth century, before the country had converted to Christianity. Long debated by scholars as to whether it's a straight history or a complex moral tale, it tells of the landowner **Hrafnkel**, a hard-working but headstrong devotee of the pagan fertility god Freyr, who settled **Hrafnkelsdalur**, a valley 35km due west of Lögurinn. Here he built the farm **Aðalból**, and dedicated a shrine and half his livestock to Freyr – including his favourite stallion, the dark-maned **Freyfaxi**, which he forbade anyone but himself to ride on pain of death.

Inevitably, somebody did. Hrafnkel's shepherd, **Einar**, borrowed Freyfaxi to track down some errant ewes, and caught in the act, was duly felled by Hrafnkel's axe. Looking for legal help, Einar's father Þorbjörn enlisted his sharp-witted nephew **Sámur**, who reluctantly took the case to court at the next Alþing at Þingvellir (see p.106). But nobody wanted to support a dispute against such a dangerous character as Hrafnkel, until a large party of men from the suitably distant Westfjords offered their services. As Sámur presented his case, his allies crowded around the gathering and Hrafnkel, unable to get close enough to mount a defence, was outlawed.

Disgusted, Hrafnkel returned home where he ignored his sentence, but Sámur and the Westfjorders followed him in secret and descended on his homestead early one morning. Dragged out of bed, Hrafnkel was told to choose between death or giving his property to Sámur. He took the latter option, leaving Aðalból and moving east over the Lagarfljót to **Hrafnkelsstaðir**, a dilapidated farm that he was forced to buy on credit. Back at Aðalból, Sámur drowned Freyfaxi as the unlucky cause of the dispute; hearing about this, Hrafnkel renounced his god.

Over the next six years Hrafnkel laboured hard to build up his new property and, his former arrogance deflated, became a wealthy and respected figure. Meanwhile, Sámur's noble brother **Eyvind** returned from a long overseas trip and decided to visit Sámur at Aðalból. Riding past Hrafnkelsstaðir, Eyvind was spotted by one of Hrafnkel's servants who goaded her master into taking revenge against his persecutor's brother. Hrafnkel and his men cut Eyvind down in a bog and then launched a raid on Aðalból, capturing Sámur and giving him the same choices that Sámur had given him: to die or hand over the farm. Like Hrafnkel, Sámur chose to live and – having vainly tried to reinvolve his friends in the Westfjords – retired unhappily to his former estate. For his part, Hrafnkel retained his power and influence and stayed at Aðalból until his death.

1966, replaced a structure from Þorvarður's time whose original **wooden doors**, carved with mythical creatures and knights on horseback, are now in Reykjavík's National Museum – replicas are on the inside of the current doors.

Heading north up the lake, **Skriðuklaustur** (daily May–Aug 10am–6pm) was the site of a medieval monastery and is now graced by a distinctive stone house built in the 1930s by novelist **Gunnar Gunnarsson**, whose bronze bust adorns the front lawn. There's a gallery here, along with the popular ⚘ *Klausturkaffi* **café-restaurant**, a good place to break your circuit for a home-made cake or light meal.

Hengifoss

Next comes the junction with **Route 910** to Snæfell and Kárahnjúkar (see p.286); by this point the lakeside is very open, with scattered homesteads and stone **rettir pens** set amongst good grazing land. Directly opposite Hrafnkelsstaðir – if you crossed at the main bridge you'll more or less end up here – a good-sized parking bay and notice boards mark the start of an hour-long walking track up to **Hengifoss**, whose 118-metre drop makes it Iceland's third-highest falls. On the way, the lesser **Litlifoss** has wild rock formations of basalt columns, bent in all directions, while Hengifoss itself drops over cliffs layered in distinct black and red bands, composed of compressed ash falling in separate volcanic eruptions.

The final 35km back along the lake to Egilsstaðir from Hengifoss is fairly bland, passing a few old turf farmhouses before rejoining the Ringroad just north of town at the hamlet of **Fellabær**.

Kárahnjúkar and Snæfell

The highland southwest of Egilsstaðir forms a huge, wild and impressively bleak expanse of moorland running right up to the edge of **Vatnajökull** (for more on which, see p.296). The main landmark out this way is the permanently snow-capped, sharply ridged peak of **Snæfell** which, at 1833m, is the highest freestanding mountain in Iceland, formed from the eroded core of a long-extinct stratovolcano. While climbing Snæfell needs experience and equipment, you can get to within 10km of its base – and see heaps of wildlife – on the way to the **Kárahnjúkar hydro dam**, built to provide power for an aluminium smelter down on the coast in Reyðarfjörður (see p.292).

Route 910 provides a sixty-kilometre-long surfaced road from Lögurinn lake to Kárahnjúkar; in summer it's accessible to conventional vehicles but parts are badly potholed and there are no facilities out here if something goes wrong, so keep your speed down and your eyes open. If you've got a four-wheel-drive, note that there are also several tracks off Route 910 to Snæfell, Vatnajökull and beyond. There's **no bus** service into the region, though you might be able to set up a tour from Egilsstaðir – see p.281 for operators.

If you're four-wheel-driving or hiking in the area, bring all **supplies** with you; **maps** of the region include Landmælingar Íslands' *Austurland* 1:250,000 and Mál og menning's excellent *Lónsöræfi* 1:100,000 (if you're planning to hike down to Lónsöræfi).

Lögurinn to Snæfell

Route 910 zigzags steeply uphill from Lögurinn's shore and out onto a high, gently undulating moorland; on cloudless days there are fantastic views back over the lake and then, as the miles pass by, of Snæfell and **Heiðubreiðalindur** (see p.286) gradually rising up out of the horizon ahead. Keep eyes peeled for **reindeer**, geese and whooper swans, all of which breed and feed among the boggy pasture up here.

After about 40km you should be around the junction of the four-wheel-drive **F909** to Snæfell itself; the mountain is only 10km south as the raven flies but rather more once you start weaving around the outlying peaks and fording rivers along the way. Once there, a thirty-kilometre-long track **circuits Snæfell's base** via three **huts** and **campgrounds**, on the northeast (closest), southeast and western flanks. The last is run by Ferðafélag Íslands (bookings ☎853 9098, Ⓦwww.fi.is; toilets, water and showers), and marks the start of the long hike **south to Lónsöræfi** – for more on which, see the box on p.299.

Kárahnjúkar

Kárahnjúkar, a highland area located on the headwaters of the Jökulsá á Dal at the northeastern edge of the Vatnajökull ice cap, was one of Europe's most pristine environments, a prime summer nesting site for pink-footed geese. This all changed in 2003, when construction began on a **hydroelectric dam** across the river where it flowed into the dramatic **Dimmugljúfur** canyon, backflooding to create a huge new lake, **Hálslón**, which extends 45km south to Vatnajökull itself. At 630-megawatts, the project has almost doubled Iceland's hydroelectric output, but the cost to the country's environmental heritage – not to mention its reputation – has been immense.

Route 910 terminates at the dam site around 20km past the Snæfell road; the road suddenly narrows before crossing the two-hundred-metre-high **dam wall**. Park the car on the far side for views down into Dimmugljúfur, which forms a long, narrow, jagged tear in the landscape, clearly caused by a single, violent earthquake: you have to ponder the wisdom of building a dam on what is patently a highly unstable area. Also note the dam's **spillway**; in late summer, melting ice around Vatnajökull fills Hálslón beyond capacity, and the overflow creates an artificial waterfall here known as **Kárahnjúkafoss**.

Húsey and Bakkagerði

North of Egilsstaðir, a broad, waterlogged valley contains the last stages of the silt-laden Lagarfljót and Jökulsá á Brú as they wind their final 50km to the coast at **Héraðsflói**, an equally wide bay. Strewn with wildflowers, the lowland moors along the way are a prime place to see reindeer in autumn and spring, and birds in summer, while the coast has **seals** all through the year. If you fancy a few days amongst it all, head for the beautifully isolated farmstead of **Húsey**, though you'll also cross Héraðsflói en route to tiny **Bakkagerði** at the very top of the Eastfjords, an appealing place with excellent hiking potential.

Húsey

To explore Héraðsflói's western stretches, head 20km northwest of Egilsstaðir along the Ringroad, then follow **Route 925** 30km coastwards to a tongue of land between the Jökulsá á Brú and the Lagarfljót. These flat heaths are known as **Hróarstunga**, liberally populated by wading birds, ducks, swans, geese, skuas and sheep. You'll find all of these at the working farm and self-catering IYHA **hostel** of ⚑ *Húsey* (☎ 471 3010, ⓦ www.husey.de; sleeping-bag accommodation 2250kr), an excellent place to spend a few days observing an Icelandic farm in action and getting to know the region. The farm breeds **horses** and rents them by the hour, day or week, and can set up riding packages including accommodation and meals. Along with netting for salmon and trout, the farm is one of the last in Iceland still to hunt seals, selling the skins and meat – though they'll point you in the right direction if you want to see them in the wild. Without your own transport, you can reach Húsey by calling them in advance to arrange a pickup from the 925 junction.

Bakkagerði

BAKKAGERÐI, also known as **Borgarfjörður Eystri**, is an isolated community of just 120 people, overlooking a wide fjord 70km northeast of Egilsstaðir. Backed by mountains, it's a charming location, steeped in local lore, with some of the Eastfjords' most rewarding hiking trails. Without your own transport, catch the **mail van** from Egilsstaðir at 11am (Mon–Fri; ☎ 894 8305), which also functions as the village post office.

Route 94 from Egilsstaðir runs north, via tiny **Eiðar** (comprising an agricultural college and huge radio mast), out towards Heraðsflói, before bending eastwards

Bakkagerði has become quite a hiking haven in recent years, with a good number of **marked trails** around the place. However, the possibility of dense summer fogs and atrocious weather with heavy snow on higher ground make it essential to ensure you're properly equipped, and to seek local advice before setting out.

Prominent behind Bakkagerði, **Dyrfjöll**, the "Door Mountain", gets its name from the huge gap in its sharp-peaked, 1136-metre-high basalt crest. This is another abode of local spirits, this time mischievous imps that emerge around Christmas to tie cows' tails together. A round-trip from town would be a major hike, though you could arrange a lift up to the top of the pass at **Geldingafjall** on the Egilsstaðir road, from where there's a marked track around the upper reaches of the mountain, and then down to the end of the valley south of town – a full day's walk.

A good introduction to the area is to hike 4km or so west to the next bay of **Brúnavík**, whose steeply sloping valley was farmed until being abandoned in the 1940s. This is a story typical of the whole northern Eastfjords; as the herring industry fizzled out after World War II, and roads and services began to bypass the region, farms founded in Settlement times were given up as people moved on. There's a small shelter shed here today, and a further rough trail over loose-sided fells to **Breiðavík**, where there's a hiking **hut** and campground with water and toilets (bookings ⊕868 5813, ©ferdafelag@egilsstadir.is; 2600kr) and a seven-kilometre-long **jeep track** northwest back to town – the round-trip via Brúnavík and Breiðavík takes about fourteen hours.

It's also possible to spend a few days hiking **to Seyðisfjörður**, initially following another jeep track south down the valley from Bakkagerði. One of the highlights is about 10km along where you cross a saddle below **Hvítserkur**, a pink rhyolite mountain, wonderfully streaked with darker bands and stripes. There's another **hut** (same phone and facilities) at the head of the next valley over, whose lush meadows once supported four farms, and remains of a church on the bay here, **Húsavík**. Then it's over a steep hillside to the next fjord, **Loðmundarfjörður**, most of whose population clung on into the 1970s. A partly restored church remains, built in 1891, though there is little else. Loðmundarfjörður marks the end of the jeep track, but hikers can follow a rough trail through a pass over **Hjálmárdalsheiði** and then down to Seyðisfjörður.

past a network of fragmented ponds and lagoons favoured by nesting **red-throated divers** (loons) and plenty of ducks and wildfowl. It then cuts up the flanks of **Geldingafjall** before a steep descent on the far side to the coast. Njardvík, the bay here, is sided in dangerously loose cliffs, a hazard attributed to the malevolent local spirit **Naddi**, who – despite being pushed into the sea by a fourteenth-century farmer – remains active, judging by the state of the road: keep an eye out for a protective cross by the roadside with the Latin inscription *Effigiem Christi qui transis pronus honora* ("You who hurry past, honour Christ's image"). By now, you're rounding the edge of **Dyrfjöll**, a spiky rhyolite mountain which rises behind Bakkagerði, and reach the village itself within a few kilometres.

The village and around

Bakkagerði sits at the mouth of a ten-kilometre-long valley running south, with Dyrfjöll to the west, and steep-sided, colourful fells to the east; a slowly dwindling population just about gets by on fishing and sheep farming. The core of the village is its main **harbour**, where a jetty marks the fish-processing plant and Fuglaskoðunarhús **bird hide** overlooking a black shingle beach strewn with seaweed and patrolled by the usual seashore suspects. Across the road, behind the blocky

Fjarðarborg school, **Kjarvalsstofa gallery** (daily noon–6pm; 500kr) displays the works of the late Icelandic painter **Jóhannes Kjarval**, who grew up here and often incorporated local landscapes into his work. About 500m around the harbour from here, the **church** is a standard nineteenth-century wood and corrugated iron affair, with an altarpiece in sunset hues by Kjarval depicting the Sermon on the Mount as delivered atop **Álfaborg**, the rocky hill behind. Álfaborg means "elf-town" and, according to folklore, is home to Iceland's fairy queen.

If you need a further sea bird hit, follow the bay road for 5km from town to **Hafnarholm**, by Bakkagerði's tiny fishing harbour – worth checking out in its own right to see if any of the bizarre-looking **Greenland shark** (source of the notorious speciality *hákarl*; see p.40) have been landed. Here, a set of wooden steps leads up to an **observation platform** (summer 10am–10pm) with views out over the headland and an adjacent outcrop of rock. Although there are plenty of fulmars and kittiwakes here, it's the **puffins** which are the real draw; they return from their fishing expeditions during the afternoon when your chance of seeing them is greatest.

Practicalities

Bakkagerði's services are extremely limited: there's only a **bank** and a **fuel station-cum-store**, both near the jetty. The **campground** is between the church and Álfaborg (free, with toilets and showers; ☎472 9999); while **beds** are available at the unreliable *Ásbyrgi Youth Hostel* (☎472 9962, @borgarfjordur@hostel.is; sleeping-bag accommodation 2600kr) and friendly ☩ *Borg* (☎472 9870 or 894 4470; sleeping-bag accommodation 2500kr, beds 3600kr), on the main road before the church. They can also arrange drop-off/pick ups for hiking trails, and four-wheel-drive **tours** for 5000kr an hour.

Opposite the church and towards the sea, the *Álfa Café* (Mon–Fri 11am–8pm, Sat & Sun 1–8pm) serves waffles, soups and coffee. There's similar fare available too across from the fuel station at *Fjarðarborg* (June–Aug); otherwise the **supermarket** is the only source of food.

The Eastfjords

The Eastfjords cover a 120-kilometre stretch of eastern Iceland's twisted coastline between Bakkagerði in the north and southern Berufjörður, with many of the fjords – none of which is particularly large – sporting small villages, mostly given over to fishing. The fjord scenery can be vivid, particularly in summer, with the villages sitting between flat blue sea and steep, steel-grey mountains, their peaks dusted in snow and lower slopes covered in greenery and flowers. Aside from **Bakkagerði**, covered on pp.287–289, highlights include **Seyðisfjörður**, for its Norwegian-style wooden houses and international ferry, and, right at the fjords' southern end near the town of **Djúpivogur**, the sea-bird-infested island of **Papey** – believed to have been a former retreat for Christian monks.

There isn't a continuous road linking the fjords, so you'll have to backtrack to check out the entire coast: north from Egilsstaðir is the road to Bakkagerði; east is Seyðisfjörður; and southeast are separate routes to Reyðarfjörður and around the rest of the region. You can also bypass most of the Eastfjords by taking the Ringroad south from Egilsstaðir, which cuts down through the wonderfully stark **Skriðadalur** and **Breiðdalur** valleys to rejoin the coastal road at Breiðdalsvík. Regular **buses** connect Egilsstaðir with all the Eastfjord villages, though not necessarily every day. Almost everywhere has accommodation, a bank, post office, supermarket and swimming pool, though, as usual, services might be limited outside the main season and it's always worth phoning ahead to check.

Seyðisfjörður

Twenty-five kilometres east of Egilsstaðir over a good mountain road (Route 93), **SEYÐISFJÖRÐUR** is an attractive town set at the base of a long, tight fjord. It has a strong Norwegian heritage: first settled by a tenth-century Norwegian named Bjólf, Seyðisfjörður was established as a herring port a thousand years later by entrepreneurs from Norway, who also imported the town's wooden architecture. During its herring heyday, Seyðisfjörður looked set to become Iceland's largest port, but geography limited its expansion. Used as a US naval base during World War II, the town remains an active fishing and processing centre, with a continuing Nordic link embodied by the Faroese-operated **ferry** *Norröna*, which calls in every Thursday on its Iceland–Faroes–Denmark route. The town's summer rhythms follow the ferry schedule and it's generally busy only on Wednesdays, when an afternoon craft **market** is laid on for departing visitors.

Scattered along a kilometre-long crescent of road, Seyðisfjörður sports a smart, neatly arranged core of older wood and corrugated-iron houses backed by steep fjord walls and greenery. The town is split by the small mouth of the shallow **Fjarðará** as it empties into the fjord – marked by a short bridge – with Bláa kirkjan, the **Blue Church**, and surrounding older buildings to the north, and the ferry terminal and most amenities to the south. The church is one of the nicest examples of Seyðisfjörður's chocolate-box architecture, painted in pastel hues and hosting classical **concerts** on Wednesday evenings in summer. South of the river, Austurvegur runs east along the waterfront, where you'll find a cannon salvaged from the 1944 wreck of the *El Grillo*, a British oil carrier hit by a German bomb. Another 250m up along the waterfront takes you past the ferry terminal to Tækniminjasafn, the **Technology Museum of East Iceland** (June to mid–Sept daily 11am–5pm; mid-Sept to May Mon–Fri 1–4pm; 600kr, free on Fri), whose

▲ Seyðisfjörður

collection of historical exhibits is outshone by the imposing museum itself, built in 1894 as east Iceland's first telegraph office.

Some hikes

One popular walk starts by following the road along the north side of the fjord for a couple of kilometres to the **Vestdalsá**, the first real river you'll encounter on the way. Just before you reach it, a trail heads uphill along **Vestadalur**, a valley leading up into the hills to a small lake, Vestdalsvatn, past several pretty waterfalls; allow five hours to make the return hike from town.

In the opposite direction, take the coastal track past the Technology Museum for 8km along the south side of the fjord to the site of **Þórarinsstaðir**, a former farm where archeologists unearthed the foundations of a church dating from the eleventh century, believed to be the oldest such remains in the country. Not much further on, **Eyrar** is yet another abandoned farm, though here the ruins are far more substantial; it's hard to believe now, but this was once one of the region's busiest settlements. Experienced hikers can spend an extra half-day walking south across mountains from here to the narrow and virtually uninhabited **Mjóifjörður**, the next fjord south, where there's **cabin accommodation** at *Sólbrekka* (T 476 0020, @mjoi@simnet.is) for four people (10,500kr per night available all year) or sleeping-bag accommodation (2200kr per person between June and mid-August only) and Route 953 back towards Egilsstaðir.

Seyðisfjörður practicalities

Egilsstaðir-Seyðisfjörður **buses** (T 472 1515) run year-round; between late May and August there are two buses a day (Mon–Fri), with an extra service running on Wednesday and Thursday to cope with passengers taking the *Norröna*. The ferry terminal (T 472 1111, W www.smyril-line.com) is at Strandarbakki off Ferjuleira, where you can make bookings and also buy Icelandic bus passes (see Basics, p.31). Seyðisfjörður's **tourist information office** (summer Mon–Fri 9am–5pm; T 472 1551, W www.sfk.is) is located here too; at weekends and in winter try the office at Hrafnargata 44 (T 470 2308).

The **bank** (with ATM) and **post office** (Mon–Fri 9am–4.30pm) are opposite the ferry terminal on Hafnargata, with a **supermarket** 100m down the road near the bridge. For alcohol, the **vínbúð** is hidden away inside the *Shell* station, next to the bank, at Hafnargata 2a. The **swimming pool** (Mon–Fri 6.30–8.30am & 5–9pm, Sat 11am–4pm) is located one block inland from *Hótel Seyðisfjörður* (see below) on Suðurgata. For **food**, both hotel restaurants are highly recommended for a full meal, with mains from around 2500kr. Otherwise try the *Kaffi Lára*, opposite the *Hótel Aldan*, for cakes and coffee; the tiny **cinema** at Austurvegur 15; and at the Skaftafell Cultural Centre (Tues–Fri 11am–3pm, Sun 3–6pm; T 692 8711), opposite the ferry terminal on Hafnargata, whose **internet café** serves light meals.

Accommodation

Accommodation is only likely to be in short supply on ferry days. The **campsite** (T 472 1521), with showers and toilets, is just north over the river.

Hafaldan Youth Hostel Ránargata 9, 500m north of town overlooking the harbour T 472 1410, @seydisfjordur@hostel.is. A friendly place with a well-equipped kitchen, warm, wood-panelled rooms, and great views over the fjord. They also operate another old building down in the town, but you need to check in here first. Dorm beds 2600kr, **❶**

Hótel Aldan Norðurgata 2 T 472 1277, W www.hotelaldan.com. A heritage-listed gem, one of Seyðisfjörður's original Norwegian wooden kit-homes that housed the town's bank for almost a century and oozes old-fashioned charm. Excellent restaurant and bar. **❷**

Hótel Seyðisfjörður Austurvegur 3 T 472 1460, W www.hotelaldan.com. Another nice old wooden building, which once served as the local post office; it's owned by the *Aldan* management. ❸ **Skálanes** Mouth of the fjord, about 15km from town ⓦ www.skalanes.com. Wild and remote private nature reserve, with accommodation inside a modernized 1920s farmhouse. Two nights' accommodation, meals and short guided walks cost 63,000kr for two.

Fjarðabyggð: Reyðarfjörður, Eskifjörður and Neskaupstaður

The Eastfjords' middle reaches, known as **Fjarðabyggð**, comprise the three relatively large fishing villages of **Reyðarfjörður**, **Eskifjörður** and **Neskaupstaður**, linked by the sixty-kilometre Route 92 from Egilsstaðir. During the summer, there are two **buses** in each direction (Mon–Fri) and one on Saturday between Egilsstaðir and Neskaupstaður; at other times call ☎477 1713 or check the timetable at ⓦ www.austfjardaleid.is.

Though there isn't really a huge amount to drag you into the region, Fjarðabyggð has a pleasant character despite being at the centre of the **aluminium smelter** row and the ensuing environmental damage at Kárahnjúkar (see p.286). As you leave Reyðarfjörður, 6km east towards Eskifjörður, you'll drive past the plant in question; the project is very popular locally due to the bright job prospects and this is not somewhere to start airing negative views about it.

Reyðarfjörður

Around 20km from Egilsstaðir, **REYÐARFJÖRÐUR** is a functional port surrounded by imposing mountains, their tops ground flat by now-vanished glaciers. The **Fjarðaal aluminium smelter** has brought employment, a huge new sports centre and an upbeat air to town, but the only real point of interest here is Stríðárasafnið, the **Icelandic Wartime Museum** (June–Aug daily 1–5pm; 600kr), whose collection of photos and mannequins in period clothes is located back towards the hills off Austurvegur at the end of Heiðarvegur.

North of Reyðarfjörður, **Grænafell** isn't particularly high at 581m, but is accessible along a two-hour track that climbs up through a narrow gorge to reveal a broad fjord panorama from the top. Try also to track down the grave of **Völva**, which according to local tales was a supernatural being who watches over the town – the name is applied throughout Nordic countries to a range of benevolent female spirits.

Route 92 runs through Reyðarfjörður as the town's seven-hundred-metre-long main street; the west half is called Búðareyri, and the eastern end Austurvegur. Most of the town's services are along Búðareyri, including the post office, bank and **bus stop**. Opposite the post office on Hafnargata, there's a small shopping complex housing a **supermarket** and **vínbúð**. At present, **accommodation** is polarized between the **free campground** (☎470 9090), right on Reyðarfjörður's western boundary, and the small *Fjarðahótel* next to the post office on Búðareyri (☎474 1600, ⓦ www.fjardarhotel.is; ❸). For **food**, head to *Café Kosy* or adjacent *Tærgesen* **restaurant-bar** on Búðurgata.

Eskifjörður

Set in its own mini-fjord 15km east of Reyðarfjörður, **ESKIFJÖRÐUR** reeks of fish and revels in fishing, managing to maintain a busy fleet despite the fact that most other Eastfjord towns have fallen on hard times. Road junctions are marked by huge propellers and anchors salvaged from trawlers; the fishing fleet is either clogging up the harbour or out on business somewhere between Finland and Ireland; and the town's centre is focused around a huge **fish-freezing plant** whose walls are covered in bright murals. Unsurprisingly, across from the freezing plant you'll also find Sjóminjasafn, the **Maritime Museum** (June–Aug daily 1–5pm;

600kr; ☎476 1179), atmospherically housed in an early nineteenth-century warehouse made of dark, creosoted timber, and full of seafaring memorabilia – a skiff, models of bigger boats, nets, and bits and pieces from the sea. The only other diversion in the town itself is a **swimming pool** (Mon–Fri 6.30am–8pm, Sat & Sun 10am–6pm) at the opposite end of the main road, beside the N1 fuel station.

Though appearing from a distance to be spread out along the fjord shore, Eskifjörður's centre is very compact, with a **post office** (Mon–Fri 9am–4.30pm), a **bank**, a **bus stop** and **supermarket** within 50m of the freezing plant on Strandgata. Around 200m west along Strandgata, Tanni Travel (☎476 1399, ⓦwww .tannitravel.is) offers limited tourist **information**.

For somewhere to stay, the **free campground** is out at the entrance to the village opposite the N1 station on Bleiksárhlíð, while in town your options are along Strandgata at *Mjóeyri* (☎477 1247, ⓦwww.mjoeyri.is; sleeping-bag accommodation 2600kr; ❷) or *Kaffihúsið Eskifjörður* (☎477 1064; ❷), both characterful old guesthouses. **Food and drink** are served up at *Kaffihúsið Eskifjörður* daily noon–11pm.

Neskaupstaður

A further 23km northeast of Eskifjörður, **NESKAUPSTAÐUR** curls around the northern side of **Norðfjörður** at the end of Route 92. It's Iceland's easternmost town and the Eastfjords' largest settlement, but again an insubstantial one. The setting is splendid, however, the town backed by tall, avalanche-prone fells all around, facing across the fjord; judging by the number of antlers hung over front doors, there's also a healthy reindeer population up in the hills.

Not to be outdone by its neighbours, the town sports two museums, both on main street Egilsbraut: the **Museum of Natural History** (June–Aug daily 1–6pm; 600kr), which has a rock collection upstairs and various stuffed and mounted fauna downstairs; and a **Maritime Museum** (same details), which gives a potted history of the town's seafaring traditions with fading black and white photographs and assorted nautical bits and bobs – something for a rainy day only. Otherwise, Neskaupstaður is probably best seen as the starting point for a difficult **hike** southeast to **Gerpir**, a sheer set of cliffs marking Iceland's easternmost point and famed for their sea-bird colonies – rocks here are also some of the oldest in the country at thirteen million years. You'll need to be completely self-sufficient to do the hike; contact Tanni Travel in Eskifjörður (see above) for more information about the routes and finding a guide.

Most of Neskaupstaður's facilities are near the harbour on Egilsbraut: the **bus stop**, two **banks** and the Samkaup **supermarket** are here, with the **vínbúð** immediately opposite. The **post office** is two streets back from the bus stop on Þiljuvellir.

The **free campground** is up above town, underneath the avalanche defences. Otherwise, try the summer-only *Edda* hotel at Nesgata 40 (☎444 4860, ⓦwww .hoteledda.is; ❷) or the blue-painted, snug *Hótel Capitano* (☎477 1800 or 861 4747, ⓦwww.hotelcapitano.is; ❷), inside a restored old building in the centre of town at Hafnarbraut 50, which has an excellent **restaurant**. The convivial ⅍ *Nesbær Café* (Mon–Fri 9am–6pm, Sat 10am–6pm, Sun 1–5pm), near the hotel on Hafnarbraut, has home-made cakes, sandwiches, coffee and an unusually good choice of teas, plus light meals; it also acts as a basic **tourist information office**.

The southern fjords

South of Reyðarfjörður the Eastfjords begin to open up, and the mountains – if no lower than before – have room to move into the background, softening the scenery until the fjords themselves fizzle out 160km further on. From Reyðarfjörður, a new tunnel slices through the mountains into the upper reaches of Daladalur, cutting out a lengthy detour around the headland of Hafnarnes in order to reach the successively smaller hamlets of **Fáskrúðsfjörður**, **Stöðvarfjörður** and **Breiðdalsvík** – all connected by daily **buses** (Ⓦ www.austfjardaleid.is) from Egilsstaðir. The Ringroad meets up with Route 96 at Breiðdalsvík and continues around the coast to the Eastfjords' finale at **Djúpivogur** (on the Egilsstaðir–Höfn bus run). In fair weather, the afternoon trip out from Djúpivogur to **Papey** is one of the Eastfjords' highlights, not to be missed.

Fáskrúðsfjörður

Thanks to a six-kilometre-long tunnel under the rocky heights of Hallberutindur (1136m) you can now drive direct from Reyðarfjörður to its southern neighbour, **FÁSKRÚÐSFJÖRÐUR**. This quiet, elongated hamlet was, until the early twentieth century, a busy seasonal base for fishing fleets from northern **France**, and the French even established stores, a hospital and consulate here. Today, other than the bilingual street names which pepper the village, the French connection is most tangible during the **Franskir dagir festival** in late July (details on Ⓦ www .austurbyggd.is), which celebrates all things French with four days of singing, dancing and, naturally, feasting. There's more on the subject at the **Fransmenn á Íslandi museum** (June–Aug daily 10am–6pm; Ⓦ www.fransmenn.net), in the centre of the village at Búðavegur 8, which contains a jumble of black and white photographs of the French glory days alongside other Gallic flotsam. At the far seaward end of the village, a French **cemetery** encircled by a white fence is a reminder of how many French and Belgian fishermen lost their lives off Fáskrúðs-fjörður during the village's heyday; the path down to the cemetery begins opposite the Welcome to Fáskrúðsfjörður sign.

Set back from the sea, Búðavegur is the kilometre-long main street, where you'll find the **bank**, **post office** and **supermarket** all within spitting distance of Fáskrúðsfjörður's main **accommodation** prospect, the wooden *Hótel Bjarg* (Ⓣ 475 1466; ❸) at Skólavegur 49. The only other option is the **free campsite**, at the western exit to the town. The hotel **restaurant** has a reasonable grill menu and a bar, or try the summertime *Café Súmarlina* at Búðavegur 59, which serves light meals and sandwiches. *Hótel Bjarg* can also organize half-day **boat trips** out to the three small islands of Andey (very flat), Æðey and the high, wind-sharpened Skrúður, famed for its gannet colonies.

Stöðvarfjörður

Another 25km of fjord scenery as you head southwards lands you at **STÖÐVARFJÖRÐUR**, a small spot with a diminutive harbour. If you're here in spring, you're likely to see snow-white ptarmigans wandering fearlessly down the streets, eating ornamental berries in people's front gardens. Every-thing of note can be found on the through road, Fjarðarbraut: on the west side of town, **Gallerí Snærós**, at no. 42, displays graphic work and ceramics by local artists Sólrún Friðriksdóttir and Ríkhardur Vattingoyer; while **Petra Steina-safn** (May–Sept daily 9am–6pm; 600kr) is an extraordinary private collection of thousands of rocks and mineral samples from all over the place, accumulated over a lifetime of fossicking by elderly Petra Sveinsdóttir, who doesn't speak any English.

Aside from the **campsite** just back towards Fáskrúðsfjörður, the only **place to stay** is on the hill above town at *Kirkjubær* (Ⓣ 475 8819 or 892 3319, Ⓦ www .simnet.is/birgiral; 2500kr) at Fjarðarbraut 37a, a wooden church, moved to its current location in 1925 and now converted into a comfortable, self-catering lodge sleeping ten; they also hire out fishing gear and boats. For **food** try the simple restaurant-cum-store, *Brekkan*, on the main road adjacent to the gallery which serves no-nonsense fry-ups and fish dishes. The **bus stop** and all other services are huddled together near the N1 fuel station on Fjarðabraut.

Breiðdalsvík

A final 18km south past Stöðvarfjörður and just off the highway overlooking the sea, **BREIÐDALSVÍK** marks the point where the Ringroad begins its journey south around the coast, so you might need to change **buses** here: local services (Ⓦwww.austfjardaleid.is) head back north through the Eastfjords to Egilsstaðir; while Ringroad buses (Ⓦwww.trex.is) follow the Ringroad, either inland to Egilsstaðir, or south along the coast to Djúpivogur and Höfn.

The village itself comprises the standard knot of essentials, including the friendly *Hótel Bláfell* and adjoining **restaurant** at Sólvöllur 14 (Ⓣ470 6770, Ⓦwww.hotelblafell.is; ❷), though little else. However, a better choice of **accommodation** and food can be found 1km east of the village, on the Ringroad at Þverhamar, where a sizeable timber building resembling a Swiss chalet houses the German-run ⚒*Café Margret* (Ⓣ475 6625, Ⓔcafemargret@simnet.is; ❸). There are just four rooms here, overlooking the fjord; the **café** rustles up mouth-watering home-made German cakes and main meals including chicken breast for 2300kr, lamb chops at 2550kr and fishy main courses for around 2900kr.

Djúpivogur

The coastal road winds a further 26km past some steep basalt cliffs to Berufjörður and *Berunes* **IYHA hostel** (Ⓣ478 8988 or 869 7227, Ⓔberunes@hostel.is; breakfast available; camping 500kr, sleeping-bag accommodation 2600kr, ❶), set in an exposed position facing distant mountains, which float on the horizon like icebergs. Ask at the hostel about **hiking** routes in the area – some are quite challenging. Not far up the road, **Gautavík** is where the fiery Norwegian evangelist Þangbrand (see p.323) landed in Iceland in the late tenth century to convert the country to Christianity.

Set slightly off the main road, at the southern tip of Berufjörður, **DJÚPIVOGUR**, 64km from Breiðdalsvík, is the southernmost of the Eastfjord settlements, founded by German traders in 1589, and now a tiny, pretty village surrounding a sheltered harbour. On one side of the harbour, the welcoming ⚒*Hótel Framtíð* at Vogaland 4 (Ⓣ478 8887, Ⓦwww.simnet.is/framtid; doubles ❸) is a characterful wooden structure from 1906 wrapped in corrugated iron, offering rooms in the main building, plus self-contained cabins out the back. They also run the town **campsite**, set up on the hill behind the harbour, whose excellent facilities include showers, kitchen and a dining area.

Opposite the hotel is *Langabúð* (June–Aug Sun–Thurs 10am–6pm, Fri & Sat 10am–11.30pm; 500kr; Ⓦwww.rikardssafn.is), a long wooden building that has variously served as a store, warehouse, slaughterhouse, managers' residence and meeting hall since its construction in 1850, and currently houses a **folk museum** featuring household goods, stuffed birds, a mineral collection and a section devoted to local sculptor **Ríkarður Jónsson** (1888–1977).

Between the two museums, the *Við Voginn* **café** serves burgers and chips in various guises, and the hotel has a **restaurant-bar** decorated with old black and white photographs of Djúpivógur from the early 1900s; the soup and fish of the day deal is good value at 2350kr. The **supermarket** (Mon–Fri 11am–6pm, Sat 11am–2pm) is next to the church, on the main road into the village. For the **swimming pool**, head up the hill behind the hotel and take the first left.

The **boat to Papey** (☎478 8838, ✉papey@djupivogur.is) departs from the wooden pier near *Langabúð* daily June to Sept 15 at 1pm, and the four-hour round trip costs 5600kr. It takes about forty minutes to reach the island, slowing down along the way to take in a small shelf of rock favoured by slumbering **seals**. Approaching Papey's green, hummocky form, the boat is further slowed by incredible numbers of swimming sea birds, mostly guillemots, razorbills, and – especially – **puffins**, which flap frantically out of the way or circle overhead in their thousands like a swarm of insects. After landing, you get an hour-long **guided tour** of the two-square-kilometre island, which is mostly flat and somewhat boggy, with a 58-metre apex topped by a lighthouse, and a few cliffs dropping sharply into the water. According to tradition, it was first settled by monks fleeing the ninth-century Viking expansion – Papey means "Monks' Island" – and excavations here during the early twentieth century uncovered three ancient **wooden crosses**. The island has been sporadically farmed, with a wooden **church** built around 1807 – said to be Iceland's smallest, and chained down against fierce winter winds – and more recent turf and timber farm buildings as evidence, though the only present tenants are the birds and a few sheep. Bring a camera for the puffins; you can get closer to them here than just about anywhere else in Iceland.

The southeast: Vatnajökull

About 50km south of Djúpivogur the fjords finally recede into the background and you enter the altogether different world of **southeastern Iceland**, a coastal band between the Eastfjords and Vík dominated by Europe's largest ice cap, **Vatnajökull**. Covering eight thousand square kilometres, almost 150km broad and up to a kilometre thick, Vatnajökull's vast size gradually sinks in as it floats inland for hour after hour as you drive past, its numerous glacier tongues flowing in slow motion from the heights to sea level, grinding out a black gravelly coastline as they go. The recently created **Vatnajökull National Park** (see box opposite) protects the region, though it's still accessible by hiking, four-wheel-driving or even by snowmobile. Flying is perhaps the only way to absorb Vatnajökull's full immensity: glaring ice sheets shadowed in lilac; pale blue tarns; and grey, needle-sharp *nunataks* – mountain peaks – poking through the ice.

Given Vatnajökull's proximity, Iceland's "mini ice-age" between 1200 and 1900 hit the southeast especially hard – not to mention the devastating **jökulhlaups** (see p.306) that flood out from beneath Vatnajökull's icy skirt from time to time – and it remains a thinly settled area, even though all glaciers here are actually **retreating** as the climate warms once more. Following the Ringroad through the region, Vatnajökull's eastern flank is accessed at **Lónsöræfi**, a private reserve managed by **Stafafell farm**, close to the southeast's main town of **Höfn**. Continuing southwest, the ice cap's southern glaciers and adjacent heaths can be explored at **Skaftafell National Park**, after which you cross the **Skeiðarársandur**, a huge glacier-induced wilderness between Vatnajökull and the sea. On the far side and moving away from Vatnajökull, **Kirkjubæjarklaustur** is the only other settlement in the region, near where lava fields and craters at **Lakagígar** stand testament to one of Iceland's most violent volcanic events.

Vatnajökull National Park

The truly vast **Vantnajökull National Park** (ⓦwww.vatnajokulsthjodgardur.is) covers 12,000 square kilometres of unspoiled wilderness – an extraordinary eleven percent of Iceland's total landmass. Areas of special interest within its borders include **Skaftafell National Park** (see p.303) – site of the National Park Headquarters – Stafafell and **Lónsöræfi reserve** (p.297), the **Lakagígar** crater rows (p.307), the **Askja** caldera (p.317), **Snæfell** near Kárahnjúkar (p.286) and **Jökulsárgljúfur National Park** (p.268), including Dettifoss and Ásbyrgi.

The regional **airport** is at Höfn, with regular flights to Reykjavík. The main road through the region is the Ringroad (Route 1), making Höfn, Kirkjubæjarklaustur and the rest of the coastal band accessible by **bus** from Reykjavík year-round, and from Egilsstaðir between June and August. From mid-June until early September, an exciting alternative from Reykjavík is to take a bus along the Interior's **Fjallabak route** via Landmannalaugur and Lakagígar to Kirkjubæjarklaustur – see p.307 for more on this. Once here, there are endless **hiking** opportunities, and plenty of **tours** on offer.

Lón and Höfn

Lón is a glacial river valley whose thirty-kilometre-wide estuary is framed by **Eystrahorn** and **Vestrahorn**, two prominent spikes of granite to the east and west. The central **Jökulsá í Lóni** is a typical glacial flow, its broad gravel bed crisscrossed by intertwined streams that are crystal clear and shallow in winter but flow murky and fast with increased snowmelt in summer. A sandbar across the mouth of the bay has silted the estuary up into lagoons – *lón* in Icelandic – with good trout fishing, thousands of whooper swans nesting on the eastern side below Eystrahorn, and reindeer herds descending from the upper fells in winter. Inland, the heights above the valley are **Lónsöræfi**, the Wilderness of Lón, an area of streams, moor and fractured rhyolite hills, capped by Vatnajökull's eastern edge – though this is invisible from the main road. It's beautiful **hiking** country, where you could spend a couple of days or more on remote tracks, all incorporated into the private **Lónsöræfi reserve** accessed through **Stafafell farm**. Southwest of Lón, **Höfn** is a transit point and somewhere to dry off and stock up before heading off to attack the score of glaciers further west.

Stafafell and Lónsöræfi

Halfway across Lón and just east of the river, a short road off the Ringroad heads inland to **Stafafell farm**, behind which the **Lónsöræfi reserve** stretches back into the mountains. Stafafell has been settled for a long time, and the unassuming **church** here, surrounded by birch trees, was founded a generation after the tenth-century Norwegian missionary **Þangbrand** – armed with a sword, and a crucifix instead of a shield – killed Stafafell's pagan owner in a duel. Þangbrand went on to spread the Christian message across Iceland, surviving attacks by sorcery and a berserker in the process, dividing the country and forcing the Alþing to restore unity by accepting Christianity as the national religion in 1000.

Besides the church, Stafafell comprises farm buildings and a slightly tatty **hostel** (ⓣ478 1717, ⓦwww.eldhorn.is/stafafell; camping 600kr, sleeping-bag accommodation 2000kr, ❶) with warm two- to four-bed rooms, showers, kitchen and TV, set just where hills begin to rise off the estuary flats. **Meals** can be arranged,

▲ Stafafell farm, Lón

but otherwise bring all your own supplies, as the nearest shops are 20km away in Höfn. The helpful, mildly eccentric manager can advise and provide guides for **treks** in Lónsöræfi, and also runs horseriding and four-wheel-drive **tours**. In summer, passing buses will drop off and collect on the highway; in winter, the manager can pick up guests from Höfn with advance warning.

Hiking in Lónsöræfi

Access into Lónsöræfi reserve from Stafafell is either on jeep tracks, or along the dozen or so hiking trails, which cover everything from return walks of a few hours' duration to the week-long trek northeast to Snæfell and Egilsstaðir. However long you're going for, take some warm clothing, food, water and a tent; weather or navigation errors can see even day-walks accidentally extended. Without a guide, you'll also need Mál og menning's *Lónsöræfi* 1:100,000 **map** and advice from the farm about conditions on the longer routes – the reserve's waterways are all glacier-fed, making for unpredictable flow rates in summer.

A short, easy hike follows **marker pegs** uphill behind the hostel onto the moor, above but away from the east side of the Jökulsá í Lóni river. It's slightly boggy heathland, with spongy cushions of moss, low birch thickets and hummocks of gravel; there's a tight grouping of fells looming to the northeast, while the west is more open. Following a general northwest bearing, after a couple of hours you'll find yourself above the shattered, orange and grey rhyolite sides of the **Grákinn valley**; scramble west down the scree and then crisscross the stream to where the valley appears to dead-end in a wall of dark cliffs. Push through a short canyon and exit to the Jökulsá í Lóni, which you follow southeast downstream along a dull jeep track to the highway and the farm. In all, the walk takes four to five hours; just watch out for where the marker pegs may have fallen over.

If you don't head back through Grákinn, the above route continues – unmarked – into the reserve and most of the other trails; the next **campground** in this direction is around three hours past Grákinn at **Eskifell**, with the famed **Illikambur** area near Vatnajökull's eastern flanks a further 5–6 hours beyond. For details of this hike, which can be continued right through **to Snæfell** outside the reserve, see the box opposite.

Höfn

Emerging from the tunnel north of Vestrahorn on the Ringroad around 15km west of Stafafell, you're suddenly confronted by the first roadside view of Vatnajökull, a hazy white streak on the horizon with more sharply defined glaciers sliding seawards. Enjoying a prime position before these glacial tongues and perched on a narrow neck of land, the regional centre of **HÖFN** is the biggest place for miles around. Vatnajökull's offshoots certainly make a splendid backdrop – at least on days when the pernicious **fogs** abate – though otherwise Höfn's main function is as a staging post for the southeast, with a bus station, airport and organized tours onto the ice cap.

The western half of the bay over which Höfn presides, **Hornafjörður**, offered good landing for vessels in Viking times, and is the reason that the place exists at all. Höfn began life in 1863 as a tiny trading post east at Papafjörður in Lón, but went into a decline with the advent of modern vessels, whose deep keels prevented them from landing in the shallow bay. Faced with the prospect of having to ride all the way to Reykjavík for supplies, the traders moved shop to deeper anchorage at Hornafjörður, naming the spot Höfn (simply meaning "harbour"); expansion followed the 1950s fishing boom and the establishment of a fish-freezing plant, still the largest local employer.

You can get to grips with all this – or just take shelter in wet weather – at Höfn's Byggðasafn **museum** (June to Sept 1 daily 1–6pm; free), housed in the original store just up from the bus station on Hafnarbraut. There's also a **Glacier Exhibition** (May & Sept daily 1–6pm; June–Aug daily 9am–9pm; Oct–April Mon–Fri 1–4pm; 700kr) in the same building as the tourist office (see below) at Hafnarbraut

Lónsöræfi to Snæfell

The **hiking trail** from Stafafell in Lónsöræfi to Snæfell takes at least four days, with another three to Egilsstaðir – or arrange a pickup from Snæfell with Tanni Travel (see p.282). Factor in a couple of extra days for rest or casual exploration along the way, especially after the lengthy final section to Snæfell. While the hike isn't especially hard, this is a remote area: don't hike alone, and bring everything you'll need with you. There's one short glacier traverse, requiring a little experience; otherwise you just need to be fit. Ferðafélag Íslands, the Iceland Touring Association (Ⓦwww.fi.is), does this trip every year, should you want to join a **tour**; they also operate many of the **huts** along the way.

Instead of descending into Grákinn (see opposite), continue northwest along the edge of the fells before crossing westwards over the multi-streamed Jökulsá í Lóni to a hut and campground at **Eskifell**. From here, you follow an ever-tightening gorge, cut by the headwaters of the Lóni, due north to another hut and campground at **Illikambur** (bookings Ⓣ699 1424; water; 2600kr), around 25km from Stafafell, where there's a high concentration of day-walks along side-gorges and up nearby peaks, including a route west up to Rauðhamar for views down onto Öxarfellsjökull, Vatnajökull's easternmost extension.

Back on the main track, around 10km north of Illikambur is **Víðidalur**, an attractive valley with a campground to the south and lakeside hut 2km to the northwest at **Kollumúlvatn** (Ⓣ863 5813; no amenities; 2000kr), where there are further glacial views and trails northwest to a collection of wind-scoured outcrops known as **Tröllakrókar**, "troll spires". The next 17km follows Vatnajökull's northeastern edge to the **Geldingafell** hut (Ⓣ863 5813; no amenities; 2600kr); from here, the final stage to Snæfell is a lengthy 35km (avoiding unfordable rivers), first westwards over the tip of **Eyjabakkajökull**, then bearing north at Litla-Snæfell to the Ferðafélag Íslands' hut on Snæfell's west side. For more on Snæfell and the route to Egilsstaðir, see p.286.

30, whose best feature is a nine-minute-long film of the 1996 eruption under Grímsvotn and the subsequent *jökulhlaup* flash flood (see p.306).

For the best views of the glaciers behind Höfn, head through town, past the harbour and out to the seafront at grassy, hummocky **Ósland**, a protected nature reserve. Don't walk out here in summer unless you fancy being attacked by several thousand nesting **arctic terns**, but in a car you can reach a small hillock capped by a weird abstract sculpture in concrete and bronze, where it's safe to get out and admire the scenery.

Arrival and information

Most of what you need in Höfn lies along a 700m stretch of the main road **Hafnarbraut**, which runs south through the middle of town and down to the harbour. From June to August **buses** (℡587 6000, ⓦwww.trex.is) stop at the campsite on Hafnarbraut (close to the junction with Vesturbraut); the rest of the year they use *Hótel Höfn* as their terminus. There are year-round services west along the Ringroad to Skaftafell, Kirkjubæjarklaustur, and through to Reykjavík (daily in summer, otherwise three weekly); and from June to August daily via Djúpivogur and Breiðdalsvík to Egilsstaðir. **Hornafjörður airport** (℡562 4200) is 6km west, with flights year-round to Reykjavík; you'll have to hire a **taxi** (1500kr) from the desk here to reach town.

Höfn's **tourist information office**, at Hafnarbraut 30 (June–Aug daily 8am–noon & 4–8pm; ℡478 2665, ⓦwww.hornafjordur.is), is a well-informed place with regional maps, brochures and **internet** access (200kr per hour); there's also a toaster, microwave, kettle and indoor seating. All other services are south along Hafnarbraut towards the harbour, including two **banks** (with ATMs), a **supermarket** (daily 9am–11pm), the **post office** (Mon–Fri 1–4.30pm) and a new **swimming pool** (Mon–Fri 7–9am & 4–8pm, Sat & Sun 9am–3pm; 350kr).

Accommodation, eating and drinking

Höfn's excellent 荼**campsite** (℡895 3991, Ⓔcamping@simnet.is; 750kr pp) is at the tourist office/summer bus stop and has showers, laundry and plenty of space. The other budget options are the *Nýibær* **IYHA hostel** near the harbour at Hafnarbraut 8 (℡478 1736, Ⓔhofn@hostel.is; sleeping-bag accommodation 2600kr), and the cosy *Hvammur* guesthouse facing the water nearby at Ránarslóð 2 (℡478 1503, ⓦwww.hvammurinn.is; ❷). The town's most upmarket option is *Hótel Höfn*, west on Víkurbraut (℡478 1240, ⓦwww.hotelhofn.is; ❹), a comfortable but characterless modern pile where rooms #201 and #301 have the best views of the glacier. For **farmstay** accommodation, *Árnanes*, near the airport (℡478 1550, ⓦwww.arnanes .is; sleeping-bag accommodation 4200kr, doubles with or without bath ❷–❸) has self-contained cabins as well as rooms in the farmhouse itself.

For **eating**, ☕ *Kaffi Hornið* at Hafnabraut 42 and nearby *Víkin* at Víkurbraut 2 offer coffee, cakes, burgers, pizza and a range of pasta and grills in pleasant surrounds; the *Víkin* also has a **bar**. The *Ósinn* restaurant inside *Hótel Höfn* is pricier, though its regular all-you-can-eat buffets for around 1800kr are extremely popular with locals; ask at reception for details. Höfn's most ambitious option is *Humarhöfnin* (☎478 1200, ◍www.humarhofnin.is) at Hafnabraut 4, near the Youth Hostel, a **lobster restaurant** whose menu extends to include lamb and fish dishes.

To Skaftafell National Park

It is 125km west along the Ringroad from Höfn to **Skaftafell National Park**, with Vatnajökull – or rather, its score of outrunning glaciers – staying with you the whole way, never more than a few kilometres from the roadside. With the clear atmosphere playing tricks with your eyes and making it difficult to judge scale, it is only by the length of time it takes to pass them that you realize how huge these glaciers are, scored and scarred with crevasses and with a light powder of white snow covering the blue-green ice of the glacier tongues themselves.

From Höfn and the road west you can see four of these glaciers at once – from east to west they're Hoffellsjökull, Fláajökull, Heinabergsjökull and **Skálafell-sjökull**. This last is the destination of glacier day-trips from Höfn (though if you've a four-wheel-drive you can turn up here yourself), with the 16km, bumpy and steep Route F985 leaving the Ringroad 45km from Höfn and ascending to the snowline at the *Jöklasel* **restaurant**, somewhere to fork out a fortune for a cake and coffee and gaze down to the coast. This is also the departure point for **rides onto the ice** in either an enclosed and sedate snowcat, or an open-air, speedy two-seater snowmobile (also called a skiddoo). These are certainly not cheap at 12,000kr for just over an hour, but it's great fun tearing across a frozen, empty horizon at upwards of 40km an hour. You'll reach the top of Skálafellsjökull and at least get an idea of Vatnajökull's extent; the usual destination is **Brókarbotnstindur**, a sharp-edged *nunatak* with great views west across a deep valley to more tall peaks and ice. Warm clothing, crash helmet and full instruction are provided (bringing sunglasses is a good idea), but it's best to come a month either side of the main season – in July and August they have over three hundred people a day up here.

Jökulsárlón to Skaftafell

Southwest of the Route F985 junction, the road is forced ever closer to the sea by the encroaching glaciers, with **accommodation** 7km along at *Vagnsstaðir* (☎478 1048, ◍glacierjeeps@simnet.is; sleeping-bag 2600kr); they offer **jeep trips** onto the glacier and the bird-infested coast is within easy walking distance.

After another 30km, the Ringroad reaches a short bridge spanning the mouth of **Jökulsárlón**, Glacier River Lagoon. This large pool between the nose of **Breiðamerkurjökull** and the sea formed after the glacier began shrinking rapidly in the 1940s, and is chock-full of smallish, powder-blue icebergs which have split off Breiðamerkurjökull's front and float idly in the lake as if performing some slow ballet. All transport stops for a view, and you can make thirty-minute **boat trips** (☎478 2222; May 15 to Sept 15; 3100kr) in fat-bellied craft, or just go for a walk along the shore to spot **seals** and soak up the somehow soulful atmosphere. A **café** (daily in summer 9am–7pm) here serves inexpensive snacks.

Once you've seen the lagoon, make sure you cross the road and walk down to the black-sand **beach**. The seafront here is littered with clear, incredibly sculpted **ice**

boulders, the remains of the icebergs which have washed down the kilometre-long **Jökulsár** (Iceland's shortest river) and into the sea – a very memorable sight on such a desolate shore.

Breiðamerkursandur and Öræfi

From here the road continues southwest for another 30km, the coastal strip comprising the black gravel and thin grass glaze of **Breiðamerkursandur**, with the surf breaking on shingle just metres from the road. This provides ideal nesting grounds for **great skuas**, avian pirates resembling brown, bulky gulls who chase and harass other sea birds until they drop their catches – or simply gang up on weaker birds and kill them. Skuas are best watched from a distance as they take exception to being disturbed while raising their young. At the end of the *sandur* the road bends sharply northwest at a fuel station and small supermarket, as you round the base of **Öræfajökull**, a glacier covering the Öræfi volcano, whose devastating eruption in 1362 covered the whole region in tephra and caused its abandonment. Öræfi's protruding peak, **Hvannadalshnúkur**, is the highest point in Iceland at 2199m; if you fancy a crack at the summit, contact ⚑ Mountain Guides (☎894 2959, Ⓦwww.mountainguide.is), which offers a fifteen-hour ascent of Hvannadalshnúkur for the fit and fearless (19,900kr), though you don't need previous mountaineering experience.

Ingólfshöfði

Jutting 10km out to sea at this point is the flat prong of **Ingólfshöfði**, said to be where Iceland's first official settler, **Ingólfur Arnarson** (see p.322), landed. Tipped by a lighthouse, Ingólfshöfði's soft soil and low cliffs attract summer colonies of razorbills, guillemots, greater skua and – especially – **puffins**. Between June and September, *Hofsnes* **farm** runs excellent three-hour-long ⚑ **tours** (☎894 0894; June–Aug Mon–Sat 12pm; 3000kr) out to Ingólfshöfði; you're towed out across huge black-sand dunes in a tractor-driven wagon, then get a guided tour of the grassy headland, where there's a memorial stone to Ingólfur and more puffins and skuas than your camera can handle. Just give it a miss if the weather's bad, as there's nowhere to shelter from the rain along the way. Hofsnes is south off the Ringroad; turn off where you see a sign advertising the tours.

If you want to stay in the area, try *Litla Hof*, which is a self-catering **farmstay** 5km up the road (☎478 1670, Ⓔhof@vortex.is; sleeping-bag accommodation 2400kr, ❸), with a nineteenth-century **turf church** that was built on the site of a pagan temple.

Svínafell

The final twenty-kilometre run up to Skaftafell crosses the easternmost fringe of Skeiðarársandur (see p.305), a desert of rubble and boulders with the massive spread of Skeiðarárjökull – one of Vatnajökull's largest, most active glaciers – filling the distance but seeming to recede the closer you come. Just short of the national park, and sitting within a few hundred metres of the snout of Svínafellsjökull, modern farmhouses mark out **Svínafell** farm and **campsite** (☎478 1765, Ⓔflosihf@simnet .is; 850kr pp), which has the area's only **pool** (July daily 1–9pm). According to **Njál's Saga**, Svínafell was home to Flosi, the man who headed the burning of Njál and his family; it was also where Njal's son-in-law Kári finally forgave Flosi in the tale's closing chapter. See pp.126–127 for the full story.

A couple of kilometres past Svínafell at Freysnes, *Fosshótel Skaftafell* (☎478 1945, Ⓦwww.fosshotel.is; ❹) is an ordinary, modern **hotel** on the Ringroad. Rooms here are overly pink and flowery with cheap wooden panels and flooring; bizarrely for such a prime location they don't have views of the glacier. From here, it's just a few minutes drive to the Skaftafell National Park.

Skaftafell National Park

Bordered by Öræfajökull to the east and Skeiðarárjökull to the west, **Skaftafell National Park** covers 1700 square kilometres of barren lowland *sandurs*, highland slopes brimming with wildflowers, sharp mountain ridges and, of course, glaciers. The most accessible part of the park is **Skaftafellsheiði**, a high tongue of moorland protruding from between **Skaftafellsjökull** to the southeast, and northerly **Morsárjökull**. This is one of Iceland's premier **hiking** venues, with a mass of relatively easy paths of anything from an hour to a full day in length running over the highlands, or along the valleys exposed by the retreating ice.

Hikers should always take the **weather** into account – low cloud, rain and fog can move in quickly – and carry Landmælingar Íslands *Skaftafell* map, which has 1:100,000 and 1:25,000 sheets covering the Skaftafellsheiði area. For a more adventurous take on the area, contact Mountain Guides (☎587 9999, ⓦwww .mountainguide.is), whose staff arrange introductory three-hour **ice-climbing** tours on local glaciers (11,900kr including equipment).

Park practicalities

Your first port of call is Skaftafell's excellent **Visitor Centre**, which is also the **Vatnajökull National Park Headquarters** (June to Sept daily 9am–7pm;

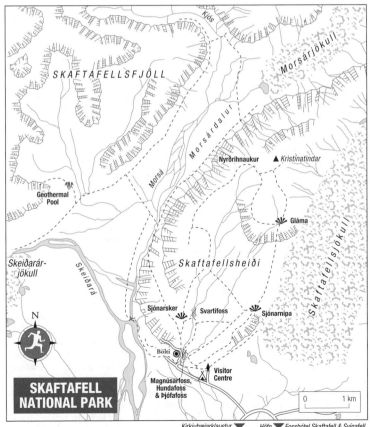

kilometres north off the Ringroad at the foot of Skaftafellsheiði. The building is wired for **wi-fi** and you can also buy **maps**, get a light meal at the **café** and spend an hour watching films and browsing displays about the park.

The adjacent huge **campsite** (750kr) has toilets, showers (400kr extra) and laundry; note that camping out in the park itself needs prior permission from the park office. The only other local **accommodation** is *Bölti* (⊤478 1626, ⓕ478 2426; sleeping-bag accommodation 2800kr), whose six-bunk cabins and tiny turf-roofed kitchen are perched on Skaftafellsheiði's upper front, with beautiful views seawards – it's popular and cheap, so book ahead. Otherwise, head east to Svínafell or the *Fosshótel Skaftafell* (see p.302).

Buses (ⓦwww.trex.is) travelling year-round along the Ringroad between Reykjavík and Höfn stop at the Visitor Centre. From mid-June until early September, you can also reach Reykjavík on daily buses inland via **Landmannalaugar** (ⓦwww.re.is; see p.123); in July and August there are return day-trips from Skaftafell, via Kirkjubæjarklaustur, to **Lakagígar** (ⓦwww.re.is; see p.307).

Skaftafellsjökull and Skaftafellsheiði

One of Skaftafell's shortest walks runs from the Visitor Centre to the front of **Skaftafellsjökull** itself, an easy thirty minutes through low scrub around the base of yellow cliffs where ravens tumble overhead. The woods end at a pool and stream formed from glacial meltwater, beyond which stretch ice-shattered shingle and the four-metre-high front of the glacier, streaked with mud and grit and surprisingly unattractive. Crevasses, and the generally unstable nature of glacier extremities, make it inadvisable to climb onto the tongue unless you've previous experience.

Most of Skaftafell's trails are up top on **Skaftafellsheiði**, and the following clockwise circuit takes upwards of six hours – though you can easily just walk part of it. The first place to aim for is pretty **Svartifoss**, the Black Falls, named after the dark, underhanging hexagonal columns that the water drops over, which inspired the architecture of Reykjavík's National Theatre. Depending on the track you've taken, you might have to cross below the falls here to the west bank, heading towards **Sjónarsker**, a stony 310-metre ridge where the trail to Morsárdalur diverges (see below) – it makes a good general orientation point, as you can see from the coast right up to Vatnajökull from here. Heading due north the path weaves through knee-high birch thickets, silent except for bird calls, towards **Skerhóll**'s steep front, and then climbs the gently sloping rear of this platform. Next comes a short ascent up to **Nyrðrihnaukur**, a long grassy crest off which you can spy downwards on Morsárdalur's picturesque spread of crumbly grey cliffs, flat valley floor with intertwined streams, and encroaching glaciers.

By now you're about two hours from Svartifoss, right at the foot of **Kristínatindar**, a scree-covered peak rising 1125m to a jagged set of pinnacles. One trail heads eastwards around its south side, but you can also hike on unmarked trails up and over Kristínatindar itself, starting from where the main path curves into a "bowl" between the two main peaks – the ascent is nowhere near as hard as it looks, though tiring enough. You emerge onto an icy saddle, the wind suddenly tearing into your face, with the main peak on your left (difficult in very strong winds) and the minor summit to the right. You want to do this on a good day, when the views are magnificent: the mountain is surrounded on three sides by ice, its wedge-like spine splitting Vatnajökull's outflow into the two glaciers which run either side of it – eastern Skaftafellsjökull is closer, a broad, white ribbon, crinkled and ribbed with the vast pressures squeezing it forward. The trail heads down towards it – you have to cast around to find the steep, indistinct track – landing you at **Gláma**, at the top of the sheer-sided valley filled by Skaftafellsjökull, where the trail meets the marked track around Kristínatindar. From here, you simply follow the stony cliff edge for an hour or so south to **Sjónarnípa**, a vantage above the glacier's front, where the path divides to either continue along the edge back to the campsite via birch scrub at **Austurbrekka**, or crosses southwest over the moor to Svartifoss.

To Morsárdalur

Skaftafell's other main track is out to **Morsárdalur**, a ten-kilometre-long, flat-bottomed valley left in Morsárjökull's wake. From Sjórnarsker (see above), the path descends to the flat valley floor, where you have a couple of options: either follow the east side of the valley up to Morsárjökull's noisy front; or cross over to the west side at **Bæjarstaðarskógar**, a small wood of willows and birches, close to a sublime **geothermal pool** just big enough for two people. To reach the pool from the woodland, first wade across the narrow river coming down Austurdalur and the Réttargil ravine, continue over the river flowing down from Vesturdalur and then take the well-trodden path which leads up the western side of the Vesturdalur river (see the map on p.303 for the precise location). You should allow five hours to complete the return hike from the Visitor Centre.

A less steep option to reach Bæjarstaðaskógur and the geothermal pool from the Visitor Centre is to cross the new **bridge** over the Morsá, at the foot of the Hrafnagil ravine, and then follow the stony west bank of the Morsá up towards the original bridge opposite Bæjarstaðaskógur.

Alternatively, once at Bæjarstaðaskógur, you can head in the opposite direction up the Morsárdalur valley and bear west in front of the glacier for **Kjós**, a strikingly beautiful canyon of bare, fractured boulders and sharp yellow crests, which peak at 1000m. Again, give yourself at least six hours for the return hike.

Across Skeiðarársandur to Kirkjubæjarklaustur

West of Skaftafell, the highway skirts the massive crescent edge of **Skeiðarárjökull**, the most mobile glacier in Iceland, whose twenty-kilometre-wide front is so vast that it somehow manages to turn its 1000m drop off the top of Vatnajökull into what appears to be a gentle descent. Over the centuries, the scouring action from Skeiðarárjökull and other glaciers running west off Öræfajökull, combined with titanic outflows from the volcanic glacial lakes Grænalón and Grímsvötn, have created **Skeiðarársandur**, and much of the 66km of highway between Skaftafell and the tiny hamlet of **Kirkjubæjarklaustur** is spent scudding over this bleak gravel desert, which stretches 15km south from the road to the sea, and where winds can whip up sandstorms strong enough to strip the paint off your car. Surprisingly, then, Skeiðarársandur is the largest European nesting ground for the greater skua – keep an eye open, too, for **arctic foxes**, which feed on the birds. Near Kirkjubæjarklaustur, you can detour inland to take in the stark gorges and glacial rivers of **Núpsstaðarskógur**, and to **Lakagígar**, the site of Iceland's most destructive volcanic event of historic times.

Núpsstaðarskógur and on to Kirkjubæjarklaustur

Nearing Skeiðárarjökull's western end, the huge red and black outcrop of **Lómagnúpur** gradually rises up out of the scenery, marking the glacier's former limit before it began to retreat a century ago. In doing so, it allowed access to

Grænalón, Grímsvötn and jökulhlaups

The complex network of turbulent, ever-shifting glacial rivers flowing out from underneath Skeiðarárjökull was such an obstacle to road building that it was only with the construction of a series of bridges here in 1975 that the Ringroad around Iceland was completed – prior to which, anyone living to the east had to travel to Reykjavík via inland roads or Akureyri. These bridges – including **Skeiðarárbrú**, Iceland's longest – had to be designed to cope with **jökulhlaups**, massive floods that erupt out from under Vatnajökull regularly and carry untold tonnes of boulders, gravel, ice and water before them. One cause of these is **Grænalón**, a lake formed by a short river whose outlet is blocked by the western side of Skeiðárarjökull, damming a two-hundred-metre-deep valley; every few years the lake fills enough to float the glacier dam wall and empties.

Far more destructive, however, is **Grímsvötn**, a crater lake above a smouldering volcano buried 400m under Vatnajökull's ice cap. Like Grænalón, Grímsvötn fills and empties every few years, but in October 1996 a force-five earthquake signalled abnormal activity under Vatnajökull and over the next few days the ice cap's surface gradually sagged and collapsed inwards to reveal a six-kilometre-long volcanic vent. For ten days the volcano erupted continuously, blowing steam, ash and smoke 6km into the sky, and melting enough ice to fill Grímsvotn. Then, at 8am on November 5, Grímsvötn suddenly drained out underneath Skeiðarárjökull, sending three billion litres of water spewing across Skeiðarársandur in a five-metre-high wave, sweeping away 7km of road and – despite design precautions – demolishing or badly damaging several bridges, including Skeiðarárbrú. Fourteen hours later the flood rate was peaking at 45,000 cubic metres per second, and when the waters subsided a day later, the *sandur* was dotted with house-sized chunks of ice ripped off the front of Skeiðarárjökull. Aside from the barren scenery, there's very little evidence for any of this today – the ice has long gone and the bridges are repaired – though if you're heading to Skaftafell, look out for the twisted remains of the original Skeiðarárbrú, which are on display by the roadside.

Núpsstaðarskógur, a highly scenic valley with sheer cliffs and twisted glacial streams stretching 15km north along the side of the glacier towards Grænalón. You'll need a high-clearance four-wheel-drive to negotiate the fords on the way in, so it's best to line up transport for camping, or join a tour from *Hvoll* (see below).

Back on the Ringroad and just west of the **Núpsstaðarskógur** turning at the foot of Lómagnúpur, have a quick look at **Núpsstaður**, a neat line of **turf-covered buildings** including an eighteenth-century stone farmhouse and an older church. This was once considered the most remote place in all Iceland: before Höfn existed, the closest ports were at Djúpivogur and Eyrarbakki near Selfoss, and so anyone wanting to shift their goods around had to first load them onto a pack-horse and head inland via the Fjallabak region. The buildings themselves are fairly unremarkable, but the stark location evokes the hardships of farm life in Iceland a century ago. There's summer-only **accommodation** about 5km further west and south off the road at *Hvoll* (☎487 4785, @hvoll@hostel.is; sleeping-bag accommodation 2600kr), an IYHA hostel with a kitchen, where you can arrange day-trips to Núpsstaðarskógur.

Past Núpsstaður, the scenery changes quickly as you finally leave Vatnajökull behind, hugging a band of low cliffs inland fronted by rounded hummocks rising over grassland and decayed lavafields, though *sandurs* still persist to the south. Around 15km along at **Foss**, you can see how the cliffs were pressed down under the weight of now vanished ice, with a thin waterfall falling over the lowest edge above the farm. Across the road, a short walking track from a parking area circuits a pile of twisted hexagonal trachyte known as **Dverghammrar**, the Dwarf Cliffs, whose form indicates rapid and uneven cooling.

Kirkjubæjarklaustur, Lakagígar and around

The only place of any size between Höfn and Vík, **KIRKJUBÆJARKLAUSTUR** is best used as a base from which to launch an assault on nearby attractions. The tiny township sits at the foot of an escarpment on the **Skaftá**, whose circuitous path originates on the western side of Vatnajökull and is flanked by lavafields from eruptions by **Lakagígar** in 1783, centred some 75km to the northwest (see below).

Kirkjubæjarklaustur (the tongue-twisting name indicates a now-vanished convent) has had religious associations since Irish monks set up camp here before the Settlement; a **Benedictine convent** was later established in 1186, though two of its nuns had the misfortune to be burned at the stake for heresy. But it was during the Lakagígar eruptions that the town's church achieved national fame: as lava flows edged into the town, the pastor, **Jón Steingrímsson**, delivered what became known as the "Fire Sermon", and the lava halted. The modern **church**, sided in granite slabs halfway down Kirkjubæjarklaustur's single street, has an unusual facade resembling a ski lodge. It's possible to climb the escarpment behind by means of a chain, and from the top there's a fine view southwest over Landbrot, a collection of a thousand-odd **pseudocraters** (for more on these, see p.332), formed when lava flowed over a lake during another eruption in 950. For a final geological hit, walk a kilometre or so along the road heading north from town, to where you'll find a field paved in a small cross section of hexagonal basalt "tiles" known as **Kirkjugólf**, or "Church Floor".

Kirkjubæjarklaustur practicalities

Kirkjubæjarklaustur is more or less a single street stretching for 500m west off the highway as it kinks over the river; first comes the **bus stop** and fuel station, then a tiny complex containing a **bank** (with ATM), **post office** and **supermarket** (Mon–Sat 9am–9pm). Past this is the church, with a **tourist information** office (☎487 4620, ⒲ www.klaustur.is; mid-June to Aug daily 10am–3pm) opposite, though it's not of great use. Kirkjubæjarklaustur's **campsite** (☎487 4612; 750kr), with toilets and showers, is behind the shopping complex, while the Icelandair-run *Hótel Klaustur* (☎487 4900, ⒲ www.icehotel.is; ❸) is up past the information office at Klausturvegur 6, with the **pool** (Mon–Thurs 10am–7pm, Fri 10am–8.30pm, Sat & Sun noon–4pm; 300kr) behind. For **meals**, head to *Systrakaffi* in the complex, which serves expensive pizzas (from 2100kr) and an assortment of snacks and coffee – the fuel-station café is a poor alternative.

Buses (⒲ www.trex.is) head year-round in both directions along the Ringroad. From mid-June until early September you can also pick up day trips running from Skaftafell to **Lakagígar** (see below) and **Fjallabak** buses heading inland to Eldgjá and Landmannalaugar (see p.123).

Lakagígar

Reached off the highway along a 45-kilometre jeep track some 5km west of Kirkjubæjarklaustur, **Lakagígar** – the Laki Craters – are evidence of the most catastrophic volcanic event in Iceland's recorded history. In June 1783, the earth here split into a 25-kilometre-long **fissure** that, over the next seven months, poured out a continuous thick blanket of poisonous ash and smoke and enough lava to cover six hundred square kilometres. So thick were the ash clouds that they reached as far as northern Europe, where they caused poor harvests; in Iceland, however, there were no harvests at all, and livestock dropped dead, poisoned by eating fluorine-tainted grass. Over the next three years Iceland's population plummeted by a quarter – through starvation, earthquakes and an outbreak of smallpox – to just 38,000 people, at which point the Danish government considered evacuating the survivors to Jutland.

A succession of difficult river crossings means that you can only get to Lakagígar on **tours** (⒲ www.re.is, ☎580 5400), which run daily through July and August from Skaftafell via Kirkjubæjarklaustur. It's certainly worth the journey to see the succession of low, black craters surrounded by a still sterile landscape, though the flows themselves are largely covered in a carpet of thick, spongy green moss. Pick of the scenery is on the journey in at **Fagrifoss**, the Beautiful Falls, and the view from atop Laki itself (818m), which takes in an incomprehensible expanse of lava.

West to Vík
As you head west out of Kirkjubærjarklaustur, a big orange sign warns of sandstorms.Once past the Landbrot pseudo-crater fields and the Lakagígar road, you head over the dismal **Eldhraun** – another of Laki's lava legacies – for the final 60km to Vík and the southwest. It's not an exciting journey: around 23km along you pass Eystriásar farm, which marks the eastern end of the Fjallabak route through the southern Interior via Landmannalaugur (see p.123), after which Vík is a brief drive away across the equally eventless Mýrdalssandur.

Travel details

Buses

Buses run along the Ringroad between Reykjavík and Höfn and between Egilsstaðir and Akureyri year-round; the service is daily from June until August, with a restricted service at other times. Between September and May – when Ringroad services terminate at Höfn and Egilsstaðir – there are no buses between these two places. We have shown the winter/summer frequencies below separated by /.
Breiðdalsvík to: Djúpivogur (3 weekly/1 daily; 1hr); Egilsstaðir (3 weekly/1 daily; 2hr); Fáskrúðs-fjörður (daily; 50min); Höfn (3 weekly/1 daily; 2hr 15min); Stöðvarfjörður (daily; 20min).
Djúpivogur to: Breiðdalsvík (3 weekly/1 daily; 1hr); Egilsstaðir (3 weekly/1 daily; 2hr 20min); Höfn (3 weekly/1 daily; 1hr 15min).
Egilsstaðir to: Akureyri (4 weekly/1 daily; 4hr); Breiðdalsvík (3 weekly/1 daily; 2hr); Djúpivogur (3 weekly/1 daily; 2hr 20min); Eskifjörður (daily; 45min); Fáskrúðsfjörður (daily; 1hr 10min); Höfn (3 weekly/1 daily; 3hr 45min); Neskaupstaður (daily; 1hr 10min); Reyðarfjörður (daily; 30min); Seyðisfjörður (3 daily; 25min); Stöðvarfjörður (daily; 1hr 40min).
Eskifjörður to: Egilsstaðir (daily; 45min); Neskaup-staður (2 daily; 25min); Reyðarfjörður (2 daily; 15min).
Fáskrúðsfjörður to: Breiðdalsvík (daily; 50min); Egilsstaðir (daily; 1hr 10min); Stöðvarfjörður (daily; 30min).
Höfn to: Breiðdalsvík (3 weekly/1 daily; 2hr 15min); Djúpivogur (3 weekly/1 daily; 1hr 15min); Egilsstaðir (1 daily; 3hr 45min); Jökulsárlón (3 weekly/1 daily; 1hr 30min); Kirkjubæjarklaustur (3 weekly/1 daily; 3hr); Reykjavík (3 weekly/1 daily; 8hr 30min); Selfoss (3 weekly/1 daily; 7hr 30min);

Skaftafell (3 weekly/1 daily; 2hr 40min); Skógar (3 weekly/1 daily; 5hr 45min); Vík (3 weekly/1 daily; 3hr 50min).
Kirkjubæjarklaustur to: Höfn (3 weekly/1 daily; 3hr); Jökulsárlón (3 weekly/1 daily; 2hr); Reykjavík (3 weekly/1 daily; 6hr 30min); Selfoss (3 weekly/1 daily; 5hr 30min); Skaftafell (3 weekly/1 daily; 1hr 5min); Skógar (3 weekly/1 daily; 2hr); Vík (3 weekly/1 daily; 1hr 20min).
Neskaupstaður to: Egilsstaðir (daily; 1hr 10min); Eskifjörður (2 daily; 25min); Reyðarfjörður (2 daily; 35min).
Reyðarfjörður to: Egilsstaðir (daily; 30min); Eskifjörður (daily; 15min); Neskaupstaður (2 daily; 35min).
Seyðisfjörður to: Egilsstaðir (3 daily; 25min).
Skaftafell to: Höfn (3 weekly/1 daily; 2hr 40min); Kirkjubærjarklaustur (3 weekly/1 daily; 1hr 5min); Reykjavík (3 weekly/1 daily; 5hr 30min); Selfoss (3 weekly/1 daily; 4hr 30min); Skógar (3 weekly/1 daily; 3hr 50min); Vík (3 weekly/1 daily; 2hr 20min).
Stöðvarfjörður to: Breiðdalsvík (daily; 20min); Egilsstaðir (daily; 1hr 40min); Fáskrúðsfjörður (daily; 30min).

Flights

Egilsstaðir to: Reykjavík (daily; 1hr).
Höfn to: Reykjavík (daily; 55min).

Ferries

The *Norröna* ferry operates all year but the frequencies and times below apply between mid-May and mid-September.
Seyðisfjörður to: Hanstholm, Denmark (weekly, 2 days); Tórshavn, Faroe Islands (weekly, 16hr).

8

The Interior

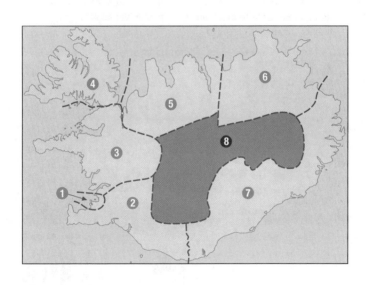

CHAPTER 8 # Highlights

✳ **Sprengisandur** The classic Interior trip, to where outlaws were once banished – an unremittingly bleak and barren desert stretching to a horizon tipped with ice caps. See p.314

✳ **Hveravellir** Unexpected splash of green and a bathable hot spring in the middle of the wilderness, and a great place to break an Interior traverse. See p.315

✳ **Askja** Massive caldera rimmed by rough, snowy peaks, where you can swim in a flooded crater, the remnants of a colossal eruption in 1875. See p.317

✳ **Kverkfjöll** Extremely remote and difficult-to-reach ice caves, hollowed out by hot springs welling up under the northwestern edge of the mighty Vatnajökull ice cap. See p.318

▲ Hiking on Kverkfjöll

The Interior

Nothing you might see elsewhere in Iceland prepares you for the stark, desolate, raw beauty of the barren upland plateau (500–900m) that is the **Interior** (known in Icelandic as *hálendið* or "highlands"), Europe's last true wilderness. The strength and unpredictability of the elements here means that the country's heart is a desolate and uninhabited place, with no towns or villages, just cinematic vistas of seemingly infinite plains, glacial rivers and lavafields punctuated only by ice caps, volcanoes and jagged mountains, all reminiscent of lunar landscapes – this is, after all, where the *Apollo* **astronauts** came to train for their moon landing. Sheep are virtually the only living things that manage to survive here, but pasture and vegetation, where they do exist, comprise only scattered clumps of ragged grass, and it's a daunting task for the farmers who venture out into this no-man's-land to round up their livestock every autumn.

Historically, routes through the Interior were forged in Viking times as a shortcut for those making the journey on horseback to the annual law-making sessions at Þingvellir, though the region later provided refuge – if you can call it that – for **outlaws**, who are said to have been pardoned in the unlikely event that they managed to survive here for twenty years. Today, with the advent of the Ringroad and direct flights to Reykjavík from all corners of the country, the need to traverse this area has long gone, and there are **no roads**, just tracks (the main ones are listed on p.314) marked by stakes, and hardly any bridges across the rivers, causing some hairy moments when they are forded. The **weather**, too, is Iceland at its most elemental. Not only can fierce winds whip up the surface layer of loose grit in a matter of seconds, turning a beautiful sunny spell into a blinding haze of sand and dirt, but snowstorms are common even in July and August – the summer here is very short indeed, barely a matter of weeks, the winter long and severe, when the tracks are blocked by deep snowdrifts and closed to traffic. Every year, the Interior claims victims through drownings, snowstorms or simple disappearance.

Of all the various tracks, only two **Interior routes** actually cross the whole way between north and south Iceland. The most dramatically barren of these is **Sprengisandur** (F26), which leads from the Þjórsá, east of Selfoss, to the Bárðardalur valley between Akureyri and Lake Mývatn – it's also possible to approach Sprengisandur from Skagafjörður on the F752 and from Akureyri on the F821. The alternative is **Kjölur** (Route 35), from Gullfoss to the Blöndudalur valley south of Blönduós, which has less dramatic scenery but is the only route on which you might be able to use normal cars. Other routes lead into the Interior but don't offer a complete traverse: there's the western **Kaldidalur** route (F550) between Borgafjörður and Þingvellir (see box, p.106); east of Lake Mývatn, the F88 follows

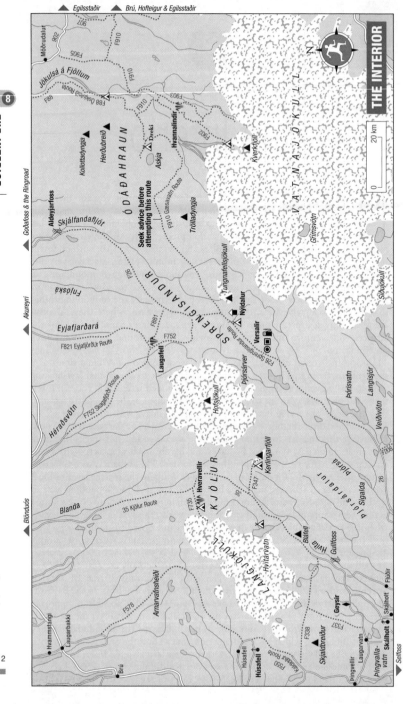

Móðrudalur

F905

907

F910

F910

F910

Jökulsá á Fjöllum

F88 Öskjuleið Route

F903

F910

F902

Dreki

Hvannalindir

Askja

Kverkfjöll

ÓÐÁÐAHRAUN

Herðubreið

Kollóttadyngja

V A T N A J Ö K U L L

Aldeyjarfoss

Skjálfandafljót

Seek advice before
attempting this route

F910 Gæsavatn Route

Trölladyngja

Grímsvötn

Síðujökull

Fnjóská

26

S P R E N G I S A N D U R

Tungnafellsjökull

F881

Eyjafjarðará

F821 Eyjafjörður Route

Nýidalur

F752

Versalir

F752 Skagafjörður Route

Laugafell

F24 Sprengisandur Route

Héraðsvötn

Hofsjökull

Þjórsárver

Þórisvatn

Langisjór

Veiðivötn

Blanda

35 Kjölur Route

Hveravellir

K J Ö L U R

F735

F347

Kerlingarfjöll

35

Þjórsá

Sigalda

26

F208

Þórisvatn

Arnarvatnsheiði

F578

L A N G J Ö K U L L

Hvítárvatn

Bláfell

Hvítá

Gullfoss

Hvammstangi

Laugarbakki

Húsafell

F550

F338

Skjaldbreiður

F337

Geysir

Skálholt

Brú

Þingvellir

Þingvalla-
vatn

Laugarvatn

Flúðir

N

20 km

0

the course of the mighty Jökulsá á Fjöllum south to the **Askja caldera**, from near where the F902 continues towards **Kverkfjöll**; heading inland from Egilsstaðir, the recently sealed Route 910 heads towards **Snæfell** (en route to Karahnjúkar, see p.286), before becoming the F910 and kinking northwest to join the F88, while the **Fjallabak route** runs behind the south coast's ice caps (see box, p.123).

The Interior is best traversed in safety on **bus tours**, though even then it's a bumpy ride. Should you decide instead to cross the Interior under your own steam, it's essential to be properly prepared before departure; note too that the majority of routes are fully accessible only by **four-wheel-drives**, and that when on them, you should stick to them: off-road driving is not only illegal, but carries substantial fines and does irreparable damage to the land.

Bus tours and tickets

There are four main **bus tours** across the Interior in summer. All the trips listed below last a day unless otherwise stated, though it is possible to hop off the buses at any of their stops – there's at least one hut and campsite on each route – and get back on another service another day. Unless otherwise stated, all the **fares** below are one-way.

From early July to late August three buses every week cross between Reykjavík and Mývatn via **Sprengisandur** (Reykjavík–Landmannalaugar 5,500kr; Landmannalaugar–Mývatn 9,000kr) in two stages, overnighting at Landmannalaugar's hot springs (see p.123), where you might have to camp. The more straightforward day-trip between Reykjavík and Akureyri over **Kjölur** runs daily from late June until August (Ⓦwww.trex.is or Ⓦwww.sba.is; 9,900kr). Round-trips to **Askja** leave from Mývatn on Monday, Wednesday and Friday from late June to mid-July and the last two weeks of August, with daily services from mid-July to mid-August (Ⓦwww.askjatours.is; 14,000kr). Lastly, a three-day excursion to **Kverkfjöll** runs out of Mývatn, Akureyri and Húsavík every Monday from early July until late August, and includes two nights' accommodation and a day's walking on a glacier (Ⓦwww.sba.is; 25,000kr round trip).

Self-driving, cycling and hiking

Any self-driving, cycling or hiking trip through the Interior must be carefully planned and considered. Never underestimate the extreme conditions, climatic and geological, which you may encounter en route. Read the relevant sections in Basics on pp.34–35, especially regarding **weather** and **road conditions**, and take everything you'll need with you, including a **compass** – at times it can be difficult to determine a route where several sets of car tracks meet.

Driving, check your **car insurance** policy, as four-wheel-drives aren't usually covered for breakdowns when crossing rivers and most rental cars are not allowed to cross the Interior at all, even via the relatively easy Kjölur route. **Essential equipment** for drivers includes a tow rope, shovel, basic spare parts – and a rudimentary knowledge of how the engine works. It's best to travel in groups of two or more vehicles, and remember to carry plenty of **fuel**, as consumption in low-range gears can be half as much again as on well-surfaced roads. Never venture from the marked tracks – the off-road tyre marks you'll see here and there, made by illegal off-roaders, take years to heal and only worsen the country's uphill struggle against soil erosion. Don't expect to find many bridges either – you'll need some previous experience of tackling glacial river crossings before you set out.

The only Interior route that **cyclists and hikers** can tackle unaided is the Kjölur track, since there are no rivers to wade through while heavily laden with packs and cycles, and the terrain is less severe. If you are planning on using other routes, you'll have to hitch rides over the more difficult rivers with passing

Average opening dates of Interior routes	
These **official opening times** for routes can vary according to the weather.	
Askja/Öskjuleið (F88) June 20	**Kjölur** (35) June 20
Eyjafjörður (F821) July 20	**Kverkfjöll** (F902) June 20
Fjallabaksleið (F208) July 2	**Skagafjörður** (F752) July 14
Landmannalaugar–Eldgjá (F208) July 2	**Sprengisandur** (F26) June 29
Kaldidalur (F550) June 15	

transport, so will probably spend longer on your journey than you intended – making it all the more vital that you carry excess food and water.

Overnight huts and camping

The mainstay of accommodation in the Interior is the network of **overnight huts**, or *sæluhús*, open all year and run by Ferdafélag Íslands, the Touring Club of Iceland (see p.45). Marked on maps of the Interior, the huts are very busy during summer, and it's essential to book them well in advance. Although they differ – the better ones have self-catering facilities and running water – you'll always need to bring your own sleeping bag and all sleeping space is in dorms. The huts are located in two main areas in the Interior: south and east of Langjökull, on and close to the Kjölur route; and north of Vatnajökull around Askja and Kverkfjöll. We've given contact numbers in the guide text; costs are around 2500kr per person per night.

If you're **camping** make sure to take enough tent pegs with you to anchor down your tent since the wind that howls uninterrupted across the Interior plain can be truly ferocious – among seasoned Iceland-travellers, tales of blown-away tents are alarmingly common. **Campsites** (around 750kr), some of which have running water, are at Hveravellir and Hvítárnes, for the Kjölur route; at Nýidalur, for the Sprengisandur route; and at Herðubreiðarlindir, Dyngjufjöll (Dreki) and Kverk-fjöll, on the Askja and Kverkfjöll routes.

Across Sprengisandur: the F26

Featuring the most desolate terrain found in Iceland, the **Sprengisandur** trip runs from Reykjavík to Mývatn, initially taking the Ringroad to Hella before turning inland and following the course of the Ytri-Rangá river. The Interior section of this route, from Sigalda to Godafoss, covers 244km. On coach trips, you pass within 10km of the foot of Hekla near **Þórisvatn**, a lake whose waters find their outlet in the Þjórsá river and feed a hydroelectric power station. After this, the route climbs into the stony highlands between Hofsjökull and the western edge of the mighty Vatnajökull, which mark the beginning of Sprengisandur proper, an incredible journey through mile after mile of grey sand, stones and rocks that have lain untouched for thousands of years. The enduring image is of nothingness: the glaciers and mountains that fringe the desolation seem a long way off.

Glacial rivers are periodically crossed until you reach **Nýidalur**, where the route's sole **campsite** and **hut** (July & August only; ☎854 1194) occupies a lonely, cold and windswept spot at 800m, right on the base of **Tungnafellsjökull**'s tiny, isolated ice cap. The Nýidalur valley leads southeast around the glacier from here towards Vatnajökull, only 20km distant; while well away to the west below Hofsjökull are the **Þjórsárver** wetlands, breeding ground of many of the world's population of pink-footed geese.

Three kilometres past Nýidalur comes the turn for the **Gæsavatn route** (F910), which weaves its way over some quite appalling terrain and through an alarming number of rivers, around the north of Vatnajökull, to meet the F88 to Askja. Get local advice if you're thinking of taking this route, and only travel in convoy. Otherwise, the F26 continues due north across Sprengisandur to the grey waters of **Fjórðungsvatn**, which marks the turn for the F752 Skagafjörður route, via the **Laugafell** hot springs and overnight hut (☎462 2720), to Varmahlíd and the Ringroad. Then, slowly, the Sprengisandur route gains traces of green, passing a blaze of twisted basalt columns and lively waterfall at **Aldeyjarfoss** before descending into the Bárðardalur valley, whose scattered farms seem positively lively after hours spent looking at barren waste. The road down from Bárðardalur hits the Ringroad close to Goðafoss, where coaches turn right for Mývatn. Allow at least eight hours if you're driving Sprengisandur yourself – which is nothing compared with the week it took for the first car to traverse it in 1933.

Across Kjölur: Route 35

Kjölur (also known as Kjalvegur) is the more direct of the two inland routes between north and south Iceland, and the one known for longest: its discovery is recorded in the *Book of Settlements*. Considered safer than Sprengisandur, though abandoned for a while after the death of a large party in 1780, it qualifies as a highway if any Interior route can claim to be, with buses, coaches, four-wheel-drives and even ordinary family sedans bouncing along it during the summer months. But beware before risking your own (or a hire) car, as Kjölur's rough gravel surface is still quite capable of shredding tyres, tearing off exhausts and puncturing sumps: keep your speed down, especially if driving conventional, low-slung vehicles. The unsealed section, from the Ringroad near Blönduós south through to Gullfoss, is around 200km; if driving yourself, allow at least five hours.

To Hveravellir

Turning off the Ringroad some 30km east from Blönduós, you head south past a power station into an area of moorland and lakes, with ice caps and black-streaked mountains ahead, which soon cedes to the Interior's classic vistas of grey sands and stones. For much of its duration, the route follows the line of barbed-wire fencing erected to keep the sheep from the west separate from those in the east and restrict the spread of disease (someone is actually employed to ride back and forth along the fence to check that it hasn't been breached). **Kjölur** itself, the highest point on the route, is a broad rocky pass between the massive ices heets of Langjökull and Hofsjökull. Here the F735 leads around 2km west to a grassy depression in the landscape at **Hveravellir hot springs**, where you'll find a campsite and well-appointed overnight 🏠 **huts** (⊕ www.hveravellir.is). The only bathable **pool** is a small, waist-deep affair next to one of the huts, above which boardwalks head up a calcified slope to where hotter springs, encrusted with sulphur, bubble, belch and occasionally erupt violently. One of these is named **Eyvindarhver**, after the outlaw Eyvindur (see p.317) who lived here for two years and used the spring to boil up sheep for his dinner. In summer, the springs can get busy, so try to time your dip to avoid scheduled daily bus arrivals in the early afternoon – or stay overnight and have the springs almost to yourself.

Hveravellir to Gullfoss and Reykjavík

South of here the road runs rougher as it passes between **Hofsjökull** to the east, whose ice cap presses down on a black plateau, and Hrútfell, an outpost of Langjökull.

The Kjölurvegur trek

The **Kjölurvegur** trek is an excellent two- to three-day hike from Hveravellir to the glacial lake of Hvítárvatn, following the original Kjölur route that ran west of the present Route 35, hugging the slopes of **Langjökull**: it's punctuated by overnight huts roughly four to six hours' walk apart. From the springs, follow the F735 west towards the glacier and after roughly 14km, at the *Þjófadalir* overnight hut, the jeep track peters out into a walking path as it swings southeast, around the tiny Hrútfell glacier, for another overnight hut at *Þverbrekknamúli*. From here, it's a further straightforward hike of around four to six hours to reach the *Hvítárnes* hut, an idyllic if somewhat lonely place to break the journey – the hut is supposedly haunted by a young woman who lived hereabouts when the area was farmed, though only men who sleep in a certain bed in the hut will see her, apparently. From the hut, it's an easy eight-kilometre walk back to Route 35 and the bus to either Reykjavík or Akureyri passing the beautiful **Hvítárvatn** glacial lake, at the foot of Langjökull, on the way.

Around 28km south of the Hveravellir junction, the F347 heads 10km southeast to the tumble of peaks at **Kerlingarfjöll**, where there's 🏠 **accommodation** from June 15 until September 30 (☎852 5132, 🌐www.kerlingarfjoll.is; camping 750k, sleeping-bag accommodation 2500kr, chalet beds 6000kr) and a **restaurant**.

Continuing down Route 35 the road runs closer to Langjökull and **Hvítarvatn**, stage on the Kjölurvegur (see box below) and source of the Hvítá, which flows down to Gullfoss. Heathland surrounding the lakeshore is said to harbour some ninety species of Alpine plant, and you can often see **icebergs**, calved off the front of the Norðurjökull glacier, floating in the serene, pale-blue lake. Once across a substantial **bridge** over the river's headwaters, the road climbs up beside **Bláfell** and then you're suddenly on a plateau with a view extending southwest over green river plains almost to the sea. The road improves, too, and it's only a further 25km downhill run from here to **Gullfoss**, whose spray is visible in the distance like a puff of smoke. Tours pause briefly at Gullfoss (see p.114), Geysir (see p.113) and often Þingvellir (see p.106) on the way to Reykjavík, fitting in these Golden Circle attractions.

Herðubreið and Askja: the F88

The 1682-metre-high, crownlike formation of **Herðubreið** towers over the surrounding **Ódáðahraun** (Desert of Misdeeds), a featureless lavafield north of Vatnajökull. You can get within a few kilometres of the mountain on the F88 Askja route (Öskjuleið in Icelandic), which leaves the Ringroad not far east of Mývatn and heads south, via Herðubreið, to **Askja**, a vast flooded caldera in the middle of the lavafield.

To Herðubreið

Marked by wooden posts and tyre tracks weaving off across the usual black gravel plains, the F88 initially follows the west bank of the glacial **Jökulsá á Fjöllum** (see p.268) until reaching **Herðubreiðarlindir**, an oasis of poor grass and hot springs between the river and Herðubreið, where there's a **campsite** and overnight **hut** with kitchen and toilets (☎462 2720). On the edge of the encircling lava, a small stream wells out through a wall of lava blocks that conceal **Eyvindur's cave**, said to have been inhabited by this resourceful outlaw during the harsh winter of 1774–75. During this time he survived on dried horsemeat and the bitter roots of angelica plants, which grow in profusion nearby – he always considered this the worst experience of his entire twenty years on the run (see box below).

Other sights in the area include a small gorge along the river some 6km upstream; and **Herðubreið** itself, a brown, snow-streaked cone whose base is about 5km west over the lava – a surprisingly tiring hike over what appears to be flat ground – with a difficult trail to the **summit** from the west side. A third option is a two-day **hike to Askja**: from the hut, follow the path around the mountain until it meets the trail up to the summit, then turn due west, away from the mountain, heading for the shield volcano of **Kollóttadyngja**, where there's an overnight hut *Bræðrafell* (bookings ☏ 462 2720) – allow roughly six hours to cover the 17km here from Herðubreiðarlindir. The route on the second day (20km; 6hr) leads due south from Bræðrafell across the lava to the foot of the Askja caldera and the overnight hut at Drekagil (see below).

Herðubreið to Askja

Back on the F88, the tracks veers west away from the river towards the black and contorted **Dyngjufjöll** mountains which rim Askja's eastern edge. There's another basic **cabin** and campsite here at **Drekagil** (bookings ☏ 462 2720), a small, rough canyon which you can follow for a short way, then the track continues for a final 8km to a walking track to Askja itself. **Askja** is a partially flooded, eight-kilometre-wide crater formed from a collapsed subterranean magma chamber, source of the prehistoric outflows which drained out over the land and caused the grim and forbidding surrounds. There have been more recent eruptions, too: in 1875, a colossal explosion here vapourized two cubic kilometres of rock with such force that dust and gravel fell on Denmark; land between here and the coast at Vopnafjörður was buried under drifts of yellow pumice up to two metres deep, which poisoned the soil and sterilized the region – some two thousand local farmers emigrated to Canada as a result. The last big outflow of lava here was in the 1960s, and it's over this that you walk up into the caldera and south to the 217-metre-deep lake, **Öskuvatn**, which half-fills Askja.

Eyvindur and Halla

Iceland's most famous **outlaws** since saga times were the seventeenth-century **Eyvindur** and his harsh-tempered wife, **Halla**. They are the only Icelandic outlaws to have managed twenty years on the run, thus earning themselves a pardon; many places around Iceland are named after Eyvindur, showing just how much he had to keep moving.

Once on the run, Eyvindur and Halla abandoned their farm in the West Fjords and set up at Hveravellir (see p.315), robbing travellers and stealing sheep from nearby properties. Eventually chased on by a vengeful posse, they shifted south to the Þjórsá west of Hekla for a few years – the easiest time of his outlawry, so Eyvindur later said – then to remoter pastures on the Sprengisandur, which at that time hadn't been crossed for many years. Caught after stealing a horse, Eyvindur and Halla were held at Mývatn's church, from where Eyvindur managed to escape by asking to be untied so that he could pray. As luck would have it, a thick fog came down and he was able to hide nearby until people had given up looking for him, thinking him far away. He then stole another horse and rode it south to Herðubreiðarlindir (see p.316), where he somehow survived an appalling winter in a "cave" he built into the lava here. Later on, he met Halla again and they drifted around the country, always just managing to evade capture but forced by hunger or pursuit to kill their infant children. Tradition has it that after being pardoned they returned to their farm, where they died in the late seventeenth century.

On Askja's north shore, **Viti** is a smaller flooded crater marking the site of the 1875 catastrophe, before which the vent was described by one local traveller as "a complete Devil's cauldron from which all living things fly; horses quake with mortal fear and can hardly stand when taken to the brink". It's more docile today; you can scramble down its steep sides, dotted with sulphur springs, to bathe in the opaque blue-white waters, which can be a little tepid sometimes but perfect for a quick dip.

From Askja, the F910 wiggles around the northern flank of Vatnajökull to join the F26 Sprengisandur route north of Nýidalur (see p.314), but this should only be driven in convoy and after seeking local advice.

Routes to Kverkfjöll

The main route to the ice-covered Kverkfjöll begins by turning south off the Ringroad halfway between Lake Mývatn and Vopnafjörður, and following Route 901 for 8km to tiny **Möðrudalur**. Twenty kilometres south of Möðrudalur, the route links up with the F910, leading over the Kreppá, which is bridged, to the junctions with the F902 and F903. The latter leads to the hot springs of **Hvann-alindir**, an oasis where the outlaw Eyvindur fashioned a rough shelter using lava blocks around a hollow on the edge of the lavafield. He also built a sheep pen with a covered passageway to the nearby stream, so the animals could drink without being spotted and hence not give away his location. Both can still be found but are well concealed, as Eyvindur intended.

Beyond the springs, route F903 joins up with its neighbour to the north, the F902, before reaching **Kverkfjöll** via a maze of ash hills. There's a campsite and an **overnight hut** here (☎853 6236) overlooking the braided streams of the Jökulsá á Fjöllum's upper reaches. Low white clouds hover overhead during the long hard slog up the dormant volcano, which erupted to devastating effect in the fifteenth century, and once at the top these are revealed to be steam issuing from deep fissures in the ice. Nearby sulphur springs, hissing like boiling kettles, prevent ice from forming in their immediate area and the bare yellow earth is in stark contrast to the surroundings. The outstanding views from the glacier take in the entire expanse of Ódáðahraun lavafield, the Dyngjufjöll mountains, Herðubreið mountains, and even the jagged peaks that mark the distant northern coast.

Jökulsá á Fjöllum rises from hot springs under Vatnajökull, and its heat forms an **ice cave**, 5km from the hut. Some daylight penetrates a few metres into the cave, but visibility rapidly diminishes in the thick, damp fog that fills it. The walls and roof are sculpted by constantly dripping water, and the debris embedded in the ice gives a marbled effect. Be warned, however, that entering ice caves is always **dangerous**, due to the possibility of cave-ins. Not far from here the slopes of the glacier are climbable, but they shouldn't be attempted without a guide.

Travel details

Buses

Akureyri to: Reykjavík, via Kjölur (1 daily late June to Aug; 9hr).

Mývatn to: Askja (3 weekly late June to Aug, daily mid-July to mid-Aug; 12hr return); Kverkfjöll

(1 weekly early July to late Aug; 3 days return); Reykjavík, via Sprengisandur (three weekly early July to late Aug; 2 days).

Reykjavík to: Akureyri, via Kjölur (1 daily late June to Aug; 9hr); Mývatn, via Sprengisandur (three weekly early July to late Aug; 2 days).

Contexts

Contexts

History

I celand is not only one of the more geologically recent places on earth, it was also among the last to be colonized. European seafarers may have known that something lay out beyond Scotland as far back as 300 BC, when the historian Pytheas of Marseille wrote about "Ultima Thule" – possibly Iceland – a northern land on the edge of a frozen ocean, where it never became dark in summer.

It wasn't until considerably later, however, that Iceland was regularly visited by outsiders, let alone settled, and it's still unclear who might have been the first to try. Whoever they were, the first arrivals would have found the country much the same as it appears today, but well forested with willow and birch, and with no large animals.

Discovery

Much of the uncertainty in deciding who discovered Iceland, and when it happened, is down to the lack of archeological and written records. **Roman** coins from around 300 AD, found at several sites along Iceland's south coast, provide the earliest evidence of visitors, and suggest that ships from Britain – which was then a Roman colony and just a week's sail away – made landfall here from time to time. These coins could have been brought in at a later date, however, and no other Roman artefacts or camps have been found. Similarly, the age of a **Norse** homestead on Heimaey in the Westman Islands is disputed; archeologists date it to the seventh century, but medieval Icelandic historians – accurate enough in other matters – state that it was founded two hundred years later. It is also believed that by the late eighth century **Irish** monks, having already colonized the Faroes, were visiting Iceland regularly, seeking solitude and, according to contemporary accounts, believing that they had rediscovered Pytheas' Ultima Thule. Oral tradition and place names link them to certain spots around the country – such as Papey, "Monks' Island" in the east – but they left no hard evidence behind them and were driven out over the next century by new invaders, the **Vikings**.

Vikings were Scandinavian adventurers, armed with the fastest ships of the time and forced by politics and a land shortage at home to seek their fortune overseas through war and piracy. They had already exploded into Britain and Ireland in the 790s, which is why Irish monks had sought out Iceland as a more peaceful place to live. Though a few Vikings may have been Christian, the majority believed in the **Norse gods**, the Æsir, which included Óðinn, the creator of mankind; his wild and adventurous hammer-wielding son Þór; and Freyr, the god of fertility and farming. The Æsir themselves were children of the first beings, the Giants, who had also created dwarfs and elves; they lived above the world in Ásgarður, where the great hall Valhalla housed the souls of Champions, men killed in warfare. The Champions awaited Ragnarok, when they would join the Æsir in a final massive battle against the Frost Giants, in which the world would be totally destroyed. Fearsome in battle, honour was everything to the Vikings, and the faintest slur could start a century-long blood feud between families.

According to tradition, the Vikings came across Iceland by accident when a certain mid-ninth-century freebooter named **Naddoddur** lost his way to the Faroes and landed on the eastern coast of what he called **Snæland**, or Snowland. He didn't stay long, but his reports of this new country were followed up by the

Swede **Garðar Svavarsson**, who circumnavigated Iceland in around 860, wintering at modern-day Húsavík in the northeast, where two of his slaves escaped and may have settled. At about the same time, **Flóki Vilgerðarson** left his home in Norway intending to colonize Snæland, which he was led to by following his pet ravens – hence his other name, Hrafna-Flóki, Raven-Flóki. But a hard winter in the northwest killed all his livestock; climbing a mountain he saw a fjord on the other side choked with ice and, frustrated, he renamed the country **Ísland**, Iceland, and returned to Norway.

Settlement

Despite Flóki's experiences, the idea of so much free space proved tempting to two other Norwegians, **Ingólfur Arnarson** and his brother-in-law **Hjörleifur Hróðmarsson**, who had lost their own lands in Norway as compensation for killing the son of a local earl. Around 870 they set sail with their households and possessions for Iceland, intending to settle there permanently. When they came within sight of land, Ingólfur dedicated his wooden **seat-posts** – the cherished symbol of his being head of a household – to his gods and threw them overboard, vowing to found his new home at the spot where they washed up. While his slaves searched for them, Ingólfur spent three years exploring Iceland's southern coast, wintering first at Ingólfshöfði (near Skaftafell), Hjörleifshöfði (just east of Vík), and then at Ingólfsfjall (Selfoss). The posts were duly found in a southwestern bay and there Ingólfur built his homestead in 874, naming the place **Reykjavík** ("Smoky Bay") after the steam rising off nearby hot springs, and becoming Iceland's first official resident.

Although Hjörleifur had meanwhile been murdered by his own Irish slaves, things went well for Ingólfur and this attracted other migrants to Iceland, who spent the next sixty years snapping up vacant land in what has become known as the **Settlement**, or Landnám. These first Icelanders, who were mostly Norwegian, were primarily **farmers**, importing their pagan beliefs along with sheep, horses, and crops such as barley, while also clearing forests to create pasture and provide timber for buildings and ships. While it was available, a man could take as much land as he could light fires around in one day, while a woman could have the area she could lead a heifer around in the same time. Landowners became local **chieftains**, whose religious responsibilities earned them the title of *goðar*, or priests, and who sorted out their differences through negotiations at regional **assemblies** (*þing*) – or if these failed, by fighting. Conditions must have been very favourable compared to those in Norway, however, as by 930, when the last areas of the country were claimed, an estimated 60,000 people already lived in Iceland – a figure not exceeded until the nineteenth century.

The Commonwealth: 930–1262 AD

By the early tenth century, Iceland was firmly occupied and had begun to see itself as an independent nation in need of national government. The chieftains rejected the idea of a paramount leader, and instead decided, in 930, on a **Commonwealth** governed by a national assembly, or **Alþing**, which came to be held for two weeks every summer at **Þingvellir** in southwestern Iceland. Here laws were recited publicly by a **lawspeaker**, and disputes settled by four regional courts, with a supreme court formed early in the eleventh century. Legal settlement typically involved payment to the injured party or their family; the highest punishment was not death but being declared an **outlaw**, thus being exiled from Iceland. Courts had no power to enforce decisions, however, only make recommendations, and though they held great public authority, in practice their decisions could be ignored – something which was to undermine the Commonwealth in later years.

The first century of the Commonwealth was very much a golden era, however: the country was united, resources were rich, and farming profitable. This was the **Saga Age**, the time when the first generations of Icelanders were carving out great names for themselves in events that passed into oral lore and would only later be written down.

Contact with the outside world continued too, and – in the same way that Iceland itself was discovered – Icelandic seafarers came across their own new worlds. In 980, Eiríkur Þorvaldsson (better known in English as **Erik the Red**) was outlawed for killing his neighbour and sailed from the Westfjords to follow up earlier reports of land to the northwest. He found a barren, treeless coastline, then returned to Iceland to whip up support for colonizing what he called **Greenland** – a misleading name, chosen deliberately to arouse interest. Enough people were hooked to emigrate along with Eiríkur, and two settlements were founded in Western Greenland which lasted until the sixteenth century. And it was from Greenland that Eiríkur's son **Leifur Eiríksson** heard that land had been sighted even further west, and set sail around the year 1000 to discover Baffin Island, Labrador, and "**Vínland**", an as-yet unidentified area of the north American coast. A couple of attempts made by others to colonize these distant lands came to nothing, however, and America was then forgottenabout by Europeans until Columbus rediscovered it.

The Coming of Christianity

Meanwhile, the late tenth century had seen Norway convert to **Catholicism** under the fiery king **Ólafur Tryggvason**. Ólafur then sent the missionary **Þangbrand** to evangelize Iceland, where – despite having to physically battle strong resistance from pagan stalwarts – he baptized several influential chieftains. Back in Norway, Þangbrand's unfavourable reports infuriated Ólafur, who was only prevented from executing all Icelanders in the country by the Icelandic chieftain **Gizur the White**, who promised to champion the new religion at home. Gizur mustered his forces and rode to the Alþing in 1000, where civil war was only averted by the lawspeaker **Þorgeir**, who – having made pagan and Christian alike swear to accept his decision – chose Christianity as Iceland's official religion, though pagans were initially allowed to maintain their beliefs in private. Gizur the White's son **Ísleifur** became Iceland's first **bishop** in 1056, and his homestead at **Skálholt** near Þingvellir was made the bishop's seat, with a second, northern diocese founded in 1106 at **Hólar**.

The new religion brought gradual changes with it, notably the introduction in 1097 of **tithes** – property taxes – to fund churches. As their wealth increased, churches founded **monasteries** and **schools**, bringing education and the beginnings of **literature**: Iceland's laws were first written down in 1117; and in 1130 the church commissioned Ari the Learned to compile the **Íslendingabók**, a compendium of the Icelandic people and their lineages. Importantly, Ari wrote not in Latin, the usual language of education and the Church at the time, but in

Icelandic, an expression of national identity that was followed by almost all later Icelandic writers.

Collapse of the Commonwealth

Despite these benefits, several factors were beginning to undermine the Alþing's authority. During the twelfth century, for instance, life in Iceland became much tougher. The country's unstable geology made itself felt for the first time with the **eruption** of the volcano Hekla in southern Iceland in 1104, which buried around twenty farms. **Tree felling** had also become so extensive that there was no longer enough timber for ship building; the effects of subsequent **erosion** were compounded by overgrazing and the beginnings of a **"mini ice-age"**, which was to last until the late nineteenth century and caused Iceland's glaciers to expand over previously settled areas – all of which reduced available farmland and made the country dependent on **imports**.

Meanwhile, the tithes were dividing Iceland's formerly egalitarian society. With its taxes, the Church became rich and politically powerful, as did chieftains who owned Church lands or had become priests, and so took a share of the tithes. These chieftains formed a new elite group of **aristocrats**, who bought out their poorer neighbours and so concentrated land ownership, wealth and inherent political power in the hands of just a few clans. At the same time, in 1152 the Icelandic Church came under the jurisdiction of the **Archbishop of Nidaros** in Norway (modern-day Trondheim), giving the expansionist Norwegian throne a lever to start pressuring Iceland to accept its authority. Backed by the Archbishop and **Þorlákur Þórhallsson**, bishop at Skálholt from 1179 and later beatified as Iceland's first saint, the Church began to demand freedom from secular laws.

The Alþing's lack of effective power now became clear, as it proved unable to deal with the Church's demands, or the fighting that was breaking out between the six biggest clans as they battled for political supremacy. The period from 1220 is known as the **Sturlung Age** after the most powerful of these clans, led by the historian, lawspeaker and wily politician **Snorri Sturluson**. Travelling to Norway in 1218, Snorri became a retainer of King Hákon Hákonarson, and returned to Iceland in 1220 to promote Norwegian interests. But his methods were slow, and in 1235 the king sent Snorri's nephew, **Sturla Sighvatsson**, to Iceland to win it over for Norway, by force if necessary. In the ensuing **civil war**, forces led in part by **Gissur Þorvaldsson**, head of the Haukadalur clan, killed Sturla and virtually wiped out the Sturlungs at the battle of **Örlygsstaðir** in 1238. Snorri escaped by being in Norway at the time, but was killed by Gissur after his return.

Amid this violence, Iceland was also experiencing a literary flowering: Snorri Sturluson wrote the **Prose Eddas**, containing much of what is known about Norse mythology; his relative Sturla Þordarson compiled the **Book of Settlements Expanded**, accounts of the original landowners and their lives; and it was during this period that the **sagas** were composed, romanticizing the nobler events of the early Commonwealth. Meanwhile the war continued, and by 1246 only two chieftains were left standing: Gissur Þorvaldsson, who held the south of the country; and Sturla's brother **Þordur**, who controlled the north. Rather than fight, they let King Hákon decide who should govern; the king chose Þordur, who ruled Iceland until 1250, sharing power with the two bishops – also Norwegian appointees. In the end, the bishop at Hólar denounced Þordur for putting his own interests before Norway's, and the king replaced him with Gissur who, after a further decade of skirmishes, finally persuaded Icelanders that the only way to obtain lasting peace was by accepting **Norwegian sovereignty**. In 1262, Iceland's chieftains signed the *Gamli sáttmáli* or **Old Treaty**, which allowed Iceland to keep its laws and promised that the Norwegian king would maintain order, in exchange for taxes and replacing the chieftainships with government officials. While the treaty didn't give Norway absolute control of the country, and demanded a return for Icelandic obedience, it marked the beginnings of seven centuries of foreign rule.

Decline, the English Century and the Reformation

With the Alþing discredited by over forty years of conflict, Iceland turned to Norway to help draft a new constitution. The **Jónsbók** of 1280 was the result, a set of laws that were to remain partly in force until the nineteenth century. The country was to be overseen by a **governor**, with twelve regional **sheriffs** acting as local administrators; all officials would be Icelanders, though appointed by Norway. The Alþing would still meet as a national court, retaining some legislative power, but its decisions would have to be approved by the king.

The new system should have brought a much-needed period of stability to Iceland, but it was not always administered as planned – officials often abused their position, leading to several **revolts**, such as when the brutal governor Smiður Andrésson was killed by farmers in 1361. At the same time, the fourteenth century heralded a further succession of **natural disasters**: severe winters wiped out crops and livestock; Hekla became active again; and the volcano under Öræfajökull in the southeast exploded in 1362, covering a third of the country in ash. But most devastating was the **Plague** or Black Death, which had ravaged Europe in the 1350s and arrived in Iceland in 1402, killing half of the population in the following two years. Compared with this, it seems inconsequential that the Danish "lady king" **Margrete I** had meanwhile absorbed the Norwegian throne under the **Kalmar Union** of 1397, thereby placing Iceland in Denmark's hands.

The English Century

While all this was going on, the underlying struggles between landowners, the Church and the king were escalating, typified by events during what is known as the **English Century**. At the time there was growing demand in Europe for dried **cod**, which after 1400 became a major Icelandic export, exchanged for linen, wine and grain. **Fishing** – formerly a secondary income – boomed, providing a new source of funds for coastal landowners. Soon English and German vessels were vying for trade with Iceland and even beginning to fish themselves; the English gained the ascendancy after setting up a base on the Westman Islands (where they also indulged in kidnapping and piracy), and managing to get an English bishop – **John Craxton** – appointed to Hólar in the 1420s. Denmark, alarmed at England's rising influence and the taxes it was losing through uncontrolled trade, appointed its own **Jón Gerreksson** as bishop at Skálholt, although this violent man – who had his own military and spent his time levying illegal taxes and harassing his neighbours – ended up being murdered in 1433.

Trying to restore order, Denmark passed laws stopping the Church from raising illegal taxes and banning the English from Iceland. The English response was to kill the Icelandic governor in 1467, so the Danish king encouraged the German trading organization known as the **Hanseatic League** to establish trading bases in the country – a popular move, as the League had better goods than the English and gave better prices. The English returned with cannons, a forceful stance that after 1490 gained them the right to fish Icelandic waters as long as they paid tolls to Denmark. All went well until 1532, when trouble flared between German and English vessels at the trading post at **Grindavík** on the southwestern Reykjanes Peninsula, culminating in the death of the English leader. English involvement in Iceland dropped off sharply after this, leaving Icelandic trade in the hands of Danish and German interests.

The Reformation and its effects

The Church, which by now had complete jurisdiction over Iceland's lands, and profitable stakes in farming and fishing, became even more powerful in 1533 when the two bishops – **Jón Arason** and **Ögmundur Pálsson** – were appointed as joint governors of the country. But outside Iceland, a new Christian view first proposed by the German Martin Luther in 1517 had been gaining ground. **Lutherism** revolted against what was seen as the Catholic Church's growing obsession with material rather than spiritual profits, and encouraged a break with Rome as the head of the Church – a suggestion that European monarchs realized would therefore place the Church's riches and influence in their hands.

During the 1530s, all Scandinavia became Lutheran, and converts were already making headway in Iceland, though threatened with excommunication by the bishops. In 1539, the Danish king **Christian III** ordered the Icelandic governor to appropriate Church lands, which led to the murder of one of his sheriffs and a subsequent military expedition to Iceland to force conversion to Lutherism. This was headed by **Gissur Einarsson**, a former protégé of Ögmundur but covert Lutheran, who replaced Ögmundur as bishop at Skálholt in 1542. A skilful diplomat, he encouraged Lutherism without, by and large, antagonizing Catholics. His appointment left Jón Arason at Hólar as the last Catholic bishop in Scandinavia, and on Gissur's death in 1548, Arason unsuccessfully pushed his own Catholic candidate for Skálholt, an act that got him declared an outlaw. Gathering a band of supporters, Arason marched south and captured Skálholt, but was subsequently defeated and executed along with two of his sons on November 7, 1550, allowing Lutherism to be imposed across the entire country.

The consequences of the Reformation were severe, with the new faith forced on an initially unwilling population, who – in common with many other countries at the time – may have disagreed with Catholic abuses of power but not with Catholicism itself. The Danish king acquired all Church holdings and their revenues, profits from which had previously stayed in Iceland; monasteries were abolished and, deprived of funds, the Church found it hard to sponsor education – though it did manage to publish a translation of the Bible in 1584, the first book printed in Icelandic.

Politically, too, the Church was now an instrument of the king, and the Danish crown gained a far more direct hold on the country. Technically, however, Iceland remained an independent state through its treaty with Norway, but in 1661 King **Frederick III** declared his rule absolute over all Danish lands, and the following year sent an armed ambassador to Iceland to make its people swear allegiance. During an assembly at **Bessastaðir**, near Reykjavík, the Alþing's lawspeaker and Skálholt's bishop were forced to submit, removing their final vestiges of authority and handing complete control of the country to the Danish crown.

In the meantime, Iceland's economy – still based on farming and fishing – suffered a severe blow through the **Trade Monopoly** of 1602. This restricted all trade between Iceland and the outside world to a select few Danish merchants, who charged steeply for their goods, while giving poor prices for Icelandic products. By 1700, the monopoly had ruined the country, creating a poor, dispirited population of tenant farmers and landless labourers. Fishing was also on the wane, partly because a shortage of timber meant that Iceland's vessels were basic and small, and easily out-competed by foreign boats. Aside from a fruitless attempt to introduce **reindeer** as livestock, the only concrete action taken to redress trade imbalances was made by the bailiff **Skúli Magnússon**, who in 1752 founded a company at Reykjavík – still just a small farming settlement at the time – to improve agricultural practices and modernize the wool and fishing industries. Though the company was only moderately successful, its warehouses became the core of Reykjavík town, soon to become Iceland's largest settlement and de facto capital.

Unfortunately, a fresh wave of disasters now swept the country, the worst of which was the catastrophic **Laki Eruptions** of 1783–84 in the southeast. Poisonous fallout from Laki wrecked farming over the entire country, and the ensuing **famine** reduced the population to just 38,000. Denmark briefly considered evacuating the survivors to Jutland, but in the end settled for easing the economy by replacing the trade monopoly with a **Free Trade Charter** in 1787, which allowed Iceland to do business with a greater range of Danish merchants. Another effect of the eruptions were accompanying **earthquakes** which knocked over the church at Skálholt and caused subsidence at the Alþing site; the bishopric was moved to Reykjavík, and the Alþing – which by now only met irregularly to discuss minor matters – was finally dissolved.

Nationalism

European political upheavals during the early nineteenth-century Napoleonic Wars had little effect on Iceland, though there was brief excitement in 1809 when opportunistic Danish interpreter **Jörgen Jörgensen** deposed the governor and ran the country for the summer. However, the increasingly liberal political climate that followed the war encouraged **nationalism** throughout Europe and was championed in Iceland by the romantic poet **Jónas Hallgrímsson** and historian **Jón Sigurðsson**, a descendent of Snorri Sturluson, who pushed for free trade and autonomy from Denmark. Bowing to popular demand, the Danish king reconstituted the Alþing at Reykjavík in 1843, which met every other year and had twenty elected regional members of parliament and six representatives of the king. Jón Sigurðsson was amongst the first members elected.

Even greater changes were on the way, sparked by the French Revolution of 1789, after which Europe's other royal families began to cede real power in order to avoid a similar fate. Following uprisings in Denmark, the **monarchy** there became constitutional in 1848, allowing Jón Sigurðsson to point out that Iceland's 1662 oath of allegiance to the king as an absolute ruler was therefore no longer valid, and that the Old Treaty was now back in force. This didn't make him popular with the king, a situation exacerbated when he led the defeat of a bill at the Alþing, in 1851, that would have legally incorporated Iceland into Denmark. Sigurðsson also managed to have remaining trade restrictions finally lifted four years later, an act which did more than anything else to improve life in Iceland by bringing in modern farm implements and wood for boats at affordable prices, while allowing the profitable export of livestock, wool and fish.

In 1871 Denmark politically **annexed** Iceland, an event that, though not accepted by Icelanders, gave them a favourable **new constitution**. Broadly speaking, this returned full legislative powers to the Alþing and was ratified by King Christian IX himself, while attending celebrations at Þingvellir in 1874 to mark a thousand years since Settlement. Home control of lawmaking saw further benefits to living conditions: the tithe system was abolished; infrastructure improved; schooling was made compulsory; improvements in boats and fishing equipment caused the growth of port towns; and farmers formed the first Icelandic co-operatives to deal directly with foreign suppliers. There followed a sizeable population boom, despite heavy **emigration** to Canada and the US during the late nineteenth century following another spate of harsh weather, the eruption of Víti in the Askja caldera in northeastern Iceland (see p.318), disease and livestock problems.

Home Rule, Union and Independence

The concept of total political autonomy from Denmark grew from ideas planted by Jón Sigurðsson before his death in 1879. By 1900, differences in the way this could be achieved led to the formation of **political parties**, who in 1904 pressured the king into granting Home Rule under the **Home Rule Party** led by **Hannes Hafstein**. Hafstein's decade in office saw the start of trends that were to continue throughout the century: an emerging middle class led a gradual **population shift** from the land to towns, communications picked up with the introduction of telephones in 1906, and new technologies were adopted for farming and fishing, boosting output. Workers also founded the first unions, and women were granted rights to an equal education and allowed to vote in 1915.

Hafstein's biggest defeat came in 1908 when the Alþing rejected the **Draft Constitution**, a proposal to make Iceland an independent state under the Danish king. Yet a decade later, a referendum found ninety percent of voters approved of the idea, and in December 1918, Iceland entered into the **Act of Union** with Denmark, where it received recognition as an independent state while still accepting the Danish king as monarch.

World War I itself bypassed Iceland, though during the war the country profited from the high export prices paid for fish, meat, and **wool** (in great demand in Europe for military uniforms). As **World War II** loomed however, Iceland – dependent on trade with both Britain and Germany – decided to stay neutral, but, after the outbreak of hostilities in 1939, the country's strategic North Atlantic location meant that, neutral or not, it was simply a matter of time before either Germany or Britain invaded. The **British** were first, landing unopposed in May 1940, so gaining a vital supply point for the Allies' North Atlantic operations. The following year **US forces** replaced the British with the approval of the Alþing, on condition that they respected Icelandic sovereignty and left once hostilities were over.

Though fighting never came to Iceland itself, World War II was to trigger the end of foreign rule. When Germany invaded Denmark in 1940 the Alþing decided that, as the king could no longer govern, the Act of Union should be dissolved and therefore that Iceland should declare its full **independence**. The formal ratification took some time, however, as the government was in disarray, with none of the four political parties holding a parliamentary majority. In the end, acting regent **Sveinn Björnsson** founded an apolitical government, which finally proclaimed independence from Denmark on June 17, 1944, with Björnsson elected as the first president of the **Icelandic Republic**.

The Republic: from 1944 onwards

One of the biggest challenges for the new republic came immediately after the war. The US troops departed in 1946 as requested, but as the **Cold War** between the Soviet and Western powers began to take shape Iceland felt uncertain about its lack of defence. With neither the population nor desire to form its own military, in 1949 the Alþing voted that Iceland should instead join the US, Britain and others as part of **NATO**, the North Atlantic Treaty Organization, and in 1951 agreed to have US forces operate an airforce base at **Keflavík**, using facilities the US had already built during World War II. Though the need for defence was widely accepted, the idea of having foreign influence back in Iceland after having only just got rid of it for the first time in seven hundred years was not popular, and the decision to join NATO caused a **riot** in Reykjavík.

The country has also had to deal with a rather different defence matter: that of preserving its **fish stocks**, and hence most of its export earnings, in the face of foreign competition. Following skirmishes dating right back to the English Century (see p.325), in 1896 Iceland's **territorial waters** – the area from which it could exclude foreign vessels – had been set as extending three nautical miles from land. As commercial fishing picked up again after World War II, fish stocks through the Atlantic declined, and most countries increased their territorial limits. In 1958, Iceland declared a twelve-mile limit which Britain protested, sending in naval boats to protect its trawlers fishing in these new Icelandic waters in the first act of the **Cod Wars**. These flared on and off for the next thirty years, with Iceland continuing to expand its claims as fish stocks continued to dwindle, and employing its coastguard to cut the cables of any foreign trawlers that were caught poaching. Things came to a head in 1975, when Iceland declared a two-hundred-mile limit around its shores, at which point Britain broke off diplomatic relations and ordered its Navy to ram Icelandic coastguard boats, which happened on several occasions. The situation was only resolved in 1985, when international laws justified Iceland's position by granting the two-hundred-mile limit to all countries involved in the dispute.

Domestically, Iceland has become predominantly urban since 1944, with around two-thirds of the population living in the Greater Reykjavík area, and just 24,000 remaining on the land as farmers. Standards of living are now equal to any European country – in fact, with little industry and low pollution levels, Icelanders are in some ways better off. Virtually all Icelanders are literate and well educated, and communications are as good as they can be given the natural conditions – the Ringroad around the country was completed in 1974, and Iceland's per-capita usage of **computers** and the internet is one of the world's highest. New technologies, such as the harnessing of **hydro** and **geothermal energy** for electricity, heating and growing **hothouse** foods, have also been enthusiastically embraced.

On the downside, **fishing** as the single main source of export earnings created a very sensitive economy while a reliance on **imports** lead to high prices, with many people needing more than one job in order to make ends meet. The runaway inflation of the 1970s (in part caused by the 1973 eruption of the volcano on Heimaey, which disrupted the season's fishing) was capped, though at the cost of rising **unemployment** figures. After decades of stability and prosperity since then, however, disaster struck in October 2008 with the **collapse of the banking system**. Since the late 1990s, Iceland had sought to diversify its heavily fishing-oriented economy by investing in **banking**, which initially created incredibly high profits: suddenly a few mega-wealthy Icelanders were buying up everything from English soccer clubs to European supermarkets; and foreign investors, tempted by the **fifteen percent** interest rates that Icelandic banks were using to counter rising inflation, began pouring in money. But this only accelerated inflation and hikes in interest rates, causing the exchange rate to lose touch with economic reality while giving the Icelanders an illusion of wealth.

Meanwhile, the Icelandic banks continued to buy up foreign assets, until these were valued at ten times Iceland's actual economy. This meant the Icelandic government couldn't guarantee the banks and, when the bubble burst in 2008, the consequences for the whole country were disastrous. The banks were nationalized, unemployment and inflation soared and the exchange rate collapsed. Living standards fell, too, leaving one in five households bankrupt. A series of public protests brought about the fall of Geir Haarde's rightwing government in January 2009 (see Chapter 1, p.72), which was replaced by the new leftwing administration of Prime Minister, Jóhanna Sigurðardóttir. In a bid to restore credibility and stability to the economy, it lost no time in applying to join the European Union in July 2009, following approval by the Alþing. Tricky negotiations are expected on the subject of Iceland's sole use of its territorial waters for fishing, which is at odds with the EU's Common Fisheries Policy. The target date for membership is 2012, though the issue must first be approved by a national referendum whose outcome is less than certain.

Landscape and geology

Iceland's lunar landscapes are one of the country's prime attractions, but its apparently ancient facade is in fact an illusion. Geologically, Iceland is very young, with its oldest rocks dating back a mere fourteen million years, to a time in the Earth's history when the dinosaurs had long gone and humans were yet to evolve.

The reason that its landscape appears so raw is because Iceland sits on a geological hot spot on the mid-Atlantic ridge, where the **Eurasian** and **American continental plates** are drifting east and west apart from each other. As they do so, Iceland is continually tearing down the middle, allowing **magma** (molten rock from the Earth's core) to well upwards towards the surface. When the surface cracks – in an earthquake, for instance – magma erupts through as a volcano, and when groundwater seeps down to magma levels it boils and returns to the surface as a **thermal spring**, or even a **geyser**.

Almost all such geological activity in Iceland is located over this mid-Atlantictear, which stretches northeast in a wide band across the country, taking in everything between the Reykjanes Peninsula, the Westman Islands and Mýrdalsjökull in the southwest, and Mývatn and Þórshöfn in the northeast. As this band is where volcanoes are creating all the new land, it's here that you'll find the most recent rocks; conversely, the oldest, most geologically stable parts of the country are around Ísafjörður in the Westfjords and Gerpir cliffs in Iceland's extreme east.

At the same time, Iceland is close enough to the Arctic for its higher mountains and plateaux – most of which are in the south of the country – to have become permanently ice-capped, forming extensive **glaciers**. Melt from around their edges contributes to many of Iceland's **rivers**, which are further fed by **underground springs** – also the source of the country's largest **lakes**. Cold, dry air formed by sub-zero temperatures over the ice caps is also responsible for some of the weird **atmospheric effects** you'll encounter here, while others have an extraterrestrial origin.

Volcanoes

Though Iceland's volcanoes share a common origin, they form many different types, based on the chemical composition of their magma, which flows out of the volcano as **lava**. Where the lava is very fluid and the eruption is slow and continuous, the lava builds up to form a wide, flattened cone known as a **shield volcano**, a type that takes its name from the Skjaldbreiður (Shield-broad) volcano at Þingvellir. Where an eruption is violent, the lava is thrown out as a fine spray, cooling in mid-air and forming cones of ash or **tephra**, a cover-all name for volcanic ejecta; typical examples of tephra cones are found at Mývatn's Hverfjall, and Eldfell on Heimaey in the Westman Islands. Relatively rare in Iceland, **strato volcanoes** are tall, regular cones built from very long-term lava and tephra accumulations; westerly Snæfellsjökull is a good example, though the country's most consistently active volcano, Hekla, has formed in a similar manner but along a line of craters rather than a single vent.

Crater rows are one of the country's most common volcanic formations, caused when lava erupts at points along a lengthy **fissure**, such as occurred at Leirhnjukur north of Mývatn in the 1970s, and Lakagígar in southeast Iceland during the 1780s. Both eruptions produced a string of low, multiple cones and large quantities of lava – in Lakagígar's case, flows covered six hundred square kilometres. **Submarine eruptions** also occur off Iceland and are how the Westman Islands originally formed, as demonstrated by the creation of the new island of Surtsey in the 1960s. Looking like mini-volcanoes but actually nothing of the sort, aptly named **pseudocraters** – like those at Mývatn and Kirkjubæjarklaustur – form when lava flows over damp ground, vapourising the water beneath, which explodes through the soft rock as a giant blister.

Most **rocks** in Iceland were created in volcanic eruptions, and two common forms are easily identifiable. **Basalt** forms fluid lava solidifying into dark rock, weathered expanses of which cover the Reykjanes Peninsula and elsewhere. Where basaltic lavas cool rapidly – by flowing into a river or the sea, for instance – they form characteristic hexagonal pillars, with excellent examples at Svartifoss in Skaftafell National Park and Hjálparfoss at Þórsárdalur. In contrast, **rhyolite** forms a very thick lava, which often builds up into dome-like volcanoes such as Mælifell on the Snæfellsnes Peninsula. Cooled, it normally produces distinctively crumbly, grey, yellow and pink rocks, typified by the peaks of the central Landmannalaugar region, though in some cases rhyolite solidifies into black, glass-like **obsidian** (best seen at Hrafntinnusker, on the Laugavegur hiking trail). Types of tephra to look for include black or red, gravel-like **scoria**; solidified lava foam or **pumice**, which is light enough to float on water; and **bombs**, spherical or elongated twists of rock formed when semi-congealed lava is thrown high into the air and hardens as it spins – they can be as big as a football but are usually fist-sized.

Aside from their cones and lava fields, volcanoes affect the landscape in other ways. Historically, dense clouds of tephra have destroyed farms and farmland on a number of occasions – such as the twelfth-century eruption of Hekla that buried Stöng in Þórsárdalur, or the 1875 explosion of Viti, at Askja. Volcanic activity under ice caps can also cause catastrophic flash floods known as **jökulhlaups**, the most recent being at Grímsvötn in 1996. On the other hand, extinct volcano craters often become flooded themselves and form lakes, or **maars**; one of the biggest is Öskjuvatn in the Askja caldera, but there are also smaller examples at Grænvatn on the Reykjanes Peninsula and Kerið crater near Selfoss.

Thermal springs and geysers

Thermal springs are found all over Iceland, sometimes emerging at ground level literally as a hot-water spring – such as at Hveragerði – or flooding natural depressions or crevasses to form hot pools, which can be found at Mývatn and Landmannalaugur. In some cases the water emerges from the ground as steam through a vent; where this mixes with clay, boiling mud pits or **solfataras** are formed, of which the most extensive are those at Hverarönd, east of Mývatn. Natural steam is harnessed in Iceland to drive turbines and generate **geothermal power**, and also as heating for homes and hothouses.

While geysers tap into the same subterranean hot water as thermal springs, nobody is quite sure exactly why they erupt – it's either a gradual buildup of water pressure or a subterranean hiccup. Since the Krísuvík geyser blew itself to pieces in 1999, Iceland's only example of note is at Geysir, northeast of Selfoss (see p.113).

Glaciers, rivers and lakes

Glaciers can be thought of as giant, frozen rivers or waterfalls that move downhill under their own colossal weight. Usually movement is slow – maybe a few centimetres a year – though some can shift a metre or more annually. In Iceland, they're all associated with ice caps, the biggest of which, **Vatnajökull** (which more or less means Glacial Sea), spreads over 150km across the country's southeast. These caps sit atop plateaux, with a few isolated rocky peaks or **nunataks** poking through the ice, off which scores of glaciers descend to lower levels.

Deeper glacial ice is often distinctly blue, caused by the air being squeezed out from between the ice crystals by the weight of the ice above. However, glaciers are also full of debris, either from falls of volcanic ash, or simply from the way they grind down the rocks underneath them into fine gravel or sand. As this dark grit and gravel nears the surface of the glacier it warms up in the sunlight, causing surrounding ice to melt, exposing the gravel and thereby making the front of most Icelandic glaciers appear very "dirty". The debris ultimately is carried away from the glacier by streams or rivers which are also the product of glacial friction, and deposited as desert-like **sandurs**, such as those that occupy much of Iceland's southeastern coastline.

It's also possible to see the effects that the glaciers themselves leave on the landscape, as both ice caps and glaciers were formerly far more extensive than they appear today. During previous ice ages – the last of which ended around 12,000 years ago – much of the country was beneath the ice, but there has been considerable fluctuation in glacier limits even in recorded times, and at present most are **shrinking**. The intricate inlets of the Eastfjords and Westfjords were carved by vanished glaciers, as were the characteristically flat-topped mountains known as **móbergs** southeast of Mývatn. Former glacialvalleys – typically broad and rounded – can be seen along the Ringroad southwest of Akureyri; and Iceland's most mobile glacier, Skeiðarárjökull in Skaftafell National Park, has been retreating over the last eighty years leaving raised **moraine** gravel ridges in its wake.

The majority of Iceland's **rivers** are fairly short, glacial-fed affairs, though two of the largest – the **Hvíta** in the southwest, and northeastern **Jökulsá á Fjöllum** – each exceed a respectable 200km in length. Both have quite spectacular stretches where they have carved **canyons** and **waterfalls** out of the landscape: at Gullfoss on the Hvíta; and Dettifoss and Ásbergi along the Jökulsá. Icelandic **lakes** are not especially large and tend to be caused – as with Mývatn or Þingvallavatn – when lava walls dam a spring-fed outflow, causing it to back-flood.

Atmospheric phenomena

One of the strangest features of being in Iceland during the summer is the extremely **long days**. The northernmost part of the mainland is actually just outside the Arctic Circle, and so the sun does set (briefly) even on the longest day of the year, though you can cross over to the little island of Grímsey, whose northern tip is inside the Arctic and so enjoys midnight sun for a few days of the year. Conversely, winter days are correspondingly short, with the sun barely getting above the horizon for three months of the year.

One consequence of Iceland's often cold, dry atmosphere is that – on sunny days at least – it can play serious tricks on your sense of scale. Massive objects such as mountains and glaciers seem to stay the same size, or even shrink, the closer you come to them, and sometimes phantom hills or peaks appear on the horizon. Another effect – best viewed on cold, clear nights – is the **northern lights**, or **Aurora Borealis**, which form huge, shifting sheets of green or red in the winter skies. They're caused by the solar wind bringing electrically charged particles into contact with the Earth's atmosphere, and you'll have to be in luck to catch a really good show – they improve the further north you travel.

Wildlife and the environment

CONTEXTS | Wildlife and the environment

Iceland's first settlers found a land whose coastal fringe, compared with today, was relatively well wooded; there were virtually no land mammals, but birdlife and fish stocks were abundant and the volcanic soil was reasonably fertile. Over a thousand years of farming has brought great changes: big trees are a rare sight, fish stocks have plummeted, and introduced mammals have contributed to erosion and other problems, but a growing regard for Iceland's natural heritage is beginning to redress the imbalance, and the country's natural history remains very much alive.

Flora

Though fossils indicate that around twelve million years ago Iceland had stands of maples and other broad-leaved trees, dawn redwood and even giant sequoias, subsequent ice ages had wiped these out long before humans ever landed here. It's likely that the Vikings found woods mostly comprising **dwarf birch** and **willow** that you still see here today. Both can grow up to 10m or so in height, but generally form shrub-like thickets – original forests, however, would have been fairly extensive, reaching from the coast up into highland valleys. Clearances for timber and pasture have reduced Iceland's tree cover to just one percent of the land, though since 1994 over four million trees – including commercial stands of **pine** – have been planted in an attempt to restore levels to pre-Settlement estimates.

The most widespread flora – **mosses** and **lichens** – tend to get overlooked, but they cover almost every lava flow and cliff in the country and provide a colourful mosaic of greens, greys and oranges, especially after rain has darkened the surrounding rocks. **Flowering plants** are most obvious in midsummer, and include the very common, blue vertical spikes of **arctic lupins**, introduced from North America to help reduce erosion; the tiny magenta flowers and spongy green clumps of **arctic river beauty** and **thyme** (which you can also identify from its smell); fluffy **cottongrass** growing in boggy areas; the cauliflower-shaped, yellow-green flower heads of **angelica**, often covered in flies; blue **harebells**; and yellow **kingcups** and **dandelions**. In early autumn, **berries** are also plentiful, and many people collect them to eat.

Mammals

The **arctic fox**, which feeds almost exclusively on birds, was the only land mammal in Iceland when the first settlers arrived. Common throughout Iceland, they're chubbier than European foxes, with short, rounded ears, bushy tail, and a coat that turns white in winter. **Polar bears** have never flourished here, though every decade one or two float over on ice floes from Greenland (which is probably how foxes first arrived too), only to be shot as a dangerous pest by the first person who sees them.

Domestic animals arrived with the Vikings. The **Icelandic horse** is a unique breed descended from medieval Norwegian stock, as none have been imported since the tenth century. Cattle numbers are fairly low, but **sheep** outnumber the human population by four to one. **Reindeer** were introduced from Norway and Finland in the late seventeenth century for hunting purposes – today they're restricted to eastern Iceland, where they stick to high-altitude pasture in summer, descending to coastal areas in winter. Iceland's cold climate has limited the spread of smaller vermin such as **rats** and **mice**, which were unintentionally brought in on boats and only occur around human habitations; escaped **rabbits** have recently established themselves around Reykjavík and on Heimaey, however. **Minks** have also broken out of fur farms and seem to be surviving in the wild, much to the detriment of native birdlife.

Offshore, Iceland has a number of **whale** species. Traditionally, their valuable meat, bones and teeth were most frequently obtained from washed-up corpses, and – as described in *Eyrbyggja Saga* (see p.341) – battles were even fought over the rights to their carcasses. **Commercial whaling** began in the nineteenth century, and resumed after a fifteen-year-long moratorium ended in 2003, though numbers remain high and you've a good chance of seeing some if you put to sea. Most common are a couple of species of **dolphin** and the five-metre-long **pilot whale**, but there are also substantial numbers of far larger **fin whales**, **sei whales** and **minke whales**, all of which feed by straining plankton from sea water through moustache-like baleen plates inside their mouths. Far less common are **orca** (also known as killer whales), square-headed **sperm whales**, and **blue whales**, which reach 30m in length and are the largest known animal ever to have lived.

Grey and harbour **seals** are found in Iceland, with the biggest numbers seen around the north coast and off the Westman Islands. Both seal species are also hunted, despite being depicted as almost human in Icelandic folktales, appearing as "were-seals" who have human families on land and seal families in the sea. According to these stories, if you walk along a beach and find a seal following you out from shore, it may be looking to see if you're one of its children.

Birds

Iceland has some three hundred recorded bird species, of which around eighty breed regularly. The **gyrfalcon**, a large bird of prey with variable grey-white plumage, is a national icon, once appearing on the Icelandic coat of arms and exported for hunting purposes until the nineteenth century. They're not common, but occur throughout mountainous country; rather oddly, in folklore the gyrfalcon is said to be brother to the ptarmigan, its main source of food. Another spectacular bird of prey is the huge **white-tailed sea eagle**, whose numbers have recently rebounded following a low point in the 1980s, when birds took poison baits intended for escaped minks. Around forty pairs breed annually in the Westfjords, though juveniles travel quite widely over the country.

The **ptarmigan** is a plump game bird, plentiful across Iceland wherever there is low scrub or trees. They're well camouflaged, patterned a mottled brown to blend with summer vegetation, and changing – with the exception of black tail feathers and a red wattle around the eye – to snow-white plumage in winter. Aside from being preyed upon year-round by foxes and gyrfalcons, ptarmigan are also a traditional Christmas food, eaten instead of turkey. Their population

Below is a partial list of **Icelandic birds**, with English and Icelandic names (US names are given in brackets where they differ substantially from British usage). You won't have to be an ardent twitcher to clock up most of these, though a couple of less widespread species are also included. Some of these are pictured on pp.22–24.

Arctic skua	Kjói	Oystercatcher	Tjaldur
Arctic tern	Kría	Pink-footed goose	Heiðagæs
Barnacle goose	Helsingi	Pintail	Grafönd
Barrow's goldeneye	Húsönd	Ptarmigan	Rjúpa
Black guillemot	Teista	Puffin	Lundi
Black-headed gull	Hettumáfur	Purple sandpiper	Sendlingur
Black-tailed godwit	Jaðrakan	Raven	Hrafn
Black-throated diver (Loon)	Himbrimi	Razorbill	Álka
		Red-necked (Northern) phalarope	Óðinshani
Brünnich's guillemot (Thick-billed murre)	Stuttnefja	Red-throated diver	Lómur
Cormorant	Dílaskarfur	Redpoll	Auðnutittlingur
Dunlin	Lóuþræll	Redshank	Stelkur
Eider	Æðarfugl	Redwing	Skógarþröstur
Fulmar	Fýll	Ringed plover	Sandlóa
Gannet	Súla	Scaup	Duggönd
Golden plover	Heiðlóa	Scoter	Hrafnsönd
Goosander	Gulönd	Shag	Toppskarfur
Great auk*	Geirfugl	Short-eared owl	Brandugla
Great skua	Skúmur	Slavonian grebe	Flórgoði
Greater black-backed gull	Svartbakur	Snipe	Hrossagaukur
		Snow bunting	Snjótittlingur
Guillemot (Murre)	Langvía	Starling	Stari
Gyrfalcon	Fálki	Storm petrel	Stormsvala
Harlequin duck	Straumönd	Teal	Urtönd
Herring gull	Silfurmáfur	Tufted duck	Skúfönd
Iceland gull	Bjartmáfur	Turnstone	Tildra
Kittiwake	Rita	Wheatear	Steindepill
Lesser black-backed gull	Sílamáfur	White wagtail	Maríuerla
		White-tailed sea eagle	Haförn
Little auk (Dovekie)	Haftyrðill	Whooper swan	Álft
Longtail duck (Old squaw)	Hávella	Widgeon	Rauðhöfðaönd
Mallard	Stokkönd	Wren	Músarrindill
Meadow pipit	Þúfutittlingur		
Merganser	Toppönd	*Extinct	
Merlin	Smyrill		

goes through boom-and-bust cycles, and in bad years Christmas ptarmigan have to be brought in from Scotland, allowing Icelanders to bemoan the flavour of imported birds.

Other common heathland birds include the **golden plover**, a migrant whose mournful piping is eagerly awaited in Iceland as the harbinger of summer; long-legged **redshank** and **godwit**; and **snipe**, identified by their long beaks, zigzag flight, and strange "buzzing" noise made by two stiffened tail feathers which protrude at right angles to its body. In fields and estuaries you'll see **pink-footed geese**, the most common of Iceland's wildfowl species, with **whooper swans** resident even in downtown Reykjavík. Similarly widespread are **raven**, held by some Icelanders to be highly intelligent, though often associated in tales with portents of doom. Norse mythology describes Óðinn as having two ravens called Huginn (the Thinker) and Muninn (the Rememberer), who report to him on the state of the world; and folklore holds that the congregations of ravens commonly seen in autumn are dividing up Iceland's farms between them, so that each pair will have a home over winter.

Many of Iceland's **ducks** are coastal, though you can see almost all recorded species either on or around Mývatn, a lake in the northeast. **Eider** are probably the most famous Icelandic duck, known for their warm down, but birders will want to clock up **harlequin** and **barrow's goldeneye**, which occur nowhere else in Europe; for more about these species and others, see the box opposite.

Of all the country's birdlife, however, it's the huge, noisy, teeming **sea-bird colonies** which really stick in the mind. There are several types of gull – including the uniformly pale **Iceland gull**, and slight, graceful **kittiwake** – but far more common are narrow winged, stumpy **fulmars**, which look gull-like but are actually related to albatrosses. They nest in half-burrows or overhangs on steep slopes and cliffs, and are relatively fearless, often allowing you to approach fairly close – come too near, however, and they spit a foul-smelling oil from their double-chambered beak.

In summer, flat, open places around the coast are utilized by colossal numbers of ground-nesting **arctic terns**, small, white birds with narrow wings, trailing tails, black caps and bright red beaks. It's interesting to watch the activity in a tern colony, but bear in mind that the birds relentlessly attack anything that threatens their eggs or chicks. **Skuas** are heavily built, brown birds with nasty tempers and a piratic lifestyle – they chase and harass weaker sea birds into dropping their catches. Like terns, they also nest on the ground

▲ Puffin, Látrabjarg cliffs

in vast colonies across the southeastern coastal *sandurs*, and are equally defensive of their territory.

Iceland's equivalent to penguins are the similar-looking **auks**, a family that includes **guillemot** (murre), **razorbill** and **puffin**. Like penguins, these hunt fish, live in huge seaside colonies, and have black and white plumage. Unlike penguins, however, they can also fly. Auks' **beaks** are distinctively specialized: long and pointed in guillemots; mid-length and broad in razorbills; and colourfully striped, sail-shaped in puffins – all aids to their specific fishing techniques. The best place to see puffins is on Heimaey in the Westman Islands – for more on them see p.140 – but you'll find other auks anywhere around Iceland where there are suitable nesting cliffs. One exception is the Arctic-dwelling **little auk**, or dovekie, now seen only rarely on Grímsey, Iceland's northernmost outpost.

Books and sagas

With a population of barely over a quarter of a million, Iceland boasts more writers per capita than any other country in the world. The long dark winter months are said to be the reason so many folk put pen to paper, and native-language books on all matters Icelandic can be found in shops across the country. Conversely, as the Icelandic-language market is so small, prices can be inordinately high – specialist publications cost the equivalent of hundreds of dollars, and even a popular-fiction paperback comes in at around 3000kr.

On the other hand, the **sagas** and associated literature have been widely translated into English – Penguin Books, Everyman and Oxford University Press publish a good range of the longer sagas and their own compilations of the shorter tales, some of which are reviewed below (with the publisher of specific compilations indicated in brackets). Icelandic Review also publishes a series of collections of folk tales, lesser sagas, and mythologies, available in bookshops across Iceland.

There's an increasing amount of **contemporary fiction** available in English, too, though it's not always easy to find outside of Iceland. Foreign books about Iceland remain, unfortunately, remarkably scant, and often lapse into "land of fire and ice"-style clichés.

History and culture

Þráinn Bertelsson *My Self & I*. Fine autobiography by one of Iceland's most respected film directors and writers, focusing on growing up in 1950s Reykjavík as Iceland was rediscovering itself in the wake of new-found independence.

Johannes Brøndsted *The Vikings*. Solid overview of the causes and motivation of the Viking explosion through Europe, focusing mostly on Scandinavia rather than Iceland but giving heaps of details – backed up by archeology – about religion, customs and daily life.

Jesse Byock *Viking Age Iceland*. A bit academic in character but helpfully fills in background on the environment, politics and peoples of Iceland's "Viking republic".

Victoria Clark *The Far Farers*. Lively, if slightly shallow account of Clark's attempt to foot-step the route that took an Icelander named Thorvald to Jerusalem, reinforcing how worldly and well travelled many Vikings were.

Hugleikur Dagsson *Avoid Us* (aka *Should You Be Laughing at This?*). Daggson's cartoon strips of stick-figures engaged in outrageous activities have made him a national icon in Iceland; on publication in English, The *Irish Sun* tabloid clamoured "Ban This Sick Book". Not for the easily offended – his strip runs in the free English-language magazine *Reykjavík Grapevine*.

David Roberts *Iceland Land of the Sagas*. Beautiful glossy pictures by photographer Jon Krakauer accompany the rich text in this coffee-table book of Iceland.

Anna Yates *Leifur Eiríksson and Vínland the Good*. An excellent and readable account of the discovery of North America by Icelandic Vikings. A thorough argument of where exactly Vínland is accompanies debate on why the Norse settlements in North America died out.

Modern fiction

Frans G. Bengtsson *The Long Ships*. Buckle your swash for this lusty novel of Viking times, as the irrepressible hero Orm hacks and pillages his way across northern Europe. Though not set in Iceland, it evokes the period with historical accuracy while never letting up on the rollocking, good-humoured pace.

Einar Már Guðmundsson *Angels of the Universe*. A sad, challenging story of a young man's descent into schizophrenia and the way society treats him, based on the life of the author's brother. Difficult reading at times but never patronizing or pointlessly grim – a great work.

Hallgrímur Helgason *101 Reykjavík*. A wry look at the undemanding values of a modern urban existence, centring on the self-inflicted crisis-ridden life of Reykjavík resident Hlynur Björn, a 30-year-old slacker living at home with his mother. It's also been made into a film that catches the book's humour superbly.

Arnaldur Indriðason *Jar City* (aka *Tainted Blood*). Known in Icelandic as *Mýrin*, this gritty thriller with a uniquely Icelandic twist to the plot introduced the misanthropic Reykjavík detective Erlendur and launched Indriðason's massive success as a crime writer. Others in the series include *Silence of the Grave*, *The Draining Lake* and *Arctic Chill*.

Einar Kárason *Devil's Island*. First in a trilogy of novels set in 1950s Reykjavík, seen through the eyes of an eccentric family housed in an abandoned US army barracks. Lively, satirical and sharp, it has also been made into a film.

Halldór Laxness *Independent People*. Nobel Prize-winning novel about the toils and troubles of the dirt-poor but comically stubborn sheep-farmer Bjartur to live free and unbeholden to any man. A potentially downbeat tale of haves and have-nots, lifted by humorous undercurrents, a lack of bitterness, and real humanity.

Yrsa Sigurðardóttir *Last Rituals*. Well-above-average murder mystery set in modern Reykjavík but descending into a dark world of witchcraft and folklore. Inevitably living in the shadow of Arnarldur Indriðason's novels, but coping well.

Sjón *The Blue Fox*. Lyrical poem written by one-time Björk collaborator about two apparently unconnected events taking place during a nineteenth-century winter's day, and ultimately exploring Icelandic folklore and relationships with the land.

Travel and wildlife

W.H. Auden and Louis MacNeice *Letters from Iceland*. Amusing and unorthodox travelogue, the result of a summer journey the young poets undertook through Iceland in 1936. Especially enjoyable are the irreverent comments about local people, politicians and literature.

Sigurður Ægisson *Icelandic Whales*. Slim, pocket-sized guide to the 23 species recorded from Icelandic waters, well illustrated and with entertaining, informative text.

Mark Cawardine *Iceland Nature's Meeting Place*. Plenty of colour photos and maps in this wildlife guide, which provides useful information for the amateur naturalist. Advice, too, on where to go to see individual species of birds.

Rob Hume *RSPB Birds of Britain & Europe*. A mine of superlative photographs covering most of the birds you're likely to encounter in Iceland; invaluable for accurate identification in the field or just handy for some background reading.

Mark Kurlansky *Cod*. Entertaining and offbeat account of the cod in history, and a trade in it which reached from Iceland to the US and Spain. A good number of recipes too, if you want to see what all the fuss was about.

Tim Moore *Frost on my Moustache*. Highly enjoyable account of the

author's attempts to follow in the footsteps of adventurer Lord Dufferin, who sailed to Iceland in 1856. A critical and well-observed account of the Icelandic nation makes this book a must-read.

Saga of the Volsungs Penguin. Said to have inspired Tolkien's *Lord of the Rings* and Wagner's *Ring* cycle, this epic delves deep into Norse mythology and the eternal pitfalls of human nature as it follows the adventures of Sigurd the Dragon Slayer.

Sagas and classics

Icelanders will tell you that the greatest of the **sagas** contain everything you need to know about life, and getting acquainted with them certainly reveals something of the culture and history of Iceland. No other ancient literature matches them for their hard-boiled style, laconic but gripping delivery, or their trademark theme of individuals caught in inexorable, often terrible fates.

The word *saga* itself simply means "thing told", and they cover a range of subjects. They were written anonymously between the twelfth and fifteenth centuries, often long after the events they describe; Snorri Sturluson – the thirteenth-century historian and politician – is the only known **author** of any of the sagas, with the *Heimskringla* and *Egil's Saga* attributed to him. All this leaves scholars to debate whether the sagas are historically accurate, or historical novels written to extol the virtues of an earlier age. But none of this really matters – what makes the sagas great is that, even today, they feel immediate and believable.

The most characteristic group of sagas are the so-called "Sagas of Icelanders", which deal mostly with the events of Settlement and the early Commonwealth (around 870–1050). They read like histories, being set in real places (many of which still bear the same name today), and usually begin with a series of genealogies establishing the "historical" origins of the main characters. Some are biographies of individuals, such as in **Egil's Saga** (see p.158) or **Grettir's Saga**. Many tell of long-running feuds, from origin to conclusion; **Njal's Saga** (see p.126) is the greatest of these, but **Eyrbyggja Saga** and the short but impressive **Hrafnkel's Saga** (see p.285) are other good examples. There are also a few that focus on a particular area – most famous is the tragic love story recounted in **Laxdæla Saga** (see p.169).

Other sagas range widely in theme, from chivalric stories of knights in armour and outright romances (often influenced by contemporary foreign literature, or even Homer), to folklore, lives of the saints and Icelandic bishops, and far more historical works such as the **Vinland Sagas**, the massive saga of the Sturlung age (**Sturlunga Saga**), or Snorri Sturluson's **Heimskringla**, the history of the Norse Kings.

The saga manuscripts were first recognized for what they were and collected together by just one man, **Árni Magnuson** (1663–1730). As the Icelanders became increasingly poor under Danish rule, many manuscripts could be found stuffing holes in farmhouse walls, and Arni Magnusson made it his mission to save them and take them to Copenhagen for storage. Once there, however, many were destroyed in a fire, though Arni managed to save some himself. Following Iceland's independence in 1944, a strong political movement arose to return the manuscripts from Copenhagen and an institute was established to receive them. Such was the political importance attached to these priceless artefacts that some were brought back by gunboat (for more on this, see p.77).

Egil's Saga A powerful and lucid narrative, unmatched for the vivid presence of the central figure, Egil, a mean, mischief-making, murdering poet and grandson of a reputed werewolf, whose last wish in old age is to cause a violent riot at the Alþing by publicly scattering his hoarded cash.

Eirík the Red and other Iceland Sagas Oxford University Press. The tale of one of Iceland's most notorious Viking heroes, whose son went on to discover North America, plus some shorter period pieces –*Hrafnkel*'s and the *Vopnafjörd* sagas are the most coherent.

Eyrbyggja Saga A strange and often unsettling story, mixing historical events with tales of ghosts, Viking ceremony and family intrigue, while mapping out the shadowy life of Snorri Þórgrimsson, who advocated the introduction of Christianity in 1000. Uneven, but with some great set pieces and character sketches.

Laxdæla Saga One of the world's great tragic love stories, following the lives of the families sharing a river valley, and the consequences of Gudrún Ósvifsdottir's forced marriage to her lover's best friend.

Njal's Saga The longest of all the sagas, this is a compelling, visceral account of the schemings and person-alities involved in a fifty-year medieval feud, full of bloodshed, pride and falls, and laconic humour.

Robert Kellog and Jane Smiley *The Sagas of Icelanders* Allen Lane Penguin. Hefty compendium of a dozen key sagas, including *Laxdæla*, *Egil's*, *Hrafn-kel's* and the *Vinland Sagas* but strangely omitting that of *Njál*. Comprehensive explanatory text and a few less well-known short stories flesh

out the era – and the tale of Auðun and his bear is a gem.

Sagas of Warrior-Poets Penguin. Being a poet brought respect in Viking times, but poets typically suffered from thorny temperaments, often bringing unhappy fates. The most famous is portrayed in *Egil's Saga*, but this collection of shorter tales also emphasizes the poet's lot – the best here is the wonderfully named saga of *Gunnlaug Serpent-tongue*.

Seven Viking Romances Penguin. Unlike the moral, realistic sagas, these contemporary tales stretch belief a bit and have fun along the way, as warriors outwit gods, overcome monsters and vast armies, and get up to all sorts of bawdy mischief. Tellingly, this always happens away from Iceland – and reliable witnesses.

Snorri Sturluson *King Harald's Saga* Penguin. Part of the *Heimskringla*, recording the turbulent life of King Harald of Norway, felled in battle at Stamford Bridge in Yorkshire, when invading England in 1066, just three weeks before the Battle of Hastings – had he won, English history might have been very different.

Snorri Sturluson *The Prose Edda*. The *Prose Edda* contain almost all of what is known about Norse mythology, so for the details on everything from the creation of the Æsir to the events leading to Ragnarok, read this book. The other source of Norse myths is the difficult *Poetic Edda*, an earlier compila-tion of even older poetry fragments.

The Vinland Sagas Two versions of the Viking discovery of Greenland and North America ("Vinland"), recounted in *Saga of the Greenlanders* and *Eirik the Red's Saga*.

Language

Language

Icelandic

Icelandic is an oddly archaic language, heavy with declensions, genders and cases, not to mention Norse peculiarities. Whereas the other principal members of the North Germanic group of languages, Danish, Norwegian and Swedish, lost much of their grammar over time, Icelandic has proudly maintained features that make even the most polyglottal language student cough and splutter.

It is also one of the most linguistically pure languages in Europe in terms of **vocabulary**, and a campaign to rid the language of foreign (mostly English) words has led to the coining of many new, purely Icelandic words and phrases, devised by a committee of linguistic experts. Modern inventions especially have been given names from existing Icelandic words, such as *sími* for telephone (literally "long thread"), hence *farsími* ("travelling long thread") for "mobile phone", and *tölva* ("number prophetess") for computer; and even *fara á puttanu* ("to travel on the thumb") for "to hitchhike". Perhaps worryingly there's no Icelandic word for "interesting", the closest term being *gaman* – "fun". Dogs also speak Icelandic and can quite clearly be heard to say *voff* (small children will refer to a dog as a *voffi*) while cows on the other hand say *mö*.

Icelandic has also maintained many old names for European cities that were in use at the time of the Settlement, such as Dyflinni (Dublin), Jórvík (York, in Britain, hence Nýa Jórvík for New York) and Lundúnir (London).

Anyone learning Icelandic will also have to grapple with a mind-blowing use of grammatical cases for the most straightforward of activities: "to open a door", for instance, requires the accusative case (*opna dyrnar*), while "to close a door" takes the dative case (*loka dyrunum*). Not only that, but "door" is plural in Icelandic, as is the word for Christmas, *jólin*, hence *jólin eru í desember*, literally "Christmasses are in December" (as opposed to the English "Christmas is in December"). Thankfully, there are no dialects anywhere in the country.

Basic grammar

There are 32 **letters** in the Icelandic alphabet. Accented á, é, í, ó, ú and ý count as separate letters. Letters Þ/þ, Æ/æ and Ö/ö come at the end of the alphabet in that order, while Ð/ð comes after d. Hence a dictionary entry for *mögulegur* comes after *morgunn*.

Verbs come in many classes and are either strong and characterized by a vowel change (*tek*, *tók*, *tekinn*: "take", "took", "taken") or weak (*tala*, *talaði*: "speak", "spoke"), without a vowel shift. Verb endings agree with **pronouns**, which are as follows: *ég* ("I"), *þú* ("you", singular), *hann* ("he"), *hún* ("she"), *það* ("it"), *við* ("we"), *þið* ("you", plural), *þeir* ("you", masculine plural), *þaer* ("you", feminine plural), *þau* ("you", neuter or mixed gender plural).

Icelandic **nouns** can have one of three genders (masculine, feminine or neuter) and can appear in any one of four different grammatical cases (nominative, accusative, genitive and dative). For example, the masculine word *fjörður*, meaning "a fjord", is *fjörður* in the nominative case, *fjörð* in the accusative case, *fjarðar* in the genitive and *firði* in the dative case. The case of a noun is determined by many factors, including the use of a preceding preposition, for instance, *í Reykjavík* ("in Reykjavík") but *til Reykjavíkur* ("to Reykjavík").

Vowels also have an unnerving ability to shift – for example, *hér er amma* ("here is grandma") but *ég sé ömmu* ("I see grandma"). This even happens with proper nouns: *þetta er Lada* ("this is a Lada car") but *ég á Lödu* ("I own a Lada"). There is no **indefinite article** in Icelandic with the result that *fjörður* can mean both "fjord" and "a fjord". The **definite article**, as in the other Scandinavian languages, is suffixed to the noun; for example, *maður* means "a man", but *maðurinn* means "the man". The definite article is declined according to the gender and number of the noun.

Adjectives generally precede the noun they qualify and are inflected according to the gender and case gender of the noun. The strong declension is used with indefinite nouns, as in *góður maður* – "a good man". Definite nouns (those with the definite article or other determinatives) require the weak declension, so *góði maðurinn*, "the good man".

Names and numbers

Icelanders take the forename of their father as the first part of their own **surname**, plus the Icelandic word for son (*son*) or daughter (*dóttir*). For example, the son of a man whose forename is Jón will have Jónsson as a surname; a daughter of the same man will have Jónsdóttir as a surname. A family of four in Iceland will therefore have four different surnames, which can certainly throw things into confusion when they travel abroad. When asking someone's surname Icelanders will enquire "*hvers son er Kristbjörn?*" ("Whose son is Kristbjörn?") for example, to which the reply might be "*hann er Egils son*" ("He's Egil's son"). Formally or informally, Icelanders are always addressed by their forename and are listed accordingly in the telephone directory.

When giving their **addresses**, Icelanders put their street names in the dative case but their town and country in the nominative case. They decline their own names, for instance, *ég tala við Önnu* – "I'm speaking to Anna" (*Önnu* is the accusative, genitive and dative form of "*Anna*") and *bókin er eftir Ingibjörgu Sigurðardóttur* – "the book is by Ingibjörg Sigurðardóttir".

When **counting**, the nominative masculine form of the numerals is used, i.e. *einn, tveir, þrír, fjórir*. However, **street numbers** and the **time** are given in the neuter form. It's a good idea to familiarize yourself with the feminine and neuter forms because they are frequently used in shops and restaurants, since *króna* (plural: *krónur*) and *þúsund* (thousand: plural *þúsundir*) are feminine, while *hundrað* (hundred: plural *hundruð*) is neuter. Note, however, that *tvö hundruð þrjátíu og ein króna* where *tvö* is neuter to agree with *hundruð* but *ein* is feminine and singular to agree with *króna*.

Learning Icelandic

In theory, the Germanic roots of English and Icelandic, coupled with over two centuries of Norse influence in England during the Viking era, should make Icelandic a fairly easy language for English speakers to learn. It doesn't – and any foreigner who has mastered even a smattering of the language will find Icelandic jaws dropping at his every turn. Conversely, most Icelanders speak excellent

English, and young people in particular are only too keen to try out turns of phrase on you.

If you want to teach yourself **Icelandic**, however, your best bet is the widely available and excellent *Colloquial Icelandic* by Daisy L. Neijmann, a thoroughly contemporary and well-constructed beginners' course accompanied by a couple of cassettes. There is only one Icelandic reference work in English on the subject of **grammar**, *Icelandic Grammar, Texts and Glossary*, by Stefán Einarsson. Originally published in 1945 and still printed today in paperback, it offers a very thorough if somewhat stodgy analysis of the language.

Dictionaries and phrasebooks

Dictionaries are exceptionally thin on the ground outside Iceland, but the pocket sized *Icelandic–English, English–Icelandic Dictionary*, published by Hippocrene Books, New York, is good for basic reference and is fairly easy to get hold of. German-speakers have the best option, with *Universal-Wörterbuch Isländisch* (Langenscheidt) being by far the best small dictionary. Larger dictionaries are best bought in Iceland, where they are much less expensive.

Of the **phrasebooks**, most useful is Berlitz's *Scandinavian Phrase Book and Dictionary*, which includes a hundred-page section on Icelandic.

Pronunciation

Stress in Icelandic is always on the first syllable. Below is a guide to the pronunciation of Icelandic vowels and consonants – some have no equivalent in English, but the nearest sound has been given to facilitate pronunciation.

Vowels

a	as is **father**		ó	as in **sow**
á	as in **cow**		u	like u in **cute**
e	as in g**e**t or a**i**r, depending on whether long or short		ú	as in f**oo**l
			y	see "i", above
			ý	see "í" above
é	like **yeah**		æ	as is **eye**
i	as in h**i**t		au	as in French f**eui**lle
í	as in l**ea**n		ei	as in h**ay**
ö	as in f**ur**			

Consonants

As in English except:

j	as in **yet**	f before l or n	pronounced **b**, eg Keflavík
ll and rl	like the Welsh **ll**, or **dl** pronounced together in English as in sa**ddl**e	rn	pronounced as **dn**

Note that Icelandic Þ/þ is the same as English "th" in thing. And Icelandic Ð/ð is the same as English "th" in **this**.

Useful words and phrases

Basic phrases

Yes	Já
No	Nei
Hello	Halló/hæ
How are you?	Hvað segirðú?
Fine, thanks	Allt fint, takk
Goodbye	Bless/bæ
Good morning/ afternoon	Góðan dag
Good night	Góða nótt
Today/tomorrow	Í dag/á morgun
Tonight	Í kvöld
Please	Afsakið
Thank you	Takk fyrir
I'd like...	Ég ætla að fá...
Excuse me	Fyrirgefðu
Here you are	Gerið svo vel (plural)/gerðu svo vel (singular)
Don't mention it	Ekkert að þakka
Sorry? (as in "what did you say?")	Ha?/hvað sagðir þú?
Where/when?	Hvar/hvenær?
What/why?	Hvað/hvers vegna?
Who/how?	Hver/hvernig?
How much?	Hvað mikið?
I don't know	Ég veit ekki
Do you know (a fact)?	Veistu...?
Is there/are there...?	Er/eru...?
With/without	Með/án
And/not	Og/ekki
Something/nothing	Eitthvað/ekkert
Here/there	Hér/þar
Near/far	Nálægt/fjarlægt

This/that	Þetta/það
Now/later	Núna/seinna
More/less	Meiri/minni
Big/little	Stór/lítill/smár
Open/closed	Opið/lokað
Men/women	Karlmenn/kvenmenn
Toilet	Snyrting
Gentlemen/ladies	Herrar/konur
Bank	Banki
Post office	Pósthús
Stamp(s)	Frímerki
Where are you from?	Hvaðan ertu?
I'm from...	Ég er frá...
...America	...Bandaríkjunum
...Australia	...Ástralíu
...Britain	...Bretlandi
...Canada	...Kanada
...England	...Englandi
...Ireland	...Írlandi
...New Zealand	...Nyja Sjálandi
...Scotland	...Skotlandi
...Wales	...Wales
What's your name?	Hvað heitirðu?
My name is	Ég heiti
How do you say... in Icelandic?	Hvernig segir maður ...á íslensku?
Do you speak English?	Talarðu ensku?
I don't understand	Ég skil ekki
Could you speak more slowly?	Gætirðu talað hægar?
How much is it?	Hvað kostar þetta?
Can I pay, please?	Ég ætla að borga?
The bill/check, please	Reikninginn, takk

Getting around

How do I get to...?	Hvernig kemst ég til...?
Left/right	Vinstri/hægri
Straight ahead/back	Beint áfram/tilbaka
Bus (in towns)	Strætó

Bus (long distance)	Rúta
Where is the bus station?	Hvar er biðstöðin?
Where is the bus stop?	Hvar er strætóstöðin?

Does this bus go to...?	Fer þessi rúta (strætó) til...?	Is this the road to...?	Er þetta leiðin til...?
What time does it leave?	Hvenær fer hún?	Where are you going?	Hvert ertu að fara?
What time does it arrive?	Hvenær kemur hún til?	I'm going to...	Ég er að fara til...
When is the next bus to...?	Hvenær fer næsta rúta (strætó) til...?	Here's great, thanks	Hérna er ágætt, takk
Can you let me know when we get to...?	Gætirðu sagt mér þegar við komum til...?	Stop here, please	Stansaðu hérna, takk
Is anyone sitting here?	Er þetta sæti laust?	Single ticket to...	Einn miða, aðra leiðina til...
		Return ticket to...	Einn miða, báðar leiðir til...

Accommodation

Where's the youth hostel?	Hvar er farfuglaheimilið?	Can I see it?	Má ég sjá það?
Is there a hotel/ guesthouse round here?	Er hótel/gistiheimili hér nálægt?	I'll take it	Ég ætla að taka það
I'd like a single/ double room...	Gæti ég fengið einsmanns herbergi/ tveggjamanna herbergi...	How much is it a night?	Hvað kostar nóttin?
		It's too expensive	Það er of dýrt
		Do you have anything cheaper?	Áttu eitthvað ódýrara?
...with a bath/ shower	...með baði/sturtu	Can I leave the bags here until...?	Má ég geyma farangurinn hérna þangað til...?
Bed	Rúm	Can I camp here?	Má ég tjalda hérna?

Days and months

Days and months are never capitalized. Days are declinable but months are not.

Monday	mánudagur	March	mars
Tuesday	þriðjudagur	April	apríl
Wednesday	miðvikudagur	May	maí
Thursday	fimmtudagur	June	júní
Friday	föstudagur	July	júlí
Saturday	laugardagur	August	ágúst
Sunday	sunnudagur	September	september
		October	október
January	janúar	November	nóvember
February	febrúar	December	desember

Numbers

1	einn	5	fimm
2	tveir	6	sex
3	þrír	7	sjö
4	fjórir	8	átta

9	níu	31	þrjátíu og einn
10	tíu	40	fjörutíu
11	ellefu	50	fimmtíu
12	tólf	60	sextíu
13	þrettán	70	sjötíu
14	fjórtán	80	áttatíu
15	fimmtán	90	níutíu
16	sextán	100	hundrað
17	sautján	101	hundrað og einn
18	átján	110	hundrað og tuttugu
19	nítján	200	tvö hundruð
20	tuttugu	500	fimm hundruð
21	tuttugu og einn	1000	þúsund
22	tuttugu og tveir	1,000,000	milljón
30	þrjátíu		

Numerals

Numerals 1–4 are all inflected as follows:

1	Masculine	Feminine	Neuter
Nominative	einn	ein	eitt
Accusative	einn	eina	eitt
Genitive	eins	einnar	eins
Dative	einum	einni	einu

2	Masculine	Feminine	Neuter
Nominative	tveir	tvær	tvö
Accusative	tvo	tvær	tvö
Genitive	tveggja	tveggja	tveggja
Dative	tveimur	tveimur	tveimur

3	Masculine	Feminine	Neuter
Nominative	þrír	þrjár	þrjú
Accusative	þrjá	þrjár	þrjú
Genitive	þriggja	þriggja	þriggja
Dative	þremur	þremur	þremur

4	Masculine	Feminine	Neuter
Nominative	fjórir	fjórar	fjögur
Accusative	fjóra	fjórar	fjögur
Genitive	fjögra	fjögra	fjögra
Dative	fjórum	fjórum	fjórum

Glossary

Á river

Áætlun timetable

Ás small hill

Bær farm

Bíll car

Bjarg cliff, rock

Brú bridge

Dalur valley

Djúp deep inlet, long fjord

Drangur rock column

Ey island

Eyri sand spit

Fell/fjall mountain

Ferja ferry

Fjörður fjord

Fljót large river

Flói bay

Flugvöllur airport

Foss waterfall

Gata street

Gil ravine, gill (ghyll)

Gisting accommodation

Gjá ravine

Heiði heath

Herbergi room

Hnjúkur peak

Höfði headland

Hraðbanki cash machine (ATM)

Hraun lava

Hver hot spring

Jökull glacier

Kirkja church

Laug warm pool

Lón lagoon

Reykur smoke

Rúta long-distance coach

Staður place

Strætó city bus

Tjörn lake, pond

Trachyte igneous rock, usually light grey and with a rough surface

Vatn lake

Vegur road

Vík bay

Völlur plain, flatland

Travel
store

Travel

Andorra The Pyrenees, Pyrenees & Andorra Map, Spain
Antigua The Caribbean
Argentina Argentina, Argentina Map, Buenos Aires, South America on a Budget
Aruba The Caribbean
Australia Australia, Australia Map, East Coast Australia, Melbourne, Sydney, Tasmania
Austria Austria, Europe on a Budget, Vienna
Bahamas The Bahamas, The Caribbean
Barbados Barbados DIR, The Caribbean
Belgium Belgium & Luxembourg, Bruges DIR, Brussels, Brussels Map, Europe on a Budget
Belize Belize, Central America on a Budget, Guatemala & Belize Map
Benin West Africa
Bolivia Bolivia, South America on a Budget
Brazil Brazil, Rio, South America on a Budget
British Virgin Islands The Caribbean
Brunei Malaysia, Singapore & Brunei [1 title], Southeast Asia on a Budget
Bulgaria Bulgaria, Europe on a Budget
Burkina Faso West Africa
Cambodia Cambodia, Southeast Asia on a Budget, Vietnam, Laos & Cambodia Map [1 Map]
Cameroon West Africa
Canada Canada, Pacific Northwest, Toronto, Toronto Map, Vancouver
Cape Verde West Africa
Cayman Islands The Caribbean
Chile Chile, Chile Map, South America on a Budget
China Beijing, China,

Hong Kong & Macau, Hong Kong & Macau DIR, Shanghai
Colombia South America on a Budget
Costa Rica Central America on a Budget, Costa Rica, Costa Rica & Panama Map
Croatia Croatia, Croatia Map, Europe on a Budget
Cuba Cuba, Cuba Map, The Caribbean, Havana
Cyprus Cyprus, Cyprus Map
Czech Republic The Czech Republic, Czech & Slovak Republics, Europe on a Budget, Prague, Prague DIR, Prague Map
Denmark Copenhagen, Denmark, Europe on a Budget, Scandinavia
Dominica The Caribbean
Dominican Republic Dominican Republic, The Caribbean
Ecuador Ecuador, South America on a Budget
Egypt Egypt, Egypt Map
El Salvador Central America on a Budget
England Britain, Camping in Britain, Devon & Cornwall, Dorset, Hampshire and The Isle of Wight [1 title], England, Europe on a Budget, The Lake District, London, London DIR, London Map, London Mini Guide, Walks In London & Southeast England
Estonia The Baltic States, Europe on a Budget
Fiji Fiji
Finland Europe on a Budget, Finland, Scandinavia
France Brittany & Normandy, Corsica, Corsica Map, The Dordogne & the Lot, Europe on a Budget, France, France Map, Languedoc & Roussillon, The Loire, Paris, Paris DIR,

Paris Map, Paris Mini Guide, Provence & the Côte d'Azur, The Pyrenees, Pyrenees & Andorra Map
French Guiana South America on a Budget
Gambia The Gambia, West Africa
Germany Berlin, Berlin Map, Europe on a Budget, Germany, Germany Map
Ghana West Africa
Gibraltar Spain
Greece Athens Map, Crete, Crete Map, Europe on a Budget, Greece, Greece Map, Greek Islands, Ionian Islands
Guadeloupe The Caribbean
Guatemala Central America on a Budget, Guatemala, Guatemala & Belize Map
Guinea West Africa
Guinea-Bissau West Africa
Guyana South America on a Budget
Holland see The Netherlands
Honduras Central America on a Budget
Hungary Budapest, Europe on a Budget, Hungary
Iceland Iceland, Iceland Map
India Goa, India, India Map, Kerala, Rajasthan, Delhi & Agra [1 title], South India, South India Map
Indonesia Bali & Lombok, Southeast Asia on a Budget
Ireland Dublin DIR, Dublin Map, Europe on a Budget, Ireland, Ireland Map
Israel Jerusalem
Italy Europe on a Budget, Florence DIR, Florence & Siena Map, Florence & the best of Tuscany, Italy, The Italian Lakes, Naples & the Amalfi Coast, Rome, Rome DIR, Rome Map, Sardinia, Sicily, Sicily Map, Tuscany & Umbria, Tuscany Map,

Venice, Venice DIR, Venice Map
Jamaica Jamaica, The Caribbean
Japan Japan, Tokyo
Jordan Jordan
Kenya Kenya, Kenya Map
Korea Korea
Laos Laos, Southeast Asia on a Budget, Vietnam, Laos & Cambodia Map [1 Map]
Latvia The Baltic States, Europe on a Budget
Lithuania The Baltic States, Europe on a Budget
Luxembourg Belgium & Luxembourg, Europe on a Budget
Malaysia Malaysia Map, Malaysia, Singapore & Brunei [1 title], Southeast Asia on a Budget
Mali West Africa
Malta Malta & Gozo DIR
Martinique The Caribbean
Mauritania West Africa
Mexico Baja California, Baja California, Cancún & Cozumel DIR, Mexico, Mexico Map, Yucatán, Yucatán Peninsula Map
Monaco France, Provence & the Côte d'Azur
Montenegro Montenegro
Morocco Europe on a Budget, Marrakesh DIR, Marrakesh Map, Morocco, Morocco Map,
Nepal Nepal
Netherlands Amsterdam, Amsterdam DIR, Amsterdam Map, Europe on a Budget, The Netherlands
Netherlands Antilles The Caribbean
New Zealand New Zealand, New Zealand Map

DIR: Rough Guide **DIRECTIONS** for short breaks

Available from all good bookstores

For more information go to www.roughguides.com

Small print and

Index

A Rough Guide to Rough Guides

Published in 1982, the first Rough Guide – to Greece – was a student scheme that became a publishing phenomenon. Mark Ellingham, a recent graduate in English from Bristol University, had been travelling in Greece the previous summer and couldn't find the right guidebook. With a small group of friends he wrote his own guide, combining a highly contemporary, journalistic style with a thoroughly practical approach to travellers' needs.

The immediate success of the book spawned a series that rapidly covered dozens of destinations. And, in addition to impecunious backpackers, Rough Guides soon acquired a much broader and older readership that relished the guides' wit and inquisitiveness as much as their enthusiastic, critical approach and value-for-money ethos.

These days, Rough Guides include recommendations from shoestring to luxury and cover more than 200 destinations around the globe, including almost every country in the Americas and Europe, more than half of Africa and most of Asia and Australasia. Our ever-growing team of authors and photographers is spread all over the world, particularly in Europe, the US and Australia.

In the early 1990s, Rough Guides branched out of travel, with the publication of Rough Guides to World Music, Classical Music and the Internet. All three have become benchmark titles in their fields, spearheading the publication of a wide range of books under the Rough Guide name.

Including the travel series, Rough Guides now number more than 350 titles, covering: phrasebooks, waterproof maps, music guides from Opera to Heavy Metal, reference works as diverse as Conspiracy Theories and Shakespeare, and popular culture books from iPods to Poker. Rough Guides also produce a series of more than 120 World Music CDs in partnership with World Music Network.

Visit www.roughguides.com to see our latest publications.

Rough Guide credits

Text editor: Anna Streiffert Limerick
Layout: Umesh Aggarwal
Cartography: Maxine Repath
Picture editor: Emily Taylor
Production: Rebecca Short
Proofreader: Susanah Wight
Cover design: Dan May and Chloë Roberts
Photographer: David Leffman
Editorial: **London** Ruth Blackmore, Andy Turner, Keith Drew, Edward Aves, Alice Park, Lucy White, Jo Kirby, James Smart, Natasha Foges, Róisín Cameron, James Rice, Lara Kavanagh, Emma Traynor, Emma Gibbs, Kathryn Lane, Monica Woods, Mani Ramaswamy, Harry Wilson, Lucy Cowie, Alison Roberts, Joe Staines, Peter Buckley, Matthew Milton, Tracy Hopkins, Ruth Tidball; **Delhi** Madhavi Singh, Karen D'Souza, Lubna Shaheen
Design & Pictures: **London** Scott Stickland, Diana Jarvis, Mark Thomas, Nicole Newman, Sarah Cummins; **Delhi** Ajay Verma, Jessica Subramanian, Ankur Guha, Pradeep Thapliyal, Sachin Tanwar, Anita Singh, Nikhil Agarwal, Sachin Gupta.

Production: Liz Cherry
Cartography: **London** Ed Wright, Katie Lloyd-Jones; **Delhi** Rajesh Chhibber, Ashutosh Bharti, Rajesh Mishra, Animesh Pathak, Jasbir Sandhu, Karobi Gogoi, Alakananda Roy, Swati Handoo, Deshpal Dabas
Online: **London** Faye Hellon, Jeanette Angell, Fergus Day, Justine Bright, Clare Bryson, Aine Fearon, Adrian Low, Ezgi Celebi; **Delhi** Amit Verma, Rahul Kumar, Narender Kumar, Ravi Yadav, Debojit Borah, Rakesh Kumar, Ganesh Sharma, Shisir Basumatari
Marketing & Publicity: **London** Liz Statham, Jess Carter, Vivienne Watton, Anna Paynton, Rachel Sprackett, Laura Vipond; **New York** Katy Ball, Judi Powers; **Delhi** Ragini Govind
Reference Director: Andrew Lockett
Operations Assistant: Becky Doyle
Operations Manager: Helen Atkinson
Publishing Director (Travel): Clare Currie
Commercial Manager: Gino Magnotta
Managing Director: John Duhigg

Publishing information

This fourth edition published June 2010 by
Rough Guides Ltd,
80 Strand, London WC2R 0RL
14 Local Shopping Centre, Panchsheel Park, New Delhi 110017, India
Distributed by the Penguin Group
Penguin Books Ltd,
80 Strand, London WC2R 0RL
Penguin Group (USA)
375 Hudson Street, NY 10014, USA
Penguin Group (Australia)
250 Camberwell Road, Camberwell, Victoria 3124, Australia
Penguin Group (Canada)
195 Harry Walker Parkway N, Newmarket, ON, L3Y 7B3 Canada
Penguin Group (NZ)
67 Apollo Drive, Mairangi Bay, Auckland 1310, New Zealand
Cover concept by Peter Dyer.

Typeset in Bembo and Helvetica to an original design by Henry Iles.
Printed in Singapore
© David Leffman and James Proctor, 2010
Maps © Rough Guides

368pp includes index
A catalogue record for this book is available from the British Library
ISBN: 978-1-84836-461-5

Help us update

We've gone to a lot of effort to ensure that the fourth edition of **The Rough Guide to Iceland** is accurate and up-to-date. However, things change – places get "discovered", opening hours are notoriously fickle, restaurants and rooms raise prices or lower standards. If you feel we've got it wrong or left something out, we'd like to know, and if you can remember the address, the price, the hours, the phone number, so much the better.

Please send your comments with the subject line "**Rough Guide Iceland Update**" to © mail @roughguides.com. We'll credit all contributions and send a copy of the next edition (or any other Rough Guide if you prefer) for the very best emails.

Have your questions answered and tell others about your trip at ® www.roughguides.com

Acknowledgements

David: For Narrell, with love. Massive thanks to Njóla and Álfrún for company, the car and accommodation in Iceland; and to Sue & Mark, Chris & Karen and Katherine & Jonathon in the UK for more of the same.

James would like to thank: Georgina at Discover the World whose behind the scenes efforts with

this trip were much appreciated; in Reykjavík, Kristbjörn and Ólafur for their friendship and help in getting to grips with Iceland's new economic reality; Sigga Gróa at the Icelandic Tourist Board and her letter; Siggi in Hólmavík who knows everything there is to know about the West Fjords; and everyone else I met on my travels around the country.

Readers' letters

Thanks to all the readers who have taken the time to write in with comments and suggestions (and apologies if we've inadvertently omitted or misspelt anyone's name):

Mirjam Blekkenhorst, Alix Branch, Stuart Brock, Robert Brown, Giorgos Chaziris, Kim Erle, Stephen Frew, Alison Gale, Anna Hildur, Anne & David Jewell, Amy Kelly, Liesbeth Lijnzaad & Liesbeth Schellens, Karen Pass, Debbie Sheppard & Michelle Claxton, Tom, Ilse Vogels, Susan Woolard.

Photo credits

All photos © Rough Guides except the following:

SMALL PRINT

www.roughguides.com

Index

Map entries are in colour.
Entries beginning with Þ and Ö are listed at the end of the index.

www.roughguides.com

INDEX

F

G

H

Map symbols

maps are listed in the full index using coloured text

---	Chapter division boundary
===	Major road
===	Minor road
===	Pedestrianized road
·········	4-wheel-drive road
=====	Tunnel
——	Tracks
----	Footpath/hiking trail
▬▬▬	River/canal
— —	Ferry route
⌒	Bridge/tunnel
✦	Point of interest
◉	Accommodation
▣	Restaurant/pub
✈	Airport
✗	Airstrip
★	Bus stop
ⵔ	Lighthouse
⋏	Campsite
⌂	Hut
�	Rift
⳾	Cliff
/|\	Hill
⌃⌃	Mountains
▲	Peak
ⵛ	Waterfall

⚘	Spring
⚘	Viewpoint
/⍫	Volcano
◔	Crater
⌓	Cave
⚡	Skiing
⊙	Statue
∴	Ruins
♟	Museum
♜	Fort
⛳	Golf course
◉	Swimming pool
⛽	Petrol station
P	Parking
ⓘ	Tourist office
✉	Post office
@	Internet
ⵜ	Church (regional maps)
⬭	Stadium
✚	Church (town maps)
▮	Building
⊞	Cemetery
▦	Park/forest
▨	Glacier
▦	Beach
⫘	Lava flow

So now we've told you about the things not to miss, the best places to stay, the top restaurants, the liveliest bars and the most spectacular sights, it only seems fair to tell you about the best travel insurance around